KEY INDICATORS
FOR ASIA AND THE PACIFIC
2019
50TH EDITION

ADB

ASIAN DEVELOPMENT BANK

Some rights reserved. Published in 2019.

ISBN 978-92-9261-724-0 (print), 978-92-9261-725-7 (electronic)
ISSN 0116-3000
Publication Stock No. FLS190428-3
DOI: http://dx.doi.org/10.22617/FLS190428-3

The views expressed in this publication are those of the authors and do not necessarily reflect the views and policies of the Asian Development Bank (ADB) or its Board of Governors or the governments they represent.

ADB does not guarantee the accuracy of the data included in this publication and accepts no responsibility for any consequence of their use. The mention of specific companies or products of manufacturers does not imply that they are endorsed or recommended by ADB in preference to others of a similar nature that are not mentioned.

By making any designation of or reference to a particular territory or geographic area, or by using the term "country" in this document, ADB does not intend to make any judgments as to the legal or other status of any territory or area.

Please contact pubsmarketing@adb.org if you have questions or comments with respect to content, or if you wish to obtain copyright permission for your intended use that does not fall within these terms, or for permission to use the ADB logo.

Notes:
In this publication, "$" refers to US dollars.
Corrigenda to ADB publications may be found at http://www.adb.org/publications/corrigenda

Cover photo:
Cover design by Marjorie G. Ofaga. On the cover: The design for this publication is inspired by the symbolism associated with butterflies, representing transformation and change. The emergence of new technologies has spearheaded a switch from traditional methods of collecting and compiling data to a more innovative statistical ecosystem. This digital transformation has expanded the possibilities for enhanced human-data interaction, paving the way to a better understanding of our world.

Contents

Tables

PART II: Regional Trends and Tables

Population

PART III: Global Value Chains

Tables

Figures

Foreword

This edition of *Key Indicators for Asia and the Pacific* marks 50 years of the flagship statistical publication of the Asian Development Bank (ADB). In July 1969, *Key Indicators of Developing Member Countries of ADB* was first published as an internal reference document, providing data on each of the 17 developing economies that were ADB members at the time.

Just as we have seen many changes across our region over half a century, *Key Indicators for Asia and the Pacific* has reflected these changes. Today, the publication contains a comprehensive set of economic, social, and environmental statistics, including indicators of the Sustainable Development Goals (SDG). Covering the 49 regional members of ADB, *Key Indicators for Asia and the Pacific* now reaches out to a broad audience that includes policymakers, development practitioners, government officials, researchers, students, and the general public. Beginning this year, the publication's vitally important data will also be accessible in a user-friendly digitized format.

Data in this 2019 edition of *Key Indicators for Asia and the Pacific*—prepared for the first time by ADB's newly formed Statistics and Data Innovation Unit—show that development across Asia and the Pacific has been impressive on many fronts. The number of people in our region living in extreme poverty declined from 1.1 billion in 2002 to 264 million in 2015. The maternal mortality ratio was halved in the period from 2000 to 2015, and an average of about 90% of children were enrolled in primary school in 2017. The region's share of global gross domestic product (in current United States dollars) surpassed one-third in 2018, while international trade has become a growing source of regional integration, as economies across Asia and the Pacific strengthen, broaden, and diversify their participation in global value chains.

While the region has done remarkably well, the indicators presented here also remind us of the many challenges that lie ahead. Economic growth throughout Asia and the Pacific has generally been accompanied by a rise in carbon dioxide emissions; cities are affected by air pollution; and, in some economies, more than half the urban population is living in slums or informal settlements. The proportion of elderly people in the total population reached an average of 8.6% across all ADB regional members in 2018, while the number of women participating in national parliaments is below gender parity. The SDG indicators highlight the need to expand access to safe water and sanitation facilities, and to ensure that all people have safe, nutritious, and sufficient food to eat all year round.

Effective governance depends on accurate and timely data to support evidence-based policymaking. This requires investment in data development and statistical capacity building. The special supplement to *Key Indicators for Asia and the Pacific 2019* presents results from one such capacity-building initiative by ADB. It provides a quantitative assessment of the benefits of using handheld digital devices for survey data collection and management, with the traditional pen and paper interviewing method as a basis for comparison.

In the 50th year of this publication, ADB again acknowledges the ongoing relationships with statistical partners in our regional member economies, who provide us with the most recent data from their official sources. We are also indebted to those international agencies from which the data in many of the publication's tables are sourced. We hope that *Key Indicators for Asia and the Pacific* will remain a valuable resource for data on major development issues well into the future. As always, we welcome feedback from our users on both the content and structure of the publication.

Takehiko Nakao
President
Asian Development Bank

Acknowledgments

This 50th edition of *Key Indicators for Asia and the Pacific 2019* was prepared by the newly established Statistics and Data Innovation Unit (EROD-SDI) within the Economic Research and Regional Cooperation Department (ERCD) at the Asian Development Bank (ADB). The publication team was led by Stefan Schipper, under the overall direction of Kaushal Joshi. Pamela Lapitan, Melissa Pascua, and Eric Suan provided technical and coordination support in preparing the data and tables.

The statistical tables that present development indicators for ADB's regional member economies in Parts I and II of the printed publication, and the 49 tables for individual economies available online, were prepared by EROD-SDI staff and consultants, under the supervision of Kaushal Joshi, Mahinthan Joseph Mariasingham, Arturo Martinez Jr., Lakshman Nagraj Rao, and Stefan Schipper. The research team included Raymond Adofina, Nalwino Billones, Joseph Albert Nino Bulan, Ephraim Cuya, Criselda De Dios, Madeline Dumaua-Cabauatan, Anna Marie Fernando, Karen Firshan, Patricia Georgina Gonzales, Pamela Lapitan, Melissa Pascua, Lea Rotairo, Iva Sebastian, Christian Flora Mae Soco, Eric Suan, and Mic Ivan Vito Sumilang. Proofreading of statistical tables was done by Ma. Roselia Babalo, Oth Marulou Gagni, and Aileen Gatson. The analysis of Sustainable Development Goal indicators and regional trends was prepared by Kevin Donahue and Stefan Schipper. The statistical tables and analytical reports for Parts I and II were reviewed by Kaushal Joshi, Mahinthan Joseph Mariasingham, Arturo Martinez Jr., Lakshman Nagraj Rao, and Stefan Schipper. Mahinthan Joseph Mariasingham led the team comprising Kristina Baris, John Arvin Bernabe, Donald Jay Bertulfo, Marc Alvin Ermino, Krizia Anne Garay, Janine Elora Lazatin, Julieta Magallanes, Sarah Mae Manuel, Dianne Lara Monis, Clara Delos Santos, and Jonarie Vergara, which prepared the statistical tables for Part III. Monelle Capistrano and Ana Francesca Rosales provided valuable comments on the analysis of Part III, which was prepared by John Arvin Bernabe, Donald Jay Bertulfo, and Janine Elora Lazatin, under the guidance of Mahinthan Joseph Mariasingham.

We greatly appreciate the contributions from ERCD's statistical partners—ADB regional members and international organizations—who shared their data for the statistical tables on Sustainable Development Goal indicators (Part I), regional tables (Part II), global value chains (Part III), and individual economy tables. ADB resident missions in Afghanistan, Armenia, Azerbaijan, Bangladesh, Bhutan, Cambodia, Georgia, India, Indonesia, Kazakhstan, the Kyrgyz Republic, the Lao People's Democratic Republic, Myanmar, Mongolia, Nepal, Pakistan, Papua New Guinea, the People's Republic of China, Sri Lanka, Tajikistan, Thailand, Timor-Leste, Turkmenistan, Uzbekistan, and Viet Nam provided support in compiling the data from their respective countries. ADB's Japanese Representative Office, Pacific Liaison and Coordination Office, Philippines Country Office, and Pacific Subregional Office also provided help in data compilation. We greatly appreciate the continuing cooperation of the governments of ADB member economies and other international agencies.

Paul Dent edited the publication. The cover was designed by Marjorie Ofaga, winner of the *Key Indicators for Asia and the Pacific 2019* cover design contest. Rhommell Rico led the typesetting process, and provided technical support for the preparation of all promotional and awareness materials. Joseph Manglicmot assisted in typesetting. Staff from ADB's Office of Information Systems and Technology provided database management and technology support, while the Logistics Management Unit of the Office of Administrative Services facilitated the timely and smooth production of *Key Indicators for Asia and the Pacific 2019*. The publishing team in ADB's Department of Communications provided general guidance on production issues, and organized promotional and awareness activities.

Yasuyuki Sawada
Chief Economist and Director General
Asian Development Bank

Statistical Partners

The preparation and publication of *Key Indicators for Asia and the Pacific 2019* would not have been possible without the support, assistance, and cooperation of partners in the regional members of the Asian Development Bank and the invaluable contributions of international, private, and nongovernment organizations. These partners—who shared their data, knowledge, expertise, and other information—help provide the Asian Development Bank, policymakers, and other data users with a better understanding of the performance of economies across Asia and the Pacific, so that better policies can be formulated to improve the quality of life for people in this part of the world.

REGIONAL MEMBERS

Afghanistan	Da Afghanistan Bank (http://dab.gov.af/) Ministry of Finance (http://mof.gov.af/en) National Statistics and Information Authority (https://nsia.gov.af/home)
Armenia	Central Bank of Armenia (http://www.cba.am/en) Ministry of Finance (http://www.minfin.am/en/) Statistical Committee of the Republic of Armenia (http://www.armstat.am/en)
Australia	Australian Bureau of Statistics (http://www.abs.gov.au) Department of the Environment and Energy (http://www.environment.gov.au/) Reserve Bank of Australia (http://www.rba.gov.au)
Azerbaijan	Central Bank of the Republic of Azerbaijan (https://www.cbar.az/en) State Statistical Committee of the Republic of Azerbaijan (http://www.stat.gov.az/?lang=en)
Bangladesh	Bangladesh Bank (https://www.bb.org.bd) Bangladesh Bureau of Statistics (http://www.bbs.gov.bd) Ministry of Finance (https://www.mof.gov.bd/en)
Bhutan	Ministry of Finance (https://www.mof.gov.bt) Ministry of Labour and Human Resources (http://www.molhr.gov.bt/molhr) National Statistics Bureau (http://www.nsb.gov.bt/main/main.php) Royal Monetary Authority of Bhutan (https://www.rma.org.bt)
Brunei Darussalam	Autoriti Monetari Brunei Darussalam (http://www.ambd.gov.bn) Department of Economic Planning and Development (http://www.depd.gov.bn) Ministry of Finance and Economy (http://www.mofe.gov.bn)
Cambodia	Ministry of Economy and Finance (http://www.mef.gov.kh) National Bank of Cambodia (http://www.nbc.org.kh) National Institute of Statistics (http://www.nis.gov.kh)

China, People's Republic of	National Bureau of Statistics of China (http://www.stats.gov.cn/english) The People's Bank of China (http://www.pbc.gov.cn) State Administration of Foreign Exchange (http://www.safe.gov.cn)
Cook Islands	Cook Islands Statistics Office (http://www.mfem.gov.ck/statistics) Ministry of Finance and Economic Management (http://www.mfem.gov.ck)
Fiji	Bureau of Statistics (http://www.statsfiji.gov.fj) Reserve Bank of Fiji (http://www.rbf.gov.fj/) Ministry of Economy (http://www.economy.gov.fj)
Georgia	Ministry of Finance of Georgia (http://mof.ge/en/) National Bank of Georgia (http://www.nbg.gov.ge) National Statistics Office of Georgia (http://www.geostat.ge/en)
Hong Kong, China	Census and Statistics Department (http://www.censtatd.gov.hk) Hong Kong Monetary Authority (https://www.hkma.gov.hk) Financial Services and the Treasury Bureau (https://www.fstb.gov.hk/)
India	Central Statistics Office (http://mospi.nic.in) Ministry of Finance (http://finmin.nic.in) Reserve Bank of India (http://www.rbi.org.in)
Indonesia	Bank Indonesia (http://www.bi.go.id/web) Badan Pusat Statistik-Statistics Indonesia (http://www.bps.go.id) Ministry of Energy and Mineral Resources (http://www.esdm.go.id) Ministry of Finance (https://www.kemenkeu.go.id) PT Pertamina (Persero) (http://barata.com/en/)
Japan	Bank of Japan (http://www.boj.or.jp/en) Economic and Social Research Institute (http://www.esri.go.jp) Japan Customs (http://www.customs.go.jp/english/) Japan Statistics Bureau (http://www.stat.go.jp/english) Ministry of Economy, Trade and Industry (http://www.meti.go.jp) Ministry of Finance (http://www.mof.go.jp) The Institute of Energy Economics, Japan (http://oil-info.ieej.or.jp/)
Kazakhstan	Committee on Statistics, Ministry of National Economy of the Republic of Kazakhstan (http://www.stat.gov.kz) Ministry of Finance of the Republic of Kazakhstan (http://www.minfin.gov.kz/) National Bank of Kazakhstan (https://nationalbank.kz)
Kiribati	Kiribati National Statistics Office (http://www.mfed.gov.ki/our-work/national-statistics-office)

Korea, Republic of	Bank of Korea (https://bok.or.kr) Ministry of Economy and Finance (formerly Ministry of Strategy and Finance) (https://english.moef.go.kr) Statistics Korea (http://kostat.go.kr)
Kyrgyz Republic	National Bank of the Kyrgyz Republic (https://www.nbkr.kg) National Statistical Committee of the Kyrgyz Republic (http://www.stat.kg)
Lao People's Democratic Republic	Bank of the Lao PDR (http://www.bol.gov.la) Lao Statistics Bureau (http://www.lsb.gov.la) Ministry of Finance (http://www.mof.gov.la)
Malaysia	Bank Negara Malaysia (http://www.bnm.gov.my) Department of Statistics Malaysia (http://www.dosm.gov.my) Ministry of Finance Malaysia (http://www.treasury.gov.my)
Maldives	National Bureau of Statistics (http://statisticsmaldives.gov.mv/) Maldives Monetary Authority (http://www.mma.gov.mv)
Marshall Islands	Economic Policy, Planning and Statistics Office (https://www.rmieppso.org/)
Micronesia, Federated States of	Division of Statistics (http://www.fsmstats.fm/) States of Department of Resources and Development (http://www.fsmrd.fm/)
Mongolia	Central Bank of Mongolia (https://www.mongolbank.mn/eng) National Statistics Office of Mongolia (https://en.nso.mn)
Myanmar	Central Bank of Myanmar (http://www.cbm.gov.mm/) Central Statistical Organization (https://www.csostat.gov.mm) Ministry of National Planning and Economic Development (https://www.mnped.gov.mm)
Nauru	Ministry of Finance and Economic Planning (http://www.naurugov.nr) Nauru Bureau of Statistics (https://nauru.prism.spc.int)
Nepal	Central Bureau of Statistics (https://cbs.gov.np) Ministry of Energy, Water Resources and Irrigation (http://www.moewri.gov.np/en/) Ministry of Finance (https://www.mof.gov.np) Nepal Rastra Bank (https://www.nrb.org.np)

New Zealand	Ministry of Business, Innovation and Employment https://www.mbie.govt.nz)
	Reserve Bank of New Zealand (https://www.rbnz.govt.nz/)
	Stats NZ Tatauranga Aotearoa (https://www.stats.govt.nz/)
Niue	Statistics Niue (https://niue.prism.spc.int/)
Pakistan	Ministry of Finance (http://www.finance.gov.pk)
	Pakistan Bureau of Statistics (http://www.pbs.gov.pk)
	State Bank of Pakistan (http://www.sbp.org.pk)
Palau	Bureau of Budget and Planning, Ministry of Finance (http://palaugov.pw/budgetandplanning/)
Papua New Guinea	Bank of Papua New Guinea (https://www.bankpng.gov.pg)
	Department of Treasury (http://www.treasury.gov.pg)
	National Statistical Office (https://www.nso.gov.pg)
Philippines	Bangko Sentral ng Pilipinas (http://www.bsp.gov.ph)
	Bureau of Local Government Finance (http://www.blgf.gov.ph)
	Bureau of the Treasury (http://www.treasury.gov.ph)
	Department of Budget and Management (http://www.dbm.gov.ph)
	Department of Energy (https://www.doe.gov.ph)
	Philippine Statistics Authority (http://www.psa.gov.ph)
Samoa	Samoa Bureau of Statistics (http://www.sbs.gov.ws)
	Central Bank of Samoa (https://www.cbs.gov.ws)
Singapore	Department of Statistics (http://www.singstat.gov.sg)
	Enterprise Singapore (formerly International Enterprise Singapore) (http://www.enterprisesg.gov.sg)
	Ministry of Finance (http://www.mof.gov.sg)
	Ministry of Manpower (http://www.mom.gov.sg)
	Ministry of Trade and Industry (http://www.mti.gov.sg)
	Monetary Authority of Singapore (http://www.mas.gov.sg)
Solomon Islands	Central Bank of Solomon Islands (http://www.cbsi.com.sb)
	Solomon Islands National Statistics Office (https://www.statistics.gov.sb)
Sri Lanka	Central Bank of Sri Lanka (https://www.cbsl.gov.lk)
	Department of Census and Statistics (http://www.statistics.gov.lk)

Taipei,China	Central bank of Taipei,China (https://www.cbc.gov.tw)
	Directorate-General of Budget, Accounting and Statistics (https://eng.dgbas.gov.tw)
	Ministry of Finance (https://www.mof.gov.tw)
Tajikistan	National Bank of Tajikistan (http://www.nbt.tj)
	Agency on Statistics under President of the Republic of Tajikistan (https://www.stat.tj)
Thailand	Bank of Thailand (http://www.bot.or.th)
	Ministry of Finance (http://www2.mof.go.th)
	National Economic and Social Development Board (http://www.nesdb.go.th/nesdb_en)
	National Statistical Office (http://web.nso.go.th)
Timor-Leste	Central Bank of Timor-Leste (http://www.bancocentral.tl)
	Ministry of Finance (http://www.mof.gov.tl)
	General Directorate of Statistics (http://www.statistics.gov.tl)
Tonga	Ministry of Finance and National Planning (http://www.finance.gov.to)
	National Reserve Bank of Tonga (http://www.reservebank.to)
	Department of Statistics (http://www.spc.int/prism/tonga)
Turkmenistan	Central Bank of Turkmenistan (http://www.cbt.tm/en/)
	Ministry of Finance and Economy of Turkmenistan (http://www.minfin.gov.tm/)
	State Committee of Turkmenistan on Statistics (formerly the National Institute of State Statistics and Information of Turkmenistan) (http://www.stat.gov.tm)
Tuvalu	Central Statistics Division (https://tuvalu.prism.spc.int)
Uzbekistan	Cabinet of Ministers (https://www.gov.uz/en/pages/executive_office)
	Central Bank of Uzbekistan (http://www.cbu.uz)
	Ministry of Finance of the Republic of Uzbekistan (http://www.mf.gov.uz)
	State Statistical Committee of the Republic of Uzbekistan(http://www.stat.uz)
Vanuatu	Department of Finance and Treasury (https://doft.gov.vu)
	Reserve Bank of Vanuatu (http://www.rbv.gov.vu)
	Vanuatu National Statistics Office (http://www.vnso.gov.vu)
Viet Nam	General Statistics Office (http://www.gso.gov.vn)
	Ministry of Finance (http://www.mof.gov.vn)
	State Bank of Viet Nam (http://www.sbv.gov.vn)

INTERNATIONAL, PRIVATE, AND NONGOVERNMENT ORGANIZATIONS

Association of Southeast Asian Nations
Food and Agriculture Organization of the United Nations
International Labour Organization
International Monetary Fund
International Telecommunication Union
Interstate Statistical Committee of the Commonwealth of Independent States
Joint United Nations Programme on HIV/AIDS
Organisation for Economic Co-operation and Development
Secretariat of the Pacific Community
Transparency International
UNESCO Institute for Statistics
United Nations Children's Fund
United Nations Conference on Trade and Development
United Nations Department of Economic and Social Affairs
United Nations Development Programme
United Nations Economic Commission for Europe
United Nations Economic and Social Commission for Asia and the Pacific
United Nations Educational, Scientific and Cultural Organization
United Nations Environment Programme
United Nations Human Settlements Programme
United Nations Office on Drugs and Crime
United Nations Population Division
United Nations Statistics Division
United Nations World Tourism Organization
United States Census Bureau
World Bank
World Health Organization
WHO/UNICEF Joint Monitoring Programme for Water Supply, Sanitation and Hygiene
World Trade Organization

Guide for Users

Key Indicators for Asia and the Pacific 2019 begins with a Highlights section that presents key messages from various parts of the publication.

Part I comprises the data tables and brief analyses of trends of select indicators for the Sustainable Development Goals (SDGs) for which data are available. The indicators are presented according to the United Nations SDG global indicator framework.

Part II explores trends in social, economic, and environmental developments in member economies of the Asian Development Bank (ADB) across Asia and the Pacific. These assessments are grouped into eight themes: People; Economy and Output; Money, Finance, and Prices; Globalization; Transport and Communications; Energy and Electricity; Environment; and Government and Governance. Each theme is further analyzed by specific indicators, which are presented in the 100 regional tables that are incorporated into Part II of the publication.

The 17 SDGs in Part I and the 8 themes in Part II start with a short commentary, complemented by figures and charts describing the status of economies with respect to key trends of select targets and indicators. The scales used in some figures and charts are adjusted to show very small numbers. In addition, figures and charts appearing in this publication are also provided with a digital object identifier to facilitate easier access to data. Both Part I and Part II also present discussion boxes on how to approach important measurement issues for select indicators.

The SDGs and regional tables presented in Part I and II cover 49 national economies across Asia and the Pacific, all of which are members of ADB. The term "country," used interchangeably with economy, is not intended to make any judgment as to the legal or other status of any territory or area. The 49 economies have been broadly grouped into developing ADB member economies and developed ADB member economies. The term "developing Asia" refers to the 46 developing member economies of ADB, including Niue as new member of ADB in 2019. The developed economies refer to Australia, Japan, and New Zealand. Based on ADB's geographic operations, the 46 developing ADB member economies are divided into 5 subregions within the Asia and Pacific region. These subregions are Central and West Asia, East Asia, the Pacific, South Asia, and Southeast Asia. Economies are listed alphabetically within each subregion. The term "regional members", often used interchangeably with Asia and the Pacific, refers to all 49 ADB members, both developing and developed. Indicators are shown for the most recent year (usually 2018) or period for which data are available and, in most tables, for a starting year or period (usually 2000). Depending on available data, the starting point may be a year from 2000 to 2008 (usually the year closest to 2000), and the most recent year may be a year from 2009 to 2018 (usually the year closest to 2018). There may, however, be some exceptions to these general principles. In the tables, aggregates for subregions include economies with available data and are shown if the indicator is available for more than half of the economies and if more than two-thirds of the reference population is represented.

Part III contains select indicators for depicting participation by economies of Asia and the Pacific in global value chains (GVCs), and the sector-specific comparative advantage of each economy in terms of exports. Typical indicators of international trade, which mainly refer to the value of exports and imports of goods and services, can be traced back to the traditional trading of final goods across borders. Today's globalization has made many economies more open to trade, providing opportunities for firms to scale up production and allocate their resources more efficiently by moving production chains across borders where there is comparative advantage. GVC analysis provides detailed cross-border trading transactions of inputs used in different stages of production—from raw materials, to intermediate inputs, to the final products purchased by the end consumers.

This publication is also available on ADB's website at www.kidb.adb.org, along with individual statistical tables for each of the 49 ADB regional members, and time series for the indicators presented in Part I and II. Data for the SDG indicators, regional tables, and individual member tables are mainly obtained from two sources: (i) ADB's statistical partners linked to regional member economies, and (ii) international statistical agencies, particularly from the United Nations SDG Indicators Global Database, a master set of data prepared by the Department of Economic and Social Affairs of the United Nations Secretariat. The term "economy source", cited as a source in some tables, refers to data provided by the statistical partners linked to the ADB regional member economies.

The data presented for indicators in Part I are from either official country sources, the SDG Indicators Global Database, or databases maintained by international agencies that, based on their areas of expertise, prepared one or more of the series of statistical indicators included in the SDG Indicators Global Database. The data presented in Part III are mainly drawn from the ADB Multiregion Input–Output Tables Database.

Data produced and disseminated by international agencies are generally based on data produced and disseminated by an individual economy (including data adjusted by the economy to meet international standards). However, it should be noted that national data may be compiled using national standards and practices and, as such, international agencies often adjust the data for international comparability. In such cases, data disseminated by the international agencies may differ from data available from national sources. In other cases, when data for a specific year, or set of years, are not available; or they are available from multiple national sources (surveys,

administrative data sources, and other sources); or when there are data quality issues; the relevant international agency may estimate the data. Some indicators are regularly produced for the purpose of global monitoring by the designated agency and there are no corresponding data at the national level (e.g., population living on less than $1.90 at 2011 purchasing power parity). In other cases, the differences between data from national and international agencies may be because the most recent and/or revised data available at the national level are not yet available with the relevant international agency. Some data gaps are filled by supplementing or deriving data collected through sample surveys financed and carried out by international agencies. For example, many of the health indicators are estimated using data from the Multiple Indicator Cluster Surveys and Demographic and Health Surveys.

ADB exercises due care and caution in collecting data before publication. Nevertheless, data from international sources presented in this publication may differ from those available within individual member economies. Thus, for a detailed description of how the indicators are compiled by the international agencies, readers may refer to the metadata available from databases of the individual international agencies, or the SDG Indicators Global Database website for metadata of SDG indicators. Comparable and standardized national data gathered through a robust data-reporting mechanism of the international agencies should be the basis for all data in the global monitoring databases, and global indicators should be produced in full consultation with national statistical agencies.

Data obtained from ADB member economies are comparable to the extent that the ADB members follow standard statistical concepts, definitions, and estimation methods recommended by the United Nations and other applicable international agencies. Nevertheless, member economies invariably develop and use their own concepts, definitions, and estimation methodologies to suit their individual circumstances, and these may not necessarily comply with recommended international standards. Therefore, even though attempts are made to present the data in a comparable and uniform format, the data are subject to variations in the statistical methods used by individual economies, so full comparability may not be possible. These variations are reflected in the footnotes of the statistical tables, or noted in the Data Issues and Comparability sections. Moreover, the aggregates shown in some tables for the developing ADB member economies and ADB regional members are treated as approximations of the actual total or average, or growth rates, due to missing data from the primary source. No attempt has been made to impute the missing data.

The data published by ADB do not constitute any form of advice or recommendation. For answers to any questions on the data, users of this publication are requested to seek advice from the relevant data source or organization.

Fiscal Year

There are 24 regional members of the Asian Development Bank with fiscal years that do not coincide with the calendar year. Whenever statistical series (for example, national accounts or government finance) are compiled on the basis of a fiscal year, these series are presented in the column for the single-year during which most of the fiscal year occurred. The 24 fiscal year definitions for 2018 are outlined below.

Regional Member	Fiscal Year	Year Caption
Afghanistan (fiscal year since 2013)	21 December 2017 to 20 December 2018	2018
Brunei Darussalam (fiscal year since 2002) Hong Kong, China India Japan Myanmar New Zealand Singapore	1 April 2018 to 31 March 2019	2018
Fiji	1 August 2017 to 31 July 2018	2018
Australia Bangladesh Bhutan Cook Islands Kiribati Nauru Pakistan Samoa Tonga	1 July 2017 to 30 June 2018	2018
Nepal	16 July 2017 to 15 July 2018	2018
Lao People's Democratic Republic Marshall Islands Micronesia, Federated States of Palau Thailand	1 October 2017 to 30 September 2018	2018

Key Symbols

...	data not available
–	magnitude equals zero
(-/+) 0 or 0.0	magnitude is less than half of unit employed
*	provisional/preliminary/estimate/budget figure
|	marks break in series
>	greater than
<	less than
≥	greater than or equal to
≤	less than or equal to
n.a.	not applicable
%	percentage

Units of Measurement

kg	kilogram
kl	kiloliter
km	kilometer
km^2	square kilometer
kWh	kilowatt-hour
kt	kiloton
ktoe	kiloton of oil equivalent
L	liter
m^3	cubic meter
mj	megajoule
PM	particulate matter
teu	twenty-foot equivalent unit
t	metric ton
tj	terajoule
$\mu g/m^3$	micrograms per cubic meter

Abbreviations

ADB	Asian Development Bank
BPM5	Balance of Payments Manual (Fifth Edition)
BPM6	Balance of Payments and International Investment Position Manual (Sixth Edition)
CIF	cost, insurance, and freight
CO_2	carbon dioxide
CPI	consumer price index
DHS	Demographic and Health Survey
ESCAP	Economic and Social Commission for Asia and the Pacific
FAO	Food and Agriculture Organization of the United Nations
FDI	foreign direct investment
FOB	free on board
FVA	foreign value added
GDP	gross domestic product
GNI	gross national income
GVC	global value chain
IDA	International Development Association
ILO	International Labour Organization
IMF	International Monetary Fund
ISIC	International Standard Industrial Classification
MICS	Multiple Indicator Cluster Surveys
MMR	maternal mortality ratio
MOF	Ministry of Finance
NPL	nonperforming loan
NSO	national statistics office; national statistical office
NSS	national statistical service
ODA	official development assistance
OECD	Organisation for Economic Co-operation and Development
PLI	price level index
PPP	purchasing power parity
UN	United Nations
UNDESA	United Nations Department of Economic and Social Affairs
UNICEF	United Nations Children's Fund
UNSD	United Nations Statistics Division

Unless otherwise indicated, "$" refers to United States dollars.

HIGHLIGHTS

Part I. Sustainable Development Goals

The 17 Sustainable Development Goals (SDGs) to be achieved by 2030, along with their 232 related indicators, provide a global policy framework toward ending all forms of poverty, fighting inequality, and tackling climate change, while ensuring that no person is left behind as economies of the world grow and prosper. A summary of trends for selected SDG indicators across economies in Asia and the Pacific is presented here.

- In developing Asia, the proportion of people living on less than $1.90 a day (at 2011 purchasing power parity) fell from 33.7% in 2002 to 7.0% in 2015. In absolute terms, this represented a decline in people living in extreme poverty from 1.11 billion to 264 million.

- Poor food security can result in cases of severe malnutrition, which in turn can lead to stunting (i.e., being too short for one's age). Since 2000, the prevalence of stunting in children below the age of 5 years has fallen in 26 of the 30 ADB developing member economies with available data for this indicator.

- The number of women in Asia and the Pacific dying during pregnancy or childbirth, or soon after childbirth, fell from 264 per 100,000 live births in 2000 to 123 per 100,000 live births in 2015. All subregions within the Asia and Pacific region experienced a reduction in maternal deaths during the review period, with South Asia reporting the largest drop.

- The under-5 mortality rate across Asia and the Pacific declined from 69 deaths per 1,000 live births in 2000 to 31 deaths per 1,000 live births in 2017. This rate fell in 46 of the 47 economies with available data for the review period.

- In Asia and the Pacific, significant gaps persist in ensuring women's full participation in political leadership. The threshold of 20% women's representation in national parliaments was surpassed in only one-third of economies with available data in 2018.

- Since 2000, there has been an increase in the proportion of people with access to safely managed drinking water services in 21 of the 25 economies with available data for this indicator. However, the proportion of the population using safely managed drinking water services exceeded 90% in only 8 economies in 2017, and urban–rural disparities persisted in 9 of the 10 economies with disaggregated data available.

- Of the 14 economies with available data on sanitation from 2000 to 2017, the share of the population benefiting from safely managed sanitation services increased in 11 economies, decreased in 2 economies, and remained unchanged at 100% in Singapore. In 2017, 4 of the 14 economies had more than 90% of the population using safely managed sanitation services, but another 4 economies reported usage of such services at below 50% of the population.

- The proportion of the population across Asia and the Pacific with access to electricity exceeded 90% in 38 of the 48 economies with available data for 2017, compared with only 20 economies in 2000.

- Of the 30 developing member economies with available data on unemployment in 2017 (or the most recent year), all but 1 had a higher rate of unemployment among people aged 15–24 years than among people aged 25 years and older. Of these, 13 economies had an employment gap between the two age groups that exceeded 10 percentage points.

- Household expenditure (or income) per capita rose for the bottom 40% of the total population in 17 of the 18 developing member economies with available data during the most recent 5-year assessment period. The average annual growth rates in the per capita household expenditure of the bottom 40% outpaced the per capita household expenditure growth of the total population in 11 of the 18 reporting economies.

- In 2016, air pollution—as measured by the annual mean of the daily concentrations of fine suspended particles equal to or less than 2.5 microns in diameter—exceeded the maximum recommended value by the World Health Organization in urban areas in all but 4 of the 43 economies with available data. Among Asia and the Pacific's 10 largest economies in terms of population in 2016, the highest levels of air pollution in urban areas were found in India, Bangladesh, and Pakistan.

- Domestic material consumption measures the total amount of material directly used in production processes within an economy. Economies in Asia and the Pacific more than doubled their aggregate domestic material consumption from 23.7 billion metric tons in 2000 to 53.6 billion metric tons in 2017. The region's highest per capita domestic material consumption in 2017 were found in Australia, Mongolia, and Singapore.

- The Sendai Framework helps governments substantially reduce disaster risk and minimize the loss of lives, livelihoods, and health experienced as a result of natural disasters. Self-assessment on the alignment of national disaster risk reduction strategies with the Sendai Framework in 2017 and 2018 showed that 3 of the 16 economies in Asia and the Pacific with such strategies were in comprehensive alignment with the framework, while another 8 economies had at least a moderate alignment.

- From 2000 to 2018, 46 of the 48 regional economies with available data reported a decline in their respective score on the Red List Index, a measure of change in aggregate extinction risk across groups of species. Nepal and Niue each experienced a marginal increase in their scores during the review period.

- For 2000–2004 and 2011–2017, the number of victims of intentional homicide per 100,000 people fell in 29 of the 37 regional economies with available data. The largest declines in the intentional homicide rate occurred in Kazakhstan, Mongolia, and Thailand.

- The aggregate value of annual financial and technical assistance increased in 35 of the 41 developing economies with available data for 2000–2008 and 2009–2017. The largest amounts of average annual financial and technical assistance during 2009–2017 went to Afghanistan ($1,405 million), Indonesia ($1,310 million), and Pakistan ($894 million).

- The financial resources devoted to statistical capacity building increased in 17 of the 41 developing member economies with available data for the decade preceding 2016. The largest increases in resources dedicated to statistical capacity building (in current dollars) were observed in in Uzbekistan ($1.73 million), the Solomon Islands ($1.28 million), and Nepal ($1.01 million).

Part II. Region at a Glance

Each year, ADB presents data on social, economic, and environmental developments in its member economies from across the Asia and Pacific region. These indicators are grouped into eight themes: People; Economy and Output; Money, Finance, and Prices; Globalization; Transport and Communications; Energy and Electricity; Environment; and Government and Governance. Each of these themes has a brief analysis of key trends of select indicators highlighting important recent developments in Asia and the Pacific.

People

- The combined population of the 49 regional members of ADB reached 4,180 million in 2018, accounting for nearly 55% of the global population. Among the world's 10 most populous national economies in 2018, there were 6 in Asia and the Pacific: the People's Republic of China (PRC) with 1,395 million people, India with 1,332 million, Indonesia with 265 million, Pakistan with 213 million, Bangladesh with 165 million, and Japan with 127 million.

- The region's population is gradually aging amid increased life expectancy and decreasing fertility rates. In 2018, the average ratio of the elderly population (65 years and older) to the total population reached 8.6% across all ADB regional members, up from 5.9% in 2000.

- Economies in the region are increasing access to primary education. In 2017 (or the most recent year for which data are available), 30 of the 35 ADB developing member economies with available data had a primary education attainment ratio that met or exceeded 90% for both boys and girls. By comparison, in 2000 (or the earliest year for which data are available), only 20 of the 35 economies had achieved this same measure of primary education attainment. Of the economies reporting in 2017, showing an improvement in primary education attainment compared to 2000 (or the earliest year available), and having data for both boys and girls, more than two-thirds reported that the gain for girls exceeded that for boys.

Economy and Output

- Asia and the Pacific's share of global gross domestic product (GDP) at purchasing power parity increased from 30.3% in 2000 to 42.8% in 2018. Whereas when measured in terms of current United States dollars, the region's share of global GDP surpassed one-third in 2018.

- In 2018, the five largest economies in Asia and the Pacific in terms of GDP at purchasing power parity were the PRC, India, Japan, Indonesia, and the Republic of Korea. All five economies experienced positive GDP growth each year from 2016 to 2018, with India having the highest growth rate in each of the 3 years.

- Capital formation comprises fixed investment in the form of buildings, civil engineering, machinery, and equipment, as well as changes in inventories. In 2018, of the 37 economies with available data, 21 reported capital formation that was more than a quarter of GDP.

Money, Finance, and Prices

- In 25 of 47 reporting economies across Asia and the Pacific, consumer price inflation accelerated from 2017 to 2018, while in 22 economies it decelerated. Rising oil prices and falling exchange rates contributed to an acceleration in inflation in some developing member economies, while falling prices for food and nonalcoholic beverages slowed inflation in others.

- In 2018, the money supply expanded on an annual basis in 38 of the 39 economies with available data.

- During and after the global financial crisis, the value of nonperforming bank loans—as well as the percentage of nonperforming loans as a share of total gross loans—rose across the region. Subsequent years have seen a gradual recovery. From 2010 to 2017, the percentage of nonperforming loans as a share of total gross loans fell in 22 of the 31 economies with available data.

Globalization

- The aggregate of remittances to developing member economies in Asia and the Pacific reached $297.1 billion in 2018, up significantly from $35.5 billion in 2000. Among the region's top recipients of remittances, India, the PRC, and the Philippines were ranked first, second, and fourth in the world, respectively. In 2018, remittances accounted for at least 10% of GDP in one-quarter of ADB's developing member economies.

- Foreign direct investment in Asia and the Pacific totaled $541.9 billion in 2017, up more than threefold since 2000. The region's aggregate foreign direct investment in 2017 accounted for 29.2% of the global total, compared with 12.4% in 2000.

- Economies in Asia and the Pacific are exporting an increasing share of their goods to other economies within the region. Among the 48 regional economies, 40 increased their intraregional share of merchandise exports from 2000 to 2018. On an aggregate basis, intraregional exports as a share of the region's total exports rose from 50.8% in 2000 to 57.7% in 2018.

- Merchandise exports from Asia and the Pacific rose to $7 trillion in 2018. The region's share of total global merchandise exports was 36.1% in 2018, up from 28.7% in 2000.

Transport and Communications

- Asia and the Pacific is extending its lead as the busiest region in the world in terms of passenger air traffic, accounting for about 34% of the global total in 2017. In 29 of the 35 developing economies with available data, air carrier departures increased from 2000 to 2017. By economy, the most air carrier departures in 2017 were in the PRC (4.36 million); India (1.03 million); Indonesia (0.92 million); Taipei,China (0.51 million); and the Republic of Korea (0.50 million).

- The proportion of households in Asia and the Pacific with internet access rose from about 28% in 2010 to more than 48% in 2017. The corresponding internet penetration rates for males and females were 47.9% and 39.7%, respectively, signaling that a digital gender divide persists.

Energy and Electricity

- From 2000 to 2016, Asia and the Pacific's five most populous economies all increased their energy efficiency, as measured by the amount of GDP per unit use of energy (i.e., one petajoule). The largest increases in GDP per petajoule were in India ($76.1 million per petajoule) and Bangladesh ($73.7 million per petajoule).

- The region's aggregate energy production increased to 33.7% of the global total in 2016, compared with 24.6% in 2000. In 2016, the PRC contributed 49.3% of the region's energy production. The region's next largest energy producers and their respective regional production shares in 2016 were India (12.1%), Indonesia (9.8%), and Australia (8.5%).

- Of the 44 regional economies with available data for 2016, 29 were net energy importers. Compared with their respective positions in 2000 (or the earliest year for which data are available), the Lao People's Democratic Republic, Mongolia, and Timor-Leste had all switched from being net energy importers to being net energy exporters by 2016.

Environment

- In 2016, 15 of 46 reporting economies in Asia and the Pacific increased their total forested land, 14 economies experienced a decrease, and 17 experienced no change. The region's highest rates of reforestation in 2016 occurred in the Philippines (3.0%), Azerbaijan (2.3%), and the Lao People's Democratic Republic (1.0%).

- Economic growth in the region has been accompanied by a rise in carbon dioxide (CO_2) emissions. In 2014, Asia and the Pacific accounted for nearly half of all global CO_2 emissions. The top five emitters—the PRC, India, Japan, the Republic of Korea, and Indonesia—together accounted for more than 90% of the region's total. From 2000 to 2014, only 7 of the 47 regional economies with available data were successful in reducing CO_2 emissions on a per capita basis.

Government and Governance

- The ratio of government taxes to GDP rose between 2017 and 2018 in 13 of the 23 reporting economies. In eight economies, a decrease in the government taxes-to-GDP ratio occurred, and in 2 regional economies the government taxes-to-GDP ratio remained unchanged between 2017 and 2018. The largest increases were observed in Tonga (4.9 percentage points), Mongolia (2.6 percentage points), and Uzbekistan (2.4 percentage points). The largest decreases were observed in Nauru (–5.4 percentage points), Bangladesh (–1.7 percentage points), and the Maldives (–1.1 percentage points).

- Comparing 2018 with 2005, there were 30 economies in Asia and the Pacific with available data that reduced the number of days required to start a business, 4 economies in which there was an increase, and 3 economies with no change. The high-income economies of New Zealand (0.5 days); Hong Kong, China (1.5 days); and Singapore (1.5 days) had the shortest times required to start a business among all regional members in 2018.

Part III. Global Value Chains

ADB utilizes global value chain statistics derived from multi-regional input-output tables to describe the role of Asia and the Pacific in global production networks. This year, *Key Indicators for Asia and the Pacific* features the flow of domestic value-added via forward linkages to depict the evolving dynamics of production networks across Asia. Domestic value-added via forward linkages measures the amount of domestic value-added that is generated from the production of total exports.

- Asia has been growing as a source of, and destination for, domestic value-added in exports. In 2000, 23.0% of the world's total domestic value-added via forward linkages came from Asia, while 19.7% of the world's total domestic value-added was received by Asia. By 2018, Asia was contributing 30.2% to the world's total domestic value-added generation and absorbing 26.0% of the total domestic value-added sent around the world.

- Intraregional trade remains important for Asia, especially as its dependence on North America (defined here as the United States and Canada) as a trade partner appears to be diminishing. Up to 33.5 % of domestic value-added generated in Asia stayed within the region in 2018, while 39.0%

of total domestic value-added absorbed in Asia originated from within the region. Comparing 2000 to 2018, Asia sent a smaller share of its generated domestic value-added to North America, while North America's contribution to total domestic value-added flowing into Asia also declined.

- When assessing all sectors, the People's Republic of China (PRC) had overtaken Japan as the largest source of intraregional domestic value-added outflows by 2018, while the subregion comprising Southeast Asia plus Fiji had become the largest destination for total intraregional domestic value-added inflows. In 2000, Japan was the largest source of intraregional domestic value-added, while East Asia was the largest destination for domestic value-added.

- In the primary sector, Southeast Asia plus Fiji was the largest source of intraregional domestic value-added in 2000, while Japan was the largest destination. By 2018, the PRC had become the leading source of intraregional domestic value-added in the primary sector, generating 46.3% of intraregional domestic value-added outflows. Meanwhile, Southeast Asia plus Fiji became the top destination for primary sector intraregional domestic value-added in 2018, with the PRC being its major source.

- In the low-technology industrial sector, intraregional domestic value-added in 2000 was more or less evenly generated by the PRC, Japan, East Asia, and Southeast Asia plus Fiji. However, by 2018, the PRC had emerged as the region's source hub for the sector, followed by Southeast Asia plus Fiji. In terms of destinations for intraregional domestic value-added in this sector, Southeast Asia plus Fiji had replaced Japan as the region's

largest by 2018. Also noticeable was the rise of India and economies in South Asia and Central & West Asia as destinations for low-technology industrial sector intraregional domestic value-added.

- In the medium- to high-technology industrial sector, Japan was Asia's largest source of intraregional domestic value-added in 2000, but East Asia had surpassed it by 2018. Meanwhile, the PRC rose to become the region's largest destination of intraregional domestic value-added flows for the sector in 2018, exceeding those going to East Asia and Southeast Asia plus Fiji, which were the region's leading destinations in 2000. India, South Asia, and Central & West Asia were also receiving increased volumes of medium- to high-technology industrial sector domestic value-added inflows by 2018, with most of the inflows coming from the PRC.

- In the business services sectors, the PRC and Southeast Asia plus Fiji were the largest sources of intraregional domestic value added in 2018, replacing Japan and East Asia. While East Asia and Southeast Asia plus Fiji remained the destination hubs for the sector's intraregional domestic value-added flows, the share of inflows to the PRC also increased as East Asia's and Japan's shares declined.

- In the personal and public services sector, the PRC had surpassed Japan as the region's leading source of intraregional domestic value-added by 2018. While the PRC replaced East Asia as the region's destination hub, the destinations for the sector's intraregional flows in 2018 were more diversified than those in 2000, with flows from India to the PRC representing the single highest movement of total intraregional domestic value-added.

PART I

Sustainable Development Goals Trends and Tables

Sustainable Development Goals—Data Stories

The United Nations (UN) Sustainable Development Goals (SDGs) were adopted in September 2015 to set targets for global development that would be achieved by 2030. Economies in Asia and the Pacific are working toward achieving the 17 goals and 169 targets that comprise the SDG framework. A total of 232 statistical indicators are used to track the progress of individual economies toward meeting the SDGs.[1]

The SDGs were developed through a participatory process.[2] A key feature of the SDGs, when compared with the Millennium Development Goals, is their increased emphasis on level of disaggregation by income, sex, age, race, ethnicity, migratory status, and disability status. Responses to a 2017 survey conducted by the Asian Development Bank (ADB) and the United Nations Economic and Social Commission for Asia and the Pacific (UNESCAP) suggested that, while disaggregation by location was available for several SDG indicators, disaggregation was less common by sex and often absent for disabled persons and indigenous peoples.[3]

The SDG indicator framework comprises a three-tier classification system based on data availability and whether the methodology is well established. Tier I indicators are those with a clearly established methodology and where data are being regularly collected by many economies. Tier II indicators are those with an established methodology, but where data are not regularly collected by many economies. Tier III indicators have neither established standards nor estimation methodologies. Of the 232 SDG indicators, 82 belong to Tier I, 61 belong to Tier II, and 84 belong to Tier III. The remaining 5 indicators fall under multiple tiers.

Data availability is an area of concern for tracking progress in achieving the SDGs. It is also vital to the design, implementation, and monitoring of national development plans. A lack of resources devoted to the development of statistics at the economy level is often a primary constraint to sufficient data being available (PARIS21 2017). The Cape Town Global Action Plan for Sustainable Development Data, which was adopted by the UN Statistical Commission in March 2017, appeals for a commitment from governments to provide the funding necessary to upgrade national statistical systems, use a combination of traditional and innovative data sources, and harness strategic partnerships with an array of stakeholders (UN 2017).

Part I of *Key Indicators for Asia and the Pacific 2019* seeks to contribute to improved data availability in Asia and the Pacific. It provides a status update for ADB's 49 regional member economies on their progress toward achievement of the Sustainable Development Agenda. In addition to the data tables, the discussions for select SDG indicators are accompanied by supporting data stories and charts. Most of the statistics presented in the tables and charts are presented for two data points from 2000 to 2018. Data gaps and other data-related issues are also considered to inform any related policy actions.

---

1   In May 2018, the UN Statistical Commission approved the revised list of 232 indicators, which is the framework in place today for tracking progress toward achievement of the SDGs. Further refinements to the SDG indicators are expected.

2   As an example of this participatory process, the UN conducted an online survey asking citizens of the world to identify areas that they would like to see addressed in the SDGs.

3   In 2017, ADB and UNESCAP undertook a survey of 22 selected national statistics offices from ADB and UNESCAP member economies on their experience with SDG data compilation.

SDG 1. End poverty in all its forms everywhere

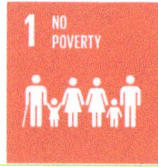

Developing Asia has made major gains in reducing extreme poverty since 2002, but more than one-quarter of a billion people still live in extreme poverty.

Eradicating extreme poverty throughout Asia and the Pacific has been one of region's greatest challenges. Those mired in such conditions struggle to meet basic needs, and often lack access to appropriate healthcare, education, clean water, and sanitation.

In developing Asia, the percentage of people living in extreme poverty—as measured by surviving on less than $1.90 per day at 2011 purchasing power parity—fell significantly in the early part of the new millennium, from 33.7% in 2002 to 7.0% in 2015 (Figure 1.1.1). In absolute terms, this represented a decline from 1.11 billion people in extreme poverty to 264 million. The overwhelming majority of this decline occurred in East Asia (from 409 million people to 10 million) and South Asia (from 505 million to 202 million).

Extreme poverty fell in every subregion of Asia and the Pacific over the review period: Central and West Asia (from 29.3% in 2002 to 5.5% in 2015), East Asia (from 31.9% to 0.7%), the Pacific (from 45.6% to 25.0%), South Asia (from 39.7% to 13.3%), and Southeast Asia (from 24.7% to 5.5%).

The proportion of the world's population living in extreme poverty fell from 25.6% in 2002 to 10.0% in 2015, largely due to the reduction in extreme poverty in developing Asia.

Figure 1.1.1: Proportion and Number of People Living in Extreme Poverty

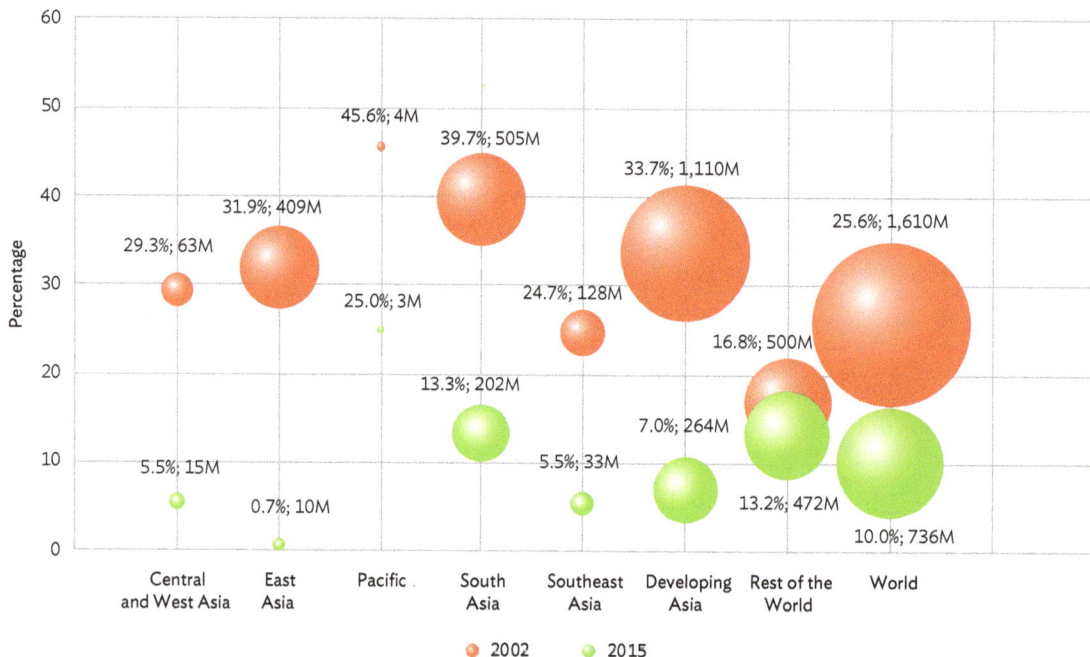

M = million.

Note: The size of the bubbles refer to the number of people living in extreme poverty, and the numbers next to the bubbles indicate the proportion of population in extreme poverty and the number of extreme poor in millions.

Source: Asian Development Bank estimates using World Bank. PovcalNet Database: http://iresearch.worldbank.org/PovcalNet/home.aspx (accessed 24 September 2018).

Proportion of the "working poor" to total population falling throughout developing Asia

Across developing Asia in 2018, the proportion of the employed population living in extreme poverty (i.e., the "working poor") was less than 5% in 15 of the 27 economies with available data for this indicator. The share of the working poor as a percentage of the total population exceeded 20% in 6 economies (Figure 1.1.2). The smallest proportions of the employed population living in extreme poverty in 2018 were found in Azerbaijan (0.02%), Mongolia (0.12%), and Sri Lanka (0.15%). The largest shares were observed in Afghanistan (37.6%), Uzbekistan (27.1%), and Papua New Guinea (PNG) (26.3%).

Figure 1.1.2: Proportion of Employed Population Living below the International Poverty Line

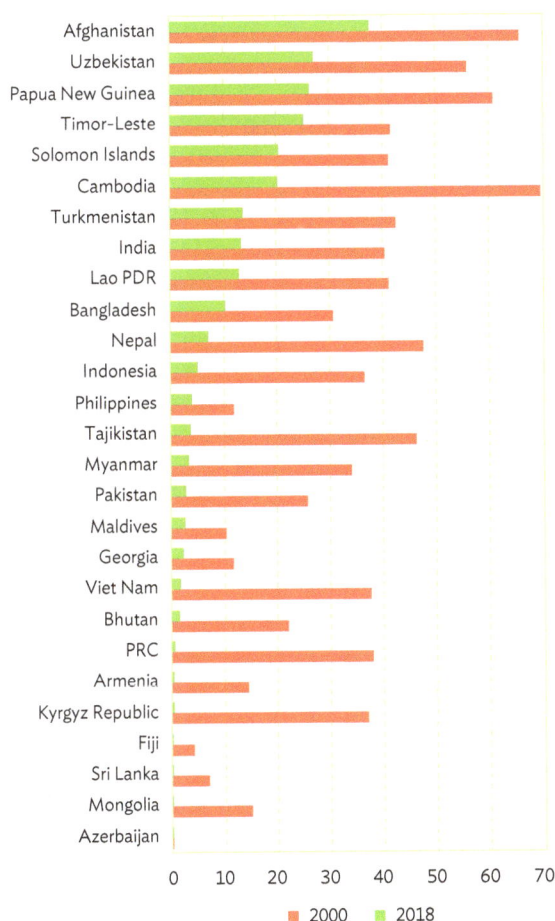

(%)

■ 2000 ■ 2018

Lao PDR= Lao People's Democratic Republic, PRC= People's Republic of China.
Note: Only economies with values greater than zero for both years are included.
Source: ILOSTAT. International Labour Organisation (accessed 18 July 2019).

From 2000 to 2018, the share of the working poor as a percentage of the total population fell in all of the 27 reporting economies. The largest declines occurred in Cambodia (49.3 percentage points), Tajikistan (42.4 percentage points), and Nepal (40.3 percentage points).

SDG 2. End hunger, achieve food security and improved nutrition, and promote sustainable agriculture

In spite of reductions in undernourishment in more than four-fifths of economies in Asia and the Pacific since 2000, hunger persists in the region

According to the UN, the rates of reducing undernourishment in Asia and the Pacific have slowed significantly in recent years, risking progress toward the SDG target to eradicate hunger by 2030 (FAO 2018). Investments in agriculture are needed to increase productivity and sustainability in food production systems.

Of the 37 regional economies with available data, 31 experienced a decline in the prevalence of undernourishment in the total population from 2000 to 2017 (Figure 1.2.1). The largest reductions during the review period occurred in Myanmar (37.7 percentage points), Mongolia (21.7 percentage points), and the Lao People's Democratic Republic (21.2 percentage points).

In 2017, the prevalence of undernourishment in the total population was below 10.0% in 26 of the 37 reporting economies, compared with only 14 of 37 in 2000. The prevalence of undernourishment was lowest—at a rate of 2.5% or below—in Australia; Azerbaijan; Hong Kong, China; Japan; Kazakhstan; Malaysia; New Zealand; and the Republic of Korea. The highest rates of undernourishment in 2017 were observed in Afghanistan (29.8%), Timor-Leste (24.9%), and Pakistan (20.3%).

Figure 1.2.1: Prevalence of Undernourishment in Select Economies of Asia and the Pacific
(% of total population)

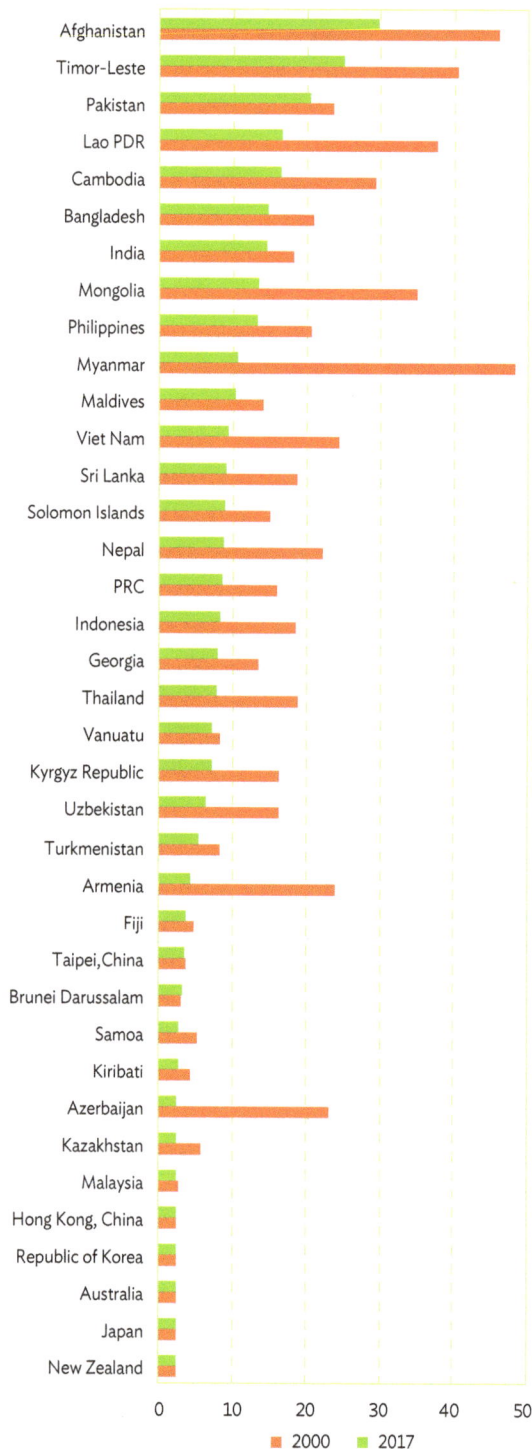

Afghanistan
Timor-Leste
Pakistan
Lao PDR
Cambodia
Bangladesh
India
Mongolia
Philippines
Myanmar
Maldives
Viet Nam
Sri Lanka
Solomon Islands
Nepal
PRC
Indonesia
Georgia
Thailand
Vanuatu
Kyrgyz Republic
Uzbekistan
Turkmenistan
Armenia
Fiji
Taipei,China
Brunei Darussalam
Samoa
Kiribati
Azerbaijan
Kazakhstan
Malaysia
Hong Kong, China
Republic of Korea
Australia
Japan
New Zealand

0   10   20   30   40   50

■ 2000   ■ 2017

Lao PDR = Lao People's Democratic Republic, PRC = People's Republic of China.
Note: 2000 values refer to 3-year average for 1999–2001; 2017 values refer to 3-year average for 2016–2018; and data with values smaller than 2.5% are presented as 2.5%.
Source: Table 1.2.1, Key Indicators for Asia and the Pacific 2019.

The prevalence of stunting has fallen since 2000 in more than 85% of developing member economies for which data are available

Poor food security and severe malnutrition have led to millions of Asian and Pacific islander children being stunted (i.e., too short for their age). The prevalence of stunting in children below the age of 5 years exceeded 25% in 15 of the 30 developing member economies with available data for 2016 (or another recent year)(Figure 1.2.2). The highest rates of stunting were found in Timor-Leste (50.9%), PNG (49.5%), and the Lao PDR (44.2%).

The prevalence of stunting in children below the age of 5 years fell in 26 of the 30 reporting economies that had two data points available for comparison (ranging from 2000 to 2008 and 2009 to 2016). The 3 economies in which the prevalence of stunting increased over the review period were PNG (5.6 percentage points), Malaysia (3.5 percentage points), and Vanuatu (2.8 percentage points), while there was no change to this indicator in the Republic of Korea.

SDG 3. Ensure healthy lives and promote well-being for all at all ages

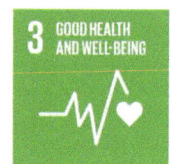

Maternal mortality more than halved across Asia and the Pacific

In Asia and the Pacific, the ratio of women dying during pregnancy, childbirth, or soon after fell from 264 deaths per 100,000 live births in 2000 to 123 deaths per 100,000 live births in 2015. This compares with world averages of 341 and 216 in 2000 and 2015, respectively (Table 1.3.1).

All subregions of Asia and the Pacific experienced a reduction in the maternal mortality ratio (MMR) from 2000 to 2015. South Asia reported

Figure 1.2.2: Prevalence of Stunting among Children under 5 Years of Age

(%)

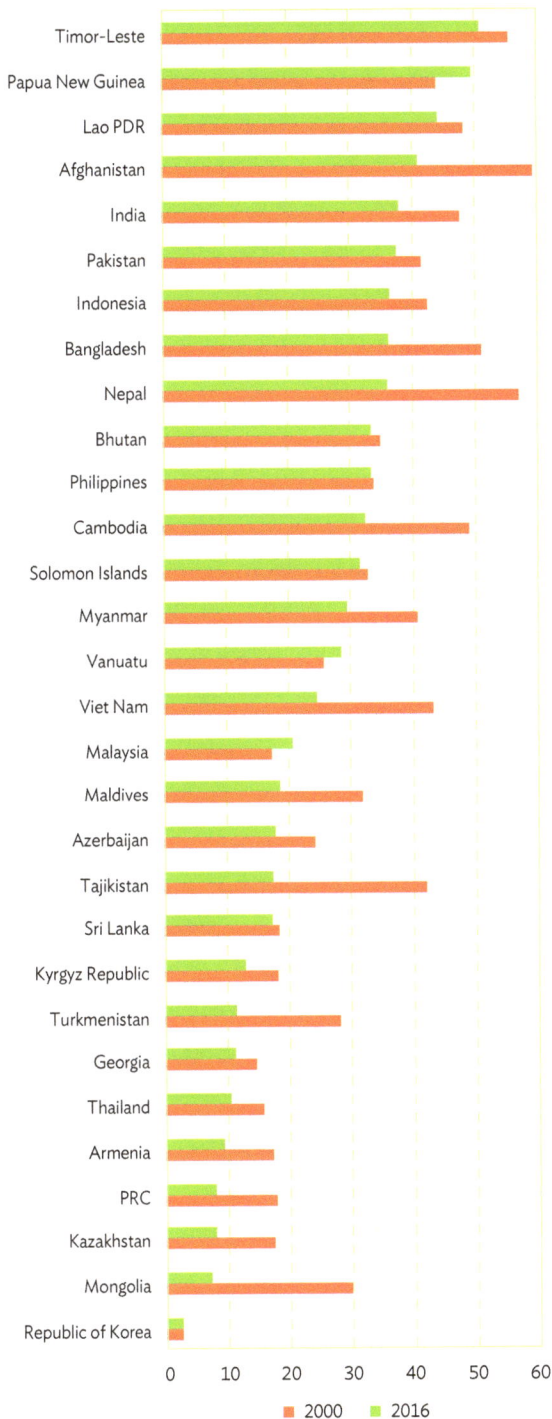

Lao PDR = Lao People's Democratic Republic, PRC = People's Republic of China.

Note: 2000 values refer to available data between 2000 and 2008; and 2016 values refer to available data between 2009 and 2018. Only economies with data for both years 2000 and 2016 are included. "Stunting" is when a child is too short compared to the average height for his or her age.

Source: Table 1.2.1, Key Indicators for Asia and the Pacific 2019.

the largest drop (203 fewer maternal deaths per 100,000 live births), followed by Central and West Asia (192) and the Pacific (154) (Table 1.3.1).

From 2000 to 2015, the MMR decreased in 39 of the 43 regional economies with available data (Table 1.3.1). The exceptions were in the Kyrgyz Republic (from 74 maternal deaths per 100,000 live births in 2000 to 76 in 2015); Taipei,China (from 8 to 10); Tonga (from 97 to 124); and Uzbekistan (from 34 to 36).

Afghanistan experienced the largest decline in its MMR, with 704 fewer maternal deaths per 100,000 live births in 2015 than in 2000. It was followed by Timor-Leste (479), the Lao PDR (349), and Cambodia (323), Nepal (290) and Bhutan (275). Economies with fewer than 20 maternal deaths per 100,000 live births in 2015 included Hong Kong, China (2); Japan (5); Australia (6); Singapore (10); Taipei,China (10); the Republic of Korea (11); New Zealand (11); and Kazakhstan (12) (Table 1.3.1).

In economies where maternal deaths were low, there was a high proportion of births attended by skilled health personnel. Conversely, in those economies where maternal deaths were high, there was a low proportion of births attended by medical professionals (Figure 1.3.1).

Figure 1.3.1: Maternal Mortality Ratios and Proportion of Births Attended by Skilled Health Personnel

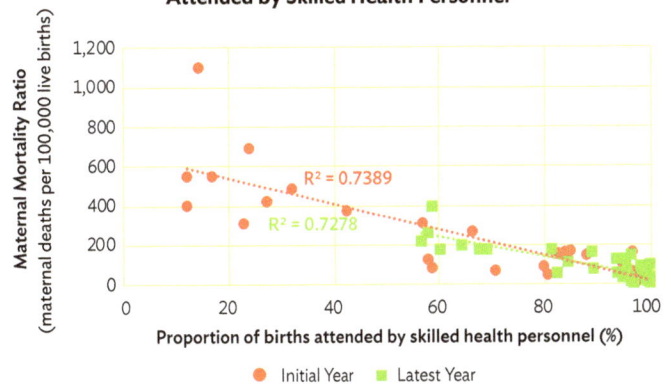

Note: Initial year refers to 2000–2007 and latest year refers to 2009–2018.

Source: Table 1.3.1, Key Indicators for Asia and the Pacific 2019.

The under-5 mortality rate fell in 46 out of 47 economies between 2000 and 2017.

The under-5 mortality rate in Asia and the Pacific fell from 69 deaths per 1,000 live births in 2000 to 31 deaths per 1,000 live births in 2017. This compares with world averages of 77 and 39 in 2000 and 2017, respectively.

By subregion, South Asia experienced the largest decline in under-5 mortality (52 fewer deaths per 1,000 live births), followed by Central and West Asia (41), East Asia (27), the Pacific (24), and Southeast Asia (22) as shown in Figure 1.3.2. For the 3 developed economies in Asia and the Pacific, the average decline during the review period was 2 fewer deaths per 1,000 live births.

The under-5 mortality rate fell during the review period in 46 out of the 47 regional economies with available data. The largest reductions occurred in Cambodia (78 fewer deaths per 1,000 live births), Afghanistan (61), Timor-Leste (60), and Bangladesh (55) as can be observed in Table 1.3.1. Fiji was the only economy in which the under-5 mortality rate increased, from 23 deaths per 1,000 live births in 2000 to 25 in 2017.

**Figure 1.3.2: Under-5 Mortality Rate
by Region and Subregion of Asia and the Pacific**
(per 1,000 live births)

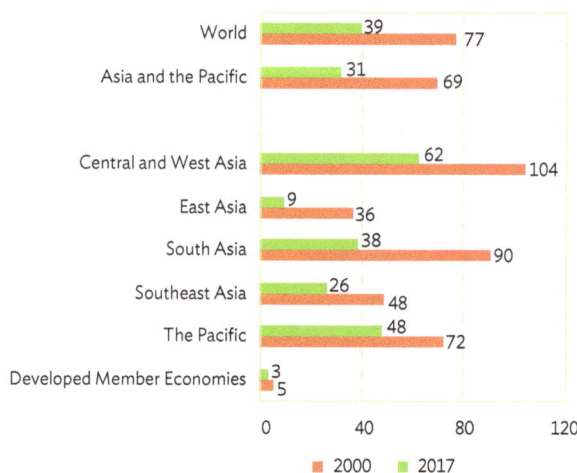

Source: Table 1.3.1, Key Indicators for Asia and the Pacific 2019.

SDG 4. Ensure inclusive and equitable quality education and promote lifelong learning opportunities for all

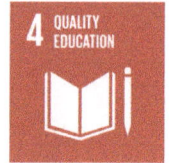

Participation rates in pre-primary education for both boys and girls exceed 90% in two-fifths of developing member economies

Early childhood education is critical to laying a strong foundation for future development and lifelong learning. Among the developing economies of Asia and the Pacific, 14 of the 32 economies with available data for 2017 (or another recent year) had at least 90% of both boys and girls participating in organized learning 1 year before the official entrance age to primary school (Figure 1.4.1). For boys in developing economies, 100% participation rates in preprimary education were observed in Hong Kong, China; Palau; and Viet Nam. For girls, 100% preprimary participation rates were observed in the Cook Islands, Indonesia, Niue, and Tuvalu.

Participation rates below 50% for both boys and girls were found in 6 of the 32 economies reporting for 2017 (or the most recent year for which data are available). These economies, and their respective preprimary participation rates for each sex, were Bangladesh (35.3% for boys and 35.4% for girls), Cambodia (42.5% and 43.6%), Samoa (34.9% and 39.1%), Tajikistan (13.4% and 11.6%), Timor-Leste (32.8% and 33.5%), and Uzbekistan (37.4% and 36.4%).

**Figure 1.4.1: Participation Rate
in Preprimary Learning[a] by Sex of Child, 2017[b]
(%)**

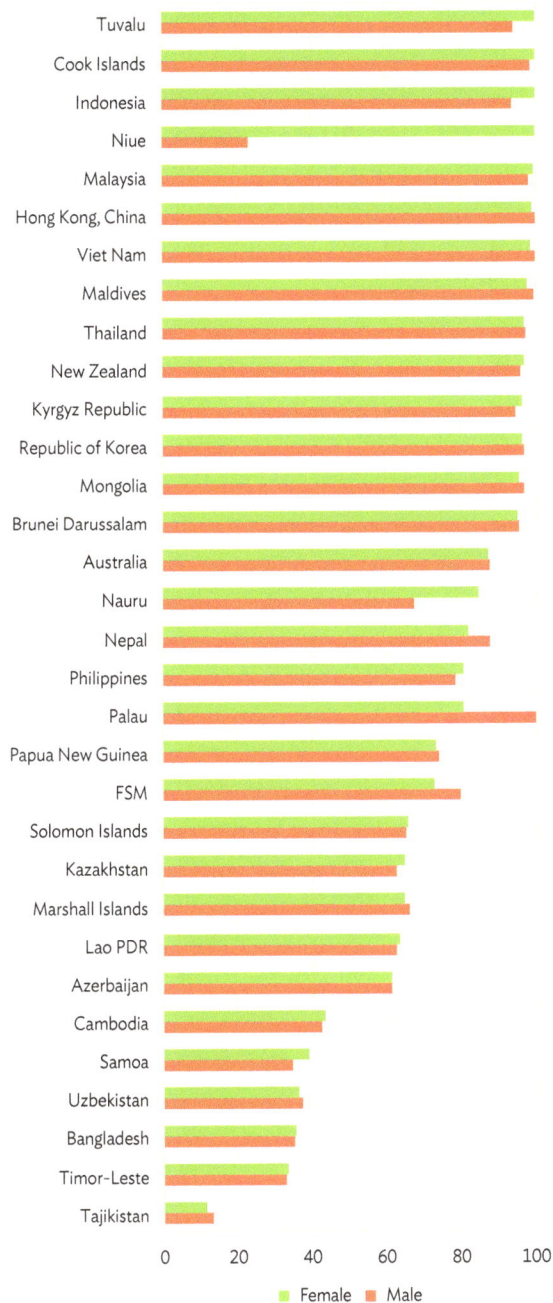

FSM = Federated States of Micronesia, Lao PDR = Lao People's Democratic Republic.
a   Participation in organized learning 1 year before the official entrance age to primary school.
b   For Kazakhstan, data refer to 2018; for the Cook Islands, the Republic of Korea, the Marshall Islands, Nauru, Papua New Guinea, the Philippines, and Tuvalu data refer to 2016; for Niue, Malaysia, the FSM, and Solomon Islands, data refer to 2015; for Palau, data refer to 2014; for Cambodia, data refer to 2012; and for Bangladesh, data refer to 2010.
Source: Table 1.4.1, Key Indicators for Asia and the Pacific 2019.

In 15 of the 32 reporting economies, the preprimary participation rate for girls lagged behind that of boys. The biggest gaps were found in Palau (19.6 percentage points), the Federated States of Micronesia (7.0 percentage points), and Nepal (5.5 percentage points).

Providing qualified primary school teachers is a priority in most economies

Primary school teachers play a key role in ensuring the quality of children's education. While national minimum training requirements can vary widely across economies, all primary education teachers should receive adequate and relevant pedagogical training, both pre-service and in-service, required for teaching at the relevant level.

Comparing 2000 (or another early year) with 2017 (or another recent year), 15 of the 23 regional economies with available data increased the proportion of primary education teachers receiving the minimum organized training. The largest increases in this proportion over the review period were achieved in Nepal (from 15.4% to 97.3%), Kyrgyz Republic (from 52.0% to 95.4%), and Myanmar (from 62.7% to 97.8%). The largest declines in the proportion of primary education teachers receiving the minimum organized training were in Kiribati (from 93.9% to 72.7%), Fiji (from 97.8% to 90.1%), and Bangladesh (from 53.4% to 50.4%).

In 2017 (or the most recent year for which data are available), the proportion of primary education teachers receiving the minimum organized training exceeded 90% in 19 of the 23 reporting economies with available data for both 2000 and 2017 (Figure 1.4.2). This compares favorably with 2000 (or the earliest year for which data are available), when only 10 of the 23 economies met the 90% threshold.

Figure 1.4.2: Proportion of Teachers in Primary Education Who Have Received at Least the Minimum Organized Teacher Training (%)

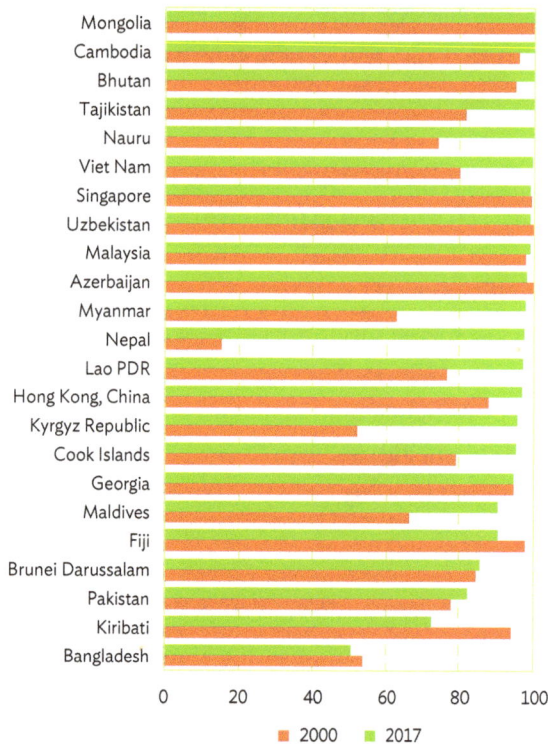

Mongolia, Cambodia, Bhutan, Tajikistan, Nauru, Viet Nam, Singapore, Uzbekistan, Malaysia, Azerbaijan, Myanmar, Nepal, Lao PDR, Hong Kong, China, Kyrgyz Republic, Cook Islands, Georgia, Maldives, Fiji, Brunei Darussalam, Pakistan, Kiribati, Bangladesh

■ 2000   ■ 2017

Lao PDR = Lao People's Democratic Republic.
Note: 2000 values refer to available data between 2000 and 2008; and 2017 values refer to available data between 2009 and 2018. Only economies with data for both years 2000 and 2017 are included.
Source: Table 1.4.2, Key Indicators for Asia and the Pacific 2019.

SDG 5. Achieve gender equality and empower all women and girls

5 GENDER EQUALITY

At least 20% of women aged 20–24 years old were married or in a union before the age of 18 in 11 of 29 regional economies

Early-age marriage can compromise the education outcomes of a girl or young woman. It can impact her employment prospects; the type, arrangements, and conditions of her future work; her overall well-being; and the health of her offspring (Nour 2009).

In 11 of the 29 regional economies with available data, at least 20% of women between the ages of 20 and 24 years had been married or in a union before the age of 18 (Table 1.5.1). Bangladesh (58.6%) reported the largest proportion of women aged 20–24 being married or in a union before the age of 18 (Figure 1.5.1). More than a quarter of women between the ages of 20 and 24 years were married or in a union before the age of 18 in Nepal (39.5%), Afghanistan (34.8%), the Lao PDR (32.7%), India (27.3%), and Bhutan (25.8%).

Women's representation in the national parliament exceeds 30% in only 3 economies

Sustainable development and societies in general can be strengthened by providing women and girls with equal access to education, health care,

Figure 1.5.1: Proportion of Women Who Were Married or in a Union before Age 15 or Age 18
(% of all women aged 20–24 years)

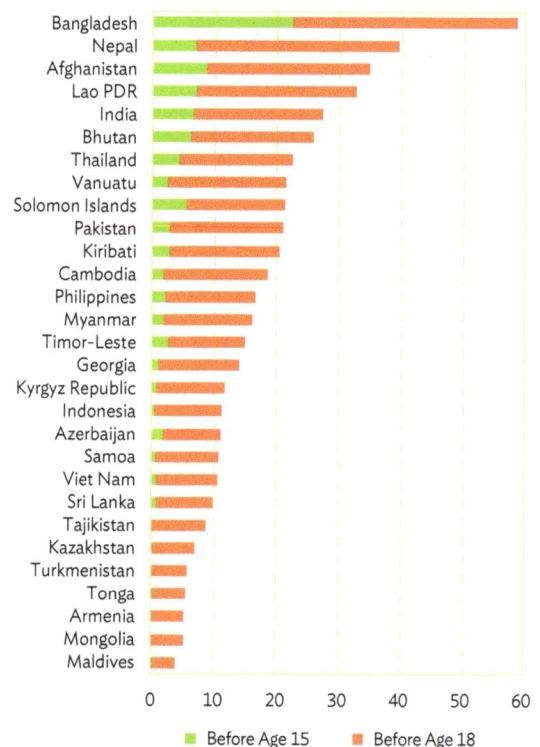

Bangladesh, Nepal, Afghanistan, Lao PDR, India, Bhutan, Thailand, Vanuatu, Solomon Islands, Pakistan, Kiribati, Cambodia, Philippines, Myanmar, Timor-Leste, Georgia, Kyrgyz Republic, Indonesia, Azerbaijan, Samoa, Viet Nam, Sri Lanka, Tajikistan, Kazakhstan, Turkmenistan, Tonga, Armenia, Mongolia, Maldives

■ Before Age 15   ■ Before Age 18

Lao PDR = Lao People's Democratic Republic.
Note: The percentages shown are based on economy data for the most recent year from 2009 to 2018.
Source: Table 1.5.1, Key Indicators for Asia and the Pacific 2019.

decent work, and representation in political and economic decision-making processes. Unfortunately, no economy in Asia and the Pacific was even remotely close to 50% representation of women in their national parliaments in 2018 (Figure 1.5.2). In fact, only 3 of the 45 economies with available data had female parliamentary representation exceeding 30%: New Zealand (38.3%), Nepal (32.7%), and Timor-Leste (32.3%). A threshold of 15% for women's representation was surpassed in only 25 of the 45 economies reporting in 2018, while 13 economies failed to achieve a 10% threshold.

Figure 1.5.2: Proportion of Seats in National Parliament Held by Women, 2018

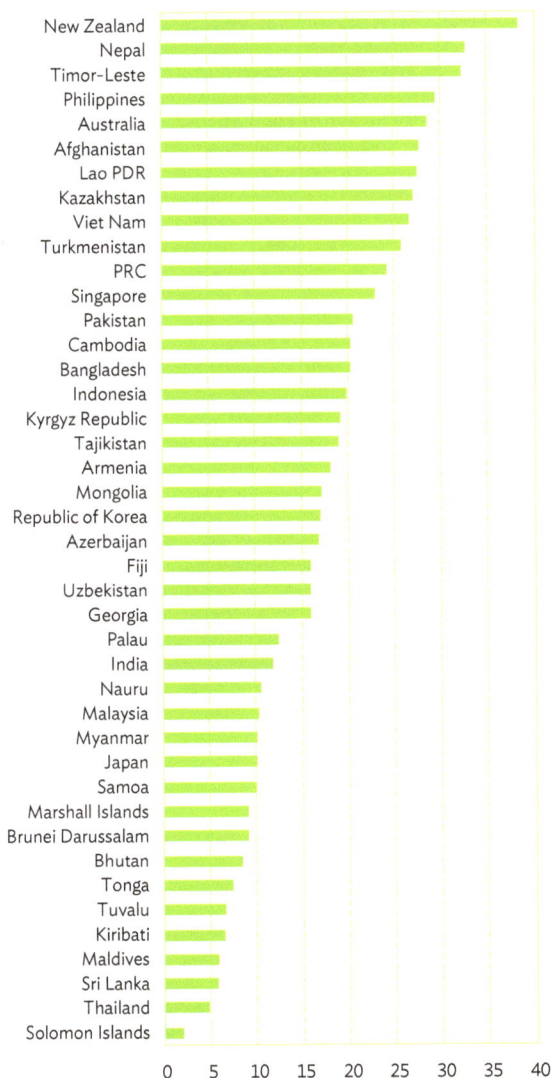

(%)

Lao PDR = Lao People's Democratic Republic, PRC= People's Republic of China.

Note: The Federated States of Micronesia, Papua New Guinea, and Vanuatu have zero representation and are not shown in the figure.

Source: Table 1.5.1, Key Indicators for Asia and the Pacific 2019.

A UN assessment of female participation in local governance in Asia and the Pacific showed that, as with national level data, female participation at the local level is far below gender parity levels. A shortage of women in elected local leadership posts implies that fewer women will continue into higher elected offices, at both the local and national level (ADB and UN Women 2018).

SDG 6. Ensure availability and sustainable management of water and sanitation for all

Economies are doing more to provide safe drinking water, but rural areas still lag

There is sufficient fresh water on the planet to provide clean water for all. Yet, millions of people die every year from diseases associated with inadequate water supply, sanitation, and hygiene. Proper management of water and sanitation services is needed to reduce the risk of contracting preventable diseases.

In 2017, the proportion of the population using safely managed drinking water services exceeded 90% in only 8 of the 25 regional economies with available data (Figure 1.6.1). Among these 8 economies, the proportion reached 100% in Hong Kong, China; New Zealand; and Singapore. Conversely, the proportion of the population using safely managed drinking water services was below 50% in 9 economies.

Since 2000, all but 3 of the 25 reporting economies have made progress in providing safely managed drinking water services. Over the review period, the largest increases in the proportion of the population using such services were in Armenia (56.9 percentage points), Kazakhstan (32.0 percentage points), and Turkmenistan (28.0 percentage points).

Among the 10 reporting economies with data disaggregated into urban and rural areas, 9 had a higher share of the population using safely managed drinking water services in urban areas than in rural areas. The biggest discrepancies were observed in Uzbekistan (urban coverage 55.0 percentage points higher than rural coverage), Cambodia (39.9 percentage points), and the Kyrgyz Republic (39.6 percentage points). The exception was Bangladesh, where rural areas had greater access to safely managed drinking water services than did urban areas (by a difference of 16.9 percentage points).

The share of the population receiving safely managed sanitation services increased in 11 of 14 reporting economies between 2000 and 2017

Inadequate sanitation can negatively impact food security, livelihood choices, and educational opportunities. Only 4 of the 14 regional economies with available data for 2017 had more than 90% of the population using safely managed sanitation services. Coverage of such services reached or approached 100% in Singapore (100.0%), the Republic of Korea (99.9%), and Japan (98.8%) as shown in Figure 1.6.2. However, the share of the population accessing safely managed sanitation services in 2017 was below 50% in 4 of the 14 reporting economies.

From 2000 to 2017, 11 of the 14 economies increased the share of the population benefiting from safely managed sanitation services, 2 experienced a decline, and 1 remain unchanged (Singapore's

Figure 1.6.1: Proportion of the Population Using Safely Managed Drinking Water Services, 2017

(%)

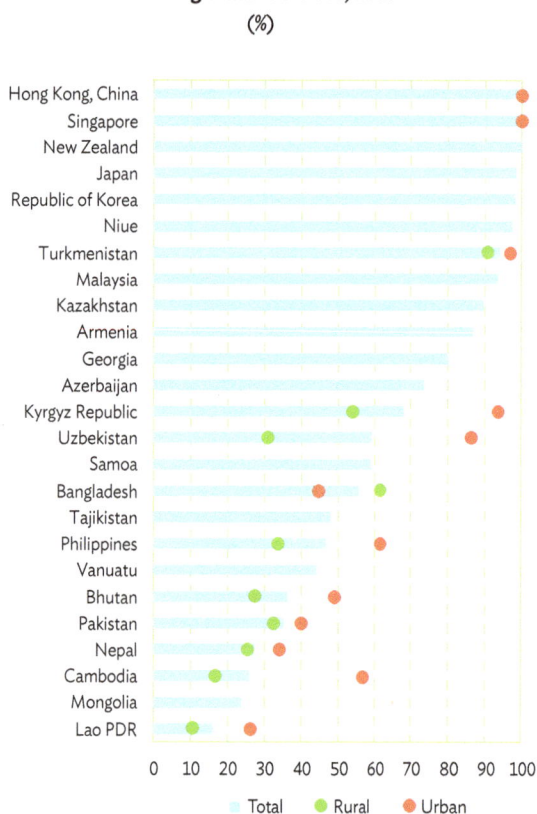

Lao PDR = Lao People's Democratic Republic.
Note: This figure excludes economies that provided only urban and/or rural data, with no national totals provided.
Source: Table 1.6.1, Key Indicators for Asia and the Pacific 2019.

Figure 1.6.2: Proportion of Population Using Safely Managed Sanitation Services, 2017

(%)

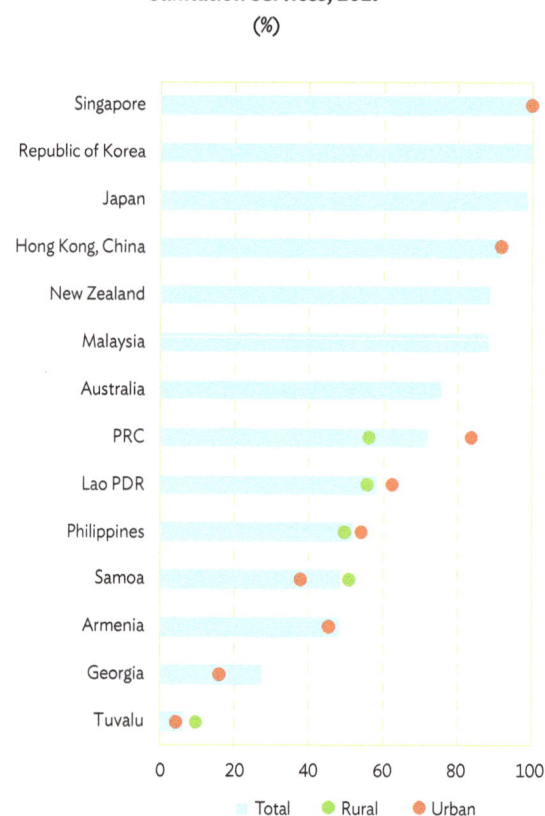

PRC = People's Republic of China, Lao PDR = Lao People's Democratic Republic.
Note: This figure excludes economies that provided only urban and/or rural data, with no national totals provided.
Source: Table 1.6.1, Key Indicators for Asia and the Pacific 2019.

sanitation coverage was stable at 100%.). The largest increases during the review period were in the People's Republic of China (PRC) (45.5 percentage points), the Lao PDR (36.2 percentage points), and the Republic of Korea (14.0 percentage points).

Among the 5 reporting economies with data disaggregated into urban and rural areas, 3 had a higher share of the population using safely managed sanitation services in urban areas, while 2 had a higher share in rural areas. The biggest discrepancy in sanitation services coverage in favor of urban areas was observed in the PRC (27.6 percentage points). The biggest discrepancy in favor of rural areas was in Samoa (13.2 percentage points).

SDG 7. Ensure access to affordable, reliable, sustainable, and modern energy for all

Economies in Asia and the Pacific have significantly expanded access to electricity since 2000.

Universal access to energy, improved energy efficiency, and the increased use of renewable energy support the development of sustainable and inclusive communities, while also strengthening resilience to climate change and other environmental hazards. Public and private investments in energy generation and distribution are needed globally, and greater emphasis should be placed on equitable regulatory frameworks and innovative business models.

Across economies of Asia and the Pacific, the proportion of the population with access to electricity exceeded 90% in 38 of the 48 economies with available data for 2017. This compares with 20 of 46 economies in 2000 (Table 1.7.1). No economy

had electricity coverage below 50% of the population in 2017, compared with 12 economies in 2000.

From 2000 to 2017, the largest gains in expanding access to electricity across the population occurred in Afghanistan (74.7 percentage points), Cambodia (72.5 percentage points), and Nepal (68.4 percentage points) as shown in Figure 1.7.1.

Figure 1.7.1: Proportion of the Population with Access to Electricity (%)

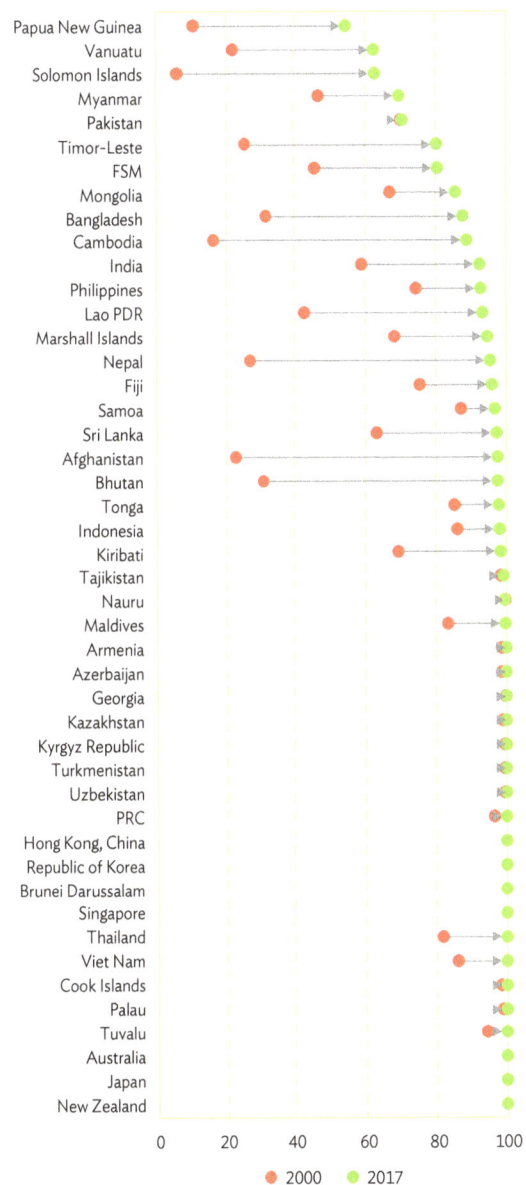

● 2000   ● 2017

FSM = Federated States of Micronesia, Lao PDR = Lao People's Democratic Republic, PRC = People's Republic of China.
Source: Table 1.7.1, Key Indicators for Asia and the Pacific 2019.

Access to clean fuels and technology has broadly risen across the region since 2000, with a handful of economies lagging behind

In 16 of the 47 regional economies with available data on clean energy in 2017, more than 90% of the population had access to clean fuels and technology for cooking, heating, or lighting (Figure 1.7.2). This compares with 9 economies in 2000.

Figure 1.7.2: Proportion of Population with Primary Reliance on Clean Fuels and Technology

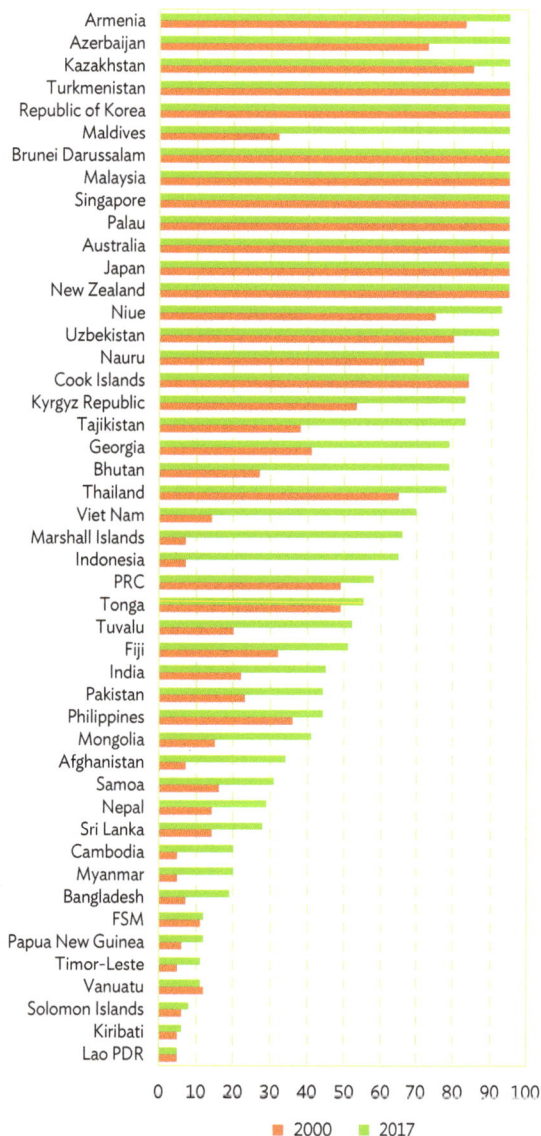

(%)

FSM = Federated States of Micronesia, Lao PDR = Lao People's Democratic Republic, PRC = People's Republic of China.
Note: Data with values greater than 95% are presented as 95% and values smaller than 5% are presented as 5%.
Source: Table 1.7.1, Key Indicators for Asia and the Pacific 2019.

From 2000 to 2017, the largest increases in the share of the population with access to clean energy occurred in Maldives (63.0 percentage points), the Marshall Islands (59.0 percentage points), and Indonesia (58.0 percentage points).

Conversely, the share of the population with access to clean energy was below 20% in 8 of the 46 reporting economies.

SDG 8. Promote sustained, inclusive, and sustainable economic growth; full and productive employment; and decent work for all

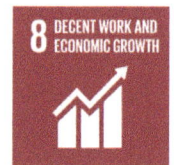

Age and gender gaps persist in job markets across Asia and the Pacific

Employment provides individuals with income and (in many cases) access to social protection coverage, unemployment benefits, pensions, and maternity leave. Yet, those in vulnerable forms of employment, such as the self-employed and contributing family workers, generally lack access to these benefits (ILO 2018).

Of the 30 economies with available data for 2017 (or another recent year), all but 1 (Kazakhstan) had a higher rate of unemployment among the population aged 15–24 years than among the population aged 25 years and older (Figure 1.8.1). Moreover, there were 13 economies with an employment gap between the two age groups that exceeded 10 percentage points. The most significant gaps were in Kiribati (33.1 percentage points), Armenia (22.7 percentage points), and Samoa (21.9 percentage points).

Among the population aged 15 years and older, there was a gender gap in unemployment in favor of males in 19 of the 34 economies with available data for 2017 (or another recent year) (Table 1.8.2). In economies where there was a gender gap in unemployment in favor of girls and women in 2017 (or another recent year), the largest gaps were in the Lao PDR (3.0 percentage points), Turkmenistan (3.0 percentage points), and Georgia (2.3 percentage points).

Closing the age and gender gaps in employment will require investments in youth education, increasing opportunities for girls and women to enroll in education and enter labor markets, promoting efficient school-to-work transition programs, and creating decent jobs (ILO 2017).

SDG 9. Build resilient infrastructure, promote inclusive and sustainable industrialization, and foster innovation

Manufacturing value added per capita increased in around 75% of economies in Asia and the Pacific since 2000, signaling progress in industrialization across most of the region.

Manufacturing value-added is used to assess an economy's level of industrialization. Its share as a percentage of gross domestic product (GDP) reflects manufacturing's significance in an economy, as the jobs created by an expanding manufacturing sector can support an economy's overall development.

From 2000 to 2018, an increase in manufacturing value-added per capita was observed in 34 of the 46 economies with available data (Figure 1.9.1). Among the developing economies, the biggest gains (in constant 2010 United States dollars) occurred in the Republic of Korea ($4,371 per capita), Singapore ($2,348), and Turkmenistan ($2,118). The largest declines occurred in Brunei Darussalam ($1,499); Hong Kong, China ($389); and Samoa ($120).

In 2018, manufacturing value-added per capita exceeded $1,000 (in constant 2010 United States dollars) in 9 developing economies, led by Singapore ($9,358), the Republic of Korea ($7,769), and Brunei Darussalam ($4,738). Conversely, manufacturing value-added per capita was below $100 in 8 economies.

Figure 1.8.1: Unemployment Rate by Age Group, 2017 or Most Recent Year Prior (%)

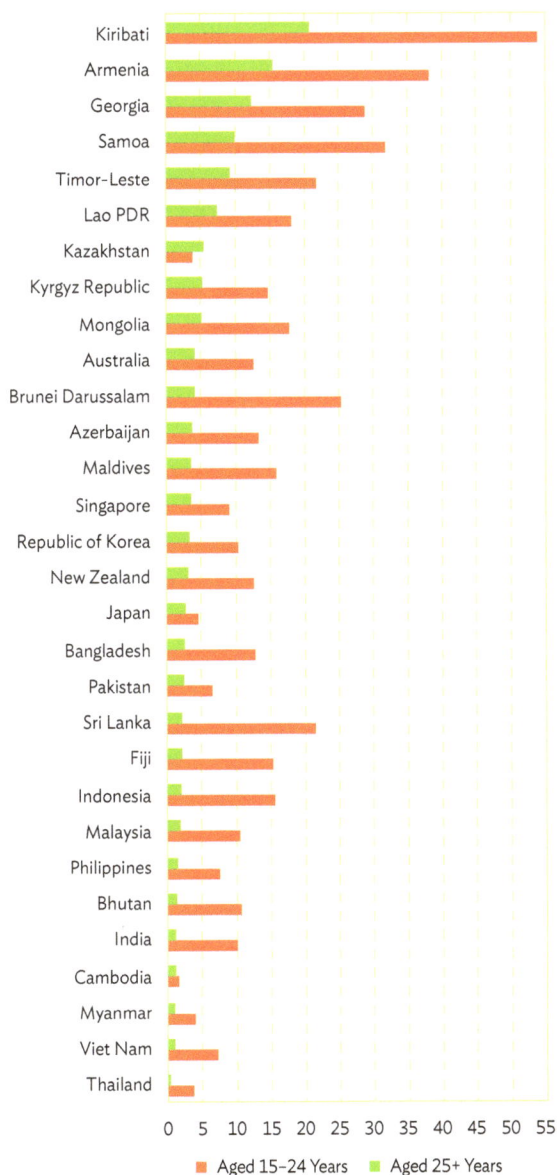

Aged 15–24 Years   Aged 25+ Years

Lao PDR = Lao People's Democratic Republic.
Note: For Fiji, Malaysia, Maldives, Singapore, and Sri Lanka, data refer to 2016; for Azerbaijan, Bhutan, and Pakistan, data refer to 2015; for Brunei Darussalam, data refers to 2014; for Kazakhstan and Timor-Leste, data refer to 2013; for Cambodia and India, data refer to 2012; for Kiribati, data refers to 2010.
Source: Table 1.8.2, Key Indicators for Asia and the Pacific 2019.

Figure 1.9.1: Manufacturing Value-Added per Capita
(constant 2010 $)

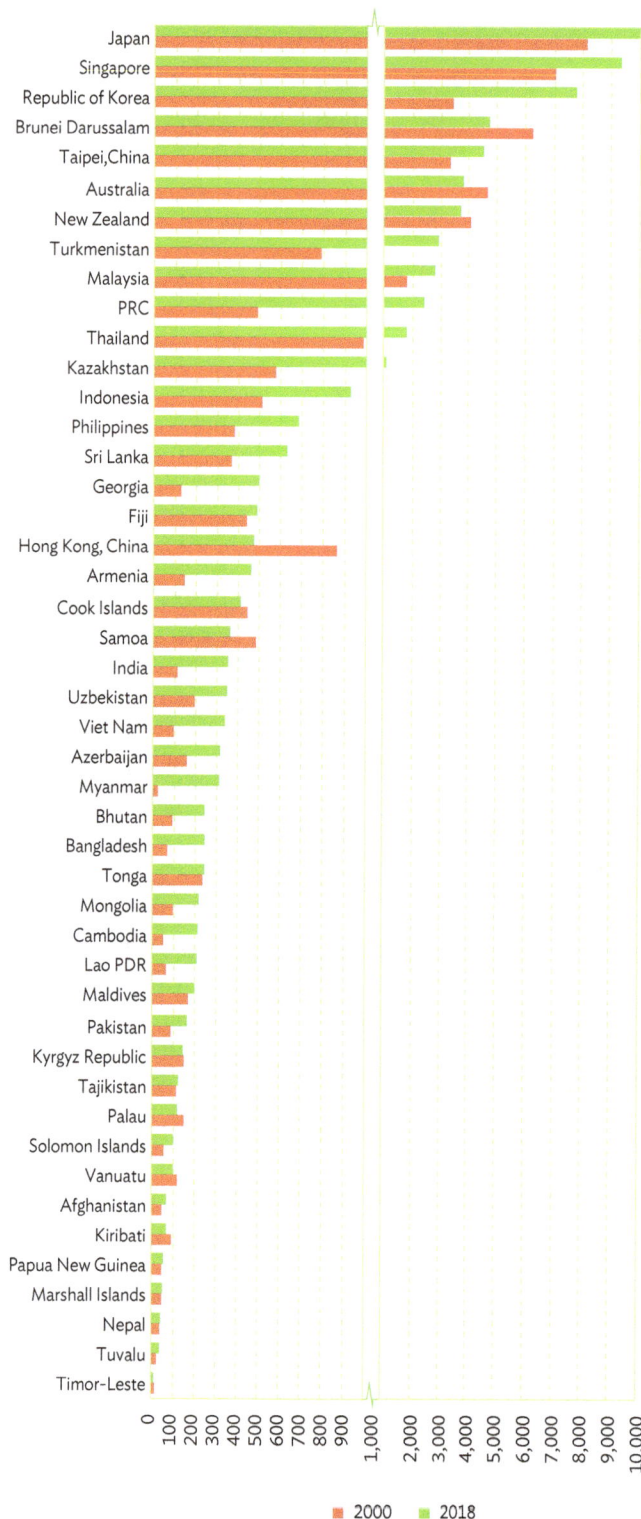

Japan
Singapore
Republic of Korea
Brunei Darussalam
Taipei,China
Australia
New Zealand
Turkmenistan
Malaysia
PRC
Thailand
Kazakhstan
Indonesia
Philippines
Sri Lanka
Georgia
Fiji
Hong Kong, China
Armenia
Cook Islands
Samoa
India
Uzbekistan
Viet Nam
Azerbaijan
Myanmar
Bhutan
Bangladesh
Tonga
Mongolia
Cambodia
Lao PDR
Maldives
Pakistan
Kyrgyz Republic
Tajikistan
Palau
Solomon Islands
Vanuatu
Afghanistan
Kiribati
Papua New Guinea
Marshall Islands
Nepal
Tuvalu
Timor-Leste

0 100 200 300 400 500 600 700 800 900 1,000 2,000 3,000 4,000 5,000 6,000 7,000 8,000 9,000 10,000

■ 2000 ■ 2018

$ = United States dollars, Lao PDR = Lao People's Democratic Republic,
PRC = People's Republic of China.
Note: For 2000, data for Taipei,China refer to 2001. Only economies with data
          for both years 2000 and 2018 are included.
Source: Table 1.9.2, Key Indicators for Asia and the Pacific 2019.

While Asia and the Pacific's aggregate carbon dioxide (CO_2) emissions have risen, CO_2 emissions per unit of manufacturing value added declined in a majority of regional economies between 2000 and 2016.

The adoption of clean and environmentally sound technologies and industrial processes promotes resource-use efficiency and reduces carbon dioxide (CO_2) emissions.

Across Asia and the Pacific, emissions—in term of kilograms (kg) of CO_2 equivalent—per unit of manufacturing value-added declined in 18 of the 30 regional economies with data available for both 2000 and 2016 (Figure 1.9.2). The biggest declines per unit of manufacturing value-added (in 2010 constant United States dollars) occurred in Uzbekistan (2.2 kg of CO_2 equivalent), Myanmar (2.0 kg), and Armenia (1.3 kg). The largest increases were in Nepal (1.4 kg of CO_2 equivalent); Hong Kong, China (1.2 kg); and Viet Nam (0.5 kg).

In 2016, the economies with the highest levels of CO_2 emissions per unit of manufacturing value-added were Nepal (2.6 kg of CO_2 equivalent), Viet Nam (2.3 kg), and Kazakhstan (2.2 kg). In 2000, the three highest emitters in terms of CO_2 equivalent per unit of manufacturing value-added were Uzbekistan (3.2 kg of CO_2 equivalent), Mongolia (2.2 kg), and Kazakhstan (2.1 kg).

SDG 10. Reduce inequality within and among countries

Household expenditure on the rise among the bottom 40% low-income sections of the population

Growth in household expenditure (or income) per capita was assessed over varying periods for each economy, usually periods of 5 or 6 years falling within 2008 and 2017.

Figure 1.9.2: Carbon Dioxide Emissions per Unit of Manufacturing Value-Added
(kg of CO_2 per constant 2010 $)

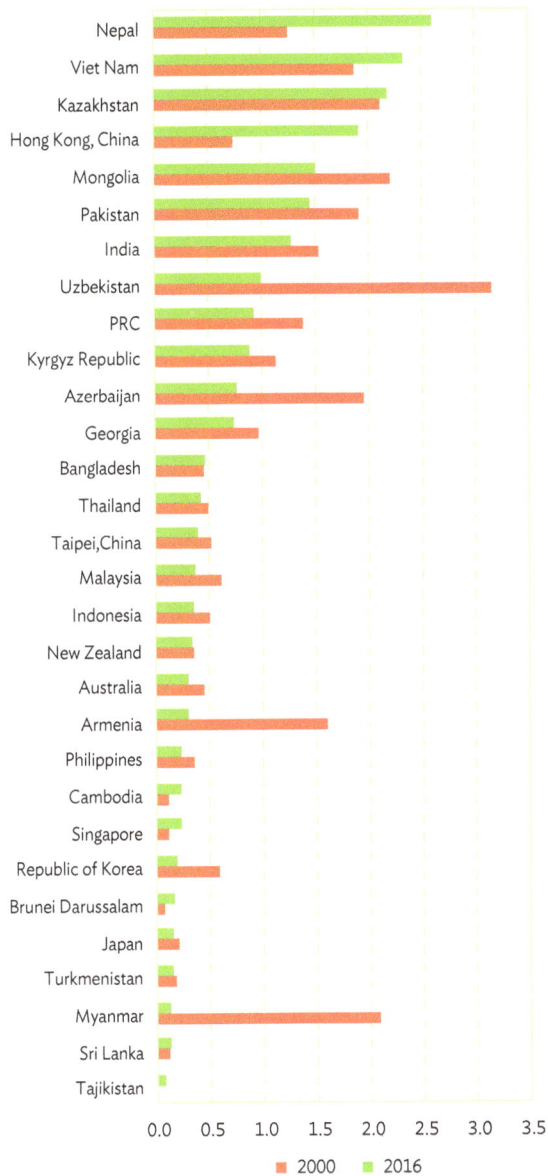

■ 2000   ■ 2016

$ = United States dollars, CO_2 = carbon dioxide, kg = kilogram,
PRC = People's Republic of China.
Note: Only economies with available data for both years 2000 and 2016 are included.
Source: Table 1.9.3, Key Indicators for Asia and the Pacific 2019.

Figure 1.10.1: Growth Rates of Household Expenditure or Income per Capita, 2009–2017
(%)

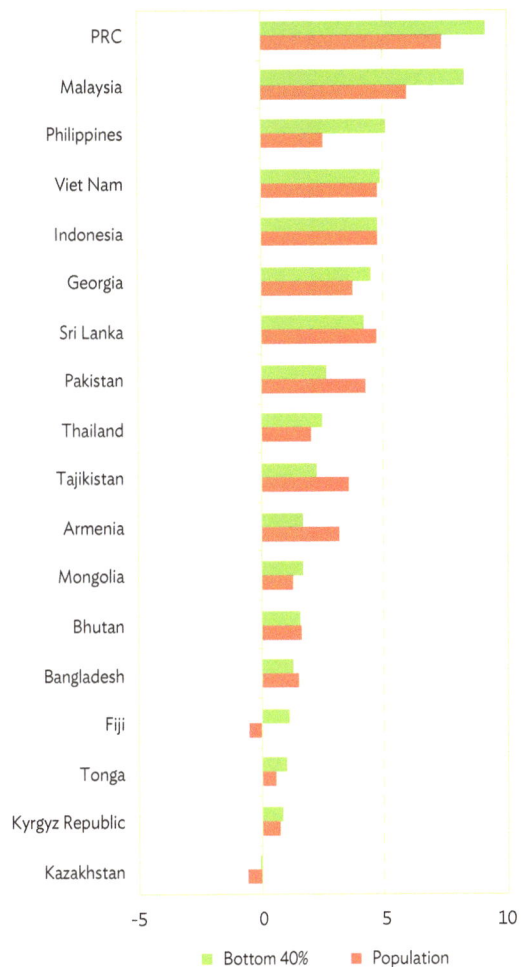

■ Bottom 40%   ■ Population

PRC = People's Republic of China.
Note: "Bottom 40%" refers to individuals within the lowest 40 percentile band in terms of income. Growth in household expenditure or income per capita is assessed over varying periods for each economy, usually periods of 5 or 6 years falling within 2009 and 2017. Growth rates refer to latest available data for over about a five-year period. Only economies with data for both the bottom 40% and the total population are included.
Source: Table 1.10.1, Key Indicators for Asia and the Pacific 2019.

Of the 18 developing economies with available data, household expenditure (or income) per capita rose for the bottom 40% of the total population in 17 economies (Figure 1.10.1). Kazakhstan was the exception, with a negligible average annual decline of 0.02%. The biggest gains during the review period were in the PRC (9.1% average annual growth), Malaysia (8.3%), and the Philippines (5.1%).

Over the review period, average annual growth rates in household expenditure (or income) per capita among the bottom 40% outpaced the annual growth rates for the total population in 11 of the 18 reporting economies. The largest increases in favor of the bottom 40% occurred in the Philippines (2.6 percentage points), Malaysia (2.4 percentage points), the PRC (1.7 percentage points), and Fiji (1.7 percentage points).

The economies in which the average annual growth rates in household expenditure (or income) per capita among the bottom 40% lagged behind the growth rates for the total population were Armenia (–1.5 percentage points), Pakistan (–1.5 percentage points), and Tajikistan (–1.3 percentage points).

SDG 11. Make cities and human settlements inclusive, safe, resilient, and sustainable

Individual economies have made major gains since 2000 in reducing the share of the urban population living in slums

Lack of access to basic services is a common constraint in informal settlements and slums, contributing to the persistence of poverty and posing a challenge for sustainable and inclusive urbanization. The UN estimates that about one-quarter of all urban residents, or 1 billion people, live in slums, with an additional 600 million living in inadequate housing (UN-Habitat 2016).

Among the 13 developing economies with data available for both 2000 (or 2005) and 2016 (or 2014), those with the highest rates of the urban population living in slums, informal settlements, or inadequate housing in 2016 were Myanmar (56.6%), Nepal (51.0%), and Bangladesh (49.4%) as shown in Figure 1.11.1.

Among the 13 reporting economies, the largest reductions in the percentage of the urban population living in slums, informal settlements, or inadequate housing over the review period were in the Lao PDR (58.5 percentage points), Viet Nam (34.4 percentage points), and Cambodia (31.2 percentage points), with an increase of 11.0 percentage points noted in Myanmar.

Figure 1.11.1: Proportion of Urban Population Living in Slums, 2000 and 2016
(%)

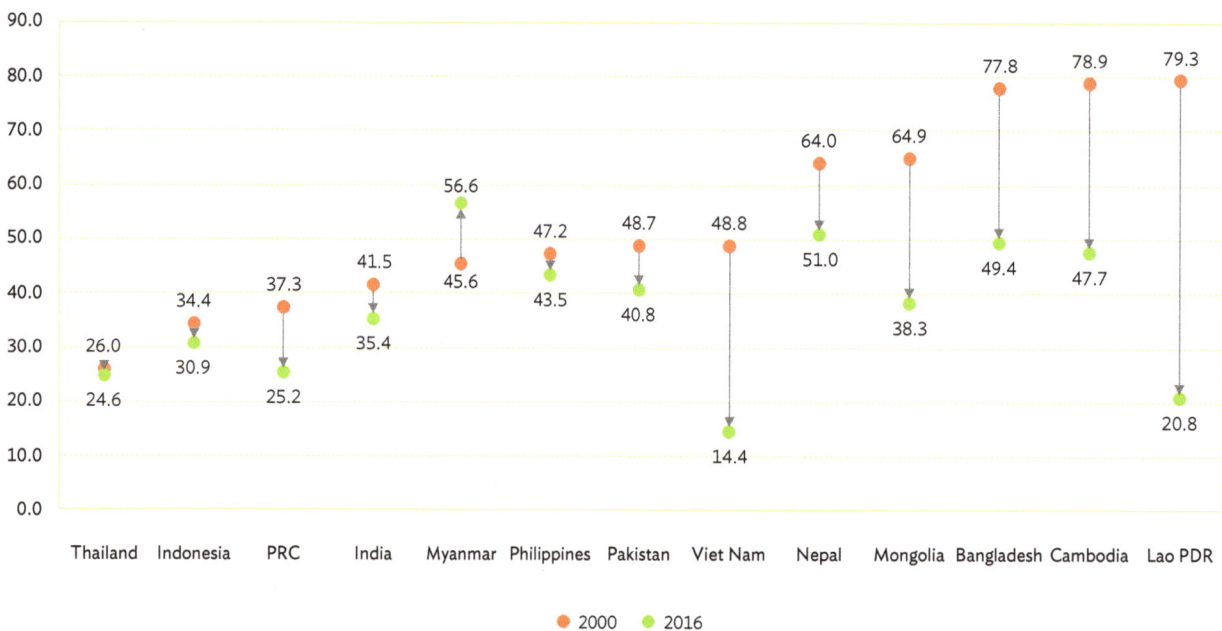

Lao PDR = Lao People's Democratic Republic, PRC = People's Republic of China.
Note: Only economies with available data for both 2000 and 2016 are included. For reference year 2000, data for Cambodia, the Lao PDR, Myanmar, and Thailand refer to 2005. For reference year 2016, data for PRC refer to 2014.
Source: Table 1.11.1, Key Indicators for Asia and the Pacific 2019.

Air pollution is dangerously high in urban areas of highly populated economies

Particulate matter with a diameter equal to or less than 2.5 microns ($PM_{2.5}$) is the most commonly used pollutant in studies on health effects caused by exposure to air pollution. The primary sources of particulate matter include the combustion of fossil fuels for industry, transportation, and power generation, as well as household activities such as heating, cooking, and lighting (WHO 2018).

In 2016, the annual mean of the daily concentrations of fine suspended particles equal to or less than $PM_{2.5}$ in urban areas exceeded 10 micrograms per cubic meter [$\mu g/m^3$]—the maximum recommended value by the World Health Organization (WHO 2018)—in all but 4 of the 43 economies in Asia and the Pacific with available data (Table 1.11.1). These 4 economies, and their respective annual means, were Brunei Darussalam (5.8 [$\mu g/m^3$]), New Zealand (5.8 $\mu g/m^3$), Australia (7.3 $\mu g/m^3$), and Maldives (7.7 $\mu g/m^3$). The regional economies with the highest annual means of daily concentrations of $PM_{2.5}$ in urban areas were Nepal (99.5 $\mu g/m^3$), India (68.0 $\mu g/m^3$), and Afghanistan (59.9 $\mu g/m^3$).

When considering the 10 largest economies in Asia and the Pacific in terms of population, 4 of the 5 most populous had the highest annual means of daily concentrations of $PM_{2.5}$ in urban areas in 2016: India (68.0 $\mu g/m^3$), Bangladesh (58.6 $\mu g/m^3$), Pakistan (56.2 $\mu g/m^3$), and the PRC (51.0 $\mu g/m^3$) as shown in Figure 1.11.2. In 9 of the region's 10 most populous economies, air pollution levels in urban areas exceeded the economy's overall level of air pollution. Myanmar was the exception, as its annual mean of daily concentrations of $PM_{2.5}$ in urban areas (34.6 $\mu g/m^3$) was just slightly below the level for all of Myanmar (34.7 $\mu g/m^3$).

Figure 1.11.2: Annual Mean Levels of Fine Particulate Matter in Cities of Asia and the Pacific's Most Populous Economies, 2016 ($\mu g/m^3$)

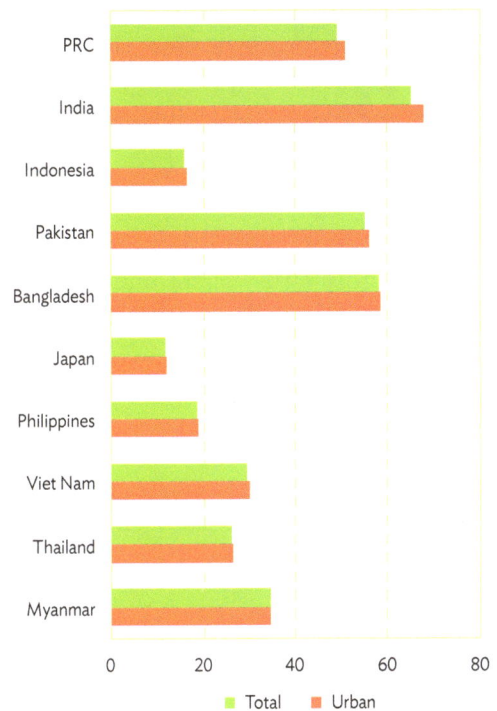

μg = microgram, m^3 = cubic meter, PRC = People's Republic of China.
Note: Fine particulate matter is classified as matter with a diameter equal to or less than 2.5 microns in diameter (PM2.5). The graph covers cities in the 10 most populous economies of Asia and the Pacific.
Sources: Table 1.11.1 and Table 2.1.1, Key Indicators for Asia and the Pacific 2019.

SDG 12. Ensure sustainable consumption and production patterns

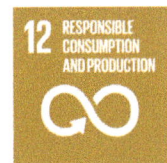

There is a strong correlation in Asia and the Pacific between an economy's material footprint per capita and GDP per capita.

Material footprint is the quantity of material extraction that is required to meet the consumption of an economy. Therefore, an economy's total material footprint is the sum of the material footprint for biomass, fossil fuels, metal ores, and nonmetal ores.

The aggregate material footprint of economies in Asia and the Pacific more than doubled from 2000 to 2017, rising from 20.7 billion metric tons (t) to 47.0 billion t (Table 1.12.1). The regional economies with the largest material footprints in 2017 were the PRC (27.7 billion t), India (6.1 billion t), and Japan (3.1 billion t).

Figure 1.12.1 shows a strong correlation between material footprint per capita and GDP per capita in 2017. The economies with the largest material footprint per capita in 2017 were the high-income economies of Singapore (73.0 t), Australia (43.0 t), and the Republic of Korea (26.4 t). The economies with the smallest material footprints on a per capita basis in 2017 were Afghanistan (1.2 t), Myanmar (1.5 t), and Bangladesh (2.4 t).

Of the 36 regional economies with data available for both 2000 and 2017, only Japan showed a reduction in its material footprint per capita, decreasing from 27.8 t in 2000 to 24.6 t in 2017.

Aggregate domestic material consumption has more than doubled in Asia and the Pacific since 2000, although about one-fifth of the region's economies have reduced their domestic material consumption on a per capita basis.

Domestic material consumption measures the total amount of material directly used in production processes within an economy.

On an aggregate basis, domestic material consumption in Asia and the Pacific more than doubled from 23.7 billion metric tons (t) in 2000 to 53.6 billion t in 2017 (Table 1.12.1). The region's most populous economy, the PRC, accounted for half the region's total in 2000 and about two-thirds of it in 2017.

On a per capita basis, 3 regional economies had a domestic material consumption over 30 t in 2017: Australia (37.9 t), Mongolia (34.5 t), and Singapore (32.6 t) as shown in Figure 1.12.2. The lowest levels of domestic material consumption per capita were in Tuvalu (1.1 t), Palau (1.2 t), and Afghanistan (1.9 t).

Figure 1.12.1: Material Footprint per Capita and Gross Domestic Product per Capita, 2017

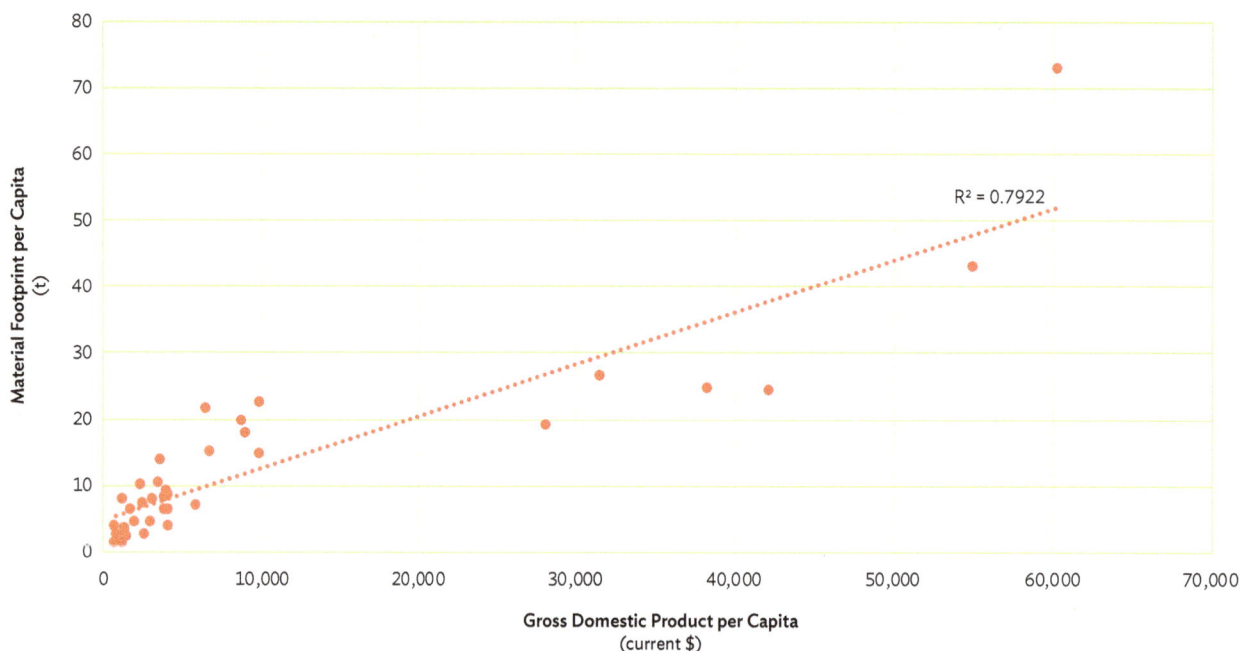

t = metric ton, $ = United States dollars.
Sources: Table 1.12.1 and Table 2.2.5, Key Indicators for Asia and the Pacific 2019.

Figure 1.12.2: Domestic Material Consumption per Capita (t)

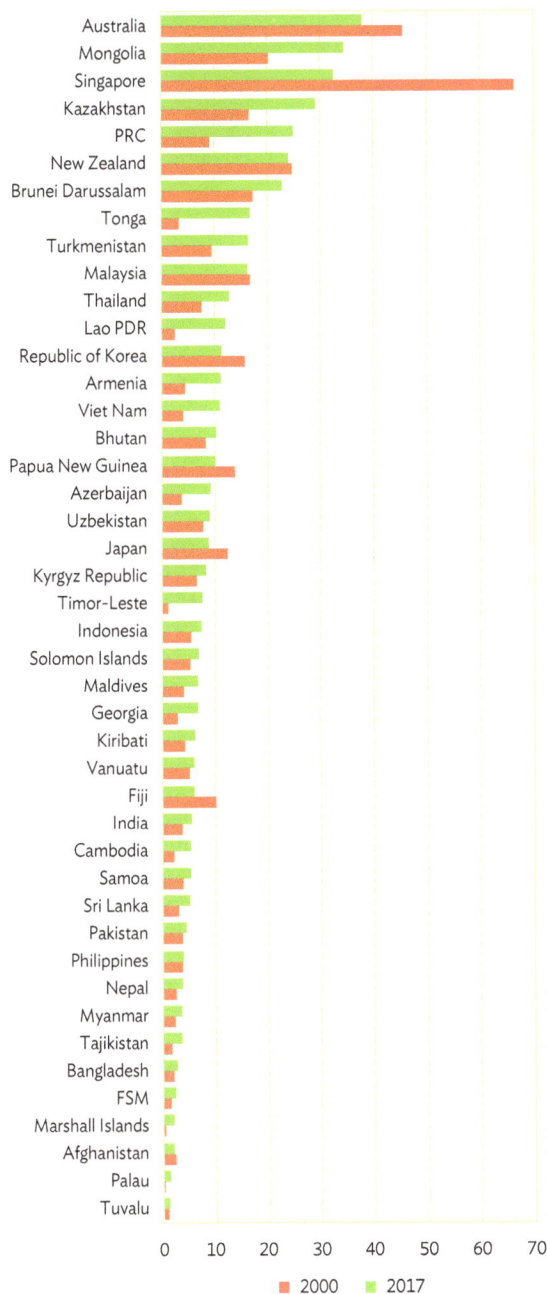

FSM = Federated States of Micronesia, Lao PDR = Lao People's Democratic Republic, PRC = People's Republic of China, t = metric ton.
Source: Table 1.12.1, Key Indicators for Asia and the Pacific 2019.

From 2000 to 2017, the largest increases in domestic material consumption per capita occurred in the PRC (15.7 t), Mongolia (14.1 t), and Tonga (13.5 t). Reductions in domestic material consumption per capita over the review period were realized in 9 of the 44 economies with available data. The economies with reductions were led by Singapore (–33.8 t), Australia (–7.6 t), and the Republic of Korea (–4.4 t).

SDG 13. Take urgent action to combat climate change and its impacts

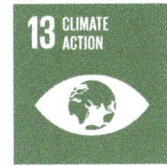

13 CLIMATE ACTION

Economies across Asia and the Pacific are developing sound disaster risk reduction strategies

The Sendai Framework for Disaster Risk Reduction, 2015–2030 recognizes the state (central government) as having primary responsibility for reducing disaster risk, while also sharing this responsibility with local governments, the private sector, and other stakeholders. The framework can help governments substantially reduce disaster risk and minimize the loss of lives, livelihoods, and health as may be experienced as a result of natural disasters.[4]

Figure 1.13.1 outlines the results of self-assessments conducted by 16 economies in Asia and the Pacific on how well their national disaster risk reduction strategies align with the Sendai Framework. The results show that, in 2018 (or the most recent year for which data are available), 3 of the 15 economies achieved a score of 1.0, indicating comprehensive alignment with the framework. These economies were Armenia, Georgia, Japan, the Republic of Korea, and Mongolia. Another 8 economies had a score of 0.5 or higher, reflecting at least a moderate alignment with the framework. Note that Malaysia's self-assessment returned a score of 0, so it is not included in Figure 1.13.1.

---

4   For more information on the Sendai Framework for Disaster Risk Reduction, go to https://www.unisdr.org/we/coordinate/sendai-framework.

Figure 1.13.1: Score Measuring Alignment of National Disaster Risk Strategy with Sendai Framework, 2018

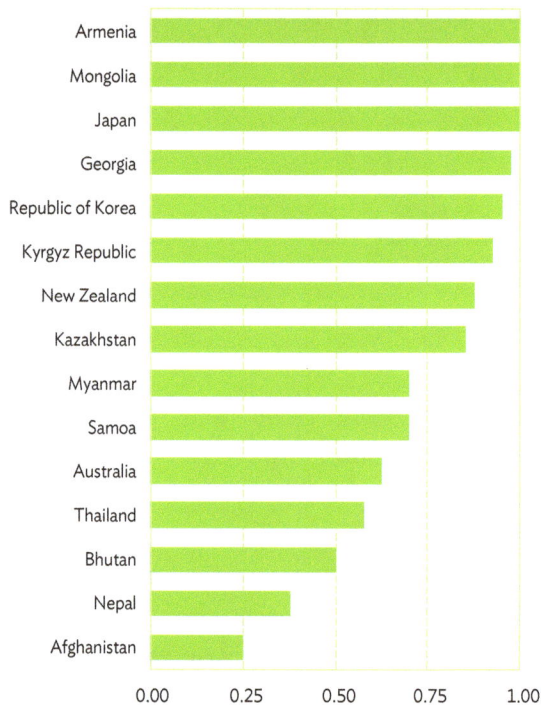

Notes: The economies shown have undertaken adoption and implementation of national disaster risk reduction strategies in line with the Sendai Framework. Scores indicate the compliance of alignment with the framework, based on self-assessments of the economy using 10 criteria for monitoring the progress of national national disaster risk reduction strategies. The score ranges are as follows: 1 = comprehensive alignment, 0.75 = substantial alignment, 0.50 = moderate alignment, 0.25 = limited alignment, 0 = no alignment. Malaysia has a score of "0" and not shown in the figure. For Afghanistan, Armenia, Mongolia, Myanmar, and the Republic of Korea, data refer to 2017.
Source: Table 1.13.1, Key Indicators for Asia and the Pacific 2019.

SDG 14. Conserve and sustainably use the oceans, seas, and marine resources for sustainable development

More than half of all reporting economies protect less than 1% of their total marine areas

About 71 percent of the Earth's surface is covered by water, and the oceans hold about 96.5% of all Earth's water (USGS 2019). As they play a critical role in our planet's overall health, our existence is threatened by the deterioration of seas and oceans as a result of overexploitation, pollution, and the impacts of climate change. SDG 14 stresses that careful environmental management is needed to curtail (and ultimately reverse) declines in biodiversity, rebuild depleted fish stocks, and reduce ocean acidification in order to ensure the long-term, sustainable use of marine resources.[5]

Some economies in Asia and the Pacific have taken bold measures to protect their marine resources. In 2018, the proportion of protected area to total marine area exceeded 80% in the Cook Islands (100.0%) and Palau (83.0%) as shown in Figure 1.14.1. The next highest proportions of protected marine resources were in Australia (40.6%), New Zealand (29.7%), and Kiribati (11.8%).

However, of the 37 regional economies with available data on marine areas in 2018, 32 had protected areas covering less than the SDG target of 10%, which is to be met in 2020. More alarmingly, 19 economies had extended protection to less than 1% of their total marine area in 2018.

---

5   For more information on SDG 14 and its associated targets, go to https://www.un.org/sustainabledevelopment/oceans/.

Figure 1.14.1: Proportion of Protected Marine Area to Total Marine Area, 2018

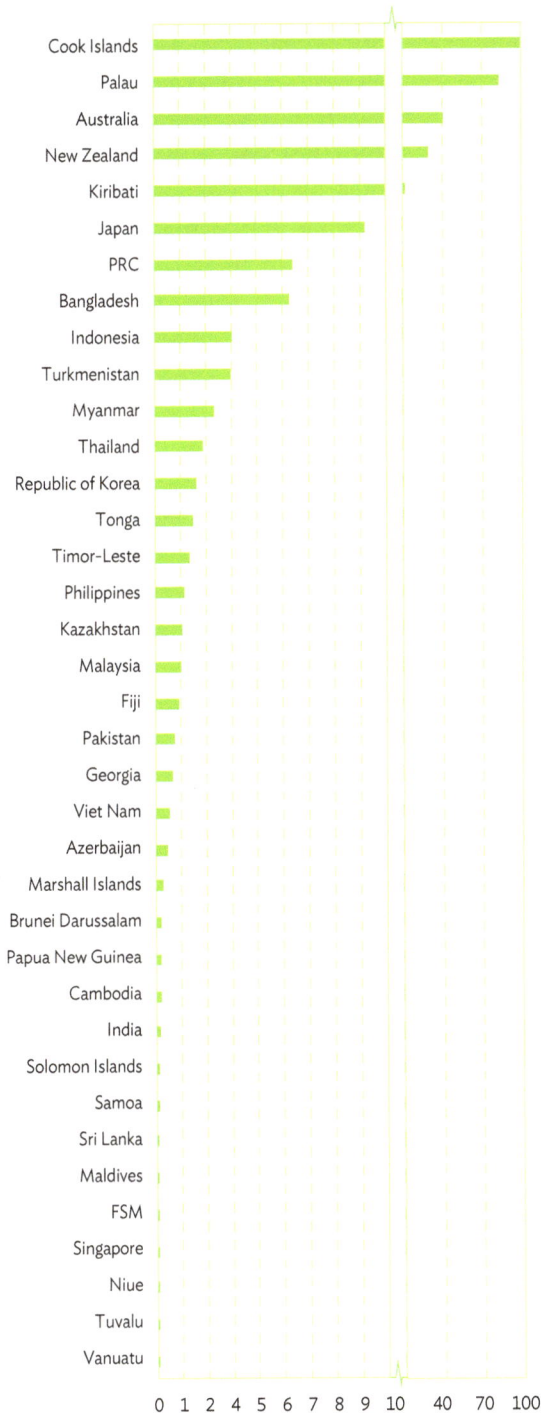

(%)

FSM = Federated States of Micronesia, PRC = People's Republic of China.
Source: Table 1.14.1, Key Indicators for Asia and the Pacific 2019.

SDG 15. Protect, restore, and promote sustainable use of terrestrial ecosystems; sustainably manage forests; combat desertification; halt and reverse land degradation; and halt biodiversity loss

15 LIFE ON LAND

Overexploitation of forest resources remains a risk for a number of regional economies

Forests cover more than 30% of the Earth's land surface. They are on the front line in the struggle against climate change—absorbing and storing massive amounts of carbon dioxide (CO_2)—and their preservation is key to protecting biodiversity.[6]

Forested areas as a proportion of an economy's total land exceeded 30% in 25 of the 46 economies of Asia and the Pacific with available data for 2016 (Figure 1.15.1). The highest proportions were in the FSM (91.9%), Palau (87.6%), and the Lao PDR (82.1%) as shown in Figure 1.15.1. Conversely, the economies with the lowest proportions of forested land to total land in 2016 were Nauru (0.0%), Kazakhstan (1.2%), and Pakistan (1.9%).

From 2000 to 2016, 17 of the 46 reporting economies experienced an increase in the proportion of forested land to total land, with the largest gains occurring in the Lao PDR (10.5 percentage points), Viet Nam (10.4 percentage points), and Bhutan (7.0 percentage points). The biggest decreases occurred in Cambodia (–12.6 percentage points), Timor-Leste (–12.1 percentage points), and Myanmar (–9.7 percentage points) (Table1.15.1).

---

6   For more information about the role of forests in the Earth's environment, go to https://www.un-redd.org/forest-facts.

Figure 1.15.1: Proportion of Forested Area to Total Land Area, 2016
(%)

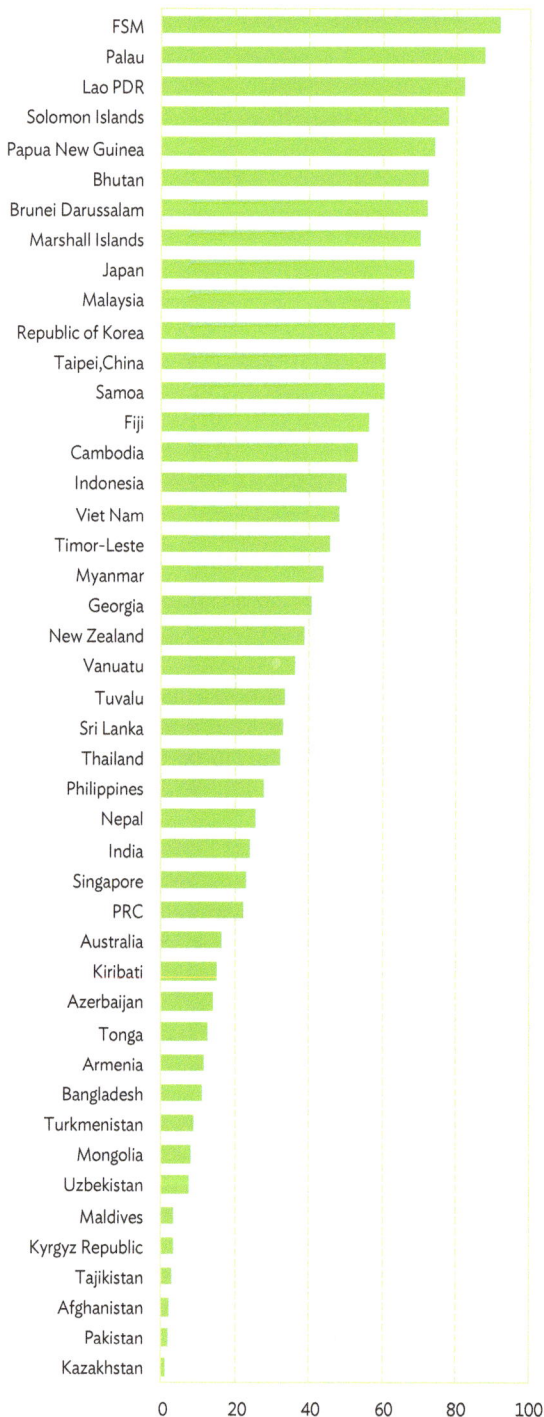

Economy	

FSM
Palau
Lao PDR
Solomon Islands
Papua New Guinea
Bhutan
Brunei Darussalam
Marshall Islands
Japan
Malaysia
Republic of Korea
Taipei,China
Samoa
Fiji
Cambodia
Indonesia
Viet Nam
Timor-Leste
Myanmar
Georgia
New Zealand
Vanuatu
Tuvalu
Sri Lanka
Thailand
Philippines
Nepal
India
Singapore
PRC
Australia
Kiribati
Azerbaijan
Tonga
Armenia
Bangladesh
Turkmenistan
Mongolia
Uzbekistan
Maldives
Kyrgyz Republic
Tajikistan
Afghanistan
Pakistan
Kazakhstan

0   20   40   60   80   100

FSM = Federated States of Micronesia, Lao PDR = Lao People's Democratic Republic, PRC = People's Republic of China.
Note: Nauru has 0 forest area and is not included in the figure. For Taipei,China, data refer to 2017.
Source: Table 1.15.1, Key Indicators for Asia and the Pacific 2019.

Extinction risks rising in almost every economy of Asia and the Pacific

The Red List Index is a composite measure representing aggregate survival probability (the inverse of extinction risk) for all birds, mammals, amphibians, corals, and cycads occurring within an economy, weighted by the fraction of each species' distribution occurring within that economy. Index values can range from 0.0 (indicating all species are categorized as "extinct") to 1.0 (indicating all species are categorized as "least concern").

In 2018, 26 of the 48 regional economies with available data garnered a score of at least 0.8 on the Red List Index, down from 37 economies in 2000 (Figure 1.15.2). The highest Red List Index scores in 2018 were recorded in the Central Western economies of Tajikistan (0.99), the Kyrgyz Republic (0.98), Turkmenistan (0.97), and Uzbekistan (0.97).

There were 8 economies that scored 0.7 or lower on the Red List Index in 2018: the FSM (0.69), India (0.68), Malaysia (0.68), Fiji (0.67), Vanuatu (0.66), the Philippines (0.64), New Zealand (0.63), and Sri Lanka (0.56).

Over the review period, all 48 reporting economies, apart from Nepal (0.82 to 0.83) and Niue (0.76 to 0.77), experienced a decline in their scores. The largest declines were recorded in Palau (0.91 to 0.73), Malaysia (0.83 to 0.68), and Sri Lanka (0.66 to 0.56).

**Figure 1.15.2: Red List Index Scores
for Select Economies of Asia and the Pacific**

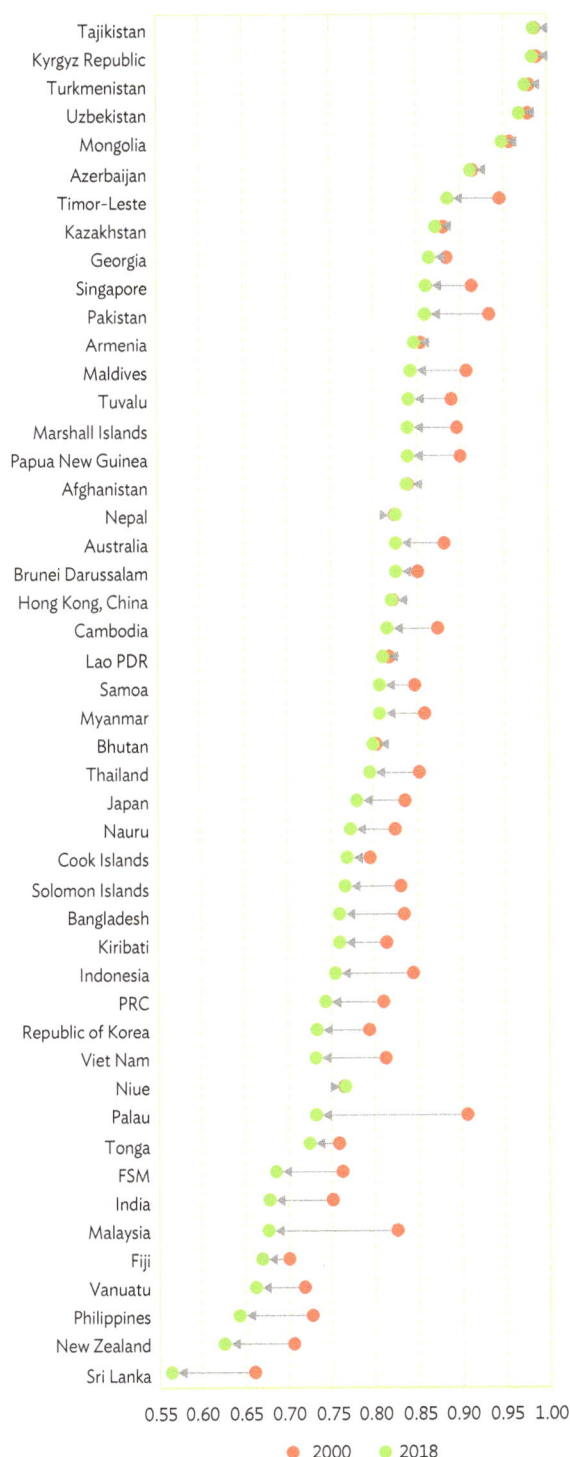

Tajikistan
Kyrgyz Republic
Turkmenistan
Uzbekistan
Mongolia
Azerbaijan
Timor-Leste
Kazakhstan
Georgia
Singapore
Pakistan
Armenia
Maldives
Tuvalu
Marshall Islands
Papua New Guinea
Afghanistan
Nepal
Australia
Brunei Darussalam
Hong Kong, China
Cambodia
Lao PDR
Samoa
Myanmar
Bhutan
Thailand
Japan
Nauru
Cook Islands
Solomon Islands
Bangladesh
Kiribati
Indonesia
PRC
Republic of Korea
Viet Nam
Niue
Palau
Tonga
FSM
India
Malaysia
Fiji
Vanuatu
Philippines
New Zealand
Sri Lanka

0.55 0.60 0.65 0.70 0.75 0.80 0.85 0.90 0.95 1.00

● 2000   ● 2018

FSM = Federated States of Micronesia, Lao PDR = Lao People's Democratic Republic,
PRC = People's Republic of China.
Note: Index values range from 0.0 (indicating all species are categorized as
           "extinct") to 1.0 (indicating all species are categorized as "least concern").
Source: Table 1.15.1, Key Indicators for Asia and the Pacific 2019.

SDG 16. Promote peaceful and inclusive societies for sustainable development; provide access to justice for all; and build effective, accountable, and inclusive institutions at all levels

Intentional homicide reduced in around 80% of Asian and Pacific economies

Effective, transparent, and accountable institutions are needed at all levels to promote peaceful and inclusive societies, including the reduction of intentional homicides.

Comparing 2000–2004 with 2011–2017, the number of victims of intentional homicide per 100,000 people fell in 29 of the 37 regional economies with available data (Figure 1.16.1). The largest declines in the intentional homicide rate occurred in Kazakhstan[7] (–10.4), Mongolia (–7.7), and Thailand (–5.0). The largest increases were in the Pacific economies of Tuvalu (18.6)[8], Kiribati (3.9), PNG (1.7), and Timor-Leste (1.6).

In 2017 (or the most recent year for which data are available), the lowest rates of intentional homicide per 100,000 people were in Japan (0.2); Singapore (0.2); and Hong Kong, China (0.3). The highest rates were in Tuvalu (18.6), PNG (10.0), and the Philippines (8.4).

---

7   Per the UN Office on Drugs and Crime, counting rules changes in the time series are not specified. The changes in methodology were not accounted
    for in the statement.
8   The population of Tuvalu in 2017 was around 11,000 people. The indicator is presented per 100,000 population. Therefore, one victim of intentional
    homicide could lead to a spike in the rate for Tuvalu.

More than 20% of firms in 19 of 32 developing member economies reported being solicited for a bribe by a public official within the most recent year for which data are available.

Corruption can be challenging to assess and quantify. As one measure, the World Bank asks firms if they have been solicited by public officials for gifts or informal payments. By doing so, the World Bank seeks to determine the bribery prevalence rate in an economy in the context of service delivery and other transactions.

Across a review period in which the most recent year of available data ranged from 2009 to 2018, the proportion of firms reporting that they had been solicited by public officials for gifts or informal payments exceeded 20% in 19 of 32 economies (Figure 1.16.2). The lowest levels of reported bribery solicitations occurred in Bhutan (0.9%), Georgia (2.2%), and the FSM (4.5%).

Figure 1.16.1: Number of Victims of Intentional Homicide per 100,000 Population

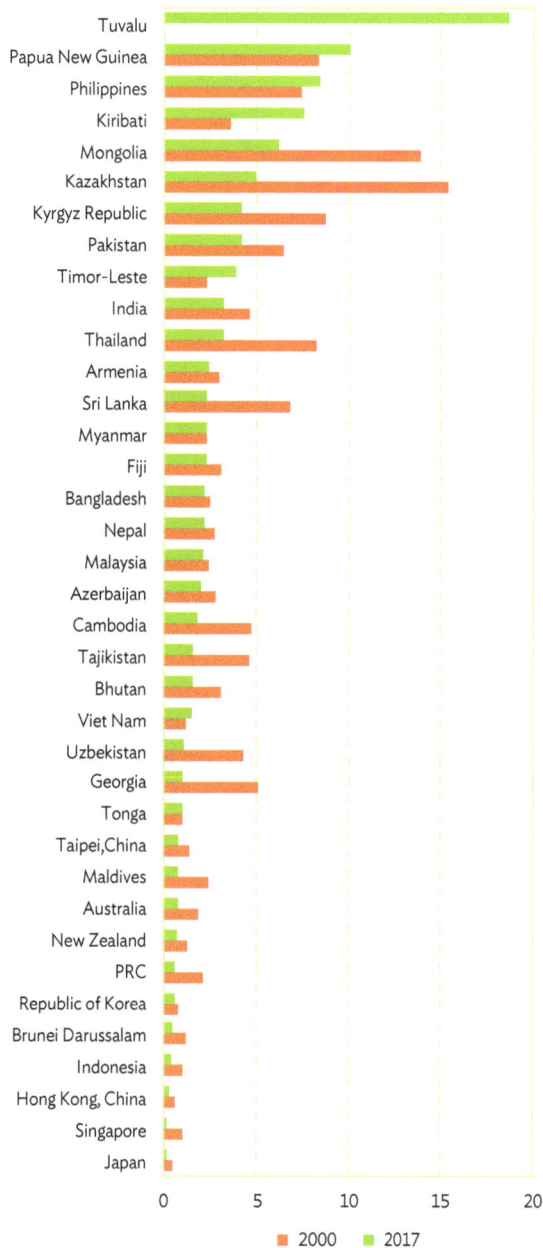

Figure 1.16.2: Proportion of Firms Experiencing at Least One Bribe Payment Request
(%)

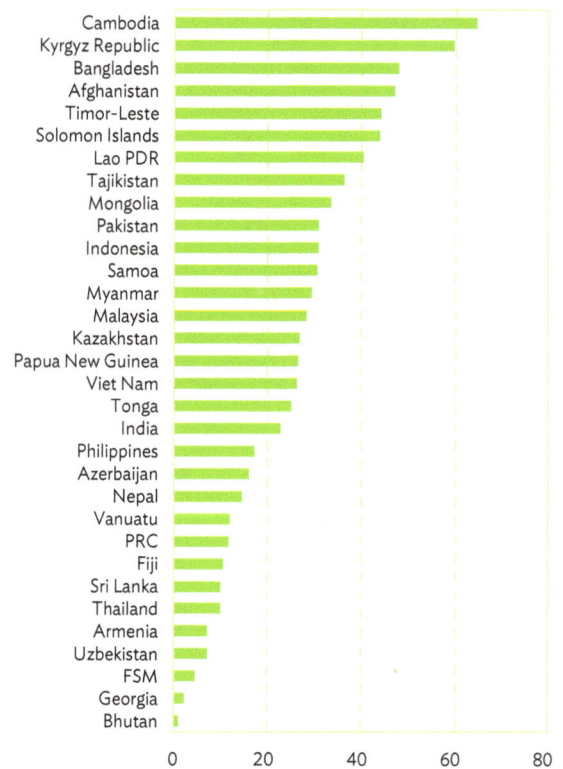

PRC = People's Republic of China.
Note: This chart includes economies with available data for both 2000 and 2017. For 2000, data included are for 2000 to 2004. For 2017, data included are for 2011 to 2017. For 2000, Tuvalu has zero recorded data for the number of victims of intentional homicide.
Source: Table 1.16.1, Key Indicators for Asia and the Pacific 2019.

FSM = Federated States of Micronesia, Lao PDR = Lao People's Democratic Republic, PRC = People's Republic of China.
Note: The percentages shown are based on economy data for the most recent year from 2009 to 2018.
Source: Table 1.16.1, Key Indicators for Asia and the Pacific 2019.

SDG 17. Strengthen the means of implementation and revitalize the Global Partnership for Sustainable Development

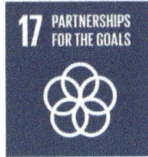

Financial and technical assistance doubled in one-third of reporting economies

Helping the most vulnerable communities requires partnerships between governments, the private sector, and civil society to efficiently mobilize and redirect public and private resources to deliver on sustainable development objectives.

When comparing annual averages of the periods 2000–2008 and 2009–2017, the value (in constant 2017 United States dollars) of financial and technical assistance increased in 35 of the 41 developing economies of Asia and the Pacific with available data (Figure 1.17.1). The largest amounts of average annual financial and technical assistance during 2009–2017 went to Afghanistan ($1,405 million), Indonesia ($1,310 million), and Pakistan ($894 million).

From 2000–2008 to 2009–2017, the value of average financial and technical assistance more than doubled in 14 of the 41 reporting economies. In absolute (constant 2017 United States dollars) terms, the largest increases occurred in Afghanistan ($843 million), Indonesia ($669 million), and Pakistan ($529 million). The largest absolute declines were in the FSM ($17 million), the Solomon Islands ($11 million), and the Marshall Islands ($9 million).

Figure 1.17.1: Dollar Value of Financial and Technical Assistance Committed to Developing Countries
(constant 2017 $ million)

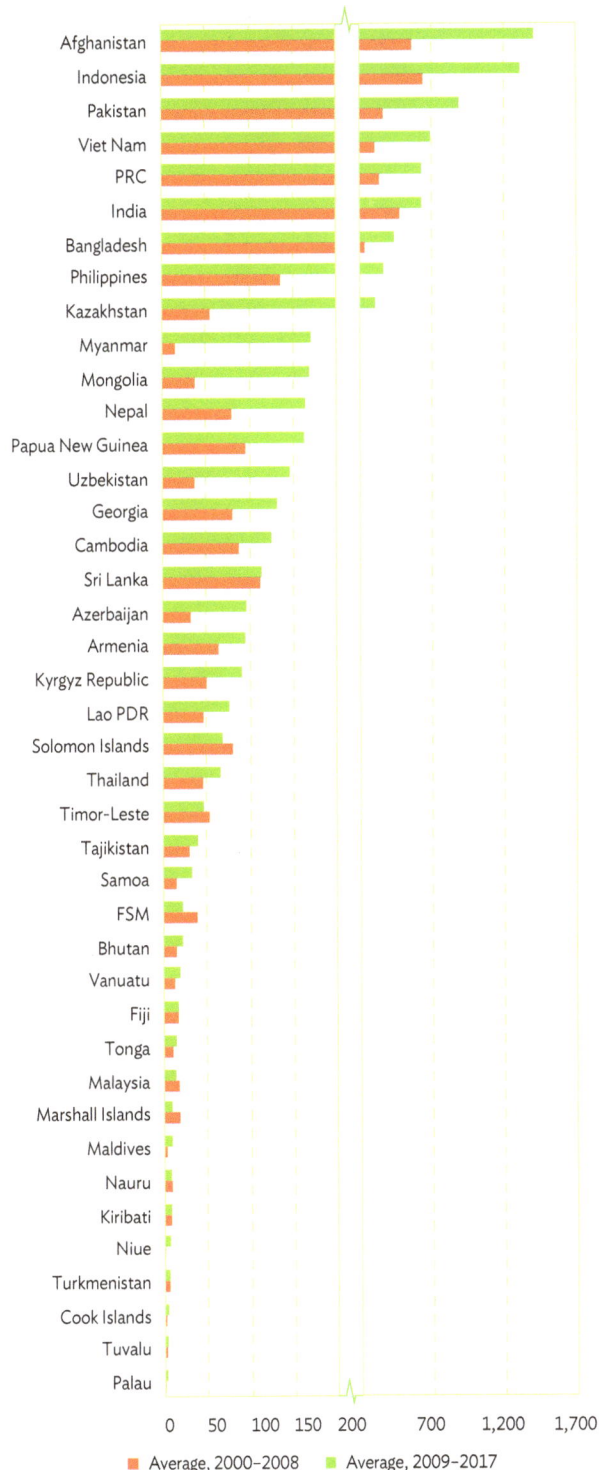

$ = United States dollars, FSM = Federated States of Micronesia, Lao PDR = Lao People's Democratic Republic, PRC = People's Republic of China.
Note: Totals include assistance through North-South, South-South, and triangular cooperation.
Source: Table 1.17.1, Key Indicators for Asia and the Pacific 2019.

High-quality statistical data is imperative for improving development effectiveness, yet the amount of all resources made available to strengthen statistical capacity increased only in about 40% of regional economies over the past decade

Financing better-quality statistical data, and increasing transparency in monitoring and accountability, will help improve development effectiveness. However, many developing economies in Asia and the Pacific need support from partners to build institutional capacity and improve data collection activities.

In 2016, the highest levels of financial resources (in current United States dollars) dedicated to statistical capacity building were observed in Cambodia ($2.22 million), Uzbekistan ($2.00 million), and Myanmar ($1.84 million) as shown in Figure 1.17.2.

From 2006 (or the earliest year for which data are available) to 2016, the dollar value of all resources made available for strengthening statistical capacity increased in only 17 of the 41 developing economies with available data. The largest increases (in current United States dollars) were in Uzbekistan ($1.73 million), the Solomon Islands ($1.28 million), and Nepal ($1.01 million).

1.17.2: Value of All Resources Made Available to Strengthen Statistical Capacity in Developing Countries
(current $)

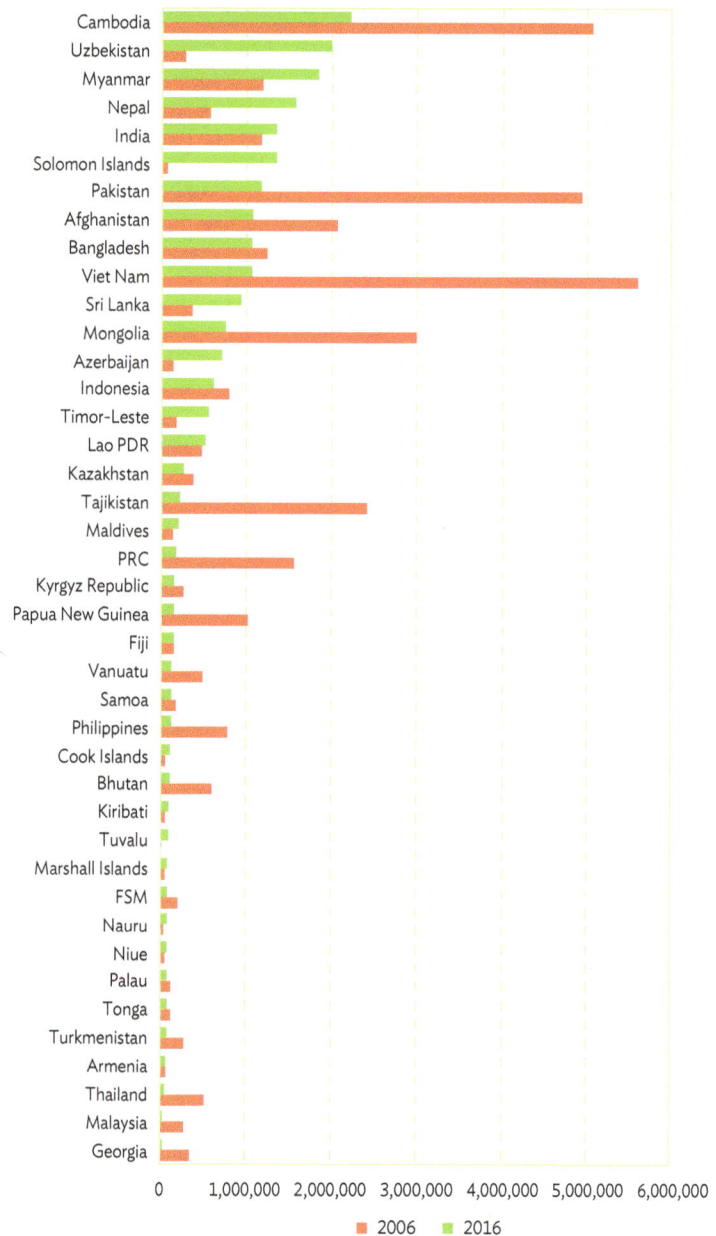

■ 2006   ■ 2016

$ = United States dollars, FSM = Federated States of Micronesia, Lao PDR = Lao People's Democratic Republic, PRC = People's Republic of China.
Note: For Kiribati, Nauru, and Tuvalu, data for 2007 are presented instead of 2006. For Niue, data for 2008 are presented instead of 2006.
Source: Table 1.17.1, Key Indicators for Asia and the Pacific 2019.

Data Gaps and Other Data-Related Issues

New and huge data demands. The approved framework for global monitoring of the SDGs consists of 232 indicators with greater disaggregation than the Millennium Development Goals and across a wider spectrum of topics. This requires national statistical systems and the global statistical system to work closely with each other to identify strategies to produce more disaggregated and better-quality data. Currently, national statistical systems, with the assistance of their governments and the development community, are working toward addressing these data demands across all tiers of the SDG indicators.

Limited data availability for SDG indicators. Since the launch of the SDGs in 2015, significant progress has been made toward closing the gap in data and their timely availability. However, there is scope for further improvement. An assessment undertaken by ADB and the United Nations Economic and Social Commission for Asia and the Pacific (UNESCAP) on the extent of data availability for the SDG indicators across Asia and the Pacific revealed that only 52% of the SDG indicators had some data (ADB and UNESCAP 2017). Moreover, an assessment made by UNESCAP revealed that 11% of Tier I indicators, 34% of Tier II indicators, and 93% of Tier III indicators do not have any data available. Only 26% of all SDG indicators are amenable to trend analysis at the regional level, with two or more data points available for these indicators for 50% or more economies in Asia and the Pacific.

There may be disparities in data availability for SDG indicators across economic, social, and environmental dimensions as national statistics offices prioritize data production on economic indicators. Further, SDG indicators with social dimensions that overlap with indicators for the Millennium Development Goals would be expected to have relatively good data availability. Most national statistics offices across Asia and the Pacific conduct population and housing censuses every decade, and

such sources provide baseline data for socioeconomic information requirements, including SDG indicators with economic and social dimensions. Aside from censuses, data (and updates) on SDG indicators are sourced from household surveys—such as labor force surveys, household income and expenditure surveys, demographic and health surveys, establishment surveys, and agriculture surveys—as well as from administrative reporting systems, but the frequency of data on SDG indicators would depend on the regularity of these data collection activities.

Gaps in data granularity. Since the principle of the SDGs is to leave no one behind, many of the SDG indicators require disaggregation by location, sex, gender, age, income, ethnicity, migration status, disability status, and other relevant dimensions. Granular data can illustrate disparities within and across economies. However, the extent to which specific groups are disproportionately at risk—for example, to lack of housing and security of tenure in slums—is currently difficult to decipher given the lack of data disaggregation and interlinkages across indicators. Sex disaggregations, even for basic indicators such as extreme poverty rates based on the $1.90 a day (at 2011 purchasing power parity) level, are not currently available. Similarly, poverty numbers are currently unavailable for vulnerable groups, such as persons with disabilities or indigenous peoples, since the sample surveys that form the basis for poverty calculations are only designed to obtain an overall picture of welfare conditions. To obtain poverty data for groups that have a small share of the total population, investments in population registers and/or special surveys need to be made.

With the growing use of information and communication technology, innovative data sources such as big data and crowdsourced data can potentially address gaps in data granularity in monitoring the SDGs. Unlike censuses, sample surveys, and administrative reporting systems (all of which have well-defined target populations), some types of big data may not represent underlying populations of interest. Careful attention is needed when complementing surveys and other conventional data sources with big data to ensure that reliable statistical inferences can be made (Cox, Kartsonaki, and Keogh 2018).

Lack of data comparability. SDG indicators, such as the proportion of the urban population living in slums or the proportion of the population with access to safely managed sanitation services, require data on housing conditions that may not be fully comparable across economies due to differences in definitions. Comparisons across economies are likewise difficult for urban-rural disaggregation of SDG indicators due to variations in the definition of "urban" and "rural" across time and economies.

Sparse data and irregular frequency. Indicators that provide a useful description of income inequality, such as the growth in household income of those in the bottom 40th percentile of income distribution in relation to national averages, are only currently available for a few economies. Indicators on material footprint and domestic material consumption, which are widely accepted as strategic sustainability indicators of production and consumption, are not produced annually. Data to monitor progress made toward addressing climate change are sparse.

Frequency is also of concern. For example, data on the coverage of protected areas in relation to total marine areas are not collected regularly, alongside other challenges such as the difficulty in determining whether a site conforms to the definition of a protected area. Further, some protected areas are not assigned management categories. While access to remote-sensing data has improved in recent years, these data have their own limitations in assessing land use. For example, forest regrowth cannot easily be detected with remote-sensing techniques.

Data limitations. While the indicators included in the framework for monitoring the SDGs are carefully chosen, they may have some limitations. The labor share in GDP, for instance, does not include the income of the self-employed, and yet a sizeable proportion of the employed population in developing Asia is made up of people who are self-employed. Current measures of poverty used by economies are largely based on income or consumption data, while the SDG indicators include a multidimensional poverty measure, which has yet to be tested on a wider scale.

Cities face many challenges in relation to pollution, traffic, and inadequate housing for the poor, and these challenges are further fueled by migration and population growth, changes in family structures, inequalities of opportunity for excluded groups, and rising insecurity. The interconnectedness of these issues is not easy to explore using currently available data.

With regard to the Red List Index, since the composite index is aggregated across multiple taxonomic groups, it can be updated annually, but the index does not adequately capture the deteriorating status of common species that are abundant and widespread although declining gradually. Other indicators for monitoring many targets under SDG 15 are also sparsely available. The absence of a framework for monitoring terrestrial ecosystems, low data availability, and the lack of good-quality data all have ecological implications and these issues must be carefully addressed.

Measurement errors. The quality of data for all the SDG indicators needs to be considered when uncovering trends and patterns, as data are subject to measurement issues. Farmer self-reports of land area and production are known to have significant biases (Dillon and Rao 2018). The calculation of mortality rates in children under the age of 5 years requires complete counts of live births and child deaths by a precise age, which are not always available due to lacking civil registration systems in some developing economies of Asia and the Pacific. Maternal deaths are likewise not always accounted for given incomplete or inaccurate records on causes of death. The measurement of quality education is a challenge given the lack of standard definitions for minimum competency. Anthropometric measures of malnutrition (including stunted heights) are subject to measurement errors and issues around reference standards (i.e., local versus international standards). Access to safely managed drinking water services, access to safely managed sanitation, and information on hygiene crucially depend on more and better data, particularly administrative data sources (WHO and UNICEF 2017).

As far as international support for statistics development is concerned, full coverage of all statistical capacity development programs cannot be guaranteed in the data compiled by PARIS21 for measuring the dollar-value of such support. Double counting of projects may happen. The data may also be inflated by including project totals for multisector projects. Further, donor-side commitments do not necessarily translate to actual disbursements to the economies slated for official development assistance.

Reliability of data on SDG indicators depends on the quality of the underlying data sources. Economies need to increase investment, look for innovative data sources, and form strategic partnerships with a range of stakeholders to ensure that data quality, comparability, measurement, and timeliness can be enhanced. The result will be good development data that can be used for evidence-based policymaking, which will in turn translate into better outcomes in sustainable development.

References

Asian Development Bank (ADB) and the United Nations Economic and Social Commission for Asia and the Pacific (UNESCAP). 2017. *Asia-Pacific Sustainable Development Goals Outlook.* http://sdgasiapacific.net/download/AP_SDG_Outlook.pdf.

ADB and United Nations (UN) Women. 2018. *Gender Equality and the Sustainable Development Goals in Asia and the Pacific: Baseline and Pathways for Transformative Change by 2030.* Bangkok.

D.R. Cox, C. Kartsonaki, and R. H.Keogh. 2018. Big Data: Some Statistical Issues. *Statistics & Probability Letters* Volume 136, May 2018, pp. 111–115.

A. Dillon and L.N. Rao. 2018. Land Measurement Bias: Comparisons from Global Positioning System, Self-Reports, and Satellite Data. Asian Development Bank, Economics Working Paper Series. No. 540.

European Union and United Nations Human Settlements Programme (UN-Habitat). 2016. *The State of European Cities: Cities Leading the Way to a Better Future.* Brussels, Belgium: European Commission.

Food and Agriculture Organization of the United Nations (FAO). 2018. *The State of Food Security.* Rome.

International Labour Organization (ILO). 2017. *Global Employment Trends for Youth 2017: Paths To a Better Working Future.* Geneva.

International Labour Organization (ILO). 2018. *World Employment and Social Outlook: Trends 2018.* Geneva, Switzerland: ILO.

N.M. Nour. 2009. Child Marriage: A Silent Health and Human Rights. *Reviews in Obstetrics & Gynecology.* 2 (1). pp. 51–56.

Secretariat of the Partnership in Statistics for Development in the 21st Century (PARIS21). 2017. Partner Report on Support to Statistics PRESS 2017. Paris, France: PARIS21.

United Nations Statistical Commission (UNSC). 2017. *Cape Town Global Action Plan for Sustainable Development Data.* New York. https://unstats.un.org/sdgs/hlg/Cape_Town_Global_Action_Plan_for_Sustainable_Development_Data.pdf.

United States Geological Survey (USGS). 2019. *How Much Water is There on Earth?.* Reston, Virginia. https://www.usgs.gov/special-topic/water-science-school/science/how-much-water-there-earth?qt-science_center_objects=0#qt-science_center_objects.

World Health Organization (WHO) and United Nations Children's Fund (UNICEF). 2017. *Progress on Drinking Water, Sanitation and Hygiene: 2017 Update and SDG Baselines.* Geneva.

World Health Organization (WHO). 2018. Ambient (Outdoor) Air Quality and Health. Geneva. https://www.who.int/news-room/fact-sheets/detail/ambient-(outdoor)-air-quality-and-health.

Goal 1. End poverty in all its forms everywhere

Table 1.1.1: Selected Indicators for Sustainable Development Goal 1—No Poverty

ADB Regional Member	Target 1.1: By 2030, eradicate extreme poverty for all people everywhere, measured as people living below the international poverty line of $1.90 a day (2011 PPP)							
	1.1.1a: Proportion of Population Living below the $1.90 a Day (2011 PPP) Poverty Line[a,b] (%)				1.1.1b: Proportion of Employed Population Living below the International Poverty Line, by Age Group and Sex[b,c] (%)			
					2018			
					Age Group			
					15+			15–24	25+
	2000		2017		Total	Female	Male		
Developing ADB Member Economies									
Central and West Asia									
Afghanistan	...		...		37.6	39.99	36.3	39.2	36.9
Armenia	19.3	(2001)	1.4		0.4	0.5	0.4	0.6	0.4
Azerbaijan[d]	2.7	(2001)	...		0.0	0.0	0.0	0.0	0.0
Georgia	19.4		5.0		2.2	2.0	2.4	2.9	2.2
Kazakhstan	10.3	(2001)	0.0		0.0	0.0	0.0	0.0	0.0
Kyrgyz Republic	42.1		1.5		0.3	0.2	0.4	0.3	0.3
Pakistan	28.6	(2001)	3.9	(2015)	2.8	3.4	2.7	3.1	2.8
Tajikistan	30.8	(2003)	4.8	(2015)	3.8	3.6	3.9	3.6	3.9
Turkmenistan	...		...		13.7	10.6	16.1	15.6	13.4
Uzbekistan[d]	62.0		...		27.1	23.5	29.7	27.7	27.0
East Asia									
China, People's Republic of	31.7	(2002)	0.7	(2015)	0.6	0.6	0.6	0.8	0.6
Hong Kong, China[f]	...		...		–	–	–	–	–
Korea, Republic of[f]	0.2	(2006)	0.2	(2012)	–	–	–	–	–
Mongolia	9.7	(2002)	0.6	(2016)	0.1	0.1	0.1	0.2	0.1
Taipei,China	...		...		0.0	0.0	0.0	0.1	0.0
South Asia									
Bangladesh	34.8		14.8	(2016)	10.4	11.9	9.8	11.8	10.1
Bhutan	17.6	(2003)	1.5		1.6	2.0	1.3	2.8	1.4
India	38.2	(2004)	21.2	(2011)	13.4	15.2	12.9	17.4	12.8
Maldives	10.0	(2002)	7.3	(2009)	2.7	3.6	2.4	3.6	2.6
Nepal	46.1	(2003)	15.0	(2010)	7.2	7.2	7.2	7.2	7.2
Sri Lanka	8.3	(2002)	0.8	(2016)	0.2	0.1	0.2	0.2	0.1
Southeast Asia									
Brunei Darussalam	...		...		–	–	–	–	–
Cambodia	...		...		20.3	20.3	20.3	23.4	19.4
Indonesia	39.3		5.7		5.2	5.2	5.2	5.3	5.1
Lao People's Democratic Republic	33.8	(2002)	22.7	(2012)	13.1	12.3	13.8	17.8	11.7
Malaysia	0.4	(2004)	0.0	(2015)	0.0	0.0	0.0	0.0	0.0
Myanmar	...		6.2	(2015)	3.3	3.6	3.2	4.2	3.1
Philippines	14.5		7.8	(2015)	4.1	3.3	4.5	5.1	3.8
Singapore	...		...		–	–	–	–	–
Thailand	2.5		0.0		0.0	0.0	0.0	0.0	0.0
Viet Nam	38.0	(2002)	2.0	(2016)	1.6	1.7	1.5	3.1	1.4
The Pacific									
Cook Islands	...		...		...	...	...	...	...
Fiji	4.9	(2002)	1.4	(2013)	0.2	0.3	0.2	0.3	0.2
Kiribati	12.9	(2006)	...		...	...	...	...	...
Marshall Islands	...		...		...	...	...	...	...
Micronesia, Federated States of	8.1	(2005)	15.4	(2013)	...	...	...	...	...
Nauru	...		...		...	...	...	...	...
Niue	...		...		...	...	...	...	...
Palau	...		...		...	...	...	...	...
Papua New Guinea	...		38.0	(2009)	26.3	28.1	24.6	30.9	25.0
Samoa	2.0	(2002)	1.1	(2013)	...	...	...	...	...
Solomon Islands	45.6	(2005)	25.1	(2013)	20.6	20.8	20.5	25.0	19.0
Timor-Leste	46.0	(2001)	30.7	(2014)	25.2	24.6	25.4	31.0	24.3
Tonga	2.8	(2001)	1.0	(2015)	...	...	...	...	...
Tuvalu	...		3.3	(2010)	...	...	...	...	...
Vanuatu	...		13.1	(2010)	...	...	...	...	...
Developed ADB Member Economies									
Australia	...		...		...	...	...	...	...
Japan	...		...		...	...	...	...	...
New Zealand	...		...		...	...	...	...	...

continued on next page

Table 1.1.1: Selected Indicators for Sustainable Development Goal 1—No Poverty (continued)

ADB Regional Member	Target 1.2: By 2030, reduce at least by half the proportion of men, women, and children of all ages living in poverty in all its dimensions according to national definitions					
	1.2.1: Proportion of Population Living below the National Poverty Line, by Urban–Rural Location[a] (%)					
	2000			2017		
	Total	Urban	Rural	Total	Urban	Rural
Developing ADB Member Economies						
Central and West Asia						
Afghanistan	33.7 (2007)	25.7 (2007)	35.7 (2007)	54.5 (2016)	41.6 (2016)	58.6 (2016)
Armenia	53.5 (2004)	...	...	25.7	25.0	26.8
Azerbaijan[d]	49.0 (2001)	...	...	5.4	...	...
Georgia	34.3 [e] (2004)	34.4 [e] (2004)	34.1 [e] (2004)	20.1 [e] (2018)	18.0 [e] (2018)	23.1 [e] (2018)
Kazakhstan	46.7 (2001)	36.0 (2001)	59.4 (2001)	4.3 (2018)	...	...
Kyrgyz Republic	62.6	53.3	67.6	22.4 (2018)	...	...
Pakistan	64.3 (2001)	50.0 (2001)	70.2 (2001)	24.3 * (2015)	12.5 * (2015)	30.7 * (2015)
Tajikistan	72.4 (2003)	68.8 (2003)	73.8 (2003)	29.5	...	...
Turkmenistan	...	...	...	...	...	...
Uzbekistan[d]	...	...	...	11.4 (2018)	...	...
East Asia						
China, People's Republic of	...	...	49.8	...	...	3.1
Hong Kong, China[f]	...	...	...	14.7	...	...
Korea, Republic of[f]	...	...	...	17.4	...	...
Mongolia	36.1 (2003)	30.3 (2003)	43.4 (2003)	28.4 (2018)	27.2 (2018)	30.8 (2018)
Taipei,China	0.7 [g]	...	...	1.4 [g]	...	...
South Asia						
Bangladesh	48.9	35.2	52.3	21.8 * (2018)		
Bhutan	23.2 (2007)	1.7 (2007)	30.9 (2007)	8.2	0.8	11.9
India	37.2 [h] (2004)	25.7 [h] (2004)	41.8 [h] (2004)	21.9 [h] (2011)	13.7 [h] (2011)	25.7 [h] (2011)
Maldives	21.0 (2002)	...	...	8.2 [i] (2016)	...	...
Nepal	30.9 (2003)	9.6 (2003)	34.6 (2003)	25.2 (2010)	15.5 (2010)	27.4 (2010)
Sri Lanka	22.7 (2002)	7.9 (2002)	24.7 (2002)	4.1 (2016)	1.9 (2016)	4.3 (2016)
Southeast Asia						
Brunei Darussalam	...	...	...	...	...	...
Cambodia	47.8 (2007)	...	53.2 (2007)	12.9 (2018)	...	14.0 (2018)
Indonesia	19.1 [j]	14.6 [j]	22.4 [j]	9.4 [k] (2019)	6.7 [k] (2019)	12.9 [k] (2019)
Lao People's Democratic Republic	33.5 (2002)	19.7 (2002)	37.6 (2002)	23.2 (2012)	10.0 (2012)	28.6 (2012)
Malaysia	5.1 (2002)	2.0 (2002)	11.4 (2002)	0.4 (2016)	0.2 (2016)	1.0 (2016)
Myanmar	48.2 (2005)	32.2 (2005)	53.9 (2005)	24.8	11.3	30.2
Philippines	26.6 (2006)	...	...	21.6 (2015)	...	...
Singapore	...	...	...	...	...	...
Thailand	42.3	22.2	51.4	7.9	...	...
Viet Nam	28.9 (2002)	6.6 (2002)	35.6 (2002)	5.8 (2016)	2.0 (2016)	7.5 (2016)
The Pacific						
Cook Islands	28.4 [l] (2006)	...	...	...	...	...
Fiji	35.0 [l] (2002)	28.0 [l] (2002)	40.0 [l] (2002)	28.1 [l] (2013)	19.8 [l] (2013)	36.7 [l] (2013)
Kiribati	21.8 [l] (2006)	...	...	...	...	...
Marshall Islands	52.7 [l] (2002)	...	...	...	...	...
Micronesia, Federated States of	31.4 [l] (2005)	...	...	41.2 [l] (2013)	...	...
Nauru	25.1 [l] (2006)	...	...	24.0 [l] (2013)	...	...
Niue	13.0 [l] (2002)	...	...	...	...	...
Palau	24.9 [l] (2006)	...	...	...	...	...
Papua New Guinea	...	...	...	37.5 *	...	...
Samoa	22.9 [l] (2002)	...	...	18.8 [l] (2013)	...	...
Solomon Islands	23.0 [m] (2005)	...	...	12.7 [m] (2012)	9.1 [m] (2012)	13.6 [m] (2012)
Timor-Leste	50.3 (2007)	37.7 (2007)	54.8 (2007)	41.8 (2014)	28.3 (2014)	47.1 (2014)
Tonga	16.2 [l] (2001)	...	...	22.1 [l],* (2015)	...	...
Tuvalu	21.2 [l] (2004)	...	...	26.3 [l] (2010)	24.8 [l] (2010)	27.5 [l] (2010)
Vanuatu	13.0 [l] (2006)	...	11.5 (2006)	12.7 [l] (2010)	...	10.0 [l] (2010)
Developed ADB Member Economies						
Australia	...	...	...	...	...	...
Japan	...	...	...	...	...	...
New Zealand	...	...	...	...	...	...

... = data not available, * = provisional/preliminary/estimate/budget figure, 0.0 = magnitude is less than half of unit employed or true zero, ADB = Asian Development Bank, PPP = purchasing power parity.

a   For indicator 1.1.1a and indicator 1.2.1, the year indicated in the table refers to the year when the household survey data were collected. For economies in which the household survey data collection period bridged 2 calendar years, the table reports the first year.

b   For indicator 1.1.1a, data are consumption-based, except for Malaysia, where data are income-based. For indicator 1.1.1a and indicator 1.1.1b, the estimates are based on the international poverty line of $1.90 a day (2011 PPP).

c   Data are taken from International Labour Organization modelled estimates and projections.

d   For Indicator 1.1.1a, the latest available estimate for Azerbaijan is for 2005: 0.0%. For Uzbekistan, the latest available estimate is for 2003: 62.1%.

e   Refers to absolute poverty or the share of the population under the absolute poverty line.

f   For indicator 1.2.1, the earliest available estimate for Hong Kong, China is for 2009: 16.0%. For the Republic of Korea, the earliest available estimate is for 2012: 18.6%. For Hong Kong, China, data refer to the poverty rate after policy intervention (recurrent cash). For the Republic of Korea, data refer to the relative poverty rate.

g   Refers to the percentage of the low-income population to the total population.

h   Based on Tendulkar methodology, using mixed reference period.

i   Based on half the median of total consumption expenditure equivalent to Maldivian Rufiyaa 74.

j   Reference period is February 2000.

k   Reference period is March 2019.

l   Data refer to the percentage of the population living below the basic-needs poverty line.

m   Refers to the poverty headcount ratio using the upper poverty line.

Sources: For indicator 1.1.1a: World Bank. PovcalNet Database. http://iresearch.worldbank.org/PovcalNet/povDuplicateWB.aspx (accessed 3 June 2019); and United Nations Statistics Division. Sustainable Development Goals (SDGs), SDG Indicators, Global Database. http://unstats.un.org/sdgs/indicators/database/ (accessed 13 July 2019). For indicator 1.1.1b: International Labour Organisation. ILOSTAT. http://www.ilo.org/ilostat (accessed 18 July 2019). For indicator 1.2.1: Economy sources; World Bank. World Development Indicators. http://databank.worldbank.org/data/reports.aspx?source=world-development-indicators (accessed 3 June 2019); and Secretariat of the Pacific Community. National Minimum Development Indicators. https://www.spc.int/nmdi/ (accessed 15 July 2019).

Sustainable Development Goals

Table 1.2.1: Selected Indicators for Sustainable Development Goal 2—Zero Hunger

Target 2.1: By 2030, end hunger and ensure access by all people, in particular the poor and people in vulnerable situations, including infants, to safe, nutritious, and sufficient food all year round

Target 2.2: By 2030, end all forms of malnutrition, including achieving, by 2025, the internationally agreed targets on stunting and wasting in children under 5 years of age, and address the nutritional needs of adolescent girls, pregnant and lactating women, and older persons

ADB Regional Member	2.1.1: Prevalence of Undernourishment (%)		2.2.1: Prevalence of Stunting among Children under 5 Years of Age[a] (%)		2.2.2c: Prevalence of Malnutrition (Overweight) among Children under 5 Years of Age[a] (%)		2.2.2d: Prevalence of Malnutrition (Wasting) among Children under 5 Years of Age[a] (%)	
	2000[b]	2017[c]	2000	2016	2000	2016	2000	2016
Developing ADB Member Economies								
Central and West Asia								
Afghanistan	46.1	29.8	59.3 (2004)	40.9 (2013)	4.6 (2004)	5.4 (2013)	8.6 (2004)	9.5 (2013)
Armenia	23.8	4.3	17.3	9.4	15.7	13.7	2.5	4.5
Azerbaijan	23.0	<2.5	24.2	17.8 (2013)	6.2	14.1 (2013)	9.0	3.2 (2013)
Georgia	13.5	7.9	14.6 (2005)	11.3 (2009)	20.8 (2005)	19.9 (2009)	3.0 (2005)	1.6 (2009)
Kazakhstan	5.8	<2.5	17.5 (2006)	8.0 (2015)	16.9 (2006)	9.3 (2015)	4.9 (2006)	3.1 (2015)
Kyrgyz Republic	16.3	7.1	18.1 (2006)	12.9 (2014)	10.7 (2006)	7.0 (2014)	3.4 (2006)	2.8 (2014)
Pakistan	23.4	20.3	41.5 (2001)	37.6 (2018)	4.8 (2001)	2.5 (2018)	14.2 (2001)	7.1 (2018)
Tajikistan	...	...	42.1	17.5 (2017)	6.7 (2005)	3.3 (2017)	9.4	5.6 (2017)
Turkmenistan	8.2	5.4	28.1	11.5 (2015)	4.5 (2006)	5.9 (2015)	7.1	4.2 (2015)
Uzbekistan	16.2	6.3	24.9 (2002)	...	10.9 (2002)	...	9.0 (2002)	...
East Asia								
China, People's Republic of	15.9	8.5	17.8	8.1 (2013)	3.4	9.1 (2013)	2.5	1.9 (2013)
Hong Kong, China	<2.5	<2.5	...	...	...	...	...	...
Korea, Republic of	<2.5	<2.5	2.5 (2003)	2.5 (2010)	6.2 (2003)	7.3 (2010)	0.9 (2003)	1.2 (2010)
Mongolia	35.1	13.4	29.8	7.3	12.7	11.7	7.1	1.3
Taipei,China	3.7	3.5	...	...	...	...	...	...
South Asia								
Bangladesh	20.8	14.7	51.1	36.2 (2014)	0.9	1.6 (2014)	12.5	14.4 (2014)
Bhutan	...	...	34.9 (2008)	33.5 (2010)	4.4 (2008)	7.6 (2010)	4.7 (2008)	5.9 (2010)
India	18.2	14.5	47.8 (2006)	37.9 (2015)	1.9 (2006)	2.4 (2015)	20.0 (2006)	20.8 (2015)
Maldives	14.0	10.3	31.9 (2001)	18.6 (2009)	3.9 (2001)	6.1 (2009)	13.4 (2001)	10.8 (2009)
Nepal	22.0	8.7	57.1 (2001)	36.0	0.7 (2001)	1.2	11.3 (2001)	9.6
Sri Lanka	18.6	9.0	18.4	17.3	1.0	2.0	15.5	15.1
Southeast Asia								
Brunei Darussalam	3.1	3.2	...	19.7 (2009)	...	8.3 (2009)	...	2.9 (2009)
Cambodia	29.3	16.4	49.0	32.4 (2014)	4.0	2.2 (2014)	17.1	9.8 (2014)
Indonesia	18.5	8.3	42.4	36.4 (2013)	1.5	11.5 (2013)	5.5	13.5 (2013)
Lao People's Democratic Republic	37.7	16.5	48.2	44.2 (2011)	2.7	2.0 (2011)	17.5	6.4 (2011)
Malaysia	2.8	2.5	17.2 (2006)	20.7	...	6.0	...	11.5
Myanmar	48.3	10.6	40.8	29.4	2.4	1.5	10.7	6.6
Philippines	20.4	13.3	33.8 (2003)	33.4 (2015)	2.4 (2003)	3.9 (2015)	6.0 (2003)	7.1 (2015)
Singapore	...	...	4.4	...	2.6	...	3.6	...
Thailand	18.8	7.8	15.7 (2006)	10.5	8.0 (2006)	8.2	4.7 (2006)	5.4
Viet Nam	24.3	9.3	43.2	24.6 (2015)	2.6	5.3 (2015)	6.1	6.4 (2015)
The Pacific								
Cook Islands	...	...	...	...	...	...	...	...
Fiji	4.8	3.7	7.5 (2004)	...	5.1 (2004)	...	6.3 (2004)	...
Kiribati	4.4	2.7	...	...	...	...	...	...
Marshall Islands	...	...	...	34.8 (2017)	...	4.1 (2017)	...	3.6 (2017)
Micronesia, Federated States of	...	...	...	...	...	...	...	...
Nauru	...	...	24.0 (2007)	...	2.8 (2007)	...	1.0 (2007)	...
Niue	...	...	...	...	...	...	...	...
Palau	...	...	...	...	...	...	...	...
Papua New Guinea	...	...	43.9 (2005)	49.5 (2010)	3.4 (2005)	13.7 (2010)	4.4 (2005)	14.1 (2010)
Samoa	5.3	2.7	...	4.9 (2014)	...	5.3 (2014)	...	3.9 (2014)
Solomon Islands	15.0	8.9	32.8 (2007)	31.6 (2015)	2.5 (2007)	4.5 (2015)	4.3 (2007)	8.5 (2015)
Timor-Leste	40.4	24.9	55.7 (2002)	50.9 (2013)	5.7 (2002)	1.4 (2013)	13.7 (2002)	10.5 (2013)
Tonga	...	...	...	8.1 (2012)	...	17.3 (2012)	...	5.2 (2012)
Tuvalu	...	...	10.0 (2007)	...	6.3 (2007)	...	3.3 (2007)	...
Vanuatu	8.2	7.2	25.7 (2007)	28.5 (2013)	4.7 (2007)	4.6 (2013)	5.9 (2007)	4.4 (2013)
Developed ADB Member Economies								
Australia	<2.5	<2.5	2.0 (2007)	...	7.7 (2007)	...	... (2007)	...
Japan	<2.5	<2.5	...	7.1 (2010)	...	1.5 (2010)	...	2.3 (2010)
New Zealand	<2.5	<2.5	...	...	...	...	...	...

... = data not available, < = less than, ADB = Asian Development Bank.

a According to the World Health Organization, for some economies the estimates were adjusted where necessary to be nationally representative and to cover the age range 0–5 years, which might result in slight differences in prevalence from the survey results reported. Estimates for some economies are also "pending reanalysis." Details can be found in the "Notes" column of the joint child malnutrition dataset.

b Data refer to 3-year average for 1999–2001.

c Data refer to 3-year average for 2016–2018.

Sources: For Indicator 2.1.1: Food and Agriculture Organization of the United Nations. FAOSTAT. http://www.fao.org/faostat/ (accessed 24 July 2019). For Indicator 2.2.1, Indicator 2.2.2c, and Indicator 2.2.2d: United Nations Statistics Division. Sustainable Development Goals (SDGs), SDG Indicators, Global Database. https://unstats.un.org/sdgs/indicators/database/ (accessed 8 July 2019).

Goal 2. End hunger, achieve food security and improved nutrition, and promote sustainable agriculture

Table 1.2.2: Selected Indicators for Sustainable Development Goal 2—Improved Agricultural Investment

ADB Regional Member	Target 2.a: Increase investment, including through enhanced international cooperation, in rural infrastructure, agricultural research and extension services, technology development, and plant and livestock gene banks in order to enhance agricultural productive capacity in developing countries, in particular least developed countries			
	2.a.1: The Agriculture Orientation Index for Government Expenditures		2.a.2: Total Official Flows to the Agriculture Sector[a] (constant 2017 $ million)	
	2001	2017	2000	2017
Developing ADB Member Economies				
Central and West Asia				
Afghanistan	0.1 (2003)	0.2 (2015)	4.3	324.8
Armenia	...	0.2	15.1	112.7
Azerbaijan	0.4 (2008)	0.5 (2015)	74.3	10.7
Georgia	0.1 (2003)	0.3	36.5	51.6
Kazakhstan	0.4	0.4	3.6	43.8
Kyrgyz Republic	0.1	0.1 (2016)	80.9	21.7
Pakistan	0.0	0.0 (2016)	58.1	275.3
Tajikistan	...	...	23.2	29.3
Turkmenistan	...	...	0.0	1.1
Uzbekistan	...	0.6	0.2	110.7
East Asia				
China, People's Republic of	0.3 (2007)	0.3	327.6	447.2
Hong Kong, China	...	...	...	...
Korea, Republic of	1.5	2.1 (2016)	...	...
Mongolia	0.2	0.1 (2015)	4.3	33.0
Taipei,China	...	...	...	...
South Asia				
Bangladesh	0.2	0.4 (2016)	333.6	280.0
Bhutan	0.3	0.8	5.8	19.5
India	0.2	0.3 (2016)	221.1	632.4
Maldives	0.2	0.0	0.0	4.9
Nepal	0.2 (2002)	0.4	69.5	135.1
Sri Lanka	0.4	0.7	51.9	53.6
Southeast Asia				
Brunei Darussalam	...	...	...	...
Cambodia	...	...	158.8	106.3
Indonesia	0.2 (2004)	0.1 (2013)	194.1	355.9
Lao People's Democratic Republic	...	...	27.9	86.4
Malaysia	0.4	0.3	8.6	3.7
Myanmar	...	0.1	2.1	193.8
Philippines	0.3	0.3	355.4	150.0
Singapore	2.0	11.4	...	...
Thailand	0.9	0.7	28.0	7.4
Viet Nam	0.1 (2006)	0.2 (2014)	103.8	297.1
The Pacific				
Cook Islands	0.4 (2005)	0.4 (2013)	0.0	0.2
Fiji	0.3 (2005)	0.4 (2016)	1.0	17.3
Kiribati	...	...	7.7	4.2
Marshall Islands	0.1 (2008)	0.1	3.3	1.2
Micronesia, Federated States of	...	0.2	9.7	2.1
Nauru	...	...	0.2 (2003)	0.4
Niue	...	...	0.0 (2002)	0.1
Palau	0.1 (2008)	0.2	0.2	3.0
Papua New Guinea	0.1	...	58.6	22.4
Samoa	...	0.7	2.7	13.3
Solomon Islands	...	0.1 (2015)	3.4	13.9
Timor-Leste	1.2 (2008)	0.2 (2015)	8.8	32.5
Tonga	...	...	0.2	1.7
Tuvalu	...	...	7.3 (2001)	7.7
Vanuatu	0.1 (2005)	0.2 (2012)	3.7	8.4
Developed ADB Member Economies				
Australia	0.2	0.2	...	...
Japan	...	...	...	...
New Zealand	0.3 (2004)	...	...	...

... = data not available, 0.0 = magnitude is less than half of unit employed, $ = United States dollars, ADB = Asian Development Bank.

a   Total official flows refer to official development assistance plus other official flows. Data refer to gross disbursements.

Sources: Food and Agriculture Organization of the United Nations. FAOSTAT. http://www.fao.org/faostat/ (accessed 1 August 2019); and United Nations Statistics Division. Sustainable Development Goals (SDGs), SDG Indicators, Global Database. https://unstats.un.org/sdgs/indicators/database/ (accessed 8 July 2019).

Goal 3. Ensure healthy lives and promote well-being for all at all ages

Table 1.3.1: Selected Indicators for Sustainable Development Goal 3—Maternal and Child Health

| ADB Regional Member | Target 3.1: By 2030, reduce the global maternal mortality ratio to less than 70 per 100,000 live births | | | | Target 3.2: By 2030, end preventable deaths of newborns and children under 5 years of age, with all countries aiming to reduce neonatal mortality to at least as low as 12 per 1,000 live births and under-5 mortality to at least as low as 25 per 1,000 live births | | | |
| | 3.1.1: Maternal Mortality Ratio (per 100,000 live births)[a] | | 3.1.2: Proportion of Births Attended by Skilled Health Personnel (%)[b] | | 3.2.1: Under-5 Mortality Rate (per 1,000 live births)[a] | | 3.2.2: Neonatal Mortality Rate (per 1,000 live births)[a] | |
	2000	2015	2000	2017	2000	2017	2000	2017
Developing ADB Member Economies								
Central and West Asia	**366**	**174**			**104**	**62**	**53**	**36**
Afghanistan	1,100	396	14.3 [c] (2003)	58.8 [d] (2018)	129	68	61	39
Armenia	40	25	96.8 [c]	99.8 [d] (2016)	30	13	16	7
Azerbaijan	48	25	80.7 [c]	99.8 [e]	75	23	34	12
Georgia	37	36	95.5 [e]	99.9 [c] (2016)	35	11	22	7
Kazakhstan	65	12	98.3 [e]	99.4 [c] (2015)	43	10	21	5
Kyrgyz Republic	74	76	98.6 [e]	98.4 [c] (2014)	50	20	22	11
Pakistan	306	178	23.0 [c] (2002)	69.3 [c] (2018)	113	75	60	44
Tajikistan	68	32	70.7 [c]	94.8 [c]	88	34	28	15
Turkmenistan	59	42	97.2 [c]	100.0 [c] (2016)	81	47	30	21
Uzbekistan	34	36	94.9 [c]	100.0 [e] (2015)	62	23	28	12
East Asia	**57**	**27**			**36**	**9**	**21**	**5**
China, People's Republic of	58	27	96.6 [e]	99.9 [e] (2016)	37	9	21	5
Hong Kong, China	6	2 * (2018)	...	...	...	...	2 [f]	1 [f]
Korea, Republic of	16	11	99.9 [g]	100.0 [g] (2015)	8	3	3	2
Mongolia	161	44	96.6 [e]	98.9 [c] (2013)	64	17	25	9
Taipei,China	8	10 (2017)	...	...	...	...	3	2
South Asia	**377**	**174**			**90**	**38**	**44**	**23**
Bangladesh	399	176	12.1 [d]	67.8 [c]	87	32	42	18
Bhutan	423	148	27.3 [e]	96.4 [e] (2018)	78	31	32	17
India	374	174	42.5 [d]	81.4 [d] (2016)	92	39	45	24
Maldives	163	68	84.0 [c] (2004)	95.6 [c] (2014)	44	8	25	5
Nepal	548	258	11.9 [c]	58.0 [d] (2016)	82	34	41	21
Sri Lanka	57	30	96.0 [d]	...	17	9	10	6
Southeast Asia	**200**	**110**			**48**	**26**	**21**	**13**
Brunei Darussalam	31	23	99.2 [e]	99.8 [e]	12	11	5	5
Cambodia	484	161	31.8 [c]	89.0 [d] (2014)	107	29	35	15
Indonesia	265	126	66.3 [d] (2003)	93.6 [c] (2018)	52	25	22	12
Lao People's Democratic Republic	546	197	16.7 [c]	64.4 [c]	113	63	40	28
Malaysia	58	40	96.6 [e]	99.5 [e] (2016)	10	8	5	4
Myanmar	308	178	57.0 [c] (2001)	60.2 [d] (2016)	90	49	38	24
Philippines	124	114	58.0 [c]	84.4 [c]	39	28	17	14
Singapore	18	10	99.7 [g]	99.6 [g]	4	3	2	1
Thailand	25	20	99.3 [e]	99.1 [d] (2016)	22	10	12	5
Viet Nam	81	54	58.8 [c]	93.8 [c] (2014)	30	21	15	11
The Pacific	**346**	**192**			**72**	**48**	**27**	**21**
Cook Islands	...	...	98.0 [d]	100.0 [e] (2009)	17	8	9	4
Fiji	42	30	96.9 [g]	99.8 [e] (2016)	23	25	9	11
Kiribati	166	90	85.0 [d]	98.3 [e] (2010)	71	55	29	23
Marshall Islands	...	...	86.2 [c] (2007)	92.4 [c]	41	34	18	16
Micronesia, Federated States of	153	100	82.8 [c]	100.0 [e] (2009)	54	32	25	17
Nauru	...	...	97.4 [d] (2007)	...	41	33	25	21
Niue	...	...	100.0 [d]	100.0 [c] (2011)	23	22	12	11
Palau	...	...	100.0 [d]	100.0 [c]	27	15	14	8
Papua New Guinea	342	215	39.0 [e] (2004)	...	78	53	30	24
Samoa	93	51	80.0 [d]	82.5 [d] (2014)	22	17	12	9
Solomon Islands	214	114	85.5 [d] (2007)	86.2 [d] (2015)	30	21	13	9
Timor-Leste	694	215	24.0 [d] (2002)	56.7 [d] (2016)	108	48	37	21
Tonga	97	124	95.0 [d]	95.5 [c] (2012)	18	16	8	7
Tuvalu	...	...	100.0 [d]	...	42	25	25	16
Vanuatu	144	78	88.0 [d]	89.4 [d] (2013)	29	27	12	12
Developed ADB Member Economies	**10**	**5**			**5**	**3**	**2**	**1**
Australia	9	6	99.3 [g]	97.0 [g] (2016)	6	4	4	2
Japan	10	5	99.8 [g]	99.9 [g]	5	3	2	1
New Zealand	12	11	97.3 [g]	96.3 [g] (2015)	7	5	4	3
DEVELOPING ADB MEMBER ECONOMIES	**269**	**126**			**71**	**32**	**35**	**18**
ALL ADB REGIONAL MEMBERS	**264**	**123**			**69**	**31**	**35**	**18**
WORLD	**341**	**216**			**77**	**39**	**31**	**18**

... = data not available, * = provisional, preliminary, ADB = Asian Development Bank.

a   Regional aggregates are weighted averages estimated using population of annual live births for the respective year headings. The data for maternal, under-5, and neonatal deaths are from United Nations Statistics Division databases. Aggregates are derived for reporting economies only. Aggregates for East Asia exclude Hong Kong, China and Taipei,China.
b   Based on population-based national household survey data and routine health systems.
c   Estimates are aligned with the standard definition of doctor, nurse, and/or midwife.
d   Includes other health personnel not in alignment with the standard definition.
e   No clear definition of health personnel.
f   Calculated based on known births and deaths.
g   Institutional birth including all deliveries that occurred at a health facility.

Sources: For Indicator 3.1.1: United Nations Statistics Division. Sustainable Development Goals (SDGs), SDG Indicators, Global Database. https://unstats.un.org/sdgs/indicators/database/ (accessed 8 July 2019). For Hong Kong, China: Government of the Hong Kong Special Administrative Region of the People's Republic of China, Centre for Health Protection. https://www.chp.gov.hk/en/statistics/data/10/27/110.html (accessed 22 July 2019); and Department of Health. Annual Report 2014/2015. https://www.dh.gov.hk/english/pub_rec/pub_rec_ar/pdf/1415/supplementary_table2014.pdf (accessed 22 July 2019). For Taipei,China: Government of Taipei,China, Directorate-General of Budget, Accounting and Statistics. https://eng.dgbas.gov.tw/public/data/dgbas03/bs2/yearbook_eng/Yearbook2017.pdf (accessed 22 July 2019). For Indicators 3.1.2 and 3.2.1: United Nations Statistics Division. SDGs, SDG Indicators, Global Database. https://unstats.un.org/sdgs/indicators/database/ (accessed 8 July 2019). For Indicator 3.2.2: United Nations Statistics Division. SDGs, SDG Indicators, Global Database. https://unstats.un.org/sdgs/indicators/database/ (accessed 8 July 2019). For Hong Kong, China: Government of the Hong Kong Special Administrative Region of the People's Republic of China, Department of Health. Annual Report 2014/2015. https://www.chp.gov.hk/en/statistics/data/10/27/110.html (accessed 22 July 2019); and Health Facts of Hong Kong 2018 Edition. https://www.dh.gov.hk/english/statistics/statistics_hs/files/Health_Statistics_pamphlet_E.pdf (accessed 22 July 2019). For Taipei,China: Government of Taipei,China, Ministry of Health and Welfare. 2017 Statistics of Causes of Deaths. https://www.mohw.gov.tw/cp-3961-42866-2.html accessed 22 July 2019).

Table 1.3.2: Selected Indicators for Sustainable Development Goal 3—Incidence of Communicable Diseases

| ADB Regional Member | Target 3.3: By 2030, end the epidemics of AIDS, tuberculosis, malaria, and neglected tropical diseases; and combat hepatitis, water-borne diseases, and other communicable diseases | | | | | |
| | 3.3.1: Number of New HIV Infections (per 1,000 uninfected population) | | 3.3.2: Tuberculosis Incidence (per 100,000 population) | | 3.3.3: Malaria Incidence (per 1,000 population) | |
	2000	2018	2000	2017	2000	2017
Developing ADB Member Economies						
Central and West Asia						
Afghanistan	0.01	0.02	190.0	189.0	92.6	23.0
Armenia	0.10	0.06	54.0	36.0	0.0	–
Azerbaijan	0.05	0.08 (2017)	80.0	67.0	8.2	–
Georgia	0.06	0.18	254.0	86.0	5.2	–
Kazakhstan	0.02	0.14	166.0	66.0	–	–
Kyrgyz Republic	0.03	0.09	244.0	144.0	0.0	–
Pakistan	<0.01	0.11	275.0	267.0	6.9	4.9
Tajikistan	0.08	0.09	219.0	85.0	9.2	–
Turkmenistan	...	...	112.0	43.0	0.0	–
Uzbekistan	0.08	0.16	99.0	73.0	0.1	–
East Asia						
China, People's Republic of	...	...	109.0	63.0	0.0	–
Hong Kong, China	...	...	104.0	67.0	...	...
Korea, Republic of	...	...	49.0	70.0	1.3	0.1
Mongolia	0.01	0.01	428.0	428.0	...	...
Taipei,China	...	...	...	...	...	...
South Asia						
Bangladesh	<0.01	0.01	221.0	221.0	5.6	1.9
Bhutan	0.25	0.11	249.0	134.0	14.0	0.0
India	0.19	0.10 (2017)	289.0	204.0	22.8	7.7
Maldives	...	...	59.0	39.0	...	...
Nepal	0.19	0.03	163.0	152.0	7.4	0.5
Sri Lanka	0.02	0.01	66.0	64.0	48.6	–
Southeast Asia						
Brunei Darussalam	...	...	106.0	64.0	...	...
Cambodia	0.88	0.05	575.0	326.0	100.5	18.4
Indonesia	0.11	0.17	370.0	319.0	8.3	5.8
Lao People's Democratic Republic	0.16	0.08	330.0	168.0	62.7	5.8
Malaysia	0.27	0.18	75.0	93.0	13.7	0.1
Myanmar	0.58	0.20	411.0	358.0	49.3	3.7
Philippines	<0.01	0.13	590.0	554.0	2.7	0.3
Singapore	0.09	0.04	51.0	47.0	...	...
Thailand	0.64	0.09	241.0	156.0	6.6	0.8
Viet Nam	0.30	0.06	197.0	129.0	3.5	0.1
The Pacific						
Cook Islands	...	...	6.3	–	...	...
Fiji	...	...	22.0	49.0	...	...
Kiribati	...	...	373.0	413.0	...	...
Marshall Islands	...	...	81.0	480.0	...	...
Micronesia, Federated States of	...	...	106.0	165.0	...	...
Nauru	...	...	46.0	91.0	...	...
Niue	...	...	–	71.0	...	...
Palau	...	...	65.0	106.0	...	...
Papua New Guinea	0.84	0.26	432.0	432.0	273.5	181.9
Samoa	...	...	28.0	18.0	...	...
Solomon Islands	...	...	91.0	76.0	623.2	171.0
Timor-Leste	...	...	498.0 (2002)	498.0	214.7	0.1
Tonga	...	...	28.0	12.0	...	...
Tuvalu	...	...	195.0	236.0	...	...
Vanuatu	...	...	110.0	51.0	125.4	8.2
Developed ADB Member Economies						
Australia	0.05	0.04	6.3	6.8	...	...
Japan	0.01	0.01	36.0	15.0	...	...
New Zealand	0.03	0.03	10.0	7.5	...	...

... = data not available, < = less than, – = magnitude equals zero, 0.0 = magnitude is less than half of unit employed, ADB = Asian Development Bank.

Sources: For Indicator 3.3.1: The Joint United Nations Programme on HIV/AIDS. http://aidsinfo.unaids.org/ (accessed 18 July 2019). For Azerbaijan and India: United Nations Statistics Division. Sustainable Development Goals (SDGs), SDG Indicators, Global Database. http://unstats.un.org/sdgs/indicators/database/ (accessed 8 July 2019). For Indicators 3.3.2 and 3.3.3: United Nations Statistics Division. SDGs, SDG Indicators, Global Database. http://unstats.un.org/sdgs/indicators/database/ (accessed 8 July 2019).

Goal 3. Ensure healthy lives and promote well-being for all at all ages

Table 1.3.3: Selected Indicators for Sustainable Development Goal 3—Mortality Rates, Health

ADB Regional Member	Target 3.4: By 2030, reduce by one third premature mortality from noncommunicable diseases through prevention and treatment, and promote mental health and well-being					Target 3.6: By 2020, halve the number of global deaths and injuries from road traffic accidents	
	3.4.1: Mortality Rate Attributed to Cardiovascular Disease, Cancer, Diabetes, or Chronic Respiratory Disease (%)		3.4.2 Suicide Mortality Rate[a] (per 100,000 population) 2016			3.6.1: Death Rate Due to Road Traffic Injuries (per 100,000 population)	
	2000	2016	Total	Female	Male	2000	2016
Developing ADB Member Economies							
Central and West Asia							
Afghanistan	34.4	29.8	4.7	1.5	7.6	15.7	15.1
Armenia	27.8	22.3	6.6	2.8	10.8	20.6	17.1
Azerbaijan	29.3	22.2	2.6	1.1	4.2	7.9	8.7
Georgia	24.7	24.9	8.2	2.7	14.2	10.5	15.3
Kazakhstan	39.1	26.8	22.5	7.6	38.3	14.1	17.6
Kyrgyz Republic	31.4	24.9	8.3	3.5	13.2	12.0	15.4
Pakistan	26.7	24.7	2.9	3.0	2.7	14.8	14.3
Tajikistan	27.3	25.3	2.5	1.3	3.7	19.7	18.1
Turkmenistan	34.0	29.5	6.7	3.5	10.1	18.0	14.5
Uzbekistan	29.3	24.5	7.4	4.8	9.9	9.7	11.5
East Asia							
China, People's Republic of	21.5	17.0	9.7	10.3	9.1	18.0	18.2
Hong Kong, China	...	...	...	...	...	2.4	1.4 (2018)
Korea, Republic of	16.5	7.8	26.9	15.4	38.4	26.4	9.8
Mongolia	38.9	30.2	13.0	3.5	22.6	18.7	16.5
Taipei,China	...	...	16.4 (2017)	...	...	...	...
South Asia							
Bangladesh	21.4	21.6	5.9	7.0	4.7	14.3	15.3
Bhutan	30.8	23.3	11.4	8.5	14.0	16.5	17.4
India	26.6	23.3	16.3	14.7	17.8	16.3	22.6
Maldives	26.8	13.4	2.3	1.3	3.0	2.9	0.9
Nepal	27.3	21.8	8.8	7.9	9.7	16.9	15.9
Sri Lanka	21.5	17.4	14.6	6.4	23.5	18.3	14.9
Southeast Asia							
Brunei Darussalam	20.5	16.6	4.6	2.7	6.4	16.3	8.0 (2013)
Cambodia	25.5	21.1	5.3	2.9	7.8	17.8	17.8
Indonesia	26.3	26.4	3.4	2.0	4.8	15.2	12.2
Lao People's Democratic Republic	29.2	27.0	8.6	5.7	11.4	14.0	16.6
Malaysia	20.3	17.2	5.5	3.2	7.8	26.6	23.6
Myanmar	25.0	24.2	7.8	9.5	5.9	21.8	19.9
Philippines	26.8	26.8	3.2	2.0	4.3	9.9	12.3
Singapore	16.8	9.3	9.9	6.1	13.8	6.7	2.8
Thailand	19.2	14.5	14.4	5.9	23.4	37.7	32.7
Viet Nam	18.6	17.1	7.3	3.7	10.9	23.6	26.4
The Pacific							
Cook Islands	...	...	...	...	...	5.6	17.3
Fiji	36.4	30.6	5.0	2.4	7.5	9.6	9.6
Kiribati	29.5	28.4	14.4	5.0	24.1	8.5	4.4
Marshall Islands	...	...	...	...	...	17.3	5.7 (2013)
Micronesia, Federated States of	27.4	26.1	11.1	6.3	15.8	16.8	1.9
Nauru	...	...	...	...	...	19.9	...
Niue	...	...	...	...	...	–	...
Palau	...	...	...	...	...	15.6	4.8 (2013)
Papua New Guinea	31.2	30.0	6.0	3.3	8.6	17.3	14.2
Samoa	29.5	20.6	4.4	1.9	6.7	16.6	11.3
Solomon Islands	31.2	23.8	4.7	2.6	6.8	18.7	17.4
Timor-Leste	26.8	19.9	4.6	2.9	6.2	17.1	12.7
Tonga	26.1	23.3	3.5	2.7	4.3	15.3	16.8
Tuvalu	...	...	...	...	...	21.2	...
Vanuatu	27.9	23.3	4.5	2.2	6.6	15.7	15.9
Developed ADB Member Economies							
Australia	13.1	9.1	13.2	7.0	19.5	9.5	5.6
Japan	11.4	8.4	18.5	11.4	26.0	12.3	4.1
New Zealand	15.9	10.1	12.1	6.6	17.9	12.1	7.8

continued on next page

Goal 3. Ensure healthy lives and promote well-being for all at all ages

Table 1.3.3: Selected Indicators for Sustainable Development Goal 3—Mortality Rates, Health (*continued*)

ADB Regional Member	3.7.1: Proportion of Women of Reproductive Age (Aged 15-49 Years) Who Have Their Need for Family Planning Satisfied with Modern Methods		3.7.2: Adolescent Birth Rate (Aged 15-19 Years) per 1,000 Women in That Age Group		3.8.1: Coverage of Essential Health Services[b] (index in a unitless scale of 0 to 100)	3.9.1: Mortality Rate Attributed to Household and Ambient Air Pollution (per 100,000 population)	3.9.2: Mortality Rate Attributed to Unsafe Water, Unsafe Sanitation, and Lack of Hygiene (per 100,000 population)
	2000	2016	2000	2016	2015	2016	2016
Developing ADB Member Economies							
Central and West Asia							
Afghanistan	...	42.2	193.8	77.2 (2014)	34.0	95.0	13.9
Armenia	28.3	36.9	31.6	24.0	67.0	81.0	0.2
Azerbaijan	17.8 (2001)	...	29.0	52.8	64.0	55.0	1.1
Georgia	30.8	52.8 (2010)	39.9	43.6	66.0	184.0	0.2
Kazakhstan	...	79.4 (2018)	33.0	24.9 (2017)	71.0	57.0	0.4
Kyrgyz Republic	...	66.2 (2014)	34.7	33.9 (2017)	66.0	74.0	0.8
Pakistan	33.3 (2001)	48.5 (2018)	83.0	46.0	40.0	113.0	19.6
Tajikistan	...	44.8 (2017)	37.3	54.3	65.0	70.0	2.7
Turkmenistan	70.9	75.6	26.1	28.0 (2014)	67.0	51.0	4.0
Uzbekistan	...	...	21.1	29.5 (2010)	72.0	54.0	0.4
East Asia							
China, People's Republic of	96.6 (2001)	...	6.0	9.2 (2015)	76.0	140.0	0.6
Hong Kong, China	...	...	5.0	2.9 (2015)	...	...	...
Korea, Republic of	...	...	2.5	1.3	>=80	35.0	1.8
Mongolia	79.3 (2003)	65.2 (2013)	27.3	30.1 (2017)	63.0	97.0	1.3
Taipei,China	...	...	...	...	...	...	...
South Asia							
Bangladesh	60.2	72.6 (2014)	134.0	78.0	46.0	103.0	11.9
Bhutan	...	84.6 (2010)	61.7	28.4 (2012)	59.0	88.0	3.9
India	61.7 (2004)	67.2	79.1	10.7	56.0	141.0	18.6
Maldives	...	42.5 (2009)	28.9	9.8	55.0	14.0	0.3
Nepal	52.8 (2001)	56.0 (2017)	71.0	88.2 (2015)	46.0	133.0	19.8
Sri Lanka	56.1	74.3	30.3	21.0 (2015)	62.0	89.0	1.2
Southeast Asia							
Brunei Darussalam	...	...	31.2	11.4 (2015)	>=80	9.0	–
Cambodia	33.0	56.5 (2014)	52.0 (2003)	57.4 (2013)	55.0	87.0	6.5
Indonesia	77.1 (2003)	77.6 (2017)	54.0	48.0 (2010)	49.0	81.0	7.1
Lao People's Democratic Republic	40.3	71.6 (2017)	76.0 (2004)	83.4	48.0	110.0	11.3
Malaysia	...	...	12.0	10.0	70.0	35.0	0.4
Myanmar	56.0 (2001)	74.9	22.7	36.0 (2014)	60.0	116.0	12.6
Philippines	46.5 (2003)	52.5 (2017)	55.0 (2001)	46.9	58.0	117.0	4.2
Singapore	...	...	7.7	2.7 (2015)	>=80	39.0	0.1
Thailand	94.8 (2006)	89.2	31.1	42.5	75.0	85.0	3.5
Viet Nam	66.6 (2002)	69.6 (2014)	24.0	30.1 (2014)	73.0	65.0	1.6
The Pacific							
Cook Islands	...	...	47.0 (2001)	67.0 (2015)	...	...	...
Fiji	...	...	34.8 (2002)	40.0 (2014)	66.0	76.0	2.9
Kiribati	...	35.8 (2009)	42.0	49.0 (2010)	40.0	88.0	16.7
Marshall Islands	80.5 (2007)	...	127.0 (2005)	84.5 (2011)	...	...	...
Micronesia, Federated States of	...	...	57.9	44.0 (2009)	60.0	93.0	3.6
Nauru	42.5 (2007)	...	71.0	94.0 (2015)	...	...	...
Niue	...	...	34.9 (2001)	20.0 (2011)	...	...	...
Palau	...	...	23.0 (2001)	27.0 (2015)	...	...	...
Papua New Guinea	40.6 (2007)	...	70.0	...	41.0	90.0	16.3
Samoa	...	39.4 (2014)	33.6 (2001)	39.2 (2011)	56.0	62.0	1.5
Solomon Islands	60.0 (2007)	38.0 (2015)	70.0 (2004)	78.0 (2013)	50.0	67.0	6.2
Timor-Leste	...	37.4	78.3 (2001)	41.9 (2015)	47.0	77.0	9.9
Tonga	...	47.9 (2012)	18.7	30.0 (2011)	62.0	57.0	1.4
Tuvalu	41.0 (2007)	...	42.0 (2007)	28.0 (2012)	...	...	...
Vanuatu	...	50.7 (2013)	...	78.0 (2011)	56.0	76.0	10.4
Developed ADB Member Economies							
Australia	...	...	17.8	10.4	>=80	17.0	0.1
Japan	...	...	5.4	3.7	80.0	43.0	0.2
New Zealand	...	...	28.2	14.9 (2017)	>=80	14.0	0.1

... = data not available, ≥ = greater than or equal to, – = magnitude equals zero, ADB = Asian Development Bank.

a   Data refers to crude suicide rates (per 100,000 population).

b   The universal health coverage service coverage index is a single indicator that is calculated based on tracer indicators (some of which are proxies of service coverage) to monitor coverage of essential health services. For presentation purposes, index values of 80 and over are reported as "≥80" to avoid comparisons that are not meaningful. This should not be interpreted as a target.

Sources: For Indicators 3.4.1, 3.4.2, 3.7.1, 3.7.2, 3.8.1, and 3.9.2: United Nations Statistics Division. Sustainable Development Goals (SDGs), SDG Indicators, Global Database. https://unstats.un.org/sdgs/indicators/database/ (accessed 8 July 2019). For Indicator 3.4.2 for Taipei,China: Government of Taipei,China. Cause of Death Statistics. https://www.mohw.gov.tw/lp-3961-2.html (accessed 22 July 2019). For Indicator 3.6.1: For 2000: United Nations Statistics Division. Sustainable Development Goals (SDGs), SDG Indicators, Global Database. https://unstats.un.org/sdgs/indicators/database/ (accessed 8 July 2019). For 2016: World Health Organization. Global Health Observatory Data Repository. http://apps.who.int/gho/data/node.main.A997?lang=en (accessed 22 July 2019). For Hong Kong, China: Government of the Hong Kong Special Administrative Region of the People's Republic of China. Road Traffic Accident Statistics. https://www.td.gov.hk/en/road_safety/road_traffic_accident_statistics/accident_trend_since_1953/index.html (accessed 22 July 2019).

Goal 4. Ensure inclusive and equitable quality education and promote lifelong learning opportunities for all

Table 1.4.1: Selected Indicators for Sustainable Development Goal 4—Early Childhood Education

Target 4.2: By 2030, ensure that all girls and boys have access to quality early childhood development, care, and preprimary education, so that they are ready for primary education

4.2.2: Participation Rate in Organized Learning (1 Year before the Official Primary Entry Age)[a,b] (%)

ADB Regional Member	2000 Total	2000 Female	2000 Male	2017 Total	2017 Female	2017 Male
Developing ADB Member Economies						
Central and West Asia						
Afghanistan	...	...	...	...	...	...
Armenia	...	...	...	...	...	...
Azerbaijan	15.8	16.1	15.6	61.3	61.4	61.2
Georgia	46.1 (2004)	49.1 (2004)	43.4 (2004)	...	...	...
Kazakhstan	...	...	...	63.9 (2018)	65.0 (2018)	62.7 (2018)
Kyrgyz Republic	42.4	43.2	41.6	95.4	96.3	94.5
Pakistan	...	...	...	...	...	...
Tajikistan	...	...	...	12.5	11.6	13.4
Turkmenistan	...	...	...	...	...	...
Uzbekistan	...	...	...	36.9	36.4	37.4
East Asia						
China, People's Republic of	...	...	...	...	...	...
Hong Kong, China	...	...	...	99.5	99.0	100.0
Korea, Republic of	49.6 (2005)	49.6 (2005)	49.6 (2005)	96.4 (2016)	96.1 (2016)	96.6 (2016)
Mongolia	96.5 (2007)	100.0 (2007)	93.1 (2007)	96.0	95.5	96.6
Taipei,China	...	...	...	...	...	...
South Asia						
Bangladesh	...	...	...	35.3 (2010)	35.4 (2010)	35.3 (2010)
Bhutan	...	...	...	...	...	...
India	...	...	...	...	...	...
Maldives	69.5	70.0	69.1	98.5	97.4	99.5
Nepal	...	...	...	84.9	82.1	87.6
Sri Lanka	...	...	...	...	...	...
Southeast Asia						
Brunei Darussalam	97.5 (2006)	95.0 (2006)	100.0 (2006)	95.1	94.8	95.3
Cambodia	26.6 (2006)	27.2 (2006)	26.0 (2006)	43.0 (2012)	43.6 (2012)	42.5 (2012)
Indonesia	...	...	...	96.8	100.0	93.7
Lao People's Democratic Republic	...	...	...	63.1	63.6	62.6
Malaysia	76.9 (2002)	79.3 (2002)	74.6 (2002)	98.6 (2015)	99.3 (2015)	98.0 (2015)
Myanmar	...	...	...	...	...	...
Philippines	24.0 (2001)	23.8 (2001)	24.1 (2001)	79.6 (2016)	80.7 (2016)	78.6 (2016)
Singapore	...	...	...	...	...	...
Thailand	98.9 (2006)	100.0 (2006)	97.9 (2006)	97.0	96.8	97.1
Viet Nam	78.7 (2006)	...	...	99.3	98.5	100.0
The Pacific						
Cook Islands	...	...	...	99.1 (2016)	100.0 (2016)	98.3 (2016)
Fiji	48.6 (2004)	50.2 (2004)	47.1 (2004)	...	...	...
Kiribati	...	...	...	...	...	...
Marshall Islands	...	...	...	65.6 (2016)	64.8 (2016)	66.4 (2016)
Micronesia, Federated States of	...	...	...	76.4 (2015)	72.8 (2015)	79.8 (2015)
Nauru	89.4 (2007)	78.5 (2007)	100.0 (2007)	74.8 (2016)	84.3 (2016)	67.3 (2016)
Niue	...	...	...	55.7 (2015)	100.0 (2015)	23.2 (2015)
Palau	...	...	...	90.4 (2014)	80.4 (2014)	100.0 (2014)
Papua New Guinea	...	...	...	73.5 (2016)	73.1 (2016)	73.9 (2016)
Samoa	...	...	...	36.9	39.1	34.9
Solomon Islands	...	...	...	65.4 (2015)	65.7 (2015)	65.1 (2015)
Timor-Leste	...	...	...	33.1	33.5	32.8
Tonga	...	...	...	...	...	...
Tuvalu	...	...	...	97.0 (2016)	100.0 (2016)	94.2 (2016)
Vanuatu	...	...	...	...	...	...
Developed ADB Member Economies						
Australia	52.6 (2001)	53.3 (2001)	52.0 (2001)	87.4	87.1	87.7
Japan	...	...	...	...	...	...
New Zealand	...	...	...	96.2	96.5	95.8

... = data not available, ADB = Asian Development Bank.
a Covers participation in early childhood education and primary education.
b The indicator measures the exposure of children to organized learning, but not to the intensity of the learning programs.
Source: United Nations Statistics Division. Sustainable Development Goals (SDGs), SDG Indicators, Global Database. https://unstats.un.org/sdgs/indicators/database/ (accessed 8 July 2019).

Goal 4. Ensure inclusive and equitable quality education and promote lifelong learning opportunities for all

Table 1.4.2: Selected Indicators for Sustainable Development Goal 4—Teacher Training and Supply

Target 4.c: By 2030, substantially increase the supply of qualified teachers, including through international cooperation for teacher training in developing countries, especially least developed countries and small island developing states

ADB Regional Member	4.c.1a: Proportion of Teachers in Preprimary Education Who Have Received at least the Minimum Organized Teacher Training (% of total teachers)		4.c.1b: Proportion of Teachers in Primary Education Who Have Received at least the Minimum Organized Teacher Training (% of total teachers)		4.c.1c: Proportion of Teachers in Lower Secondary Education Who Have Received at least the Minimum Organized Teacher Training (% of total teachers)		4.c.1d: Proportion of Teachers in Upper Secondary Education Who Have Received at least the Minimum Organized Teacher Training (% of total teachers)	
	2000	2017	2000	2017	2000	2017	2000	2017
Developing ADB Member Economies								
Central and West Asia								
Afghanistan	...	...	...	...	...	...	...	...
Armenia	97.1 (2002)	82.0	66.7 (2004)	...	...	...	...	...
Azerbaijan	79.1	88.4	99.9	98.0	...	97.6	...	...
Georgia	99.1	...	94.7	94.6 (2009)	76.8	94.6 (2009)	93.0	94.8 (2009)
Kazakhstan	...	100.0 (2014)	...	100.0 (2018)	...	...	...	...
Kyrgyz Republic	32.1	46.2 (2011)	52.0 (2003)	95.4	...	...	...	...
Pakistan	...	...	78.0 (2004)	82.5 (2015)	...	54.5	...	...
Tajikistan	91.3 (2001)	100.0 (2016)	81.6 (2001)	100.0	94.0 (2003)	...	94.3 (2003)	...
Turkmenistan	...	...	...	...	...	...	...	...
Uzbekistan	100.0 (2006)	98.5	100.0 (2006)	98.9	...	99.0	...	93.4
East Asia								
China, People's Republic of	...	...	...	...	...	...	...	...
Hong Kong, China	...	...	87.5	96.9	...	...	...	...
Korea, Republic of	...	...	...	...	...	...	...	...
Mongolia	100.0	100.0	100.0	100.0 (2016)	100.0	...	100.0	...
Taipei,China	...	...	...	...	...	...	...	...
South Asia								
Bangladesh	...	...	53.4 (2005)	50.4	36.8	67.2 (2016)	22.4	58.5 (2016)
Bhutan	93.8	100.0	94.8	100.0	93.5 (2005)	100.0	72.2 (2008)	100.0
India	...	...	...	69.8	...	76.6	...	...
Maldives	47.2	87.9	66.5	90.1	76.3	96.8	54.3 (2002)	...
Nepal	72.6 (2008)	88.7	15.4 (2001)	97.3	32.6	89.5	28.5 (2002)	88.0
Sri Lanka	...	...	...	85.5	...	84.5	...	79.8
Southeast Asia								
Brunei Darussalam	64.4 (2005)	59.1	84.5 (2005)	85.3	...	92.1	...	89.1
Cambodia	98.1 (2001)	100.0	95.9 (2001)	100.0	99.7 (2001)	100.0 (2016)	99.1 (2001)	...
Indonesia	...	...	...	...	...	...	...	...
Lao People's Democratic Republic	83.1	90.1	76.7	97.0	98.5	94.7	95.6	98.4
Malaysia	...	91.0	97.9	98.9	...	...	...	...
Myanmar	50.3 (2006)	97.9	62.7	97.8 (2016)	62.1	93.6	97.1	91.9
Philippines	...	100.0 (2016)	...	100.0 (2016)	...	100.0 (2016)	...	100.0 (2016)
Singapore	...	...	99.2 (2007)	99.0 (2016)	...	...	...	...
Thailand	...	...	...	100.0	...	100.0 (2015)	...	100.0 (2015)
Viet Nam	50.5	98.8	80.0	99.7	86.3	99.0	...	...
The Pacific								
Cook Islands	60.9 (2005)	78.1 (2016)	79.2 (2007)	95.3 (2016)	...	...	...	...
Fiji	...	...	97.8 (2008)	90.1 (2016)	...	100.0 (2012)	94.8 (2008)	85.7 (2016)
Kiribati	...	...	93.9 (2005)	72.7 (2016)	83.6 (2005)	86.7 (2014)	43.1 (2005)	...
Marshall Islands	100.0 (2002)	...	...	...	...	...	...	...
Micronesia, Federated States of	...	...	...	...	...	...	...	...
Nauru	77.5 (2006)	100.0 (2016)	74.2 (2007)	100.0 (2016)	...	100.0 (2016)	...	100.0 (2016)
Niue	...	100.0 (2016)	...	92.3 (2016)	...	80.0 (2016)	...	100.0 (2015)
Palau	...	...	...	...	...	...	...	...
Papua New Guinea	...	...	...	...	...	100.0 (2012)	...	100.0 (2012)
Samoa	...	100.0	...	...	...	...	...	79.5 (2016)
Solomon Islands	...	59.5 (2014)	...	74.1	...	86.6	...	63.0 (2015)
Timor-Leste	...	...	...	...	...	...	...	...
Tonga	...	100.0 (2012)	...	92.5 (2015)	...	...	...	...
Tuvalu	...	87.9 (2016)	...	76.6 (2016)	...	52.4 (2016)	...	34.6 (2016)
Vanuatu	100.0 (2007)	46.0 (2015)	100.0 (2007)	...	...	21.5 (2015)	...	...
Developed ADB Member Economies								
Australia	...	...	...	...	...	...	...	...
Japan	...	...	...	...	...	...	...	...
New Zealand	...	...	...	...	...	...	...	...

... = data not available, ADB = Asian Development Bank.

Source: United Nations Statistics Division. Sustainable Development Goals (SDGs), SDG Indicators, Global Database. https://unstats.un.org/sdgs/indicators/database/ (accessed 8 July 2019).

Goal 5. Achieve gender equality and empower all women and girls

Table 1.5.1: Selected Indicators for Sustainable Development Goal 5—Early Marriage and Women in Leadership

ADB Regional Member	Target 5.3: Eliminate all harmful practices such as child, early, and forced marriage, and female genital mutilation				Target 5.5: Ensure women's full and effective participation in, and equal opportunities for leadership at, all levels of decision-making in political, economic, and public life		
	5.3.1: Proportion of Women Aged 20-24 Years Who Were Married or in a Union (%)				5.5.1.a: Proportion of Seats Held by Women in National Parliaments (%)		5.5.2: Proportion of Women in Managerial Positions (%)
	Before Age 15		Before Age 18				
	2000	2016	2000	2016	2000	2018	2017
Developing ADB Member Economies							
Central and West Asia							
Afghanistan	...	8.8 (2015)	...	34.8 (2015)	27.3 (2006)	27.7	...
Armenia	...	0.0	...	5.3	3.1	18.1	28.7
Azerbaijan	...	1.9 (2011)	...	11.0 (2011)	10.4	16.8	34.5
Georgia	...	1.1 (2010)	...	14.0 (2010)	7.2	16.0	32.0
Kazakhstan	...	0.2 (2015)	...	7.0 (2015)	10.4	27.1	37.1 (2015)
Kyrgyz Republic	...	0.9 (2014)	...	11.6 (2014)	1.4	19.2	36.2
Pakistan	...	2.8 (2013)	...	21.0 (2013)	21.6 (2003)	20.6	2.9 (2016)
Tajikistan	...	0.1 (2017)	...	8.7 (2017)	15.0	19.0	14.8 (2009)
Turkmenistan	...	0.0	...	5.7	26.0	25.8	...
Uzbekistan	0.3 (2006)	...	7.2 (2006)	...	6.8	16.0	...
East Asia							
China, People's Republic of	...	...	...	...	21.8	24.2	...
Hong Kong, China	...	...	...	...	...	...	...
Korea, Republic of	...	...	...	...	3.7	17.0	12.3
Mongolia	...	0.1 (2013)	...	5.2 (2013)	7.9	17.1	42.5
Taipei,China	...	...	...	...	...	...	...
South Asia							
Bangladesh	...	22.4 (2014)	...	58.6 (2014)	9.1	20.3	10.7
Bhutan	...	6.2 (2010)	...	25.8 (2010)	2.0	8.5	18.5 (2015)
India	...	6.6	...	27.3	9.0	11.8	12.9 (2012)
Maldives	...	0.3 (2009)	...	3.9 (2009)	6.0	5.9	19.6 (2016)
Nepal	...	7.0	...	39.5	5.9	32.7	...
Sri Lanka	...	0.9	...	9.8	4.9	5.8	27.6
Southeast Asia							
Brunei Darussalam	...	...	...	...	...	9.1	33.6 (2014)
Cambodia	...	1.9 (2014)	...	18.5 (2014)	8.2	20.3	30.9 (2012)
Indonesia	...	0.6 (2018)	...	11.2 (2018)	8.0	19.8	27.5
Lao People's Democratic Republic	...	7.1 (2017)	...	32.7 (2017)	21.2	27.5	59.0
Malaysia	...	...	...	...	7.3	10.4	20.4 (2016)
Myanmar	...	1.9 (2015)	...	16.0 (2015)	...	10.2	35.6
Philippines	...	2.2 (2017)	...	16.5 (2017)	12.4	29.5	51.5
Singapore	...	...	...	...	4.3	23.0	34.5
Thailand	...	4.4 (2015)	...	22.5 (2015)	5.6	4.8	32.7 (2016)
Viet Nam	...	0.9 (2014)	...	10.6 (2014)	26.0	26.7	27.2
The Pacific							
Cook Islands	...	...	...	...	...	...	...
Fiji	...	...	...	...	11.3	16.0	38.9 (2016)
Kiribati	...	2.8 (2009)	...	20.3 (2009)	4.9	6.5	36.5 (2010)
Marshall Islands	5.5 (2007)	...	26.3 (2007)	...	3.0	9.1	...
Micronesia, Federated States of	...	...	...	...	–	–	...
Nauru	1.9 (2007)	...	26.8 (2007)	...	–	10.5	...
Niue	...	...	...	...	...	...	...
Palau	...	...	...	...	–	12.5	...
Papua New Guinea	2.1 (2006)	...	21.3 (2006)	...	1.8	–	18.1 (2010)
Samoa	...	0.7 (2014)	...	10.8 (2014)	8.2	10.0	43.1
Solomon Islands	...	5.6 (2015)	...	21.3 (2015)	2.0	2.0	...
Timor-Leste	...	2.6	...	14.9	26.1 (2003)	32.3	32.9 (2013)
Tonga	...	0.3 (2012)	...	5.6 (2012)	–	7.4	...
Tuvalu	0.0 (2007)	...	9.9 (2007)	...	–	6.7	...
Vanuatu	...	2.5 (2013)	...	21.4 (2013)	–	–	28.5 (2009)
Developed ADB Member Economies							
Australia	...	...	...	...	22.4	28.7	36.6 (2016)
Japan	...	...	...	...	4.6	10.1	13.2
New Zealand	...	...	...	...	29.2	38.3	...

... = data not available, – = magnitude equals zero, 0.0 = magnitude is less than half of unit employed, ADB = Asian Development Bank.

Sources: United Nations Statistics Division. Sustainable Development Goals (SDGs), SDG Indicators, Global Database. https://unstats.un.org/sdgs/indicators/database (accessed 8 July 2019). For Tajikistan for indicator 5.5.1a: Inter-Parliamentary Union. Women in National Parliaments. http://archive.ipu.org/wmn-e/classif-arc.htm (accessed 24 July 2019).

Goal 6. Ensure availability and sustainable management of water and sanitation for all

Table 1.6.1: Selected Indicators for Sustainable Development Goal 6—Clean Water and Sanitation

| ADB Regional Member | Target 6.1: By 2030, achieve universal and equitable access to safe and affordable drinking water for all 6.1.1: Proportion of Population Using Safely Managed Drinking Water Services (%) | | | | | |
| | 2000 | | | 2017 | | |
	Total	Urban	Rural	Total	Urban	Rural
Developing ADB Member Economies						
Central and West Asia						
Afghanistan	...	...	...	...	...	...
Armenia	29.6	...	...	86.5	...	...
Azerbaijan	49.7	...	...	73.6	...	...
Georgia	74.6	...	...	80.0	...	...
Kazakhstan	57.5	...	...	89.5	...	...
Kyrgyz Republic	46.4	80.4	27.8	68.2	93.5	53.9
Pakistan	37.9	50.6	31.6	35.3	40.0	32.6
Tajikistan	35.2	...	...	47.9	...	...
Turkmenistan	65.9	84.4	50.2	93.9	96.9	90.7
Uzbekistan	56.3	84.2	32.5	58.9	86.1	31.1
East Asia						
China, People's Republic of	...	93.3	...	...	92.3	...
Hong Kong, China	79.4	79.4	...	100.0	100.0	...
Korea, Republic of	96.8 (2002)	...	...	98.2	...	...
Mongolia	22.3	...	...	23.7	...	...
Taipei,China	...	...	...	...	...	...
South Asia						
Bangladesh	55.9	44.6	59.4	55.4	44.6	61.5
Bhutan	28.6	48.6	21.7	36.2	48.9	27.6
India	...	...	19.6	...	...	56.0
Maldives	...	...	...	...	...	...
Nepal	23.9	34.9	22.2	27.2	34.1	25.6
Sri Lanka	...	86.1	...	...	90.8	...
Southeast Asia						
Brunei Darussalam	...	...	...	...	...	...
Cambodia	16.9	43.4	10.8	25.8	56.6	16.7
Indonesia	...	...	...	...	...	...
Lao People's Democratic Republic	5.1	21.5	0.5	16.1	26.3	10.8
Malaysia	93.0	...	...	93.3	...	...
Myanmar	...	...	...	...	...	...
Philippines	36.0	53.1	21.4	46.7	61.5	33.7
Singapore	100.0	100.0	...	100.0	100.0	...
Thailand	...	...	...	...	...	...
Viet Nam	...	...	...	...	...	...
The Pacific						
Cook Islands	...	...	...	...	...	...
Fiji	...	...	...	...	...	...
Kiribati	...	...	...	...	...	...
Marshall Islands	...	...	...	...	...	...
Micronesia, Federated States of	...	...	...	...	...	...
Nauru	...	...	...	...	...	...
Niue	98.2	...	...	97.2	...	...
Palau	...	...	...	...	...	...
Papua New Guinea	...	...	...	...	...	...
Samoa	57.1	...	...	58.8	...	...
Solomon Islands	...	...	...	...	...	...
Timor-Leste	...	...	...	...	...	...
Tonga	...	...	...	...	...	...
Tuvalu	...	49.2 (2001)	...	...	49.8	...
Vanuatu	39.6	...	...	44.1	...	...
Developed ADB Member Economies						
Australia	...	98.2	...	...	98.8	...
Japan	97.9	...	...	98.5	...	...
New Zealand	78.1	...	...	100.0	...	...

continued on next page

Goal 6. Ensure availability and sustainable management of water and sanitation for all

Table 1.6.1: Selected Indicators for Sustainable Development Goal 6—Clean Water and Sanitation (continued)

ADB Regional Member	Target 6.2: By 2030, achieve access to adequate and equitable sanitation and hygiene for all and end open defecation, paying special attention to the needs of women and girls and those in vulnerable situations 6.2.1a: Proportion of Population Using Safely Managed Sanitation Services (%)					
	2000			2017		
	Total	Urban	Rural	Total	Urban	Rural
Developing ADB Member Economies						
Central and West Asia						
Afghanistan	...	...	...	...	...	...
Armenia	47.4	45.4	...	48.2	45.3	...
Azerbaijan	...	70.2	...	...	92.2	...
Georgia	22.1	5.1	...	27.2	15.9	...
Kazakhstan	...	92.8	...	...	90.5	...
Kyrgyz Republic	...	...	...	...	...	...
Pakistan	...	...	...	...	...	...
Tajikistan	...	...	...	...	...	...
Turkmenistan	...	...	...	...	...	...
Uzbekistan	...	...	...	...	...	...
East Asia						
China, People's Republic of	26.6	29.4	25.0	72.1	83.7	56.1
Hong Kong, China	92.1	92.1	...	91.8	91.8	...
Korea, Republic of	85.9	...	...	99.9	...	...
Mongolia	...	...	...	...	...	...
Taipei,China	...	...	...	...	...	...
South Asia						
Bangladesh	...	...	13.8	...	...	32.3
Bhutan	...	...	...	...	...	...
India	...	...	1.6	...	...	39.0
Maldives	...	...	...	...	...	...
Nepal	...	...	...	...	...	...
Sri Lanka	...	...	...	...	...	...
Southeast Asia						
Brunei Darussalam	...	...	...	...	...	...
Cambodia	...	...	...	...	...	...
Indonesia	...	...	...	...	...	...
Lao People's Democratic Republic	21.8	45.9	15.0	58.1	62.4	55.8
Malaysia	77.8	...	...	88.6	...	...
Myanmar	...	...	...	...	...	...
Philippines	41.5	48.3	35.7	51.6	54.0	49.6
Singapore	100.0	100.0	...	100.0	100.0	...
Thailand	...	...	...	...	...	...
Viet Nam	...	...	...	...	...	...
The Pacific						
Cook Islands	...	...	...	...	...	...
Fiji	...	...	...	...	...	...
Kiribati	...	...	...	...	...	...
Marshall Islands	...	...	...	...	...	...
Micronesia, Federated States of	...	...	...	...	...	...
Nauru	...	...	...	...	...	...
Niue	...	...	...	...	...	...
Palau	...	...	...	...	...	...
Papua New Guinea	...	...	...	...	...	...
Samoa	49.4	40.5	52.0	48.5	37.7	50.9
Solomon Islands	...	...	...	...	...	...
Timor-Leste	...	...	...	...	...	...
Tonga	...	...	...	...	...	...
Tuvalu	4.7 (2001)	5.2 (2001)	4.3 (2001)	6.3	4.2	9.7
Vanuatu	...	...	...	...	...	...
Developed ADB Member Economies						
Australia	64.2	...	...	75.6	...	...
Japan	97.4	...	...	98.8	...	...
New Zealand	78.6	...	...	88.7	...	...

continued on next page

Goal 6. Ensure availability and sustainable management of water and sanitation for all

Table 1.6.1: Selected Indicators for Sustainable Development Goal 6—Clean Water and Sanitation (continued)

ADB Regional Member	Target 6.4: By 2030, substantially increase water-use efficiency across all sectors and ensure sustainable withdrawals and supply of freshwater to address water scarcity and substantially reduce the number of people suffering from water scarcity				Target 6.a: By 2030, expand international cooperation and capacity-building support to developing countries in water- and sanitation-related activities and programmes, including water harvesting, desalination, water efficiency, wastewater treatment, and recycling and reuse technologies			
	6.4.2: Level of Water Stress, Freshwater Withdrawal as a Proportion of Available Freshwater Resources (%)				6.a.1: Amount of Water- and Sanitation-Related Official Development Assistance Part of a Government-Coordinated Spending Plan ($ million)			
	2000		2015		2000		2017	
Developing ADB Member Economies								
Central and West Asia								
Afghanistan	54.8		...		4.3		93.5	
Armenia	...		64.2		12.9		79.2	
Azerbaijan	...		56.4		49.5		84.2	
Georgia	...		5.9	(2010)	0.8		68.4	
Kazakhstan	...		27.7	(2010)	7.2		0.7	
Kyrgyz Republic	50.0	(2005)	...		13.9		11.9	
Pakistan	...		112.5	(2010)	14.8		263.1	
Tajikistan	73.9	(2005)	...		15.5		24.5	
Turkmenistan	143.6	(2005)	...		0.0		0.2	(2011)
Uzbekistan	...		136.9		2.2		64.2	
East Asia								
China, People's Republic of	...		43.4		971.4		90.4	
Hong Kong, China	...		...		...		...	
Korea, Republic of	84.8	(2005)	...		...		...	
Mongolia	...		3.4		0.3		10.8	
Taipei,China	...		...		...		...	
South Asia								
Bangladesh	...		5.7	(2010)	84.4		283.5	
Bhutan	...		1.4	(2010)	5.7		11.8	
India	...		66.5	(2010)	172.7		659.4	
Maldives	...		15.7	(2010)	0.6	(2001)	3.2	
Nepal	8.3	(2005)	...		59.0		179.4	
Sri Lanka	90.8	(2005)	...		32.0		144.5	
Southeast Asia								
Brunei Darussalam	...		...		...		...	
Cambodia	1.0	(2005)	...		23.3		162.3	
Indonesia	...		28.0		84.1		121.8	
Lao People's Democratic Republic	2.3	(2005)	...		37.3		65.8	
Malaysia	5.7	(2005)	...		526.1		1.7	
Myanmar	5.8		...		1.4		74.6	
Philippines	...		26.0		20.0		70.4	
Singapore	...		...		...		...	
Thailand	23.0	(2005)	...		77.9		2.6	
Viet Nam	18.1	(2005)	...		224.9		533.2	
The Pacific								
Cook Islands	...		...		0.4		3.5	
Fiji	0.5	(2005)	...		0.4		2.7	
Kiribati	...		...		0.1		10.1	
Marshall Islands	...		...		0.1		2.0	
Micronesia, Federated States of	...		...		0.0	(2003)	1.2	
Nauru	...		...		0.1		0.1	
Niue	...		...		0.1	(2002)	0.0	
Palau	...		...		0.0	(2003)	5.2	
Papua New Guinea	0.1	(2005)	...		12.8		28.0	
Samoa	...		...		0.3		14.4	
Solomon Islands	...		...		2.2		10.6	
Timor-Leste	28.3	(2005)	...		3.9		5.9	
Tonga	...		...		10.3		2.4	
Tuvalu	...		...		0.1		1.0	
Vanuatu	...		...		0.1		2.2	
Developed ADB Member Economies								
Australia	...		6.2		...		...	
Japan	...		37.3	(2010)	...		...	
New Zealand	...		4.2	(2010)	...		...	

... = data not available, 0.0 = magnitude is less than half of unit employed, $ = United States dollars, ADB = Asian Development Bank.
Source: United Nations Statistics Division. Sustainable Development Goals (SDGs), SDG Indicators, Global Database. https://unstats.un.org/sdgs/indicators/database/ (accessed 8 July 2019).

Goal 7. Ensure access to affordable, reliable, sustainable and modern energy for all

Table 1.7.1: Selected Indicators for Sustainable Development Goal 7—Affordable and Clean Energy

ADB Regional Member	7.1.1: Proportion of Population with Access to Electricity (%) Total 2000	Total 2017	Urban 2000	Urban 2017	Rural 2000	Rural 2017	7.1.2: Clean Fuels (%) 2000	2017	7.2.1: Renewable (%) 2000	2016	7.3.1: Energy Intensity (MJ/$) 2000	2016
Developing ADB Member Economies												
Central and West Asia												
Afghanistan	23.0 a	97.7	74.0 a	99.5	8.0 a	97.1	7.0	34.0	54.2	20.8	1.7	2.3
Armenia	98.9	100.0	99.1	100.0	98.5	100.0	83.0	>95	7.2	14.0	9.4	5.3
Azerbaijan	98.9	100.0	99.7	100.0	98.1	100.0	73.0	>95	2.1	1.9	13.2	3.8
Georgia	99.9 b	100.0	100.0 b	100.0	99.8 b	100.0	41.0	79.0	47.3	28.1	8.3	5.8
Kazakhstan	99.1	100.0	99.7	100.0	98.3	100.0	85.0	>95	2.5	2.0	10.1	8.2
Kyrgyz Republic	99.7	100.0	99.9	100.0	99.6	100.0	53.0	83.0	35.2	21.9	9.6	8.0
Pakistan	70.4	70.8	93.8	100.0	58.9	54.1	23.0	44.0	51.0	45.6	5.5	4.3
Tajikistan	98.5	99.3	99.7	99.2	98.0	99.3	38.0	83.0	62.4	43.9	12.3	5.0
Turkmenistan	99.6	100.0	99.7	100.0	99.5	100.0	>95	>95	0.1	0.1	25.9	13.0
Uzbekistan	99.6	100.0	99.9	100.0	99.3	100.0	80.0	92.0	1.2	3.2	34.5	8.2
East Asia												
China, People's Republic of	96.6	100.0	...	100.0	94.7	100.0	49.0	58.0	29.6	12.6	10.1	6.2
Hong Kong, China	100.0	100.0	100.0	100.0	100.0	100.0	...	...	0.6	0.8	2.5	1.5
Korea, Republic of	100.0	100.0	100.0	100.0	100.0	100.0	>95	>95	0.7	2.6	8.1	6.6
Mongolia	67.3	85.9	99.2	99.8	24.8	55.7	15.0	41.0	5.7	3.3	9.0	6.0
Taipei,China	...	...	...	...	...	...	...	...	1.3	2.1 c	...	...
South Asia												
Bangladesh	32.0	88.0	81.2	99.5	16.7	81.3	7.0	19.0	59.0	34.0	3.6	3.1
Bhutan	31.2	97.7	96.7	99.1	8.8	96.8	27.0	79.0	91.4	84.8	21.8	10.0
India	59.4	92.6	88.7	99.2	48.1	89.3	22.0	45.0	51.8	34.0	7.0	4.5
Maldives	83.8	99.8	99.7	99.7	77.7	99.9	32.0	>95	2.3	1.1	2.4	3.4
Nepal	27.2	95.5	83.9	98.7	18.4	94.7	14.0	29.0	88.3	79.2	9.3	8.1
Sri Lanka	63.6 d	97.5	85.3 d	100.0	58.7 d	97.0	14.0	28.0	64.2	50.9	3.4	2.0
Southeast Asia												
Brunei Darussalam	100.0	100.0	100.0	100.0	100.0	100.0	>95	>95	–	0.0	3.7	4.1
Cambodia	16.6	89.1	60.6	99.1	6.6	86.1	<5	20.0	81.1	62.7	8.5	5.8
Indonesia	86.3	98.1	95.4	100.0	79.5	95.7	7.0	65.0	45.6	37.2	5.3	3.4
Lao People's Democratic Republic	43.1	93.6	96.0	99.5	28.2	90.5	<5	<5	81.6	51.9	4.4	5.9
Malaysia	...	100.0	...	100.0	...	100.0	>95	>95	6.7	6.2	5.4	4.7
Myanmar	47.0 b	69.8	83.4 b	92.6	33.3 b	59.9	<5	20.0	80.2	68.0	8.9	2.9
Philippines	74.8	93.0	89.7	96.4	61.9	90.0	36.0	44.0	34.9	24.0	5.1	3.1
Singapore	100.0	100.0	100.0	100.0	100.0	100.0	>95	>95	0.3	0.7	3.8	2.5
Thailand	82.1	100.0	99.9	100.0	74.0	100.0	65.0	78.0	22.0	21.8	5.2	5.4
Viet Nam	86.3	100.0	99.0	100.0	82.2	100.0	14.0	70.0	58.0	32.7	5.9	6.1
The Pacific												
Cook Islands	98.6 b	100.0	98.5	100.0	–	–	84.0	84.0	–	1.9	...	...
Fiji	75.8	96.0	91.4	99.9	61.4	91.1	32.0	51.0	52.2	24.4	4.0	4.4
Kiribati	69.7	98.6	93.6	88.7	51.2	100.0	<5	6.0	56.5	45.4	5.5	6.5
Marshall Islands	68.5	94.8	89.2	95.6	23.3	91.8	7.0	66.0	19.6	11.8	10.5	11.2
Micronesia, Federated States of	46.0	80.8	70.0	93.7	39.1	77.0	11.0	12.0	1.2	1.6	5.6	6.3
Nauru	99.8	99.6	98.1	99.7	98.1	99.7	72.0	92.0	16.4	31.4	17.1	4.1
Niue	...	100.0	...	100.0	...	0.0	75.0	93.0	0.6	22.1	...	...
Palau	98.9	100.0	99.7	100.0	97.0	100.0	>95	>95	–	0.0	12.2	10.4
Papua New Guinea	11.2	54.4	63.1	81.0	3.3	50.4	6.0	12.0	66.4	50.3	6.5	6.0
Samoa	87.3	96.8	98.6	100.0	84.2	96.1	16.0	31.0	42.5	27.3	4.2	4.1
Solomon Islands	6.6	62.9	59.1	73.8	0.0	59.6	6.0	8.0	66.9	65.7	7.3	4.4
Timor-Leste	25.6	80.4	70.9	100.0	10.8	71.9	<5	11.0	48.3	19.2	1.3	0.8
Tonga	85.4	98.0	97.0	98.9	81.9	97.7	49.0	55.0	2.5	2.0	3.2	3.2
Tuvalu	94.6	100.0	95.4	100.0	94.0	100.0	20.0	52.0	–	11.8	3.4	3.8
Vanuatu	22.3	62.8	78.4	92.7	6.8	52.7	12.0	11.0	48.7	33.7	4.0	4.0
Developed ADB Member Economies												
Australia	100.0	100.0	100.0	100.0	100.0	100.0	>95	>95	8.4	9.3	6.7	5.0
Japan	100.0	100.0	100.0	100.0	100.0	100.0	>95	>95	3.9	6.6	5.0	3.7
New Zealand	100.0	100.0	100.0	100.0	100.0	100.0	>95	>95	29.0	32.8	6.7	5.2

... = data not available, – = magnitude equals zero, 0.0 = magnitude is less than half of unit employed, $ = United States dollars, ADB = Asian Development Bank, GDP = gross domestic product, MJ = megajoule, PPP = purchasing power parity.

a Data is for 2005.
b Data is for 2002.
c Data is for 2015.
d Data is for 2001.
e Data is for 2006.

Sources: United Nations Statistics Division. Sustainable Development Goals (SDGs), SDG Indicators, Global Database. http://unstats.un.org/sdgs/indicators/database/ (accessed 8 July 2019). For Taipei,China: World Bank. Sustainable Energy for All Database. http://databank.worldbank.org/data/source/sustainable-energy-for-all# (accessed 19 July 2019).

Goal 8. Promote sustained, inclusive, and sustainable economic growth; full and productive employment; and decent work for all

Table 1.8.1: Selected Indicators for Sustainable Development Goal 8—Decent Work and Economic Growth

ADB Regional Member	Target 8.1: Sustain per capita economic growth in accordance with national circumstances and, in particular, at least 7% gross domestic product per annum in the least developed countries 8.1.1: Annual Growth Rate of Real GDP per Capita at Constant 2010 $ (%)		Target 8.2: Achieve higher levels of economic productivity through diversification, technological upgrading and innovation, including through a focus on high-value added and labor-intensive sectors 8.2.1: Annual Growth Rate of Real GDP per Employed Person at Constant 2011 $ (%)	
	2000	2017	2000	2018
Developing ADB Member Economies				
Central and West Asia				
Afghanistan	-8.8	0.0	-8.2	-0.1
Armenia	6.6	7.3	6.1	4.3
Azerbaijan	10.2	-0.9	10.3	1.6
Georgia	2.9	5.2	2.4	5.2
Kazakhstan	10.6	2.8	9.4	3.2
Kyrgyz Republic	4.2	3.0	2.1	3.0
Pakistan	1.9	3.6	0.3	2.9
Tajikistan	6.5	4.8	4.5	3.8
Turkmenistan	4.3	4.7	1.8	4.7
Uzbekistan	2.5	3.7	-0.4	4.8
East Asia				
China, People's Republic of	7.8	6.4	7.3	6.7
Hong Kong, China	6.3	3.0	4.4	2.7
Korea, Republic of	8.1	2.7	4.5	2.3
Mongolia	0.2	3.4	-1.5	2.2
Taipei,China	...	...	...	...
South Asia				
Bangladesh	3.9	6.2	2.4	5.2
Bhutan	5.7	4.7	2.3	7.6
India	2.2	5.5	1.7	5.8
Maldives	1.7	4.8	-1.9	2.5
Nepal	4.2	6.3	4.3	1.9
Sri Lanka	5.3	2.9	5.1	4.6
Southeast Asia				
Brunei Darussalam	0.7	0.0	-0.8	6.5
Cambodia	6.4	5.4	7.5	5.2
Indonesia	3.5	3.9	3.3	3.8
Lao People's Democratic Republic	4.1	5.3	3.5	4.4
Malaysia	6.4	4.4	5.3	3.1
Myanmar	12.4	5.9	12.3	6.3
Philippines	2.2	5.1	1.8	4.2
Singapore	6.2	2.1	4.6	1.4
Thailand	3.4	3.7	1.7	3.1
Viet Nam	5.6	5.7	4.3	5.6
The Pacific				
Cook Islands	13.9	1.9	...	...
Fiji	-2.3	2.3	-2.0	3.1
Kiribati	10.1	1.3	...	...
Marshall Islands	5.8	2.4	...	...
Micronesia, Federated States of	5.0	1.4	...	...
Nauru	-6.8	3.9	...	...
Niue	...	...	...	...
Palau	-2.7	-4.7	...	...
Papua New Guinea	-4.9	-3.5	-6.0	0.9
Samoa	6.6	-1.1	8.1	1.3
Solomon Islands	-16.5	1.5	-18.2	0.6
Timor-Leste	12.6	-10.0	18.9	-0.3
Tonga	2.6	1.9	3.4	1.8
Tuvalu	12.4	5.0	...	...
Vanuatu	3.1	1.3	3.6	1.8
Developed ADB Member Economies				
Australia	0.9	1.6	1.4	1.3
Japan	2.6	2.0	3.1	1.6
New Zealand	1.2	1.8	-0.2	0.6

... = data not available, 0.0 or -0.0 = magnitude is less than half of unit employed, $ = United States dollars, ADB = Asian Development Bank, GDP = gross domestic product

Source: United Nations Statistics Division. Sustainable Development Goals (SDGs), SDG Indicators, Global Database. http://unstats.un.org/sdgs/indicators/database/ (accessed 8 July 2019).

Goal 8. Promote sustained, inclusive, and sustainable economic growth; full and productive employment; and decent work for all

Table 1.8.2: Selected Indicators for Sustainable Development Goal 8—Unemployment

ADB Regional Member	Target 8.5: By 2030, achieve full and productive employment and decent work for all women and men, including for young people and persons with disabilities, and equal pay for work of equal value 8.5.2a: Unemployment Rate for Age Group 15+, by Sex (%)					
	2000			2017		
	Total	Female	Male	Total	Female	Male
Developing ADB Member Economies						
Central and West Asia						
Afghanistan	...	...	...	...	...	...
Armenia	9.8 (2007)	9.8 (2007)	9.9 (2007)	17.7	17.5	17.9
Azerbaijan	11.8	12.7	10.9	5.0	5.9	4.1
Georgia	10.8	10.5	11.1	13.9	12.7	15.0
Kazakhstan	12.8	12.1 (2001)	8.9 (2001)	4.9	5.9 (2013)	4.6 (2013)
Kyrgyz Republic	7.5	14.3 (2002)	11.2 (2002)	6.9	8.9	5.6
Pakistan	0.6 (2006)	0.3 (2006)	0.6 (2006)	3.6 (2015)	6.1 (2015)	2.8 (2015)
Tajikistan	...	...	...	11.5 (2009)	10.5 (2009)	12.3 (2009)
Turkmenistan	...	...	...	4.0 (2010)	2.3 (2010)	5.3 (2010)
Uzbekistan	5.0 (2007)	...	...	5.2 (2016)	...	...
East Asia						
China, People's Republic of	...	...	...	...	...	...
Hong Kong, China	...	...	...	...	...	...
Korea, Republic of	4.4	3.6	5.0	3.7	3.6	3.8
Mongolia	6.8 (2003)	6.4 (2003)	7.1 (2003)	6.4	5.7	7.0
Taipei,China	...	...	...	...	...	...
South Asia						
Bangladesh	3.3	3.3	3.2	4.4	6.7	3.3
Bhutan	1.9 (2001)	3.2 (2001)	1.3 (2001)	2.5 (2015)	3.2 (2015)	1.8 (2015)
India	2.7	2.4	2.9	2.7 (2012)	3.7 (2012)	2.4 (2012)
Maldives	2.0	2.7	1.6	6.1 (2016)	5.6 (2016)	6.4 (2016)
Nepal	1.3 (2008)	1.1 (2008)	1.6 (2008)	...	...	...
Sri Lanka	7.7	11.4	5.9	4.2	7.0 (2016)	2.9 (2016)
Southeast Asia						
Brunei Darussalam	...	...	...	7.0 (2014)	7.9 (2014)	6.3 (2014)
Cambodia	2.5	2.8	2.1	0.2 (2014)	0.2 (2014)	0.2 (2014)
Indonesia	...	...	...	4.2	3.9	4.4
Lao People's Democratic Republic	...	...	...	9.4	7.8	10.8
Malaysia	3.0	3.1	3.0	3.4	3.9 (2016)	3.1 (2016)
Myanmar	...	...	...	1.6	2.0	1.2
Philippines	3.7 (2001)	4.0 (2001)	3.5 (2001)	2.6	2.7	2.5
Singapore	3.7	3.5	3.9	4.1 (2016)	4.5 (2016)	3.8 (2016)
Thailand	2.4	2.3	2.4	0.7 (2016)	0.7 (2016)	0.7 (2016)
Viet Nam	2.3	2.1	2.4	1.9	1.7	2.1
The Pacific						
Cook Islands	...	...	...	...	...	...
Fiji	4.7 (2004)	6.0 (2004)	4.1 (2004)	4.3 (2016)	5.5 (2016)	3.7 (2016)
Kiribati	14.7 (2005)	18.2 (2005)	12.3 (2005)	30.6 (2010)	34.1 (2010)	27.6 (2010)
Marshall Islands	25.4 (2005)	...	...	...	...	...
Micronesia, Federated States of	...	...	...	...	...	...
Nauru	...	...	...	23.0 (2011)	25.5 (2011)	21.4 (2011)
Niue	...	...	...	...	...	...
Palau	3.3	3.5	3.1	...	...	...
Papua New Guinea	2.9	...	...	...	...	...
Samoa	5.0 (2001)	6.2 (2001)	4.4 (2001)	14.5	21.3	10.6
Solomon Islands	...	...	...	2.0 (2009)	1.8 (2009)	2.3 (2009)
Timor-Leste	...	...	...	11.0 (2013)	10.6 (2013)	11.2 (2013)
Tonga	5.2 (2003)	7.4 (2003)	3.8 (2003)	...	...	...
Tuvalu	6.5 (2002)	8.6 (2002)	5.0 (2002)	...	...	...
Vanuatu	...	...	...	...	...	...
Developed ADB Member Economies						
Australia	6.3	6.1	6.5	5.6	5.7	5.5
Japan	4.7	4.5	4.9	2.8	2.7	3.0
New Zealand	6.1	6.0	6.3	4.7	5.2	4.3

continued on next page

Sustainable Development Goals

Goal 8. Promote sustained, inclusive, and sustainable economic growth; full and productive employment; and decent work for all

Table 1.8.2: Selected Indicators for Sustainable Development Goal 8—Unemployment (continued)

ADB Regional Member	Target 8.5: By 2030, achieve full and productive employment and decent work for all women and men, including for young people and persons with disabilities, and equal pay for work of equal value 8.5.2b: Unemployment Rate for Age Group 15-24, by Sex (%)					
	2000			2017		
	Total	Female	Male	Total	Female	Male
Developing ADB Member Economies						
Central and West Asia						
Afghanistan	...	...	...	...	...	...
Armenia	11.7 (2007)	10.1 (2007)	12.6 (2007)	38.2	44.8	32.8
Azerbaijan	14.0 (2007)	10.5 (2007)	18.2 (2007)	13.4 (2015)	15.8 (2015)	11.4 (2015)
Georgia	21.1	20.5	21.6	28.9	32.8	26.3
Kazakhstan	17.3 (2002)	19.3 (2002)	15.7 (2002)	3.9 (2013)	4.3 (2013)	3.6 (2013)
Kyrgyz Republic	20.1 (2002)	21.2 (2002)	19.3 (2002)	14.8	21.0	11.7
Pakistan	0.9 (2006)	0.6 (2006)	1.0 (2006)	6.6 (2015)	9.4 (2015)	5.7 (2015)
Tajikistan	...	...	...	...	...	...
Turkmenistan	...	...	...	...	...	...
Uzbekistan	...	...	...	...	...	...
East Asia						
China, People's Republic of	...	...	...	...	...	...
Hong Kong, China	...	...	...	...	...	...
Korea, Republic of	10.8	9.0	13.6	10.4	9.7	11.3
Mongolia	9.8 (2008)	8.8 (2008)	10.6 (2008)	17.9	22.6	15.0
Taipei,China	...	...	...	...	...	...
South Asia						
Bangladesh	10.7	10.3	11.1	12.8	16.8	10.8
Bhutan	...	...	...	10.7 (2015)	12.7 (2015)	8.2 (2015)
India	8.1	7.0	8.4	10.1 (2012)	12.0 (2012)	9.5 (2012)
Maldives	4.4	5.1	4.0	15.9 (2016)	12.1 (2016)	19.1 (2016)
Nepal	2.2 (2008)	1.6 (2008)	2.9 (2008)	...	...	...
Sri Lanka	23.7	30.8	19.9	21.6 (2016)	29.2 (2016)	17.1 (2016)
Southeast Asia						
Brunei Darussalam	...	...	...	25.4 (2014)	28.1 (2014)	23.5 (2014)
Cambodia	...	...	...	1.6 (2012)	1.4 (2012)	1.8 (2012)
Indonesia	...	...	...	15.6	15.6	15.6
Lao People's Democratic Republic	...	...	...	18.2	15.5	20.8
Malaysia	10.9 (2007)	11.5 (2007)	10.5 (2007)	10.5 (2016)	11.4 (2016)	9.8 (2016)
Myanmar	...	...	...	4.0	4.8	3.3
Philippines	9.7 (2001)	12.8 (2001)	7.9 (2001)	7.5	8.9	6.6
Singapore	7.7 (2001)	10.7 (2001)	5.1 (2001)	9.1 (2016)	12.5 (2016)	6.2 (2016)
Thailand	6.6	6.0	7.0	3.7 (2016)	4.7 (2016)	3.0 (2016)
Viet Nam	4.6 (2004)	4.9 (2004)	4.4 (2004)	7.3	7.3	7.3
The Pacific						
Cook Islands	...	...	...	...	...	...
Fiji	9.8 (2005)	16.0 (2005)	7.1 (2005)	15.4 (2016)	22.4 (2016)	11.9 (2016)
Kiribati	39.3 (2005)	41.6 (2005)	37.2 (2005)	54.0 (2010)	61.8 (2010)	47.6 (2010)
Marshall Islands	...	...	...	...	...	...
Micronesia, Federated States of	...	...	...	...	...	...
Nauru	...	...	...	...	...	...
Niue	...	...	...	...	...	...
Palau	9.6	10.6	8.8	...	...	...
Papua New Guinea	5.3	...	...	...	...	...
Samoa	12.2 (2001)	15.5 (2001)	10.6 (2001)	31.9	43.4	24.6
Solomon Islands	...	...	...	...	...	...
Timor-Leste	...	...	...	21.8 (2013)	16.7 (2013)	25.1 (2013)
Tonga	...	...	...	...	...	...
Tuvalu	...	...	...	...	...	...
Vanuatu	...	...	...	...	...	...
Developed ADB Member Economies						
Australia	12.1	11.2	12.9	12.6	11.5	13.7
Japan	9.1	7.9	10.2	4.6	4.5	4.7
New Zealand	13.5	12.4	14.5	12.7	13.0	12.4

continued on next page

Goal 8. Promote sustained, inclusive, and sustainable economic growth; full and productive employment; and decent work for all

Table 1.8.2: Selected Indicators for Sustainable Development Goal 8—Unemployment (continued)

ADB Regional Member	Target 8.5: By 2030, achieve full and productive employment and decent work for all women and men, including for young people and persons with disabilities, and equal pay for work of equal value					
	8.5.2c: Unemployment Rate for Age Group 25+, by Sex (%)					
	2000			2017		
	Total	Female	Male	Total	Female	Male
Developing ADB Member Economies						
Central and West Asia						
Afghanistan	...	...	...	...	...	...
Armenia	9.6 (2007)	9.7 (2007)	9.5 (2007)	15.5	14.7	16.2
Azerbaijan	5.2 (2007)	4.3 (2007)	6.1 (2007)	3.8 (2015)	4.6 (2015)	3.0 (2015)
Georgia	9.7	9.5	9.8	12.4	11.0	13.7
Kazakhstan	7.9 (2002)	9.9 (2002)	6.0 (2002)	5.4 (2013)	6.1 (2013)	4.7 (2013)
Kyrgyz Republic	10.4 (2002)	12.4 (2002)	8.8 (2002)	5.3	6.9	4.2
Pakistan	0.4 (2006)	0.2 (2006)	0.5 (2006)	2.5 (2015)	4.8 (2015)	1.8 (2015)
Tajikistan	...	...	...	...	...	...
Turkmenistan	...	...	...	...	...	...
Uzbekistan	...	...	...	...	...	...
East Asia						
China, People's Republic of	...	...	...	...	...	...
Hong Kong, China	...	...	...	...	...	...
Korea, Republic of	3.7	2.7	4.3	3.3	3.0	3.5
Mongolia	4.7 (2008)	4.6 (2008)	4.9 (2008)	5.2	4.3	6.1
Taipei,China	...	...	...	...	...	...
South Asia						
Bangladesh	0.9	0.7	1.0	2.6	4.4	1.8
Bhutan	...	...	...	1.3 (2015)	1.6 (2015)	1.1 (2015)
India	1.2	1.1	1.3	1.2 (2012)	2.1 (2012)	0.9 (2012)
Maldives	1.1	1.8	0.8	3.6 (2016)	3.7 (2016)	3.6 (2016)
Nepal	1.0 (2008)	0.9 (2008)	1.1 (2008)	...	...	...
Sri Lanka	3.5	6.2	2.2	2.2 (2016)	4.1 (2016)	1.1 (2016)
Southeast Asia						
Brunei Darussalam	...	...	...	4.1 (2014)	4.9 (2014)	3.5 (2014)
Cambodia	...	...	...	1.2 (2012)	1.0 (2012)	1.3 (2012)
Indonesia	...	...	...	2.0	1.7	2.2
Lao People's Democratic Republic	...	...	...	7.4	5.9	8.6
Malaysia	1.4 (2007)	1.3 (2007)	1.5 (2007)	1.9 (2016)	2.3 (2016)	1.7 (2016)
Myanmar	...	...	...	1.0	1.3	0.7
Philippines	2.0 (2001)	1.7 (2001)	2.2 (2001)	1.5	1.5	1.5
Singapore	3.3 (2001)	3.0 (2001)	3.5 (2001)	3.6 (2016)	3.7 (2016)	3.6 (2016)
Thailand	1.5	1.5	1.4	0.3 (2016)	0.3 (2016)	0.4 (2016)
Viet Nam	1.5 (2004)	1.8 (2004)	1.1 (2004)	1.0	0.9	1.2
The Pacific						
Cook Islands	...	...	...	...	...	...
Fiji	2.6 (2005)	2.7 (2005)	2.5 (2005)	2.2 (2016)	2.4 (2016)	2.2 (2016)
Kiribati	7.9 (2005)	10.1 (2005)	6.5 (2005)	20.9 (2010)	22.8 (2010)	19.2 (2010)
Marshall Islands	...	...	...	...	...	...
Micronesia, Federated States of	...	...	...	...	...	...
Nauru	...	...	...	...	...	...
Niue	...	...	...	...	...	...
Palau	2.6	2.8	2.5	...	...	...
Papua New Guinea	2.1	...	...	...	...	...
Samoa	2.7 (2001)	3.0 (2001)	2.6 (2001)	10.0	15.1	7.3
Solomon Islands	...	...	...	...	...	...
Timor-Leste	...	...	...	9.3 (2013)	9.5 (2013)	9.3 (2013)
Tonga	...	...	...	...	...	...
Tuvalu	...	...	...	...	...	...
Vanuatu	...	...	...	...	...	...
Developed ADB Member Economies						
Australia	4.9	4.7	5.1	4.2	4.5	4.0
Japan	4.2	3.9	4.3	2.7	2.5	2.8
New Zealand	4.6	4.6	4.6	3.2	3.8	2.7

... = data not available, ADB = Asian Development Bank.

Source: United Nations Statistics Division. Sustainable Development Goals (SDGs), SDG Indicators, Global Database. https://unstats.un.org/sdgs/indicators/database/ (accessed 8 July 2019).

Goal 8. Promote sustained, inclusive, and sustainable economic growth; full and productive employment; and decent work for all

Table 1.8.3: Selected Indicators for Sustainable Development Goal 8—Youth Participation in Education and Work, Child Labor

ADB Regional Member	Target 8.6: By 2020, substantially reduce the proportion of youth not in employment, education, or training				Target 8.7: Take immediate and effective measures to eradicate forced labor, end modern slavery and human trafficking, and secure the prohibition and elimination of the worst forms of child labor, including recruitment and use of child soldiers; and, by 2025, end child labor in all its forms					
	8.6.1: Proportion of Youth (Aged 15–24 Years) not in Education, Employment, or Training (%)				8.7.1: Proportion of Children (Aged 5–17 Years) Engaged in Child Labor, 2015 (%)					
	2000		2017		Total		Female		Male	
Developing ADB Member Economies										
Central and West Asia										
Afghanistan	...		...		16.6	(2013)	12.6	(2013)	20.3	(2013)
Armenia	...		36.6		3.9		2.7		4.9	
Azerbaijan	...		...		...		...		...	
Georgia	...		...		1.5		0.9		2.1	
Kazakhstan	18.6	(2001)	9.5	(2016)	...		...		...	
Kyrgyz Republic	...		21.0		15.3	(2014)	13.8	(2014)	17.3	(2014)
Pakistan	36.2	(2006)	30.4	(2015)	...		...		...	
Tajikistan	...		42.2	(2009)	...		...		...	
Turkmenistan	...		...		0.3		0.1		0.4	
Uzbekistan	...		...		...		...		...	
East Asia										
China, People's Republic of	...		...		...		...		...	
Hong Kong, China	...		...		...		...		...	
Korea, Republic of	...		...		...		...		...	
Mongolia	18.5	(2006)	19.8		9.4	(2013)	7.2	(2013)	11.5	(2013)
Taipei,China	...		...		...		...		...	
South Asia										
Bangladesh	31.0	(2005)	27.4		5.9	(2013)	5.2	(2013)	6.4	(2013)
Bhutan	...		...		1.7	(2010)	1.7	(2010)	1.6	(2010)
India	32.2		27.5	(2012)	4.3	(2012)	3.1	(2012)	5.3	(2012)
Maldives	...		23.5	(2016)	...		...		...	
Nepal	23.4	(2008)	...		19.0	(2014)	19.3	(2014)	19.2	(2014)
Sri Lanka	...		27.7	(2014)	...		...		...	
Southeast Asia										
Brunei Darussalam	...		17.2	(2014)	...		...		...	
Cambodia	...		12.7	(2012)	11.5	(2012)	12.2	(2012)	10.8	(2012)
Indonesia	29.4		21.5		...		...		...	
Lao People's Democratic Republic	...		42.1		11.4	(2010)	12.9	(2010)	9.9	(2010)
Malaysia	...		11.7	(2016)	...		...		...	
Myanmar	...		17.4		...		...		...	
Philippines	24.7	(2006)	21.7		4.3	(2011)	3.5	(2011)	5.1	(2011)
Singapore	...		4.3		...		...		...	
Thailand	...		15.0	(2016)	...		...		...	
Viet Nam	10.6	(2007)	9.7	(2014)	12.1	(2014)	12.5	(2014)	11.9	(2014)
The Pacific										
Cook Islands	...		...		...		...		...	
Fiji	20.6	(2005)	20.1	(2016)	...		...		...	
Kiribati	...		...		...		...		...	
Marshall Islands	...		...		...		...		...	
Micronesia, Federated States of	...		...		...		...		...	
Nauru	...		...		...		...		...	
Niue	...		...		...		...		...	
Palau	27.2		...		...		...		...	
Papua New Guinea	...		27.7	(2010)	...		...		...	
Samoa	...		37.9		...		...		...	
Solomon Islands	...		...		13.8		13.8		13.8	
Timor-Leste	...		24.3	(2013)	...		...		...	
Tonga	...		...		...		...		...	
Tuvalu	...		...		...		...		...	
Vanuatu	...		...		15.0	(2013)	15.8	(2013)	14.2	(2013)
Developed ADB Member Economies										
Australia	...		9.8	(2015)	...		...		...	
Japan	...		3.3		...		...		...	
New Zealand	10.8	(2004)	11.8		...		...		...	

... = data not available, ADB = Asian Development Bank.

Source: United Nations Statistics Division. Sustainable Development Goals (SDGs), SDG Indicators, Global Database. https://unstats.un.org/sdgs/indicators/database/ (accessed 8 July 2019).

Goal 8. Promote sustained, inclusive, and sustainable economic growth; full and productive employment; and decent work for all

Table 1.8.4: Selected Indicators for Sustainable Development Goal 8—Access to Banking, Insurance, and Financial Services; and Trade

ADB Regional Member	Target 8.10: Strengthen the capacity of domestic financial institutions to encourage and expand access to banking, insurance, and financial services for all				8.10.2: Proportion of Adults (15 Years and Older) with an Account at a Bank or Other Financial Institution or with a Mobile-Money Service Provider (%)	
	8.10.1: Number of Commercial Bank Branches and ATMs per 100,000 Adults					
	Commercial Bank Branches		ATMs			
	2004	2017	2004	2017	2011	2017
Developing ADB Member Economies						
Central and West Asia						
Afghanistan	0.4	2.1	0.0	1.3	9.0	14.9
Armenia	10.8	23.1	3.0	63.7	17.5	47.8
Azerbaijan	6.5	10.7 (2015)	17.1 (2006)	32.1	14.9	28.6
Georgia	9.5	33.2	2.0	75.9	33.0	61.2
Kazakhstan	3.7	2.8	10.0	74.6	42.1	58.7
Kyrgyz Republic	5.1	8.1	0.6	33.4	3.8	39.9
Pakistan	7.7	10.6	0.8	10.4	10.3	21.3
Tajikistan	4.9	6.5 (2013)	0.6 (2005)	10.3 (2013)	2.5	47.0
Turkmenistan	...	...	...	...	0.4	40.6
Uzbekistan	39.2	38.2	0.9	24.1	22.5	37.1
East Asia						
China, People's Republic of	...	8.8	9.6 (2006)	84.2	63.8	80.2
Hong Kong, China	23.6	21.1	...	50.7 (2016)	88.7	95.3
Korea, Republic of	16.8	15.5	208.2	271.9 (2016)	93.1	94.9
Mongolia	40.0	70.4 (2016)	9.9 (2008)	88.6 (2016)	77.7	93.0
Taipei,China	...	...	...	...	...	...
South Asia						
Bangladesh	6.9	8.6	0.1	8.1	31.7	50.1
Bhutan	14.4	17.0	0.5	36.6	...	33.7
India	9.0	14.7	2.3 (2005)	22.1	35.2	79.9
Maldives	10.1	15.6	7.2	35.0	...	...
Nepal	2.6	11.4	...	10.3	25.3	45.4
Sri Lanka	8.8	18.6 (2015)	9.4 (2007)	17.2 (2015)	68.5	73.7
Southeast Asia						
Brunei Darussalam	21.0	18.2	34.9	68.5	...	...
Cambodia	2.3 (2006)	7.5	0.0 (2005)	16.7	3.7	21.7
Indonesia	5.2	16.9	8.6	55.6	19.6	48.9
Lao People's Democratic Republic	...	3.1	2.6 (2008)	26.1	26.8	29.1
Malaysia	14.1	10.1	27.1	46.8	66.2	85.3
Myanmar	1.8	4.7	...	4.4	...	26.0
Philippines	8.2	9.1	10.3	28.3	26.6	34.5
Singapore	11.7	8.5	47.9	65.2	98.2	97.9
Thailand	7.8	11.9	19.9	117.3	72.7	81.6
Viet Nam	3.3 (2008)	3.4	1.4	24.3	21.4	30.8
The Pacific						
Cook Islands	...	...	...	...	...	...
Fiji	9.3	11.6	19.0	50.2	...	...
Kiribati	...	5.7 (2013)	...	14.3 (2013)	...	...
Marshall Islands	11.8	20.3 (2016)	2.9 (2007)	5.8 (2016)	...	...
Micronesia, Federated States of	12.3	14.2	3.1	14.2	...	...
Nauru	...	...	...	...	...	...
Niue	...	...	...	...	...	...
Palau	...	...	30.9 (2007)	45.8	...	...
Papua New Guinea	1.8	1.5	3.8	8.8	...	...
Samoa	17.6	22.5	12.1	49.8	...	...
Solomon Islands	7.5	4.3	1.5	12.0	...	...
Timor-Leste	1.2	5.3	2.1 (2008)	12.6	...	...
Tonga	24.2	28.9	22.5	36.1	...	...
Tuvalu	...	...	...	...	...	...
Vanuatu	19.6	21.4 (2015)	4.9	39.9 (2015)	...	...
Developed ADB Member Economies						
Australia	30.7	29.6	139.6	162.0	99.1	99.5
Japan	34.6	34.0	124.4	127.8	96.4	98.2
New Zealand	35.0	27.3	59.0	65.9	99.4	99.2

... = data not available, 0.0 = magnitude is less than half of unit employed, ADB = Asian Development Bank.

Source: United Nations Statistics Division. Sustainable Development Goals (SDGs), SDG Indicators, Global Database. http://unstats.un.org/sdgs/indicators/database/ (accessed 8 July 2019).

Goal 9. Build resilient infrastructure, promote inclusive and sustainable industrialization, and foster innovation

Table 1.9.1: Selected Indicators for Sustainable Development Goal 9—Road and Rail Transport, Passenger and Freight Volume

| ADB Regional Member | Target 9.1: Develop quality, reliable, sustainable and resilient infrastructure, including regional and transborder infrastructure, to support economic development and human well-being, with a focus on affordable and equitable access for all | | | |
	9.1.2: Passenger Volume, by Road Transport (passenger-km million) 2017	9.1.2: Freight Volume, by Road Transport (t-km million) 2017	9.1.2: Passenger Volume, by Rail Transport (passenger-km million) 2017	9.1.2: Freight Volume, by Rail Transport (t-km million) 2017
Developing ADB Member Economies				
Central and West Asia				
Afghanistan	28,050.6	8,060.3	0.4	–
Armenia	14,587.2	1,736.6	43.2	343.8
Azerbaijan	63,138.7	10,993.7	912.1	10,996.5
Georgia	20,283.5	1,741.6	51.4	2,270.2
Kazakhstan	65,242.3	191,652.1	413.2	259,481.0
Kyrgyz Republic	10,445.6	4,765.5	2.7	154.3
Pakistan	442,575.6	341,086.4	84.3	56,418.3
Tajikistan	13,908.4	2,847.9	1.3	73.6
Turkmenistan	31,283.4	6,095.0	0.3	11,734.0
Uzbekistan	84,312.2	33,062.2	705.6	21,618.6
East Asia				
China, People's Republic of	4,053,259.5	7,168,249.2	1,305,450.5	2,543,045.7
Hong Kong, China	38,636.6	10,665.7	2,630.9	11,295.2
Korea, Republic of	379,629.5	198,410.5	140,776.1	11,726.6
Mongolia	7,360.9	14,393.4	17,162.8	22,662.5
Taipei,China	...	...	...	...
South Asia				
Bangladesh	214,466.5	21,894.1	82,290.9	7,889.0
Bhutan	748.3	1,207.6	5,419.4	–
India	2,123,246.4	2,204,061.9	705,580.9	573,788.2
Maldives	2,113.6	53.4	2,978.2	–
Nepal	18,293.4	6,528.6	3,489.8	–
Sri Lanka	24,113.9	9,343.4	115,991.7	437.5
Southeast Asia				
Brunei Darussalam	49.6	891.2	7,131.3	–
Cambodia	14,900.7	9,699.8	21,769.7	1,566.5
Indonesia	228,384.2	329,869.7	593,963.0	5,539.5
Lao People's Democratic Republic	8,024.4	19,084.2	14,513.9	
Malaysia	44,529.0	98,324.7	168,479.1	6,527.0
Myanmar	51,442.9	14,517.0	27,094.8	4,057.2
Philippines	154,173.2	47,828.8	274,605.5	–
Singapore	22,522.6	567.7	103,818.6	662.5
Thailand	120,694.3	184,681.1	332,528.2	23,477.7
Viet Nam	122,902.0	118,524.8	186,146.3	3,358.0
The Pacific				
Cook Islands	87.0	–	3.4	–
Fiji	2,672.7	442.7	317.0	–
Kiribati	326.7	19.5	11.8	–
Marshall Islands	679.4	–	8.7	–
Micronesia, Federated States of	536.7	34.2	37.4	–
Nauru	41.4	–	1.6	–
Niue	4.1	–	0.2	–
Palau	194.4	24.6	120.4	–
Papua New Guinea	15,871.6	3,954.1	816.6	–
Samoa	1,213.0	1.3	115.7	–
Solomon Islands	1,932.7	0.4	89.8	–
Timor-Leste	156.5	–	–	–
Tonga	736.2	54.5	82.1	–
Tuvalu	54.6	3.1	4.3	–
Vanuatu	1,687.2	1.5	157.1	–
Developed ADB Member Economies				
Australia	98,606.9	262,176.7	21,698.8	418,843.4
Japan	869,989.0	209,997.1	428,851.8	28,708.0
New Zealand	18,602.1	16,717.1	5,367.2	10,316.8

... = data not available, ADB = Asian Development Bank, km = kilometer, t = metric ton.

Source: United Nations Statistics Division. Sustainable Development Goals (SDGs), SDG Indicators, Global Database. http://unstats.un.org/sdgs/indicators/database/ (accessed 8 July 2019).

Goal 9. Build resilient infrastructure, promote inclusive and sustainable industrialization, and foster innovation

Table 1.9.2: Selected Indicators for Sustainable Development Goal 9—Growth in Manufacturing

ADB Regional Member	Target 9.2: Promote inclusive and sustainable industrialization; and, by 2030, significantly raise industry's share of employment and GDP, in line with national circumstances, and double its share in least developed countries					
	9.2.1: Manufacturing Value Added[a]				9.2.2: Manufacturing Employment as a Proportion of Total Employment (%)	
	As a Proportion of GDP (%)		Per Capita (at constant 2010 $)			
	2000	2018	2000	2018	2000	2017
Developing ADB Member Economies						
Central and West Asia						
Afghanistan	17.2	11.0	46.3	68.8	4.6 (2008)	6.8 (2012)
Armenia	9.9	9.7	146.2	459.0	10.7 (2002)	9.1
Azerbaijan	9.6	5.5	158.1	315.9	4.6	5.2
Georgia	9.6	11.5	128.6	495.2	5.9	5.9
Kazakhstan	13.0	10.0	575.1	1,110.2	7.7 (2001)	6.4 (2015)
Kyrgyz Republic	23.2	13.2	151.0	145.8	6.4	10.1
Pakistan	10.1	13.2	83.9	164.8	11.5	15.3 (2016)
Tajikistan	27.1	12.1	113.4	120.7	4.7 (2004)	5.5 (2009)
Turkmenistan	33.0	38.0	786.1	2,904.5	...	...
Uzbekistan	24.1	16.6	195.6	350.1	...	...
East Asia						
China, People's Republic of	28.2	31.2	489.3	2,383.3	...	...
Hong Kong, China	3.8	1.2	862.6	473.3	...	...
Korea, Republic of	22.7	28.8	3,397.6	7,769.0	20.3	16.9
Mongolia	5.9	5.1	93.9	215.8	6.8	7.5
Taipei,China	24.6	21.4	3,314.8 (2001)	4,530.6	27.7 (2001)	26.8 (2018)
South Asia						
Bangladesh	13.5	21.1	67.4	244.2	7.3	14.4
Bhutan	7.6	7.9	90.8	245.3	2.0 (2005)	6.5 (2015)
India	15.2	17.0	114.0	353.0	10.7	12.5 (2012)
Maldives	2.9	2.3	165.4	200.6	12.9	11.0 (2016)
Nepal	8.1	5.5	37.5	42.9	...	...
Sri Lanka	20.1	15.5	366.2	630.0	16.5 (2002)	19.3
Southeast Asia						
Brunei Darussalam	17.4	14.9	6,237.5	4,738.3	...	3.7 (2014)
Cambodia	11.5	17.7	49.3	212.1	7.0	17.4 (2012)
Indonesia	23.8	21.6	510.5	928.0	13.0	14.1
Lao People's Democratic Republic	9.1	11.1	61.7	207.0	...	7.9
Malaysia	25.8	23.3	1,807.8	2,768.3	22.8	16.9 (2016)
Myanmar	8.5	23.9	24.5	314.1	...	10.5
Philippines	23.7	22.6	380.2	684.4	10.0	8.6
Singapore	20.4	17.2	7,010.3	9,358.1	20.7	14.4 (2015)
Thailand	28.5	27.7	985.1	1,784.8	14.7 (2002)	16.7 (2016)
Viet Nam	12.8	17.5	95.9	338.7	9.2	17.4
The Pacific						
Cook Islands	3.5	2.4	441.5	410.9	...	...
Fiji	13.3	11.2	439.8	490.1	13.7 (2005)	5.6 (2016)
Kiribati	5.1	4.0	91.8	67.7	1.6	13.2 (2010)
Marshall Islands	1.8	1.3	47.6	48.0	...	0.7 (2010)
Micronesia, Federated States of	...	...	...	...	...	...
Nauru	...	...	...	...	...	...
Niue	...	...	...	...	...	...
Palau	1.5	1.2	150.9	118.8	0.7	...
Papua New Guinea	2.5	2.4	43.9	54.2	1.1	1.8 (2010)
Samoa	16.9	9.0	481.8	362.1	...	6.8
Solomon Islands	4.9	6.8	52.4	101.3	...	...
Timor-Leste	1.9	0.3	15.0	7.1	...	5.5 (2013)
Tonga	7.1	6.1	234.6	242.2	24.7 (2003)	...
Tuvalu	0.8	1.0	24.1	36.2	...	...
Vanuatu	4.3	3.2	117.2	97.5	...	1.9 (2009)
Developed ADB Member Economies						
Australia	9.3	5.9	4,677.3	3,809.9	12.1	7.2
Japan	19.4	21.2	8,154.7	10,366.1	20.5	16.1
New Zealand	14.1	9.6	4,081.3	3,712.8	15.8	9.8

... = data not available, $ = United States dollars, ADB = Asian Development Bank, GDP = gross domestic product.

a   United Nations Statistics Division data used for indicator 9.2.1 were calculated from GDP, manufacturing value added, and population data.

Sources: United Nations Statistics Division. Sustainable Development Goals (SDGs), SDG Indicators, Global Database. https://unstats.un.org/sdgs/indicators/database/ (accessed 8 July 2019); and United Nations Industrial Development Organization. Statistics Data Portal. https://stat.unido.org/SDG (accessed 22 July 2019).

Goal 9. Build resilient infrastructure, promote inclusive and sustainable industrialization, and foster innovation

Table 1.9.3: Selected Indicators for Sustainable Development Goal 9—Carbon Dioxide Emissions

ADB Regional Member	Target 9.4: By 2030, upgrade infrastructure and retrofit industries to make them sustainable, with increased resource-use efficiency and greater adoption of clean and environmentally sound technologies and industrial processes, with all countries taking action in accordance with their respective capabilities			
	9.4.1: Carbon Dioxide Emissions[a]			
	Per Unit of GDP (PPP) (kg of CO_2 equivalent per constant 2010 $)		Per Unit of Manufacturing Value Added (kg of CO_2 equivalent per constant 2010 $)	
	2000	2016	2000	2016
Developing ADB Member Economies				
Central and West Asia				
Afghanistan	...	...	...	...
Armenia	0.4	0.2	1.6	0.3
Azerbaijan	0.8	0.2	2.0	0.8
Georgia	0.3	0.3	1.0	0.7
Kazakhstan	0.8	0.6	2.1	2.2
Kyrgyz Republic	0.5	0.5	1.1	0.9
Pakistan	0.2	0.2	1.9	1.5
Tajikistan	0.3	0.2	–	0.1
Turkmenistan	1.6	0.8	0.2	0.2
Uzbekistan	1.9	0.5	3.2	1.0
East Asia				
China, People's Republic of	0.7	0.5	1.4	0.9
Hong Kong, China	0.2	0.1	0.7	1.9
Korea, Republic of	0.4	0.3	0.6	0.2
Mongolia	0.8	0.5	2.2	1.5
Taipei,China	...	...	0.5	0.4
South Asia				
Bangladesh	0.1	0.1	0.5	0.5
Bhutan	...	...	...	...
India	0.3	0.3	1.5	1.3
Maldives	...	...	...	...
Nepal	0.1	0.1	1.3	2.6
Sri Lanka	0.1	0.1	0.1	0.1
Southeast Asia				
Brunei Darussalam	0.2	0.2	0.1	0.2
Cambodia	0.1	0.2	0.1	0.2
Indonesia	0.2	0.2	0.5	0.4
Lao People's Democratic Republic	...	...	...	...
Malaysia	0.3	0.3	0.6	0.4
Myanmar	0.2	0.1	2.1	0.1
Philippines	0.2	0.2	0.4	0.2
Singapore	0.2	0.1	0.1	0.2
Thailand	0.3	0.2	0.5	0.4
Viet Nam	0.2	0.4	1.9	2.3
The Pacific				
Cook Islands	...	...	...	...
Fiji	...	...	...	...
Kiribati	...	...	...	...
Marshall Islands	...	...	...	...
Micronesia, Federated States of	...	...	...	...
Nauru	...	...	...	...
Niue	...	...	...	...
Palau	...	...	...	...
Papua New Guinea	...	...	...	...
Samoa	...	...	...	...
Solomon Islands	...	...	...	...
Timor-Leste	...	...	...	...
Tonga	...	...	...	...
Tuvalu	...	...	...	...
Vanuatu	...	...	...	...
Developed ADB Member Economies				
Australia	0.5	0.4	0.5	0.3
Japan	0.3	0.2	0.2	0.2
New Zealand	0.3	0.2	0.4	0.4

... = data not available, – = magnitude equals zero, $ = United States dollar, ADB = Asian Development Bank, CO_2 = carbon dioxide, GDP = gross domestic product, kg = kilogram, PPP = purchasing power parity.

a Refers to carbon dioxide emissions from fuel combustion.

Sources: United Nations Statistics Division. Sustainable Development Goals (SDGs), SDG Indicators, Global Database. https://unstats.un.org/sdgs/indicators/database/ (accessed 8 July 2019); and United Nations Industrial Development Organization. Statistics Data Portal. https://stat.unido.org/SDG (accessed 23 July 2019).

Goal 9. Build resilient infrastructure, promote inclusive and sustainable industrialization, and foster innovation

Table 1.9.4: Selected Indicators for Sustainable Development Goal 9—Research and Development

ADB Regional Member	Target 9.5: Enhance scientific research, upgrade the technological capabilities of industrial sectors in all countries, in particular developing countries, including, by 2030, encouraging innovation and substantially increasing the number of research and development workers per 1 million people and public and private research and development spending							
	9.5.1: Research and Development Expenditure as a Proportion of GDP (%)				9.5.2: Researchers (Full-Time Equivalent) (per million inhabitants)			
	2000		2017		2000		2017	
Developing ADB Member Economies								
Central and West Asia								
Afghanistan	...		...		...		...	
Armenia	0.19		0.23		...		...	
Azerbaijan	0.34		0.19		...		...	
Georgia	0.22		0.29		...		1,773	
Kazakhstan	0.18		0.13		553	(2007)	870	
Kyrgyz Republic	0.16		0.11		...		...	
Pakistan	0.13		0.24		345	(2005)	515	
Tajikistan	0.09	(2001)	0.12		...		...	
Turkmenistan	...		...		...		...	
Uzbekistan	0.36		0.19		1,030	(2002)	651	
East Asia								
China, People's Republic of	0.89		2.13		719		2,862	
Hong Kong, China	0.46		0.80		1,471		4,052	
Korea, Republic of	2.18		4.55		2,914		9,242	
Mongolia	0.19		0.13		...		...	
Taipei,China	...		...		...		...	
South Asia								
Bangladesh	...		...		...		...	
Bhutan	...		...		...		...	
India	0.77		0.62	(2015)	302		404	(2015)
Maldives	...		...		...		...	
Nepal	0.05	(2008)	0.30	(2010)	265	(2002)	...	
Sri Lanka	0.14		0.11	(2015)	283	(2004)	264	(2015)
Southeast Asia								
Brunei Darussalam	0.02	(2002)	...		404	(2002)	...	
Cambodia	0.05	(2002)	0.12	(2015)	39	(2002)	122	(2015)
Indonesia	0.07		0.24		266		245	
Lao People's Democratic Republic	0.04	(2002)	...		49	(2002)	...	
Malaysia	0.47		1.44	(2016)	434		2,859	(2016)
Myanmar	0.11		0.03		94	(2001)	59	
Philippines	0.14	(2002)	0.14	(2013)	113	(2003)	270	(2013)
Singapore	1.82		2.22	(2016)	4,948		7,808	(2014)
Thailand	0.24		0.78	(2016)	504	(2001)	1,632	(2016)
Viet Nam	0.19	(2002)	0.53		139	(2002)	887	
The Pacific								
Cook Islands	...		...		...		...	
Fiji	...		...		...		...	
Kiribati	...		...		...		...	
Marshall Islands	...		...		...		...	
Micronesia, Federated States of	...		...		...		...	
Nauru	...		...		...		...	
Niue	...		...		...		...	
Palau	...		...		...		...	
Papua New Guinea	...		0.03	(2016)	...		73	(2016)
Samoa	...		...		...		...	
Solomon Islands	...		...		...		...	
Timor-Leste	...		...		...		...	
Tonga	...		...		...		...	
Tuvalu	...		...		...		...	
Vanuatu	...		...		...		...	
Developed ADB Member Economies								
Australia	1.58		1.92	(2015)	5,015		6,682	(2010)
Japan	2.91		3.20		7,032		6,987	
New Zealand	1.10	(2001)	1.26	(2015)	3,829	(2001)	5,721	(2015)

... = data not available, ADB = Asian Development Bank, GDP = gross domestic product.

Sources: United Nations Statistics Division. Sustainable Development Goals (SDGs), SDG Indicators, Global Database. https://unstats.un.org/sdgs/indicators/database/ (accessed 8 July 2019); and United Nations Educational, Scientific and Cultural Organization Institute for Statistics. Sustainable Development Goals. http://data.uis.unesco.org/# (accessed 29 July 2019).

Goal 9. Build resilient infrastructure, promote inclusive and sustainable industrialization, and foster innovation

Table 1.9.5: Selected Indicators for Sustainable Development Goal 9—Official International Support and Industry Value Added

ADB Regional Member	Target 9.a: Facilitate sustainable and resilient infrastructure development in developing countries through enhanced financial, technological, and technical support to African countries, least developed countries, landlocked developing countries, and small-island developing States		Target 9.b: Support domestic technology development, research and innovation in developing countries, including by ensuring a conducive policy environment for, inter alia, industrial diversification, and value addition to commodities	
	9.a.1: Total Official International Support to Infrastructure[a] (constant 2016 $ million)		9.b.1: Proportion of Medium and High-Tech Industry Value Added in Total Value Added (%)	
	2000	2017	2000	2016
Developing ADB Member Economies				
Central and West Asia				
Afghanistan	0.4	500.5	13.6	9.5
Armenia	134.0	290.1	9.5	4.5
Azerbaijan	24.1	1,160.1	16.5	20.3
Georgia	141.7	422.6	21.4	11.5
Kazakhstan	239.8	392.6	5.2	14.2
Kyrgyz Republic	92.2	118.5	5.9	3.0
Pakistan	477.7	1,755.4	25.2	24.6
Tajikistan	16.5	143.8	2.7	2.2
Turkmenistan	1.8	10.8	...	...
Uzbekistan	47.1	582.6	...	...
East Asia				
China, People's Republic of	2,283.4	2,401.5	42.9	41.5
Hong Kong, China	...	...	39.5	37.4
Korea, Republic of	...	...	58.9	63.7
Mongolia	115.2	402.9	2.5	5.6
Taipei,China	...	...	56.2	68.9
South Asia				
Bangladesh	626.1	2,207.7	21.1	9.8
Bhutan	30.8	39.3	...	...
India	2,996.7	6,277.5	41.3	38.8
Maldives	11.5	23.3	2.6	2.6
Nepal	114.3	324.4	12.1	8.4
Sri Lanka	75.5	465.5	9.4	7.6
Southeast Asia				
Brunei Darussalam	...	...	3.3	3.3
Cambodia	44.4	371.0	0.3	0.3
Indonesia	108.7	2,513.3	35.7	35.1
Lao People's Democratic Republic	73.4	150.4	13.6	13.6
Malaysia	568.5	4.3	51.2	44.1
Myanmar	0.0	400.3	12.4	6.6
Philippines	781.8	292.1	38.1	44.7
Singapore	...	...	78.5	78.1
Thailand	693.1	429.1	37.9	40.7
Viet Nam	1,111.3	2,325.3	23.5	37.8
The Pacific				
Cook Islands	1.0	7.7	...	...
Fiji	0.2	16.9	8.5	7.1
Kiribati	1.5	24.5	...	...
Marshall Islands	3.2	100.9	...	...
Micronesia, Federated States of	5.0	8.6	...	...
Nauru	0.0 (2002)	4.5	...	...
Niue	0.5	2.3	...	...
Palau	0.2	12.3	...	...
Papua New Guinea	218.4	196.7	12.6	12.6
Samoa	3.2	60.5	...	...
Solomon Islands	9.1	44.7	...	...
Timor-Leste	2.5	62.1	...	...
Tonga	5.0	34.5	1.6	1.6
Tuvalu	0.0 (2002)	9.8	...	...
Vanuatu	9.7	54.5	...	...
Developed ADB Member Economies				
Australia	...	...	27.2	27.0
Japan	...	...	52.0	56.2
New Zealand	...	...	12.5	18.5

... = data not available, 0.0 = magnitude is less than half of unit employed, $ = United States dollars, ADB = Asian Development Bank.

a Gross disbursements of total official development assistance and other official flows from all donors in support of infrastructure.

Sources: United Nations Statistics Division. Sustainable Development Goals (SDGs), SDG Indicators, Global Database. http://unstats.un.org/sdgs/indicators/database/ (accessed 8 July 2019); and United Nations Industrial Development Organization. Statistics Data Portal. https://stat.unido.org/SDG (accessed 23 July 2019).

Goal 9. Build resilient infrastructure, promote inclusive and sustainable industrialization, and foster innovation

Table 1.9.6: Selected Indicators for Sustainable Development Goal 9—Coverage by Mobile Networks

ADB Regional Member	Target 9.c: Significantly increase access to information and communications technology and strive to provide universal and affordable access to the Internet in least developed countries by 2020					
	9.c.1a: Proportion of Population Covered by 2G Mobile Networks (%)		9.c.1b: Proportion of Population Covered by 3G Mobile Networks (%)		9.c.1c: Proportion of Population Covered by LTE Mobile Networks (%)	
	2000	2017	2008	2017	2012	2017
Developing ADB Member Economies						
Central and West Asia						
Afghanistan	72.0 (2007)	90.0	...	46.0	– (2014)	5.0
Armenia	38.0 (2001)	100.0	81.1 (2009)	100.0	17.5	90.1
Azerbaijan	93.5	100.0	32.2 (2009)	96.3	6.7	42.0
Georgia	79.0 (2001)	100.0	...	100.0	8.9 (2013)	99.7
Kazakhstan	94.0 (2001)	96.6	...	87.5	2.7	72.5
Kyrgyz Republic	5.2 (2004)	99.1	...	75.0	0.5 (2014)	50.0
Pakistan	27.1 (2001)	88.0	...	72.0	–	67.0
Tajikistan	– (2001)	90.0	...	90.0	8.4	80.0
Turkmenistan	12.4 (2001)	95.8	...	75.8	6.0 (2013)	67.0
Uzbekistan	75.0 (2002)	98.4	...	75.0	1.0 (2014)	43.0
East Asia						
China, People's Republic of	50.0 (2001)	99.5	...	98.0	10.0 (2013)	98.0
Hong Kong, China	100.0	100.0	99.0 (2009)	99.0	91.7	99.0
Korea, Republic of	99.0	99.9	99.0 (2007)	99.9	99.0 (2014)	99.9
Mongolia	58.0	99.0	39.9	95.0	...	21.0
Taipei,China	...	...	...	...	...	...
South Asia						
Bangladesh	40.0 (2001)	99.5	...	92.8	59.0 (2014)	67.0
Bhutan	5.4 (2005)	98.0	15.0 (2010)	88.0	5.0 (2013)	55.0
India	21.1 (2001)	97.0	– (2007)	88.0	2.0 (2014)	88.0
Maldives	40.0	100.0	41.8 (2009)	100.0	11.4 (2013)	100.0
Nepal	10.0 (2006)	92.5	20.4 (2009)	54.1	– (2014)	15.5
Sri Lanka	57.9 (2001)	99.7	...	88.0	5.0	48.0
Southeast Asia						
Brunei Darussalam	...	99.3	...	92.7	5.0 (2013)	90.0
Cambodia	80.0	99.0	43.0 (2009)	83.9	9.0 (2014)	57.5
Indonesia	89.0	98.6	...	93.8	5.0 (2013)	90.4
Lao People's Democratic Republic	55.0 (2005)	98.0	– (2007)	78.0	2.0 (2014)	9.0
Malaysia	95.0 (2001)	96.2	74.0 (2009)	96.2	15.0 (2013)	92.0
Myanmar	10.0 (2006)	90.5	...	90.5	– (2014)	29.5
Philippines	70.0	95.0	69.0 (2009)	93.0	6.0	80.0
Singapore	100.0	100.0	99.8 (2007)	100.0	99.0 (2014)	100.0
Thailand	25.9 (2005)	98.0	...	98.0	– (2014)	98.0
Viet Nam	70.0 (2006)	99.5	...	98.0	– (2014)	95.0
The Pacific						
Cook Islands	...	100.0	...	55.0	...	55.0
Fiji	40.0	96.0	...	96.0	15.0 (2014)	96.0
Kiribati	...	45.0	...	48.0	10.0 (2013)	45.0
Marshall Islands	...	65.0	...	...	...	...
Micronesia, Federated States of	–	80.0	...	15.0	...	–
Nauru	...	98.0	98.0 (2010)	98.0	– (2014)	30.0
Niue	...	...	...	– (2015)	...	...
Palau	30.0 (2005)	98.0 (2015)	...	88.0 (2016)	...	...
Papua New Guinea	...	89.0	...	64.4	7.0 (2014)	50.0
Samoa	...	97.0	...	91.0	...	49.0
Solomon Islands	35.0	94.0	...	25.0	...	19.0
Timor-Leste	38.0 (2003)	96.5	...	96.5	...	20.0
Tonga	70.0 (2001)	98.0	...	95.0	– (2014)	65.0
Tuvalu	15.0 (2004)	48.0	...	48.0	...	–
Vanuatu	20.0 (2002)	98.0	...	98.0	...	33.0
Developed ADB Member Economies						
Australia	95.6	99.4	98.8	99.4	52.2	99.0
Japan	99.0	99.9	...	99.9	84.0	99.0
New Zealand	97.0	98.0	97.0	98.0	50.0 (2014)	94.0

... = data not available, – = magnitude equals zero, ADB = Asian Development Bank, LTE = Long-Term Evolution.

Source: United Nations Statistics Division. Sustainable Development Goals (SDGs), SDG Indicators, Global Database. http://unstats.un.org/sdgs/indicators/database/ (accessed 8 July 2019).

Goal 10. Reduce inequality within and among countries

Table 1.10.1: Selected Indicators for Sustainable Development Goal 10—Household Expenditure or Income Growth

ADB Regional Member	Target 10.1: By 2030, progressively achieve and sustain income growth of the bottom 40% of the population at a rate higher than the national average			
	10.1.1a: Growth Rates of Household Expenditure or Income per Capita among the Bottom 40% of the Population[a,b] (%)		10.1.1b: Growth Rates of Household Expenditure or Income per Capita[a,b] (%)	
Developing ADB Member Economies				
Central and West Asia				
Afghanistan	...		...	
Armenia	1.8	(2012–2017)	3.2	(2012–2017)
Azerbaijan	...		...	
Georgia	4.5	(2012–2017)	3.8	(2012–2017)
Kazakhstan	–0.0	(2012–2017)	–0.6	(2012–2017)
Kyrgyz Republic	0.9	(2012–2017)	0.8	(2012–2017)
Pakistan	2.7	(2010–2015)	4.3	(2010–2015)
Tajikistan	2.3	(2009–2015)	3.6	(2009–2015)
Turkmenistan	...		...	
Uzbekistan	...		...	
East Asia				
China, People's Republic of	9.1	(2013–2015)	7.4	(2013–2015)
Hong Kong, China	...		...	
Korea, Republic of	...		...	
Mongolia	1.7	(2010–2016)	1.3	(2010–2016)
Taipei,China	...		...	
South Asia				
Bangladesh	1.4	(2010–2016)	1.5	(2010–2016)
Bhutan	1.6	(2012–2017)	1.7	(2012–2017)
India	...		...	
Maldives	...		...	
Nepal	...		...	
Sri Lanka	4.2	(2012–2016)	4.7	(2012–2016)
Southeast Asia				
Brunei Darussalam	...		...	
Cambodia	...		...	
Indonesia	4.8	(2015–2017)	4.8	(2015–2017)
Lao People's Democratic Republic	...		...	
Malaysia	8.3	(2011–2015)	6.0	(2011–2015)
Myanmar	...		...	
Philippines	5.1	(2012–2015)	2.6	(2012–2015)
Singapore	...		...	
Thailand	2.5	(2014–2017)	2.1	(2014–2017)
Viet Nam	4.9	(2012–2016)	4.8	(2012–2016)
The Pacific				
Cook Islands	...		...	
Fiji	1.2	(2008–2013)	–0.5	(2008–2013)
Kiribati	...		...	
Marshall Islands	...		...	
Micronesia, Federated States of	...		...	
Nauru	...		...	
Niue	...		...	
Palau	...		...	
Papua New Guinea	...		...	
Samoa	...		...	
Solomon Islands	...		...	
Timor-Leste	...		...	
Tonga	1.0	(2009–2015)	0.6	(2009–2015)
Tuvalu	...		...	
Vanuatu	...		...	
Developed ADB Member Economies				
Australia	...		...	
Japan	...		...	
New Zealand	...		...	

... = data not available, –0.0 = magnitude is less than half of unit employed, ADB=Asian Development Bank.

a   Based on real mean per capita consumption or income measured at 2011 purchasing power parity, using the PovcalNet database (http://iresearch.worldbank.org/PovcalNet). Data reported are based on consumption, except for Malaysia and the Philippines, which are based on income.

b   For the data collection periods, the initial year refers to the nearest survey collected 5 years before the most recent survey available; only surveys collected between 3 and 7 years before the most recent survey are considered. The final year refers to the most recent survey available between 2014 and 2018.

Source: United Nations Statistics Division. Sustainable Development Goals (SDGs), SDG Indicators, Global Database. https://unstats.un.org/sdgs/indicators/database/ (accessed 8 July 2019).

Goal 11. Make cities and human settlements inclusive, safe, resilient, and sustainable

Table 1.11.1: Selected Indicators for Sustainable Development Goal 11—Sustainable Cities and Environment

ADB Regional Member	Target 11.1: By 2030, ensure access for all to adequate, safe, and affordable housing and basic services, and upgrade slums 11.1.1: Proportion of Urban Population Living in Slums, Informal Settlements, or Inadequate Housing (%)		Target 11.5: By 2030, significantly reduce the number of deaths and the number of people affected, and substantially decrease the direct economic losses relative to global gross domestic product caused by disasters, including water-related disasters, with a focus on protecting the poor and people in vulnerable situations 11.5.2: Direct Economic Loss Attributed to Disasters ($ million)	Target 11.6: By 2030, reduce the adverse per capita environmental impact of cities, including by paying special attention to air quality and municipal and other waste management 11.6.2: Annual Mean Levels (µg/m³) of Fine Particulate Matter (e.g. $PM_{2.5}$ and PM_{10}) in Cities (Population Weighted)	
	2000	2016	2018	Total 2016	Urban 2016
Developing ADB Member Economies					
Central and West Asia					
Afghanistan	...	71.3	52.2 (2017)	53.2	59.9
Armenia	...	9.3	13.4 (2017)	30.5	32.9
Azerbaijan	...	...	...	18.2	18.5
Georgia	...	34.1	0.4 (2017)	21.2	24.0
Kazakhstan	...	...	5.0	11.3	14.5
Kyrgyz Republic	...	9.7	14.9	18.1	17.4
Pakistan	48.7	40.8	17.5	55.2	56.2
Tajikistan	...	26.0	6.4	40.0	42.8
Turkmenistan	...	...	...	19.0	24.2
Uzbekistan	...	52.2	...	25.3	28.9
East Asia					
China, People's Republic of	37.3	25.2 (2014)	...	49.2	51.0
Hong Kong, China	...	...	...	...	...
Korea, Republic of	...	...	171.9 (2017)	24.6	24.7
Mongolia	64.9	38.3	149.4 (2017)	40.4	49.5
Taipei,China	...	...	...	...	...
South Asia					
Bangladesh	77.8	49.4	...	58.3	58.6
Bhutan	...	...	1.8	35.3	35.4
India	41.5	35.4	...	65.2	68.0
Maldives	...	32.1	...	7.6	7.7
Nepal	64.0	51.0	32.2	94.3	99.5
Sri Lanka	...	...	272.1	15.2	15.1
Southeast Asia					
Brunei Darussalam	...	...	...	5.8	5.8
Cambodia	78.9 (2005)	47.7	60.9 (2017)	24.0	24.9
Indonesia	34.4	30.9	600.7	15.6	16.4
Lao People's Democratic Republic	79.3 (2005)	20.8	11.2 (2012)	24.5	25.5
Malaysia	...	...	354.8	16.0	17.3
Myanmar	45.6 (2005)	56.6	1,249.6 (2017)	34.7	34.6
Philippines	47.2	43.5	...	18.4	18.7
Singapore	...	...	...	18.3	18.3
Thailand	26.0 (2005)	24.6	...	26.2	26.6
Viet Nam	48.8	14.4	945.0 (2010)	29.7	30.1
The Pacific					
Cook Islands	...	...	– (2010)	12.0	...
Fiji	...	10.8	50.3	10.2	10.5
Kiribati	...	...	0.3 (2014)	10.5	10.9
Marshall Islands	...	...	0.4 (2014)	9.4	...
Micronesia, Federated States of	...	...	...	10.2	10.5
Nauru	...	...	...	12.5	12.5
Niue	...	...	...	11.5	...
Palau	...	...	5.6 (2012)	12.2	12.4
Papua New Guinea	...	...	1.6 (2013)	10.9	11.5
Samoa	...	...	25.8 (2009)	10.6	10.9
Solomon Islands	...	...	11.9 (2013)	10.7	11.5
Timor-Leste	...	34.0	1.7 (2016)	17.9	18.2
Tonga	...	...	8.0	10.1	10.2
Tuvalu	...	...	...	11.4	...
Vanuatu	...	...	0.2 (2014)	10.3	11.0
Developed ADB Member Economies					
Australia	...	...	169.9	7.2	7.3
Japan	...	...	...	11.4	11.8
New Zealand	...	...	120.8	5.7	5.8

... = data not available, – = magnitude equals zero, $ = United States dollars, ADB = Asian Development Bank, m³ = cubic meter, PM = particulate matter, µg = microgram.

Source: United Nations Statistics Division. Sustainable Development Goals (SDGs), SDG Indicators, Global Database. https://unstats.un.org/sdgs/indicators/database/ (accessed 8 July 2019).

Goal 12. Ensure sustainable consumption and production patterns

Table 1.12.1: Selected Indicators for Sustainable Development Goal 12—Responsible Consumption and Production

ADB Regional Member	Target 12.2: By 2030, achieve the sustainable management and efficient use of natural resources							
	12.2.1: Material Footprint				12.2.2: Domestic Material Consumption			
	All (t million)		Per Capita (t)		All (t million)		Per Capita (t)	
	2000	2017	2000	2017	2000	2017	2000	2017
Developing ADB Member Economies								
Central and West Asia								
Afghanistan	11.9	42.6	0.6	1.2	46.0	67.9	2.3	1.9
Armenia	7.2	24.0	2.3	8.2	13.8	32.5	4.5	11.1
Azerbaijan	20.4	61.8	2.5	6.3	30.1	90.1	3.7	9.2
Georgia	14.2	35.6	3.0	9.1	13.3	26.5	2.8	6.8
Kazakhstan	172.8	325.2	11.5	17.9	249.3	530.4	16.6	29.1
Kyrgyz Republic	29.2	48.1	5.9	8.0	32.0	50.6	6.5	8.4
Pakistan	354.7	627.0	2.6	3.2	514.2	875.8	3.7	4.4
Tajikistan	4.5	33.3	0.7	3.7	10.2	31.2	1.6	3.5
Turkmenistan	45.0	124.3	10.0	21.6	43.4	94.9	9.6	16.5
Uzbekistan	115.4	197.4	4.6	6.2	195.5	289.2	7.9	9.1
East Asia								
China, People's Republic of	8,864.7	27,670.5	6.9	19.6	11,782.8	35,101.0	9.2	24.9
Hong Kong, China	...	...	...	...	...	...	...	...
Korea, Republic of	1,056.5	1,346.1	22.3	26.4	746.1	576.9	15.7	11.3
Mongolia	9.1	42.6	3.8	13.9	49.0	106.2	20.4	34.5
Taipei,China	...	...	...	...	...	...	...	...
South Asia								
Bangladesh	228.2	387.7	1.7	2.4	254.4	435.7	1.9	2.6
Bhutan	2.6	8.4	4.5	10.4	4.7	8.4	8.3	10.4
India	2,941.9	6,135.9	2.8	4.6	3,866.5	7,403.2	3.7	5.5
Maldives	1.8	6.4	6.3	14.6	1.2	3.0	4.1	6.8
Nepal	30.3	79.2	1.3	2.7	61.7	111.6	2.6	3.8
Sri Lanka	37.0	79.7	2.0	3.8	57.9	107.4	3.1	5.1
Southeast Asia								
Brunei Darussalam	4.2	8.2	12.6	19.1	5.8	9.8	17.3	22.9
Cambodia	20.2	57.2	1.7	3.6	26.9	84.6	2.2	5.3
Indonesia	711.4	1,643.6	3.4	6.2	1,156.3	1,972.5	5.5	7.5
Lao People's Democratic Republic	6.7	50.6	1.3	7.4	13.7	82.2	2.6	12.0
Malaysia	445.0	714.9	19.2	22.6	387.9	517.8	16.7	16.4
Myanmar	24.5	79.9	0.5	1.5	106.9	187.6	2.3	3.5
Philippines	311.9	455.5	4.0	4.3	295.0	415.7	3.8	4.0
Singapore	200.2	417.0	51.1	73.0	259.8	186.1	66.4	32.6
Thailand	487.8	1,029.0	7.7	14.9	477.3	879.1	7.6	12.7
Viet Nam	274.9	956.6	3.4	10.0	332.2	1,049.5	4.1	11.0
The Pacific								
Cook Islands	...	...	...	...	...	...	...	...
Fiji	4.4	6.4	5.4	7.0	8.1	5.5	10.0	6.1
Kiribati	...	...	...	...	0.4	0.7	4.2	6.3
Marshall Islands	...	...	...	...	0.0	0.1	0.4	2.0
Micronesia, Federated States of	...	...	...	...	0.2	0.2	1.4	2.3
Nauru	...	...	...	...	...	...	...	...
Niue	...	...	...	...	...	...	...	...
Palau	...	...	...	...	0.0	0.0	0.2	1.2
Papua New Guinea	11.6	21.3	2.1	2.6	76.9	83.8	13.8	10.2
Samoa	0.7	1.7	4.1	8.4	0.7	1.0	4.0	5.3
Solomon Islands	...	...	...	...	2.2	4.3	5.4	7.0
Timor-Leste	...	...	...	...	0.9	10.0	1.1	7.7
Tonga	...	...	...	...	0.3	1.8	3.4	16.9
Tuvalu	...	...	...	...	0.0	0.0	0.9	1.1
Vanuatu	0.6	2.2	3.4	7.9	1.0	1.7	5.3	6.1
Developed ADB Member Economies								
Australia	643.6	1,050.7	33.8	43.0	868.2	927.3	45.5	37.9
Japan	3,539.6	3,138.5	27.8	24.6	1,571.5	1,139.9	12.3	8.9
New Zealand	82.0	114.5	21.2	24.3	95.7	113.3	24.8	24.1

... = data not available, 0.0 = magnitude is less than half of unit employed, ADB = Asian Development Bank, t = metric ton.

Source: For Indicator 12.2.1: Organisation for Economic Co-operation and Development. OECD Statistics - Material Resources. hhttps://stats.oecd.org/ (accessed 22 July 2019). For Indicator 12.2.2: United Nations Statistics Division. Sustainable Development Goals (SDGs), SDG Indicators, Global Database. https://unstats.un.org/sdgs/indicators/database/ (accessed 8 July 2019).

Goal 13. Take urgent action to combat climate change and its impacts

Table 1.13.1: Selected Indicators for Sustainable Development Goal 13—Impact of Disasters and Risk Reduction Strategies

| ADB Regional Member | Target 13.1: Strengthen resilience and adaptive capacity to climate-related hazards and natural disasters in all countries | | | | 13.1.2: Countries that Adopt and Implement National Disaster Risk Reduction Strategies in Line with the Sendai Framework for Disaster Risk Reduction 2015–2030[a] |
| | 13.1.1.a: Number of Persons Affected by Disaster | | 13.1.1.b: Number of Deaths Due to Disaster | | |
	2005	2018	2005	2018	2018
Developing ADB Member Economies					
Central and West Asia					
Afghanistan	...	24,644 (2017)	...	17 (2017)	0.25 (2017)
Armenia	...	8,228 (2017)	...	302 (2017)	1.00 (2017)
Azerbaijan	...	...	...	...	...
Georgia	...	103 (2017)	...	2	0.98
Kazakhstan	496	15,743	6	1	0.85
Kyrgyz Republic	1,105	1,105 (2017)	1 (2006)	7	0.93
Pakistan	4,121,220	6,817	45,275	137	...
Tajikistan	...	1,193	...	12	...
Turkmenistan	...	...	...	...	...
Uzbekistan	...	...	...	...	...
East Asia					
China, People's Republic of	...	6,493,721	...	589	...
Hong Kong, China	...	...	...	...	...
Korea, Republic of	...	22,089 (2017)	...	68 (2017)	0.95 (2017)
Mongolia	...	8,514 (2017)	193	204 (2017)	1.00 (2017)
Taipei,China	...	...	...	...	...
South Asia					
Bangladesh	...	12,384,370 (2017)	...	716 (2017)	...
Bhutan	...	244	...	12	0.50
India	...	...	...	...	...
Maldives	1,012	...	1	...	...
Nepal	294,950 (2006)	64,256	599 (2006)	478	0.38
Sri Lanka	55,910	103,403	123	250	...
Southeast Asia					
Brunei Darussalam	...	...	...	...	...
Cambodia	15,243	43,067 (2017)	29	98 (2017)	...
Indonesia	569,620	11,094,891	1,960	3,369	...
Lao People's Democratic Republic	730,208	5,254 (2012)	19	19 (2012)	...
Malaysia	10,158	51,298	14	31 (2017)	–
Myanmar	38,837	1,023,154 (2017)	17	554 (2017)	0.70 (2017)
Philippines	...	5,562,065	...	255	...
Singapore	...	...	...	...	...
Thailand	...	142,780	...	81	0.58
Viet Nam	108,432	651,751 (2010)	675	60 (2010)	...
The Pacific					
Cook Islands	1,681	4,443 (2010)	...	3 (2010)	...
Fiji	60 (2006)	155,726	3	8	...
Kiribati	...	176 (2014)	...	...	...
Marshall Islands	96 (2008)	280 (2014)	...	...	...
Micronesia, Federated States of	...	...	...	10 (2015)	...
Nauru	...	...	...	...	...
Niue	...	...	...	...	...
Palau	...	1,528 (2012)	...	...	...
Papua New Guinea	2	264 (2013)	4	30 (2015)	...
Samoa	270 (2008)	6,332 (2009)	18	1 (2014)	0.70
Solomon Islands	21,343 (2007)	4,800 (2013)	138 (2007)	22 (2014)	...
Timor-Leste	2,388 (2006)	805 (2016)	1 (2007)	3 (2016)	...
Tonga	7 (2006)	86,275	...	1 (2014)	...
Tuvalu	...	...	...	...	...
Vanuatu	4 (2007)	152 (2014)	2 (2006)	11 (2015)	...
Developed ADB Member Economies					
Australia	...	25,022	...	1	0.63
Japan	...	199,903 (2016)	...	136 (2017)	1.00
New Zealand	...	547	...	1 (2017)	0.88

... = data not available, – = magnitude equals zero, ADB = Asian Development Bank.

a Economies displaying data in this column have adopted and implemented national disaster risk reduction strategies. Data refers to the score for adoption and implementation of national disaster risk reduction strategies in line with the Sendai Framework. The scores indicate the compliance of alignment of national strategies with the Sendai Framework, based on self-assessments of the economy using 10 criteria for monitoring the progress of national national disaster risk reduction strategies. The score ranges are as follows: 1 = comprehensive alignment, 0.75 = substantial alignment, 0.50 = moderate alignment, 0.25 = limited alignment, 0 = no alignment.

Source: United Nations Statistics Division. Sustainable Development Goals (SDGs), SDG Indicators, Global Database. https://unstats.un.org/sdgs/indicators/database/ (accessed 8 July 2019).

Goal 14. Conserve and sustainably use the oceans, seas, and marine resources for sustainable development

Table 1.14.1: Selected Indicators for Sustainable Development Goal 14—Life Below Water

ADB Regional Member	Target 14.5: By 2020, conserve at least 10% of coastal and marine areas, consistent with national and international law and based on the best available scientific information		
	14.5.1.a: Average Proportion of Marine Key Biodiversity Areas Covered by Protected Areas (%)	14.5.1.b: Coverage of Protected Areas in Relation to Marine Areas (Exclusive Economic Zones) (%)	14.5.1.c: Protected Marine Areas (Exclusive Economic Zones) (km²)
	2018	2018	2018
Developing ADB Member Economies			
Central and West Asia			
Afghanistan	...	...	...
Armenia	...	...	...
Azerbaijan	...	0.4	345.4
Georgia	26.5	0.7	153.0
Kazakhstan	...	1.0	1,249.5
Kyrgyz Republic	...	...	...
Pakistan	39.3	0.8	1,707.4
Tajikistan	...	...	...
Turkmenistan	...	3.0	2,331.8
Uzbekistan	...	...	...
East Asia			
China, People's Republic of	21.7	5.4	47,502.6
Hong Kong, China	43.6	...	62.8
Korea, Republic of	24.2	1.6	5,308.8
Mongolia	...	...	...
Taipei,China	...	...	...
South Asia			
Bangladesh	34.5	5.3	4,458.4
Bhutan	...	...	...
India	37.7	0.2	3,962.3
Maldives	–	0.1	474.9
Nepal	...	...	...
Sri Lanka	43.4	0.1	398.6
Southeast Asia			
Brunei Darussalam	60.9	0.2	51.6
Cambodia	19.2	0.2	89.1
Indonesia	23.4	3.1	181,846.6
Lao People's Democratic Republic	...	...	...
Malaysia	28.5	1.0	4,709.0
Myanmar	21.4	2.3	11,964.4
Philippines	44.2	1.2	21,267.4
Singapore	3.3	0.0	0.1
Thailand	60.4	1.9	5,773.8
Viet Nam	44.2	0.6	3,630.3
The Pacific			
Cook Islands	28.3	100.0	1,972,774.8
Fiji	15.9	0.9	11,959.0
Kiribati	40.2	11.8	408,793.3
Marshall Islands	12.3	0.3	5,388.4
Micronesia, Federated States of	1.6	0.0	475.1
Nauru	–	...	...
Niue	...	0.0	36.9
Palau	...	83.0	504,690.9
Papua New Guinea	1.9	0.2	4,585.5
Samoa	11.9	0.1	114.8
Solomon Islands	9.4	0.1	1,900.4
Timor-Leste	18.8	1.4	584.1
Tonga	5.9	1.5	10,055.2
Tuvalu	...	0.0	62.1
Vanuatu	4.7	0.0	47.5
Developed ADB Member Economies			
Australia	66.0	40.6	3,014,642.6
Japan	73.5	8.2	331,976.8
New Zealand	44.6	29.7	1,221,615.5

... = data not available, – = magnitude equals zero, 0.0 = magnitude is less than half of unit employed, ADB = Asian Development Bank, km² = square kilometer.

Source: United Nations Statistics Division. Sustainable Development Goals (SDGs), SDG Indicators, Global Database. https://unstats.un.org/sdgs/indicators/database/ (accessed 8 July 2019).

Goal 15. Protect, restore, and promote sustainable use of terrestrial ecosystems; sustainably manage forests; combat desertification and halt and reverse land degradation; and halt biodiversity loss

Table 1.15.1: Selected Indicators for Sustainable Development Goal 15—Protection of Ecosystems and Biodiversity

ADB Regional Member	Target 15.1: By 2020, ensure the conservation, restoration, and sustainable use of terrestrial and inland freshwater ecosystems and their services, in particular forests, wetlands, mountains, and drylands, in line with obligations under international agreements						Target 15.4: By 2030, ensure the conservation of mountain ecosystems, including their biodiversity, in order to enhance their capacity to provide benefits that are essential for sustainable development		Target 15.5: Take urgent and significant action to reduce the degradation of natural habitats, halt the loss of biodiversity and, by 2020, protect and prevent the extinction of threatened species	
	15.1.1: Forest Area as a Proportion of Total Land Area (%)		15.1.2: Proportion of Important Sites for Terrestrial and Freshwater Biodiversity that are Covered by Protected Areas				15.4.1: Coverage by Protected Areas of Important Sites for Mountain Biodiversity (%)		15.5.1: Red List Index[a]	
			Terrestrial (%)		Freshwater (%)					
	2000	2016	2000	2018	2000	2018	2000	2018	2000	2018
Developing ADB Member Economies										
Central and West Asia										
Afghanistan	2.07	2.07	0.0	6.1	0.1	0.1	0.1	12.3	0.84	0.84
Armenia	11.7	11.7	22.1	30.5	25.1	26.9	17.5	28.0	0.85	0.85
Azerbaijan	10.6	14.1	20.4	39.4	6.1	24.5	30.5	58.8	0.91	0.91
Georgia	39.7	40.6	15.4	28.4	1.8	27.3	15.6	30.1	0.88	0.86
Kazakhstan	1.3	1.2	9.6	16.3	8.4	17.4	28.0	30.2	0.88	0.87
Kyrgyz Republic	4.5	3.3	21.7	22.6	29.8	31.1	28.5	30.2	0.99	0.98
Pakistan	2.7	1.9	35.0	36.6	36.3	37.0	36.0	36.0	0.93	0.86
Tajikistan	2.9	3.0	17.6	21.0	27.2	34.6	15.9	19.5	0.99	0.99
Turkmenistan	8.8	8.8	14.4	14.6	12.7	13.1	21.3	21.3	0.98	0.97
Uzbekistan	7.6	7.5	11.1	15.9	1.8	10.4	37.5	37.5	0.98	0.97
East Asia										
China, People's Republic of	18.8	22.3	44.2	47.6	31.1	36.1	62.2	65.0	0.81	0.74
Hong Kong, China	...	...	...	...	...	...	...	...	0.82	0.82
Korea, Republic of	65.2	63.4	25.3	36.6	29.7	36.8	...	...	0.79	0.73
Mongolia	7.5	8.0	33.1	43.7	30.7	42.1	42.5	47.0	0.96	0.95
Taipei,China	58.1 (2001)	60.7 (2017)	...	...	...	...	...	...	...	...
South Asia										
Bangladesh	11.3	11.0	37.8	48.0	20.8	20.8	...	...	0.83	0.76
Bhutan	65.5	72.5	38.6	42.9	23.1	34.3	38.6	42.9	0.80	0.80
India	22.0	23.8	21.7	26.1	13.2	15.2	28.0	35.4	0.75	0.68
Maldives	3.3	3.3	–	–	...	...	...	...	0.91	0.84
Nepal	27.2	25.4	42.2	54.6	21.9	36.5	57.1	67.1	0.82	0.83
Sri Lanka	35.0	32.9	41.6	49.8	72.6	79.9	25.9	40.2	0.66	0.56
Southeast Asia										
Brunei Darussalam	75.3	72.1	62.9	62.9	50.0	50.0	...	...	0.85	0.82
Cambodia	65.4	52.9	35.8	39.5	28.0	33.0	92.3	92.3	0.87	0.82
Indonesia	54.9	49.9	19.2	23.5	33.0	39.3	19.8	23.4	0.84	0.75
Lao People's Democratic Republic	71.6	82.1	44.0	45.5	19.9	19.9	56.7	56.7	0.82	0.81
Malaysia	65.7	67.6	38.9	39.5	76.6	76.6	37.3	37.6	0.83	0.68
Myanmar	53.4	43.6	15.6	22.9	14.8	18.5	23.3	42.2	0.86	0.81
Philippines	23.6	27.8	29.9	41.7	48.1	48.1	28.3	43.9	0.73	0.64
Singapore	24.4	23.1	19.0	21.1	...	...	...	...	0.91	0.86
Thailand	33.3	32.2	67.2	71.7	43.4	43.6	85.6	91.9	0.85	0.79
Viet Nam	37.7	48.1	12.0	40.9	11.6	33.2	13.3	48.1	0.81	0.73
The Pacific										
Cook Islands	...	...	...	...	...	...	...	...	0.79	0.77
Fiji	53.7	55.9	2.9	4.9	–	0.1	5.7	11.4	0.70	0.67
Kiribati	15.0	15.0	12.5	52.5	...	...	...	...	0.81	0.76
Marshall Islands	70.2	70.2	–	25.4	...	...	...	...	0.90	0.84
Micronesia, Federated States of	91.2	91.9	1.3	1.3	...	...	–	–	0.76	0.69
Nauru	–	–	–	–	...	...	...	...	0.82	0.77
Niue	...	...	...	...	...	...	...	...	0.76	0.77
Palau	86.1	87.6	0.0	36.6	...	...	...	...	0.91	0.73
Papua New Guinea	74.2	74.1	6.9	7.3	...	...	6.3	6.8	0.90	0.84
Samoa	60.4	60.4	16.3	36.5	...	...	19.0	51.3	0.85	0.81
Solomon Islands	81.0	77.9	3.9	9.5	...	...	0.3	0.3	0.83	0.77
Timor-Leste	57.4	45.4	14.9	38.7	...	...	13.5	42.0	0.95	0.89
Tonga	12.5	12.5	0.7	9.3	...	...	...	...	0.76	0.72
Tuvalu	33.3	33.3	...	...	...	...	...	...	0.89	0.84
Vanuatu	36.1	36.1	6.2	6.4	...	...	9.2	9.3	0.72	0.66
Developed ADB Member Economies										
Australia	16.8	16.3	34.9	54.3	24.1	35.1	59.6	82.5	0.88	0.83
Japan	68.3	68.5	59.9	68.5	60.8	67.0	71.4	74.3	0.84	0.78
New Zealand	38.5	38.6	40.2	44.3	20.0	26.7	20.9	29.0	0.71	0.63

... = data not available, 0.0 = magnitude is less than half of unit employed, – = magnitude equals zero, ADB = Asian Development Bank.

a The Red List Index midpoint value ranges from 1, which means all species are categorized as 'Least Concern' hence that none are expected to go extinct in the near future, to 0 meaning all species are categorized as 'Extinct'. The index therefore indicates how far the set of species has moved overall towards extinction.

Source: For Indicator 15.1.1, Indicator 15.1.2, and Indicator 15.4.1: United Nations Environment Programme. Environment Live Statistics. https://environmentlive.unep.org/ statistics (accessed 7 August 2019). For Indicator 15.1.1 for Taipei,China: Directorate-General of Budget, Accounting and Statistics. https://eng.stat.gov.tw/ (accessed 22 July 2019). For Indicator 15.5.1: United Nations Statistics Division. Sustainable Development Goals (SDGs), SDG Indicators, Global Database. https://unstats. un.org/sdgs/indicators/database/ (accessed 8 July 2019).

Goal 16. Promote peaceful and inclusive societies for sustainable development; provide access to justice for all; and build effective, accountable, and inclusive institutions at all levels

Table 1.16.1: Selected Indicators for Sustainable Development Goal 16—Peace, Justice, and Strong Institutions

ADB Regional Member	Target 16.1: Significantly reduce all forms of violence and related death rates everywhere — 16.1.1: Number of Victims of Intentional Homicide (per 100,000 population)				Target 16.3: Promote the rule of law at the national and international levels and ensure equal access to justice for all — 16.3.2: Unsentenced Detainees as a Proportion of Overall Prison Population (%)			Target 16.5: Substantially reduce corruption and bribery in all their forms — 16.5.2: Proportion of Firms Experiencing at least One Bribe Payment Request (%)		Target 16.9: By 2030, provide legal identity for all, including birth registration — 16.9.1: Proportion of Children Under 5 Years of Age Whose Births have been Registered with a Civil Authority[a] (%)	
	2000		2017		2005[b]	2017[c]		2013		2017	
Developing ADB Member Economies											
Central and West Asia											
Afghanistan	...		7.1		81.0	30.8		46.8	(2014)	42.3	(2015)
Armenia	3.0		2.4		28.1	32.1		7.1		99.3	(2016)
Azerbaijan	2.8		2.0		12.0	17.2		15.9		...	
Georgia	5.1		1.0	(2016)	52.9	13.1		2.2		99.6	(2015)
Kazakhstan	15.4 [d]		5.0 [d]		15.6	15.1		26.7		99.7	(2015)
Kyrgyz Republic	8.7		4.2		16.2	18.4		59.8		97.7	(2014)
Pakistan	6.4		4.2		57.8	67.0		30.8		33.6	(2013)
Tajikistan	4.6		1.6	(2011)	...	...		36.3		95.8	
Turkmenistan	5.9		...		...	...		...		99.6	(2016)
Uzbekistan	4.3		1.1		...	...		7.0		...	
East Asia											
China, People's Republic of	2.1		0.6		...	...		11.6	(2012)	...	
Hong Kong, China	0.6		0.3		11.5	20.3		...		...	
Korea, Republic of	0.8		0.6		34.2	35.7		...		...	
Mongolia	13.9	(2003)	6.2		18.8	19.8		33.4		99.3	(2013)
Taipei,China	1.4	(2001)	0.8	(2015)	...	...		...		...	
South Asia											
Bangladesh	2.5		2.2		64.0	78.5		47.7		20.2	(2014)
Bhutan	3.1		1.6		...	...		0.9	(2015)	99.9	(2010)
India	4.6		3.2	(2016)	67.9	67.2		22.7	(2014)	79.7	(2016)
Maldives	2.4	(2001)	0.8	(2013)	...	...		...		92.5	(2009)
Nepal	2.7		2.2	(2016)	...	...		14.4		56.2	(2016)
Sri Lanka	6.8 [d]	(2003)	2.3 [d]		52.4	55.3		10.0	(2011)	...	
Southeast Asia											
Brunei Darussalam	1.2		0.5	(2013)	7.2	7.1		...		...	
Cambodia	4.7		1.8	(2011)	32.6	28.3		64.7	(2016)	73.3	(2014)
Indonesia	1.0		0.4		46.6	32.0		30.6	(2015)	71.9	(2018)
Lao People's Democratic Republic	...		...		...	...		40.3	(2018)	73.0	
Malaysia	2.4		2.1	(2013)	33.8	29.3		28.2	(2015)	...	
Myanmar	2.3		2.3	(2016)	...	...		29.3	(2016)	81.3	(2016)
Philippines	7.4 [d]		8.4 [d]		66.7	73.0		17.2	(2015)	91.8	
Singapore	1.0		0.2		4.1	10.9		...		...	
Thailand	8.2		3.2	(2016)	24.6	18.2		9.9	(2016)	99.5	(2016)
Viet Nam	1.2	(2001)	1.5	(2011)	...	...		26.1	(2015)	96.1	(2014)
The Pacific											
Cook Islands	...		3.5	(2012)	3.7	17.7		...		...	
Fiji	3.1	(2003)	2.3	(2014)	8.7	28.0		10.5	(2009)	...	
Kiribati	3.6		7.5	(2012)	2.6	5.1		...		93.5	(2009)
Marshall Islands	...		...		...	...		...		83.8	
Micronesia, Federated States of	...		...		...	...		4.5	(2009)	...	
Nauru	...		...		...	...		...		95.9	(2013)
Niue	...		...		...	...		...		...	
Palau	...		...		...	...		...		...	
Papua New Guinea	8.3		10.0	(2010)	31.3	38.1		26.4	(2015)	...	
Samoa	...		3.1	(2013)	...	...		30.5	(2009)	58.6	(2014)
Solomon Islands	4.4	(2004)	...		35.4	50.2		43.8	(2015)	88.0	(2015)
Timor-Leste	2.3	(2004)	3.9	(2015)	64.7	24.0		44.2	(2015)	60.4	(2016)
Tonga	1.0		1.0	(2012)	2.6	7.4		24.9	(2009)	93.4	(2012)
Tuvalu	–	(2002)	18.6	(2012)	...	...		...		...	
Vanuatu	...		...		22.5	20.4		11.9	(2009)	43.4	(2013)
Developed ADB Member Economies											
Australia	1.9		0.8		20.4	30.1		...		100.0	(2013)
Japan	0.5		0.2		15.0	11.1		...		100.0	(2013)
New Zealand	1.3 [d]		0.7 [d]		18.4	22.3		...		100.0	(2014)

... = data not available, – = magnitude equals zero, ADB = Asian Development Bank.

a Changes in the definition of birth registration were made from the second and third rounds of Multiple Indicator Cluster Surveys (MICS2 and MICS3) to the fourth round (MICS4). In order to allow for comparability with the latter round, data from MICS2 and MICS3 on birth registration were recalculated according to the MICS4 indicator definition. Therefore, the recalculated data presented here may differ from estimates included in MICS2 and MICS3 national reports.

b For 2005, data refer to a 3-year average for 2003–2005.

c For 2017, data refer to a 3-year average for 2015–2017.

d For Kazakhstan, the Philippines, and Sri Lanka: Changes in definitions and/or counting rules are reported by the Member State to indicate a break in the time series. For New Zealand: For 2000–2006, data refer to offences; for 2007 onward, data refer to victims of intentional homicide.

Sources: For Indicator 16.1.1: United Nations Office on Drugs and Crime. Statistics Online. https://dataunodc.un.org/ (accessed 24 July 2019). For Indicators 16.3.2, 16.5.2, and 16.9.1: United Nations Statistics Division. Sustainable Development Goals (SDGs), SDG Indicators, Global Database. https://unstats.un.org/sdgs/indicators/database/ (accessed 8 July 2019).

Goal 17. Strengthen the means of implementation and revitalize the Global Partnership for Sustainable Development

Table 1.17.1: Selected Indicators for Sustainable Development Goal 17—Financial Sustainability of Developing Countries

| ADB Regional Member | Target 17.4: Assist developing countries in attaining long-term debt sustainability through coordinated policies aimed at fostering debt financing, debt relief, and debt restructuring, as appropriate, and address the external debt of highly indebted poor countries to reduce debt distress | | Target 17.9: Enhance international support for implementing effective and targeted capacity-building in developing countries to support national plans to implement all the Sustainable Development Goals, including through North-South, South-South, and triangular cooperation | |
| | 17.4.1: Debt Service as a Proportion of Exports of Goods and Services (%) | | 17.9.1: Dollar Value of Financial and Technical Assistance Committed to Developing Countries[a] (constant 2017 $ million) | |
	2000	2017	Average, 2000–2008	Average, 2009–2017
Developing ADB Member Economies				
Central and West Asia				
Afghanistan	0.5 (2008)	3.8	562.1	1,404.7
Armenia	8.2	5.3	64.9	94.0
Azerbaijan	5.5	7.6	32.1	95.7
Georgia	12.2	6.7	80.5	130.6
Kazakhstan	8.8	3.3	55.7	303.5
Kyrgyz Republic	9.8	6.1	50.9	90.5
Pakistan	21.1	20.1	364.7	893.9
Tajikistan	9.1 (2002)	6.5	29.8	40.5
Turkmenistan	...	...	6.1	6.2
Uzbekistan	...	...	37.1	145.6
East Asia				
China, People's Republic of	7.1	0.6	332.4	630.6
Hong Kong, China	...	...	...	...
Korea, Republic of	...	...	...	...
Mongolia	6.5	4.2	38.2	169.0
Taipei,China	...	...	...	...
South Asia				
Bangladesh	10.3	3.5	235.7	439.8
Bhutan	2.5 (2006)	10.1	15.1	22.4
India	15.4	2.9	477.9	627.9
Maldives	4.0	2.4	3.6	9.2
Nepal	7.4	7.4	79.4	163.8
Sri Lanka	10.9	19.3	111.3	112.5
Southeast Asia				
Brunei Darussalam	...	...	87.2	124.5
Cambodia	0.7	1.3	641.1	1,310.1
Indonesia	11.2	9.2	47.1	76.5
Lao People's Democratic Republic	7.9	8.9	17.7	14.0
Malaysia	...	...	15.7	171.1
Myanmar	1.0	5.1	135.0	362.8
Philippines	14.6	5.3	...	...
Singapore	...	...	46.1	66.2
Thailand	5.8	0.2	305.9	690.2
Viet Nam	7.2	1.4		
The Pacific				
Cook Islands	...	...	2.3	4.4
Fiji	2.5	2.3	16.6	16.9
Kiribati	...	...	8.6	8.8
Marshall Islands	...	...	18.4	9.2
Micronesia, Federated States of	...	...	39.3	22.6
Nauru	...	...	9.2	8.8
Niue	...	...	1.7	6.7
Palau	...	...	1.7	3.2
Papua New Guinea	8.0	1.3	95.2	162.0
Samoa	5.5 (2004)	8.9	15.7	33.6
Solomon Islands	2.8	1.5	80.2	69.0
Timor-Leste	– (2006)	0.1	53.9	47.4
Tonga	9.8 (2001)	9.9	10.6	14.4
Tuvalu	...	...	3.3	4.0
Vanuatu	1.4	2.0 (2016)	13.3	19.4
Developed ADB Member Economies				
Australia	...	...	...	...
Japan	...	...	...	...
New Zealand	...	...	...	...

... = data not available, $ = United States dollars, ADB = Asian Development Bank.

a   Technical assistance includes assistance through North-South, South-South, and triangular cooperation. United Nations Statistics Division dataset and metadata refer to this indicator as total official development assistance (gross disbursements) for technical cooperation.

Sources: For Indicator 17.4.1: World Bank. World Development Indicators. https://data.worldbank.org (accessed 19 July 2019). For Indicator 17.9.1: United Nations Statistics Division. Sustainable Development Goals (SDGs), SDG Indicators, Global Database. http://unstats.un.org/sdgs/indicators/database/ (accessed 8 July 2019).

Goal 17. Strengthen the means of implementation and revitalize the Global Partnership for Sustainable Development

Table 1.17.2: Selected Indicators for Sustainable Development Goal 17—Statistical Capacity Building

ADB Regional Member	Target 17.18: By 2020, enhance capacity-building support to developing countries, including for least developed countries and small island developing states, to increase significantly the availability of high-quality, timely, and reliable data disaggregated by income, gender, age, race, ethnicity, migratory status, disability, geographic location, and other characteristics relevant in national contexts	Target 17.19: By 2030, build on existing initiatives to develop measurements of progress on sustainable development that complement gross domestic product and support statistical capacity-building in developing countries		
	17.18.3: Availability of National Statistical Plan[a]	17.19.1: Value of All Resources Made Available to Strengthen Statistical Capacity in Developing Countries (current $)		17.19.2: Countries that Have Conducted at Least One Population and Housing Census in the Past 10 Years[b]
	2018	2006	2016	2018
Developing ADB Member Economies				
Central and West Asia				
Afghanistan	B	2,069,400.0	1,068,881.9	...
Armenia	A, B, C, D	56,731.7	62,246.8	2011
Azerbaijan	...	140,534.9	712,524.1	2009
Georgia	A, B, C	342,978.7	20,550.5	2014
Kazakhstan	A, B, C	372,625.0	257,878.3	2009
Kyrgyz Republic	A, B, C, D	260,060.6	154,417.3	2009
Pakistan	A, B, C	4,933,085.6	1,172,347.8	2017
Tajikistan	C, D, E	2,411,705.8	219,524.2	2010
Turkmenistan	...	279,722.6	73,769.5	2012
Uzbekistan	A, B, C, D, E	272,261.8	2,002,363.0	...
East Asia				
China, People's Republic of	A, B, C	1,568,187.0	180,924.5	2010
Hong Kong, China	A, B, C	...	...	2016
Korea, Republic of	B, C	...	...	2015
Mongolia	A, B, C, D	2,994,147.0	754,892.8	2010
Taipei,China	...	...	...	2010
South Asia				
Bangladesh	A, B, C, D	1,245,957.7	1,057,761.7	2011
Bhutan	A, B, D	598,515.6	105,675.9	2016
India	B, C	1,171,518.6	1,355,733.6	2011
Maldives	B, C	136,444.6	208,525.1	2014
Nepal	B, C, D	568,917.5	1,582,385.8	2011
Sri Lanka	D	361,402.2	938,315.0	2012
Southeast Asia				
Brunei Darussalam	A, C	...	4,978.0	2011
Cambodia	C, D	5,058,884.8	2,219,806.6	2008
Indonesia	...	795,895.3	615,634.0	2010
Lao People's Democratic Republic	B	468,513.1	507,017.1	2015
Malaysia	...	274,242.8	21,288.2	2010
Myanmar	B	1,187,054.1	1,843,609.9	2014
Philippines	B	773,000.7	114,773.8	2015
Singapore	A, B, C	...	...	2010
Thailand	A, B, C	510,883.2	43,542.2	2010
Viet Nam	B	5,598,915.4	1,055,629.5	2009
The Pacific				
Cook Islands	B	43,363.3	108,442.6	2016
Fiji	...	151,154.8	147,500.5	2017
Kiribati	...	50,302.5 (2007)	92,853.0	2015
Marshall Islands	...	53,283.3	79,617.9	2011
Micronesia, Federated States of	...	210,191.8	79,617.9	2010
Nauru	...	34,046.5 (2007)	79,617.9	2011
Niue	...	44,967.1 (2008)	79,617.9	2011
Palau	...	120,972.2	79,617.9	2015
Papua New Guinea	...	1,018,702.0	150,531.7	2011
Samoa	B	174,911.1	118,212.8	2016
Solomon Islands	B	66,377.7	1,348,830.7	2009
Timor-Leste	B	172,795.8	553,476.0	2015
Tonga	...	123,480.6	79,617.9	2016
Tuvalu	...	7,618.0 (2007)	89,360.3	2012
Vanuatu	C	489,116.6	125,678.4	2016
Developed ADB Member Economies				
Australia	A, B, C	...	...	2016
Japan	...	...	...	2015
New Zealand	A, B, C, E	...	...	2013

... = data not available, $ = United States dollars, ADB = Asian Development Bank.

a   A = a national statistical plan fully funded, B = a national statistical plan under implementation, C = a national statistical plan with funding from government, D = a national statistical plan with funding from donors, E = a national statistical plan with funding from others.

b   Refers to the most recent year in which a population and housing census was conducted.

Sources: United Nations Statistics Division. Sustainable Development Goals (SDGs), SDG Indicators, Global Database. http://unstats.un.org/sdgs/indicators/database/ (accessed 8 July 2019). For Taipei,China: Government of Taipei,China. Directorate-General of Budget, Accounting and Statistics. https://eng.stat.gov.tw/ (accessed 19 July 2019).

PART II

Regional Trends and Tables

Regional Tables and Trends—Data Stories

Part II of *Key Indicators for Asia and the Pacific 2019* contains 100 tables depicting social, economic, and environmental trends and developments in the 49 member economies of the Asian Development Bank (ADB) located in the Asia and the Pacific region. These statistical tables are grouped into eight themes, each with a short commentary highlighting important recent developments regarding select indicators. Each theme concludes with a section on data issues and comparability, wherein issues surrounding the collection and presentation of indicators are detailed.

The eight themes are People; Economy and Output; Money, Finance, and Prices; Globalization; Transport and Communications; Energy and Electricity; Environment; and Government and Governance.

Data patterns for the key indicators are summarized and/or visualized through charts and figures. These charts and figures compare indicators across ADB member economies and depict the most recent year for which data are available, which is generally 2018. In some cases, the most recent year for which data are available is compared to either the previous year (e.g., 2017) or an earlier year (e.g., 2000 or 2005). Such comparisons help the reader identify regional, subregional, and economy-level trends.

I.   People

People brings together standard demographic indicators such as population size and age structure, as well as primary education attainment levels. The regional tables in this section present data on birth, death, and fertility rates; age dependency ratios; urbanization and employment; poverty and inequality; health and education resources; international migration; and the Human Development Index.

Pace of population growth slows across Asia and the Pacific

The total population of the Asia and Pacific region reached 4,180 million in 2018, up from 3,435 million in 2000. The region's share of the global population gradually decreased from 55.9% in 2000 to 54.8% in 2018, as annual population growth rates over the review period slowed in all the subregions within Asia and the Pacific, except in Central and West Asia (Figure 2.1.1).

In 2018, annual population growth rates in the Pacific (2.6%), Central and West Asia (2.5%), and South Asia (1.2%) exceeded the global average (1.1%), while annual population growth was 1.1% in Southeast Asia and 0.4% in East Asia. Populations in developed ADB member economies expanded at an average of only 0.1% in 2018.

The most populous subregion in 2018 was South Asia (1,549 million). This was followed by East Asia (1,481 million), Southeast Asia (649 million), Central and West Asia (332 million), and the Pacific (13 million). In 2018, the aggregate population of the region's three developed member economies—Australia, Japan, and New Zealand—was 156 million.

According to the United Nations (UN), India is projected to overtake the People's Republic of China (PRC) as the world's most populous economy by 2027 (UN 2019a). Together, the two economies' populations comprised 35.7% of the global total in 2018. Among the world's 10 most populous countries in 2018, 6 were located in Asia and the Pacific: the PRC (1,395 million), India (1,332 million), Indonesia (265 million), Pakistan (213 million), Bangladesh (165 million), and Japan (127 million). The ADB member economies with the smallest populations in 2018 were all located in the Pacific: Niue (1,700), Nauru (11,400), and Tuvalu (11,600).

Girls are benefitting from education expansion across the region

In the 1970s, Asia and the Pacific was home to two-thirds of the world's out-of-school children. Today, about 90% of children, on average, are enrolled at the primary school level in economies across the region.[1]

In 2017 (or the most recent year for which data are available), 30 of the 35 ADB developing member economies with available data had a primary education attainment ratio that met or exceeded 90% for both boys and girls.[2] By comparison, in 2000 (or

---

[1]   For more information on education issues in Asia and the Pacific, go to https://www.adb.org/sectors/education/issues.

[2]   The primary education attainment ratios for boys and girls are defined as the gross intake levels for the last grade of primary education for both males and females. These calculations include all new entrants, by sex, regardless of age. Therefore, the ratios for boys and girls can exceed 100% due to inclusion in the numerator, but not in the denominator, of overaged and underaged children who enter school late or early, and/or repeat grades. For the full definition and data specifications, go to http://uis.unesco.org/en/glossary-term/gross-intake-ratio-last-grade-primary-education.

Figure 2.1.1: Distribution of Population by Global Region and by Economy in Asia and the Pacific, 2018
(%)

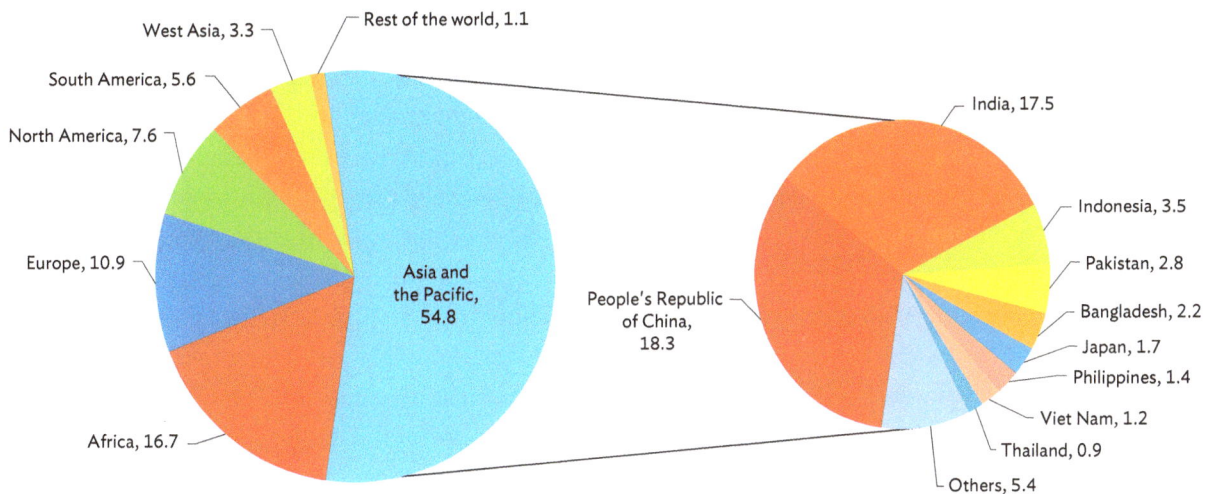

West Asia, 3.3 — Rest of the world, 1.1
South America, 5.6
North America, 7.6
Europe, 10.9
Asia and the Pacific, 54.8
Africa, 16.7

India, 17.5
Indonesia, 3.5
Pakistan, 2.8
Bangladesh, 2.2
Japan, 1.7
Philippines, 1.4
Viet Nam, 1.2
Thailand, 0.9
Others, 5.4
People's Republic of China, 18.3

Note: The aggregate for the West Asia region was adjusted to exclude Armenia, Azerbaijan, and Georgia, which are included in the total for Asia and the Pacific.
Source: Table 2.1.1, Key Indicators for Asia and the Pacific 2019.

the earliest year for which data are available), only 20 of the 35 economies had achieved this same measure of primary education attainment (Table 2.1.11).

During the review period, 28 economies increased their overall primary education attainment level (Table 2.1.11). Of these, 19 economies reported that the increase for girls exceeded that for boys, for which data are available. The largest gains in primary education attainment for girls, achieved over the review period, were observed in Nepal (60.9 percentage points), Bangladesh (56.2 percentage points), and Bhutan (53.4 percentage points) (Figure 2.1.2).

Data Issues and Comparability

Demographic data are based on vital registration records, censuses, and surveys. Since vital registration records in many ADB developing member economies are incomplete, they cannot be used for statistical purposes. In most economies, population censuses, which are used to provide more accurate estimates of population sizes, are conducted every 10 years. Population numbers in between census years are

Figure 2.1.2: Primary Education Completion Rate, by Sex:
(percentage point difference between earliest and most recently available annual data)

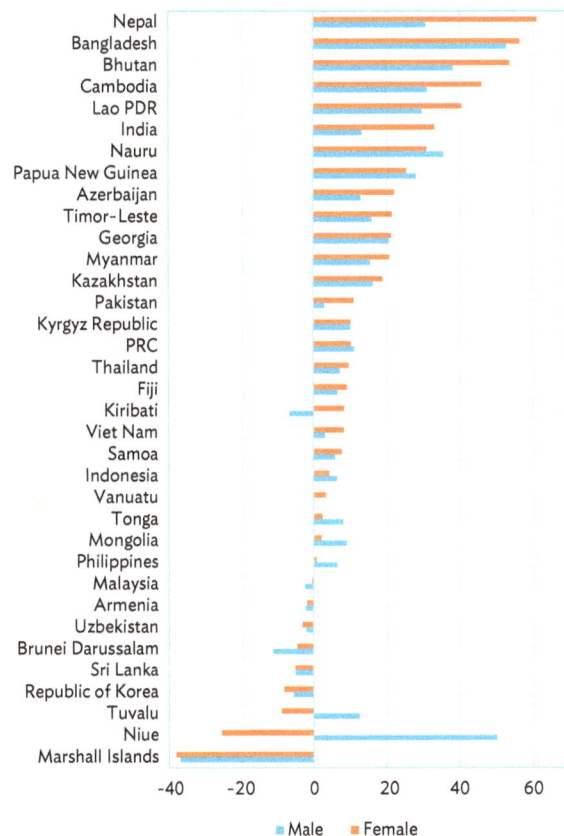

■ Male ■ Female

Lao PDR = Lao People's Democratic Republic, PRC = People's Republic of China.
Note: Earliest year refers to the period 2000 to 2008, while latest year refers to 2009 to 2018, where data are available. Only economies with available data for both earliest and latest years are included.
Source: Table 2.1.11, Key Indicators for Asia and the Pacific 2019.

products of imputation methods that use various population distributional assumptions.

The UN Department of Economics and Social Affairs' Population Division uses future trends on fertility, mortality, and international migration to project population numbers through to 2100. The medium-fertility variant included in *World Population Prospects 2019 Revision* assumes, over the remainder of the century, a decline of fertility in economies where large families are still prevalent, a slight increase of fertility in several economies where women have fewer than two live births on average over a lifetime, and continued reductions in mortality at all ages.

Urban population statistics are compiled according to each economy's national definition, as there is no agreed international standard for defining an urban area, which poses constraints in the comparability of urban and city indicators across economies. Data from *World Urbanization Prospects* are used when national estimates are not available.

Household surveys, which are the best source of labor force data, are not carried out in all economies on a regular basis. Some economies rely on census data supplemented by enterprise surveys and unemployment registration records, which are often incomplete and may refer only to formal employment. Furthermore, a breakdown by economic activities also may not be available. An initiative is underway to adopt new standards for work and employment statistics, following the recommendations of the 19th International Conference of Labour Statisticians in 2013, which included the need for more in-depth statistics on forced labor, cooperatives, and labor migration, as well as guidelines on a statistical definition of employment in the environment sector. The conceptual definitions used here are, however, based on the traditional framework.

Table 2.1.1:   Midyear Population

ADB Regional Member	Population (million)				Population Growth Rates[a] (%)			
	2000	2005	2010	2018	2000	2005	2010	2018
Developing ADB Member Economies								
Central and West Asia	**230.0**	**251.7**	**276.8**	**331.9**	**2.1**	**1.8**	**2.0**	**2.5**
Afghanistan[b]	19.5	22.1	24.5	30.1	5.0	1.9	2.1	6.6
Armenia	3.2	3.1	3.0	3.0*	-0.3	-0.6	-0.7	-0.3*
Azerbaijan	8.1	8.5	9.1	9.9	1.0	1.2	1.2	0.9
Georgia	4.1	3.9	3.8	3.7	-1.9	-0.6	-0.7	-0.0
Kazakhstan	14.9	15.1	16.3	18.3	-0.3	0.9	1.4	1.3
Kyrgyz Republic[b]	4.9	5.1	5.4	6.3	1.4	1.2	1.3	1.9
Pakistan	140.0	156.0	173.5	212.8	2.4	2.2	2.1	2.4
Tajikistan	6.2	6.8	7.5	9.0	2.3	1.2	2.5	2.1
Turkmenistan	4.5	4.8	5.1	5.9	1.1	1.1	1.6	1.6
Uzbekistan	24.7	26.2	28.6	33.0	1.4	1.2	2.9	1.8
East Asia	**1,345.7**	**1,387.8**	**1,423.4**	**1,481.2**	**0.8**	**0.6**	**0.5**	**0.4**
China, People's Republic of[b]	1,267.4	1,307.6	1,340.9	1,395.4	0.8	0.6	0.5	0.4
Hong Kong, China	6.7	6.8	7.0	7.5	0.9	0.4	0.7	0.8
Korea, Republic of	47.0	48.2	49.6	51.6	0.8	0.2	0.5	0.4
Mongolia	2.4	2.5	2.7	3.2	1.3	1.1	1.8	1.9
Taipei,China	22.2	22.7	23.1	23.6	0.8	0.4	0.3	0.1
South Asia	**1,189.6**	**1,290.5**	**1,382.6**	**1,548.6**	**1.6**	**1.5**	**1.4**	**1.2**
Bangladesh	129.3	138.6	148.6	164.6	1.4	1.4	1.3	1.2
Bhutan	0.6	0.6	0.7	0.7	1.3	1.3	1.8	1.0
India[b]	1,019.0	1,106.0	1,186.0	1,332.0	1.8	1.5	1.4	1.2
Maldives	0.3	0.3	0.4	0.5	1.5	3.3	2.3	4.2
Nepal	21.0	25.3	26.3	29.1	3.0	2.3	1.4	1.4
Sri Lanka	19.4	19.6	20.7	21.7	1.3	0.9	1.0	1.1
Southeast Asia	**512.3**	**547.8**	**588.0**	**648.9**	**1.4**	**1.3**	**1.9**	**1.1**
Brunei Darussalam	0.3	0.4	0.4	0.4	2.5	1.8	1.8	3.0
Cambodia	12.5	13.3	14.1	15.6	1.3	1.3	1.3	1.3
Indonesia	206.3	219.9	237.6	265.0	1.2	1.3	2.7	1.3
Lao People's Democratic Republic	5.1	5.6	6.0	6.8	2.0	2.0	1.5	1.4
Malaysia	23.5	26.0	28.6	32.4	2.5	2.1	1.8	1.1
Myanmar[b]	46.1	48.5	50.2	53.9	1.2	0.9	0.7	0.9
Philippines	76.8	84.7	93.1	106.6	2.3	1.9	2.3	1.6
Singapore	4.0	4.3	5.1	5.6	1.7	2.4	1.8	0.5
Thailand	60.7	63.2	65.9	67.8	0.8	0.8	0.8	0.3
Viet Nam	77.1	81.9	86.9	94.7	1.4	1.2	1.1	1.0
The Pacific[c]	**8.0**	**9.2**	**10.4**	**12.8**	**4.5**	**2.7**	**2.8**	**2.6**
Cook Islands	18.0	21.5	23.7	18.6	9.1	5.9	4.9	-4.6
Fiji	802.0	827.0	850.7	886.2	0.6	0.7	0.6	0.6
Kiribati[b]	84.5	92.5	103.1	113.0	1.7	1.8	2.2	-0.1
Marshall Islands	51.2	51.2	52.9	54.6	0.8	1.4	1.2	0.4
Micronesia, Federated States of[b]	107.0	105.6	102.8	102.6 (2017)	0.2	-0.3	-0.5	0.1 [d]
Nauru	10.1	9.5	9.7	11.4	1.0	-2.2	1.9	1.6
Niue[b]	1.9	1.6 (2006)	1.6 (2011)	1.7 (2017)	-3.7 [e]	...	...	1.1 [d]
Palau	18.9	19.8	18.3	17.5	0.3	0.8	-1.9	-2.0
Papua New Guinea	5,190.8	6,051.7	7,055.4	9,018.9	3.3	3.1	3.1	3.1
Samoa	175.2	179.9	186.4	197.7	0.9	0.5	0.8	0.7
Solomon Islands	418.6	470.1	555.5	667.0	2.3	2.3	2.6 [f]	2.1
Timor-Leste	871.6	1,026.5	1,109.6	1,324.0	1.0	3.0	1.6	2.1
Tonga	99.1	101.2	102.8	99.6	0.4	0.4	0.2	-0.5
Tuvalu	9.5	10.3	11.1	11.6	1.3	3.1	0.5	1.2
Vanuatu	190.9	214.0	239.7	284.6	2.3	2.3	2.4	2.2
Developed ADB Member Economies	**149.7**	**152.1**	**154.5**	**156.4**	**0.3**	**0.2**	**0.3**	**0.1**
Australia	19.0	20.2	22.0	25.0	1.2	1.2	1.6	1.6
Japan	126.8	127.8	128.1	126.5	0.2	0.0	0.0	-0.2
New Zealand	3.9	4.1	4.4	4.9	0.6	1.1	1.1	1.9
DEVELOPING ADB MEMBER ECONOMIES[g]	**3,285.6**	**3,487.0**	**3,681.2**	**4,023.4**	**1.3**	**1.1**	**1.2**	**1.0**
ALL ADB REGIONAL MEMBERS[g]	**3,435.3**	**3,639.1**	**3,835.6**	**4,179.9**	**1.2**	**1.1**	**1.1**	**1.0**
WORLD	**6,143.5**	**6,541.9**	**6,956.8**	**7,631.1**	**1.3**	**1.2**	**1.2**	**1.1**

0.0 = magnitude is less than half of unit employed, * = preliminary, ADB = Asian Development Bank.

a   The annual population growth rate is calculated as the percentage change in population when comparing the reference year with the year prior. For example, the population growth rates under the column heading "2018" refer to population growth from 2017 to 2018.

b   Estimates of population size are as of 1 January for the Kyrgyz Republic; 11 March for Niue; 10 June for Afghanistan; 1 April for 2000, 4 April for 2010, and 30 September for 2005 and 2017 for the Federated States of Micronesia; 1 October for India and Myanmar; 7 November for Kiribati; and 31 December for the People's Republic of China.

c   Estimates of population size for ADB developing member economies in the Pacific are expressed in thousands, while the total population for the Pacific region is expressed in millions.

d   Refers to 2017 annual population growth rate.

e   Refers to 2001 annual population growth rate.

f   Refers to 2011 annual population growth rate.

g   For reporting economies only.

Sources: Economy sources; and United Nations. World Population Prospects 2019. https://population.un.org/wpp/Download/Standard/Population/ (accessed 22 July 2019).

Table 2.1.2:   Migration and Urbanization

ADB Regional Member	Net International Migration Rate[a] (per 1,000 population)				Urban Population (% of total population)			
	2000–2005	2005–2010	2010–2015	2015–2020	2000	2005	2010	2018
Developing ADB Member Economies								
Central and West Asia								
Afghanistan	6.4	-7.6	3.3	-1.7	21.3	21.5	23.2	25.0
Armenia	-10.6	-12.5	-2.1	-1.7	64.8	64.0	63.5	63.8
Azerbaijan	0.9	1.2	0.2	0.1	51.1	52.5	53.0	52.9
Georgia	-6.9	-5.8	-4.7	-2.5	55.1	56.5	56.5	58.5
Kazakhstan	0.6	-0.4	1.9	-1.0	56.5	57.1	54.5	58.0
Kyrgyz Republic	-6.9	-2.9	-3.3	-0.6	34.7	34.8	34.1	33.9
Pakistan	-0.9	-0.4	-1.1	-1.1	33.0	34.6	36.3	36.4
Tajikistan	-4.5	-4.1	-3.4	-2.2	26.6	26.4	26.4	27.1
Turkmenistan	-5.4	-2.5	-1.9	-0.9	45.9	47.1	48.5	51.6
Uzbekistan	-1.9	-1.0	-0.4	-0.3	37.2	36.1	51.3	50.6
East Asia								
China, People's Republic of	-0.3	-0.3	-0.2	-0.2	36.2	43.0	50.0	59.6
Hong Kong, China	1.9	2.6	2.1	4.0	100.0	100.0	100.0	100.0
Korea, Republic of	0.3	-0.6	1.6	0.2	79.6	81.3	81.9	81.5
Mongolia	-1.2	-0.8	-0.3	-0.3	56.6	61.9	69.2	67.9
Taipei,China[b]	1.8	2.2	1.5	1.3	55.8	57.7	59.3	62.5
South Asia								
Bangladesh	-2.2	-4.5	-3.0	-2.3	23.1	24.2	25.9	36.6
Bhutan	2.0	-3.3	0.1	0.4	21.0	30.9	34.8	40.9
India	-0.3	-0.4	-0.4	-0.4	27.7	28.8	29.9	34.0
Maldives	11.6	10.5	28.4	22.8	27.7	33.8	36.4	39.8
Nepal	-6.2	-7.4	-15.1	1.5	14.1	14.6	16.6	20.8
Sri Lanka	-4.7	-5.2	-4.7	-4.6	18.4	18.3	18.2	18.5
Southeast Asia								
Brunei Darussalam	0.2	-1.2	-0.4	–	71.2	73.2	75.0	77.6
Cambodia	-0.6	-4.3	-2.0	-1.9	18.6	19.2	20.3	23.4
Indonesia	-1.1	-1.1	-0.4	-0.4	42.0	45.9	49.9	50.2
Lao People's Democratic Republic	-5.3	-3.7	-3.5	-2.1	22.0	27.2	30.1	35.0
Malaysia	5.5	5.7	1.7	1.6	62.0	66.5	71.0	75.6
Myanmar	-5.1	-5.4	-2.0	-3.1	27.0	27.9	28.9	30.0
Philippines	-3.0	-3.4	-1.7	-0.6	46.1	45.7	45.3	46.9
Singapore	4.5	30.7	11.8	4.7	100.0	100.0	100.0	100.0
Thailand	1.2	0.2	0.5	0.3	31.1	32.5	43.4	50.1
Viet Nam	-1.6	-1.9	-0.9	-0.8	24.2	27.1	30.5	35.7
The Pacific								
Cook Islands	...	...	...	...	65.2	71.0	73.3	75.1
Fiji	-14.4	-5.6	-12.0	-7.0	47.9	49.9	52.2	56.9
Kiribati	-4.4	-0.6	-7.7	-6.9	43.0	43.6	47.4	54.1
Marshall Islands	...	...	...	...	68.6	71.1	73.6	77.0
Micronesia, Federated States of	-23.0	-23.5	-5.7	-5.4	22.3	22.3	22.3	22.6 (2017)
Nauru	...	...	...	...	100.0	100.0	100.0	100.0
Niue	...	...	...	...	33.1	35.2	38.7	44.8
Palau	...	...	...	...	69.5	77.4	77.0	78.7 (2015)
Papua New Guinea	-2.7	1.1	-0.1	-0.1	13.2	13.1	13.0	13.2
Samoa	-17.7	-16.5	-12.8	-14.3	20.0	22.1	21.0	19.0
Solomon Islands	-3.8	-5.7	-2.8	-2.5	15.8	17.8	20.0	23.7
Timor-Leste	-5.9	-7.3	-4.9	-4.3	24.3	26.0	27.7	30.6
Tonga	-15.8	-15.2	-25.4	-7.7	23.0	23.2	23.4	22.8
Tuvalu	...	...	...	...	46.0	49.7	54.8	62.4
Vanuatu	-2.6	-2.9	1.4	0.4	21.8	23.2	24.4	25.0
Developed ADB Member Economies								
Australia	6.0	11.4	8.6	6.4	84.1 (2001)	84.6	85.7	86.8
Japan	0.3	0.4	0.6	0.6	78.6	86.0	90.8	91.6
New Zealand	6.7	2.9	4.0	3.2	83.5	83.8	83.7	84.1

... = data not available, – = magnitude equals zero, ADB = Asian Development Bank.

a   Refers to annual average. The United Nations' population estimates and projections are based on all available sources of data on population size, and levels of fertility, mortality, and international migration. Statistics on international migration are sourced from population registers and other administrative sources. These estimates and projections are made for 235 distinct national economies or areas comprising the total population of the world.

b   For urban population, refers to localities of 100,000 or more inhabitants.

Sources: Economy sources; United Nations. World Urbanization Prospects: The 2018 Revision – Data Query. https://esa.un.org/unpd/wup/DataQuery/ (accessed 20 July 2019); and United Nations. World Population Prospects 2019. https://population.un.org/wpp/Download/Standard/Migration/ (accessed 20 July 2019).

Table 2.1.3: Proportion of Total Population Aged 0–14 Years and Aged 15–64 Years[a]
(%)

ADB Regional Member	Population Aged 0–14 Years				Population Aged 15–64 Years			
	2000	2005	2010	2018	2000	2005	2010	2018
Developing ADB Member Economies								
Central and West Asia	**39.9**	**37.7**	**35.9**	**34.4**	**55.6**	**57.7**	**59.7**	**61.1**
Afghanistan	48.9	47.9	48.2	43.1	48.8	49.9	49.5	54.3
Armenia	25.8	21.5	19.5	20.6	64.2	66.6	69.5	68.1
Azerbaijan	31.1	26.2	22.8	23.4	63.0	67.2	71.3	70.4
Georgia	20.8	19.0	18.0	19.8	66.2	66.5	67.8	65.3
Kazakhstan	27.5	24.5	24.1	28.5	65.6	67.8	69.1	64.1
Kyrgyz Republic	34.9	31.0	29.9	32.4	59.6	63.4	65.6	63.2
Pakistan	42.0	40.0	37.7	35.3	54.0	55.9	58.1	60.4
Tajikistan	42.5	38.0	35.7	36.8	53.9	58.2	61.0	60.2
Turkmenistan	36.3	32.6	29.5	30.8	59.5	62.8	66.3	64.8
Uzbekistan	37.3	32.6	29.1	28.7	58.1	62.6	66.4	66.9
East Asia	**24.6**	**20.3**	**18.5**	**17.6**	**68.6**	**72.2**	**73.3**	**71.3**
China, People's Republic of	24.8	20.4	18.7	17.9	68.4	72.2	73.3	71.2
Hong Kong, China	16.9	14.3	11.9	11.9	72.1	73.4	75.1	71.2
Korea, Republic of	20.6	18.8	16.1	13.0	72.2	72.3	73.2	72.6
Mongolia	34.8	28.9	27.0	30.4	61.5	67.3	69.2	65.5
Taipei,China	21.2	19.0	15.9	12.9	70.0	71.3	73.4	72.7
South Asia	**35.0**	**32.9**	**31.0**	**27.1**	**60.7**	**62.4**	**64.0**	**66.7**
Bangladesh	37.0	34.4	32.0	27.7	59.2	61.3	63.2	67.1
Bhutan	39.8	35.1	31.2	25.8	56.3	60.5	63.7	68.2
India	34.7	32.7	30.8	27.1	60.9	62.5	64.1	66.8
Maldives	40.5	31.5	25.3	20.1	55.8	64.1	70.2	76.1
Nepal	41.0	39.3	36.3	30.4	55.3	56.4	58.7	63.9
Sri Lanka	26.8	25.6	25.4	24.2	67.0	67.6	67.2	65.3
Southeast Asia	**31.7**	**29.9**	**27.9**	**25.7**	**63.4**	**65.0**	**66.6**	**67.7**
Brunei Darussalam	30.7	27.8	26.0	23.0	67.0	69.2	70.7	72.1
Cambodia	41.6	37.1	33.3	31.2	55.3	59.5	62.9	64.2
Indonesia	30.7	29.9	28.8	26.6	64.6	65.3	66.2	67.6
Lao People's Democratic Republic	43.4	40.3	36.4	32.6	53.1	56.0	59.9	63.3
Malaysia	33.4	30.5	28.0	24.0	62.7	65.1	67.1	69.3
Myanmar	32.5	31.2	30.0	26.4	63.0	64.2	65.1	67.8
Philippines	38.5	37.1	34.0	31.0	58.3	59.4	61.9	63.9
Singapore	18.7	17.2	14.0	12.3	74.9	75.6	78.7	76.3
Thailand	24.0	21.3	19.2	17.1	69.5	71.0	71.9	71.0
Viet Nam	31.6	27.1	23.6	23.2	62.0	66.4	69.9	69.6
The Pacific	**40.0**	**39.1**	**38.0**	**35.8**	**56.8**	**57.6**	**58.4**	**60.4**
Cook Islands	34.7	31.4	27.9	26.0	59.1	61.3	63.8	63.6
Fiji	35.0	30.5	29.0	29.5	61.6	65.4	66.2	65.0
Kiribati	40.0	36.9	36.1	35.5	56.7	59.5	60.3	60.5
Marshall Islands	42.3	41.3	41.8	38.2	55.5	56.5	55.9	58.4
Micronesia, Federated States of	40.4	38.9	35.7	31.7	56.0	57.3	61.1	64.3
Nauru	40.1	37.1	35.6	39.9	58.6	61.2	63.1	57.9
Niue	30.0	25.5	24.8	21.6	60.8	64.0	63.0	64.3
Palau	23.9	24.1	20.3	20.0	70.7	70.2	73.2	71.2
Papua New Guinea	39.8	39.2	38.3	35.8	57.2	57.6	58.4	60.7
Samoa	40.8	39.6	38.3	38.3	54.8	55.6	56.7	56.9
Solomon Islands	41.9	41.3	40.8	40.2	55.2	55.7	55.9	56.2
Timor-Leste	44.9	44.7	42.5	37.8	51.7	51.6	53.4	57.9
Tonga	38.5	38.2	37.4	35.4	55.9	55.9	56.9	58.6
Tuvalu	37.1	34.3	32.0	31.3	57.0	60.1	62.7	62.3
Vanuatu	41.5	39.7	38.2	38.8	55.2	57.1	57.9	57.5
Developed ADB Member Economies	**15.8**	**14.8**	**14.4**	**13.9**	**68.0**	**66.6**	**64.7**	**60.7**
Australia	20.9	19.8	19.0	19.2	66.8	67.3	67.6	65.2
Japan	14.8	13.8	13.4	12.7	68.2	66.5	64.1	59.7
New Zealand	22.7	21.5	20.5	19.7	65.5	66.4	66.4	64.7
DEVELOPING ADB MEMBER ECONOMIES	**30.6**	**27.8**	**26.1**	**24.0**	**64.0**	**66.3**	**67.6**	**68.1**
ALL ADB REGIONAL MEMBERS	**30.0**	**27.3**	**25.6**	**23.6**	**64.1**	**66.3**	**67.5**	**67.8**
WORLD	**30.1**	**28.1**	**27.0**	**25.8**	**63.0**	**64.6**	**65.5**	**65.4**

ADB = Asian Development Bank.

a   The estimates are based on all available sources of data on population size and levels of fertility, mortality, and international migration for 235 distinct national economies or areas comprising the total population of the world.

Sources: United Nations. World Population Prospects, The 2019 Revision. https://population.un.org/wpp/ (accessed 1 July 2019). For the Cook Islands, the Marshall Islands, Nauru, Niue, Palau, and Tuvalu: The Pacific Community, Statistics for Development Division. Official communication, 3 July 2019.

Table 2.1.4:   Proportion of Total Population Aged 65 Years or Older[a], and Age Dependency Ratio

ADB Regional Member	Population Aged 65 Years and Older (% of total population)				Age Dependency Ratio for Total Population			
	2000	2005	2010	2018	2000	2005	2010	2018
Developing ADB Member Economies								
Central and West Asia	**4.4**	**4.6**	**4.5**	**4.5**	**79.7**	**73.3**	**67.6**	**63.6**
Afghanistan	2.3	2.2	2.3	2.6	104.9	100.3	102.0	84.1
Armenia	10.0	11.9	11.0	11.3	55.8	50.1	43.8	46.8
Azerbaijan	5.8	6.6	5.9	6.2	58.7	48.8	40.3	42.0
Georgia	12.9	14.5	14.2	14.9	51.0	50.4	47.5	53.0
Kazakhstan	6.8	7.7	6.8	7.4	52.4	47.4	44.6	55.9
Kyrgyz Republic	5.5	5.6	4.5	4.5	67.9	57.7	52.5	58.3
Pakistan	4.0	4.1	4.2	4.3	85.0	78.8	72.2	65.5
Tajikistan	3.6	3.8	3.3	3.0	85.6	71.9	63.9	66.1
Turkmenistan	4.3	4.6	4.1	4.4	68.2	59.2	50.7	54.4
Uzbekistan	4.6	4.8	4.5	4.4	72.1	59.8	50.7	49.5
East Asia	**6.9**	**7.6**	**8.2**	**11.1**	**45.9**	**38.6**	**36.5**	**40.3**
China, People's Republic of	6.8	7.5	8.1	10.9	46.2	38.6	36.5	40.4
Hong Kong, China	11.0	12.2	12.9	16.9	38.7	36.2	33.1	40.4
Korea, Republic of	7.2	8.9	10.7	14.4	38.5	38.3	36.6	37.7
Mongolia	3.7	3.7	3.8	4.1	62.5	48.5	44.6	52.7
Taipei,China	8.7	9.7	10.7	14.4	42.8	40.3	36.2	37.6
South Asia	**4.3**	**4.7**	**5.1**	**6.1**	**64.7**	**60.4**	**56.3**	**49.8**
Bangladesh	3.9	4.3	4.8	5.2	69.0	63.0	58.1	49.0
Bhutan	3.9	4.4	5.1	6.0	77.7	65.3	57.0	46.6
India	4.4	4.7	5.1	6.2	64.2	59.9	56.0	49.8
Maldives	3.8	4.4	4.6	3.7	79.3	56.0	42.5	31.3
Nepal	3.8	4.3	5.0	5.7	80.9	77.2	70.4	56.6
Sri Lanka	6.2	6.8	7.4	10.5	49.2	48.0	48.8	53.1
Southeast Asia	**4.9**	**5.1**	**5.5**	**6.6**	**57.8**	**53.9**	**50.1**	**47.7**
Brunei Darussalam	2.4	3.0	3.4	4.9	49.3	44.5	41.5	38.7
Cambodia	3.1	3.4	3.7	4.6	80.7	67.9	58.9	55.7
Indonesia	4.7	4.8	5.0	5.9	54.8	53.1	51.0	47.9
Lao People's Democratic Republic	3.6	3.7	3.7	4.1	88.4	78.5	67.0	57.9
Malaysia	3.9	4.4	4.9	6.7	59.4	53.5	49.0	44.2
Myanmar	4.5	4.6	4.8	5.8	58.7	55.8	53.5	47.4
Philippines	3.3	3.5	4.1	5.1	71.6	68.2	61.6	56.5
Singapore	6.4	7.2	7.3	11.5	33.5	32.3	27.0	31.1
Thailand	6.5	7.8	8.9	11.9	43.9	40.9	39.0	40.8
Viet Nam	6.4	6.5	6.5	7.3	61.3	50.7	43.1	43.8
The Pacific	**3.2**	**3.4**	**3.6**	**3.8**	**76.0**	**73.7**	**71.2**	**65.6**
Cook Islands	6.2	7.3	8.2	10.4	69.3	63.1	56.7	57.2
Fiji	3.4	4.1	4.8	5.4	62.5	53.0	51.1	53.8
Kiribati	3.3	3.5	3.6	4.0	76.3	68.0	65.7	65.3
Marshall Islands	2.1	2.2	2.3	3.5	80.0	76.9	78.8	71.3
Micronesia, Federated States of	3.6	3.9	3.2	4.0	78.6	74.7	63.7	55.5
Nauru	1.3	1.7	1.3	2.2	70.7	63.4	58.5	72.7
Niue	9.2	10.5	12.1	14.1	64.6	56.4	58.7	55.5
Palau	5.4	5.7	6.5	8.8	41.4	42.5	36.7	40.5
Papua New Guinea	3.1	3.2	3.3	3.4	74.9	73.5	71.3	64.6
Samoa	4.4	4.8	5.0	4.8	82.3	79.7	76.3	75.8
Solomon Islands	2.9	3.0	3.3	3.6	81.1	79.6	78.9	78.1
Timor-Leste	3.4	3.7	4.0	4.3	93.3	93.7	87.2	72.7
Tonga	5.6	5.9	5.7	6.0	78.9	78.9	75.8	70.6
Tuvalu	5.9	5.6	5.3	6.4	75.4	66.5	59.5	60.6
Vanuatu	3.3	3.3	3.9	3.6	81.1	75.3	72.8	73.9
Developed ADB Member Economies	**16.3**	**18.6**	**20.9**	**25.3**	**47.1**	**50.1**	**54.5**	**64.6**
Australia	12.3	12.9	13.4	15.7	49.7	48.6	47.9	53.5
Japan	17.0	19.7	22.5	27.6	46.6	50.3	55.9	67.4
New Zealand	11.8	12.1	13.1	15.7	52.7	50.6	50.5	54.6
DEVELOPING ADB MEMBER ECONOMIES	**5.5**	**5.9**	**6.3**	**7.9**	**56.4**	**50.9**	**47.9**	**46.9**
ALL ADB REGIONAL MEMBERS	**5.9**	**6.4**	**6.9**	**8.6**	**55.9**	**50.8**	**48.1**	**47.5**
WORLD	**6.9**	**7.3**	**7.6**	**8.9**	**58.7**	**54.8**	**52.8**	**53.0**

ADB = Asian Development Bank.

a The estimates are based on all available sources of data on population size and levels of fertility, mortality, and international migration for 235 distinct national economies or areas comprising the total population of the world.

Sources: For Population Aged 65 Years and Older: United Nations. World Population Prospects, The 2019 Revision. https://population.un.org/wpp/ (accessed 1 July 2019); and for the Cook Islands, the Marshall Islands, Nauru, Niue, Palau, and Tuvalu: The Pacific Community, Statistics for Development Division. Official communication, 3 July 2019. For Age Dependency Ratio for Total Population: Asian Development Bank estimates using data from the United Nations.

Table 2.1.5: Labor Force Participation Rates[a]
(%)

ADB Regional Member	2000	2005	2010	2013	2014	2015	2016	2017	2018
Developing ADB Member Economies									
Central and West Asia									
Afghanistan	...	...	49.8 (2011)	55.4	...	...	53.9	...	...
Armenia	61.4	57.7	61.2	63.4	63.1	62.5	61.0	60.9	63.6*
Azerbaijan	77.6	68.4	64.8	64.7	65.1	65.4	66.0	66.2	66.3
Georgia	65.2	62.7	63.3	65.2	65.5	66.8	66.3	65.8	63.9
Kazakhstan	66.0	69.4	71.2	71.7	70.7	69.7	70.0	69.7	70.0
Kyrgyz Republic	64.4 (2002)	64.8	64.2	62.5	62.4	62.4	61.5	60.1	59.8
Pakistan	42.8	43.7	45.9	45.7	45.5	45.2	...	...	44.3
Tajikistan	56.3	55.0	50.3	48.6	47.8	47.7	46.7	46.2	...
Turkmenistan	63.2	63.3	64.0	64.8	65.0	65.2	65.3	65.2	65.1
Uzbekistan	...	...	...	...	71.3	71.9	72.5	73.5	...
East Asia									
China, People's Republic of	77.2	73.4	71.0	70.4	70.2	69.9	69.6	69.2	68.7
Hong Kong, China	61.4	60.9	59.6	61.2	61.1	61.1	61.1	61.1	61.2
Korea, Republic of	61.2	62.2	61.1	61.7	62.7	62.8	62.9	63.2	63.1
Mongolia	62.9	63.5	61.6	61.9	62.1	61.5	60.5	61.1	61.0
Taipei,China	57.7	57.8	58.1	58.4	58.5	58.7	58.7	58.8	59.0
South Asia									
Bangladesh	54.9	58.5 (2006)	59.3	57.1	...	...	58.5	58.2	...
Bhutan[b]	56.5 (2001)	60.4	68.6	65.3	62.6	63.1	62.2	63.3	62.6
India	37.6	39.2	36.4 (2011)	...	...	...	...	...	...
Maldives[c]	47.7	57.7 (2006)	52.1	...	63.8	...	57.6	...	...
Nepal[d]	...	77.2 (2004)	74.3 (2012)	77.2	72.2	...	...	...	38.5
Sri Lanka	50.3	49.3	48.6	53.7	53.2	53.8	53.8	54.1	51.8
Southeast Asia									
Brunei Darussalam	67.9 (2001)	...	68.9 (2011)	...	65.6	...	...	62.7	...
Cambodia	65.2	74.6 (2004)	87.0	83.0	82.6	...	...	...	...
Indonesia	67.8	66.8	67.7	66.8	66.6	65.8	66.3	66.7	67.3
Lao People's Democratic Republic[e]	79.9 (2001)	66.6	79.2	...	...	...	...	40.8	...
Malaysia	65.4	63.3	63.7	67.3	67.6	67.9	67.7	68.0	68.3
Myanmar	...	...	...	...	67.0	64.7	...	61.5	62.0
Philippines	64.9	65.1	64.1	63.9	64.6	63.7	63.5	61.2	60.9
Singapore[f]	63.2	63.0	66.2	66.7	67.0	68.3	68.0	67.7	67.7
Thailand[g]	71.5	72.5	72.3	71.1	70.3	69.8	68.8	68.1	68.3
Viet Nam	...	74.7 (2007)	77.4	77.5	77.7	77.8	77.3	76.7	76.8
The Pacific									
Cook Islands	69.0 (2001)	70.2 (2006)	71.0 (2011)	...	...	...	...	...	...
Fiji	...	...	...	...	55.2	...	58.3	57.1	...
Kiribati	80.9	63.6	59.3	...	...	66.0	...	...	...
Marshall Islands	51.1	51.1	41.7 (2011)	...	...	...	...	...	...
Micronesia, Federated States of	58.6	...	57.3	49.3	...	...	...	...	...
Nauru[h]	...	...	64.0 (2011)	60.8	...	...	...	...	...
Niue	78.7 (2001)	78.0 (2006)	68.9 (2011)	...	...	...	...	68.6	...
Palau	67.5	69.1	68.1 (2012)	...	...	77.4	...	...	...
Papua New Guinea	72.0	61.0	48.2	48.0	47.5	47.1	47.1	47.1	46.8
Samoa[d]	50.6 (2001)	49.8 (2006)	41.3 (2011)	...	...	...	47.4	43.3	...
Solomon Islands	...	...	62.9 (2009)	...	...	...	...	...	...
Timor-Leste	56.0 (2001)	60.2 (2004)	41.7	30.6	...	...	...	...	...
Tonga	...	94.8 (2003)	...	...	...	...	63.7	...	...
Tuvalu	58.2 (2002)	...	59.4 (2012)	...	...	...	52.3	...	...
Vanuatu	69.6	70.3	70.4	70.4	70.4	70.6	70.5	70.5	70.5
Developed ADB Member Economies									
Australia	63.1	64.4	65.4	64.9	64.7	65.0	64.9	65.2	65.6
Japan	62.4	60.4	59.6	59.3	59.4	59.6	60.0	60.5	61.5
New Zealand	65.2	67.7	68.0	67.8	68.7	68.7	69.8	70.7	70.7

... = data not available, * = preliminary, ADB = Asian Development Bank.

a Based on varying concepts and definitions of "labor force" across economies.
b For 2005 and 2017, data are from censuses of population. For all other years, data are from labor force surveys. Thus, data prior to and after the census years may not be directly comparable with 2005 and 2017 data.
c Includes local population only.
d Figures for different years may not be directly comparable with each other due to changes in methodology and labor concepts adopted.
e For 2017, the figure is based on the 2017 Labour Force Survey conducted using the concepts defined at the 19th International Conference of Labour Statisticians and hence is not directly comparable with figures from the 2005 Census of Population and Housing and the 2010 Report on the National Child Labour Survey of the Lao People's Democratic Republic.
f Refers to Singapore residents only.
g Includes seasonally inactive labor force.
h For 2011, the figure is from the 2011 census. For 2013, the figure refers to preliminary data from the Nauru Household Income and Expenditure Survey 2012/2013. Thus, data for 2011 and 2013 may not be directly comparable.

Sources: Economy sources. For Papua New Guinea, the People's Republic of China, Turkmenistan, and Vanuatu: International Labour Organization. ILOSTAT. http://www.ilo.org/ilostat/ (accessed 23 July 2019). For the Lao People's Democratic Republic for 2001: International Labour Organization. ILOSTAT. http://www.ilo.org/ilostat/ (accessed July 2016). For the Federated States of Micronesia and Tuvalu: Secretariat of the Pacific Community. National Minimum Development Indicator Database. http://www.spc.int/nmdi/ (accessed 23 July 2019). For Timor-Leste for 2001: United Nations Development Programme. East Timor Human Development Report 2002. http://www.tl.undp.org/content/timor_leste/en/home/library/poverty/human-development-report-2002-timor-leste.html (accessed 23 July 2018).

Labor Force and Employment

Table 2.1.6:   Employment in Agriculture, Industry, and Services[a]
(% of total employment)

ADB Regional Member	Agriculture			
	2000	2005	2010	2018
Developing ADB Member Economies				
Central and West Asia				
Afghanistan	69.6 (2001)	69.6 (2004)	...	39.5 (2016)
Armenia	44.4	46.2	38.6	31.3 (2017)
Azerbaijan	39.1	38.7	38.2	36.3
Georgia[b]	52.8 (2001)	50.0	48.0	43.1 (2017)
Kazakhstan	31.4	31.9	28.3	14.1
Kyrgyz Republic	53.1	38.5	31.2	20.3
Pakistan[c]	48.4	43.0	45.0	38.5
Tajikistan	65.0	67.5	65.9	60.9 (2017)
Turkmenistan	47.6	...	...	...
Uzbekistan	34.4	29.1	26.8	27.2 (2017)
East Asia				
China, People's Republic of[d]	50.0	44.8	36.7	26.1
Hong Kong, China[e]	0.3	0.3	–	–
Korea, Republic of[f]	10.7	8.0	6.6	5.0
Mongolia	48.6	39.9	33.5	26.7
Taipei,China	7.8	5.9	5.2	4.9
South Asia				
Bangladesh	50.8	48.1 (2006)	47.5	40.6 (2017)
Bhutan[g]	46.5 (2001)	43.6	59.4	54.0
India	59.9	56.1	53.2 (2009)	...
Maldives[h]	13.7	15.9 (2007)	4.3	9.0 (2016)
Nepal	...	...	64.0 (2011)	21.5
Sri Lanka[i]	36.0	32.8	32.5	25.5
Southeast Asia				
Brunei Darussalam	...	...	...	...
Cambodia	73.7	60.3	72.3	64.3 (2014)
Indonesia	45.3	44.0	38.3	28.8
Lao People's Democratic Republic	...	76.3	72.2	31.3 (2017)
Malaysia[j]	16.7	14.6	13.6	10.6
Myanmar	...	...	...	47.6
Philippines	37.1	35.7	33.2	24.3
Singapore[k]	0.1	0.1	0.2	0.1
Thailand	44.2	38.6	38.2	32.1
Viet Nam[l]	65.1	55.1	49.5	37.7
The Pacific				
Cook Islands[m]	7.2 (2001)	4.9 (2006)	4.3 (2011)	5.3 (2016)
Fiji[n]	1.5	1.1	1.7	19.2 (2016)
Kiribati[o]	...	2.7	22.1	24.3 (2015)
Marshall Islands	6.4	3.1	13.9	6.4 (2017)
Micronesia, Federated States of	52.2	...	...	...
Nauru	...	...	...	...
Niue	9.0 (2001)	15.9 (2006)	10.4 (2011)	8.7 (2017)
Palau[p]	7.1	7.8	...	6.4 (2015)
Papua New Guinea	...	...	...	...
Samoa	39.9 (2001)	35.4 (2006)	37.0 (2011)	21.9 (2017)
Solomon Islands[q]	...	...	41.5 (2009)	...
Timor-Leste	...	...	51.0	40.5 (2013)
Tonga	...	27.9 (2006)	...	24.1 (2016)
Tuvalu	...	...	...	...
Vanuatu	...	...	...	...
Developed ADB Member Economies				
Australia	4.8	3.6	3.2	2.6
Japan	5.1	4.4	4.0	3.4
New Zealand[r]	8.8	6.9	6.7	5.8

continued on next page

Table 2.1.6: **Employment in Agriculture, Industry, and Services**[a] *(continued)*
(% of total employment)

ADB Regional Member	Industry			
	2000	2005	2010	2018
Developing ADB Member Economies				
Central and West Asia				
Afghanistan	6.2 (2001)	6.2 (2004)	...	14.8 (2016)
Armenia	20.6	15.9	17.4	16.7 (2017)
Azerbaijan	12.1	12.4	13.7	14.6
Georgia[b]	5.8 (2001)	7.5	7.2	13.2 (2017)
Kazakhstan	18.2	17.9	18.7	19.9
Kyrgyz Republic	10.5	17.6	21.1	24.8
Pakistan[c]	11.5	20.3	20.9	24.6
Tajikistan	9.1	8.7	7.9	9.1 (2017)
Turkmenistan	13.0	...	...	...
Uzbekistan	12.7	13.2	22.7	23.1 (2017)
East Asia				
China, People's Republic of[d]	22.5	23.8	28.7	27.6
Hong Kong, China[e]	19.6	14.4	11.2	11.6
Korea, Republic of[f]	20.4	26.7	25.0	25.2
Mongolia	14.1	16.8	16.2	20.6
Taipei,China	28.1	36.4	35.9	35.7
South Asia				
Bangladesh	13.1	14.6 (2006)	17.6	20.4 (2017)
Bhutan[g]	5.6 (2001)	17.2	6.6	13.1
India	16.3	18.8	21.5 (2009)	...
Maldives[h]	19.0	27.9 (2007)	9.4	18.4 (2016)
Nepal	...	...	9.5 (2011)	30.8
Sri Lanka[i]	23.6	25.4	24.6	27.9
Southeast Asia				
Brunei Darussalam	...	...	...	...
Cambodia	7.0	9.7	9.2	9.0 (2014)
Indonesia	17.4	18.8	19.3	23.2
Lao People's Democratic Republic	...	...	8.1	14.1 (2017)
Malaysia[j]	32.5	29.7	27.8	27.1
Myanmar	...	...	...	17.8
Philippines	16.2	15.4	15.0	19.1
Singapore[k]	25.7	21.7	21.8	15.9
Thailand	20.2	22.4	20.8	22.8
Viet Nam[l]	13.1	17.6	21.0	26.8
The Pacific				
Cook Islands[m]	6.0 (2001)	14.2 (2006)	11.7 (2011)	10.1 (2016)
Fiji[n]	30.8	30.8	23.9	14.4 (2016)
Kiribati[o]	...	3.2	16.1	18.2 (2015)
Marshall Islands	8.5	9.6	9.0	10.3 (2017)
Micronesia, Federated States of	...	...	...	...
Nauru	...	...	...	...
Niue	20.4 (2001)	17.1 (2006)	14.2 (2011)	14.2 (2017)
Palau[p]	0.7	2.6	...	11.7 (2015)
Papua New Guinea	...	...	...	...
Samoa	19.7 (2001)	21.8 (2006)	12.2 (2011)	15.4 (2017)
Solomon Islands[q]	...	...	13.0 (2009)	...
Timor-Leste	...	...	8.8	12.7 (2013)
Tonga	...	27.8 (2006)	...	25.6 (2016)
Tuvalu	...	...	...	...
Vanuatu	...	...	...	...
Developed ADB Member Economies				
Australia	21.5	21.1	21.0	19.7
Japan	31.2	27.5	25.4	23.9
New Zealand[r]	12.6	22.4	20.6	19.8

continued on next page

Labor Force and Employment

Table 2.1.6: **Employment in Agriculture, Industry, and Services**[a] *(continued)*
(% of total employment)

ADB Regional Member	Services			
	2000	**2005**	**2010**	**2018**
Developing ADB Member Economies				
Central and West Asia				
Afghanistan	24.2 (2001)	24.2 (2004)	...	45.7 (2016)
Armenia	35.0	37.8	44.0	51.9 (2017)
Azerbaijan	48.7	48.8	48.1	49.1
Georgia[b]	41.4 (2001)	42.5	44.8	43.7 (2017)
Kazakhstan	50.5	50.2	53.0	66.0
Kyrgyz Republic	36.5	43.9	47.7	54.9
Pakistan[c]	40.0	36.7	34.2	39.8
Tajikistan	26.0	23.9	26.3	30.0 (2017)
Turkmenistan	39.4	...	...	...
Uzbekistan	52.8	57.7	50.5	49.8 (2017)
East Asia				
China, People's Republic of[d]	27.5	31.4	34.6	46.3
Hong Kong, China[e]	79.8	85.1	88.9	87.9
Korea, Republic of[f]	68.9	65.4	68.4	69.8
Mongolia	37.2	43.3	50.2	52.7
Taipei,China	64.1	57.7	58.8	59.4
South Asia				
Bangladesh	36.2	37.6 (2006)	35.3	38.9 (2017)
Bhutan[g]	47.9 (2001)	39.2	33.7	32.9
India	23.7	25.1	25.3 (2009)	...
Maldives[h]	67.3	56.2 (2007)	86.3	72.6 (2016)
Nepal	...	...	25.7 (2011)	47.7
Sri Lanka[i]	40.3	41.8	42.9	46.6
Southeast Asia				
Brunei Darussalam	...	...	...	...
Cambodia	19.3	30.0	18.6	26.6 (2014)
Indonesia	37.3	37.3	42.3	48.0
Lao People's Democratic Republic	...	...	19.7	54.6 (2017)
Malaysia[j]	50.8	55.6	58.7	62.3
Myanmar	...	...	...	34.7
Philippines	46.7	48.1	51.8	56.6
Singapore[k]	74.2	78.2	77.9	83.9
Thailand	35.6	39.0	41.0	45.1
Viet Nam[l]	21.8	27.3	29.5	36.2
The Pacific				
Cook Islands[m]	86.7 (2001)	80.9 (2006)	84.0 (2011)	84.6 (2016)
Fiji[n]	67.7	68.1	74.4	66.4 (2016)
Kiribati[o]	...	30.7	61.8	57.5 (2015)
Marshall Islands	85.1	87.3	77.1	83.3 (2017)
Micronesia, Federated States of	...	...	...	...
Nauru	...	...	...	...
Niue	70.6 (2001)	66.9 (2006)	75.4 (2011)	77.1 (2017)
Palau[p]	92.2	89.6	...	82.0 (2015)
Papua New Guinea	...	...	...	...
Samoa	40.4 (2001)	42.8 (2006)	50.9 (2011)	62.7 (2017)
Solomon Islands[q]	...	...	44.8 (2009)	...
Timor-Leste	...	...	39.8	46.7 (2013)
Tonga	...	44.3 (2006)	...	50.3 (2016)
Tuvalu	...	...	...	...
Vanuatu	...	...	...	...
Developed ADB Member Economies				
Australia	73.7	75.3	75.9	77.6
Japan	63.7	68.1	70.5	72.7
New Zealand[r]	66.3	70.7	72.6	74.4

... = data not available; – = magnitude equals zero, ADB = Asian Development Bank.

a Data are based on varying labor force concepts and definitions adopted by different economies. Some values may not add up to 100% due to limitations on data availability.
b Prior to 2017, employment in services includes people who were engaged in construction industries.
c For 2000, employment in services includes people who were engaged in electricity, gas, and water industries.
d Refers to persons engaged in social labor and receiving remuneration or earning business income.
e Employment in services includes people who are engaged in the following sectors: electricity and gas supply; water supply; sewerage, waste management, and remediation activities.
f For 2000, employment in services includes people who are engaged in electricity, gas, water, and construction industries.
g For 2005 and 2017, data are from the census of population. For other years, data are from labor force surveys. Data prior to and after the census years may not be directly comparable to data for 2005 and 2017.
h Figures include local population only. For 2010, employment in services includes people who were engaged in industries other than agriculture, forestry, and fishing; mining and quarrying; or manufacturing industries.
i Some data may not add up because (i) for 2005 and 2011–2013, data cover all islands; (ii) for 2003, data exclude the Northern Province; (iii) for 2004, data exclude Mullaitivu and Kilinochchi districts; and (iv) for 2006–2010 and years prior to 2003, data exclude northern and eastern provinces.
j For 2005, employment in services includes people who were engaged in water supply; sewerage, waste management, and remediation activities.
k Refers to Singapore residents only.
l Refers to total number of persons engaged in any activity, regardless of age.
m Covers all wage and salary earners from all islands. For 2001, employment in services includes people who were engaged in electricity, gas, water, and construction industries.
n Refers to paid employment as of end of June, except for 2000 and 2005, which refer to end of December.
o Refers to cash work and unpaid village work. For 2005, employment figures by industry include only paid (cash work) workers, and as such, the number of employed for all industries may not add up to the total number of employed, which includes both cash workers and unpaid village workers. For 2010, employment in agriculture includes people who were engaged in mining and quarrying.
p For 2000 and 2005, employment in services includes people who were engaged in electricity, gas, water, and construction industries.
q For 2009, the figure refers to paid employment.
r For 2000, employment in services includes people who were engaged in industries other than agriculture, forestry, and fishing or manufacturing industries.

Source: Asian Development Bank estimates using data from economy sources.

Table 2.1.7: Poverty and Inequality[a]

ADB Regional Member	Proportion of Population Living on Less Than $1.90 a Day (2011 PPP) (%)		Proportion of Population Living on Less Than $3.20 a Day (2011 PPP) (%)		Income Ratio of Highest 20% to Lowest 20%[b]		Gini Coefficient	
	2000	2017	2000	2017	2000	2017	2000	2017
Developing ADB Member Economies								
Central and West Asia								
Afghanistan	...	...	...	...	...	...	...	...
Armenia	19.3 (2001)	1.4	55.6 (2001)	12.3	5.7 (2001)	5.0	0.354 (2001)	0.336
Azerbaijan[c]	2.7 (2001)	...	17.6 (2001)	...	6.0 (2001)	...	0.365 (2001)	...
Georgia	19.4	5.0	44.8	16.3	8.6	7.1	0.405	0.379
Kazakhstan	10.3 (2001)	0.0	32.3 (2001)	0.4	6.4 (2001)	3.8	0.360 (2001)	0.275
Kyrgyz Republic	42.1	1.5	77.6	19.6	4.7	3.8	0.310	0.273
Pakistan[d]	28.6 (2001)	3.9 (2015)	72.4 (2001)	34.7 (2015)	4.3 (2001)	4.8 (2015)	0.304 (2001)	0.335 (2015)
Tajikistan	30.8 (2003)	4.8 (2015)	66.8 (2003)	20.3 (2015)	5.2 (2003)	5.6 (2015)	0.327 (2003)	0.340 (2015)
Turkmenistan	...	...	...	...	...	...	...	...
Uzbekistan[e]	62.0	...	86.7	...	6.2	...	0.361	...
East Asia								
China, People's Republic of	31.7 (2002)	0.7 (2015)	57.7 (2002)	7.0 (2015)	8.6 (2002)	7.1 (2015)	0.421 (2002)	0.386 (2015)
Hong Kong, China	...	...	...	...	...	...	...	...
Korea, Republic of	0.2 (2006)	0.2 (2012)	0.5 (2006)	0.5 (2012)	5.4 (2006)	5.3 (2012)	0.317 (2006)	0.316 (2012)
Mongolia	9.7 (2002)	0.6 (2016)	33.6 (2002)	6.9 (2016)	5.4 (2002)	5.1 (2016)	0.329 (2002)	0.323 (2016)
Taipei,China[f]	...	...	...	...	4.2	3.9	0.294	0.277
South Asia								
Bangladesh	34.8	14.8 (2016)	72.7	52.9 (2016)	5.0	4.8 (2016)	0.334	0.324 (2016)
Bhutan	17.6 (2003)	1.5	45.2 (2003)	12.0	7.4 (2003)	6.6	0.409 (2003)	0.374
India[d]	38.2 (2004)	21.2 (2011)	75.2 (2004)	60.4 (2011)	5.1 (2004)	5.5 (2011)	0.344 (2004)	0.357 (2011)
Maldives[d]	10.0 (2002)	7.3 (2009)	39.2 (2002)	24.4 (2009)	7.2 (2002)	7.0 (2009)	0.413 (2002)	0.384 (2009)
Nepal[d]	46.1 (2003)	15.0 (2010)	75.5 (2003)	50.8 (2010)	7.9 (2003)	5.0 (2010)	0.438 (2003)	0.328 (2010)
Sri Lanka	8.3 (2002)	0.8 (2016)	36.0 (2002)	10.1 (2016)	7.1 (2002)	6.8 (2016)	0.410 (2002)	0.398 (2016)
Southeast Asia								
Brunei Darussalam	...	...	...	...	...	...	...	...
Cambodia	...	...	...	...	...	...	...	...
Indonesia	39.3	5.7	79.9	27.3	4.0	6.6	0.285	0.381
Lao People's Democratic Republic[d]	33.8 (2002)	22.7 (2012)	72.1 (2002)	58.7 (2012)	4.8 (2002)	5.9 (2012)	0.326 (2002)	0.364 (2012)
Malaysia	0.4 (2004)	0.0 (2015)	2.6 (2004)	0.2 (2015)	10.9 (2004)	8.2 (2015)	0.461 (2004)	0.410 (2015)
Myanmar	...	6.2 (2015)	...	29.5 (2015)	...	6.3 (2015)	...	0.381 (2015)
Philippines	14.5	7.8 (2015)	43.1	32.6 (2015)	8.0	7.2 (2015)	0.428	0.401 (2015)
Singapore	...	...	...	...	...	...	...	...
Thailand	2.5	0.0	18.6	0.5	8.0	6.0	0.428	0.365
Viet Nam	38.0 (2002)	2.0 (2016)	70.8 (2002)	8.4 (2016)	6.1 (2002)	6.2 (2016)	0.370 (2002)	0.353 (2016)
The Pacific								
Cook Islands	...	...	...	...	...	...	...	...
Fiji[d]	4.9 (2002)	1.4 (2013)	21.8 (2002)	14.1 (2013)	6.8 (2002)	6.0 (2013)	0.381 (2002)	0.367 (2013)
Kiribati	12.9 (2006)	...	34.6 (2006)	...	6.7 (2006)	...	0.370 (2006)	...
Marshall Islands	...	...	...	...	...	...	...	...
Micronesia, Federated States of	8.1 (2005)	15.4 (2013)	24.6 (2005)	38.7 (2013)	8.7 (2005)	8.4 (2013)	0.424 (2005)	0.401 (2013)
Nauru	...	...	...	...	...	...	...	...
Niue	...	...	...	...	...	...	...	...
Palau	...	...	...	...	...	...	...	...
Papua New Guinea[d]	...	38.0 (2009)	...	65.6 (2009)	...	9.3 (2009)	...	0.419 (2009)
Samoa[d]	2.0 (2002)	1.1 (2013)	11.9 (2002)	9.6 (2013)	7.6 (2002)	6.8 (2013)	0.407 (2002)	0.387 (2013)
Solomon Islands	45.6 (2005)	25.1 (2013)	70.6 (2005)	58.8 (2013)	10.4 (2005)	6.4 (2013)	0.461 (2005)	0.371 (2013)
Timor-Leste	46.0 (2001)	30.7 (2014)	75.7 (2001)	73.3 (2014)	6.0 (2001)	4.1 (2014)	0.359 (2001)	0.287 (2014)
Tonga	2.8 (2001)	1.0 (2015)	8.4 (2001)	7.5 (2015)	7.1 (2001)	6.7 (2015)	0.377 (2001)	0.376 (2015)
Tuvalu	...	3.3 (2010)	...	17.6 (2010)	...	7.0 (2010)	...	0.391 (2010)
Vanuatu	...	13.1 (2010)	...	39.2 (2010)	...	6.7 (2010)	...	0.376 (2010)
Developed ADB Member Economies								
Australia	...	...	...	...	5.5 (2001)	6.3 (2014)	0.335 (2001)	0.358 (2014)
Japan	...	...	...	...	5.4 (2008)	...	0.321 (2008)	...
New Zealand[g]	...	...	...	...	...	...	...	0.349 (2014)

... = Data not available, 0.0 = magnitude is less than half the unit employed, ADB = Asian Development Bank, PPP = purchasing power parity.

a   Poverty and inequality estimates are consumption-based except for Malaysia, which is income-based. For New Zealand, the Gini coefficient data are based on disposable income post taxes and transfers. For Taipei,China, the estimates for the Gini coefficient are based on per capita disposable income.

b   Derived from income or expenditure shares of the highest 20% and lowest 20% groups.

c   For Azerbaijan, the latest available data are for 2005: 0.0% for proportion of population below $1.90 a day (2011 PPP); 0.0% for proportion of population below $3.20 a day (2011 PPP); 3.5 for income ratio of highest 20% to lowest 20%; and 0.266 for Gini coefficient.

d   Household income and expenditure surveys for these economies were conducted in overlapping years. The table adopts the approach of the World Bank's World Development Indicators, using the initial year of the survey as the reference period for the poverty estimates.

e   For Uzbekistan, the latest available data are for 2003: 62.1% for proportion of population below $1.90 a day (2011 PPP); 86.4% for proportion of population below $3.20 a day (2011 PPP); 5.9 for income ratio of highest 20% to lowest 20%; and 0.353 for Gini coefficient.

f   For Taipei,China, the Gini coefficient reflected in the table refers to the coefficient using per capita disposable income. The estimates using disposable income of households are 0.326 for 2000 and 0.337 for 2017.

g   Using the new income definition for New Zealand, the earliest available figure for the Gini coefficient is 0.323 for 2011.

Sources: World Bank. World Development Indicators. http://data.worldbank.org/data-catalog/world-development-indicators (accessed 3 June 2019); Organisation for Economic Co-operation and Development. Income Distribution and Poverty. /stats.oecd.org/index.aspx?queryid=66670 (accessed 3 June 2019). For Taipei,China: Government of Taipei,China, Directorate-General of Budget, Accounting and Statistics. http://eng.dgbas.gov.tw/mp.asp?mp=2 (accessed 3 June 2019).

Table 2.1.8:   Human Development Index[a]

ADB Regional Member	2000	2005	2010	2013	2014	2015	2016	2017	Rank in 2017[b]
Developing ADB Member Economies									
Central and West Asia	**0.604**	**0.620**	**0.657**	**0.675**	**0.680**	**0.683**	**0.686**	**0.689**	
Afghanistan	...	0.408	0.463	0.487	0.491	0.493	0.494	0.498	168
Armenia	0.647	0.693	0.728	0.742	0.745	0.748	0.749	0.755	83
Azerbaijan	0.640	0.679	0.740	0.752	0.758	0.758	0.757	0.757	80
Georgia	0.673	0.712	0.735	0.757	0.765	0.771	0.776	0.780	70
Kazakhstan	0.685	0.747	0.765	0.788	0.793	0.797	0.797	0.800	58
Kyrgyz Republic	0.594	0.616	0.636	0.658	0.663	0.666	0.669	0.672	122
Pakistan	0.450	0.500	0.526	0.538	0.548	0.551	0.560	0.562	150
Tajikistan	0.550	0.593	0.634	0.646	0.645	0.645	0.647	0.650	127
Turkmenistan	...	...	0.673	0.692	0.697	0.701	0.705	0.706	108
Uzbekistan	0.595	0.628	0.666	0.690	0.695	0.698	0.703	0.710	105
East Asia	**0.707**	**0.774**	**0.812**	**0.830**	**0.835**	**0.838**	**0.845**	**0.847**	
China, People's Republic of	0.594	0.647	0.706	0.729	0.738	0.743	0.748	0.752	86
Hong Kong, China	0.827	0.871	0.901	0.915	0.923	0.927	0.930	0.933	7
Korea, Republic of	0.817	0.855	0.884	0.893	0.896	0.898	0.900	0.903	22
Mongolia	0.589	0.650	0.697	0.729	0.734	0.737	0.743	0.741	92
Taipei,China	...	0.846	0.873	0.882	0.882	0.885	0.903	0.907	...
South Asia	**0.540**	**0.562**	**0.606**	**0.630**	**0.638**	**0.644**	**0.649**	**0.654**	
Bangladesh	0.468	0.505	0.545	0.575	0.583	0.592	0.597	0.608	136
Bhutan	...	0.510	0.566	0.589	0.599	0.603	0.609	0.612	134
India	0.493	0.535	0.581	0.607	0.618	0.627	0.636	0.640	130
Maldives	0.606	0.631	0.671	0.696	0.705	0.710	0.712	0.717	101
Nepal	0.446	0.475	0.529	0.554	0.560	0.566	0.569	0.574	149
Sri Lanka	0.685	0.718	0.745	0.759	0.763	0.766	0.768	0.770	76
Southeast Asia	**0.614**	**0.650**	**0.684**	**0.703**	**0.707**	**0.711**	**0.715**	**0.719**	
Brunei Darussalam	0.819	0.838	0.842	0.853	0.853	0.852	0.852	0.853	39
Cambodia	0.420	0.490	0.537	0.560	0.566	0.571	0.576	0.582	146
Indonesia	0.606	0.632	0.661	0.681	0.683	0.686	0.691	0.694	116
Lao People's Democratic Republic	0.466	0.506	0.546	0.579	0.586	0.593	0.598	0.601	139
Malaysia	0.725	0.731	0.772	0.785	0.790	0.795	0.799	0.802	57
Myanmar	0.431	0.477	0.530	0.558	0.564	0.569	0.574	0.578	148
Philippines	0.624	0.650	0.665	0.685	0.689	0.693	0.696	0.699	113
Singapore	0.819	0.868	0.909	0.923	0.928	0.929	0.930	0.932	9
Thailand	0.649	0.693	0.724	0.728	0.735	0.741	0.748	0.755	83
Viet Nam	0.579	0.616	0.654	0.675	0.678	0.684	0.689	0.694	116
The Pacific	**0.584**	**0.602**	**0.632**	**0.644**	**0.645**	**0.652**	**0.653**	**0.658**	
Cook Islands	...	...	...	...	...	...	...	...	...
Fiji	0.683	0.695	0.711	0.727	0.730	0.738	0.738	0.741	92
Kiribati	0.552	0.585	0.590	0.609	0.616	0.621	0.610	0.612	134
Marshall Islands	...	...	...	...	...	...	...	0.708	106
Micronesia, Federated States of	0.552	0.582	0.608	0.619	0.618	0.627	0.627	0.627	131
Nauru	...	...	...	...	...	...	...	...	...
Niue	...	...	...	...	...	...	...	...	...
Palau	0.743	0.760	0.769	0.780	0.786	0.793	0.798	0.798	60
Papua New Guinea	0.449	0.479	0.520	0.534	0.536	0.542	0.543	0.544	153
Samoa	0.647	0.673	0.693	0.700	0.703	0.706	0.711	0.713	104
Solomon Islands	0.450	0.487	0.507	0.539	0.539	0.546	0.543	0.546	152
Timor-Leste	0.507	0.496	0.619	0.614	0.610	0.630	0.631	0.625	132
Tonga	0.673	0.693	0.712	0.716	0.717	0.721	0.724	0.726	98
Tuvalu	...	...	...	...	...	...	...	...	...
Vanuatu	...	0.572	0.591	0.597	0.598	0.599	0.600	0.603	138
Developed ADB Member Economies	**0.874**	**0.890**	**0.902**	**0.912**	**0.915**	**0.918**	**0.920**	**0.922**	
Australia	0.898	0.908	0.923	0.931	0.933	0.936	0.938	0.939	3
Japan	0.855	0.873	0.885	0.899	0.903	0.905	0.907	0.909	19
New Zealand	0.869	0.888	0.899	0.907	0.910	0.914	0.915	0.917	16

... = data not available, ADB = Asian Development Bank.

a   The regional indexes are calculated as simple averages of the indexes for their member economies.
b   Rank among the 189 national economies presented in Human Development Report 2018 of the United Nations Development Programme.

Sources: United Nations Development Programme. Human Development Data (1990–2017). http://hdr.undp.org/en/data# (accessed 4 June 2019). For Taipei,China: Government of Taipei,China, Directorate-General of Budget, Accounting and Statistics. https://eng.stat.gov.tw/ct.asp?xItem=25280&ctNode=6032&mp=5 (accessed 4 June 2019).

Table 2.1.9: Life Expectancy at Birth
(years)

ADB Regional Member	Both Sexes		Female		Male	
	2000	2017	2000	2017	2000	2017
Developing ADB Member Economies						
Central and West Asia						
Afghanistan	55.5	64.0	56.7	65.4	54.4	62.8
Armenia	71.4	74.8	74.5	77.8	68.1	71.4
Azerbaijan	66.8	72.1	69.9	75.2	63.6	69.1
Georgia	71.9	73.4	75.4	77.6	68.1	69.2
Kazakhstan	65.5	73.0	71.1	76.9	60.2	68.7
Kyrgyz Republic	68.6	71.2	72.4	75.4	64.9	67.2
Pakistan	62.7	66.6	63.6	67.7	62.0	65.6
Tajikistan	65.5	71.2	68.8	74.4	62.5	68.4
Turkmenistan	63.6	68.0	67.7	71.4	59.6	64.5
Uzbekistan	67.2	71.4	70.4	74.2	64.0	68.6
East Asia						
China, People's Republic of	72.0	76.4	73.7	78.0	70.4	74.9
Hong Kong, China	80.9	84.7	83.9	87.6	78.0	81.9
Korea, Republic of	75.9	82.6	79.7	85.7	72.3	79.7
Mongolia	62.9	69.5	65.9	73.7	60.1	65.4
Taipei,China	76.5	80.4	79.6	83.7	73.8	77.3
South Asia						
Bangladesh	65.3	72.8	65.7	74.6	65.0	71.2
Bhutan	60.8	70.6	60.9	70.9	60.6	70.3
India	62.6	68.8	63.4	70.4	61.8	67.3
Maldives	69.9	77.6	71.1	78.8	69.2	76.7
Nepal	62.4	70.6	63.4	72.2	61.3	69.0
Sri Lanka	71.0	75.5	74.9	78.8	67.5	72.1
Southeast Asia						
Brunei Darussalam	75.2	77.4	76.9	79.1	73.7	75.8
Cambodia	58.4	69.3	60.6	71.3	56.2	67.1
Indonesia	66.3	69.4	68.0	71.6	64.6	67.3
Lao People's Democratic Republic	58.9	67.0	60.3	68.6	57.5	65.4
Malaysia	72.8	75.5	75.0	77.9	70.8	73.3
Myanmar	62.1	66.7	64.2	69.1	60.1	64.4
Philippines	67.2	69.2	70.3	72.8	64.2	65.9
Singapore	78.0	82.9	80.0	85.2	76.0	80.7
Thailand	70.6	75.5	74.5	79.3	66.9	71.8
Viet Nam	73.3	76.5	78.1	81.0	68.4	71.8
The Pacific						
Cook Islands	71.9	76.2 (2018)	74.7	79.2 (2018)	69.2	73.4 (2018)
Fiji	67.6	70.4	70.2	73.6	65.2	67.5
Kiribati	64.0	66.5	67.0	69.8	61.1	63.2
Marshall Islands	68.4	73.6 (2018)	70.4	76.0 (2018)	66.6	71.4 (2018)
Micronesia, Federated States of	67.3	69.3	67.9	70.5	66.7	68.1
Nauru	60.9	67.8 (2018)	64.5	71.2 (2018)	57.4	63.6 (2018)
Niue	70.1 (2001)	73.9 (2006–2011) [a]	71.2 (2001)	75.2 (2006–2011) [a]	69.8 (2001)	72.5 (2006–2011) [a]
Palau	68.5	73.6 (2018)	71.7	77.0 (2018)	65.4	70.4 (2018)
Papua New Guinea	61.8	65.7	64.4	68.3	59.5	63.3
Samoa	69.3	75.2	72.8	78.5	66.3	72.3
Solomon Islands	63.1	71.0	64.0	72.6	62.3	69.5
Timor-Leste	59.4	69.2	60.6	71.1	58.1	67.4
Tonga	70.8	73.2	72.8	76.2	68.8	70.2
Tuvalu	61.6	67.2 (2018)	63.6	69.5 (2018)	59.7	65.0 (2018)
Vanuatu	67.4	72.3	69.3	74.7	65.9	70.2
Developed ADB Member Economies						
Australia	79.2	82.5	82.0	84.7	76.6	80.4
Japan	81.1	84.1	84.6	87.3	77.7	81.1
New Zealand	78.6	81.7	81.3	83.4	76.1	80.0
WORLD	**67.7**	**72.2**	**69.9**	**74.5**	**65.6**	**70.1**

ADB = Asian Development Bank.

a Refers to multiyear average for the intercensal years 2006–2011. Estimates are derived through an indirect technique, by applying the United Nations Mortpak.4.1 software program (MATCH), which calculates the Coale-Demeny WEST model life tables.

Sources: World Bank. World Development Indicators. http://databank.worldbank.org/data/source/world-development-indicators/preview/on# (accessed 19 June 2019). For the Cook Islands, the Marshall Islands, Nauru, Palau, and Tuvalu: United States Census Bureau Online. https://www.census.gov/data-tools/demo/idb/informationGateway.php (accessed 19 June 2019). For Niue: Statistics Niue, Department of Finance, Planning and Statistics. https://niue.prism.spc.int/ and http://prism.spc.int/images/census_reports/Niue_2011_Population_Households_Census.pdf (accessed 19 June 2019). For Taipei,China: Government of Taipei,China, Directorate-General of Budget, Accounting and Statistics. http://eng.dgbas.gov.tw/mp.asp?mp=2 (accessed 19 June 2019).

Table 2.1.10: Births, Deaths, and Fertility Rates

ADB Regional Member	Crude Birth Rate (per 1,000 people)		Crude Death Rate (per 1,000 people)		Total Fertility Rate (births per woman)	
	2000	2017	2000	2017	2000	2017
Developing ADB Member Economies						
Central and West Asia						
Afghanistan	48.4	32.5	12.0	6.6	7.5	4.5
Armenia	12.9	13.1	8.6	9.7	1.6	1.6
Azerbaijan	14.5	14.6	5.8	5.8	2.0	1.9
Georgia	12.0	13.2	9.9	13.2	1.6	2.0
Kazakhstan	14.9	21.6	10.1	7.2	1.8	2.7
Kyrgyz Republic	19.8	24.8	7.0	5.4	2.4	3.0
Pakistan	32.0	27.7	8.7	7.2	4.6	3.4
Tajikistan	30.2	28.3	7.0	5.1	3.9	3.3
Turkmenistan	23.6	24.6	7.8	7.1	2.8	2.8
Uzbekistan	21.4	22.1	5.5	5.0	2.6	2.5
East Asia						
China, People's Republic of	14.0	12.4	6.5	7.1	1.5	1.6
Hong Kong, China	8.1	7.7	5.1	6.3	1.0	1.1
Korea, Republic of	13.3	7.0	5.2	5.6	1.5	1.1
Mongolia	19.3	23.1	7.7	6.3	2.1	2.7
Taipei,China	13.8	7.7 (2018)	5.7	7.3 (2018)	1.7	1.1 (2018)
South Asia						
Bangladesh	27.6	18.6	6.9	5.3	3.2	2.1
Bhutan	28.0	17.9	8.5	6.0	3.6	2.0
India	26.5	18.8	8.7	7.3	3.3	2.3
Maldives	22.6	17.7	4.7	3.3	2.9	2.1
Nepal	32.1	19.5	8.5	6.2	4.0	2.1
Sri Lanka	18.5	15.0	7.0	7.0	2.2	2.0
Southeast Asia						
Brunei Darussalam	21.4	15.6	2.9	3.6	2.2	1.9
Cambodia	28.1	22.9	9.4	6.0	3.8	2.5
Indonesia	21.8	18.6	7.3	7.2	2.5	2.3
Lao People's Democratic Republic	31.8	23.4	9.8	6.6	4.3	2.6
Malaysia	22.0	17.0	4.5	5.0	2.8	2.0
Myanmar	24.5	17.6	9.1	8.2	2.9	2.2
Philippines	29.6	23.0	6.0	6.5	3.8	2.9
Singapore	13.7	8.9	4.5	5.0	1.6	1.2
Thailand	14.5	10.1	6.9	8.0	1.7	1.5
Viet Nam	17.5	16.5	5.5	5.8	2.0	2.0
The Pacific						
Cook Islands	23.1	13.7 (2018)	6.3	8.6 (2018)	3.2	2.2 (2018)
Fiji	24.7	19.0	6.1	7.2	3.1	2.5
Kiribati	30.6	27.9	7.6	7.0	4.1	3.6
Marshall Islands	35.0	23.8 (2018)	5.3	4.2 (2018)	4.4	3.0 (2018)
Micronesia, Federated States of	29.9	23.8	6.3	6.2	4.3	3.1
Nauru	27.9	23.2 (2018)	7.2	5.9 (2018)	3.5	2.8 (2018)
Niue	18.5 (2001)	18.4 (2006–2011)[a]	7.8 (2001)	8.9 (2006–2011)[a]	3.0 (2001)	2.2 (2006–2011)[a]
Palau	14.5	12.4	6.5	10.3	1.8	2.2 (2015)
Papua New Guinea	34.0	27.3	8.3	7.1	4.5	3.6
Samoa	30.6	24.3	6.1	5.0	4.5	3.9
Solomon Islands	35.6	28.2	7.5	4.7	4.7	3.8
Timor-Leste	43.5	34.6	9.4	5.4	7.1	5.4
Tonga	28.2	23.6	6.2	6.0	4.3	3.6
Tuvalu	24.6	23.7 (2018)	10.8	8.4 (2018)	3.6	2.9 (2018)
Vanuatu	32.4	25.5	6.2	4.8	4.4	3.2
Developed ADB Member Economies						
Australia	13.0	12.4	6.7	6.5	1.8	1.8
Japan	9.4	7.6	7.7	10.8	1.4	1.4
New Zealand	14.7	12.4	6.9	7.0	2.0	1.8
WORLD	**21.6**	**18.7**	**8.5**	**7.6**	**2.7**	**2.4**

ADB = Asian Development Bank.

a   Refers to a multiyear average for the intercensal years 2006–2011. Crude birth rate and crude death rate are calculated by dividing the average annual number of births and deaths of the intercensal period 2006–2011 by the midperiod population size of the intercensal period. For total fertility rate, the estimate is based on the average registered number of children born, by age of mother, of the intercensal period 2006–2011, and the estimated midperiod number of women of childbearing age.

Sources: World Bank. World Development Indicators. http://databank.worldbank.org/data/source/world-development-indicators/preview/on (accessed 18 June 2019). For the Cook Islands, the Marshall Islands, Nauru, and Tuvalu: United States Census Bureau Online. http://www.census.gov/ (accessed 18 June 2019). For Niue: Statistics Niue, Department of Finance, Planning and Statistics. https://niue.prism.spc.int/ and http://prism.spc.int/images/census_reports/ Niue_2011_Population_Households_Census.pdf (accessed 18 June 2019). For Taipei,China: Government of Taipei,China, Directorate-General of Budget, Accounting and Statistics. http://eng.dgbas.gov.tw/mp.asp?mp=2 (accessed 18 June 2019).

Table 2.1.11: Primary Education Completion Rate[a]
(%)

ADB Regional Member	Both Sexes		Female		Male	
	2000	2017	2000	2017	2000	2017
Developing ADB Member Economies						
Central and West Asia						
Afghanistan	...	...	...	...	...	...
Armenia	93.7 (2002)	91.6	94.1 (2002)	92.2	93.3 (2002)	91.1
Azerbaijan	89.5	107.2	85.5	107.6	93.8	106.8
Georgia	96.2	117.1	96.4	117.6	96.0	116.7
Kazakhstan	92.1	109.7 (2018)	92.0	110.9 (2018)	92.2	108.5 (2018)
Kyrgyz Republic	93.7	103.8	93.2	103.4	94.1	104.1
Pakistan	64.3 (2005)	71.3 (2016)	53.5 (2005)	64.6 (2016)	74.5 (2005)	77.6 (2016)
Tajikistan	92.7	92.4	...	92.0	...	92.7
Turkmenistan	...	...	...	...	...	...
Uzbekistan	100.4 (2001)	97.7	100.3 (2001)	97.0	100.5 (2001)	98.4
East Asia						
China, People's Republic of	89.1 (2006)	99.9 (2013)	89.0 (2006)	99.2 (2013)	89.2 (2006)	100.5 (2013)
Hong Kong, China	...	102.2	...	100.7	...	103.6
Korea, Republic of	103.2	96.1 (2016)	105.0	96.5 (2016)	101.6	95.8 (2016)
Mongolia	87.0	92.6	89.3	91.5	84.6	93.6
Taipei,China	...	...	...	...		
South Asia						
Bangladesh	64.3 (2005)	118.6	66.8 (2005)	123.0	61.9 (2005)	114.3
Bhutan	49.5	95.1	46.1	99.5	52.9	90.9
India	71.8	94.5	63.5	96.6	79.4	92.6
Maldives	...	94.7	...	91.5	...	97.8
Nepal	67.3	112.8	57.2	118.1	77.0	107.6
Sri Lanka	107.3 (2001)	101.9	106.6 (2001)	101.2	108.0 (2001)	102.7
Southeast Asia						
Brunei Darussalam	114.8	106.5	109.9	105.2	119.5	107.8
Cambodia	51.3 (2001)	89.6	46.1 (2001)	91.9	56.3 (2001)	87.3
Indonesia	93.8 (2001)	99.2	94.2 (2001)	98.5	93.4 (2001)	99.8
Lao People's Democratic Republic	67.3	102.2	61.4	101.8	73.0	102.6
Malaysia	100.6	99.2	100.7	100.3	100.5	98.1
Myanmar	78.2	96.4	75.9	96.7	80.6	96.1
Philippines	100.3 (2001)	104.0 (2016)	105.4 (2001)	106.1 (2016)	95.5 (2001)	102.0 (2016)
Singapore	...	99.8 (2016)	...	99.2 (2016)	...	100.4 (2016)
Thailand	84.9	93.4	84.3	94.1	85.4	92.7
Viet Nam	99.0	104.8 (2016)	96.6	105.0 (2016)	101.3	104.5 (2016)
The Pacific						
Cook Islands	112.0 (2007)	108.9 (2016)	...	102.1 (2016)	...	115.9 (2016)
Fiji	95.0	102.8 (2016)	93.9	103.1 (2016)	96.0	102.6 (2016)
Kiribati	99.0	99.5 (2016)	95.1	103.5 (2016)	102.7	95.8 (2016)
Marshall Islands	114.3 (2002)	76.9 (2016)	118.1 (2002)	80.0 (2016)	110.8 (2002)	74.0 (2016)
Micronesia, Federated States of	...	...	...	...	...	...
Nauru	87.0 (2001)	120.4 (2016)	90.1 (2001)	121.0 (2016)	84.3 (2001)	119.8 (2016)
Niue	105.0 (2001)	111.5 (2016)	105.6 (2001)	80.0 (2016)	104.5 (2001)	154.5 (2016)
Palau	104.5 (2004)	95.9 (2014)	...	94.7 (2014)	...	96.9 (2014)
Papua New Guinea	52.5	79.3 (2016)	48.1	73.5 (2016)	56.7	84.7 (2016)
Samoa	94.0	100.9	95.5	103.2	92.7	98.7
Solomon Islands	...	87.2	...	89.5	...	85.0
Timor-Leste	76.6 (2008)	95.3 (2016)	76.1 (2008)	97.6 (2016)	77.2 (2008)	93.1 (2016)
Tonga	105.5 (2001)	111.0 (2013)	104.0 (2001)	106.5 (2013)	107.0 (2001)	115.1 (2013)
Tuvalu	101.7 (2001)	104.0 (2016)	108.3 (2001)	98.9 (2016)	96.1 (2001)	108.7 (2016)
Vanuatu	92.1	93.8 (2013)	94.4	97.8 (2013)	89.9	90.2 (2013)
Developed ADB Member Economies						
Australia	...	...	...	...	...	...
Japan	...	100.5 (2016)	...	100.7 (2016)	...	100.3 (2016)
New Zealand	...	...	...	...	...	...

... = data not available, ADB = Asian Development Bank.

a   Represented by the total number of new entrants in the last grade of primary education, regardless of age, expressed as a percentage of the population at the theoretical age to enter the last grade of primary education.

Source: United Nations Educational, Scientific and Cultural Organization, Institute for Statistics Database. UIS.Stat. http://data.uis.unesco.org/ (accessed 20 July 2019).

Social Indicators

Table 2.1.12:   Adult (15 Years and Older) Literacy Rate
(%)

ADB Regional Member	Both Sexes		Female		Male	
	2000	2016	2000	2016	2000	2016
Developing ADB Member Economies						
Central and West Asia						
Afghanistan	...	31.7 (2011)	...	17.6 (2011)	...	45.4 (2011)
Armenia	99.4 (2001)	99.7 (2011)	99.2 (2001)	99.7 (2011)	99.7 (2001)	99.8 (2011)
Azerbaijan	99.6 (2007)	99.8	99.4 (2007)	99.7	99.8 (2007)	99.9
Georgia	99.7 (2002)	99.6 (2014)	99.6 (2002)	99.5 (2014)	99.8 (2002)	99.7 (2014)
Kazakhstan	...	99.8 (2010)	...	99.7 (2010)	...	99.8 (2010)
Kyrgyz Republic	...	99.2 (2009)	...	99.0 (2009)	...	99.5 (2009)
Pakistan	49.9 (2005)	57.0 (2014)	35.4 (2005)	44.3 (2014)	64.1 (2005)	69.1 (2014)
Tajikistan	99.5	99.8 (2014)	99.2	99.7 (2014)	99.7	99.8 (2014)
Turkmenistan	...	99.7 (2014)	...	99.6 (2014)	...	99.8 (2014)
Uzbekistan	98.6	100.0	98.1	100.0	99.2	100.0
East Asia						
China, People's Republic of	90.9	95.1 (2010)	86.5	92.7 (2010)	95.1	97.5 (2010)
Hong Kong, China	...	...	...	...	...	...
Korea, Republic of	...	...	...	...	...	...
Mongolia	97.8	98.3 (2010)	97.5	98.3 (2010)	98.0	98.2 (2010)
Taipei,China	...	...	...	...	...	...
South Asia						
Bangladesh	47.5 (2001)	72.9 (2017)	40.8 (2001)	70.1 (2017)	53.9 (2001)	75.7 (2017)
Bhutan	52.8 (2005)	57.0 (2012)	38.7 (2005)	48.0 (2012)	65.0 (2005)	66.0 (2012)
India	61.0 (2001)	69.3 (2011)	47.8 (2001)	59.3 (2011)	73.4 (2001)	78.9 (2011)
Maldives	98.4 (2006)	98.6 (2014)	98.4 (2006)	98.7 (2014)	98.4 (2006)	98.5 (2014)
Nepal	48.6 (2001)	59.6 (2011)	34.9 (2001)	48.8 (2011)	62.7 (2001)	71.7 (2011)
Sri Lanka	90.7 (2001)	91.9 (2017)	89.1 (2001)	91.0 (2017)	92.3 (2001)	93.0 (2017)
Southeast Asia						
Brunei Darussalam	92.7 (2001)	96.1 (2011)	90.2 (2001)	94.7 (2011)	95.2 (2001)	97.4 (2011)
Cambodia	73.6 (2004)	80.5 (2015)	64.1 (2004)	75.0 (2015)	84.7 (2004)	86.5 (2015)
Indonesia	90.4 (2004)	95.4	86.8 (2004)	93.6	94.0 (2004)	97.2
Lao People's Democratic Republic	69.6	84.7 (2015)	58.5	79.4 (2015)	81.4	90.0 (2015)
Malaysia	88.7	93.7	85.4	91.1	92.0	96.3
Myanmar	89.9	75.6	86.4	71.8	93.9	80.0
Philippines	92.6	96.4 (2013)	92.7	96.8 (2013)	92.5	96.0 (2013)
Singapore	92.5	97.0	88.6	95.4	96.6	98.7
Thailand	92.6	92.9 (2015)	90.5	91.2 (2015)	94.9	94.7 (2015)
Viet Nam	90.2	93.5 (2009)	86.6	91.4 (2009)	93.9	95.8 (2009)
The Pacific						
Cook Islands	...	...	...	...	...	...
Fiji	...	...	...	...	...	...
Kiribati	...	...	...	...	...	...
Marshall Islands	...	98.3 (2011)	...	98.2 (2011)	...	98.3 (2011)
Micronesia, Federated States of	...	...	...	...	...	...
Nauru	...	...	...	...	...	...
Niue	...	...	...	...	...	...
Palau	...	96.6 (2015)	...	96.3 (2015)	...	96.8 (2015)
Papua New Guinea	57.3	61.6 (2010)	50.9	57.9 (2010)	63.4	65.3 (2010)
Samoa	...	99.0 (2011)	...	99.1 (2011)	...	98.9 (2011)
Solomon Islands	...	...	...	...	...	...
Timor-Leste	37.6 (2001)	58.3 (2010)	30.0 (2001)	53.0 (2010)	45.3 (2001)	63.6 (2010)
Tonga	99.0 (2006)	99.4 (2011)	99.1 (2006)	99.4 (2011)	99.0 (2006)	99.3 (2011)
Tuvalu	...	...	...	...	...	...
Vanuatu	78.4 (2004)	84.7 (2014)	76.2 (2004)	83.2 (2014)	80.5 (2004)	86.2 (2014)
Developed ADB Member Economies						
Australia	...	...	...	...	...	...
Japan	...	...	...	...	...	...
New Zealand	...	...	...	...	...	...
WORLD	**81.5**	**86.2**	**76.4**	**82.7**	**86.6**	**89.8**

... = data not available, ADB = Asian Development Bank.

Source: United Nations Educational, Scientific and Cultural Organization, Institute for Statistics Database. UIS.Stat. http://data.uis.unesco.org/ (accessed 20 July 2019).

Table 2.1.13:   Education Resources

ADB Regional Member	Primary Pupil–Teacher Ratio		Secondary Pupil–Teacher Ratio	
	2000	2017	2000	2017
Developing ADB Member Economies				
Central and West Asia				
Afghanistan	42.3 (2006)	44.0	31.6 (2007)	38.7
Armenia	20.3 (2001)	...	...	...
Azerbaijan	18.7	15.5	...	...
Georgia	16.8	9.0	7.5	7.4
Kazakhstan	18.7 (2001)	19.6 (2018)	...	7.0 (2018)
Kyrgyz Republic	24.1	24.9	13.3	10.4
Pakistan	33.0	44.8	24.2 (2003)	19.4
Tajikistan	21.8	22.3	16.4	15.4 (2011)
Turkmenistan	...	...	...	...
Uzbekistan	21.4	21.2	11.5	10.3
East Asia				
China, People's Republic of	22.2 (2001)	16.6	17.1	13.3
Hong Kong, China	21.5	13.8	18.8 (2001)	11.5
Korea, Republic of	32.1	16.3 (2016)	21.0	13.8 (2016)
Mongolia	32.6	30.4	19.9	14.5 (2010)
Taipei,China	19.0	12.1 (2018)	17.6	12.8ª (2018)
South Asia				
Bangladesh	47.0 (2005)	30.1	38.4	34.0
Bhutan	41.1	34.6	28.1 (2005)	11.0
India	40.0	35.2 (2016)	33.6	28.5 (2016)
Maldives	22.7	10.2	15.3	...
Nepal	38.0	20.9	30.2	28.8
Sri Lanka	26.3 (2001)	22.9	...	17.4
Southeast Asia				
Brunei Darussalam	13.7	10.2	10.9	8.7
Cambodia	50.1	41.7	18.5	...
Indonesia	22.1	16.1	14.6	15.3
Lao People's Democratic Republic	30.1	22.3	21.3	18.1
Malaysia	19.6	11.7	18.4	12.3
Myanmar	32.8	23.0	31.9	26.4
Philippines	35.3	29.0 (2016)	36.4 (2001)	23.5 (2016)
Singapore	21.1 (2007)	15.1 (2016)	17.8 (2007)	11.7 (2016)
Thailand	20.8	16.2	24.0 (2001)	24.2
Viet Nam	29.5	19.6	...	...
The Pacific				
Cook Islands	17.8	17.4 (2016)	13.9	15.7 (2016)
Fiji	28.1	19.7 (2016)	20.2	19.3 (2012)
Kiribati	31.7	25.5	21.0 (2001)	...
Marshall Islands	16.9 (2002)	...	16.7 (2002)	...
Micronesia, Federated States of	...	19.7 (2015)	...	...
Nauru	21.5	40.2 (2016)	17.4	24.8 (2016)
Niue	14.7	15.5 (2016)	7.8	7.9 (2015)
Palau	15.7	...	15.1	...
Papua New Guinea	35.4	35.5 (2016)	...	34.3 (2016)
Samoa	24.0	30.2 (2010)	21.2	27.7 (2016)
Solomon Islands	...	25.8	10.1	25.9 (2012)
Timor–Leste	61.9 (2001)	31.4 (2011)	28.0 (2001)	24.3 (2011)
Tonga	22.1	21.6 (2015)	14.6	14.5 (2015)
Tuvalu	19.7	17.2 (2016)	...	8.4 (2016)
Vanuatu	22.5	26.6 (2015)	24.7	20.6 (2015)
Developed ADB Member Economies				
Australia	...	...	...	...
Japan	...	15.9 (2016)	...	11.2 (2016)
New Zealand	18.4	14.9	15.5	13.6

... = data not available, ADB = Asian Development Bank.

a   Includes those for vocational secondary schools.

Sources: United Nations Educational, Scientific and Cultural Organization, Institute for Statistics Database. UIS.Stat. http://data.uis.unesco.org/ (accessed 24 May 2019). For Taipei,China: Government of Taipei,China, Directorate-General of Budget, Accounting and Statistics. Social Indicators. http://eng.dgbas.gov.tw/ mp.asp?mp=2 (accessed 24 May 2019).

Table 2.1.14: Health Care Resources
(per 1,000 population)

ADB Regional Member	Physicians		Hospital Beds	
	2000	2017	2000	2017
Developing ADB Member Economies				
Central and West Asia				
Afghanistan	0.20 (2001)	0.28 (2016)	0.3	0.5 (2015)
Armenia	2.99	2.90 (2014)	6.4	4.2 (2015)
Azerbaijan	3.61	3.45 (2014)	8.7	4.7 (2013)
Georgia	4.67 (2008)	5.10 (2015)	4.8	2.6 (2013)
Kazakhstan	3.29	3.25 (2014)	7.2	6.7 (2013)
Kyrgyz Republic	2.48 (2008)	1.88 (2014)	7.0	4.5 (2013)
Pakistan	0.66	0.98 (2015)	0.7	0.6 (2014)
Tajikistan	2.17	1.70 (2014)	6.5	4.8 (2013)
Turkmenistan	4.35 (2002)	2.22 (2014)	9.1	7.4 (2013)
Uzbekistan	2.95	2.37 (2014)	5.3	4.0 (2013)
East Asia				
China, People's Republic of	1.24	1.79 (2015)	2.5	4.2 (2012)
Hong Kong, China	...	...	...	...
Korea, Republic of	1.69 (2004)	2.37	6.1	11.5 (2015)
Mongolia	2.75 (2002)	2.89 (2016)	7.5 (2002)	7.0 (2012)
Taipei,China	1.54 (2001)	2.25	5.7 (2001)	7.0
South Asia				
Bangladesh	0.24 (2001)	0.53	0.3 (2001)	0.8 (2015)
Bhutan	0.18 (2004)	0.37	1.6 (2001)	1.7 (2012)
India	0.53	0.78	0.7 (2002)	0.7 (2011)
Maldives	0.97 (2004)	1.04 (2016)	1.7	4.3 (2009)
Nepal	0.21 (2004)	0.65	0.2 (2001)	0.3 (2012)
Sri Lanka	0.42	0.96	2.9	3.6 (2012)
Southeast Asia				
Brunei Darussalam	1.01	1.77 (2015)	2.6	2.7 (2015)
Cambodia	0.17	0.17 (2014)	0.6 (2001)	0.8 (2015)
Indonesia	0.13 (2003)	0.38	0.6 (2002)	1.2 (2015)
Lao People's Democratic Republic	0.28	0.50 (2014)	0.9 (2002)	1.5 (2012)
Malaysia	0.70	1.51 (2015)	1.8 (2001)	1.9 (2015)
Myanmar	0.37 (2004)	0.86	0.7	0.9 (2012)
Philippines	1.22	1.28 (2010)	1.0 (2001)	1.0 (2011)
Singapore	1.43 (2001)	2.31 (2016)	2.9 (2001)	2.4 (2015)
Thailand	0.30 (2001)	0.81	2.2	2.1 (2010)
Viet Nam	0.52 (2001)	0.82 (2016)	2.4 (2001)	2.6 (2014)
The Pacific				
Cook Islands	0.77 (2001)	1.42 (2014)	6.3 (2005)	...
Fiji	0.47 (2003)	0.84 (2015)	2.1 (2004)	2.3 (2011)
Kiribati	0.25 (2008)	0.20 (2013)	1.5 (2004)	1.9 (2015)
Marshall Islands	0.60 (2007)	0.46 (2012)	...	2.7 (2010)
Micronesia, Federated States of	0.60	0.19 (2009)	2.8	3.2 (2009)
Nauru	0.99 (2004)	1.24 (2015)	3.5 (2004)	5.0 (2010)
Niue	2.22 (2003)	...	5.2 (2006)	...
Palau	1.30 (2006)	1.18 (2014)	5.9 (2006)	4.8 (2010)
Papua New Guinea	0.05	0.05 (2010)	...	...
Samoa	0.28 (2003)	0.34 (2016)	3.3	...
Solomon Islands	0.13 (2003)	0.20 (2016)	2.2 (2003)	1.4 (2012)
Timor-Leste	0.08 (2004)	0.72	...	5.9 (2010)
Tonga	0.36 (2001)	0.52 (2013)	3.2 (2001)	2.6 (2010)
Tuvalu	0.63 (2002)	0.92 (2014)	5.6 (2001)	...
Vanuatu	0.15 (2004)	0.17 (2016)	3.1 (2001)	...
Developed ADB Member Economies				
Australia	2.48 (2001)	3.59 (2016)	7.8	3.8 (2014)
Japan	2.01	2.41 (2016)	14.7	13.4 (2012)
New Zealand	2.31 (2001)	3.03 (2016)	6.2 (2002)	2.8 (2013)

... = data not available, ADB = Asian Development Bank.

Sources: For number of physicians per 1,000 population: World Health Organization. Global Health Observatory. http://apps.who.int/gho/data/node.main.
HWFGRP_0020?lang=en (accessed 27 May 2019); and for initial year data of Armenia, Azerbaijan, Kazakhstan, Timor-Leste, and Uzbekistan: World Bank.
World Development Indicators. https://data.worldbank.org/indicator/SH.MED.PHYS.ZS (accessed 27 May 2019). For number of hospital beds per 1,000
population: World Bank. World Development Indicators. https://data.worldbank.org/indicator/SH.MED.BEDS.ZS (accessed 27 May 2019); and for initial year
data of Cook Islands and Niue: World Health Organization. Global Health Observatory. http://apps.who.int/gho/data/view.main.HS07v (accessed 27 May
2019). For Taipei,China: Government of Taipei,China, Directorate-General of Budget, Accounting and Statistics. Statistical Yearbook of the Republic of China
2017. https://eng.dgbas.gov.tw/lp.asp?ctNode=2351&CtUnit=1072&BaseDSD=36&MP=2 (accessed 27 May 2019).

Table 2.1.15: Adults Aged 15 Years and Older Living with HIV[a]
('000)

ADB Regional Member	All Adults		Women	
	2000	2018	2000	2018
Developing ADB Member Economies				
Central and West Asia				
Afghanistan	1.5	6.9	<0.5	2.0
Armenia	<1.0	3.5	<0.5	1.2
Azerbaijan	...	...	...	...
Georgia	<1.0	9.3	<0.5	3.0
Kazakhstan	1.1	25.0	<0.5	9.2
Kyrgyz Republic	<1.0	8.2	<0.2	2.7
Pakistan	<0.5	160.0	<0.2	48.0
Tajikistan	1.4	12.0	<0.5	3.5
Turkmenistan	...	...	...	...
Uzbekistan	14.0	46.0	4.2	16.0
East Asia				
China, People's Republic of	...	...	...	...
Hong Kong, China	...	...	...	...
Korea, Republic of	...	...	...	...
Mongolia	<0.1	<1.0	<0.1	<0.2
Taipei,China	...	...	...	...
South Asia				
Bangladesh	<1.0	13.0	<0.5	4.8
Bhutan	<1.0	1.3	<0.2	<0.5
India	...	...	...	...
Maldives	...	...	...	...
Nepal	15.0	29.0	2.4	12.0
Sri Lanka	2.1	3.4	<0.5	1.0
Southeast Asia				
Brunei Darussalam	...	...	...	...
Cambodia	78.0	70.0	33.0	37.0
Indonesia	80.0	620.0	15.0	220.0
Lao People's Democratic Republic	...	...	...	...
Malaysia	55.0	87.0	11.0	15.0
Myanmar	150.0	230.0	34.0	87.0
Philippines	1.0	77.0	<0.2	4.6
Singapore	2.9	7.9	<0.5	<1.0
Thailand	720.0	480.0	260.0	210.0
Viet Nam	120.0	220.0	24.0	74.0
The Pacific				
Cook Islands	...	...	...	...
Fiji	...	...	...	...
Kiribati	...	...	...	...
Marshall Islands	...	...	...	...
Micronesia, Federated States of	...	...	...	...
Nauru	...	...	...	...
Niue	...	...	...	...
Palau	...	...	...	...
Papua New Guinea	19.0	42.0	10.0	25.0
Samoa	...	...	...	...
Solomon Islands	...	...	...	...
Timor-Leste	...	...	...	...
Tonga	...	...	...	...
Tuvalu	...	...	...	...
Vanuatu	...	...	...	...
Developed ADB Member Economies				
Australia	13.0	28.0	1.3	3.3
Japan	6.1	30.0	<1.0	2.8
New Zealand	1.3	3.6	<0.5	<1.0

... = data not available, < = less than, ADB = Asian Development Bank.

a   The modeled HIV estimates are calculated by the Joint United Nations Programme on HIV/AIDS (UNAIDS) using the software Spectrum developed by Avenir Health (www.avenirhealth.org), and the Estimates and Projections Package developed by the East-West Center (www.eastwestcenter.org). The UNAIDS Reference Group on Estimates, Modelling and Projections (www.epidem.org) provides technical guidance on the development of the HIV component of the software.

Source: Joint United Nations Programme on HIV/AIDS (UNAIDS). UNAIDS Database. http://aidsinfo.unaids.org/ (accessed 20 July 2019).

II. Economy and Output

Economy and Output presents figures comparing the relative size of economies, both within the Asia and Pacific region and across the world, using data on gross domestic product (GDP) expressed at purchasing power parity (PPP) and current United States (US) dollars. Regional members' economic growth rates are also discussed. Statistical tables generated from the national accounts, include GDP, value added, consumption expenditure, capital formation, exports and imports, and gross domestic saving. Other tables present production indicators and trends in external trade and domestic consumption.

Asia and the Pacific's share of global GDP at PPP exceeds that of Europe and North America combined.

Asia and the Pacific's share of global GDP at PPP has increased steadily, from 30.3% in 2000 to 37.0% in 2010 and 42.8% in 2018 (Figure 2.2.1). In fact, the region's share of global GDP in 2018 exceeded the combined share of Europe and North America. Europe's global GDP share fell from 27.2% in 2000 to 22.4% in 2018, while North America's declined from 25.3% in 2000 to 18.3% in 2018.

Across other regions of the world, the global GDP shares in 2018 of South America (5.1%), Africa (4.9%), West Asia (4.7%), and economies not belonging to any specified region (1.8%) were little changed from the respective shares of these regions in 2000 and 2010. Among these regions, the largest change during the review period occurred in South America, where global GDP share fell from 6.1% in 2000 to 5.1% in 2018.

In 2018, the five largest economies in Asia and the Pacific in terms of GDP at PPP together

Figure 2.2.1: Global Distribution of Gross Domestic Product at Purchasing Power Parity
(%)

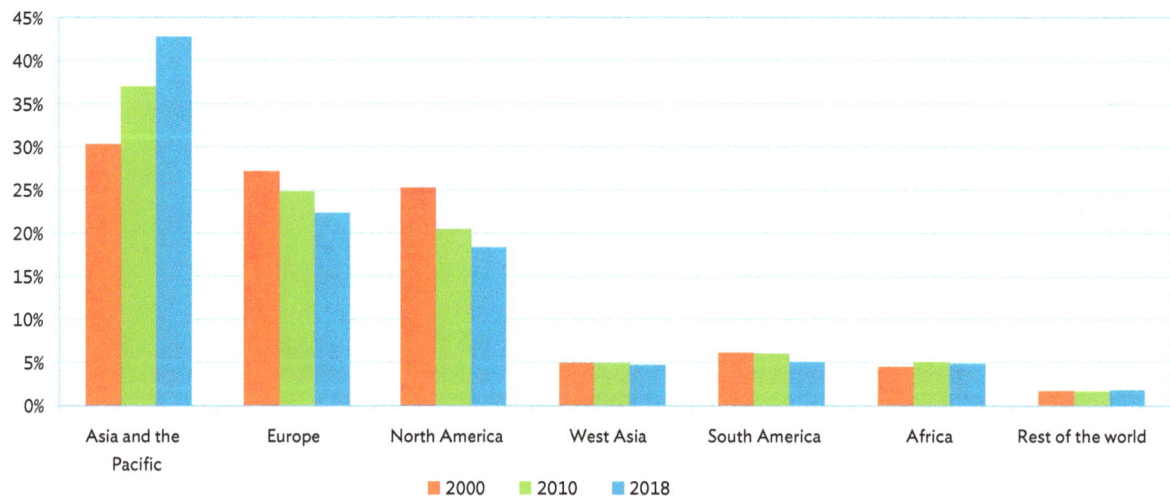

Sources: Table 2.2.1, Key Indicators for Asia and the Pacific 2019; and World Bank. World Development Indicators. http//data.worldbank.org/ (accessed 3 August 2019).

accounted for 79.7% of the region's total output. This contribution was led by the PRC (43.0%), followed by India (17.8%), Japan (9.3%), Indonesia (5.9%), and the Republic of Korea (3.8%). In 2000, these five economies accounted for 75.3% of the region's GDP at PPP, led by the PRC (24.8%) and followed by Japan (22.7%), India (15.5%), Indonesia (6.5%), and the Republic of Korea (5.8%).

India was the region's fastest-growing large economy over the last 3 years

In 2018, the five largest economies in Asia and the Pacific in terms of GDP at PPP were the PRC, India, Japan, Indonesia, and the Republic of Korea.

All five of these Asian economies posted positive GDP growth each year from 2016 to 2018, but their growth rates varied widely (Figure 2.2.2). India had the highest growth rates over the 3 years, with 8.2% in 2016, 7.2% in 2017, and 6.8% in 2018, while the high-income economies of Japan and the Republic of Korea had the lowest.

In Japan, marginal GDP growth of 0.6% was achieved in 2016. This rose to 1.9% in 2017, before falling to 0.8% in 2018. The Republic of Korea experienced moderate growth of 2.9% in 2016, 3.2% in 2017, and 2.7% in 2018.

The largest economy in the Asia and Pacific region—and, indeed, in the world—in terms of GDP at PPP was the PRC. It expanded at rates of 6.7% in 2016, 6.8% in 2017, and 6.6% in 2018. Indonesia's economy grew 5.0%, 5.1%, and 5.2% in 2016, 2017, and 2018, respectively.

Data Issues and Comparability

Indicators in this theme are derived from national accounts statistics compiled in accordance with the UN System of National Accounts. As national statistics offices gradually adopt the latest 2008 System of National Accounts framework with regard to data compilation frameworks and methodologies, these indicators will become more consistent across economies. Currently, economies in the region have

Figure 2.2.2: Growth Rates of Real Gross Domestic Product in Asia's Five Largest Economies
(%)

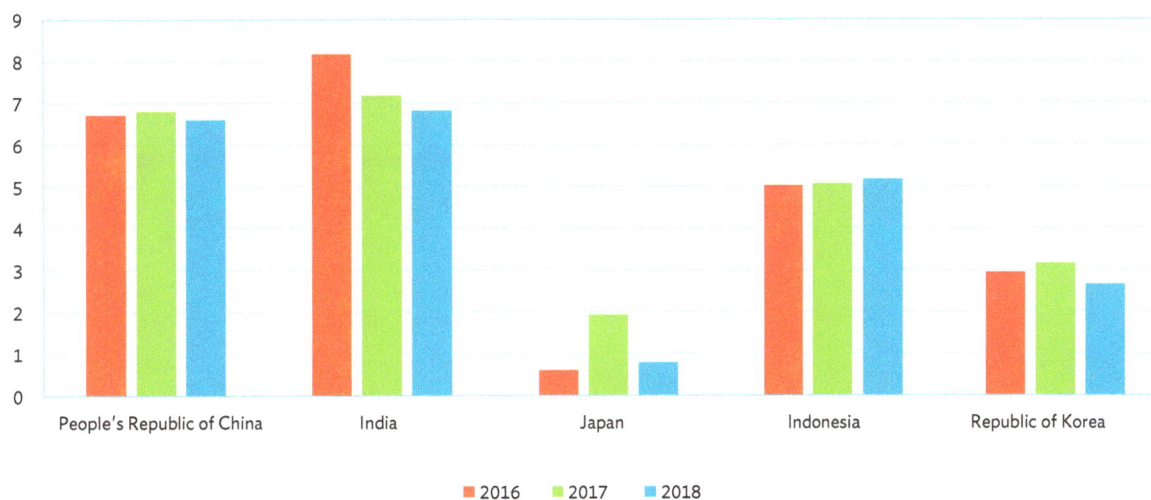

Note: Largest economies are determined in terms of gross domestic product at purchasing power parity in 2018.
Source: Table 2.2.11, Key Indicators for Asia and the Pacific 2019.

varying reference periods (e.g., calendar year versus fiscal year) and price valuation methods. Due to a lack of reliable data and limited technical and financial resources dedicated to national accounts compilation, some economies with small statistics offices are not able to provide timely estimates, while some are dependent on the estimates of external institutions.

Table 2.2.1:   Gross Domestic Product at Purchasing Power Parity
(current international dollars, million)

ADB Regional Member	2000	2005	2010	2013	2014	2015	2016	2017	2018
Developing ADB Member Economies									
Central and West Asia									
Afghanistan	21,094 (2002)	26,719	49,145	63,573	65,723	66,906	70,126	74,664	76,585
Armenia	7,144	14,228	18,892	23,190	24,479	25,532	25,863	28,331	30,477
Azerbaijan	29,486	61,179	143,821	162,121	169,809	173,428	169,953	172,695	179,085
Georgia	11,444	18,237	25,896	32,322	34,456	35,828	37,251	39,793	42,611
Kazakhstan	117,863	216,123	321,302	405,853	430,900	440,733	450,454	477,836	515,810
Kyrgyz Republic	8,086	10,902	14,890	18,486	19,590	20,571	21,691	23,142	24,492
Pakistan	427,259	603,400	715,663	841,247	897,233	949,730	1,013,179	1,091,293	1,176,498
Tajikistan	5,863	10,410	15,766	20,837	22,808	24,108	26,047	28,564	31,341
Turkmenistan	18,823	27,514	49,544	73,661	82,712	89,245	95,668	103,824	122,022
Uzbekistan	49,421	71,785	140,800	190,092	173,576	188,499	202,174	215,208	231,358
East Asia									
China, People's Republic of	3,707,488	6,624,265	12,445,651	16,779,114	18,344,523	19,820,982	21,387,607	23,266,769	25,361,730
Hong Kong, China	180,414	248,418	331,004	385,147	403,274	417,319	431,064	456,170	480,086
Korea, Republic of	872,060	1,213,618	1,572,870	1,726,903	1,792,600	1,933,849	2,018,179	2,119,722	2,220,605
Mongolia	8,881	13,612	20,483	31,897	35,063	36,281	37,107	39,789	43,446
Taipei,China	482,934	658,932	893,856	1,024,653	1,086,022	1,106,470	1,135,554	1,192,709	1,251,717
South Asia									
Bangladesh	151,802	214,078	364,054	463,397	500,782	539,303	583,983	638,430	704,165
Bhutan	1,615	2,646	4,576	5,609	5,988	6,514	7,114	7,585	7,933
India	2,318,667	3,546,543	5,487,141	6,727,353	7,362,570	8,036,327	8,787,915	9,596,835	10,474,334
Maldives	2,179	2,635	4,287	5,419	5,926	6,162	6,684	7,282	7,897
Nepal	29,088	38,478	52,569	62,803	67,824	70,827	72,023	80,150	86,755
Sri Lanka	84,781	112,660	168,758	218,576	233,759	248,090	262,055	276,168	291,459
Southeast Asia									
Brunei Darussalam	21,758	26,993	30,667	33,269	33,102	33,266	32,801	33,869	34,650
Cambodia	13,306	23,284	35,361	46,181	50,415	54,540	59,013	64,353	70,753
Indonesia	977,310	1,378,538	2,003,476	2,520,498	2,696,763	2,858,510	3,035,213	3,249,635	3,494,762
Lao People's Democratic Republic	9,981	15,860	24,421	34,455	37,779	40,959	44,315	48,233	52,543
Malaysia	300,920	424,707	581,232	715,486	772,812	833,902	877,990	945,875	1,011,337
Myanmar	47,921	98,268	182,822	237,852	261,718	283,014	302,881	329,498	357,819
Philippines	262,156	367,351	513,839	644,115	696,633	746,796	806,934	877,180	952,967
Singapore	167,813	238,071	363,321	447,490	473,741	492,656	512,797	541,878	571,494
Thailand	460,361	671,842	887,868	1,043,881	1,074,101	1,119,607	1,169,841	1,240,047	1,320,504
Viet Nam	163,686	255,824	382,022	476,764	514,852	555,113	596,038	648,742	711,219
The Pacific									
Cook Islands	...	...	...	...	...	...	...	...	...
Fiji	4,293	5,391	6,193	7,152	7,696	8,141	8,448	9,054	9,722
Kiribati	134	161	177	207	210	234	249	254	265
Marshall Islands	122	153	182	205	208	209	217	230	241
Micronesia, Federated States of	267	308	335	345	344	365	373	421	437
Nauru	...	...	65	113	157	163	182	194	189
Niue	...	...	...	...	...	...	...	...	...
Palau	190	247	241	269	287	309	324	319	317
Papua New Guinea	12,171	15,167	22,222	25,847	29,892	33,081	34,814	38,352	39,419
Samoa	534	798	1,038	1,043	1,092	1,189	1,278	1,288	1,310
Solomon Islands	392	728	989	1,122	1,162	1,200	1,250	1,319	1,394
Timor-Leste	2,297	5,764	9,646	10,629	8,025	9,783	9,960	9,220	9,694
Tonga	360	449	508	541	563	584	623	683	713
Tuvalu	23	26	30	35	36	40	45	48	50
Vanuatu	418	487	682	759	791	817	851	920	971
Developed ADB Member Economies									
Australia	504,273	664,362	866,385	1,061,628	1,100,545	1,101,971	1,145,491	1,221,574	1,288,228
Japan	3,404,300	4,045,734	4,480,784	4,967,052	4,986,566	5,136,019	5,221,770	5,319,800	5,484,024
New Zealand	83,024	106,148	135,972	160,892	168,034	172,225	183,610	193,557	203,421
DEVELOPING ADB MEMBER ECONOMIES[a]	**10,982,800**	**17,266,798**	**27,888,305**	**35,510,511**	**38,421,997**	**41,311,186**	**44,338,129**	**47,978,571**	**52,003,175**
ALL ADB REGIONAL MEMBERS[a]	**14,974,398**	**22,083,042**	**33,371,446**	**41,700,082**	**44,677,142**	**47,721,401**	**50,889,000**	**54,713,503**	**58,978,848**

... = data not available, ADB = Asian Development Bank.

a   For reporting economies only.

Source: Asian Development Bank estimates.

Table 2.2.2:   Gross Domestic Product[a]
(current $ million)

ADB Regional Member	2000	2005	2010	2013	2014	2015	2016	2017	2018
Developing ADB Member Economies									
Central and West Asia									
Afghanistan	4,285 (2002)	6,622	16,078	21,610	21,330	20,607	20,231	21,499	20,514
Armenia	1,912	4,900	9,260	11,121	11,610	10,553	10,546	11,527	12,433
Azerbaijan	5,273	13,245	52,906	74,161	75,239	53,076	37,867	40,867	46,939
Georgia	3,058	6,411	11,638	16,141	16,510	13,993	14,378	15,081	16,210
Kazakhstan	18,292	57,124	148,047	236,635	221,416	184,388	137,278	162,887	172,941
Kyrgyz Republic	1,370	2,460	4,794	7,335	7,468	6,678	6,813	7,703	8,093
Pakistan	79,097	119,739	174,508	220,269	248,949	267,035	277,521	303,092	282,346
Tajikistan	861	2,312	5,642	8,506	9,237	7,855	6,953	7,158	7,523
Turkmenistan	4,932	17,174	22,582	39,198	43,486	35,855	36,180	37,926	44,114
Uzbekistan	13,759	14,396	46,909	68,997	76,659	81,847	81,779	59,160	50,500
East Asia									
China, People's Republic of	1,211,332	2,285,960	6,087,192	9,570,468	10,438,478	11,015,560	11,137,979	12,143,563	13,608,139
Hong Kong, China	171,669	181,569	228,639	275,697	291,460	309,386	320,863	341,685	362,682
Korea, Republic of	576,179	934,901	1,144,067	1,370,795	1,484,318	1,465,773	1,500,112	1,623,901	1,720,489
Mongolia	1,137	2,523	7,189	12,582	12,227	11,750	11,187	11,426	12,980
Taipei,China	331,503	375,920	446,217	511,614	530,554	525,759	531,478	574,959	589,501
South Asia									
Bangladesh	45,468	57,627	114,508	153,505	173,062	194,466	220,837	245,633	269,628
Bhutan	439	819	1,585	1,798	1,959	2,060	2,220	2,528	...
India	484,498	837,499	1,702,346	1,917,054	2,042,939	2,146,759	2,286,229	2,625,091	2,779,692
Maldives	624	1,163	2,588	3,295	3,697	4,109	4,414	4,866	...
Nepal	5,338	8,259	16,281	18,209	20,138	20,801	20,982	25,590	27,825
Sri Lanka	16,717	24,406	56,726	74,318	79,356	80,604	82,401	88,020	88,942
Southeast Asia									
Brunei Darussalam	6,001	9,531	13,707	18,094	17,098	12,930	11,400	12,128	13,567
Cambodia	3,667	6,293	11,242	15,228	16,703	18,050	20,017	22,177	24,572
Indonesia	165,021	285,869	755,094	912,524	890,815	860,854	931,877	1,015,423	1,042,173
Lao People's Democratic Republic	1,638	2,717	6,744	11,942	13,268	14,390	15,806	16,847	17,954
Malaysia	93,790	143,534	255,017	323,276	338,066	301,355	301,255	318,955	358,579
Myanmar	...	...	...	62,140	66,300	62,543	64,590	66,491	...
Philippines	81,026	103,072	199,591	271,836	284,585	292,774	304,898	313,620	330,910
Singapore	96,077	127,808	239,808	307,576	314,864	307,997	318,057	338,399	364,146
Thailand	126,392	189,318	341,105	420,334	407,339	401,296	412,353	455,275	505,042
Viet Nam	31,173	57,633	115,932	171,222	186,205	193,241	205,276	223,780	245,214
The Pacific									
Cook Islands	92	183	241	289	319	302	310	346	374
Fiji	1,678	2,981	3,140	4,190	4,857	4,682	4,927	5,270	...
Kiribati	68	112	156	185	180	171	178	186	...
Marshall Islands	112	140	168	192	185	181	198	208	...
Micronesia, Federated States of	233	250	297	316	318	315	331	363	...
Nauru	...	31	51	102	115	90	104	116	113
Niue	8	14	18	25	27	24	25	26	30
Palau	146	184	183	223	243	280	300	286	284
Papua New Guinea	3,499	4,866	14,251	21,261	23,211	21,723	20,759	23,716	25,111
Samoa	231	434	692	764	781	787	822	825	833
Solomon Islands	286	428	696	1,015	1,047	1,027	1,093	...	...
Timor-Leste	440	1,814	3,999	5,638	4,042	3,093	2,504	2,487	...
Tonga	189	264	374	440	436	398	406	457	476
Tuvalu	14	22	31	37	37	35	40	44	...
Vanuatu	273	395	701	802	815	760	804	880	...
Developed ADB Member Economies									
Australia	383,318	704,385	1,193,596	1,483,151	1,440,948	1,220,347	1,235,745	1,352,365	1,380,500
Japan	4,887,520	4,755,410	5,700,098	5,155,717	4,850,414	4,389,475	4,926,667	4,859,951	4,970,075
New Zealand	54,444	114,723	146,584	190,786	200,835	177,207	187,853	202,276	...
DEVELOPING ADB MEMBER ECONOMIES[b]	3,589,796	5,892,925	12,262,941	17,162,959	18,381,945	18,958,217	19,366,576	21,172,468	23,050,869
ALL ADB REGIONAL MEMBERS[b]	8,915,077	11,467,442	19,303,219	23,992,612	24,874,141	24,745,247	25,716,842	27,587,060	29,401,444

... = data not available, $ = United States dollars, ADB = Asian Development Bank.

a   Gross domestic product at local currency units are obtained from economy sources and are converted to United States dollars using the official exchange rates from the International Monetary Fund. The exchange rates used are expressed as the average rate for a period of time (average of period), calculated as annual averages based on the monthly averages (local currency units relative to the United States dollar).
b   For reporting economies only.

Source: Asian Development Bank estimates.

Table 2.2.3: **Gross Domestic Product per Capita at Purchasing Power Parity**
(current international dollars)

ADB Regional Member	2000	2005	2010	2013	2014	2015	2016	2017	2018
Developing ADB Member Economies									
Central and West Asia									
Afghanistan	1,039 (2002)	1,209	2,007	2,443	2,475	2,469	2,536	2,645	2,546
Armenia	2,218	4,522	6,205	7,674	8,122	8,498	8,643	9,509	10,257
Azerbaijan	3,652	7,197	15,884	17,216	17,809	17,973	17,417	17,525	18,017
Georgia	2,807	4,673	6,839	8,694	9,264	9,618	9,993	10,674	11,434
Kazakhstan	7,919	14,268	19,685	23,824	24,924	25,123	25,315	26,491	28,223
Kyrgyz Republic	1,659	2,123	2,748	3,264	3,391	3,490	3,603	3,769	3,914
Pakistan	3,053	3,867	4,125	4,563	4,772	4,954	5,185	5,252	5,528
Tajikistan	946	1,535	2,097	2,581	2,762	2,853	3,012	3,232	3,472
Turkmenistan	4,168	5,787	9,739	13,726	15,131	16,036	16,895	18,032	20,855
Uzbekistan	2,005	2,743	4,930	6,285	5,643	6,023	6,348	6,645	7,020
East Asia									
China, People's Republic of	2,925	5,066	9,281	12,331	13,412	14,419	15,468	16,738	18,176
Hong Kong, China	27,069	36,461	47,123	53,650	55,782	57,235	58,755	61,714	64,432
Korea, Republic of	18,551	25,187	31,740	34,244	35,357	37,919	39,418	41,203	43,029
Mongolia	3,718	5,367	7,479	11,003	11,833	11,987	12,013	12,636	13,543
Taipei,China	21,769	28,990	38,627	43,892	46,404	47,158	48,289	50,634	53,084
South Asia									
Bangladesh	1,174	1,545	2,450	2,995	3,194	3,394	3,632	3,924	4,278
Bhutan	2,713	4,166	6,576	7,653	8,037	8,605	9,256	10,431	10,803
India	2,275	3,207	4,627	5,378	5,811	6,264	6,765	7,292	7,864
Maldives	8,069	7,781	10,891	12,641	13,544	13,560	14,148	14,812	15,422
Nepal	1,382	1,521	2,002	2,308	2,459	2,534	2,542	2,791	2,981
Sri Lanka	4,379	5,735	8,171	10,621	11,254	11,833	12,359	12,879	13,450
Southeast Asia									
Brunei Darussalam	66,988	75,294	79,283	82,491	81,212	80,665	78,611	78,856	78,324
Cambodia	1,068	1,748	2,503	3,147	3,392	3,623	3,870	4,167	4,523
Indonesia	4,738	6,270	8,431	10,130	10,694	11,190	11,732	12,408	13,188
Lao People's Democratic Republic	1,962	2,821	4,042	5,462	5,903	6,309	6,728	7,219	7,751
Malaysia	12,811	16,306	20,331	23,692	25,173	26,728	27,784	29,559	31,214
Myanmar	1,040	2,027	3,645	4,623	5,034	5,396	5,724	6,172	6,644
Philippines	3,415	4,338	5,517	6,559	6,975	7,353	7,816	8,362	8,940
Singapore	41,663	55,809	71,566	82,881	86,612	89,007	91,452	96,552	101,352
Thailand	7,588	10,623	13,469	15,638	16,031	16,652	17,343	18,329	19,468
Viet Nam	2,123	3,123	4,394	5,312	5,675	6,053	6,430	6,925	7,510
The Pacific									
Cook Islands	...	...	...	...	...	...	...	...	...
Fiji	5,353	6,518	7,280	8,297	8,890	9,364	9,675	10,232	10,970
Kiribati	1,587	1,741	1,714	1,933	1,930	2,125	2,229	2,249	2,348
Marshall Islands	2,377	2,982	3,444	3,834	3,875	3,883	4,014	4,224	4,410
Micronesia, Federated States of	2,492	2,919	3,257	3,380	3,368	3,566	3,642	4,106	...
Nauru	...	...	6,659	10,472	14,759	15,085	16,566	17,304	16,663
Niue	...	...	...	...	...	...	...	...	...
Palau	10,011	12,447	13,154	15,455	16,510	17,505	18,134	17,813	18,098
Papua New Guinea	2,345	2,506	3,150	3,341	3,747	4,022	4,104	4,385	4,371
Samoa	3,049	4,434	5,568	5,469	5,687	6,147	6,519	6,559	6,627
Solomon Islands	935	1,549	1,780	1,877	1,899	1,918	1,955	2,019	2,091
Timor-Leste	2,636	5,615	8,693	8,975	6,616	7,883	7,853	7,113	7,321
Tonga	3,630	4,439	4,943	5,290	5,540	5,773	6,188	6,823	7,152
Tuvalu	2,407	2,480	2,726	3,198	3,253	3,549	4,004	4,192	4,342
Vanuatu	2,188	2,275	2,846	2,956	3,013	3,040	3,124	3,303	3,411
Developed ADB Member Economies									
Australia	26,501	32,927	39,324	45,902	46,880	46,270	47,352	49,654	51,544
Japan	26,839	31,663	34,987	38,974	39,179	40,396	41,118	41,959	43,342
New Zealand	21,521	25,677	31,253	36,220	37,261	37,475	39,123	40,376	41,638
DEVELOPING ADB MEMBER ECONOMIES[a]	**3,343**	**4,952**	**7,576**	**9,307**	**9,967**	**10,608**	**11,269**	**12,044**	**12,925**
ALL ADB REGIONAL MEMBERS[a]	**4,359**	**6,068**	**8,700**	**10,503**	**11,141**	**11,783**	**12,441**	**13,217**	**14,111**

... = data not available, ADB = Asian Development Bank.

a   For reporting economies only.

Source: Asian Development Bank estimates.

National Accounts

Table 2.2.4:   Gross National Income per Capita, Atlas Method[a]
(current $)

ADB Regional Member	2000	2005	2010	2014	2015	2016	2017	2018
Developing ADB Member Economies								
Central and West Asia								
Afghanistan	...	...	510	630	600	570	550	550
Armenia	660	1,540	3,470	4,140	4,020	3,750	3,970	4,230
Azerbaijan	610	1,270	5,400	7,740	6,570	4,760	4,070	4,050
Georgia	810	1,520	3,110	4,500	4,110	3,830	3,760	4,130
Kazakhstan	1,260	2,950	7,440	12,090	11,420	8,800	7,960	7,830
Kyrgyz Republic	280	450	850	1,250	1,180	1,110	1,110	1,220
Pakistan	480	700	1,030	1,320	1,360	1,420	1,500	1,580
Tajikistan	170	320	920	1,360	1,250	1,110	1,000	1,010
Turkmenistan	600	1,590	4,070	7,200	7,030	6,820	6,380	6,740
Uzbekistan	630	530	1,340	2,210	2,440	2,660	2,350	2,020
East Asia								
China, People's Republic of	940	1,760	4,340	7,500	7,910	8,210	8,630	9,470
Hong Kong, China	26,930	28,890	33,620	40,240	41,180	42,970	46,420	50,310
Korea, Republic of	10,740	17,790	21,260	26,800	27,250	27,690	28,380	30,600
Mongolia	470	900	2,000	4,210	3,820	3,500	3,230	3,580
Taipei,China	13,922	17,644	20,034	23,369	23,075	23,039	23,895	25,371
South Asia								
Bangladesh	440	550	800	1,110	1,220	1,370	1,520	1,750
Bhutan	740	1,230	2,090	2,530	2,600	2,730	2,890	3,080
India	440	710	1,220	1,560	1,600	1,690	1,830	2,020
Maldives	2,070	3,460	5,960	7,320	7,650	8,140	8,670	9,310
Nepal	230	310	540	770	780	770	850	960
Sri Lanka	870	1,210	2,410	3,640	3,760	3,810	3,880	4,060
Southeast Asia								
Brunei Darussalam	14,680	23,090	33,300	43,130	38,830	33,160	29,890	31,020
Cambodia	300	460	750	1,020	1,060	1,140	1,230	1,380
Indonesia	580	1,220	2,530	3,620	3,430	3,400	3,530	3,840
Lao People's Democratic Republic	280	460	1,000	1,820	1,970	2,120	2,240	2,460
Malaysia	3,460	5,270	8,260	11,140	10,610	10,030	9,810	10,460
Myanmar	170 (2002)	270	850	1,230	1,200	1,200	1,200	1,310
Philippines	1,220	1,430	2,460	3,450	3,510	3,570	3,650	3,830
Singapore	23,680	28,820	44,930	56,370	53,120	52,520	54,200	58,770
Thailand	1,980	2,790	4,580	5,760	5,710	5,690	5,950	6,610
Viet Nam	410	630	1,250	1,880	1,970	2,080	2,190	2,400
The Pacific								
Cook Islands	6,129	8,475	9,349	17,088	17,157	18,347	17,360	20,026
Fiji	2,240	3,590	3,650	5,020	5,200	5,360	5,430	5,860
Kiribati	1,330	1,730	2,050	3,250	3,460	3,190	3,070	3,140
Marshall Islands	2,930	3,380	3,520	4,160	4,360	4,250	4,430	4,740
Micronesia, Federated States of	2,210	2,550	2,900	3,140	3,490	3,390	3,430	3,580
Nauru	...	...	5,810	14,730	11,830	10,730	10,820	11,240
Niue	...	8,728 (2006)	10,896 (2011)	...	...	...	14,546	...
Palau	7,420 (2002)	9,240	10,300	12,870	14,340	15,260	15,500	16,910
Papua New Guinea	570	650	1,730	2,970	2,900	2,670	2,500	2,530
Samoa	1,520 (2002)	2,310	3,200	4,050	4,080	4,130	4,120	4,190
Solomon Islands	1,010	890	900	1,840	1,870	1,820	1,830	2,000
Timor-Leste	800 (2002)	740	2,850	2,960	3,080	2,370	1,810	1,820
Tonga	2,050	2,450	3,570	4,570	4,520	4,300	4,250	4,300
Tuvalu	2,710 (2001)	3,630	4,400	4,670	5,440	5,070	4,810	5,430
Vanuatu	1,430	1,780	2,690	3,110	2,790	2,780	2,810	2,970
Developed ADB Member Economies								
Australia	21,120	30,310	46,630	65,170	60,560	54,190	51,630	53,190
Japan	36,230	40,560	43,440	43,950	38,840	37,880	38,470	41,340
New Zealand	14,080	25,440	29,690	41,650	40,600	39,410	38,470	40,820

... = data not available, $ = United States dollars, ADB = Asian Development Bank.

a   Refers to a conversion factor that averages the exchange rate for a given year and the 2 preceding years, adjusted for differences in rates of inflation between the member
    economy and the G5 economies.

Sources: World Bank. World Development Indicators Online. http://data.worldbank.org (accessed 18 July 2019). For the Cook Islands; Niue; and Taipei,China: Asian
            Development Bank estimates using Atlas method based on economy sources.

Table 2.2.5:   Gross Domestic Product per Capita
(current $)

ADB Regional Member	2000	2005	2010	2013	2014	2015	2016	2017	2018
Developing ADB Member Economies									
Central and West Asia									
Afghanistan	211 (2002)	300	657	830	803	760	732	762	682
Armenia	593	1,557	3,041	3,680	3,852	3,512	3,524	3,869	4,184
Azerbaijan	653	1,558	5,843	7,875	7,891	5,501	3,881	4,147	4,722
Georgia	750	1,643	3,073	4,342	4,439	3,756	3,857	4,045	4,350
Kazakhstan	1,229	3,771	9,070	13,891	12,807	10,511	7,715	9,030	9,462
Kyrgyz Republic	281	479	885	1,295	1,293	1,133	1,132	1,255	1,293
Pakistan	565	767	1,006	1,195	1,324	1,393	1,420	1,459	1,327
Tajikistan	139	341	750	1,053	1,119	929	804	810	833
Turkmenistan	1,092	3,612	4,439	7,304	7,955	6,443	6,390	6,587	7,540
Uzbekistan	558	550	1,642	2,281	2,492	2,615	2,568	1,827	1,532
East Asia									
China, People's Republic of	956	1,748	4,540	7,033	7,631	8,014	8,055	8,736	9,752
Hong Kong, China	25,757	26,650	32,550	38,404	40,315	42,432	43,735	46,225	48,676
Korea, Republic of	12,257	19,403	23,087	27,183	29,276	28,741	29,299	31,565	33,339
Mongolia	476	995	2,625	4,340	4,126	3,882	3,622	3,628	4,046
Taipei,China	14,943	16,539	19,283	21,916	22,670	22,408	22,601	24,409	25,000
South Asia									
Bangladesh	352	416	771	992	1,104	1,224	1,373	1,510	1,638
Bhutan	738	1,290	2,279	2,453	2,629	2,721	2,888	3,477	...
India	475	757	1,435	1,532	1,612	1,673	1,760	1,995	2,087
Maldives	2,311	3,436	6,576	7,687	8,450	9,043	9,343	9,898	...
Nepal	254	326	620	669	730	744	741	891	956
Sri Lanka	863	1,242	2,747	3,611	3,821	3,845	3,886	4,105	4,104
Southeast Asia									
Brunei Darussalam	18,477	26,587	35,437	44,865	41,947	31,354	27,322	28,238	30,667
Cambodia	294	472	796	1,038	1,124	1,199	1,313	1,436	1,571
Indonesia	800	1,300	3,177	3,667	3,533	3,370	3,602	3,877	3,933
Lao People's Democratic Republic	322	483	1,116	1,893	2,073	2,217	2,400	2,521	2,649
Malaysia	3,993	5,511	8,920	10,705	11,012	9,659	9,533	9,967	11,067
Myanmar	...	...	...	1,208	1,275	1,192	1,221	1,245	...
Philippines	1,055	1,217	2,143	2,768	2,849	2,883	2,953	2,990	3,104
Singapore	23,853	29,961	47,237	56,967	57,565	55,645	56,722	60,296	64,580
Thailand	2,083	2,994	5,174	6,297	6,079	5,968	6,113	6,730	7,446
Viet Nam	404	704	1,334	1,908	2,052	2,107	2,215	2,389	2,589
The Pacific									
Cook Islands	5,091	8,491	10,160	15,548	17,362	16,422	17,773	17,724	20,099
Fiji	2,093	3,604	3,692	4,861	5,610	5,386	5,642	5,956	...
Kiribati	799	1,212	1,515	1,726	1,654	1,554	1,598	1,641	...
Marshall Islands	2,195	2,741	3,180	3,591	3,445	3,363	3,653	3,822	...
Micronesia, Federated States of	2,179	2,370	2,886	3,096	3,113	3,080	3,235	3,536	...
Nauru	...	3,291	5,275	9,465	10,778	8,329	9,463	10,341	9,926
Niue	4,107	8,197 (2006)	13,021 (2011)	...	...	...	...	15,197	...
Palau	7,718	9,303	10,034	12,839	14,007	15,875	16,782	15,995	16,195
Papua New Guinea	674	804	2,020	2,748	2,910	2,641	2,447	2,712	2,784
Samoa	1,319	2,413	3,713	4,007	4,065	4,067	4,193	4,200	4,215
Solomon Islands	682	911	1,253	1,698	1,711	1,642	1,709	...	...
Timor-Leste	504	1,767	3,604	4,760	3,332	2,492	1,974	1,919	...
Tonga	1,907	2,607	3,636	4,310	4,291	3,935	4,032	4,562	4,777
Tuvalu	1,450	2,108	2,816	3,401	3,331	3,135	3,497	3,837	...
Vanuatu	1,432	1,846	2,923	3,124	3,104	2,828	2,952	3,161	...
Developed ADB Member Economies									
Australia	20,144	34,911	54,176	64,128	61,380	51,241	51,083	54,970	55,236
Japan	38,532	37,218	44,508	40,454	38,109	34,524	38,794	38,332	39,280
New Zealand	14,113	27,752	33,692	42,949	44,534	38,559	40,027	42,194	...
DEVELOPING ADB MEMBER ECONOMIES[a]	**1,108**	**1,714**	**3,377**	**4,498**	**4,768**	**4,868**	**4,922**	**5,315**	**5,729**
ADB REGIONAL MEMBERS[a]	**2,630**	**3,194**	**5,099**	**6,043**	**6,203**	**6,110**	**6,287**	**6,664**	**7,034**

... = data not available, $ = United States dollars, ADB = Asian Development Bank.

a   For reporting economies only.

Source: Asian Development Bank estimates using economy sources and official exchange rates from the International Monetary Fund.

National Accounts

Table 2.2.6:   Agriculture, Industry, and Services Value Added
(% of GDP[a])

ADB Regional Member	Agriculture				Industry				Services			
	2000	2005	2010	2018	2000	2005	2010	2018	2000	2005	2010	2018
Developing ADB Member Economies												
Central and West Asia												
Afghanistan	43.7 (2002)	35.2	28.8	21.4	21.7 (2002)	26.0	21.3	24.6	34.6 (2002)	38.8	49.8	54.0
Armenia	25.1	20.6	18.8	15.0	38.3	44.7	36.3	27.4	36.5	34.6	45.0	57.6
Azerbaijan	17.1	9.8	5.9	5.7	45.3	63.3	64.3	56.6	37.5	26.9	29.8	37.7
Georgia	21.9	16.7	8.4	7.7	22.4	26.8	22.2	26.3	55.7	56.5	69.4	66.0
Kazakhstan	8.6	6.6	4.7	4.6	40.1	39.2	41.9	36.9	51.3	54.2	53.4	58.6
Kyrgyz Republic	36.6	31.3	18.8	13.1	31.3	22.0	28.2	30.9	32.1	46.7	53.1	56.0
Pakistan	27.4	24.4	24.3	24.0	18.8	21.1	20.6	19.3	53.8	54.5	55.1	56.8
Tajikistan	27.3	23.8	21.8	20.9	38.4	30.7	27.9	30.1	34.3	45.6	50.3	49.0
Turkmenistan	22.9	18.8	11.5	...	41.8	37.6	60.0	...	35.2	43.6	28.5	...
Uzbekistan	34.4	29.5	32.9	32.4	23.1	29.1	25.9	32.0	42.5	41.4	41.1	35.6
East Asia												
China, People's Republic of	14.7	11.6	9.3	7.2	45.5	47.0	46.5	40.7	39.8	41.3	44.2	52.2
Hong Kong, China	0.1	0.1	0.1	0.1 (2017)	12.6	8.7	7.0	7.5 (2017)	87.3	91.3	93.0	92.4 (2017)
Korea, Republic of	4.3	2.9	2.4	2.0	38.5	37.7	37.5	37.3	57.2	59.4	60.1	60.7
Mongolia	27.4	19.8	11.6	10.8	26.0	34.9	36.1	41.6	46.6	45.3	52.3	47.6
Taipei,China	2.0	1.6	1.6	1.6	31.3	32.3	33.8	35.2	66.7	66.1	64.6	63.2
South Asia												
Bangladesh	25.5	20.1	17.8	13.8	25.3	27.2	26.1	30.2	49.2	52.6	56.0	56.0
Bhutan	27.4	23.2	17.5	18.3 (2017)	36.0	37.3	44.6	42.7 (2017)	36.6	39.5	37.9	39.1 (2017)
India	23.0	18.8	18.2	16.1	26.0	28.1	27.2	29.6	51.0	53.1	54.6	54.3
Maldives	6.9 (2001)	8.7	6.1	6.6 (2017)	13.2 (2001)	13.2	10.2	14.9 (2017)	79.9 (2001)	78.1	83.8	78.5 (2017)
Nepal	39.6	35.2	35.4	28.1	21.5	17.1	15.1	14.9	38.9	47.7	49.5	57.0
Sri Lanka	17.6	11.8	9.5	8.6	29.9	30.2	29.7	29.4	52.5	58.0	60.9	62.0
Southeast Asia												
Brunei Darussalam	1.0	0.9	0.7	1.0	63.7	71.6	67.4	62.2	35.3	27.5	31.9	36.7
Cambodia	37.8	32.4	36.0	23.5	23.0	26.4	23.3	34.4	39.1	41.2	40.7	42.1
Indonesia	15.6	13.1	14.3	13.3	45.9	46.5	43.9	41.4	38.5	40.3	41.8	45.2
Lao People's Democratic Republic	48.5	36.7	30.6	17.7	19.1	23.5	29.8	35.5	32.4	39.8	39.6	46.8
Malaysia	8.3	8.4	10.2	7.6	46.8	46.9	40.9	38.8	44.9	44.7	48.9	53.6
Myanmar	57.2	46.7	36.9	23.3 (2017)	9.7	17.5	26.5	36.3 (2017)	33.1	35.8	36.7	40.4 (2017)
Philippines	14.0	12.7	12.3	9.3	34.5	33.8	32.6	30.8	51.5	53.5	55.1	59.9
Singapore	0.1	0.1	0.0	0.0	34.8	32.9	28.2	26.6	65.1	67.1	71.8	73.3
Thailand[b]	8.5	9.2	10.5	8.1	33.7	35.5	37.1	32.4	57.8	55.3	52.4	59.5
Viet Nam	24.5	19.3	21.0	16.3	36.7	38.1	36.7	38.0	38.7	42.6	42.2	45.7
The Pacific												
Cook Islands	10.3	6.9	3.4	3.8	8.3	9.6	7.9	7.3	81.4	83.5	88.7	88.9
Fiji	16.5	14.1	11.0	12.9 (2017)	21.6	19.2	20.9	20.0 (2017)	61.9	66.8	68.1	67.1 (2017)
Kiribati	20.0	21.8	24.2	28.9 (2017)	12.2	9.3	11.9	11.6 (2017)	67.8	68.9	63.9	59.5 (2017)
Marshall Islands	10.5	9.3	15.7	16.9 (2017)	12.3	10.3	12.7	13.9 (2017)	77.1	80.5	71.6	69.3 (2017)
Micronesia, Federated States of	25.3	24.2	26.7	28.8 (2016)	8.7	5.7	7.8	6.5 (2016)	66.0	70.1	65.5	64.8 (2016)
Nauru	...	5.2	6.3	...	...	9.1	32.7	...	...	85.7	61.0	...
Niue	22.2	23.3	23.0	19.1	3.9	4.5	4.0	3.7	73.9	72.2	73.0	77.2
Palau	4.3	4.2	4.2	3.5	16.1	15.2	11.0	8.8	79.7	80.5	84.8	87.6
Papua New Guinea	35.2	34.0	20.2	17.9	40.7	44.3	34.2	40.5	24.1	21.7	45.5	41.6
Samoa	16.7	12.3	9.1	9.4	26.8	30.6	18.1	14.6	56.6	57.2	72.8	75.9
Solomon Islands	...	32.4	30.3	27.3 (2016)	...	9.5	13.3	14.7 (2016)	...	58.0	56.4	58.0 (2016)
Timor-Leste	24.2	7.4	5.7	10.4 (2017)	31.7	76.1	79.1	45.6 (2017)	44.1	16.5	15.2	44.0 (2017)
Tonga	22.2	20.0	18.2	19.5	20.7	19.0	20.0	18.7	57.1	61.0	61.8	61.8
Tuvalu	20.4	22.2	27.3	20.0 (2017)	7.4	8.3	5.7	17.8 (2017)	72.2	69.4	67.0	62.2 (2017)
Vanuatu	25.4	24.1	21.9	23.1 (2017)	12.2	8.5	13.0	11.0 (2017)	62.3	67.4	65.0	65.9 (2017)
Developed ADB Member Economies												
Australia	3.1	2.9	2.2	2.6	24.6	24.6	25.2	24.0	72.2	72.5	72.7	73.4
Japan	1.5	1.1	1.1	1.2 (2017)	32.7	30.1	28.5	29.3 (2017)	65.8	68.8	70.4	69.5 (2017)
New Zealand	8.3	4.9	7.1	6.2 (2016)	25.3	25.8	23.0	22.0 (2016)	66.4	69.3	69.9	71.8 (2016)

... = data not available, 0.0 = magnitude is less than half of the unit employed, ADB = Asian Development Bank, GDP = gross domestic product.

a   Calculated as a share of GDP at current prices.
b   For Thailand, value added for construction is included under services.

Source: Economy sources.

Table 2.2.7: Household and Government Consumption Expenditure
(% of GDP[a])

ADB Regional Member	Household Consumption				Government Consumption			
	2000	2005	2010	2018	2000	2005	2010	2018
ADB Developing Member Economies								
Central and West Asia								
Afghanistan	111.2 (2002)	115.7	97.4	78.8	7.7 (2002)	10.0	14.0	12.4
Armenia[b]	97.1	75.5	82.0	79.9	11.8	10.6	13.1	12.8
Azerbaijan	63.0	41.6	38.9	52.8	15.2	10.4	10.9	10.2
Georgia	80.5	64.6	72.3	59.3	8.5	17.3	21.1	16.6
Kazakhstan[b]	61.9	49.9	45.4	51.4	12.1	11.2	10.8	8.7
Kyrgyz Republic[b]	65.7	84.5	84.6	82.7	20.0	17.5	18.1	16.5
Pakistan[b]	75.5	78.4	79.7	82.1	8.1	7.5	10.3	12.4
Tajikistan[b]	87.7	81.1	84.7	77.9 (2017)	11.6	14.6	11.3	14.3 (2017)
Turkmenistan[b]	37.1	46.6	5.0	...	14.5	13.2	9.3	...
Uzbekistan	61.9	46.7	57.0	54.5	18.7	17.6	13.3	15.0
East Asia								
China, People's Republic of	46.7	39.8	35.6	39.4	16.6	13.9	12.9	14.9
Hong Kong, China[b]	58.6	57.5	61.4	68.3	9.4	9.2	8.9	9.9
Korea, Republic of	53.3	51.0	49.1	46.2	10.9	12.9	14.2	16.1
Mongolia	75.1	55.2	55.2	48.4	15.3	12.1	12.7	11.8
Taipei,China	55.1	56.1	53.1	53.7	15.7	15.3	14.9	14.5
South Asia								
Bangladesh	77.5	74.4	74.1	70.8	4.6	5.5	5.1	6.4
Bhutan[b]	47.7	40.4	46.6	52.8 (2017)	21.9	21.9	20.0	16.4 (2017)
India[b]	64.6	58.3	56.0	59.4	12.6	10.9	11.4	11.2
Maldives	...	...	...	...	...	...	...	...
Nepal[b]	75.9	79.5	78.6	70.5	8.9	8.9	10.0	11.7
Sri Lanka	70.9	69.0	68.5	69.8	13.7	13.1	8.5	9.0
Southeast Asia								
Brunei Darussalam[b]	24.8	22.5	14.7	19.5	25.8	18.4	22.2	24.1
Cambodia[b]	88.8	84.3	81.3	70.6	5.2	4.1	6.3	4.9
Indonesia[c]	61.7	64.4	56.2	57.0	6.5	8.1	9.0	9.0
Lao People's Democratic Republic	...	...	...	...	...	...	...	...
Malaysia[c]	43.8	44.2	48.1	57.4	10.2	11.5	12.6	12.0
Myanmar[d]	87.7	86.9	67.3	71.3 (2017)	...	...	...	...
Philippines[b]	72.2	75.0	71.6	73.8	11.4	9.0	9.7	11.9
Singapore	41.9	39.8	36.3	34.9	10.5	9.9	9.7	10.5
Thailand	53.1	54.9	51.2	47.8	13.6	13.7	15.8	16.2
Viet Nam	66.5	65.5	66.6	67.6	6.4	5.5	6.0	6.5
The Pacific								
Cook Islands	...	...	...	...	...	...	...	...
Fiji[b]	57.2	73.3	70.3	63.7 (2017)	17.3	15.9	15.0	19.8 (2017)
Kiribati	...	...	...	...	...	...	...	...
Marshall Islands	...	71.8	73.0	71.5 (2017)	...	58.0	54.8	57.1 (2017)
Micronesia, Federated States of	...	...	...	...	...	...	...	...
Nauru	...	...	...	...	...	...	...	...
Niue	...	...	...	...	...	...	...	...
Palau	...	63.6	67.7	66.6	...	31.3	37.5	32.4
Papua New Guinea[b]	44.6	48.0	...	...	16.6	16.1	...	...
Samoa	...	...	...	...	...	...	...	...
Solomon Islands	...	62.6	60.2	58.5 (2016)	...	45.3	40.7	29.7 (2016)
Timor-Leste	70.7	22.6	15.1	39.8 (2017)	111.3	13.4	22.8	35.2 (2017)
Tonga	87.3	93.0	91.3	99.6	18.2	15.5	18.1	18.8
Tuvalu	...	...	...	...	...	...	...	...
Vanuatu	62.4	65.8	60.6	60.5 (2017)	16.4	13.2	17.5	17.4 (2017)
ADB Developed Member Economies								
Australia	58.1	57.6	56.2	56.5	17.8	17.6	18.0	18.7
Japan	54.4	55.6	57.8	55.6	16.9	18.1	19.5	19.7
New Zealand	58.0	58.2	58.1	58.1	17.0	17.9	19.5	18.2

.... = data not available, ADB = Asian Development Bank, GDP = gross domestic product.

a   Calculated as a share of GDP at current prices.
b   Data for household consumption includes nonprofit institutions serving households.
c   Prior to 2010, data for household consumption includes nonprofit institutions serving households.
d   Data for household consumption includes government consumption.

Source: Economy sources.

National Accounts

Table 2.2.8:   Gross Capital Formation and Changes in Inventories
(% of GDP[a])

ADB Regional Member	Gross Capital Formation				Changes in Inventories			
	2000	2005	2010	2018	2000	2005	2010	2018
Developing ADB Member Economies								
Central and West Asia								
Afghanistan[b,c]	11.3 (2002)	21.8	17.5	22.0	...	...	5.3	21.4
Armenia	18.6	30.5	32.9	22.4	0.2	0.7	-0.6	5.7
Azerbaijan	20.7	41.5	18.1	20.1	-2.5	0.2	-0.1	-0.6
Georgia	26.6	33.5	21.6	33.3	1.1	5.4	2.3	3.9
Kazakhstan	18.1	31.0	25.4	24.7	0.8	3.0	1.0	3.3
Kyrgyz Republic	18.3	16.2	28.1	31.7	1.7	0.2	-0.7	3.8
Pakistan	17.6	17.7	15.8	16.4	1.6	1.6	1.6	1.6
Tajikistan	9.4	11.6	23.8	27.2 (2017)	2.0	0.5	-0.6	0.6 (2017)
Turkmenistan	35.4	22.9	51.9	...	...	...	...	...
Uzbekistan	19.6	26.5	26.5	40.2	-4.4	4.5	2.4	10.4
East Asia								
China, People's Republic of	34.4	41.4	47.7	44.1	1.0	0.9	2.6	1.8
Hong Kong, China	27.6	21.1	23.9	21.7	1.1	-0.3	2.1	0.2
Korea, Republic of	32.9	32.5	32.6	31.3	1.1	2.0	2.3	0.9
Mongolia	29.0	37.5	42.1	43.1	3.8	9.6	7.6	13.4
Taipei,China	27.2	24.5	25.0	21.3	0.9	0.3	1.3	0.3
South Asia								
Bangladesh[b]	23.0	24.5	26.2	31.2	...	...	...	...
Bhutan	48.7	52.0	61.7	51.3 (2017)	-1.8	-0.0	0.5	-0.1 (2017)
India	24.3	34.7	36.5	31.3	0.7	2.8	3.5	1.0
Maldives	...	...	...	...	...	...	...	...
Nepal	24.3	26.5	38.3	55.2	5.0	6.5	16.1	20.5
Sri Lanka	25.4	26.1	30.4	28.6	0.6	2.8	5.9	2.2
Southeast Asia								
Brunei Darussalam	13.1	11.4	23.7	41.1	0.1	0.0	0.2	0.2
Cambodia	17.5	20.2	17.4	23.4	-0.8	1.3	1.2	0.9
Indonesia	22.2	25.1	32.9	34.6	2.4	1.4	1.9	2.3
Lao People's Democratic Republic	...	...	...	...	...	...	...	...
Malaysia[c]	26.9	22.4	23.4	23.6	1.6	0.1	1.0	-0.6
Myanmar	12.4	13.2	23.2	34.1 (2017)	0.7	0.5	0.3	1.3 (2017)
Philippines	18.4	21.6	20.5	27.0	-3.7	1.6	0.0	0.2
Singapore	35.2	21.5	27.7	26.6	2.8	-1.7	2.1	2.5
Thailand	22.3	30.4	25.4	25.0	0.7	2.7	1.4	2.1
Viet Nam	29.6	33.8	35.7	26.5	2.0	2.5	3.0	2.7
The Pacific								
Cook Islands	...	...	...	...	...	...	...	...
Fiji	17.3	21.0	18.7	18.1 (2017)	1.9	1.4	2.9	– (2017)
Kiribati	...	...	...	...	...	...	...	...
Marshall Islands	...	19.1	42.9	22.1 (2017)	...	0.2	0.1	-0.1 (2017)
Micronesia, Federated States of	...	...	...	...	...	...	...	...
Nauru	...	...	...	...	...	...	...	...
Niue	...	...	...	...	...	...	...	...
Palau	...	42.9	24.6	26.7	...	0.4	0.7	1.2
Papua New Guinea	21.9	17.5	...	...	1.5	1.0	...	...
Samoa	...	...	...	...	...	...	...	...
Solomon Islands	...	...	...	...	...	...	...	...
Timor-Leste	28.0	4.0	12.0	22.5 (2017)	-3.7	0.0	0.0	1.0 (2017)
Tonga	20.7	22.3	30.1	27.3	0.5	0.3	0.5	0.3
Tuvalu	...	...	...	...	...	...	...	...
Vanuatu	22.9	24.1	34.7	27.9 (2017)	0.5	0.7	0.8	0.7 (2017)
Developed ADB Member Economies								
Australia	26.3	27.6	26.9	24.3	0.3	0.5	-0.2	0.1
Japan	27.3	24.7	21.3	24.4	-0.1	0.1	-0.0	0.2
New Zealand	22.0	25.4	20.1	23.7	1.2	0.7	0.4	0.3

... = data not available, -0.0 or 0.0 = magnitude is less than half of unit employed, – = magnitude equals zero, ADB = Asian Development Bank, GDP = gross domestic product.

a Computed as a share of GDP at current prices.
b Refers to gross fixed capital formation and includes data on changes in inventories.
c Changes in inventories include statistical discrepancy.

Source: Economy sources.

Table 2.2.9:   Exports and Imports of Goods and Services
(% of GDP[a])

ADB Regional Member	Exports of Goods and Services				Imports of Goods and Services			
	2000	2005	2010	2018	2000	2005	2010	2018
Developing ADB Member Economies								
Central and West Asia								
Afghanistan	29.7 (2002)	26.0	9.8	8.1	59.8 (2002)	73.6	43.9	42.8
Armenia	23.4	28.8	20.8	37.5	50.5	43.2	45.3	52.9
Azerbaijan	40.2	62.9	54.3	54.3	38.4	52.9	20.7	37.7
Georgia	23.0	33.7	35.0	55.1	39.7	51.6	52.8	66.7
Kazakhstan	56.6	53.2	44.2	38.9	49.1	44.6	29.9	26.2
Kyrgyz Republic	41.8	38.3	51.6	32.7	47.6	56.8	81.7	68.4
Pakistan	12.1	14.3	13.5	8.5	13.2	17.8	19.4	19.4
Tajikistan	92.4	54.3	26.8	15.7 (2017)	100.2	72.8	59.0	40.9 (2017)
Turkmenistan	97.2	65.0	76.3	...	82.4	47.8	44.5	...
Uzbekistan	26.5	37.9	27.9	29.1	26.7	28.7	19.7	38.7
East Asia								
China, People's Republic of	20.8	33.5	26.4	19.8	18.5	28.1	22.7	19.0
Hong Kong, China	126.0	177.5	205.3	188.3	121.6	165.2	199.4	188.2
Korea, Republic of	33.9	35.3	47.1	41.6	32.2	33.0	44.3	37.0
Mongolia	54.0	58.8	46.7	61.5	67.9	63.6	56.7	64.8
Taipei,China	51.9	60.6	70.9	66.8	49.9	56.4	63.9	56.3
South Asia								
Bangladesh	14.0	16.6	16.0	14.8	19.2	23.0	21.8	23.4
Bhutan	29.4	38.2	42.5	29.1 (2017)	48.3	64.4	70.7	49.6 (2017)
India	12.8	19.3	22.0	19.7	13.7	22.0	26.3	23.6
Maldives	...	...	...	...	...	...	...	...
Nepal	23.3	14.6	9.6	8.9	32.4	29.5	36.4	46.3
Sri Lanka	38.2	32.3	19.6	22.8	48.4	41.3	26.8	30.1
Southeast Asia								
Brunei Darussalam	67.4	70.2	67.4	51.9	35.8	27.3	28.0	42.0
Cambodia	49.8	64.1	54.1	61.6	61.8	72.7	59.5	63.3
Indonesia	41.0	34.1	24.3	21.0	30.5	29.9	22.4	22.1
Lao People's Democratic Republic	...	...	...	...	...	...	...	...
Malaysia	119.8	112.9	86.9	68.8	100.6	91.0	71.0	61.7
Myanmar	0.5	0.2	19.6	20.0 (2017)	0.6	0.1	15.1	28.0 (2017)
Philippines	51.4	46.1	34.8	31.7	53.4	51.7	36.6	44.4
Singapore	188.4	225.2	198.0	176.4	176.0	195.3	171.7	149.8
Thailand	64.8	68.4	66.5	66.8	56.5	69.5	60.8	56.5
Viet Nam	55.0	63.7	72.0	105.8	57.5	67.0	80.2	102.5
The Pacific								
Cook Islands	...	...	...	...	...	...	...	...
Fiji	65.4	54.1	57.4	50.8 (2017)	70.5	63.7	63.8	56.1 (2017)
Kiribati	...	...	...	...	...	...	...	...
Marshall Islands	...	36.7	44.0	47.4 (2017)	...	92.7	107.1	90.7 (2017)
Micronesia, Federated States of	...	...	...	...	...	...	...	...
Nauru	...	...	...	...	...	...	...	...
Niue	...	...	...	...	...	...	...	...
Palau	...	47.2	50.0	46.7	...	78.6	77.1	76.7
Papua New Guinea	66.2	74.5	...	...	49.2	56.1	...	...
Samoa	...	...	...	...	...	...	...	...
Solomon Islands	...	33.0	47.4	50.1 (2016)	...	45.2	78.7	57.3 (2016)
Timor-Leste	27.2	82.8	100.2	61.1 (2017)	139.5	23.7	50.7	59.9 (2017)
Tonga	15.4	17.7	13.2	21.6	46.8	57.8	57.9	66.7
Tuvalu	...	...	...	...	...	...	...	...
Vanuatu	34.7	45.4	46.6	47.7 (2017)	43.7	54.8	52.7	57.9 (2017)
Developed ADB Member Economies								
Australia	19.4	18.3	19.8	21.8	21.6	21.0	20.8	21.4
Japan	10.6	14.0	15.0	18.5	9.2	12.5	13.6	18.2
New Zealand	35.7	28.3	30.3	28.3	32.8	29.7	28.0	28.3

.... = data not available, ADB = Asian Development Bank, GDP = gross domestic product.

a   Computed as a share of GDP at current prices.

Source: Economy sources.

Table 2.2.10: Gross Domestic Saving
(% of GDP[a])

ADB Regional Member	2000	2005	2010	2013	2014	2015	2016	2017	2018
Developing ADB Member Economies									
Central and West Asia									
Afghanistan	-18.8 (2002)	-25.8	-11.4	7.8	7.9	5.0	8.2	12.0	8.7
Armenia	-8.9	14.0	4.9	0.9	2.4	8.8	9.2	7.7	7.3
Azerbaijan	20.4	47.5	49.8	47.8	43.7	30.9	28.5	31.1	36.7
Georgia	9.9	15.7	3.8	11.8	12.3	14.0	17.0	20.4	21.7
Kazakhstan	26.0	38.9	43.8	39.9	40.8	34.6	33.8	37.2	...
Kyrgyz Republic	14.3	-2.1	-2.7	-15.6	-13.5	-8.3	-0.2	0.8	...
Pakistan	16.5	14.2	10.0	8.2	8.2	9.3	8.7	6.8	5.5
Tajikistan	0.6	4.3	4.0	-13.6	-12.7	2.5	7.1	7.8	...
Turkmenistan	48.4	40.2	85.6	81.6	...	...	...	...	...
Uzbekistan	19.4	35.7	29.6	25.9	26.0	24.3	22.1	26.9	30.5
East Asia									
China, People's Republic of	36.8	46.8	51.4	50.0	49.7	49.1	46.7	46.1	44.9
Hong Kong, China	32.0	33.3	29.8	24.6	24.0	23.9	23.8	23.1	21.8
Korea, Republic of	34.6	34.8	35.4	34.5	34.8	36.4	36.8	37.0	35.9
Mongolia	9.6	32.7	32.1	30.7	30.4	27.4	30.5	33.7	40.8
Taipei,China	29.4	29.1	31.7	30.7	32.2	33.5	32.9	33.3	32.2
South Asia									
Bangladesh	17.9	20.0	20.8	22.0	22.1	22.2	25.0	25.3	22.8
Bhutan	29.7	25.9	33.4	24.1	21.7	17.9	29.5	22.1	...
India	...	...	...	...	...	...	...	...	...
Maldives	...	...	...	...	...	...	...	...	...
Nepal	15.2	11.6	11.5	10.6	11.9	9.2	4.1	13.4	17.8
Sri Lanka	15.4	17.9	23.1	24.6	24.2	23.6	27.4	29.0	21.2
Southeast Asia									
Brunei Darussalam	49.4	59.1	63.1	64.6	63.1	55.2	52.6	53.0	56.3
Cambodia	8.1	14.0	14.5	17.7	18.9	19.6	20.4	23.2	26.0
Indonesia	31.8	27.5	34.8	33.7	33.4	32.8	32.7	33.6	...
Lao PDR	...	...	...	...	...	...	...	...	...
Malaysia	46.1	44.3	39.3	34.5	34.3	33.0	32.6	32.4	30.6
Myanmar	12.3	13.1	32.7	33.8	22.9	23.4	24.6	25.3	...
Philippines	16.4	15.9	18.7	15.8	16.9	15.3	15.1	15.3	14.2
Singapore	47.5	51.4	54.0	53.1	52.9	52.7	53.4	53.2	53.2
Thailand	31.7	30.3	32.0	31.3	31.8	34.9	36.7	37.7	36.3
Viet Nam	27.1	29.0	27.4	28.4	27.9	25.7	24.9	25.5	26.0
The Pacific									
Cook Islands	...	...	...	...	...	...	...	...	...
Fiji	25.6	7.1	12.7	15.0	17.2	18.3	14.1	13.9	...
Kiribati	...	...	...	...	...	...	...	...	...
Marshall Islands	...	19.1	42.9	23.1	20.0	18.7	20.0	22.1	...
Micronesia, Federated States of	...	...	...	...	...	...	...	...	...
Nauru	...	...	...	...	...	...	...	...	...
Niue	...	...	...	...	...	...	...	...	...
Palau	...	3.1	-7.4	-6.1	-3.0	5.3	5.3	0.1	-1.8
Papua New Guinea	38.8	35.9	...	...	...	...	...	...	...
Samoa	...	...	...	...	...	...	...	...	...
Solomon Islands	...	...	...	...	...	...	...	...	...
Timor-Leste	-84.4	63.1	61.5	68.6	53.3	39.6	23.4	23.7	...
Tonga	-10.0	-16.3	-16.1	-19.7	-21.3	...	...	...	...
Tuvalu	...	...	...	...	...	...	...	...	...
Vanuatu	21.2	13.9	27.0	23.3	24.0	...	...	...	...
Developed ADB Member Economies									
Australia	24.1	24.8	25.8	26.6	26.3	24.7	23.1	24.7	24.8
Japan	29.0	26.8	22.9	20.9	21.4	23.3	24.2	24.9	...
New Zealand	25.0	24.0	22.4	23.6	23.7	24.1	24.2	24.3	...

.... = data not available, ADB = Asian Development Bank, GDP = gross domestic product.

a Computed as a share of GDP at current prices.

Sources: Economy sources.

Table 2.2.11:   Growth Rates of Real Gross Domestic Product
(%)

ADB Regional Member	2000	2005	2010	2013	2014	2015	2016	2017	2018
Developing ADB Member Economies									
Central and West Asia									
Afghanistan	...	9.9	3.2	6.5	3.1	-1.8	3.5	7.1	-0.2
Armenia	5.9	13.9	2.2	3.3	3.6	3.2	0.2	7.5	5.2
Azerbaijan	11.1	26.4	5.0	5.8	2.8	1.1	-3.1	0.2	1.4
Georgia	1.8	9.6	6.2	3.4	4.6	2.9	2.8	4.8	4.7
Kazakhstan	9.8	9.7	7.3	6.0	4.2	1.2	1.1	4.1	1.4
Kyrgyz Republic	5.4	-0.2	-0.5	10.9	4.0	3.9	4.3	4.7	3.5
Pakistan	3.6 (2001)	6.5	1.6	4.4	4.7	4.7	4.6	5.4	5.8
Tajikistan	8.3	6.7	6.5	7.4	6.7	6.0	6.9	7.1	...
Turkmenistan	5.5	13.0	9.2	10.2	10.3	6.5	6.2	6.5	6.2
Uzbekistan	4.0	7.0	7.3	7.6	7.2	7.4	6.1	4.5	5.1
East Asia									
China, People's Republic of	8.5	11.4	10.6	7.8	7.3	6.9	6.7	6.8	6.6
Hong Kong, China	7.7	7.4	6.8	3.1	2.8	2.4	2.2	3.8	3.0
Korea, Republic of	4.9 (2001)	4.3	6.8	3.2	3.2	2.8	2.9	3.2	2.7
Mongolia	1.1	7.3	17.3 (2011)	11.6	7.9	2.4	1.2	5.3	6.9
Taipei,China	6.4	5.4	10.6	2.2	4.0	0.8	1.5	3.1	2.6
South Asia									
Bangladesh	6.0	6.0	5.6	6.0	6.1	6.6	7.1	7.3	7.9
Bhutan	6.9	7.1	11.7	2.1	5.7	6.6	8.0	4.6	...
India	3.8	9.3	10.3	6.4	7.4	8.0	8.2	7.2	6.8
Maldives	3.8	-13.1	7.3	7.3	7.3	2.9	7.3	6.9	6.1
Nepal	6.0	3.5	4.8	4.1	6.0	3.3	0.6	8.2	6.7
Sri Lanka	6.0	6.2	8.0	3.4	5.0	5.0	4.5	3.4	3.2
Southeast Asia									
Brunei Darussalam	2.8	0.4	3.7 (2011)	-2.1	-2.5	-0.4	-2.5	1.3	0.1
Cambodia	10.7	13.3	6.0	7.4	7.1	7.0	7.0	7.0	7.5
Indonesia	4.9	5.7	6.2	5.6	5.0	4.9	5.0	5.1	5.2
Lao People's Democratic Republic	6.3	6.8	8.1	8.0	7.6	7.3	7.0	6.9	6.3
Malaysia	8.9	5.3	7.4	4.7	6.0	5.1	4.4	5.7	4.7
Myanmar	13.7	13.6	9.6	8.4	8.0	7.0	5.9	6.8	...
Philippines	4.4	4.8	7.6	7.1	6.1	6.1	6.9	6.7	6.2
Singapore	9.0	7.4	14.5	4.8	3.9	2.9	3.0	3.7	3.1
Thailand	4.5	4.2	7.5	2.7	1.0	3.1	3.4	4.0	4.1
Viet Nam	6.8	7.5	6.4	5.4	6.0	6.7	6.2	6.8	7.1
The Pacific									
Cook Islands	13.9	-1.1	-3.0	-1.4	6.2	4.0	5.7	1.9	6.6
Fiji	-1.7	-1.3	3.0	4.7	5.6	4.7	2.6	5.2	...
Kiribati	5.3	-0.0 (2006)	-0.9	4.2	-0.7	10.4	5.1	0.3	...
Marshall Islands	6.0	3.6	7.1	2.8	-0.7	-0.6	1.8	4.5	...
Micronesia, Federated States of	4.9	2.1	2.0	-3.9	-2.2	5.0	0.7	2.4	...
Nauru	...	-0.6	13.6	34.2	36.5	2.8	...	4.0	-4.0
Niue	...	8.9	0.6	6.0	4.1	4.0	3.5	2.4	6.5
Palau	6.4 (2001)	4.1	0.3	-1.4	4.4	10.1	0.8	-3.5	1.7
Papua New Guinea	-2.5	3.9	10.1	3.8	13.5	9.5	4.1	1.1	0.3
Samoa	8.6	4.7	2.4	0.8	2.6	6.7	3.7	-0.6	0.7
Solomon Islands	-14.2	7.4	9.7	2.8	1.8	2.6	3.4	...	...
Timor-Leste	9.2 (2001)	35.9	-1.2	-11.1	-25.9	20.6	0.7	-9.2	...
Tonga	-0.8	1.6	3.3	-3.1	1.9	3.1	4.8	5.4	0.2
Tuvalu	1.5 (2001)	-4.1	-3.3	4.9	1.2	9.2	5.9	5.9	...
Vanuatu	5.9	5.3	1.6	2.0	2.3	0.2	3.5	4.4	...
Developed ADB Member Economies									
Australia	3.9	3.2	2.1	2.6	2.6	2.3	2.8	2.3	2.8
Japan	2.8	1.7	4.2	2.0	0.4	1.2	0.6	1.9	0.8
New Zealand	2.9	3.3	1.5	2.6	3.7	3.6	3.6	3.2	2.7

... = data not available, -0.0 = magnitude is less than half of unit employed, ADB = Asian Development Bank.

Source: Economy sources.

Table 2.2.12:   Growth Rates of Real Gross Domestic Product per Capita
(%)

ADB Regional Member	2000	2005	2010	2013	2014	2015	2016	2017	2018
Developing ADB Member Economies									
Central and West Asia									
Afghanistan	...	7.8	1.2	4.3	1.0	-3.8	1.5	4.9	-6.3
Armenia	6.2	14.5	2.9	3.3	3.9	3.6	0.6	8.0	5.5
Azerbaijan	10.0	24.9	3.8	4.5	1.5	-0.1	-4.2	-0.8	0.5
Georgia	3.8	10.3	7.0	3.7	4.6	2.7	2.8	4.8	4.8
Kazakhstan	10.2	8.7	5.7	4.4	2.7	-0.3	-0.3	2.7	0.1
Kyrgyz Republic	4.0	-1.4	-1.8	8.7	2.0	1.8	2.2	2.7	1.5
Pakistan	1.5 (2001)	4.2	-0.5	2.3	2.6	2.7	2.6	2.9	3.3
Tajikistan	5.8	5.5	3.9	5.1	4.3	3.5	4.5	4.8	...
Turkmenistan	4.3	11.8	7.5	8.2	8.3	4.6	4.4	4.7	4.5
Uzbekistan	2.6	5.7	4.3	5.9	5.4	5.6	4.3	2.7	3.3
East Asia									
China, People's Republic of	7.7	10.7	10.1	7.3	6.7	6.4	6.1	6.2	6.2
Hong Kong, China	6.8	6.9	6.0	2.7	2.1	1.5	1.6	3.0	2.2
Korea, Republic of	...	4.1	6.3	2.7	2.6	2.3	2.4	2.8	2.3
Mongolia	-0.2	6.1	15.3 (2011)	9.4	5.6	0.2	-0.8	3.3	4.9
Taipei,China	5.6	5.0	10.3	2.0	3.8	0.6	1.3	2.9	2.5
South Asia									
Bangladesh	4.5	4.5	4.2	4.6	4.6	5.1	5.8	6.0	6.6
Bhutan	5.6	5.7	9.7	0.4	4.0	5.0	6.4	3.3	...
India	2.0	7.7	8.8	5.1	6.1	6.7	6.9	5.8	5.5
Maldives	2.3	-15.9	4.9	4.4	5.2	-0.9	3.2	2.7	1.8
Nepal	2.9	1.2	3.4	2.7	4.5	1.9	-0.8	6.8	5.2
Sri Lanka	4.6	5.3	7.0	2.6	4.0	4.0	3.3	2.2	2.1
Southeast Asia									
Brunei Darussalam	0.3	-1.3	2.0 (2011)	-3.2	-3.5	-1.6	-3.6	-1.5	-2.9
Cambodia	9.2	11.7	4.6	6.0	5.8	5.7	5.7	5.7	6.1
Indonesia	3.7	4.3	3.4	4.1	3.6	3.5	3.7	3.7	3.8
Lao People's Democratic Republic	4.2	4.7	6.6	6.5	6.1	5.7	5.5	5.3	4.8
Malaysia	6.2	3.2	5.5	2.3	4.3	3.5	3.0	4.5	3.6
Myanmar	12.4	12.6	8.9	7.5	7.0	6.1	4.9	5.8	...
Philippines	2.0	2.8	5.2	5.3	4.4	4.3	5.2	5.0	4.5
Singapore	7.2	4.8	12.5	3.2	2.6	1.7	1.6	3.6	2.6
Thailand	3.6	3.3	6.6	2.3	0.6	2.8	3.0	3.7	3.9
Viet Nam	5.3	6.3	5.3	4.3	4.9	5.5	5.1	5.7	6.0
The Pacific									
Cook Islands	4.4	-6.7	-7.5	3.4	7.3	4.0	...	...	11.7
Fiji	-2.3	-2.0	2.3	4.2	5.2	4.2	2.2	4.6	...
Kiribati	3.5	-2.2 (2006)	-3.0	2.8	-2.0	8.9	3.7	-1.0	...
Marshall Islands	5.2	2.1	5.8	2.4	-1.1	-1.0	1.4	4.2	...
Micronesia, Federated States of	4.6	2.3	2.6	-3.8	-2.2	4.8	0.6	2.4	...
Nauru	...	1.6	11.4	28.0	34.2	1.1	...	2.4	-5.5
Niue	3.9 (2001)	...	...	...	...	...	...	1.3	...
Palau	4.9 (2001)	3.2	2.2	-0.2	4.7	8.1	-0.3	-3.7	3.8
Papua New Guinea	-5.5	0.8	6.8	0.7	10.1	6.2	0.9	-2.0	-2.8
Samoa	7.6	4.2	1.6	0.0	1.9	6.0	2.4	-0.8	-0.1
Solomon Islands	-16.2	4.9	...	0.4	-0.5	0.3	1.2	...	...
Timor-Leste	6.6 (2001)	31.9	-2.7	-13.2	-27.6	17.9	-1.5	-11.1	...
Tonga	-0.8	1.6	3.3	-3.1	1.9	3.1	4.8	5.4	0.2
Tuvalu	1.1 (2001)	-7.0	-3.8	3.7	-0.0	7.9	4.6	4.7	...
Vanuatu	3.5	2.9	-0.8	-0.3	0.0	-2.1	2.0	2.2	...
Developed ADB Member Economies									
Australia	2.8	2.0	0.5	0.9	1.0	0.9	1.3	0.6	1.2
Japan	2.6	1.7	4.2	2.1	0.5	1.3	0.7	2.1	1.0
New Zealand	2.3	2.2	0.4	1.8	2.2	1.6	1.5	1.0	0.8

... = data not available, -0.0 or 0.0 = magnitude is less than half of unit employed, ADB = Asian Development Bank.

Source: Asian Development Bank estimates using economy sources.

Table 2.2.13: Growth Rates of Agriculture Real Value Added
(%)

ADB Regional Member	2000	2005	2010	2013	2014	2015	2016	2017	2018
Developing ADB Member Economies									
Central and West Asia									
Afghanistan	...	12.2	-18.0	8.3	3.7	-16.9	12.4	21.4	-10.3
Armenia	-1.0	11.2	-16.0	7.6	6.1	13.2	-5.0	-5.1	-8.5
Azerbaijan	12.1	6.7	-4.7	4.9	-2.6	6.6	2.6	4.2	4.6
Georgia	-12.0	11.7	-4.2	11.3	1.6	1.5	0.3	-3.8	0.7
Kazakhstan	-3.2	7.1	-12.9	11.2	1.3	3.5	5.4	2.8	...
Kyrgyz Republic	2.6	-4.2	-2.6	2.7	-0.5	6.2	2.9	2.2	2.7
Pakistan	-0.7 (2001)	7.0	0.2	2.7	2.5	2.1	0.2	2.1	3.8
Tajikistan	8.0 (2001)	2.8	6.8	7.7	9.2	3.4	5.2	7.6	...
Turkmenistan	-2.6	14.1	17.7	9.9	1.7	...	...	...	...
Uzbekistan	3.2	5.9	6.1	6.4	6.0	6.1	6.2	1.2	0.3
East Asia									
China, People's Republic of	2.3	5.1	4.3	3.8	4.1	3.9	3.3	4.0	3.5
Hong Kong, China[a]	0.3 (2001)	-0.2	3.9	4.9	-6.0	-6.8	-2.0	-5.2	-1.5
Korea, Republic of	0.4 (2001)	0.6	-3.6	4.2	5.1	-0.2	-5.6	2.3	1.5
Mongolia	-16.3	11.3	...	19.2	13.7	10.7	6.2	1.8	4.5
Taipei,China	1.8	-3.9	2.3	1.4	1.6	-8.4	-10.1	8.4	2.0
South Asia									
Bangladesh	7.4	2.2	6.2	2.5	4.4	3.3	2.8	3.0	4.2
Bhutan	5.4	1.1	0.9	2.4	2.4	4.9	3.9	3.4	...
India	-0.0	5.1	8.6	5.6	-0.2	0.6	6.3	5.0	2.9
Maldives	-0.8	11.4	-3.5	6.9	-0.3	-0.4	1.5	8.2	5.8
Nepal	4.9	3.5	2.0	1.1	4.5	1.1	0.2	5.2	2.8
Sri Lanka	2.3	1.8	7.0	3.2	4.6	4.7	-3.7	-0.4	4.8
Southeast Asia									
Brunei Darussalam	6.6	1.3	-2.6 (2011)	-1.2	4.7	6.4	-3.6	-1.6	-1.6
Cambodia	2.5	15.7	4.0	1.6	0.3	0.2	1.3	1.7	1.2
Indonesia	1.9	2.7	3.0	4.2	4.2	3.8	3.4	3.9	3.9
Lao People's Democratic Republic	4.2	0.7	3.2	2.8	4.1	3.6	2.8	2.9	1.3
Malaysia	6.1	2.6	2.4	2.0	2.0	1.4	-3.7	5.7	0.1
Myanmar	11.0	12.1	4.7	3.6	2.8	3.4	-0.5	1.3	...
Philippines	3.4	2.2	-0.2	1.2	1.7	0.1	-1.2	4.0	0.9
Singapore[a]	-6.0	6.9	2.7	3.5	3.3	-0.5	-0.5	-11.3	-1.4
Thailand	6.8	-0.1	-0.5	0.7	-0.3	-6.5	-1.3	3.7	5.1
Viet Nam	4.6	4.2	0.5	2.6	3.4	2.4	1.4	2.9	3.8
The Pacific									
Cook Islands	0.1	-3.5	1.9	3.9	8.5	-1.5	3.5	-13.9	-4.0
Fiji	-1.2	0.9	-2.6	6.7	1.9	2.9	-10.8	8.3	...
Kiribati	-7.2	10.4 (2006)	-3.9	-0.7	5.9	1.3	10.7	9.0	...
Marshall Islands	22.6	-9.2	28.4	3.4	-1.5	0.5	-2.4	5.3	...
Micronesia, Federated States of	7.1	4.4	-3.9	-6.4	6.0	10.7	-7.3	...	...
Nauru	...	0.3	3.7	5.3	9.5	5.2	...	1.6	...
Niue	...	8.6	-0.4	7.0	0.2	2.0	1.2	3.5	1.7
Palau	0.6 (2001)	4.3	-5.0	2.8	-5.9	-3.7	7.8	8.4	-5.2
Papua New Guinea	2.1	5.6	2.8	4.7	3.4	-2.6	2.7	7.5	3.3
Samoa	8.1	2.4	-9.0	6.4	0.7	1.9	7.1	7.1	-12.4
Solomon Islands	-17.1	-1.5	14.8	-1.3	5.8	2.5	5.8	...	...
Timor-Leste	-1.0 (2001)	2.2	4.2	-5.4	-3.6	-5.2	-1.3	-3.2	...
Tonga	-2.5	-2.1	0.5	3.7	3.1	-2.7	0.5	1.3	-1.0
Tuvalu	-2.2 (2001)	-1.1	12.8	-2.7	-0.5	-1.8	2.9	0.8	...
Vanuatu	4.3	2.3	4.8	4.8	4.2	-15.8	5.1	0.4	...
Developed ADB Member Economies									
Australia	6.7	4.3	-0.7	-0.7	1.1	1.4	-7.9	9.6	-5.1
Japan	7.3	-0.0	-5.8	0.3	-3.1	-4.5	-7.6	-1.7	...
New Zealand	3.6	5.2	-7.9	-2.6	5.5	2.6	1.3	1.0	3.1

... = data not available, -0.0 = magnitude is less than half of unit employed, ADB = Asian Development Bank.

a Refers to other goods industries comprising agriculture, forestry, and fishing; and mining and quarrying.

Source: Economy sources.

National Accounts

Table 2.2.14:   Growth Rates of Industry Real Value Added
(%)

ADB Regional Member	2000	2005	2010	2013	2014	2015	2016	2017	2018
Developing ADB Member Economies									
Central and West Asia									
Afghanistan	...	13.0	6.3	4.5	2.4	4.5	-1.8	0.9	7.6
Armenia	12.8	14.8	5.7	0.5	-2.3	2.8	-0.3	9.0	4.4
Azerbaijan	5.7	43.6	3.7	4.3	0.4	-3.4	-5.7	-3.6	-0.7
Georgia	4.9	9.6	8.2	2.4	4.6	4.1	6.2	6.5	1.0
Kazakhstan	15.3	10.7	9.5	3.1	1.5	-0.4	1.1	6.3	...
Kyrgyz Republic	8.8	-9.8	2.5	30.2	5.7	2.9	7.1	8.6	6.2
Pakistan	5.8 (2001)	6.5	3.4	0.8	4.5	5.2	5.7	5.4	5.8
Tajikistan	15.6 (2001)	7.7	5.6	4.0	14.9	16.3	22.2	7.3	...
Turkmenistan	1.0	10.6	6.0	8.0	11.6	...	...	...	...
Uzbekistan	1.8	5.3	5.5	9.8	7.4	8.3	5.9	5.4	10.5
East Asia									
China, People's Republic of	9.5	12.1	12.7	8.0	7.4	6.2	6.3	5.9	5.8
Hong Kong, China[a]	-3.8 (2001)	-1.4	7.7	1.5	7.4	2.4	3.0	-0.7	0.3
Korea, Republic of[a]	3.5 (2001)	4.4	9.6	2.8	2.9	2.4	3.1	4.2	2.2
Mongolia	1.5	4.2	8.8 (2011)	14.6	12.7	9.9	-0.4	0.7	5.8
Taipei,China[a]	7.1	7.6	20.8	1.7	7.2	-0.5	2.8	4.6	3.3
South Asia									
Bangladesh	6.2	8.3	7.0	9.6	8.2	9.7	11.1	10.2	12.1
Bhutan	7.3	3.8	12.5	3.9	3.7	8.2	6.9	2.4	...
India	6.0	9.7	7.6	3.8	7.0	9.6	7.7	5.9	6.9
Maldives	-3.8	14.3	7.3	-6.0	16.2	18.1	12.3	10.9	9.8
Nepal	8.6	3.0	4.0	2.7	7.1	1.4	-6.4	12.4	9.6
Sri Lanka	9.0	8.0	8.4	4.1	4.7	2.2	5.7	4.1	0.9
Southeast Asia									
Brunei Darussalam	3.0	-1.8	3.2 (2011)	-5.6	-4.4	-0.0	-2.9	1.5	-0.4
Cambodia	31.2	12.7	13.6	10.7	10.1	11.7	10.9	9.8	11.6
Indonesia	5.9	4.7	4.9	4.3	4.2	3.0	3.8	4.1	4.3
Lao People's Democratic Republic	9.3	10.6	17.5	7.7	7.3	7.0	12.0	11.6	7.8
Malaysia	13.6	3.6	8.4	3.6	5.9	5.2	4.3	4.7	3.2
Myanmar	21.3	19.9	18.6	11.4	12.1	8.3	8.9	9.4	...
Philippines	6.5	4.2	11.6	9.2	7.8	6.4	8.0	7.1	6.7
Singapore[a,b]	11.1	7.9	24.0	1.9	3.7	-2.7	2.7	5.6	4.9
Thailand[a,c]	4.0	4.9	10.6	1.7	0.1	1.9	2.2	2.2	2.7
Viet Nam	10.1	8.4	-9.9	5.1	6.4	9.6	7.6	8.0	8.9
The Pacific									
Cook Islands	18.2	-6.3	-8.4	-6.3	-13.5	-10.2	8.1	24.2	7.0
Fiji	-5.5	-6.7	6.5	4.4	1.2	6.9	7.6	4.4	...
Kiribati	-6.4	15.0 (2006)	9.5	16.0	-2.6	23.6	-2.4	-15.8	...
Marshall Islands	-14.6	10.1	0.1	5.8	-12.9	-4.0	16.3	13.2	...
Micronesia, Federated States of	6.6	-2.9	18.0	-19.5	-29.0	-6.1	6.9	...	...
Nauru	...	16.1	39.4	-28.5	-3.6	-17.1	...	3.1	...
Niue	...	81.4	14.4	9.7	6.1	0.9	2.3	-4.7	90.4
Palau	29.5 (2001)	7.0	5.2	-11.8	3.1	30.3	13.1	-8.4	3.0
Papua New Guinea	-0.8	4.1	12.0	2.0	39.1	35.3	8.1	-2.5	-4.2
Samoa	14.4	4.7	7.7	-2.0	1.6	8.7	-2.6	-9.7	-5.3
Solomon Islands	-29.7	-3.1	15.4	-2.0	-13.0	-5.0	0.9	...	...
Timor-Leste	-14.3 (2001)	73.9	-6.3	-14.8	-44.5	41.7	-1.1	-17.3	...
Tonga	-0.4	-2.8	11.6	-14.5	1.6	7.9	9.5	10.8	-5.8
Tuvalu	5.0 (2001)	-18.2	-41.6	40.5	-5.8	36.7	20.2	21.1	...
Vanuatu	46.4	5.3	12.6	9.8	3.2	35.3	4.3	7.1	...
Developed ADB Member Economies									
Australia[a]	...	...	...	...	...	...	...	...	...
Japan[a]	...	...	...	...	...	...	...	...	...
New Zealand[a]	...	...	...	...	...	...	...	...	...

... = data not available, -0.0 = magnitude is less than half of unit employed, ADB = Asian Development Bank.

a   National accounts are compiled using chain volume measures.
b   Industry refers to manufacturing, construction, and utilities.
c   Industry refers to mining and quarrying; manufacturing; electricity, gas, steam, and air-conditioning supply; water supply; and sewerage, waste management, and remediation activities.

Source: Economy sources.

Table 2.2.15: Growth Rates of Services Real Value Added
(%)

ADB Regional Member	2000	2005	2010	2013	2014	2015	2016	2017	2018
Developing ADB Member Economies									
Central and West Asia									
Afghanistan	...	5.4	18.1	6.4	4.0	1.4	2.3	3.3	1.2
Armenia	3.1	14.7	4.7	2.8	6.7	1.0	3.4	10.4	9.4
Azerbaijan	9.6	9.6	8.8	8.6	7.6	6.8	-0.8	3.5	3.2
Georgia	5.5	6.5	8.2	3.6	4.5	3.0	2.1	5.0	6.6
Kazakhstan	8.4	10.4	6.0	6.9	5.7	3.1	0.9	2.7	...
Kyrgyz Republic	5.8	8.4	-1.3	4.8	4.5	3.5	3.2	3.3	2.1
Pakistan	5.1 (2001)	8.1	3.2	5.1	4.5	4.4	5.7	6.5	6.4
Tajikistan	3.9 (2001)	7.7	7.1	9.4	1.7	1.9	-1.5	6.2	...
Turkmenistan	18.0	27.1	13.8	-9.2	-13.2	...	...	...	...
Uzbekistan	5.4	7.6	10.6	7.5	8.3	8.3	6.3	6.4	5.4
East Asia									
China, People's Republic of	9.8	12.4	9.7	8.3	7.8	8.2	7.7	7.9	7.6
Hong Kong, China[a]	1.8 (2001)	7.8	6.9	2.7	2.5	1.7	2.3	3.6	3.4
Korea, Republic of[a]	5.6 (2001)	4.1	4.6	3.0	2.7	2.7	3.1	2.7	3.4
Mongolia	10.5	9.7	17.8 (2011)	7.8	7.8	0.6	1.1	7.7	5.5
Taipei,China[a]	6.5	4.1	6.3	2.3	3.3	1.2	1.3	2.5	2.6
South Asia									
Bangladesh	5.5	6.4	5.5	5.5	5.6	5.8	6.3	6.7	6.4
Bhutan	8.7	14.8	12.1	1.6	8.2	8.5	9.8	6.7	...
India	5.1	10.9	9.7	7.7	9.8	9.4	8.4	8.1	7.5
Maldives	5.1	-17.7	7.3	8.8	7.0	2.4	6.7	5.2	4.7
Nepal	5.9	3.3	5.8	5.7	6.2	4.6	2.4	8.1	7.2
Sri Lanka	6.1	6.4	8.0	3.8	4.8	6.0	4.8	3.6	4.7
Southeast Asia									
Brunei Darussalam	2.5	4.1	4.9 (2011)	4.7	0.6	-1.1	-1.7	1.1	0.8
Cambodia	8.9	13.1	3.3	8.7	8.7	7.1	6.8	7.0	6.7
Indonesia	5.2	7.9	8.4	6.4	6.0	5.5	5.7	5.7	5.8
Lao People's Democratic Republic	6.9	10.8	7.6	9.7	8.1	8.0	4.7	4.4	6.9
Malaysia	6.0	7.3	7.4	6.0	6.8	5.3	5.7	6.4	6.9
Myanmar	13.4	13.1	9.5	10.3	9.1	8.7	8.1	8.3	...
Philippines	3.3	5.8	7.2	7.0	6.0	6.9	7.5	6.9	6.8
Singapore[a,b]	7.9	6.9	10.9	6.5	4.2	4.1	2.3	2.9	3.0
Thailand[a,c]	4.4	4.5	6.9	3.7	1.8	5.6	4.7	5.1	4.8
Viet Nam	5.3	8.6	-7.7	6.7	6.2	6.3	7.0	7.4	7.0
The Pacific									
Cook Islands	15.4	-0.3	-2.6	-0.6	7.6	5.4	6.6	0.6	4.0
Fiji	0.8	-17.0	2.9	4.5	7.4	3.3	0.3	3.6	...
Kiribati	1.7	0.9 (2006)	-0.1	2.6	-0.3	7.2	6.6	3.3	...
Marshall Islands	6.8	3.5	3.6	1.7	2.1	1.1	0.9	3.4	...
Micronesia, Federated States of	3.3	0.7	2.4	-0.8	-1.2	3.0	2.3	...	...
Nauru	...	-2.1	4.2	60.7	41.9	11.6	...	3.9	...
Niue	...	0.8	0.4	5.7	5.2	4.6	4.2	2.4	4.7
Palau	2.6 (2001)	2.4	-0.5	-0.4	5.7	8.6	-0.7	-2.8	2.9
Papua New Guinea	-12.7	3.6	12.4	4.3	0.9	-2.3	2.3	1.5	3.8
Samoa	6.2	5.2	3.0	0.7	3.2	6.9	4.8	0.4	3.8
Solomon Islands	-5.7	19.4	6.4	7.6	3.9	5.0	3.3	...	...
Timor-Leste	42.2 (2001)	4.3	13.7	1.3	7.8	4.7	5.7	2.7	...
Tonga	0.0	3.6	1.0	-0.5	1.4	2.7	5.7	4.0	2.7
Tuvalu	-0.5 (2001)	-4.9	2.3	0.0	2.4	7.1	2.0	3.2	...
Vanuatu	2.2	6.6	3.0	0.1	2.4	2.0	2.9	2.9	...
Developed ADB Member Economies									
Australia[a]	...	...	...	...	...	...	...	...	...
Japan[a]	...	...	...	...	...	...	...	...	...
New Zealand[a]	...	...	...	...	...	...	...	...	...

... = data not available, 0.0 = magnitude is less than half of unit employed, ADB = Asian Development Bank.

a National accounts are compiled using chain volume measures.
b Services refers to services-producing industries, including ownership of dwellings.
c Services includes construction.

Source: Economy sources.

Table 2.2.16: Growth Rates of Real Household Final Consumption
(%)

ADB Regional Member	2000	2005	2010	2013	2014	2015	2016	2017	2018
Developing ADB Member Economies									
Central and West Asia									
Afghanistan	...	...	...	...	...	...	...	...	...
Armenia[a]	8.3	8.8	3.9	0.9	1.0	-7.7	-1.0	12.4	4.8
Azerbaijan[a]	10.0	13.2	10.8	8.6	8.1	8.5	1.7	0.9	...
Georgia[a]	...	...	6.7 (2011)	-0.1	3.2	0.1	-0.6	1.3	...
Kazakhstan[a]	1.2	10.7	11.5	18.7	1.1	1.8	1.2	1.2	5.3
Kyrgyz Republic[a]	-5.0	8.3	2.7	8.0	3.0	-0.9	-0.6	6.3	3.7
Pakistan[a]	3.5 (2001)	10.8	2.2	2.1	5.6	2.9	7.6	8.7	6.3
Tajikistan[a]	8.6 (2001)	20.6	10.5	9.3	1.8	-15.1	6.4	–	...
Turkmenistan[a]	-48.3	-15.2	-61.3	...	...	...	...	...	...
Uzbekistan	...	...	51.7	10.1	10.7	11.9	9.4	3.9	4.4
East Asia									
China, People's Republic of	...	...	...	...	...	...	...	...	...
Hong Kong, China[a]	4.5	3.5	6.1	4.6	3.3	4.8	2.0	5.6	5.5
Korea, Republic of	5.8 (2001)	4.7	4.6	1.3	2.0	2.2	2.3	2.8	2.7
Mongolia	...	12.4 (2006)	15.8 (2011)	15.4	6.3	8.1	-2.6	5.5	-1.8
Taipei,China	5.1	3.3	3.8	2.4	3.2	2.9	2.4	2.6	...
South Asia									
Bangladesh	4.1	3.9	4.6	5.1	4.0	5.8	3.0	7.4	11.0
Bhutan[a]	0.4	1.3	5.5	58.0	-6.4	12.6	-5.6	5.1	...
India[a]	3.4	8.6	8.7	7.3	6.4	7.9	8.2	7.4	8.1
Maldives	...	...	...	...	...	...	...	...	...
Nepal[a]	...	4.7	6.2	2.7	4.2	2.9	-0.7	2.6	2.5
Sri Lanka	4.0	1.7	9.9 (2011)	7.8	3.7	7.5	7.4	2.5	2.3
Southeast Asia									
Brunei Darussalam[a]	-7.0	-0.6	5.4 (2011)	6.0	-3.7	5.2	-1.3	4.7	2.4
Cambodia[a]	4.9	12.2	8.8	5.8	4.5	6.0	6.8	4.6	4.6
Indonesia[b]	1.6	4.0	4.7	5.5	5.3	4.8	5.0	5.0	5.1
Lao People's Democratic Republic	...	...	...	...	...	...	...	...	...
Malaysia[b]	13.0	9.1	6.9	7.2	7.0	6.0	5.9	6.9	8.0
Myanmar[c]	4.3	14.6	2.6	13.7	11.1	4.7	2.2	4.3	...
Philippines[a]	5.2	4.4	3.4	5.6	5.6	6.3	7.1	5.9	5.6
Singapore	13.6	4.1	4.4	2.8	3.6	5.2	2.7	3.4	2.7
Thailand[a]	7.0	4.2	5.5	0.9	0.8	2.3	2.9	3.0	4.6
Viet Nam	3.1	5.8	8.2	5.2	6.1	9.3	7.3	7.3	7.3
The Pacific									
Cook Islands	...	...	...	...	...	...	...	...	...
Fiji	...	...	...	...	...	...	...	...	...
Kiribati	...	...	...	...	...	...	...	...	...
Marshall Islands	...	1.3	2.1	-3.5	0.2	1.2	6.3	9.2	...
Micronesia, Federated States of	...	...	...	...	...	...	...	...	...
Nauru	...	...	...	...	...	...	...	...	...
Niue	...	...	...	...	...	...	...	...	...
Palau	...	0.5 (2006)	-2.3	1.0	2.5	5.4	6.1	-0.5	0.2
Papua New Guinea[a]	-28.5	9.8	...	...	...	...	...	...	...
Samoa	...	...	...	...	...	...	...	...	...
Solomon Islands	...	9.3	8.7	4.8	4.8	4.4	2.2	...	...
Timor-Leste	12.9 (2001)	-1.2	5.2	3.1	6.2	2.1	6.5	4.1	...
Tonga	3.5	2.2	-1.3	4.9	2.7	5.0	5.0	4.6	5.4
Tuvalu	...	...	...	...	...	...	...	...	...
Vanuatu	...	2.4	2.6	3.5	3.9	1.3	8.9	-1.9	...
Developed ADB Member Economies									
Australia	4.3	4.5	3.3	1.8	2.4	2.3	2.8	2.4	2.8
Japan	1.8	1.2	2.3	2.4	-0.8	-0.4	-0.3	1.1	0.3
New Zealand	1.4	4.6	2.3	3.7	3.0	3.9	5.8	4.1	3.3

... = data not available, – = magnitude equals zero, ADB = Asian Development Bank.

a Includes expenditure of nonprofit institutions serving households.
b Prior to 2010, includes expenditure of nonprofit institutions serving households.
c Includes government final consumption expenditure.

Source: Economy sources.

Table 2.2.17:   Growth Rates of Real Government Consumption Expenditure
(%)

ADB Regional Member	2000	2005	2010	2013	2014	2015	2016	2017	2018
Developing ADB Member Economies									
Central and West Asia									
Afghanistan	...	...	...	7.6	-1.2	4.7	-2.4	-2.1	...
Armenia	2.8	19.0	3.9	7.6	-1.2	4.7	-2.4	-2.1	7.4
Azerbaijan	2.3	3.4	3.4	3.6	3.7	1.3	6.8	1.1	...
Georgia	...	...	1.0 (2011)	4.3	11.2	22.1	6.5	2.0	...
Kazakhstan	15.0	10.8	2.7	1.7	9.8	2.4	2.3	1.9	-14.0
Kyrgyz Republic	5.9	-2.7	-1.1	-0.4	-0.5	0.9	1.5	1.3	-0.1
Pakistan	-6.7 (2001)	3.4	-0.6	10.1	1.5	8.1	8.2	5.3	14.2
Tajikistan	10.8 (2001)	0.4	0.9	2.3	4.1	3.3	3.9	9.4	...
Turkmenistan	28.0	17.9	3.8	...	...	...	...	...	...
Uzbekistan	...	...	7.0	8.6	8.4	6.7	2.7	1.5	3.1
East Asia									
China, People's Republic of	...	...	...	...	...	...	...	...	...
Hong Kong, China	2.4	-2.6	3.4	2.7	3.1	3.4	3.4	2.8	4.2
Korea, Republic of	6.5 (2001)	5.3	5.6	4.8	4.3	3.8	4.4	3.9	5.6
Mongolia	...	...	15.3 (2011)	15.8	12.2	-4.7	10.6	-1.8	0.5
Taipei,China	0.6	0.4	1.1	-0.8	3.7	-0.1	3.6	-0.6	3.5
South Asia									
Bangladesh	0.9	7.7	6.8	5.8	7.9	8.8	8.4	7.8	15.4
Bhutan	–	2.8	7.5	-10.1	2.4	10.8	4.2	4.4	...
India	1.4	8.9	5.8	0.6	7.6	7.5	5.8	15.0	9.2
Maldives	...	...	...	...	...	...	...	...	...
Nepal	7.8 (2002)	1.2	1.3	-6.7	10.0	7.4	-0.4	10.5	13.4
Sri Lanka	5.3	12.0	-2.1 (2011)	0.1	6.0	10.2	2.3	-5.4	-5.5
Southeast Asia									
Brunei Darussalam	7.7	-1.0	5.3 (2011)	3.6	1.9	-3.6	-6.5	7.4	1.6
Cambodia	12.4	2.9	12.5	5.2	2.4	4.4	5.7	6.5	6.5
Indonesia	-0.9	6.6	0.3	6.7	1.2	5.3	-0.1	2.1	4.8
Lao People's Democratic Republic	...	...	...	...	...	...	...	...	...
Malaysia	1.6	6.5	3.4	5.8	4.4	4.5	1.1	5.5	3.3
Myanmar	...	...	...	...	...	...	...	...	...
Philippines	-1.0	2.1	4.0	5.0	3.3	7.6	9.0	6.2	13.0
Singapore	18.3	4.0	10.2	11.7	0.6	8.9	3.7	4.5	4.1
Thailand	2.8	8.0	8.9	1.5	2.8	2.5	2.2	0.1	1.8
Viet Nam	5.0	8.2	12.3	7.3	7.0	7.0	7.5	7.4	6.3
The Pacific									
Cook Islands	...	...	...	...	...	...	...	...	...
Fiji	...	...	...	...	...	...	...	...	...
Kiribati	...	...	...	...	...	...	...	...	...
Marshall Islands	...	2.1	0.3	0.3	-1.7	7.3	6.0	1.6	...
Micronesia, Federated States of	...	...	...	...	...	...	...	...	...
Nauru	...	...	...	...	...	...	...	...	...
Niue	...	...	...	...	...	...	...	...	...
Palau	...	5.9 (2006)	-1.5	1.0	1.4	1.3	4.1	-0.6	4.4
Papua New Guinea	3.7	1.1	...	...	...	...	...	...	...
Samoa	...	...	...	...	...	...	...	...	...
Solomon Islands	...	80.6	10.0	14.7	8.2	-1.4	2.0	...	...
Timor-Leste	33.8 (2001)	-28.1	2.1	-15.8	11.8	3.6	-1.2	-5.8	...
Tonga	-2.8	-1.5	-8.6	2.0	-2.3	5.6	-0.7	5.4	2.7
Tuvalu	...	...	...	...	...	...	...	...	...
Vanuatu	...	-0.1	4.3	2.2	-3.7	16.9	-1.4	19.5	...
Developed ADB Member Economies									
Australia	3.1	3.2	1.7	0.3	1.5	2.4	4.3	5.0	3.7
Japan	3.9	0.8	1.9	1.5	0.5	1.5	1.4	0.3	0.8
New Zealand	1.3	7.2	1.9	2.0	3.3	2.3	2.1	2.8	1.9

... = data not available, – = magnitude equals zero, ADB = Asian Development Bank.

Source: Economy sources.

National Accounts

Table 2.2.18:   Growth Rates of Real Gross Capital Formation
(%)

ADB Regional Member	2000	2005	2010	2013	2014	2015	2016	2017	2018
Developing ADB Member Economies									
Central and West Asia									
Afghanistan	...	...	...	...	...	...	...	...	...
Armenia	5.2	26.9	0.5	-9.1	-3.0	-1.2	-8.7	15.4	26.8
Azerbaijan	2.6	5.8	2.0	4.5	-1.7	-11.1	-19.0	-1.0	...
Georgia	...	...	28.0 (2011)	-11.7	26.9	9.3	8.1	-1.1	...
Kazakhstan	10.7	35.0	2.0	6.7	8.6	5.5	2.5	2.3	-1.3
Kyrgyz Republic	22.1	13.7	-5.2	5.1	15.7	-2.3	8.1	6.9	11.3
Pakistan	2.5 (2001)	13.2	-6.5	2.8	2.8	14.6	7.3	9.5	5.7
Tajikistan	39.2 (2001)	2.6	7.5	15.1	17.6	25.2	19.1	-0.9	...
Turkmenistan	-6.0	12.4	21.6	...	...	...	...	...	...
Uzbekistan	...	...	...	...	...	...	...	...	...
East Asia									
China, People's Republic of	...	...	...	...	...	...	...	...	...
Hong Kong, China	16.1	–	11.3	3.1	1.6	-8.1	4.0	5.2	1.3
Korea, Republic of	1.7 (2001)	2.2	17.1	1.0	3.6	6.5	6.3	10.9	-1.8
Mongolia	...	15.0 (2006)	62.8 (2011)	1.4	-30.1	-26.5	2.1	34.6	41.3
Taipei,China	9.0	1.3	35.8	3.2	4.4	1.5	0.6	-0.8	6.1
South Asia									
Bangladesh	7.3	10.7	8.6	5.4	9.9	7.1	8.9	10.1	10.5
Bhutan	26.5	-12.2	46.1	-35.7	24.4	16.5	12.0	-0.1	...
India	-5.5	16.2	14.1	-4.6	7.7	4.7	3.6	10.4	9.0
Maldives	...	...	...	...	...	...	...	...	...
Nepal	-14.0 (2002)	9.5	34.4	23.5	22.8	9.4	10.7	37.8	23.2
Sri Lanka	8.7	9.4	20.2 (2011)	-8.8	11.5	3.8	5.0	8.2	6.6
Southeast Asia									
Brunei Darussalam	6.7 (2001)	0.5	37.0 (2011)	11.9	-31.2	6.6	-11.1	8.0	28.1
Cambodia	12.7	30.7	-7.9	14.1	8.8	9.9	10.0	6.0	6.0
Indonesia	12.9	12.4	8.8	2.8	5.7	3.0	5.0	5.3	8.9
Lao People's Democratic Republic	...	...	...	...	...	...	...	...	...
Malaysia	29.2	-2.5	25.3	4.9	2.5	6.7	4.4	6.2	-3.2
Myanmar	11.3	29.8	34.6	12.3	7.5	16.1	4.3	6.8	...
Philippines	1.1	3.0	31.6	27.9	4.2	18.4	24.6	9.4	13.2
Singapore	23.6	1.3	20.0	4.9	0.8	-8.6	10.2	11.6	-2.1
Thailand	8.0	21.7	32.0	3.2	-12.3	2.1	-3.7	11.2	...
Viet Nam	10.1	11.2	10.4	5.5	8.9	9.0	9.7	9.8	8.2
The Pacific									
Cook Islands	...	...	...	...	...	...	...	...	...
Fiji	...	...	...	...	...	...	...	...	...
Kiribati	...	...	...	...	...	...	...	...	...
Marshall Islands	...	20.8	23.9	81.4	-17.7	-2.5	18.9	14.8	...
Micronesia, Federated States of	...	...	...	...	...	...	...	...	...
Nauru	...	...	...	...	...	...	...	...	...
Niue	...	...	...	...	...	...	...	...	...
Palau	...	-11.0 (2006)	3.3	-12.9	37.1	0.3	9.8	2.5	-5.0
Papua New Guinea	36.8	-9.8	...	...	...	...	...	...	...
Samoa	...	...	...	...	...	...	...	...	...
Solomon Islands	...	71.1	88.7	1.9	3.3	10.2	-5.0	...	...
Timor-Leste	10.5 (2001)	-7.8	-4.5	-20.1	3.4	-10.3	15.4	-15.0	...
Tonga	1.3	4.7	11.7	-34.8	9.3	15.0	14.7	30.3	-10.2
Tuvalu	...	...	...	...	...	...	...	...	...
Vanuatu	...	7.7	-5.2	17.0	9.0	33.2	-21.5	15.9	...
Developed ADB Member Economies									
Australia	...	...	...	...	...	...	...	...	...
Japan	3.1	2.3	3.1	3.2	3.4	2.9	-0.9	2.8	1.7
New Zealand	-3.8	4.0	7.4	8.0	8.4	2.3	4.2	3.8	2.9

... = data not available, – = magnitude equals zero, ADB = Asian Development Bank.

Source: Economy sources.

Table 2.2.19: Growth Rates of Real Exports of Goods and Services
(%)

ADB Regional Member	2000	2005	2010	2013	2014	2015	2016	2017	2018
Developing ADB Member Economies									
Central and West Asia									
Afghanistan	...	...	...	...	...	...	...	...	...
Armenia	19.0	15.9	26.5	8.6	6.4	4.9	19.1	18.7	4.6
Azerbaijan	15.4	52.8	9.1	2.1	-1.9	-0.1	11.4	-2.2	...
Georgia	...	...	15.5 (2011)	20.3	0.4	6.0	7.7	10.3	...
Kazakhstan	27.9	0.4	3.1	2.7	-2.5	-4.1	-4.5	6.4	11.5
Kyrgyz Republic	10.5	-11.0	-11.7	12.3	-6.2	-5.6	-3.8	6.1	-1.8
Pakistan	12.2 (2001)	11.7	15.7	13.6	-1.5	-6.3	-1.6	-0.8	9.9
Tajikistan	-20.8 (2001)	2.9	23.0	-10.0	–	–	–	–	...
Turkmenistan	82.7	19.2	11.7	...	...	...	...	...	...
Uzbekistan	...	...	2.1	11.1	-7.5	2.3	11.1	1.3	10.7
East Asia									
China, People's Republic of	...	...	...	...	...	...	...	...	...
Hong Kong, China	16.9	12.2	17.6	7.8	1.0	-1.4	0.7	5.9	3.8
Korea, Republic of	-1.8 (2001)	7.9	13.0	3.8	2.1	0.2	2.4	2.5	3.5
Mongolia	...	6.1 (2006)	18.2 (2011)	12.8	53.2	0.1	13.8	14.8	14.1
Taipei,China	18.0	7.6	25.7	3.5	5.9	-0.4	1.9	7.4	3.7
South Asia									
Bangladesh	14.4	15.6	0.9	2.5	3.2	-2.8	2.2	-2.3	8.1
Bhutan	3.3	34.3	7.5	3.9	-5.8	-3.5	-9.1	11.6	...
India	18.2	26.1	19.6	7.8	1.8	-5.6	5.1	4.7	12.5
Maldives	...	...	...	...	...	...	...	...	...
Nepal	-23.2 (2002)	-3.0	-10.4	10.3	18.8	6.8	-13.7	11.3	7.8
Sri Lanka	17.1	6.6	10.2 (2011)	6.6	4.3	4.7	-0.7	7.6	0.5
Southeast Asia									
Brunei Darussalam	11.9	-1.3	-3.0 (2011)	-5.7	-0.1	-9.9	-1.9	-5.3	5.7
Cambodia	30.3	16.4	20.6	14.0	11.3	7.2	8.6	5.3	5.3
Indonesia	26.5	16.6	15.3	4.2	1.1	-2.1	-1.7	8.9	6.5
Lao People's Democratic Republic	...	...	...	...	...	...	...	...	...
Malaysia	16.1	8.3	11.1	0.3	5.0	0.3	1.3	8.7	2.2
Myanmar	79.3	3.6	10.9	12.9	18.7	15.1	-0.4	19.0	...
Philippines	13.7	5.0	21.0	-1.0	12.6	8.5	11.6	19.7	13.4
Singapore	14.3	12.8	17.8	6.1	3.6	5.0	0.0	5.7	5.1
Thailand	15.8	7.8	14.2	2.7	0.3	1.6	2.8	5.4	4.2
Viet Nam	11.0 (2002)	7.8	14.6	17.4	11.6	12.6	13.9	16.7	14.3
The Pacific									
Cook Islands	...	...	...	...	...	...	...	...	...
Fiji	...	...	...	...	...	...	...	...	...
Kiribati	...	...	...	...	...	...	...	...	...
Marshall Islands	...	14.6	22.4	8.3	1.4	8.2	-8.8	8.9	...
Micronesia, Federated States of	...	...	...	...	...	...	...	...	...
Nauru	...	...	...	...	...	...	...	...	...
Niue	...	...	...	...	...	...	...	...	...
Palau	...	0.2 (2006)	5.5	-3.4	9.6	11.9	-4.1	-9.1	-7.1
Papua New Guinea	7.1	6.8	...	...	...	...	...	...	...
Samoa	...	...	...	...	...	...	...	...	...
Solomon Islands	...	10.5	34.8	-4.8	-8.9	1.8	3.6	...	...
Timor-Leste	-19.2 (2001)	74.0	-6.7	-13.4	-26.4	12.8	-9.4	-9.1	...
Tonga	-14.7	-2.8	-8.8	19.7	-21.5	7.8	34.3	-0.1	-6.6
Tuvalu	...	...	...	...	...	...	...	...	...
Vanuatu	...	7.1	0.4	4.2	-0.7	4.9	19.5	-1.1	...
Developed ADB Member Economies									
Australia	9.9	3.5	4.7	5.3	6.0	6.8	6.8	5.5	4.1
Japan	12.7	7.2	24.9	0.8	9.3	2.9	1.7	6.8	3.3
New Zealand	6.1	-0.4	2.8	0.1	4.6	5.9	1.3	3.0	3.6

... = data not available, 0.0 = magnitude is less than half of unit employed, – = magnitude equals zero, ADB = Asian Development Bank.

Source: Economy sources.

Table 2.2.20:   Growth Rates of Real Imports of Goods and Services
(%)

ADB Regional Member	2000	2005	2010	2013	2014	2015	2016	2017	2018
Developing ADB Member Economies									
Central and West Asia									
Afghanistan	...	...	...	...	...	...	...	...	...
Armenia	7.2	14.3	12.8	-2.1	-1.0	-15.1	7.6	24.6	12.7
Azerbaijan	17.3	19.8	12.4	1.1	-2.1	-0.5	11.3	-1.6	...
Georgia	...	...	17.9 (2011)	2.9	11.1	10.4	6.3	0.9	...
Kazakhstan	28.0	12.1	2.9	7.8	-4.0	-0.1	-2.0	-1.4	3.2
Kyrgyz Republic	0.4	6.5	-6.9	4.1	1.6	-13.2	-1.1	7.4	6.7
Pakistan	2.2 (2001)	39.5	4.3	1.8	0.3	-1.6	16.0	21.0	17.5
Tajikistan	-14.5 (2001)	16.5	8.0	1.1	1.0	–	–	–	...
Turkmenistan	4.1	-9.3	7.4	...	...	...	...	...	...
Uzbekistan	...	...	-6.6	8.8	0.3	-11.2	-2.2	15.5	39.4
East Asia									
China, People's Republic of	...	...	...	...	...	...	...	...	...
Hong Kong, China	17.1	9.3	18.2	8.3	1.0	-1.8	0.9	6.6	4.6
Korea, Republic of	-3.5 (2001)	7.8	17.5	1.6	1.3	2.1	5.2	8.9	0.8
Mongolia	...	6.7 (2006)	49.5 (2011)	7.6	6.8	-11.4	12.7	24.8	21.4
Taipei,China	14.9	2.9	28.0	3.4	5.7	1.1	3.1	5.3	4.9
South Asia									
Bangladesh	10.2	19.1	0.7	1.2	1.2	3.2	-7.1	2.9	27.0
Bhutan	4.2	13.0	28.7	-1.8	-3.2	16.2	-12.4	3.7	...
India	4.6	32.6	15.6	-8.1	0.9	-5.9	4.4	17.6	15.4
Maldives	...	...	...	...	...	...	...	...	...
Nepal	-15.1 (2002)	6.9	28.3	14.1	21.0	9.6	2.8	27.2	19.0
Sri Lanka	14.8	2.7	23.6 (2011)	-1.5	9.6	10.6	7.9	7.1	1.8
Southeast Asia									
Brunei Darussalam	-6.2	10.2	33.7 (2011)	14.5	-22.9	-8.9	-10.8	1.3	28.1
Cambodia	23.7	17.3	16.8	15.1	10.1	6.5	8.6	4.1	4.1
Indonesia	25.9	17.8	17.3	1.9	2.1	-6.2	-2.4	8.1	12.0
Lao People's Democratic Republic	...	...	...	...	...	...	...	...	...
Malaysia	24.4	8.9	15.6	1.7	4.0	0.8	1.4	10.2	1.3
Myanmar	-8.0	2.2	51.9	54.4	22.3	21.6	-11.4	9.4	...
Philippines	11.8	3.3	22.5	4.4	9.9	14.6	20.2	18.1	16.0
Singapore	20.0	11.6	16.3	6.5	2.8	3.4	0.1	7.5	4.7
Thailand	26.0	16.2	23.0	1.7	-5.3	0.0	-1.0	6.2	8.6
Viet Nam	15.8 (2002)	5.9	13.7	17.3	12.8	18.1	15.3	17.5	12.8
The Pacific									
Cook Islands	...	...	...	...	...	...	...	...	...
Fiji	...	...	...	...	...	...	...	...	...
Kiribati	...	...	...	...	...	...	...	...	...
Marshall Islands	...	9.6	7.6	12.0	-9.2	9.9	7.0	10.7	...
Micronesia, Federated States of	...	...	...	...	...	...	...	...	...
Nauru	...	...	...	...	...	...	...	...	...
Niue	...	...	...	...	...	...	...	...	...
Palau	...	2.0 (2006)	1.1	1.2	11.8	2.6	8.0	-1.4	-5.5
Papua New Guinea	-4.7	4.7	...	...	...	...	...	...	...
Samoa	...	...	...	...	...	...	...	...	...
Solomon Islands	...	14.0	51.7	6.6	-5.9	3.9	1.2	...	...
Timor-Leste	26.7 (2001)	-19.1	-6.6	-13.8	19.4	-15.4	-5.1	-3.3	...
Tonga	-0.6	1.8	-4.5	-2.5	0.2	23.2	9.4	5.6	1.0
Tuvalu	...	...	...	...	...	...	...	...	...
Vanuatu	...	2.9	-2.2	6.5	0.2	26.2	2.3	3.3	...
Developed ADB Member Economies									
Australia	12.0	12.5	7.1	0.3	-2.3	1.0	-0.1	4.7	7.1
Japan	9.3	6.1	11.2	3.3	8.3	0.8	-1.6	3.5	3.4
New Zealand	-1.1	4.9	11.5	8.1	7.4	2.3	5.1	7.1	4.1

... = data not available, 0.0 = magnitude is less than half of unit employed, – = magnitude equals zero, ADB = Asian Development Bank.

Source: Economy sources.

Table 2.2.21: Growth Rates of Agriculture Production Index
(%)

ADB Regional Member	2000	2005	2010	2013	2014	2015	2016	2017	2018
Developing ADB Member Economies									
Central and West Asia									
Afghanistan	-15.9	10.7	-0.8	-2.2	3.6	-3.7	5.3	...	...
Armenia	4.7	36.9	-18.3	4.3	0.3	6.1	-10.0	...	...
Azerbaijan	10.1	15.8	-0.7	1.9	-3.4	6.4	1.9	...	...
Georgia	-13.7	17.1	-6.2	19.2	-15.7	2.1	-5.2	...	...
Kazakhstan	-4.4	7.1	-10.4	9.7	1.0	3.4	5.4	3.0	3.2
Kyrgyz Republic	2.6	-4.2	-2.6	2.7	-0.5	6.2	3.1	2.4	2.7
Pakistan	1.3	-2.6	-1.9	5.5	7.4	-4.8	2.6	11.5	5.8
Tajikistan	12.6	-6.8	1.1	10.4	-1.8	6.0	-2.7	...	...
Turkmenistan	7.4	3.4	2.8	6.2	-4.0	-5.2	3.2	...	...
Uzbekistan	3.1	5.0	4.5	5.9	-2.2	6.1	6.1	1.2	0.3
East Asia									
China, People's Republic of	5.1	3.8	2.4	1.5	1.4	2.9	2.2	...	...
Hong Kong, China	2.4	13.5	0.0	0.0	-5.9	0.0	0.0	6.3	5.9
Korea, Republic of	0.8	0.6	-5.9	4.3	2.5	-1.7	-1.4	...	...
Mongolia	-1.8	-7.1	-20.2	9.4	8.6	-1.9	5.6	...	...
Taipei,China	2.2	-5.7	2.1	-1.2	1.1	-3.4	-3.6	5.4	2.8
South Asia									
Bangladesh	6.1	13.0	5.9	1.7	4.3	0.7	2.3	...	...
Bhutan	-10.2	23.5	4.5	-4.2	2.1	0.1	3.4	...	...
India	-1.1	5.7	8.6	3.8	2.7	-1.2	2.3	...	...
Maldives	5.9	-20.0	-3.9	-3.2	3.9	2.4	0.2	...	...
Nepal	5.1	2.0	1.0	-6.6	4.3	-0.2	1.4	...	...
Sri Lanka	2.3	8.7	10.5	9.5	-9.5	4.5	0.6	...	...
Southeast Asia									
Brunei Darussalam	13.0	-26.6	4.9	8.4	-0.2	2.1	-0.3	...	...
Cambodia	1.8	26.7	8.7	1.5	0.3	1.4	5.0	...	...
Indonesia	3.3	2.7	2.6	0.9	2.0	2.2	0.5	...	...
Lao People's Democratic Republic	14.3	4.0	6.9	4.4	17.1	11.0	4.0	...	...
Malaysia	3.5	4.6	0.5	1.9	-0.8	0.9	0.6	...	...
Myanmar	10.3	7.2	2.1	2.0	1.3	2.3	-0.8	0.1	...
Philippines	2.7	2.2	-0.8	0.9	-3.3	-1.3	-2.2	...	...
Singapore	-59.2	-22.8	0.5	6.7	-0.3	-2.0	4.9	...	...
Thailand	8.5	6.3 (2006)	0.9	-0.7	0.3	-3.9	0.0	7.0	6.8
Viet Nam	3.2	3.7	2.7	1.5	2.2	2.4	-1.5	...	...
The Pacific									
Cook Islands	-3.3	3.3	-2.5	3.4	-0.5	-0.2	-1.8	...	...
Fiji	-0.1	1.6	-6.9	12.1	2.2	-3.3	-2.1	...	...
Kiribati	-5.5	1.1	-48.4	-0.9	0.7	0.1	-0.2	...	...
Marshall Islands	-74.9	15.2	-5.0	6.1	0.0	-4.3	-5.6	...	...
Micronesia, Federated States of	-0.0	-3.5	-0.4	6.1	12.2	13.1	-20.8	...	...
Nauru	0.8	1.2	1.0	2.1	0.9	1.0	0.7	...	...
Niue	...	...	...	...	...	...	...	...	...
Palau	...	...	...	...	...	...	...	...	...
Papua New Guinea	3.2	1.8	-1.4	2.3	1.2	0.8	1.1	...	...
Samoa	3.1	2.1	0.0	1.5	1.1	4.1	-1.1	...	...
Solomon Islands	2.9	12.2	2.9	2.6	1.7	-0.8	-3.1	...	...
Timor-Leste	6.0	6.0	-0.7	-3.4	-0.4	0.2	-1.3	...	...
Tonga	-3.3	-0.2	-1.4	-1.0	0.8	3.6	-1.5	...	...
Tuvalu	6.1	1.4	-1.3	2.3	-0.4	0.9	1.0	...	...
Vanuatu	-4.6	1.9	24.0	6.0	-8.8	0.2	1.0	...	...
Developed ADB Member Economies									
Australia	-1.4	-0.4	-2.0	-1.0	-0.3	0.5	-3.5	...	...
Japan	-0.5	1.0	-2.4	-0.4	-0.2	-1.1	-3.8	...	...
New Zealand	6.9	-2.1	1.2	0.5	5.8	1.9	-0.8	...	...

... = data not available, -0.0 or 0.0 = magnitude is less than half of unit employed, ADB = Asian Development Bank.

Sources: Food and Agriculture Organization of the United Nations. FAOSTAT. http://foastat3.fao.org (accessed 1 July 2019). For Kazakhstan; the Kyrgyz Republic; Pakistan; Uzbekistan (2014–2018); Hong Kong, China; Taipei,China; Myanmar (2010–2017); and Thailand (2005–2018): Economy sources.

Production

Table 2.2.22:   Growth Rates of Manufacturing Production Index
(%)

ADB Regional Member	2000	2005	2010	2013	2014	2015	2016	2017	2018
Developing ADB Member Economies									
Central and West Asia									
Afghanistan	…	…	…	…	…	…	…	…	…
Armenia	…	…	…	…	…	…	…	…	…
Azerbaijan	…	…	…	…	…	…	…	…	…
Georgia	34.6 (2002)	40.6	18.5	-0.3	6.0	6.0	3.3	5.9	3.2
Kazakhstan	17.3	15.9	15.1	1.9	1.1	0.2	0.6	5.1	3.8
Kyrgyz Republic	3.4	-19.4	19.4	96.5	-33.5	-4.9	14.3	…	…
Pakistan	1.0 (2001)	18.2	0.5	4.4	5.4	3.4	3.1	5.8	5.2
Tajikistan	12.0	10.5	-6.2 (2009)	…	…	…	…	…	…
Turkmenistan	13.4	…	…	…	…	…	…	…	…
Uzbekistan	7.1	10.2 (2004)	…	…	8.2	5.9	6.9	4.2	6.4
East Asia									
China, People's Republic of	…	18.2 (2006)	16.6	10.5	9.4	7.0	6.8	7.2	6.5
Hong Kong, China	-0.5	3.0	3.6	0.1	-0.4	-1.5	-0.5	0.4	1.3
Korea, Republic of	10.4	3.3	7.9	1.7	2.9	-0.3	2.3	2.2	1.2
Mongolia	…	…	…	…	…	…	…	…	…
Taipei,China	7.8	3.2	29.7	3.4	6.8	-1.2	1.9	5.3	3.9
South Asia									
Bangladesh	4.9	8.5	6.3	11.6	9.2	10.7	13.5	11.2	15.0
Bhutan	…	…	…	…	…	…	…	…	…
India	5.3	10.3	9.0	3.6	3.8	3.0	4.1	4.6	3.6
Maldives	…	…	…	…	…	…	…	…	…
Nepal	6.5	2.6	-2.3	4.0	7.0	0.3	-13.3	17.1	10.0
Sri Lanka	…	…	…	…	…	…	…	…	…
Southeast Asia									
Brunei Darussalam	…	…	…	…	…	…	…	…	…
Cambodia	48.8	…	…	…	…	…	…	…	…
Indonesia	3.6	1.3	4.8	6.0	4.8	4.8	4.0	4.7	4.0
Lao People's Democratic Republic	…	…	…	…	…	…	…	…	…
Malaysia	24.9	5.1	11.0	4.2	6.0	4.9	4.3	6.1	4.8
Myanmar	…	…	10.1 (2011)	8.8	9.4	10.2	9.1	9.8	…
Philippines	16.0	1.1	23.3	15.2	6.2	2.4	14.5	-2.8	7.0
Singapore	15.3	9.5	29.7	1.7	2.7	-5.1	3.7	10.4	7.0
Thailand	6.9	5.0	14.2	1.9	-4.0	0.1	12.5	1.8	3.6
Viet Nam	…	…	…	2.0	1.0	1.6	0.8	2.9	-2.0
The Pacific									
Cook Islands	…	…	…	…	…	…	…	…	…
Fiji	-5.6	2.3 (2006)	7.6	5.2	-2.8	8.9	2.1	1.5	6.1
Kiribati	…	…	…	…	…	…	…	…	…
Marshall Islands	…	…	…	…	…	…	…	…	…
Micronesia, Federated States of	…	…	…	…	…	…	…	…	…
Nauru	…	…	…	…	…	…	…	…	…
Niue	…	…	…	…	…	…	…	…	…
Palau	…	…	…	…	…	…	…	…	…
Papua New Guinea	…	…	…	…	…	…	…	…	…
Samoa[a]	2.8	–	15.2	3.2	…	…	…	…	…
Solomon Islands	…	…	…	…	…	…	…	…	…
Timor-Leste	…	…	…	…	…	…	…	…	…
Tonga	…	…	…	…	…	…	…	…	…
Tuvalu	…	…	…	…	…	…	…	…	…
Vanuatu	…	…	…	…	…	…	…	…	…
Developed ADB Member Economies									
Australia	1.3	-1.0	0.5	-3.2	-1.1	-1.6	-2.2	-1.0	3.1
Japan	5.7	1.3	15.6	-0.8	1.9	-1.1	–	3.1	1.1
New Zealand	3.5	0.3	3.7	0.5	3.1	1.6	1.3	2.3	0.8

… = data not available, – = magnitude equals zero, ADB = Asian Development Bank.

a   Refers to volume indices of industrial production.

Sources: Economy sources.

III. Money, Finance, and Prices

Money, Finance, and Prices summarizes the latest statistics on consumer price inflation, the money supply, and nonperforming loans. Other monetary and financial statistics include producer price inflation, interest rates, bank lending, official exchange rates, and stock market capitalization and growth rates.

Inflation accelerated in 25 economies and decelerated in 22 economies in 2018.

In 25 of 47 economies across Asia and the Pacific with available data, consumer price inflation accelerated from 2017 to 2018, while in 22 economies it decelerated (Figure 2.3.1). Rising oil prices and falling exchange rates contributed to an acceleration in inflation among some developing member economies (ADB 2019). The largest inflation gains from 2017 to 2018 occurred in Turkmenistan (5.5 percentage points), Niue (5.1 percentage points), Uzbekistan (3.7 percentage points), and Solomon Islands (3.0 percentage points). In Turkmenistan, subsidy cuts fueled inflation at the same time as foreign exchange pressures drove up prices for imported goods (ADB 2019). In Uzbekistan, inflation reflected the ongoing impact of foreign exchange liberalization, utility price increases, the removal of price controls for bread and other basic goods, higher wages and pensions, and rapid credit growth (ADB 2019). The increase observed in Solomon Islands was driven by a reversal in the consumer price index (CPI) for food and nonalcoholic beverages, from −0.7% in 2017 to 1.9% in 2018.

The largest decreases in inflation from 2017 to 2018 were observed in Azerbaijan (−10.6 percentage points), Afghanistan (−7.0 percentage points), and Nauru (−4.0 percentage points). In Azerbaijan, a decline of 15.2 percentage points in the CPI for

Figure 2.3.1: Inflation Rates in Select Economies of Asia and the Pacific
(% annual change)

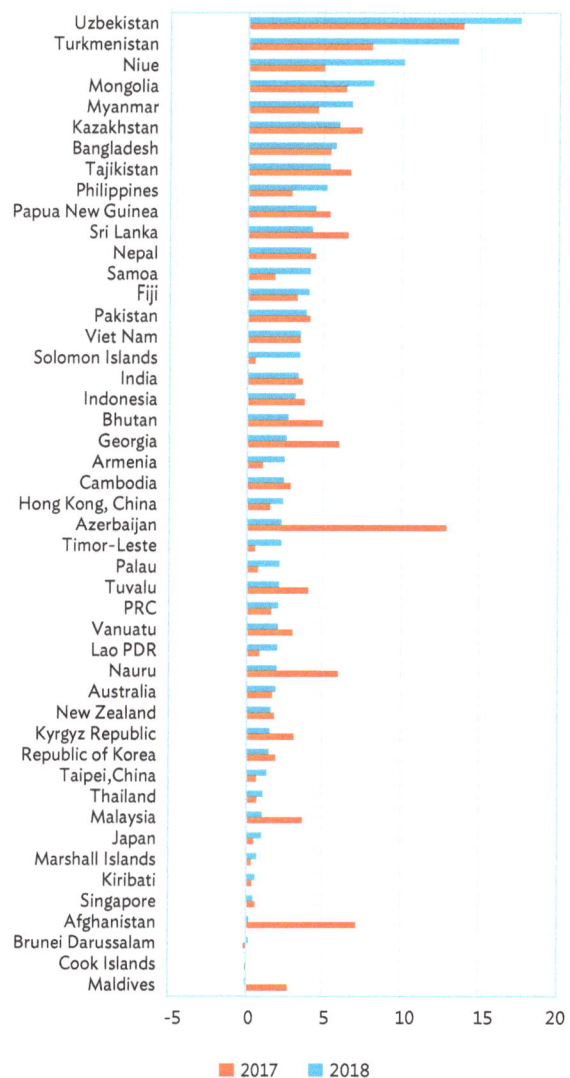

Lao PDR = Lao People's Democratic Republic, PRC = People's Republic of China.
Note: This chart includes economies with available data for both 2017 and 2018.
Source: Table 2.3.1, Key Indicators for Asia and the Pacific 2019.

food and nonalcoholic beverages lowered consumer price inflation from 12.9% in 2017 to 2.3% in 2018. In Afghanistan, the CPI for food and nonalcoholic beverages fell by 11.6 percentage points, leading to a drop in overall inflation from 7.2% in 2017 to 0.2% in 2018.

Banks' balance sheets bounce back from the global financial crisis

The global financial crisis of 2007–2008 strained the financial systems of many economies in Asia and the Pacific. During and after the crisis, the value of nonperforming bank loans—as well as the percentage of nonperforming loans as a share of total gross loans—rose across the region before gradually recovering in subsequent years.

From 2010 to 2017, the percentage of nonperforming loans as a share of total gross loans fell in 22 of the 31 economies with available data (Figure 2.3.2). The biggest improvements were seen in Afghanistan (–37.7 percentage points), Kazakhstan (–11.6 percentage points), and Maldives (–10.5 percentage points).

The largest increases from 2010 to 2017 were observed in Tajikistan (12.9 percentage points), Vanuatu (10.3 percentage points), and India (7.3 percentage points).

Data Issues and Comparability

Not all reporting economies meet the standards and classifications of the International Monetary Fund (IMF) on the compilation of monetary and financial statistics available on the fund's Dissemination Standards Bulletin Board. [3]

CPI coverage differs across economies. Most economies try to follow the Classification of Individual Consumption by Purpose guidelines, but the implementation varies across economies. In some instances, the basket of goods and services in the index is outdated or represents only urban areas (or the capital city). Other price measurements, such as the wholesale price index and the producer price index, are not available in Pacific economies.

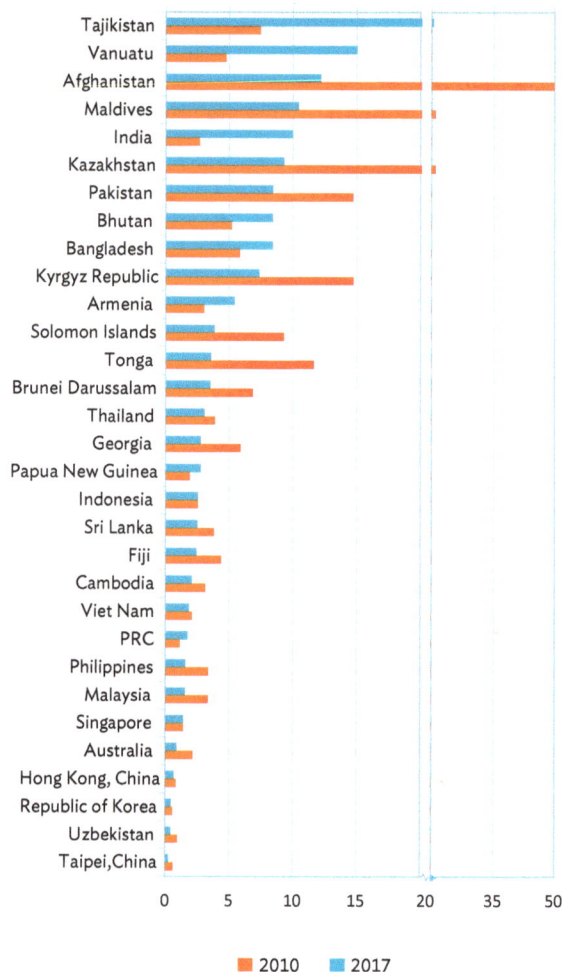

Figure 2.3.2: Nonperforming Bank Loans in Select Economies of Asia and the Pacific
(% of total gross loans)

PRC = People's Republic of China

Note: This chart includes economies with available data for both 2010 and 2017. For 2010, data included are for 2010 to 2012. For 2017, data included are for 2015 to 2017.

Source: Table 2.3.9, Key Indicators for Asia and the Pacific 2019.

---

[3]   For more information on the IMF's standards and classifications on the compilation of monetary and financial statistics, go to http://dsbb.imf.org/Pages/SDDS/StatMethod.aspx.

Broad money supply in most economies relates to M2, which includes cash, checking deposits, savings deposits, money market securities, mutual funds, and other time deposits. However, 12 of the 44 economies with available data reported M3, thereby posing limits to comparability as M3 also includes less liquid financial assets. Not all economies publish the same types of aggregates, and, even when aggregates have the same name (i.e., M1, M2, M3, etc.), their asset composition often differs significantly. For example, the definition of M2 in one economy may include time deposits with maturities of 1 year or less, whereas another economy's M2 definition may include time deposits with maturities of 2 years or less.

Finally, some economies use the central bank policy rate, while others use commercial bank rates in measuring banks' average deposit and lending rates.

Table 2.3.1: Growth Rates of Consumer Price Index[a]
(%)

ADB Regional Member	2000	2005	2010	2013	2014	2015	2016	2017	2018
Developing ADB Member Economies									
Central and West Asia									
Afghanistan	...	11.9	-4.5	6.4	5.6	-0.6	4.0	7.2	0.2
Armenia	-0.8	0.6	8.2	5.8	3.0	3.7	-1.4	1.0	2.5
Azerbaijan	1.8	9.6	5.7	2.4	1.4	4.0	12.4	12.9	2.3
Georgia	4.0	8.2	7.1	-0.5	3.1	4.0	2.1	6.0	2.6
Kazakhstan	13.2	7.6	7.1	5.8	6.7	6.6	14.6	7.4	6.0
Kyrgyz Republic	18.7	4.3	8.0	6.6	7.5	6.5	0.4	3.2	1.5
Pakistan	3.6	9.3	10.1	7.4	8.6	4.5	2.9	4.2	3.9
Tajikistan	60.6	7.1	9.8	3.7	7.4	5.1	6.1	6.7	5.4
Turkmenistan	8.0	10.7	4.4	6.8	6.0	7.4	3.6	8.0	13.6
Uzbekistan[b]	24.9	6.4	7.6	7.0	6.4	5.5	9.5	13.9	17.5
East Asia									
China, People's Republic of	0.4	1.8	3.3	2.6	2.0	1.4	2.0	1.6	2.1
Hong Kong, China	-3.7	0.8	2.3	4.3	4.4	3.0	2.4	1.5	2.4
Korea, Republic of	2.3	2.8	2.9	1.3	1.3	0.7	1.0	1.9	1.5
Mongolia	8.0 (2001)	9.5	12.9	12.5	11.0	1.9	1.3	6.4	8.1
Taipei,China	1.3	2.3	1.0	0.8	1.2	-0.3	1.4	0.6	1.4
South Asia									
Bangladesh	2.8	6.5	6.8	6.8	7.3	6.4	5.9	5.4	5.8
Bhutan	4.0	5.3	7.0	8.8	8.3	4.5	3.2	5.0	2.7
India	3.7	4.2	10.4	12.2	5.8	4.9	4.6	3.7	3.4
Maldives	-1.2	1.3	6.1	3.8	2.1	1.0	0.5	2.8	-0.1
Nepal	3.4	4.6	9.5	9.9	9.1	7.2	9.9	4.5	4.2
Sri Lanka[c]	6.2	11.0	6.2	6.9	5.1	2.2	4.0	6.5	4.3
Southeast Asia									
Brunei Darussalam	1.2	1.1	0.4	0.4	-0.2	-0.4	-0.7	-0.2	0.1
Cambodia[c]	-0.8	5.8	4.0	2.9	3.9	1.2	3.0	2.9	2.5
Indonesia[d]	3.8	10.5	5.1	7.0	6.4	6.4	3.5	3.8	3.2
Lao People's Democratic Republic	23.2	7.2	6.0	6.4	4.1	1.3	1.6	0.8	2.0
Malaysia	1.5	2.9	1.7	2.1	3.2	2.1	2.1	3.7	1.0
Myanmar	-0.2	9.4	7.7	8.9	5.0	9.5	6.9	4.6	6.8
Philippines	6.7	6.5	3.8	2.6	3.6	0.7	1.3	2.9	5.2
Singapore	1.3	0.5	2.8	2.4	1.0	-0.5	-0.5	0.6	0.4
Thailand	1.6	4.4	3.3	2.2	1.9	-0.9	0.2	0.7	1.1
Viet Nam	-0.3 (2001)	8.3	9.2	6.6	4.8	0.6	2.7	3.5	3.5
The Pacific									
Cook Islands	3.2	2.5	-0.3	1.9	2.1	1.9	-0.3	-0.1	0.0
Fiji	1.1	2.5 (2006)	3.7	2.9	0.6	1.4	3.9	3.3	4.1
Kiribati[c]	0.4	-0.3	-3.0	-1.5	2.1	0.6	1.9	0.4	0.6
Marshall Islands[c]	0.9	3.5	1.8	1.9	1.1	-2.2	-1.5	0.3	0.7
Micronesia, Federated States of	1.8	4.1	3.6	2.1	0.7	0.0	-1.0	0.2	...
Nauru	2.3	9.8	-3.1	4.1	0.3	9.8	8.2	6.0	2.0
Niue	...	0.8	5.3	-1.2	0.4	1.8	1.3	5.0	10.1
Palau	-1.8 (2001)	3.9	1.4	3.4	4.2	0.9	-1.0	0.7	2.2
Papua New Guinea	15.6	1.8	4.4 (2011)	5.0	5.2	6.0	6.7	5.4	4.5
Samoa	0.9	1.9	0.8	0.6	-0.4	0.7	1.3	1.8	4.2
Solomon Islands[c]	7.1	7.2	0.9	5.4	5.2	-0.6	0.5	0.5	3.5
Timor-Leste	...	1.6	5.2	9.5	0.8	0.6	-1.5	0.5	2.3
Tonga	6.3	8.7	3.5	0.8	2.5	-1.1	2.6	7.4	...
Tuvalu	3.9	3.2	-1.9	2.0	1.1	3.2	3.5	4.1	2.2
Vanuatu	2.5	0.8	2.8	1.5	0.8	2.5	0.8	3.1	2.1
Developed ADB Member Economies									
Australia	2.4	2.4	2.3	2.3	2.7	1.7	1.4	1.7	1.9
Japan	-0.7	-0.3	-0.7	0.3	2.8	0.8	-0.1	0.5	1.0
New Zealand	2.6	3.0	2.3	1.1	1.2	0.3	0.6	1.9	1.6

... = data not available, 0.0 = magnitude is less than half of unit employed, ADB = Asian Development Bank.

a Data refer to the whole economy, unless otherwise indicated.
b Prior to 2016, values were calculated based on variable weights. For 2016 onward, values are calculated based on fixed weights.
c Data refer to capital city.
d For 2000–2002, consumer price index data refer to the consumer price indexes for 43 cities; for 2003–2007, 45 cities; for 2008–2013, 66 cities; and for 2014–2018, 82 cities.

Source: Economy sources.

Table 2.3.2: Growth Rates of Food and Nonalcoholic Beverages Consumer Price Index[a]
(%)

ADB Regional Member	2000	2005	2010	2013	2014	2015	2016	2017	2018
Developing ADB Member Economies									
Central and West Asia									
Afghanistan	...	9.1	-9.1	5.2	10.0	-0.6	4.9	10.0	-1.6
Armenia	-5.9	0.8	9.4	5.8	1.7	3.1	-3.3	4.1	2.3
Azerbaijan	...	12.4 (2006)	7.5	2.0	0.7	4.8	13.7	17.2	2.0
Georgia	...	8.9	11.7	-0.7	5.1	4.2	1.6	6.8	2.2
Kazakhstan	16.4	8.8	5.9	4.0	5.8	5.7	12.9	8.5	4.7
Kyrgyz Republic[b]	18.5	7.0	6.5	5.3	8.2	3.7	-6.5	2.5	-2.2
Pakistan[c]	2.5 (2002)	12.5	12.6	6.7	8.6	2.6	1.0	3.3	2.8
Tajikistan	...	...	...	3.1	10.0	3.8	6.5	7.8	4.9
Turkmenistan	...	...	...	...	...	...	...	...	...
Uzbekistan	30.0	4.3	4.9	4.8	3.7	2.7	7.9	18.1	20.1
East Asia									
China, People's Republic of[d]	-2.6	2.9	7.2	4.7	3.1	2.3	4.6	-1.4	1.8
Hong Kong, China	...	2.4 (2006)	3.5	4.3	3.6	3.3	3.6	1.1	4.3
Korea, Republic of	0.8	3.1	6.4	0.9	0.3	1.6	2.3	3.4	2.8
Mongolia	8.8 (2001)	15.6	18.6	13.3	6.6	-4.8	1.7	7.3	9.1
Taipei,China	0.2	10.3	1.1	1.1	4.0	3.9	7.9	-1.8	0.6
South Asia									
Bangladesh[e]	...	...	7.7 (2012)	5.2	8.6	6.7	4.9	6.0	7.1
Bhutan	...	5.3	9.4	8.1	10.1	3.3	4.0	7.5	4.9
India	...	...	...	...	6.1	4.7	4.4	1.9	0.4
Maldives[f]	-4.8	7.8	7.5	7.2	0.7	0.5	0.6	5.6	-1.1
Nepal[g]	0.6	3.8	15.3	9.5	11.6	9.6	10.9	1.9	2.7
Sri Lanka[h]	4.5	11.4	6.9	7.9	4.3	5.5	6.1	9.2	3.4
Southeast Asia									
Brunei Darussalam	...	...	-0.0 (2011)	0.1	-0.2	0.8	-0.9	0.3	1.9
Cambodia[h]	...	...	4.3	3.9	4.9	4.0	5.6	3.4	2.5
Indonesia[i]	-4.8	10.0	9.4	12.0	...	7.2	7.2	2.1	4.2
Lao People's Democratic Republic	...	...	5.6 (2012)	12.6	6.9	4.5	4.3	-0.1	1.2
Malaysia	2.1	3.7	2.5	3.6	3.3	3.6	3.8	3.9	1.7
Myanmar	...	18.7 (2007)	7.4	6.8	6.9	13.1	9.2	4.4	6.6
Philippines	3.7 (2001)	6.4	4.0	2.5	5.9	1.8	1.6	3.0	6.8
Singapore	0.5	2.0	2.3	2.3	3.0	1.2	2.3	1.3	1.3
Thailand	-1.1	4.8	5.4	3.4	3.9	1.1	1.6	–	0.4
Viet Nam	-1.3 (2001)	11.2	10.7	2.7	4.0	1.5	2.5	-1.1	3.2
The Pacific									
Cook Islands[h, j]	3.4	1.1	2.9	2.6	3.3	-0.1	1.3	0.3	0.5
Fiji	-3.2	1.8 (2006)	4.1	3.5	1.9	4.7	6.0	-2.1	3.4
Kiribati[k]	...	6.1 (2007)	-4.6	-3.5	0.6	-0.6	1.7	1.8	-1.1
Marshall Islands[h, l]	-0.8	0.3	-1.5	2.6	2.0	2.3	-1.4	-0.3	1.5
Micronesia, Federated States of	1.1	3.4	2.2	2.6	0.8	0.8	-1.2	-1.6	...
Nauru	...	...	0.4	...	...	...	...	...	...
Niue[m]	...	1.1	8.2	-0.5	–	2.7	-0.2	3.4	0.6
Palau	-2.4 (2001)	-1.5	1.8	3.2	1.5	1.7	-3.0	1.6	3.9
Papua New Guinea	13.6	3.5	-1.0 (2011)	-0.9	4.8	4.9	5.1	2.8	0.8
Samoa	...	0.2	-6.6	0.7	-3.4	3.3	5.9	1.4	5.6
Solomon Islands[h, n]	...	...	-2.6	2.6	3.1	-2.8	0.5	-0.7	1.9
Timor-Leste	...	–	6.4	12.0	0.7	0.3	-2.1	0.9	1.7
Tonga	0.4	6.0	3.0	1.8	3.7	1.9	1.3	8.6	...
Tuvalu	1.1	5.5	-5.9	0.1	0.6	4.0	3.4	4.5	3.3
Vanuatu	2.0	0.5	4.5	1.5	1.7	3.6	2.3	6.8	3.5
Developed ADB Member Economies									
Australia[o]	2.1	1.6	1.6	0.5	1.3	2.1	0.1	1.8	-0.0
Japan	-2.4	-1.3	-0.3	-0.2	4.3	3.6	2.1	0.7	1.6
New Zealand	1.5	1.2	1.0	0.4	0.3	–	-0.6	2.1	-0.2

... = data not available, – = magnitude equals zero, -0.0 or 0.0 = magnitude is less than half of unit employed, ADB = Asian Development Bank.

a Data refer to the whole economy, unless otherwise indicated.
b For 2000–2002, refers to food and drinks, which includes alcoholic beverages.
c For 2002–2008, growth rates were calculated using price indexes for food, nonalcoholic beverages, alcoholic beverages, tobacco, and narcotics. For 2009 onward, growth rates were calculated using price indexes for food and nonalcoholic beverages only.
d For 2016 onward, excludes nonalcoholic beverages.
e Refers to food, nonalcoholic and alcoholic beverages, and tobacco.
f Prior to 2012, national and capital city consumer price indexes have the same values because the series for Maldives was linked to a previously published series for Malé. From June 2012 onward, national and capital city consumer price indexes have been compiled separately. Refers to food (including fish) and nonalcoholic beverages. Prior to 2004, also includes tobacco and narcotics.
g Refers to food and beverages. Includes nonalcoholic and alcoholic beverages.
h Refers to capital city.
i Consumer price index (CPI) data of Indonesia for 2000–2002 refer to CPI for 43 cities; for 2003–2007, 45 cities; for 2008–2013, 66 cities; and for 2014–2018, 82 cities. Refers to Indonesia's CPI group "Foodstuff" consisting of cereals, cassava, and related products; meat and related products; fresh fish; preserved fish; eggs, milk, and related products; vegetables; beans and nuts; fruits; spices; fats and oils; and other food items. The group does not include nonalcoholic and alcoholic beverages.
j Refers to fruits and vegetables; meat, poultry and fish; cereal products; soft drink and sweets; farm products, fats and oils; other food; and prepared food.
k For 2006 onward, refers to the Tarawa Retail Price Index. The index is collected data on South Tarawa, which represents data for all of Kiribati. Data refer to the weighted average of food and nonalcoholic drinks price indexes.
l Refers to food.
m For 2003–2011, data refers to food.
n For 2008–2017, excludes nonalcoholic beverages.
o Includes restaurant meals and take away and fast foods.

Source: Economy sources.

Table 2.3.3:   Growth Rates of Wholesale and/or Producer Price Indexes
(%)

ADB Regional Member	2000	2005	2010	2013	2014	2015	2016	2017	2018
Developing ADB Member Economies									
Central and West Asia									
Afghanistan	...	...	...	...	...	...	...	...	...
Armenia	0.8	7.7	22.6	4.7	8.5	-0.8	1.5	3.9	1.6
Azerbaijan	3.3 (2001)	17.3	30.5	-3.9	-5.1	-30.6	27.5	36.8	26.0
Georgia	5.8	7.5	11.3	-2.0	2.9	7.5	-0.1	11.0	6.1
Kazakhstan	38.0	23.7	25.2	-0.3	9.5	-20.5	16.8	15.3	19.0
Kyrgyz Republic	29.6	2.8	22.8	-2.1	1.5	8.8	6.4	1.7	1.5
Pakistan	1.8	6.8	13.8	7.4	8.2	-0.3	-1.0	4.0	3.5
Tajikistan	39.2	10.4	27.2	2.1	4.7	3.0	14.7	1.6	1.8
Turkmenistan	...	...	...	...	...	...	...	...	...
Uzbekistan	60.9	25.6	15.6	11.7	13.6	13.5	14.8	17.5	31.8
East Asia									
China, People's Republic of	2.8	4.9	5.5	-1.9	-1.9	-5.2	-1.4	6.3	3.5
Hong Kong, China	0.2	0.8	6.0	-3.1	-1.7	-2.7	1.3	3.8	2.0
Korea, Republic of	2.1	2.1	3.8	-1.6	-0.5	-4.0	-1.8	3.5	1.9
Mongolia	...	...	...	...	...	...	11.3	17.5	-8.1
Taipei,China	1.8	0.6	5.5	-2.4	-0.6	-8.9	-3.0	0.9	3.6
South Asia									
Bangladesh[a]	-0.4	3.4							
Bhutan	...	...	5.8 (2012)	2.7	3.0	0.6	1.2	5.8	4.7
India	7.2	4.5	9.6	5.2	1.3	-3.7	1.7	2.9	4.3
Maldives	-2.4 (2002)	4.6	3.9	0.3	2.1	-2.4	...	...	...
Nepal	1.3 (2001)	7.4	12.2	9.0	8.3	6.1	6.3	2.7	1.7
Sri Lanka	1.7	11.5	2.6	9.2	3.2	1.0	4.2	7.4	3.4
Southeast Asia									
Brunei Darussalam	...	...	...	...	...	...	...	...	...
Cambodia	...	...	...	...	...	...	...	...	...
Indonesia[b]	12.5	15.3	4.9	-1.6	5.4	4.4	7.9	4.6	5.5
Lao People's Democratic Republic	...	...	...	...	...	...	...	...	...
Malaysia	-1.8 (2001)	3.8 (2006)	12.3 (2011)	-2.7	1.5	-7.4	-1.1	6.7	-1.1
Myanmar	...	...	...	...	...	...	...	...	...
Philippines	5.8	11.4	5.9	1.6	2.7	-3.9	1.2	4.4	7.0
Singapore	10.0	9.6	4.7	-2.7	-3.3	-15.3	-6.9	7.0	6.3
Thailand	3.9	9.1	9.4	0.3	0.1	-4.1	-1.2	0.7	0.4
Viet Nam	-0.2	4.4	12.6	5.3	3.3	-0.6	-0.6	2.8	3.1
The Pacific									
Cook Islands	...	...	...	...	...	...	...	...	...
Fiji	...	...	...	...	...	...	...	...	...
Kiribati	...	...	...	...	...	...	...	...	...
Marshall Islands	...	...	...	...	...	...	...	...	...
Micronesia, Federated States of	...	...	...	...	...	...	...	...	...
Nauru	...	...	...	...	...	...	...	...	...
Niue	...	...	...	...	...	...	...	...	...
Palau	...	...	...	...	...	...	...	...	...
Papua New Guinea	...	...	...	...	...	...	...	...	...
Samoa	...	...	...	...	...	...	...	...	...
Solomon Islands	...	...	...	...	...	...	...	...	...
Timor-Leste	...	...	...	...	...	...	...	...	...
Tonga	...	...	...	...	...	...	...	...	...
Tuvalu	...	...	...	...	...	...	...	...	...
Vanuatu	...	...	...	...	...	...	...	...	...
Developed ADB Member Economies									
Australia	2.6	3.6	-0.1	1.2	2.1	1.0	1.5	1.0	1.6
Japan	0.0	1.6	-0.1	1.3	1.1	-3.0	-3.5	2.3	2.6
New Zealand	5.2	3.4	2.3	2.2	1.1	-1.3	0.8	4.8	3.4

... = data not available, 0.0 = magnitude is less than half of unit employed, ADB = Asian Development Bank.

a   For agricultural and industrial products only.
b   For 2013, change of the wholesale price index was estimated by rebasing January–October 2013 and 2012 data to 2005.

Source: Economy sources.

Table 2.3.4:   Growth Rates of Gross Domestic Product Deflator
(%)

ADB Regional Member	2000	2005	2010	2013	2014	2015	2016	2017	2018
Developing ADB Member Economies									
Central and West Asia									
Afghanistan	...	11.6	14.3	3.5	-1.0	5.1	5.2	-0.5	2.7
Armenia	-1.4	3.2	7.8	3.4	2.3	1.2	0.3	2.1	2.5
Azerbaijan	12.5	16.1	13.6	0.4	-1.3	-8.9	14.7	16.2	11.9
Georgia	4.7	7.9	8.5	-0.8	3.8	5.9	4.2	6.1	3.6
Kazakhstan	17.4	17.9	19.6	9.5	5.8	1.9	13.6	8.6	6.4
Kyrgyz Republic	27.2	7.1	10.0	3.2	8.4	3.4	6.1	6.3	1.5
Pakistan	5.3 (2001)	7.8	10.9	7.0	7.4	4.1	0.4	4.0	2.1
Tajikistan	22.7	9.5	12.4	4.3	5.5	0.2	5.2	4.9	...
Turkmenistan	21.3	7.0	2.3	1.2	0.6	-4.9	-5.0	-1.6	7.8
Uzbekistan	47.1	21.4	18.9	11.7	14.3	10.4	8.7	19.4	28.1
East Asia									
China, People's Republic of	2.0	3.8	6.7	2.2	0.8	0.1	1.1	...	...
Hong Kong, China	-3.4	-0.2	0.3	1.8	2.9	3.6	1.6	3.0	3.6
Korea, Republic of	3.5 (2001)	1.0	2.7	1.0	0.9	3.2	2.0	2.2	0.5
Mongolia	12.0	20.1	15.1 (2011)	2.9	7.4	1.7	2.2	10.6	8.7
Taipei,China	7.6	-1.5	-1.5	1.5	1.7	3.3	0.9	-1.2	-1.0
South Asia									
Bangladesh	1.9	5.1	7.1	7.2	5.7	5.9	6.7	6.3	5.6
Bhutan	3.7	5.9	6.0	5.9	7.3	3.6	4.5	5.5	...
India	3.6	4.2	9.0	6.2	3.3	2.1	3.5	3.1	4.7
Maldives	36.7 (2001)	9.2	2.9	6.4	4.6	7.9	0.1	3.2	...
Nepal	4.6	5.8	14.4	6.1	9.0	5.1	5.0	9.1	5.4
Sri Lanka	6.7	10.4	7.3	6.2	2.9	0.6	4.8	8.2	4.3
Southeast Asia									
Brunei Darussalam	29.0	18.8	5.3	-2.8	-1.8	-17.6	-9.2	5.0	9.2
Cambodia	-4.9	6.1	3.1	0.8	2.6	1.7	3.4	3.3	3.1
Indonesia	9.6	14.3	8.2	5.0	5.4	4.0	2.4	4.2	3.8
Lao People's Democratic Republic	21.8	7.8	3.1	6.5	5.7	2.3	3.0	1.8	2.0
Malaysia	-1.6 (2001)	4.0 (2006)	5.4 (2011)	0.2	2.5	-0.4	1.7	3.8	0.7
Myanmar	2.5	19.2	7.0	4.4	4.2	4.1	3.6	6.3	...
Philippines	5.7	5.8	4.2	2.0	3.2	-0.6	1.7	2.3	3.8
Singapore	3.9	1.9	1.1	-0.4	-0.3	3.2	0.8	2.6	1.8
Thailand	1.3	5.1	4.1	1.8	1.4	0.9	2.4	2.3	1.0
Viet Nam	3.4	9.0	12.1	4.8	3.7	-0.2	1.1	4.1	3.4
The Pacific									
Cook Islands	2.2	-2.6	1.9	-5.0	3.6	6.4	-2.1	-0.2	4.2
Fiji	-2.4	3.1 (2006)	2.5	2.3	4.1	3.7	4.9	0.1	...
Kiribati	3.2	5.5	1.2	0.1	4.1	2.9	7.3	-4.9	...
Marshall Islands	-2.9	2.0	1.5	0.3	-3.0	-1.4	7.1	0.5	...
Micronesia, Federated States of	1.1	2.1	3.8	0.8	2.8	-5.5	4.7	6.9	...
Nauru	...	-6.9	-18.2	-21.7	-11.8	-8.3	5.7	3.6	1.2
Niue	...	0.5	7.6	4.0	1.6	-0.3	0.5	1.9	11.2
Palau	0.8 (2001)	7.5	-0.2	7.3	4.3	4.8	6.2	-1.1	-2.5
Papua New Guinea	13.1	7.9	9.9	3.6	5.4	-3.9	3.9	8.3	8.6
Samoa	1.1	5.1	-0.0	1.2	0.5	3.7	0.9	0.6	1.7
Solomon Islands	6.9	8.8	1.8	6.8	1.9	4.0	2.9	...	...
Timor-Leste	7.8 (2001)	23.8	26.5	-4.8	-3.2	-36.6	-19.6	9.4	...
Tonga	7.4	6.7	3.7	0.8	0.9	1.4	1.7	3.0	...
Tuvalu	6.1 (2001)	0.7	2.5	2.0	4.9	4.6	7.7	1.7	...
Vanuatu	2.4	0.4	2.6	2.7	2.0	4.5	1.8	4.2	...
Developed ADB Member Economies									
Australia	2.5	3.7	1.1	-0.1	1.5	-0.7	-0.5	3.7	1.8
Japan	-1.4	-1.0	-1.9	-0.3	1.7	2.1	0.3	-0.2	-0.1
New Zealand	3.5	2.1	3.7	4.9	0.5	0.7	2.4	2.8	1.1

... = data not available; 0.0 = magnitude is less than half of unit employed, ADB = Asian Development Bank.

Source: Economy sources.

Money and Finance

Table 2.3.5:   Growth Rates of Money Supply[a]
(%)

ADB Regional Member	2000	2005	2010	2013	2014	2015	2016	2017	2018
Developing ADB Member Economies									
Central and West Asia									
Afghanistan	...	38.3 (2006)	39.3	7.1	6.0	3.7	5.5	10.4	2.6
Armenia	38.6	27.8	11.8	14.8	8.3	10.8	17.5	18.5	7.4
Azerbaijan[b]	21.8	22.3	24.3	15.0	11.8	-1.3	-1.9	9.0	5.7
Georgia[b]	39.2	27.9	30.1	24.5	13.8	19.3	20.2	14.8	14.7
Kazakhstan[b]	45.0	25.2	13.3	10.2	10.4	33.8	15.6	-1.7	7.0
Kyrgyz Republic	12.1	9.9	21.1	22.8	3.0	14.9	14.6	17.9	5.5
Pakistan	9.4	19.8	13.0	16.9	12.6	12.8	14.5	13.9	9.5
Tajikistan	43.3	62.9	17.6	18.6	3.5	12.2	56.7	36.6	10.0
Turkmenistan[b]	94.6	5.6	74.2	26.0	10.0	18.0	...	...	...
Uzbekistan	37.1	54.4	52.4	23.0	14.9	25.2	23.5	40.2	14.4
East Asia									
China, People's Republic of	12.3	16.5	19.7	13.6	11.0	13.3	11.3	9.0	8.1
Hong Kong, China	7.8	5.1	8.1	12.4	9.5	5.5	7.7	10.0	4.3
Korea, Republic of	5.2	7.0	6.0	4.6	8.1	8.2	7.1	5.1	6.7
Mongolia	17.6	34.6	62.5	24.2	12.5	-5.5	21.0	30.5	22.8
Taipei,China	6.5	6.6	5.5	5.8	6.1	5.8	3.6	3.6	2.7
South Asia									
Bangladesh	18.6	16.7	22.4	16.7	16.1	12.4	16.3	10.9	9.2
Bhutan	16.1	13.2	16.5	3.3	26.0	3.8	23.0	17.4	6.5
India[b]	16.8	21.1	16.1	13.4	10.9	10.1	10.1	9.2	10.5
Maldives	4.2	10.6	14.6	18.4	14.9	12.1	-0.2	5.2	3.4
Nepal	21.8	8.3	14.1	16.4	19.1	19.9	19.5	15.5	19.4
Sri Lanka	13.0	19.6	18.0	18.0	13.1	17.2	18.9	17.5	13.5
Southeast Asia									
Brunei Darussalam	1.9 (2002)	-4.5	4.8	1.5	3.2	-1.8	1.5	-0.4	2.8
Cambodia	26.9	16.1	20.0	14.6	30.0	14.7	17.9	23.8	24.0
Indonesia	15.6	16.3	15.4	12.8	11.9	9.0	10.0	8.3	6.3
Lao People's Democratic Republic	45.9	8.2	39.5	17.0	25.2	14.7	10.9	12.2	8.4
Malaysia[b]	5.1	8.3	6.8	7.3	7.3	3.0	3.2	4.9	8.0
Myanmar	42.2	27.3	42.5	31.4	21.0	30.7	17.4	20.5	14.6
Philippines[b]	4.6	16.8	10.0	31.8	11.2	9.4	12.8	11.9	9.5
Singapore	-2.0	6.2	8.6	4.3	3.3	1.5	8.0	3.2	3.9
Thailand	4.0	6.1	10.9	7.3	4.7	4.4	4.2	5.0	4.7
Viet Nam	56.2	29.7	33.3	18.8	17.7	16.2	18.4	15.0	12.4
The Pacific									
Cook Islands	12.2 (2001)	-0.9	0.1	-18.3	-1.0	9.5	0.1	6.4	9.9
Fiji[b]	-2.1	15.2	3.5	19.0	10.1	14.3	4.8	8.2	...
Kiribati	...	...	...	...	...	...	...	...	...
Marshall Islands	16.6	-0.8	9.4	6.8	31.0	28.6	19.9	27.8	...
Micronesia, Federated States of	...	...	...	...	...	...	...	...	...
Nauru	...	...	...	...	...	...	...	...	...
Niue	...	...	...	...	...	...	...	...	...
Palau	...	...	0.6	8.8	27.0	29.4	14.5	...	...
Papua New Guinea[b]	5.4	29.5	11.4	6.7	3.4	8.0	10.9	-0.7	-4.0
Samoa	16.4	15.6	6.4	6.4	9.6	6.0	9.2	15.2	8.8
Solomon Islands[b]	0.4	46.1	13.3	12.4	5.1	15.5	13.4	3.5	6.8
Timor-Leste	155.5 (2001)	17.6	18.2	22.9	19.9	7.1	14.2	12.1	3.1
Tonga	8.3	12.1	5.1	5.2	7.3	9.3	16.7	13.7	7.6
Tuvalu	...	...	...	...	...	...	...	...	...
Vanuatu	5.5	11.6	-6.0	-5.6	8.5	11.4	10.7	9.3	...
Developed ADB Member Economies									
Australia[b]	7.3	8.9	4.5	6.5	7.0	6.7	5.8	7.8	1.9
Japan[c]	1.9	0.4	1.9	3.4	2.8	2.5	3.2	2.9	2.2
New Zealand[d]	6.6	7.8	3.2	5.0	6.3	8.1	7.7	7.3	6.4

... = data not available, ADB = Asian Development Bank.

a Data are based on money supply M2 (M2), unless otherwise stated.
b Refers to money supply M3 (M3).
c Refers to M3, except for 2000 (M2).
d Refers to M3, except for 2016–2018 (M2).

Source: Economy sources.

Table 2.3.6:   Money Supply[a]
(% of GDP)

ADB Regional Member	2000	2005	2010	2013	2014	2015	2016	2017	2018
Developing ADB Member Economies									
Central and West Asia									
Afghanistan	11.0 (2002)	17.9	30.3	28.5	29.6	29.7	28.8	29.8	32.9
Armenia	14.7	16.3	26.3	33.9	34.7	36.8	43.0	46.4	46.2
Azerbaijan[b]	10.8	14.7	24.8	33.2	36.5	39.1	34.6	32.4	30.2
Georgia[b]	10.1	16.9	29.9	36.6	38.4	42.0	47.2	48.7	51.4
Kazakhstan[b]	15.3	27.2	38.9	32.2	32.3	41.9	42.2	36.6	35.4
Kyrgyz Republic	11.3	21.1	31.4	34.0	31.1	33.3	34.4	36.5	36.6
Pakistan	33.0	41.6	37.8	38.8	38.9	40.2	43.5	45.0	45.8
Tajikistan	5.8	11.2	12.0	13.9	12.8	13.5	18.8	22.9	22.3
Turkmenistan[b]	19.4	10.5	17.3	41.7	41.4	48.2	...	...	...
Uzbekistan	12.2	14.4	18.9	20.3	19.1	20.1	21.5	24.2	20.5
East Asia									
China, People's Republic of	134.2	158.0	176.1	186.6	191.6	203.0	209.5	205.9	202.9
Hong Kong, China	272.9	310.1	401.7	470.3	487.2	484.4	502.2	516.6	504.3
Korea, Republic of	108.6	106.7	125.5	128.0	132.9	135.5	138.3	137.8	142.6
Mongolia	21.1	37.5	48.0	49.3	47.8	43.4	50.8	56.9	60.5
Taipei,China	182.6	201.9	219.2	233.2	234.0	237.8	240.5	244.4	247.0
South Asia									
Bangladesh	31.5	40.9	45.5	50.3	52.1	52.0	52.9	51.4	49.3
Bhutan	50.8	57.8	70.5	55.2	61.4	57.7	63.0	65.6	71.2
India[b]	60.3	73.6	83.6	84.7	84.6	84.4	83.3	81.7	81.0
Maldives	41.1	45.2	47.9	46.8	47.8	48.3	44.9	42.8	40.1
Nepal	49.0	51.0	60.3	77.6	79.7	88.2	99.6	96.9	102.1
Sri Lanka	32.2	33.6	28.3	31.9	33.4	37.1	40.2	42.2	44.5
Southeast Asia									
Brunei Darussalam	77.8 (2001)	57.8	67.3	62.6	67.5	80.8	92.6	86.7	81.6
Cambodia	13.0	19.5	41.4	53.4	63.2	66.6	70.9	79.4	88.8
Indonesia	53.8	43.4	36.0	39.1	39.5	39.5	40.4	39.9	38.8
Lao People's Democratic Republic	17.4	18.7	38.0	44.5	49.0	51.2	51.5	53.1	53.1
Malaysia[b]	128.6	123.8	132.2	142.6	140.8	136.3	132.5	126.6	129.6
Myanmar	32.7	21.6	23.6	36.8	39.5	46.4	49.7	52.8	...
Philippines[b]	39.9	41.8	49.8	60.0	61.0	63.3	65.6	67.3	66.8
Singapore	103.2	103.3	123.3	128.9	128.4	122.9	127.9	124.1	122.7
Thailand	122.4	104.1	109.0	124.4	127.0	127.7	125.9	124.3	123.2
Viet Nam	50.5	75.6	129.3	122.8	131.5	143.6	158.3	163.7	166.2
The Pacific									
Cook Islands	50.1	56.4	83.1	67.2	60.9	59.3	57.7	56.2	55.6
Fiji[b]	42.4	58.9	67.6	74.2	74.7	68.9	73.3	75.0	...
Kiribati	...	...	...	...	...	...	...	...	...
Marshall Islands	54.6	52.9	60.7	47.2	64.2	84.3	92.7	112.8	...
Micronesia, Federated States of	...	...	...	...	...	...	...	...	...
Nauru	...	...	...	...	...	...	...	...	...
Niue	...	...	...	...	...	...	...	...	...
Palau	...	...	54.9	65.2	76.1	85.5	91.4	...	...
Papua New Guinea[b]	31.2	33.6	34.0	37.9	32.8	33.6	34.5	29.4	25.9
Samoa	33.5	35.7	44.2	42.3	45.0	43.1	45.0	51.9	55.1
Solomon Islands[b]	32.0	29.2	37.0	46.5	46.9	51.4	54.6	53.8	53.2
Timor-Leste	4.6	4.2	7.4	8.9	14.8	20.8	29.3	33.1	...
Tonga	29.2	39.0	40.9	44.0	45.8	48.1	52.3	53.1	...
Tuvalu	...	...	...	...	...	...	...	...	...
Vanuatu	89.7	98.6	83.3	70.9	73.7	78.5	82.5	82.9	...
Developed ADB Member Economies									
Australia[b]	65.4	73.5	94.5	101.5	104.3	109.6	113.3	115.0	111.9
Japan[c]	123.4	198.7	218.8	236.0	237.4	235.5	240.8	243.7	247.3
New Zealand[d]	86.3	98.7	110.5	114.5	116.9	120.1	102.7	103.7	106.2

... = data not available, ADB = Asian Development Bank, GDP = gross domestic product.

a   Refers to money supply M2 (M2), unless otherwise stated.
b   Refers to money supply M3 (M3).
c   Refers to M3, except for 2000 (M2).
d   Refers to M3, except for 2016–2018 (M2).

Source: Economy sources.

Money and Finance

Table 2.3.7:   Interest Rates on Savings and Time Deposits
(% per annum, period averages)

ADB Regional Member	Savings Deposits				Time Deposits[a]			
	2000	2005	2010	2018	2000	2005	2010	2018
Developing ADB Member Economies								
Central and West Asia								
Afghanistan	...	4.26 (2006)	5.42	1.60	...	4.72 (2006)	8.18	2.29
Armenia	...	...	...	...	20.72	6.66	10.70	9.38
Azerbaijan	...	...	...	...	10.40	9.38	10.96	9.79
Georgia[b]	10.98	6.79	8.71	4.28	9.85	10.23	11.60	5.82
Kazakhstan[b]	...	...	...	...	7.53	10.29	9.84	10.60
Kyrgyz Republic[c]	...	...	...	...	28.07	9.78	11.47	10.34
Pakistan[b]	5.75	1.24	5.02	4.14	7.37	4.21	7.21	4.63
Tajikistan	5.28 (2002)	3.63	3.83	1.10	14.84 (2002)	20.16	17.78	14.60
Turkmenistan	...	...	...	...	...	...	...	...
Uzbekistan[d]	...	...	...	15.94	...	...	...	16.36
East Asia								
China, People's Republic of	0.99	0.72	0.36	0.35	2.25	2.25	2.33	1.50
Hong Kong, China	4.50	0.97	0.01	0.04	5.40	1.73	0.16	0.20
Korea, Republic of	7.08	3.57	3.18	1.84	7.94	3.72	3.86	2.03
Mongolia	13.80	12.60	10.70	11.20	...	...	...	...
Taipei,China	3.50	0.55	0.24	0.23	4.98	1.77	1.03	1.05
South Asia								
Bangladesh	5.81	4.19	4.88	3.26	8.97	8.31	9.00	7.44
Bhutan[e]	6.00	4.50	4.75	5.25	9.50	6.50	6.75	7.75
India	4.00	3.50	3.50	4.00 (2016)	7.10	5.32	7.50	5.49 (2016)
Maldives[f]	5.50	2.25	2.25	1.50	6.50	4.50	3.75	4.39
Nepal	5.25	3.38	7.00	4.63	6.88	3.63	8.13	10.42
Sri Lanka	8.40	5.00	5.00	4.00	15.00	9.00	8.50	10.50
Southeast Asia								
Brunei Darussalam	...	1.01	0.47	0.35	...	1.61	0.75	0.77
Cambodia	6.13	2.08	1.18	1.14	7.20	6.83	6.58	6.11
Indonesia	8.86	4.32	3.92	1.25	12.17	10.95	7.88	6.51
Lao People's Democratic Republic	...	...	...	...	...	...	...	...
Malaysia	2.72	1.41	0.94	1.04	4.24	3.70	2.81	3.31
Myanmar	...	...	...	...	...	...	...	...
Philippines[g]	7.40	3.80	1.60	0.90	10.50	6.00	2.07	3.46
Singapore	1.30	0.24	0.14	0.16	2.45	0.76	0.48	0.45
Thailand	2.50	1.88	0.50	0.50	3.50	3.00	1.55	1.40
Viet Nam	0.20	3.00	3.00	0.54	6.24	8.40	11.50	7.09
The Pacific								
Cook Islands	...	...	...	...	...	...	...	...
Fiji	...	...	...	...	...	...	...	...
Kiribati	...	...	...	...	...	...	...	...
Marshall Islands	2.50	1.23	0.50	...	6.75	3.54	3.50	...
Micronesia, Federated States of	...	...	...	...	...	...	...	...
Nauru	...	...	...	...	...	...	...	...
Niue	...	...	...	...	...	...	...	...
Palau	...	...	0.95	0.11	...	...	0.84	0.38
Papua New Guinea	3.88	1.80	1.00	0.67	9.38	1.30	4.80	2.00
Samoa	3.00	2.75	0.88	1.00	7.35	6.38	2.25	2.90
Solomon Islands	...	...	...	...	...	...	...	...
Timor-Leste	0.20 (2002)	0.75	0.75	0.42	– (2002)	1.28	1.33	0.67
Tonga	3.15	3.36	1.52	2.42	5.13	5.93	2.97	5.24
Tuvalu	...	...	...	...	...	...	...	...
Vanuatu	...	...	...	...	...	...	...	...
Developed ADB Member Economies								
Australia	...	5.40	4.50	1.00	5.90	4.55	6.00	2.20
Japan[h]	0.09	0.01	0.04	0.00	0.24	0.03	0.10	0.03
New Zealand[i]	...	...	...	...	6.49	6.90	4.72	3.26

... = data not available, – = magnitude equals zero, 0.00 = magnitude is less than half of unit employed, ADB = Asian Development Bank.

a Refers to interest rate on time deposits of 12 months, unless otherwise indicated.
b Refers to interest rate on time deposits of over 12 months.
c Rates for time deposits refer to interest rates of commercial banks in national currency for 6–12 months.
d Refers to time deposits from 181 days to 365 days.
e Rates for time deposits refer to rates for fixed deposits of 1 year to less than 3 years.
f Refers to interest rate on time deposits of 2–3 years.
g Rates for time deposits refer to rates charged on interest-bearing deposits with maturities of over 1 year.
h Refers to time deposits from 12 months to less than 2 years, calculated as the arithmetic average of the monthly figures.
i Refers to interest rate on time deposits of 6 months.

Sources: Economy sources. For the People's Republic of China: CEIC Database. https://www.ceicdata.com/en (accessed 22 July 2019).

Table 2.3.8: Yield on Short-Term Treasury Bills and Lending Interest Rates
(% per annum, period averages)

ADB Regional Member	Yield on Short-Term Treasury Bills[a]				Lending Interest Rates			
	2000	2005	2010	2018	2000	2005	2010	2018
Developing ADB Member Economies								
Central and West Asia								
Afghanistan	...	...	...	...	...	18.0 (2006)	15.6	14.8 (2017)
Armenia[b]	20.6 (2001)	4.1	10.6	6.2	31.6	18.0	19.2	12.8
Azerbaijan	16.7	7.5	1.8	14.3 (2017)	19.7	17.0	20.7	17.4
Georgia	29.9 (2001)	12.6	9.6	7.3	...	17.6	15.8	11.1
Kazakhstan	...	...	...	...	...	...	...	...
Kyrgyz Republic	32.3	4.4	10.4	5.6	57.0	21.7	23.7	19.5
Pakistan[c]	8.4	7.2	12.5	6.0 (2017)	...	9.1	14.0	8.5
Tajikistan[d]	...	...	6.7	1.0 (2017)	1.6	23.3	23.4	29.6 (2017)
Turkmenistan	...	...	...	...	...	...	...	...
Uzbekistan	...	...	...	...	...	...	...	...
East Asia								
China, People's Republic of[e]	2.6	1.9	2.6	...	5.9	5.6	5.8	4.4
Hong Kong, China	5.9	2.7	0.2	1.3	9.3	6.2	5.0	5.0
Korea, Republic of[f]	7.1	3.6	2.7	1.4	8.5	5.6	5.5	3.7
Mongolia[g]	...	13.7	12.9 (2012)	13.9 (2017)	37.0	30.6	20.1	17.7
Taipei,China[h]	...	1.3	0.3	0.3	7.7	3.8	2.7	2.6
South Asia								
Bangladesh[d]	6.3	6.7	2.2	3.9	12.8	10.6	12.2	9.7
Bhutan[d]	7.3	3.5	2.0	2.5	16.0	14.5	13.9	14.0
India[d,i]	9.0	5.7	6.2	6.6	12.3	10.8	8.3	9.5
Maldives[j]	...	5.0 (2006)	4.9	3.5	13.0	13.0	10.4	10.7
Nepal[d]	5.3	3.0	6.9	3.6	...	...	...	...
Sri Lanka[k]	13.7 (2001)	9.0	8.6	10.1 (2017)	14.3 (2001)	10.8	10.2	11.6 (2017)
Southeast Asia								
Brunei Darussalam	...	...	...	...	5.5	5.5	5.5	5.5
Cambodia	...	...	...	...	...	...	...	...
Indonesia	...	...	...	...	18.5	14.1	13.3	10.5
Lao People's Democratic Republic[l]	29.9	18.6	8.0	...	32.0	26.8	22.6	...
Malaysia	2.9	2.5	2.6	2.8 (2016)	7.7	6.0	5.0	4.9
Myanmar	...	...	...	...	15.3	15.0	17.0	13.0
Philippines[d]	9.9	6.1	3.5	3.6	10.9	10.2	7.7	6.1
Singapore	2.2	2.1	0.3	...	5.8	5.3	5.4	5.3
Thailand[d]	2.3 (2001)	2.7	1.4	1.3	7.8	4.7	4.3	4.1
Viet Nam[m]	5.4	6.1	11.1	...	10.6	11.0	13.1	7.4
The Pacific								
Cook Islands	...	...	...	...	...	...	...	...
Fiji	3.5	1.9	3.4	1.4 (2017)	8.4	6.8	7.5	5.7 (2017)
Kiribati	...	...	...	...	...	...	...	...
Marshall Islands	...	...	...	...	...	...	...	...
Micronesia, Federated States of	...	...	...	...	15.3	16.4	15.1	16.1 (2017)
Nauru	...	...	...	...	...	...	...	...
Niue	...	...	...	...	...	...	...	...
Palau	...	...	...	...	...	...	...	...
Papua New Guinea[n]	17.0	3.8	4.6	4.7 (2017)	17.5	11.5	10.4	8.4 (2017)
Samoa	...	...	...	...	11.6 (2001)	11.4	10.7	9.0
Solomon Islands	7.0	4.5	3.7	0.5	10.3	9.3	14.4	10.7
Timor-Leste	...	...	...	...	17.4 (2002)	16.7	11.0	13.5
Tonga	...	...	...	...	11.3	11.4	11.5	8.0
Tuvalu	...	...	...	...	...	...	...	...
Vanuatu	...	...	...	...	9.9	7.5	5.5	2.7
Developed ADB Member Economies								
Australia[o]	6.0	...	4.4	...	7.7	7.3	7.3	5.3
Japan	0.2	0.0	0.1	-0.2 (2017)	2.1	1.7	1.6	1.0 (2017)
New Zealand	6.4	6.5	2.8	1.7	7.8	7.8	6.3	4.8 (2017)

... = data not available, 0.0 = magnitude is less than half of unit employed, ADB = Asian Development Bank.

a Refers to 3-month Treasury bills, unless otherwise indicated.
b Refers to average yield on 9-month to 12-month Treasury bills since March 2001.
c Refers to weighted average yield on 6-month Treasury securities.
d Refers to 91-day Treasury bills.
e Refers to 3-month Treasury bonds trading rate.
f Refers to 91-day certificates of deposit.
g Refers to weighted average rate on Treasury bills of all maturities. From December 2012 onward, refers to yield on 12-week Treasury bills.
h Refers to prime lending rates.
i Figures are for fiscal year ending March.
j Refers to rate on 28-day Treasury bills.
k Refers to weighted average rate on the last monthly issuance of 364-day Treasury bills since December 2001.
l Refers to weighted average auction rate for 12-month Treasury bills.
m Refers to average monthly yield on 360-day Treasury bills sold at auction.
n Refers to rate on 182-day Treasury bills.
o Refers to estimated closing yield in the secondary market on 13-week Treasury notes.

Sources: International Monetary Fund. International Financial Statistics. http://data.imf.org/ (accessed 5 August 2019); and Organisation for Economic Co-operation and Development. Main Economic Indicators. http://dx.doi.org/10.1787/data-00043-en (accessed 7 June 2019). For Bangladesh; Bhutan; India; and Taipei,China: Economy sources.

Money and Finance

Table 2.3.9:   Domestic Credit Provided by Banking Sector and Bank Nonperforming Loans

ADB Regional Member	Domestic Credit Provided by Banking Sector[a] (% of GDP)				Bank Nonperforming Loans[b] (% of total gross loans)	
	2000	2005	2010	2018	2010	2017
Developing ADB Member Economies						
Central and West Asia						
Afghanistan	...	-4.9 (2006)	4.8	-5.3	49.9	12.2
Armenia	11.5	8.8	27.8	62.5	3.0	5.4
Azerbaijan	9.6	11.2	23.0	13.2	...	...
Georgia	21.5	21.6	35.5	71.9	5.9	2.8
Kazakhstan	12.3	39.0	45.4	38.2	20.9	9.3
Kyrgyz Republic	12.2	13.8	12.5	22.4	14.8	7.4
Pakistan	41.6	46.5	46.2	58.3	14.7	8.4
Tajikistan	17.9	13.0	7.6	15.6	7.4	...
Turkmenistan	...	...	...	...	...	...
Uzbekistan	...	...	...	...	1.0	0.4 (2016)
East Asia						
China, People's Republic of	118.4	132.6	142.5	218.3	1.1	1.7
Hong Kong, China	134.0	139.8	195.4	252.0	0.8	0.7
Korea, Republic of	70.9	125.5	151.0	176.9	0.6	0.5 (2016)
Mongolia	9.0	26.6	25.7	65.5	...	...
Taipei,China	1.8	1.9	0.9	...	0.6	0.2
South Asia						
Bangladesh	30.2	47.7	57.4	64.1	5.8 (2011)	8.4 (2015)
Bhutan	2.9	21.8	45.6	64.0	5.2	8.4
India	52.1	59.3	73.4	72.1 (2016)	2.7 (2011)	10.0
Maldives	34.8	47.0	76.9	64.9	20.9 (2012)	10.5
Nepal	40.8	42.2	67.4	102.2	...	1.7
Sri Lanka	43.7	43.5	35.5	71.3 (2016)	3.8 (2011)	2.5
Southeast Asia						
Brunei Darussalam	38.6	10.4	22.7	28.4	6.9	3.5
Cambodia	6.4	7.2	22.7	85.7	3.1	2.1
Indonesia	60.7	46.2	34.2	47.2	2.5	2.6
Lao People's Democratic Republic	9.0	8.1	26.7	...	...	...
Malaysia	138.4	117.7	123.3	143.1	3.4	1.5
Myanmar	31.2	23.1	25.2	42.5 (2017)	...	...
Philippines	58.3	47.2	49.2	69.1	3.4	1.6
Singapore	76.5	61.0	79.6	136.6	1.4	1.4
Thailand	134.3	111.0	133.4	167.0	3.9	3.1
Viet Nam	35.1	65.4	124.7	141.9	2.1	1.8
The Pacific						
Cook Islands	...	...	...	...	...	...
Fiji	37.9	111.6	132.3	116.2 (2017)	4.4	2.4
Kiribati	...	...	...	...	...	...
Marshall Islands	...	...	...	...	...	...
Micronesia, Federated States of	-42.3	-24.5	-14.7	-46.8 (2017)	...	...
Nauru	...	...	...	...	...	...
Niue	...	...	...	...	...	...
Palau	...	...	...	...	...	...
Papua New Guinea	28.2	22.2	23.7	37.5	1.9	2.8
Samoa	18.3	31.8	63.4	76.5	...	5.3
Solomon Islands	26.5	29.4	26.8	27.9	9.3	3.8 (2016)
Timor-Leste	-7.6 (2002)	-2.5	-5.5	-10.9	...	...
Tonga	38.8	48.3	39.9	31.6	11.7 (2012)	3.6
Tuvalu	...	...	...	...	...	...
Vanuatu	35.6	44.5	63.7	52.7	4.8	15.0
Developed ADB Member Economies						
Australia	93.4	113.3	153.8	176.8	2.1	0.9
Japan	295.0	296.7	313.8	348.6 (2016)	...	...
New Zealand	108.0	126.4	150.7	154.8	...	...

... = data not available, ADB = Asian Development Bank, GDP = gross domestic product.

a   Domestic credit provided by the financial sector includes all credit to various sectors on a gross basis, with the exception of credit to the central government, which is net. The financial sector includes monetary authorities and deposit money banks, as well as other financial corporations where data are available (including corporations that do not accept transferable deposits, but do incur such liabilities as time and savings deposits). Examples of other financial corporations are finance and leasing companies, money lenders, insurance corporations, pension funds, and foreign exchange companies.

b   Bank nonperforming loans to total gross loans are the value of nonperforming loans divided by the total value of the loan portfolio (including nonperforming loans before the deduction of specific loan-loss provisions). The loan amount recorded as nonperforming should be the gross value of the loan as recorded on the balance sheet, not just the amount that is overdue.

Sources: World Bank. World Development Indicators Online. http://data.worldbank.org/ (accessed 5 August 2019). For Taipei,China: Central bank of Taipei,China. http://www.cbc.gov.tw (accessed 5 August 2019).

Table 2.3.10: Growth Rates of Stock Market Price Index[a]
(%)

ADB Regional Member	2000	2005	2010	2013	2014	2015	2016	2017	2018
Developing ADB Member Economies									
Central and West Asia									
Afghanistan	...	...	...	...	...	...	...	...	...
Armenia	...	...	...	...	...	...	...	...	...
Azerbaijan	...	...	...	...	...	...	...	...	...
Georgia	...	...	...	...	...	...	...	...	...
Kazakhstan	...	...	...	...	...	...	...	...	...
Kyrgyz Republic	...	...	...	...	...	...	...	...	...
Pakistan[b]	7.0	53.7	28.2	49.4	27.2	2.1	45.7	...	...
Tajikistan	...	...	...	...	...	...	...	...	...
Turkmenistan	...	...	...	...	...	...	...	...	...
Uzbekistan	...	...	...	...	...	...	...	...	...
East Asia									
China, People's Republic of	37.3	-22.1	3.4	-1.1	1.5	66.0	-19.0	6.7	...
Hong Kong, China	26.5	11.1	19.3	10.4	2.7	4.8	-12.0	22.3	10.2
Korea, Republic of	-8.7	28.5	23.6	1.5	1.1	1.4	-1.2	16.5	0.5
Mongolia	...	18.7	88.7	-21.0	4.2	-14.6	-14.0	33.5	30.5
Taipei,China	5.7	1.0	23.1	8.2	11.1	-0.4	-2.2	16.5	4.0
South Asia									
Bangladesh[b]	31.8	-14.9	82.8	1.1	14.0	-4.8	8.8	24.0	-13.8
Bhutan	...	...	...	...	...	...	...	...	...
India	11.2	32.6	29.8	11.4	25.2	10.9	-3.6	8.6	...
Maldives	...	51.8	-20.4	-5.3	-4.8	8.9	4.8	7.4	6.8
Nepal	...	...	...	...	...	...	...	...	...
Sri Lanka[b]	...	27.6	96.0	4.8	23.4	-5.5	-9.7	...	...
Southeast Asia									
Brunei Darussalam	...	...	...	...	...	...	...	...	...
Cambodia	...	...	...	...	...	...	...	...	...
Indonesia[b]	-38.5	16.2	46.1	-1.0	22.3	-12.1	15.3	20.0	-2.5
Lao People's Democratic Republic	...	...	...	...	...	...	...	...	...
Malaysia	21.4	6.4	27.1	8.7	5.5	-6.1	-3.8	5.0	2.2
Myanmar	...	...	...	...	...	...	...	...	...
Philippines	-6.3	17.5	43.1	16.0	1.8	5.5	0.9	8.0	0.1
Singapore	8.6	16.7	30.3	7.6	1.2	-2.5	-11.6	10.3	...
Thailand	-18.7	4.2	45.6	21.3	-0.2	0.2	-2.1	12.7	6.6
Viet Nam[b]	...	8.3	12.2	22.1	8.1	6.1	14.8	...	...
The Pacific									
Cook Islands	...	...	...	...	...	...	...	...	...
Fiji	...	13.5	-11.1	2.6	0.5	20.8	27.6	22.4	...
Kiribati	...	...	...	...	...	...	...	...	...
Marshall Islands	...	...	...	...	...	...	...	...	...
Micronesia, Federated States of	...	...	...	...	...	...	...	...	...
Nauru	...	...	...	...	...	...	...	...	...
Niue	...	...	...	...	...	...	...	...	...
Palau	...	...	...	...	...	...	...	...	...
Papua New Guinea	...	52.5	26.2	-15.3	-12.3	-6.3	...	...	...
Samoa	...	...	...	...	...	...	...	...	...
Solomon Islands	...	...	...	...	...	...	...	...	...
Timor-Leste	...	...	...	...	...	...	...	...	...
Tonga	...	...	...	...	...	...	...	...	...
Tuvalu	...	...	...	...	...	...	...	...	...
Vanuatu	...	...	...	...	...	...	...	...	...
Developed ADB Member Economies									
Australia[b]	1.7	17.6	-2.6	15.1	1.1	-2.1	7.0	7.0	-6.9
Japan	11.6	13.5	2.0	46.0	12.6	22.7	-12.6	...	...
New Zealand	2.3	19.4	9.7	25.5	14.1	12.7	17.4	11.1	14.8

... = data not available, ADB = Asian Development Bank.

a Refers to growth rates of stock market prices (period average), unless otherwise indicated.
b Refers to growth rates of end of period stock market prices.

Sources: International Monetary Fund. International Financial Statistics. http://data.imf.org/IFS (accessed 8 July 2019). For Taipei,China: Annual statistics from the stock exchange corporation in Taipei,China. http://www.twse.com.tw/en/statistics/ (accessed 8 July 2019).

Money and Finance

Table 2.3.11: Stock Market Capitalization

ADB Regional Member	Stock Market Capitalization ($ million)				Stock Market Capitalization (% of GDP)			
	2000	2005	2010	2018	2000	2005	2010	2018
Developing ADB Member Economies								
Central and West Asia								
Afghanistan	...	...	...	...	...	...	...	...
Armenia	...	...	...	...	...	...	...	...
Azerbaijan	...	...	...	...	...	...	...	...
Georgia	...	...	...	...	...	...	...	...
Kazakhstan	802	10,529	26,673	37,005	4.4	18.4	18.0	21.7
Kyrgyz Republic	...	...	...	...	...	...	...	...
Pakistan	6,625	45,317	38,007	91,864 (2016)	9.0	41.4	21.4	33.0 (2016)
Tajikistan	...	...	...	...	...	...	...	...
Turkmenistan	...	...	...	...	...	...	...	...
Uzbekistan	...	...	...	...	...	...	...	...
East Asia								
China, People's Republic of	...	401,852	4,027,840	6,324,880	...	17.6	66.2	46.5
Hong Kong, China	623,398	1,054,999	2,711,316	3,819,215	363.1	581.0	1,185.9	1,052.1
Korea, Republic of	171,262	718,011	1,091,911	1,413,717	30.5	79.9	99.8	87.3
Mongolia	...	...	...	...	...	...	...	...
Taipei,China	262,295	485,825	752,335	972,097	79.1	129.3	168.6	164.8
South Asia								
Bangladesh	2,192	3,300	41,617	77,391	4.1	4.8	36.1	28.2
Bhutan	53	101	219	393 (2017)	12.0	12.4	13.8	15.5 (2017)
India	...	553,074	1,631,830	2,083,483	...	67.4	97.4	76.4
Maldives	...	...	...	...	...	...	...	...
Nepal	...	...	...	...	...	...	...	...
Sri Lanka	1,074	5,720	19,924	15,575	6.6	23.4	35.1	17.5
Southeast Asia								
Brunei Darussalam	...	...	...	...	...	...	...	...
Cambodia	...	...	...	...	...	...	...	...
Indonesia	26,813	81,428	360,388	486,766	16.2	28.5	47.7	46.7
Lao People's Democratic Republic	...	...	...	...	...	...	...	...
Malaysia	113,156	180,518	408,689	398,019	120.6	125.8	160.3	112.3
Myanmar	...	...	...	...	...	...	...	...
Philippines	25,981	39,799	157,321	258,156	32.1	38.6	78.8	78.0
Singapore	152,826	257,340	647,226	687,257	159.1	201.3	269.9	188.7
Thailand	29,217	123,885	277,732	500,741	23.1	65.4	81.4	99.2
Viet Nam	...	...	36,855	132,653	...	...	31.8	54.2
The Pacific								
Cook Islands	...	...	...	...	...	...	...	...
Fiji	...	...	...	...	...	...	...	...
Kiribati	...	...	...	...	...	...	...	...
Marshall Islands	...	...	...	...	...	...	...	...
Micronesia, Federated States of	...	...	...	...	...	...	...	...
Nauru	...	...	...	...	...	...	...	...
Niue	...	...	...	...	...	...	...	...
Palau	...	...	...	...	...	...	...	...
Papua New Guinea	...	6,138	11,027	...	...	126.2	77.4	...
Samoa	...	...	...	...	...	...	...	...
Solomon Islands	...	...	...	...	...	...	...	...
Timor-Leste	...	...	...	...	...	...	...	...
Tonga	...	...	...	...	...	...	...	...
Tuvalu	...	...	...	...	...	...	...	...
Vanuatu	...	...	...	...	...	...	...	...
Developed ADB Member Economies								
Australia	372,794	804,015	1,454,491	1,262,800	89.8	116.0	126.9	88.2
Japan	3,157,222	4,572,901	3,827,774	5,296,811	64.6	96.2	67.2	106.6
New Zealand	18,613	40,592	43,516	86,133	35.4	35.4	29.7	42.0

... = data not available, $ = United States dollars, ADB = Asian Development Bank, GDP = gross domestic product.

Sources: World Bank. World Development Indicators Online. http://databank.worldbank.org/data (accessed 18 July 2019). For Bhutan and Taipei,China: Asian Development Bank estimates using data from economy sources.

Table 2.3.12: Official Exchange Rates
(local currency units per $, period averages)

ADB Regional Member	2000	2005	2010	2013	2014	2015	2016	2017	2018
Developing ADB Member Economies									
Central and West Asia									
Afghanistan	47.36	49.49	46.45	55.38	57.25	61.14	67.87	68.03	72.08
Armenia	539.53	457.69	373.66	409.63	415.92	477.92	480.49	482.72	482.99
Azerbaijan	0.89	0.95	0.80	0.78	0.78	1.02	1.60	1.72	1.70
Georgia	1.98	1.81	1.78	1.66	1.77	2.27	2.37	2.51	2.53
Kazakhstan	142.13	132.88	147.36	152.13	179.19	221.73	342.16	326.00	344.71
Kyrgyz Republic	47.70	41.01	45.96	48.44	53.65	64.46	69.91	68.87	68.84
Pakistan	53.65	59.51	85.19	101.63	101.10	102.77	104.77	105.46	121.82
Tajikistan	2.08	3.12	4.38	4.76	4.94	6.16	7.84	8.55	9.15
Turkmenistan	1.04	1.04	2.85	2.85	2.85	3.50	3.50	3.50	3.50
Uzbekistan[a]	236.61	1,106.10	1,578.42	2,094.99	2,310.95	2,567.99	2,965.25	5,113.88	8,069.61
East Asia									
China, People's Republic of	8.28	8.19	6.77	6.20	6.14	6.23	6.64	6.76	6.62
Hong Kong, China	7.79	7.78	7.77	7.76	7.75	7.75	7.76	7.79	7.84
Korea, Republic of	1,130.96	1,024.12	1,156.06	1,094.85	1,052.96	1,131.16	1,160.43	1,130.42	1,100.56
Mongolia	1,076.67	1,205.25	1,357.06	1,523.93	1,817.94	1,970.31	2,140.29	2,439.78	2,472.48
Taipei,China	31.23	32.17	31.64	29.77	30.37	31.90	32.32	30.44	30.16
South Asia									
Bangladesh	52.14	64.33	69.65	78.10	77.64	77.95	78.47	80.44	83.47
Bhutan	44.94	44.10	45.73	58.60	61.03	64.15	67.20	65.12	68.39
India	44.94	44.10	45.73	58.60	61.03	64.15	67.20	65.12	68.39
Maldives	11.77	12.80	12.80	15.37	15.38	15.37	15.37	15.39	15.39
Nepal	71.09	71.37	73.26	93.08	97.55	102.41	107.38	104.51	108.93
Sri Lanka	77.01	100.50	113.06	129.07	130.56	135.86	145.58	152.45	162.46
Southeast Asia									
Brunei Darussalam	1.72	1.66	1.36	1.25	1.27	1.37	1.38	1.38	1.35
Cambodia	3,840.75	4,092.50	4,184.92	4,027.25	4,037.50	4,067.75	4,058.69	4,050.58	4,051.17
Indonesia	8,421.78	9,704.74	9,090.43	10,461.24	11,865.21	13,389.41	13,308.33	13,380.83	14,236.94
Lao People's Democratic Republic	7,887.64	10,655.17	8,258.77	7,860.14	8,048.96	8,147.91	8,179.27	8,351.53	8,489.24
Malaysia	3.80	3.79	3.22	3.15	3.27	3.91	4.15	4.30	4.04
Myanmar[b]	6.52	5.82	5.63	933.57	984.35	1,162.62	1,234.87	1,360.36	1,429.81
Philippines	44.19	55.09	45.11	42.45	44.40	45.50	47.49	50.40	52.66
Singapore	1.72	1.66	1.36	1.25	1.27	1.37	1.38	1.38	1.35
Thailand	40.11	40.22	31.69	30.73	32.48	34.25	35.30	33.94	32.31
Viet Nam	14,167.75	15,858.92	18,612.92	20,933.42	21,148.00	21,697.57	21,935.00	22,370.09	22,602.05
The Pacific									
Cook Islands	2.20	1.42	1.39	1.22	1.21	1.43	1.44	1.41	1.45
Fiji	2.13	1.69	1.92	1.84	1.89	2.10	2.09	2.07	2.09
Kiribati	1.72	1.31	1.09	1.04	1.11	1.33	1.35	1.30	1.34
Marshall Islands[c]	1.00	1.00	1.00	1.00	1.00	1.00	1.00	1.00	1.00
Micronesia, Federated States of[c]	1.00	1.00	1.00	1.00	1.00	1.00	1.00	1.00	1.00
Nauru	1.72	1.31	1.09	1.04	1.11	1.33	1.35	1.30	1.34
Niue	2.20	1.42	1.39	1.22	1.21	1.43	1.44	1.41	1.45
Palau[c]	1.00	1.00	1.00	1.00	1.00	1.00	1.00	1.00	1.00
Papua New Guinea	2.78	3.10	2.72	2.24	2.46	2.77	3.13	3.19	3.28
Samoa	3.29	2.71	2.48	2.31	2.33	2.56	2.56	2.55	2.59
Solomon Islands	5.09	7.53	8.06	7.30	7.38	7.91	7.95	7.89	7.95
Timor-Leste[c]	1.00	1.00	1.00	1.00	1.00	1.00	1.00	1.00	1.00
Tonga	1.76	1.94	1.91	1.77	1.85	2.11	2.22	2.21	2.24
Tuvalu	1.72	1.31	1.09	1.04	1.11	1.33	1.35	1.30	1.34
Vanuatu	137.64	109.25	96.91	94.54	97.07	108.99	108.48	107.82	108.78
Developed ADB Member Economies									
Australia	1.72	1.31	1.09	1.04	1.11	1.33	1.35	1.30	1.34
Japan	107.77	110.22	87.78	97.60	105.94	121.04	108.79	112.17	110.42
New Zealand	2.20	1.42	1.39	1.22	1.21	1.43	1.44	1.41	1.45

$ = United States (US) dollars, ADB = Asian Development Bank.

a Data show weighted averages of the official, bank, and parallel market rates.
b From 1 April 2012 onward, the Central Bank of Myanmar adopted the managed float exchange rate regime for kyat vis-à-vis the US dollar.
c Unit of currency is the US dollar.

Sources: International Monetary Fund. International Financial Statistics. http://data.imf.org/ (accessed 26 June 2019). For Turkmenistan for 2000–2009: United Nations National Accounts Main Aggregates Database. https://unstats.un.org/unsd/snaama/resCountry.asp (accessed 22 May 2019); and for 2010–2018: Interstate Statistical Committee of the Commonwealth of Independent States. http://www.cisstat.org/eng/index.htm (accessed 6 June 2019). For Uzbekistan for 2000–2009: United Nations National Accounts Main Aggregates Database. http://unstats.un.org/unsd/snaama/resCountry.asp (accessed June 2013); for 2010–2012: Interstate Statistical Committee of the Commonwealth of Independent States. http://www.cisstat.com (accessed 15 July 2015); and for 2013–2018: Central Bank of Uzbekistan. http://cbu.uz/en/statistics/ (accessed 23 July 2019). For Taipei,China: Central bank of Taipei,China. http://www.cbc.gov.tw (accessed 26 June 2019).

Table 2.3.13:   Purchasing Power Parity Conversion Factor[a]
(local currency units per $, period averages)

ADB Regional Member	2000	2005	2010	2013	2014	2015	2016	2017	2018
Developing ADB Member Economies									
Central and West Asia									
Afghanistan	9.60 (2002)	12.27	15.20	18.82	18.58	18.83	19.58	19.59	19.31
Armenia	144.36	157.63	183.16	196.45	197.26	197.54	195.93	196.41	197.04
Azerbaijan	0.16	0.20	0.30	0.36	0.35	0.31	0.36	0.41	0.45
Georgia	0.53	0.64	0.80	0.83	0.85	0.89	0.91	0.95	0.96
Kazakhstan	22.06	35.12	67.90	88.70	92.08	92.76	104.28	111.13	115.57
Kyrgyz Republic	8.08	9.25	14.80	19.22	20.45	20.93	21.96	22.92	22.75
Pakistan	9.93	11.81	20.77	26.61	28.05	28.90	28.70	29.29	29.24
Tajikistan	0.30	0.69	1.57	1.94	2.00	2.01	2.09	2.14	2.20
Turkmenistan	0.27	0.65	1.30	1.52	1.50	1.41	1.32	1.28	1.27
Uzbekistan	65.87	221.82	525.87	760.41	1,020.61	1,115.04	1,199.44	1,405.79	1,761.40
East Asia									
China, People's Republic of	2.70	2.83	3.31	3.53	3.50	3.46	3.46	3.53	3.55
Hong Kong, China	7.41	5.68	5.37	5.55	5.60	5.75	5.78	5.84	5.92
Korea, Republic of	747.24	788.92	840.89	869.08	871.88	857.37	862.55	866.01	852.69
Mongolia	137.83	223.43	476.33	601.13	633.91	638.08	645.24	700.60	738.70
Taipei,China	21.43	18.35	15.80	14.86	14.84	15.16	15.13	14.67	14.20
South Asia									
Bangladesh	15.62	17.32	21.91	25.87	26.83	28.11	29.67	30.95	31.96
Bhutan	12.22	13.65	15.84	18.79	19.96	20.28	20.97	21.71	21.85
India	9.39	10.41	14.19	16.70	16.93	17.14	17.48	17.81	18.15
Maldives	3.37	5.65	7.73	9.34	9.60	10.25	10.15	10.28	10.28
Nepal	13.05	15.32	22.69	26.99	28.97	30.08	31.28	33.37	34.94
Sri Lanka	15.18	21.77	38.01	43.88	44.32	44.14	45.78	48.59	49.58
Southeast Asia									
Brunei Darussalam	0.48	0.59	0.61	0.68	0.65	0.53	0.48	0.49	0.53
Cambodia	1,058.37	1,106.11	1,330.50	1,327.98	1,337.63	1,346.23	1,376.69	1,395.91	1,406.93
Indonesia	1,422.04	2,012.48	3,426.11	3,787.40	3,919.40	4,032.29	4,085.95	4,181.15	4,245.60
Lao People's Democratic Republic	1,294.15	1,825.20	2,280.56	2,724.36	2,826.89	2,862.67	2,917.29	2,917.02	2,900.76
Malaysia	1.18	1.28	1.41	1.42	1.43	1.41	1.42	1.45	1.43
Myanmar	53.27	125.03	217.57	243.90	249.36	256.93	263.34	274.51	290.68
Philippines	13.66	15.46	17.52	17.91	18.14	17.84	17.94	18.02	18.29
Singapore	0.99	0.89	0.90	0.86	0.84	0.86	0.86	0.86	0.86
Thailand	11.01	11.33	12.17	12.37	12.32	12.28	12.44	12.46	12.36
Viet Nam	2,698.14	3,572.77	5,648.44	7,517.89	7,648.53	7,553.17	7,554.44	7,716.43	7,792.72
The Pacific									
Cook Islands	...	...	...	...	...	...	...	...	...
Fiji	0.83	0.93	0.97	1.08	1.19	1.21	1.22	1.20	1.18
Kiribati	0.87	0.91	0.96	0.92	0.95	0.97	0.96	0.95	0.95
Marshall Islands	0.92	0.92	0.92	0.94	0.89	0.87	0.91	0.90	0.89
Micronesia, Federated States of	0.87	0.81	0.89	0.92	0.92	0.86	0.89	0.86	0.85
Nauru	...	...	0.86	0.94	0.81	0.73	0.77	0.78	0.77
Niue	...	...	...	...	...	...	...	...	...
Palau	0.77	0.75	0.76	0.83	0.85	0.91	0.93	0.90	0.89
Papua New Guinea	0.80	1.00	1.74	1.85	1.91	1.82	1.87	1.97	2.09
Samoa	1.42	1.48	1.66	1.69	1.67	1.69	1.65	1.64	1.65
Solomon Islands	3.71	4.43	5.68	6.61	6.64	6.78	6.95	7.00	7.14
Timor-Leste	0.19	0.31	0.41	0.53	0.50	0.32	0.25	0.27	0.27
Tonga	0.92	1.14	1.40	1.44	1.43	1.44	1.44	1.47	1.49
Tuvalu	1.04	1.11	1.13	1.10	1.14	1.18	1.17	1.19	1.23
Vanuatu	90.06	88.64	99.53	99.91	100.00	101.40	102.49	103.17	103.05
Developed ADB Member Economies									
Australia	1.31	1.39	1.50	1.45	1.45	1.47	1.45	1.44	1.43
Japan	154.72	129.55	111.67	101.30	103.05	103.45	102.64	102.47	100.07
New Zealand	1.44	1.54	1.50	1.45	1.44	1.48	1.47	1.47	1.45

... = data not available, $ = United States dollars, ADB = Asian Development Bank.

a Purchasing power parity figures are extrapolated from the 2011 International Comparison Program benchmark estimates or imputed using a statistical model based on the 2011 International Comparison Program.

Sources: World Bank. World Development Indicators. http://databank.worldbank.org/data/home.aspx (accessed 23 July 2019). For Taipei,China: Asian Development Bank estimates using data from economy sources and World Bank data.

Table 2.3.14:   Price Level Indexes
(PPPs to official exchange rates, period averages, United States = 100)

ADB Regional Member	2000	2005	2010	2013	2014	2015	2016	2017	2018
Developing ADB Member Economies									
Central and West Asia									
Afghanistan	20.31 (2002)	24.78	32.72	33.99	32.45	30.80	28.85	28.80	26.79
Armenia	26.76	34.44	49.02	47.96	47.43	41.33	40.78	40.69	40.80
Azerbaijan	17.88	21.65	36.79	45.74	44.31	30.60	22.28	23.66	26.21
Georgia	26.72	35.15	44.94	49.94	47.91	39.06	38.60	37.90	38.04
Kazakhstan	15.52	26.43	46.08	58.31	51.38	41.84	30.48	34.09	33.53
Kyrgyz Republic	16.94	22.57	32.20	39.68	38.12	32.46	31.41	33.29	33.04
Pakistan	18.51	19.84	24.38	26.18	27.75	28.12	27.39	27.77	24.00
Tajikistan	14.68	22.21	35.79	40.82	40.50	32.58	26.69	25.06	24.00
Turkmenistan	26.20	62.42	45.58	53.21	52.57	40.18	37.82	36.53	36.15
Uzbekistan	27.84	20.05	33.32	36.30	44.16	43.42	40.45	27.49	21.83
East Asia									
China, People's Republic of	32.67	34.51	48.91	57.04	56.90	55.58	52.08	52.19	53.66
Hong Kong, China	95.15	73.09	69.07	71.58	72.27	74.14	74.44	74.90	75.55
Korea, Republic of	66.07	77.03	72.74	79.38	82.80	75.80	74.33	76.61	77.48
Mongolia	12.80	18.54	35.10	39.45	34.87	32.38	30.15	28.72	29.88
Taipei,China	68.64	57.05	49.92	49.93	48.85	47.52	46.80	48.21	47.10
South Asia									
Bangladesh	29.95	26.92	31.45	33.13	34.56	36.06	37.82	38.47	38.29
Bhutan	27.20	30.95	34.65	32.06	32.71	31.62	31.20	33.33	31.95
India	20.90	23.61	31.02	28.50	27.75	26.71	26.02	27.35	26.54
Maldives	28.65	44.16	60.38	60.81	62.39	66.69	66.04	66.82	66.77
Nepal	18.35	21.46	30.97	28.99	29.69	29.37	29.13	31.93	32.07
Sri Lanka	19.72	21.66	33.61	34.00	33.95	32.49	31.44	31.87	30.52
Southeast Asia									
Brunei Darussalam	27.58	35.31	44.70	54.39	51.65	38.87	34.76	35.81	39.15
Cambodia	27.56	27.03	31.79	32.97	33.13	33.10	33.92	34.46	34.73
Indonesia	16.89	20.74	37.69	36.20	33.03	30.12	30.70	31.25	29.82
Lao People's Democratic Republic	16.41	17.13	27.61	34.66	35.12	35.13	35.67	34.93	34.17
Malaysia	31.17	33.80	43.88	45.18	43.74	36.14	34.31	33.72	35.46
Myanmar[a]	7.67	20.15	36.21	26.13	25.33	22.10	21.33	20.18	20.33
Philippines	30.91	28.06	38.84	42.20	40.85	39.20	37.78	35.75	34.72
Singapore	57.25	53.68	66.00	68.73	66.46	62.52	62.02	62.45	63.72
Thailand	27.46	28.18	38.42	40.27	37.92	35.84	35.25	36.71	38.25
Viet Nam	19.04	22.53	30.35	35.91	36.17	34.81	34.44	34.49	34.48
The Pacific									
Cook Islands	...	...	...	...	...	...	...	...	...
Fiji	39.09	55.29	50.71	58.58	63.11	57.52	58.32	58.21	56.36
Kiribati	50.34	69.60	88.39	89.28	85.67	73.10	71.68	72.97	70.98
Marshall Islands	92.36	91.91	92.34	93.66	88.89	86.62	91.00	90.49	89.45
Micronesia, Federated States of	87.47	81.22	88.59	91.58	92.43	86.39	88.82	86.13	85.06
Nauru	...	...	79.20	90.38	73.03	55.21	57.12	59.76	59.57
Niue	...	...	...	...	...	...	...	...	...
Palau	77.10	74.74	76.28	83.07	84.84	90.69	92.55	89.79	89.49
Papua New Guinea	28.75	32.08	64.13	82.26	77.65	65.67	59.63	61.84	63.70
Samoa	43.25	54.43	66.69	73.27	71.48	66.16	64.31	64.04	63.60
Solomon Islands	72.94	58.83	70.40	90.46	90.10	85.63	87.41	88.79	89.76
Timor-Leste	19.14	31.47	41.46	53.04	50.37	31.61	25.14	26.98	26.63
Tonga	52.52	58.73	73.55	81.47	81.47	68.16	65.16	66.85	66.80
Tuvalu	60.24	84.98	103.30	106.36	102.40	88.35	87.34	91.52	91.55
Vanuatu	65.43	81.14	102.70	105.67	103.01	93.03	94.49	95.69	94.74
Developed ADB Member Economies									
Australia	76.01	106.02	137.77	139.71	130.93	110.74	107.88	110.71	107.16
Japan	143.57	117.54	127.21	103.80	97.27	85.46	94.35	91.36	90.63
New Zealand	65.58	108.08	107.80	118.58	119.52	102.89	102.31	104.50	100.63

... = data not available, ADB = Asian Development Bank, PPP = purchasing power parity.

a   The Central Bank of Myanmar devalued the local currency effective 1 April 2012. To achieve a consistent price series, the exchange rate used for estimating the price level index in prior years was extrapolated using the predevaluation exchange rate series.

Source: Asian Development Bank estimates using data from economy sources and World Bank data.

IV. Globalization

Globalization focuses on trends in remittances, foreign direct investment, and merchandise exports. The statistical tables cover balance of payments, external trade, international reserves, capital flows, external indebtedness, and tourism.

Remittances remain a significant and stable source of regional revenue

The aggregate of remittances to ADB developing member economies flatlined from 2014 to 2015 and actually declined in 2016 (Figure 2.4.1). However, aggregate remittances resumed their upward trend in 2017, reaching $272.2 billion, then increased again in 2018 to reach $297.1 billion. This total represents a significant rise on the $35.5 billion in aggregate remittances in 2000.

The region's top five recipients of remittances in 2018 were India ($78.6 billion), the PRC ($67.4 billion), the Philippines ($33.8 billion), Pakistan ($21.0 billion), and Viet Nam ($15.9 billion). On a global basis, India, the PRC, and the Philippines were ranked first, second, and fourth, respectively, in 2018 (World Bank 2019). Remittances accounted for at least 10.0% of GDP in 8 of the 32 economies with available data for 2018 (Table 2.4.5). These economies were led by Tonga with remittances accounting for 34.6% of GDP, the Kyrgyz Republic (33.2%), and Tajikistan (30.2%).

In comparison with remittance flows, official development assistance to economies in Asia and the Pacific has remained relatively low since 2000, totaling only $24.5 billion in 2017 (less than 10% of the region's aggregate remittances in the same year).

Figure 2.4.1: Remittances, Foreign Direct Investment, and Official Development Assistance in ADB Developing Member Economies

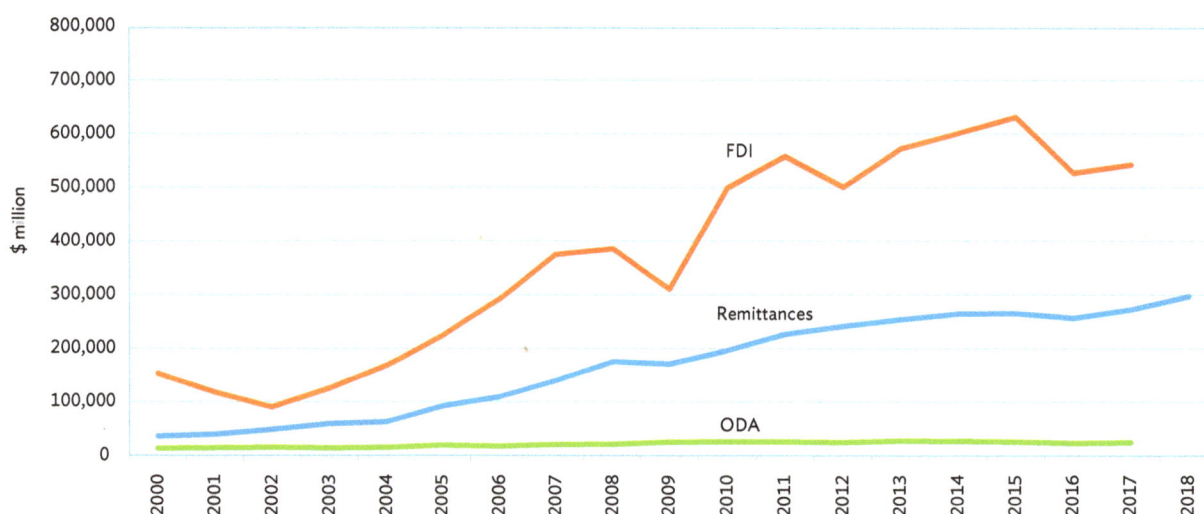

$ = United States dollars, ADB = Asian Development Bank, FDI = Foreign Direct Investment, Net Inflows; ODA = Net Official Development Assistance; Remittances = Workers' Remittances and Compensation of Employees, Receipts.
Sources: Table 2.4.4, Table 2.4.6, Table 2.4.16, Key Indicators for Asia and the Pacific 2019.

Foreign direct investment (FDI) in Asia and the Pacific climbed to $541.9 billion in 2017, more than tripling the amount of FDI in 2000. However, FDI flows were much more volatile than remittance flows during the review period, with declines observed in 2001–2002, 2009, 2012, and 2016.

The region's aggregate FDI in 2017 accounted for 29.2% of the world's total FDI, up significantly from only 12.4% in 2000. The PRC was comfortably largest recipient of FDI in Asia and the Pacific for 2018, receiving a total of $203.5 billion. It was followed by Hong Kong, China ($86.5 billion); Singapore ($82.0 billion); and Australia ($58.1 billion). These 4 economies were also among the global top 10 recipients of FDI in 2018, ranking second, fifth, sixth, and eighth, respectively (UN 2019b).

Between 2000 and 2018, economies in Asia and the Pacific exported an increasing share of their goods to other economies within the region.

Asia and Pacific's intraregional exports as a share of the region's total exports rose from 50.8% in 2000 to 57.7% in 2018 (Table 2.4.13). As a result, the region's exports to North America declined from 25.9% in 2000 to 17.5% in 2018, while exports to Europe declined from 17.6% to 16.1% over the same period.

Among 48 economies in Asia and the Pacific, 40 increased the share of merchandise exports that remained within the region (Figure 2.4.2). On the other hand, the region's largest exporter, the PRC, saw the percentage of its intraregional exports as a share of total exports fall from 51.8% in 2000 to 45.5% in 2018. The regions of the world receiving increased shares of the PRC's merchandise exports included Africa (from 1.7% in 2000 to 3.7% in 2018), South America (from 1.4% to 3.4%), the Middle East (from 2.9% to 4.5%), and Europe (from 18.4% to 19.8%).

Asia and the Pacific also received a greater share of the world's total merchandise exports, rising from 24.5% in 2000 to 33.6% in 2018. This gain occurred mainly at the expense of global exports to North America and Europe, which fell from 25.2% to 18.1% and from 42.4% to 38.1%, respectively, over the review period.

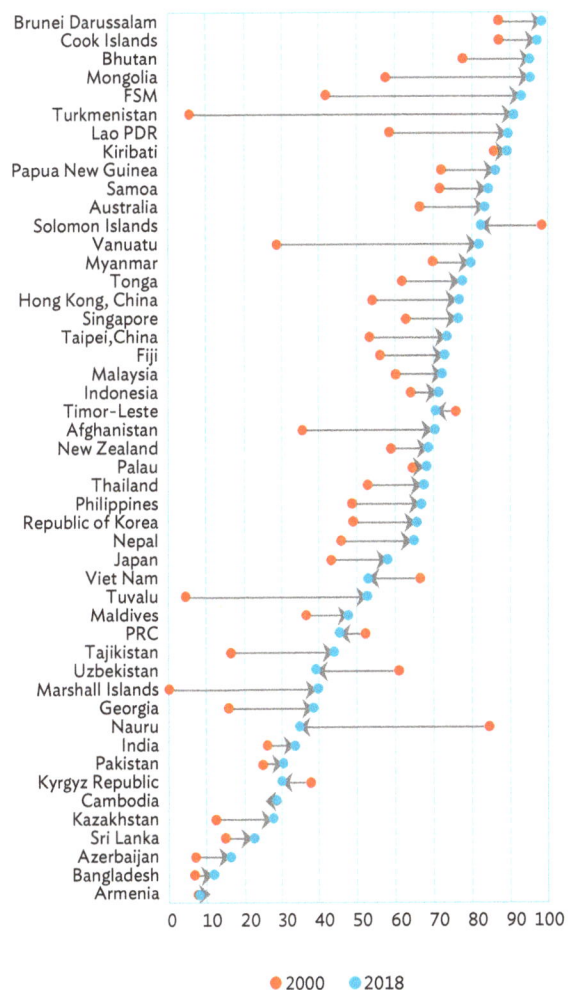

Figure 2.4.2: Intraregional Merchandise Exports in Asia and the Pacific
(% of total merchandise exports)

FSM = Federated States of Micronesia, Lao PDR = Lao People's Democratic Republic, PRC = People's Republic of China.
Source: Table 2.4.13, Key Indicators for Asia and the Pacific 2019.

Three-quarters of Asia and Pacific economies increased their share of intra-regional imports between 2000 and 2018

Among 48 economies in Asia and the Pacific, 36 increased the share of imports received from within the region from 2000 to 2018 (Figure 2.4.3). On an aggregate basis, Asia and the Pacific's intraregional merchandise imports accounted for 57.1% of total imports in 2018, up from 56.6% in 2000.

Figure 2.4.3: Intraregional Merchandise Imports
in Asia and the Pacific
(% of total merchandise imports)

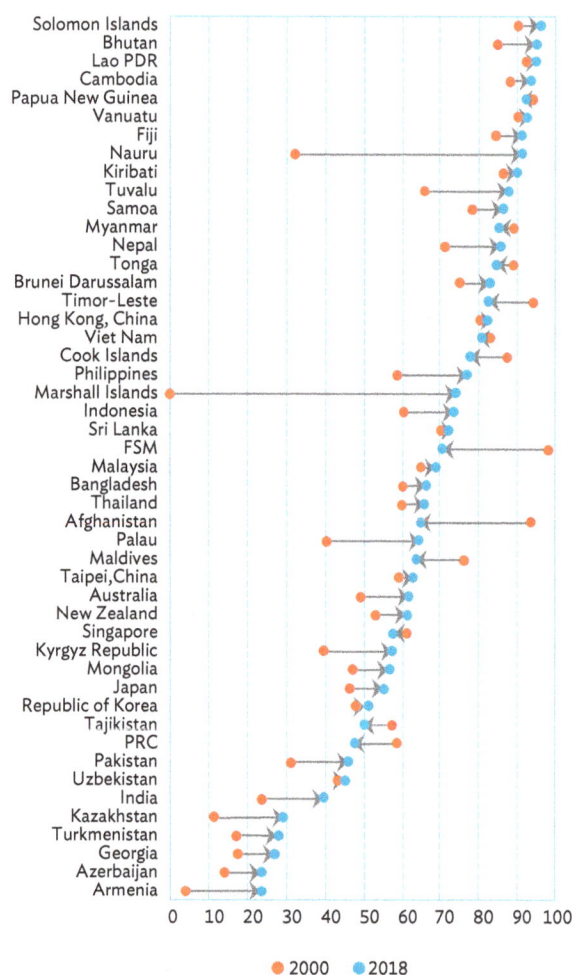

● 2000   ● 2018

FSM = Federated States of Micronesia, Lao PDR = Lao People's Democratic Republic, PRC = People's Republic of China.
Source: Table 2.4.14, Key Indicators for Asia and the Pacific 2019.

Bucking the upward trend was the region's largest importer, the PRC, whose share of imports from within Asia and the Pacific fell from 58.2% in 2000 to 47.2% in 2018. Over this period, the PRC increased its share of imports from South America (from 2.1% in 2000 to 6.6% in 2018), economies not belonging to any specified region (from 3.2% to 6.9%), the Middle East (from 4.5% to 7.6%), Africa (from 2.4% to 4.3%), and Europe (from 17.7% to 17.9%).

Afghanistan's intraregional merchandise imports as a share of its total imports also declined significantly from 2000 to 2018, falling from 93.4% to 64.9% over the review period. This decline was accounted for almost entirely by a rise of merchandise imports from the Middle East, with the proportion of total increasing from only 3.0% in 2000 to 28.3% in 2018.

Asia and the Pacific accounted for 35.7% of the world's total merchandise imports in 2018, up from 29.2% in 2000. This increase generated corresponding declines in the shares of the world's total merchandise imports by North America and Europe, which fell from 19.9% to 13.6% and from 40.6% to 38.6%, respectively, over the review period.

Total merchandise exports from Asia and the Pacific have recovered strongly

For the first time since 2009, total merchandise exports from Asia and the Pacific contracted in 2015, falling to $6.0 trillion from $6.5 trillion in 2014 (Figure 2.4.4). The region's exports fell further to $5.8 trillion in 2016, before recovering to $6.4 trillion in 2017 and rising again to $7.0 trillion in 2018. The slowdown across 2015 and 2016, along with the subsequent recovery across 2017 and 2018, mirrored the global trend in merchandise exports from 2015 to 2018.

From 2000 to 2018, merchandise exports from Asia and the Pacific experienced significant growth (Figure 2.4.4). By subregion, the following average

Figure 2.4.4: Total Merchandise Exports by Subregion within Asia and the Pacific

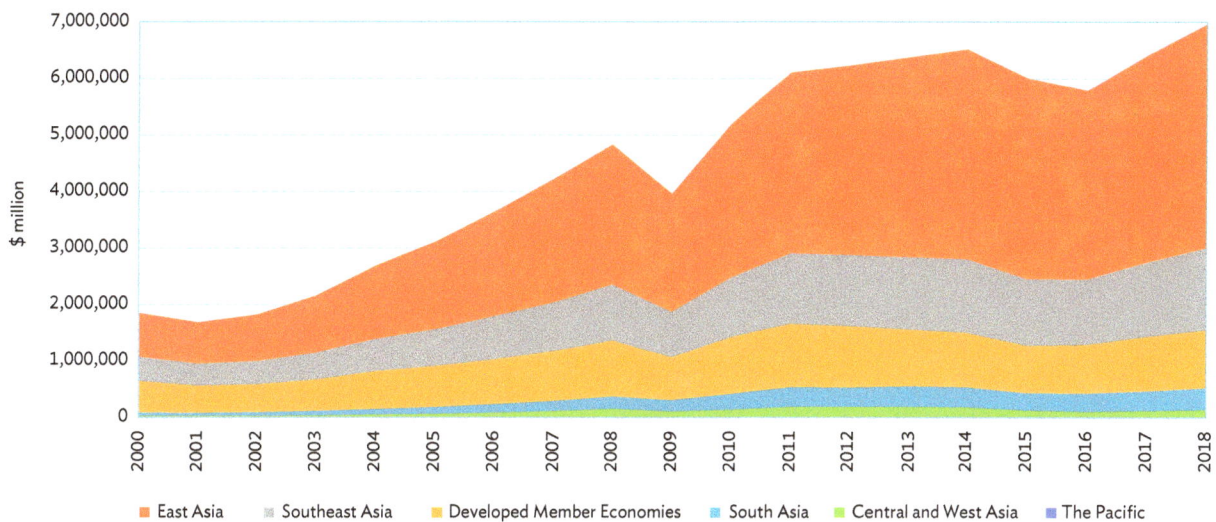

$ = United States dollars.
Source: Table 2.4.8, Key Indicators for Asia and the Pacific 2019.

annual growth rates were achieved: South Asia (32.4%), East Asia (22.9%), Central and West Asia (20.5%), the Pacific (17.7%), Southeast Asia (13.2%), and developed member economies (4.8%).

Among individual economies, Asia and the Pacific's largest exporters in 2018 were the PRC (35.7% of the regional total), Japan (10.6%), and the Republic of Korea (8.7%) as seen in Table 2.4.8. In 2000, the top three exporters, and their respective shares of regional merchandise exports, were Japan (26.0%); the PRC (13.5%); and Hong Kong, China (10.9%).

Asia and the Pacific generated 36.1% of global merchandise exports in 2018, up from 28.7% in 2000.

Data Issues and Comparability

Most of the data on international transactions presented in this section are taken from balance-of-payments statistics as reported by individual economies. IMF guidelines are followed by most governments in compiling these statistics. However, authorities have difficulty accurately recording nonofficial transactions such as migrant workers' remittances and private capital flows, which is one

of the reasons for updating the IMF's Balance of Payments Manual (BPM) to the sixth edition (BPM6) in 2009, and for aligning the BPM to the System of National Accounts 2008. A majority of economies have shifted to BPM6 while a few others continue to use either BPM5 or BPM4. This affects the comparability of data across economies.

The World Trade Organization and other international agencies closely monitor international trade statistics. Common definitions are used by all economies, with the larger economies across Asia and the Pacific using standard forms and procedures for data processing.

Data on official development assistance, other official flows, and private direct investment and other private capital are compiled by the Organisation for Economic Co-operation and Development's Development Assistance Committee. These data are standardized on a calendar-year basis for all donors, but may have discrepancies for some economies owing to the fiscal-year data available in budget documents. Donor-side commitments do not necessarily translate to actual disbursements to recipient economies of official development assistance.

Balance of Payments

Table 2.4.1:   Trade in Goods Balance
(% of GDP)

ADB Regional Member	2000	2005	2010	2013	2014	2015	2016	2017	2018
Developing ADB Member Economies									
Central and West Asia									
Afghanistan[a]	-28.4 (2002)	-65.5		-28.7	-39.9	-30.8	-36.3	-30.2	-31.4	-30.3
Armenia	-24.4	-13.0	-22.3	-19.7	-17.7	-11.2	-9.0	-11.9	-14.2
Azerbaijan	6.1	24.9	37.3	28.8	25.2	11.0	11.1	15.0	21.0
Georgia	-17.5	-19.0	-22.6	-21.7	-26.0	-28.2	-27.0	-25.2	-25.4
Kazakhstan	12.2	18.1	19.3	15.2	16.5	6.3	6.7	10.3	15.5
Kyrgyz Republic[a]	0.3	-17.0		-25.1	-37.9	-38.1	-34.3	-31.1	-30.9	-34.4
Pakistan[a]	-1.8		-3.7	-6.6	-7.0	-6.7	-6.5	-6.9	-8.8	-11.0
Tajikistan[a]	-9.5		-34.1	-43.9	-46.9	-33.2	-29.2	-27.1	-21.2	-25.1
Turkmenistan	...	11.6	9.9	10.3	9.5	-5.3	-15.6	-6.3	9.4
Uzbekistan[b]	3.6	10.1	6.4	0.5	-0.6	0.1	-0.1	1.5	-4.2
East Asia									
China, People's Republic of	2.5	5.4	3.9	3.8	4.2	5.2	4.4	3.9	2.9
Hong Kong, China	11.9	17.1	1.4	-10.1	-11.1	-7.4	-5.2	-6.7	-8.9
Korea, Republic of	2.7	3.5	4.2	5.9	5.8	8.2	7.8	7.0	6.5
Mongolia	-6.4	-3.9	-2.4	-20.7	1.5	4.8	12.0	13.0	5.2
Taipei,China	5.8	6.5	8.3	10.7	11.3	13.9	13.3	14.1	11.5
South Asia									
Bangladesh	-4.0	-5.5	-4.5	-4.7	-3.9	-3.6	-2.9	-3.8	-6.7
Bhutan[a]	-15.6	-30.7		-17.3	-19.7	-20.3	-20.2	-25.1	-18.9	-15.1
India[a]	-2.7	-6.2		-7.4	-7.9	-7.1	-6.2	-4.9	-6.0	-6.6
Maldives[a]	-37.4	-42.4	-40.9		-41.8	-45.0	-40.4	-41.8	-39.3	-45.3
Nepal[c]	-14.4	-14.6	-25.5	-27.2	-30.4	-31.3	-30.3	-33.9	-37.7
Sri Lanka[a]	-10.8	-10.3	-8.5		-10.2	-10.4	-10.4	-10.9	-11.0	-11.6
Southeast Asia									
Brunei Darussalam[a]	45.4 (2001)	50.7		45.3	38.2	43.5	22.4	18.9	19.8	...
Cambodia[a]	-14.7	-16.1		-23.9	-23.9	-23.1	-21.9	-19.2	-19.3	-23.8
Indonesia[a]	15.2		6.2	4.1	0.6	0.8	1.6	1.6	1.9	-0.0
Lao People's Democratic Republic[a]	-12.5	-12.1	-4.7		-6.6	-12.8	-14.1	-7.1	-4.7	-4.8
Malaysia[a]	22.2		23.9	15.1	9.5	10.2	9.3	8.2	8.5	8.2
Myanmar[a,d]	-0.1	0.1	0.1		0.2		-2.8	-6.1	-5.5	-9.0	...
Philippines[a]	-7.4		-11.8	-8.4	-6.5	-6.1	-8.0	-11.7	-12.8	-14.8
Singapore	16.4	37.3	26.4	25.6	27.5	30.1	27.4	27.3	27.0
Thailand	4.3	1.8	7.8	0.0	4.2	6.7	8.9	7.5	4.4
Viet Nam[a]	1.2	-4.2	-4.4	5.1		6.5	3.8	5.4	4.8	6.7
The Pacific									
Cook Islands	...	...	-25.2	-39.6	-37.2	-44.9	-49.6	-46.2	...
Fiji[a]	-14.0		-23.0	-23.5	-27.7	-21.2	-19.5	-20.2	-20.7	...
Kiribati[a]	-52.2	-62.8		-40.9	-52.4	-52.2	-52.4	-53.5	-52.9	...
Marshall Islands[c]	-54.0	-39.7	-54.0	-40.6	-39.3	-36.2	-34.1	-34.6	...
Micronesia, Federated States of	-38.2	-42.8	-43.3	-40.7	-37.0	-40.6	-33.3	-33.1	...
Nauru	...	...	33.6 (2012)	4.3	-27.1	-43.0	-37.7	-40.7	-41.6
Niue	...	-33.4 (2007)	-60.3	-43.7	-42.1	-40.2	-35.7	-43.6	-41.4
Palau	-79.1	-49.7	-45.8	-56.0	-62.4	-48.8	-44.7	-48.7	-48.6
Papua New Guinea[d]	31.4		36.8	15.6	1.1	20.6	27.0	29.5	29.1	29.7
Samoa[a]	-107.5		-28.4	-35.0	-39.5	-40.4	-35.0	-35.3	-36.3	-37.5
Solomon Islands[a]	-8.1	-5.6		-19.7	-1.7	-0.1	-0.2	0.2	0.1	0.0
Timor-Leste[a]	...	-3.9 (2006)	-7.0	-11.0	-14.9	-20.5	-21.5		-24.7	...
Tonga[e]	-44.8	-65.6	-52.6	-56.4		-56.4	-71.3	-74.6	-75.2	-81.1
Tuvalu[a]	-64.9	-40.5 (2006)	-54.3		-45.0	-47.0	-121.0	-61.0	-61.0	...
Vanuatu[a]	-18.2	-23.3	-27.1		-27.4	-24.8	-34.9	-32.5	-28.7	...
Developed ADB Member Economies									
Australia	-1.9	-2.6	-0.7	-0.2	0.6	-0.8	-1.7	0.8	0.7
Japan	2.4	2.2	1.9	-1.7	-2.0	-0.2	1.0	0.9	0.2
New Zealand	1.6	-3.0	1.4	1.2	-0.2	-1.0	-1.1	-0.9	...

... = data not available, | = marks break in series due to change in compilation methodology, 0.0 = magnitude is less than half of unit employed, ADB = Asian Development Bank, GDP = gross domestic product.

a Change in compilation methodology from the International Monetary Fund's Balance of Payments Manual (fifth edition) [BPM5] to the International Monetary Fund's Balance of Payments and International Investment Position Manual (sixth edition) [BPM6].
b Based on the International Monetary Fund's Balance of Payments Manual (fourth edition) [BPM4].
c Based on BPM5.
d Change in compilation methodology from BPM4 to BPM5.
e Change in compilation methodology from BPM4 to BPM6.

Source: Economy sources.

Table 2.4.2: **Trade in Services Balance**
(% of GDP)

ADB Regional Member	2000	2005	2010	2013	2014	2015	2016	2017	2018
Developing ADB Member Economies									
Central and West Asia									
Afghanistan[a]	-3.6 (2002)	-8.2	6.3	-3.2	-0.2	-1.0	-2.1	-3.4	-2.5
Armenia	-3.4	-3.0	-2.8	-1.1	-1.0	-0.9	-0.7	-0.2	-1.2
Azerbaijan	-4.3	-14.9	-3.3	-5.6	-8.1	-8.0	-8.3	-8.3	-4.4
Georgia	2.4	1.6	4.7	8.8	7.9	10.0	11.0	13.4	13.8
Kazakhstan	-5.3	-9.5	-4.9	-3.4	-3.1	-2.6	-2.7	-2.2	-2.7
Kyrgyz Republic[a]	-12.2	-4.9	-4.2	-0.7	-4.4	-2.8	-3.0	-1.2	-1.7
Pakistan[a]	-3.5	-2.8	-1.0	-0.7	-1.1	-1.1	-1.2	-1.4	-2.0
Tajikistan[a]	-1.7	-4.6	-0.5	-5.0	-3.1	-2.7	-2.0	-1.7	-2.9
Turkmenistan	...	...	...	...	...	...	...	...	...
Uzbekistan[b,c]	-0.5	-1.1	-1.2	-0.3	-0.1	1.3	1.4	3.1	...
East Asia									
China, People's Republic of	-0.1	0.0	-0.2	-1.3	-2.0	-2.0	-2.1	-2.1	-2.1
Hong Kong, China	-7.5	-4.9	4.4	10.7	11.3	9.8	7.5	7.8	9.0
Korea, Republic of	-0.1	-1.0	-1.2	-0.5	-0.2	-1.0	-1.2	-2.3	-1.7
Mongolia	-7.5	0.5	-4.2	-10.4	-10.5	-6.1	-12.0	-10.6	-15.2
Taipei,China	-3.8	-3.8	-2.5	-3.0	-2.2	-2.0	-1.9	-1.5	-1.2
South Asia									
Bangladesh	-1.4	-1.5	-1.1	-2.1	-2.4	-1.6	-1.2	-1.3	-1.7
Bhutan[a]	-1.8	-4.8	-4.4	-3.0	-3.3	-3.3	-2.8	-2.0	...
India[a]	0.3	2.8	2.6	3.8	3.7	3.2	3.0	3.0	2.9
Maldives[a]	33.4	6.8	34.8	57.1	59.6	49.4	40.5	35.3	...
Nepal[d]	7.2	-0.4	-1.3	0.5	1.1	1.3	0.4	0.1	0.1
Sri Lanka[a]	0.2	1.4	1.2	1.6	2.4	2.9	3.5	3.8	4.2
Southeast Asia									
Brunei Darussalam[a]	11.0 (2001)	0.6	-5.9	-13.1	-9.5	-7.8	-9.8	-5.7	...
Cambodia[a]	-0.6	2.9	9.0	11.2	10.3	9.5	8.0	8.4	9.9
Indonesia[a]	-11.1	-3.2	-1.3	-1.3	-1.1	-1.0	-0.8	-0.7	-0.7
Lao People's Democratic Republic[a]	5.1	2.5	2.4	-2.3	-2.9	-1.6	-1.2	-2.0	-1.3
Malaysia[a]	-11.1	-2.0	0.8	-0.9	-1.0	-1.8	-1.5	-1.7	-1.2
Myanmar[a,e]	-0.0	-0.1	-0.0	0.4	1.4	2.2	2.0	1.8	...
Philippines[a]	-2.3	2.1	2.9	2.6	1.6	1.9	2.3	2.8	3.2
Singapore	-4.1	-7.4	-0.1	-2.5	-4.1	-2.8	-0.8	-2.3	-0.5
Thailand	3.7	-3.6	-2.1	2.7	2.5	4.8	5.9	6.3	5.7
Viet Nam[a]	-1.8	-0.5	-2.1	-1.8	-2.1	-2.5	-2.1	-1.8	-1.5
The Pacific									
Cook Islands	...	...	41.4	33.9	32.5	37.6	44.5	43.1	...
Fiji[a]	7.1	13.4	17.1	15.0	27.8	32.8	33.6	31.9	...
Kiribati[a]	-27.4	-30.3	-25.4	-29.4	-37.1	-39.4	-36.8	-36.0	...
Marshall Islands[d]	-20.1	-21.8	-19.7	-21.5	-19.1	-19.8	-18.9	-21.8	...
Micronesia, Federated States of	-16.5	-16.3	-15.4	-12.9	-11.3	-11.7	-12.4	-10.3	...
Nauru	...	...	-13.5 (2012)	-7.4	-23.5	-13.4	-15.1	-15.2	-20.9
Niue	...	-17.5 (2007)	-40.5	4.8	8.4	13.0	13.6	16.5	21.1
Palau	13.2	16.6	19.3	27.8	32.2	32.3	25.5	21.4	19.3
Papua New Guinea[e]	-21.2	-17.8	-17.2	-16.4	-9.0	-5.4	-4.6	-5.5	-4.6
Samoa[a]	44.1	15.6	10.4	15.3	15.8	15.8	15.1	19.0	20.5
Solomon Islands[a]	-8.2	1.5	-13.8	-12.0	-10.6	-7.4	-8.4	...	...
Timor-Leste[a]	...	-10.8 (2006)	-24.0	-7.6	-14.7	-18.8	-21.0	-13.8	...
Tonga[f]	1.7	-7.3	-2.1	1.4	-0.7	1.2	4.3	5.9	6.8
Tuvalu[a]	-51.2	5.6 (2006)	-3.8	-73.0	-74.0	-95.0	-74.0	-80.0	...
Vanuatu[a]	17.1	14.9	17.6	23.3	22.7	13.5	21.7	21.8	...
Developed ADB Member Economies									
Australia	-0.2	-0.2	-0.3	-1.1	-1.1	-0.7	-0.6	-0.2	-0.3
Japan	-1.0	-0.8	-0.5	-0.7	-0.6	-0.4	-0.2	-0.1	-0.1
New Zealand	1.4	1.5	0.9	0.5	1.0	1.9	1.9	1.8	...

... = data not available, | = marks break in series due to change in compilation methodology, 0.0 = magnitude is less than half of the unit employed, ADB = Asian Development Bank, GDP = gross domestic product.

a   Change in compilation methodology from the International Monetary Fund's Balance of Payments Manual (fifth edition) [BPM5] to the International Monetary Fund's Balance of Payments and International Investment Position Manual (sixth edition) [BPM6].
b   Based on the International Monetary Fund's Balance of Payments Manual (fourth edition) [BPM4].
c   For 2005 onward, includes other goods and income.
d   Based on BPM5.
e   Change in compilation methodology from BPM4 to BPM5.
f   Change in compilation methodology from BPM4 to BPM6.

Source: Economy sources.

Balance of Payments

Table 2.4.3:   Current Account Balance
(% of GDP)

ADB Regional Member	2000	2005	2010	2013	2014	2015	2016	2017	2018
Developing ADB Member Economies									
Central and West Asia									
Afghanistan[a]	-3.5 (2002)	-2.7		-10.5	-27.5	-19.1	-24.1	-16.5	-20.9	-20.4
Armenia	-15.8	-2.5	-13.6	-7.3	-7.6	-2.6	-2.3	-2.4	-9.1
Azerbaijan	-3.2	1.3	28.4	17.6	13.9	-0.4	-3.6	4.1	12.9
Georgia	-5.8	-10.9	-10.3	-5.9	-10.8	-12.6	-13.1	-8.8	-7.7
Kazakhstan	2.0	-1.8	0.9	0.8	2.8	-3.3	-5.9	-3.1	-0.0
Kyrgyz Republic[a]	-5.5	-1.4		-6.6	-13.9	-17.2	-16.2	-11.5	-6.2	-8.7
Pakistan[a]	-0.3	-1.3	-2.3	-1.1	-1.3	-1.0	-1.8	-4.2	-6.7
Tajikistan[a]	-7.2		-12.8	-10.3	-10.4	-3.4	-6.1	-4.2	2.2	-5.0
Turkmenistan	8.4	5.1	-12.9	-7.3	-6.1	-15.6	-20.2	-10.3	3.1
Uzbekistan[b]	1.6	13.5	5.1	2.9	3.4	1.7	1.8	5.2	...
East Asia									
China, People's Republic of	1.7	5.8	3.9	1.5	2.3	2.8	1.8	1.6	0.4
Hong Kong, China	4.4	11.9	7.0	1.5	1.4	3.3	4.0	4.7	4.3
Korea, Republic of	1.8	1.3	2.4	5.6	5.6	7.2	6.5	4.6	4.4
Mongolia	-6.1	3.5	-12.3	-37.6	-15.8	-8.1	-6.3	-10.1	-17.0
Taipei,China	2.5	4.0	8.3	9.7	11.4	14.2	13.7	14.4	11.6
South Asia									
Bangladesh	-0.9	-1.0	3.7	1.6	0.8	1.8	1.9	-0.5	-3.6
Bhutan[a]	-9.4	-29.0		-20.4	-24.4	-25.2	-25.9	-29.1	-21.8	-17.7
India[a]	-0.6	-1.2		-2.8	-1.7	-1.3	-1.1	-0.6	-1.8	-2.1
Maldives[a]	-8.2	-23.5	-13.8		-3.9	-3.2	-7.4	-23.5	-21.8	-25.0
Nepal[c]	-2.2	2.0	-2.3	3.4	4.6	5.1	6.2	-0.4	-8.2
Sri Lanka[a]	-6.4	-2.7	-1.9		-3.4	-2.5	-2.3	-2.1	-2.6	-3.2
Southeast Asia									
Brunei Darussalam[a]	51.5 (2001)	47.3		36.5	20.9	30.7	16.6	12.9	16.4	...
Cambodia[a]	-2.7	-3.6		-8.7	-8.4	-8.5	-8.7	-8.4	-7.9	-11.3
Indonesia[a]	4.8		0.1	0.7	-3.2	-3.1	-2.0	-1.8	-1.6	-3.0
Lao People's Democratic Republic[a]	-0.3	-7.1	0.4		-7.9	-14.5	-15.8	-8.8	-7.5	-7.9
Malaysia[a]	9.0		14.4	10.1	3.5	4.4	3.0	2.4	2.8	2.1
Myanmar[a,d]	-0.1	0.0	0.0		-0.8		-2.9	-4.3	-2.2	-8.6	...
Philippines[a]	-2.7		1.9	3.6	4.2	3.8	2.5	-0.4	-0.7	-2.4
Singapore	11.1	23.3	22.9	15.7	18.0	17.2	17.5	16.4	17.9
Thailand	7.4	-4.0	3.4	-1.2	3.7	8.0	11.7	11.0	7.0
Viet Nam[a]	4.2	-1.0	-3.7	4.5		4.6	0.1	3.0	2.1	2.3
The Pacific									
Cook Islands	...	...	15.5	-6.2	-1.7	-0.8	1.4	2.6	...
Fiji[a]	-1.6		-7.0	-4.7	-9.7	-6.1	-3.8	-3.9	-7.1	...
Kiribati[a]	-3.2	-32.4		0.1	-4.5	31.3	32.8	10.5	38.0	...
Marshall Islands[c]	-10.9	7.6	-17.9	-10.7	-1.7	14.4	9.7	4.8	...
Micronesia, Federated States of	-13.5	-9.1	-15.7	-10.4	1.1	2.6	3.6	7.5	...
Nauru	...	...	38.1 (2012)	18.8	-13.5	-9.5	1.7	0.5	-1.8
Niue	...	-8.0 (2007)	-53.9	16.2	8.2	11.1	17.6	14.9	15.7
Palau	-49.7	-23.0	-8.8	-14.2	-17.9	-8.7	-13.6	-19.1	-16.6
Papua New Guinea[d]	10.1	13.3	-4.4	-1.5	10.4	20.2	25.0	22.5	24.3
Samoa[a]	-2.9	-6.0	-8.4	-5.9	-5.9	-1.6	-5.0	-0.8	3.0
Solomon Islands[a]	-12.9	-1.9		-20.8	-3.8	-0.6	-0.4	-0.6	-0.7	-0.5
Timor-Leste[a]	...	20.5 (2006)	42.0	43.6	27.0	6.4	-20.9		-11.4	...
Tonga[e]	-8.4	-4.2	-8.7	-15.1		-9.1	-9.1	5.2	7.0	4.4
Tuvalu[a]	54.5	-1.6 (2006)	-3.8		-7.0	3.0	-53.0	23.0	6.0	...
Vanuatu[a]	-5.0	-3.5	-5.8		-3.2	2.3	-5.3	-3.0	-9.2	...
Developed ADB Member Economies									
Australia	-5.1	-6.6	-5.0	-3.9	-3.2	-3.7	-4.7	-2.2	-2.7
Japan	2.7	3.6	3.9	0.9	0.8	3.1	4.0	4.1	3.5
New Zealand	-2.3	-7.8	-2.8	-2.5	-3.4	-2.6	-2.6	-3.0	...

... = data not available, | = marks break in series due to change in compilation methodology, 0.0 = magnitude is less than half of the unit employed, ADB = Asian Development Bank, GDP = gross domestic product.

a   Change in compilation methodology from the International Monetary Fund's Balance of Payments Manual (fifth edition) [BPM5] to the International Monetary Fund's Balance of Payments and International Investment Position Manual (sixth edition) [BPM6].
b   Based on the International Monetary Fund's Balance of Payments Manual (fourth edition) [BPM4].
c   Based on the methodology in BPM5.
d   Change in compilation methodology from BPM4 to BPM5.
e   Change in compilation methodology from BPM4 to BPM6.

Source: Economy sources.

Table 2.4.4: Workers' Remittances and Compensation of Employees, Receipts[a]
($ million)

ADB Regional Member	2000	2005	2010	2013	2014	2015	2016	2017	2018
Developing ADB Member Economies									
Central and West Asia	**1,643**	**8,018**	**20,721**	**33,741**	**34,944**	**31,083**	**30,609**	**33,514**	**35,501**
Afghanistan	...	...	362	329	250	341	368	378	384
Armenia	87	915	1,669	2,192	2,079	1,491	1,382	1,539	1,512
Azerbaijan	57	623	1,410	1,733	1,846	1,270	643	1,133	1,272
Georgia	210	446	1,184	1,945	1,986	1,459	1,521	1,794	2,034
Kazakhstan	122	62	226	207	229	194	275	355	419
Kyrgyz Republic	9	313	1,266	2,278	2,243	1,688	1,995	2,486	2,690
Pakistan	1,080	4,280	9,690	14,629	17,244	19,306	19,808	19,689	21,014
Tajikistan	79 (2002)	467	2,021	3,698	3,384	2,259	1,867	2,237	2,275
Turkmenistan	...	14 (2006)	35	40	30	16	8	2	2
Uzbekistan	...	898 (2006)	2,858	6,689	5,653	3,059	2,741	3,901	3,899
East Asia	**6,042**	**29,601**	**59,401**	**67,356**	**70,370**	**71,944**	**69,160**	**71,977**	**76,525**
China, People's Republic of	758	23,626	52,460	59,491	62,332	63,938	61,000	63,860	67,414
Hong Kong, China	136	297	340	360	372	387	399	437	469
Korea, Republic of	4,862	5,178	5,836	6,455	6,551	6,444	6,504	6,224	6,703
Mongolia	12	177	266	257	255	261	260	273	441
Taipei,China	274	323	500	792	860	915	997	1,183	1,499
South Asia	**16,092**	**29,959**	**71,929**	**95,864**	**98,319**	**97,958**	**90,231**	**96,631**	**109,685**
Bangladesh	1,969	4,642	10,850	13,867	14,988	15,296	13,574	13,498	15,496
Bhutan	...	2 (2006)	8	12	14	20	34	43	48
India	12,845	22,125	53,480	69,970	70,389	68,910	62,744	68,967	78,609
Maldives	2	2	3	3	3	4	4	4	4
Nepal	112	1,212	3,464	5,589	5,889	6,730	6,612	6,928	8,064
Sri Lanka	1,163	1,976	4,123	6,422	7,036	7,000	7,262	7,190	7,464
Southeast Asia	**11,752**	**24,900**	**42,983**	**56,157**	**60,501**	**63,376**	**65,658**	**69,302**	**74,556**
Brunei Darussalam	...	...	...	...	...	...	...	...	...
Cambodia	121	164	557	1,003	1,103	1,185	1,200	1,295	1,411
Indonesia	1,190	5,420	6,916	7,614	8,551	9,659	8,907	9,011	11,237
Lao People's Democratic Republic	1	1	42	170	188	189	189	253	271
Malaysia	342	1,117	1,103	1,423	1,580	1,644	1,604	1,648	1,663
Myanmar	102	129	115	1,644	1,864	2,005	2,346	2,565	2,754
Philippines	6,957	13,733	21,557	26,717	28,691	29,799	31,142	32,810	33,827
Singapore	...	...	...	...	...	...	...	...	...
Thailand	1,700	1,187	4,433	6,585	6,524	5,895	6,270	6,720	7,459
Viet Nam	1,340	3,150	8,260	11,000	12,000	13,000	14,000	15,000	15,934
The Pacific	**...**	**420**	**616**	**653**	**652**	**720**	**724**	**772**	**802**
Cook Islands	...	...	...	...	...	...	...	...	...
Fiji	44	203	176	204	221	251	269	274	288
Kiribati	...	13 (2006)	16	17	17	16	17	17	18
Marshall Islands	...	24	22	25	26	27	28	28	30
Micronesia, Federated States of	...	...	18	22	23	23	23	23	24
Nauru	...	...	...	...	...	...	...	...	...
Niue	...	...	...	...	...	...	...	...	...
Palau	...	1	2	2	2	2	2	2	2
Papua New Guinea	7	7	3	14	10	10	3	4	4
Samoa	...	82	139	165	141	131	131	138	142
Solomon Islands	4	7	14	21	16	19	20	16	17
Timor-Leste	...	4 (2006)	137	34	44	62	80	87	88
Tonga	53 (2001)	69	74	123	119	150	126	159	165
Tuvalu	...	5	4	4	4	4	4	4	4
Vanuatu	35	5	12	24	28	24	19	19	19
Developed ADB Member Economies	**3,514**	**2,197**	**3,919**	**5,212**	**6,331**	**5,783**	**6,160**	**6,594**	**7,610**
Australia	1,904	940	1,864	2,389	2,292	2,173	2,055	2,002	1,818
Japan	1,374	905	1,684	2,364	3,734	3,325	3,830	4,440	5,634
New Zealand	236	352	371	459	305	285	274	152	158
DEVELOPING ADB MEMBER ECONOMIES[b]	**35,530**	**92,899**	**195,650**	**253,770**	**264,786**	**265,082**	**256,381**	**272,196**	**297,070**
ALL ADB REGIONAL MEMBERS[b]	**39,044**	**95,096**	**199,570**	**258,983**	**271,116**	**270,865**	**262,541**	**278,790**	**304,679**
WORLD[b]	**119,051**	**284,762**	**469,852**	**580,511**	**603,224**	**595,831**	**589,369**	**632,727**	**689,404**

... = data not available, $ = United States dollars, ADB = Asian Development Bank.

a   For 2005 onward, figures are based on the IMF's Balance of Payments and International Investment Position Manual (sixth edition). Prior to 2005, figures are based on the IMF's Balance of Payments Manual (fifth edition).

b   For reporting economies only.

Sources: World Bank. Migration and Remittances Data. http://www.worldbank.org/en/topic/migrationremittancesdiasporaissues/brief/migration-remittances-data (accessed 3 June 2019). For Taipei,China: Central bank of Taipei,China. https://www.cbc.gov.tw/ct.asp?xItem=1061&ctNode=535&mp=2 (accessed 3 June 2019).

Balance of Payments

Table 2.4.5:   Workers' Remittances and Compensation of Employees, Receipts
(% of GDP)

ADB Regional Member	2000	2005	2010	2013	2014	2015	2016	2017	2018
Developing ADB Member Economies									
Central and West Asia									
Afghanistan	...	...	2.3	1.5	1.2	1.7	1.8	1.8	1.9
Armenia	4.6	18.7	18.0	19.7	17.9	14.1	13.1	13.3	12.2
Azerbaijan	1.1	4.7	2.7	2.3	2.5	2.4	1.7	2.8	2.7
Georgia	6.9	7.0	10.2	12.1	12.0	10.4	10.6	11.9	12.6
Kazakhstan	0.7	0.1	0.2	0.1	0.1	0.1	0.2	0.2	0.2
Kyrgyz Republic	0.6	12.7	26.4	31.1	30.0	25.3	29.3	32.3	33.2
Pakistan	1.4	3.6	5.6	6.6	6.9	7.2	7.1	6.5	7.4
Tajikistan	6.4 (2002)	20.2	35.8	43.5	36.6	28.8	26.9	31.2	30.2
Turkmenistan	...	0.1 (2006)	0.2	0.1	0.1	0.0	0.0	0.0	0.0
Uzbekistan	...	5.2 (2006)	6.1	9.7	7.4	3.7	3.4	6.6	7.7
East Asia									
China, People's Republic of	0.1	1.0	0.9	0.6	0.6	0.6	0.5	0.5	0.5
Hong Kong, China	0.1	0.2	0.1	0.1	0.1	0.1	0.1	0.1	0.1
Korea, Republic of	0.8	0.6	0.5	0.5	0.4	0.4	0.4	0.4	0.4
Mongolia	1.1	7.0	3.7	2.0	2.1	2.2	2.3	2.4	3.4
Taipei,China	0.1	0.1	0.1	0.2	0.2	0.2	0.2	0.2	0.3
South Asia									
Bangladesh	4.3	8.1	9.5	9.0	8.7	7.9	6.1	5.5	5.7
Bhutan	...	0.2 (2006)	0.5	0.7	0.7	1.0	1.5	1.7	...
India	2.7	2.6	3.1	3.6	3.4	3.2	2.7	2.6	2.8
Maldives	0.4	0.2	0.1	0.1	0.1	0.1	0.1	0.1	...
Nepal	2.1	14.7	21.3	30.7	29.2	32.4	31.5	27.1	29.0
Sri Lanka	7.0	8.1	7.3	8.6	8.9	8.7	8.8	8.2	8.4
Southeast Asia									
Brunei Darussalam	...	...	...	...	...	...	...	...	...
Cambodia	3.3	2.6	5.0	6.6	6.6	6.6	6.0	5.8	5.7
Indonesia	0.7	1.9	0.9	0.8	1.0	1.1	1.0	0.9	1.1
Lao People's Democratic Republic	0.0	0.0	0.6	1.4	1.4	1.3	1.2	1.5	1.5
Malaysia	0.4	0.8	0.4	0.4	0.5	0.5	0.5	0.5	0.5
Myanmar	...	...	...	2.6	2.8	3.2	3.6	3.9	...
Philippines	8.6	13.3	10.8	9.8	10.1	10.2	10.2	10.5	10.2
Singapore	...	...	...	...	...	...	...	...	...
Thailand	1.3	0.6	1.3	1.6	1.6	1.5	1.5	1.5	1.5
Viet Nam	4.3	5.5	7.1	6.4	6.4	6.7	6.8	6.7	6.5
The Pacific									
Cook Islands	...	...	...	...	...	...	...	...	...
Fiji	2.6	6.8	5.6	4.9	4.5	5.4	5.5	5.2	...
Kiribati	...	11.8 (2006)	10.0	9.3	9.3	9.4	9.8	9.4	...
Marshall Islands	...	16.9	13.2	12.8	14.1	15.1	14.3	13.6	...
Micronesia, Federated States of	...	...	6.1	7.0	7.3	7.4	7.0	6.4	...
Nauru	...	...	...	...	...	...	...	...	...
Niue	...	...	...	...	...	...	...	...	...
Palau	...	0.8	0.9	1.1	0.9	0.8	0.8	0.8	0.9
Papua New Guinea	0.2	0.1	0.0	0.1	0.0	0.0	0.0	0.0	0.0
Samoa	...	18.8	20.0	21.5	18.0	16.7	15.9	16.7	17.0
Solomon Islands	1.5	1.7	2.1	2.0	1.6	1.8	1.9	...	...
Timor-Leste	...	0.1 (2006)	3.4	0.6	1.1	2.0	3.2	3.5	...
Tonga	31.5 (2001)	26.1	19.8	27.9	27.3	37.6	31.1	34.7	34.6
Tuvalu	...	22.7	12.5	10.9	11.0	11.6	10.3	9.2	...
Vanuatu	12.7	1.3	1.7	3.0	3.5	3.2	2.3	2.1	...
Developed ADB Member Economies									
Australia	0.5	0.1	0.2	0.2	0.2	0.2	0.2	0.1	0.1
Japan	0.0	0.0	0.0	0.0	0.1	0.1	0.1	0.1	0.1
New Zealand	0.4	0.3	0.3	0.2	0.2	0.2	0.1	0.1	...
DEVELOPING ADB MEMBER ECONOMIES[a]	**1.0**	**1.6**	**1.6**	**1.5**	**1.4**	**1.4**	**1.3**	**1.3**	**1.3**
ALL ADB REGIONAL MEMBERS[a]	**0.4**	**0.8**	**1.0**	**1.1**	**1.1**	**1.1**	**1.0**	**1.0**	**1.0**

... = data not available, 0.0 = magnitude is less than half of unit employed, ADB = Asian Development Bank, GDP = gross domestic product.

a   For reporting economies only.

Sources: Economy sources; and World Bank. Migration and Remittances Data. http://www.worldbank.org/en/topic/migrationremittancesdiasporaissues/brief/migration-remittances-data (accessed 3 June 2019).

Table 2.4.6: Foreign Direct Investment, Net Inflows
($ million)

ADB Regional Member	2000	2005	2010	2013	2014	2015	2016	2017	2018
Developing ADB Member Economies									
Central and West Asia	**2,271**	**10,946**	**20,287**	**19,777**	**21,128**	**18,960**	**30,977**	**16,853**	**...**
Afghanistan	0	271	191	48	43	169	94	52	...
Armenia	104	292	529	346	404	178	338	250	254
Azerbaijan	130	4,476	3,353	2,619	4,430	4,048	4,500	2,867	1,403
Georgia	131	453	900	1,028	1,818	1,659	1,571	1,830	1,184
Kazakhstan	1,371	2,546	7,456	10,011	7,308	6,578	17,221	4,713	208
Kyrgyz Republic	-2	43	473	612	343	1,144	619	-107	...
Pakistan	308	2,201	2,022	1,333	1,868	1,621	2,488	2,952	2,778
Tajikistan	24	54	94	283	327	454	242	186	221
Turkmenistan	131	418	3,632	2,861	3,830	3,043	2,243	2,314	...
Uzbekistan	75	192	1,636	635	757	66	1,663	1,797	624
East Asia	**129,082**	**160,528**	**340,093**	**386,210**	**410,384**	**430,126**	**325,218**	**314,499**	**313,606**
China, People's Republic of	42,095	104,109	243,703	290,928	268,097	242,489	174,750	166,084	203,492
Hong Kong, China	70,496	40,963	82,709	76,857	129,847	181,047	133,259	125,717	86,463
Korea, Republic of	11,509	13,643	9,497	12,767	9,274	4,104	12,104	17,913	14,479
Mongolia	54	188	1,691	2,060	338	94	-4,156	1,494	2,174
Taipei,China	4,928	1,625	2,492	3,598	2,828	2,391	9,261	3,291	6,998
South Asia	**4,062**	**8,364**	**29,486**	**32,144**	**38,397**	**47,877**	**48,263**	**44,165**	**...**
Bangladesh	280	761	1,232	2,603	2,539	2,831	2,333	2,151	...
Bhutan	2 (2002)	6	75	20	24	6	12	-17	4
India	3,584	7,269	27,397	28,153	34,577	44,009	44,459	39,966	43,302
Maldives	22	53	216	361	333	298	457	493	...
Nepal	-0	2	88	74	30	52	106	196	...
Sri Lanka	173	272	478	933	894	680	897	1,375	...
Southeast Asia	**21,371**	**43,002**	**108,136**	**133,321**	**129,818**	**132,933**	**121,793**	**166,093**	**...**
Brunei Darussalam	61 (2001)	175	481	776	568	171	-151	468	...
Cambodia	118	379	1,404	2,068	1,853	1,823	2,476	2,788	3,103
Indonesia	-4,550	8,336	15,292	23,282	25,121	19,779	4,542	20,510	20,171
Lao People's Democratic Republic	34	28	279	681	868	1,078	935	1,599	...
Malaysia	3,788	3,925	10,886	11,296	10,619	9,857	13,470	9,512	...
Myanmar	255	235	901	2,255	2,175	4,084	3,278	4,002	...
Philippines	1,487	1,664	1,070	3,737	5,740	5,639	8,280	10,256	9,802
Singapore	15,515	18,090	55,076	64,390	68,698	69,775	73,553	94,811	82,039
Thailand	3,366	8,216	14,747	15,936	4,975	8,928	2,810	8,046	13,248
Viet Nam	1,298	1,954	8,000	8,900	9,200	11,800	12,600	14,100	...
The Pacific	**259**	**240**	**459**	**503**	**524**	**584**	**459**	**308**	**...**
Cook Islands	...	...	...	...	...	...	...	...	...
Fiji	1	173	178	244	378	205	392	388	342
Kiribati	1	3	-7	1	3	-1	2	1	...
Marshall Islands	126	3	-9	33	9	-5	-3	0	...
Micronesia, Federated States of	-0 (2001)	0	1	1	20	1	...	...	...
Nauru	1	1	1 (2009)	...	...	...	...	...	...
Niue	...	...	...	...	...	...	...	...	...
Palau	3	4	3	18	40	35	35	27	...
Papua New Guinea	96	32	29	18	-30	203	-40	-180	...
Samoa	-1	4	-1	14	23	27	3	9	...
Solomon Islands	2	1	166	53	21	32	37	37	...
Timor-Leste	1 (2002)	1	30	56	34	43	5	7	...
Tonga	9	6	5	6	13	13	6	-6	15
Tuvalu	-0 (2001)	-0	0	0	0	0	0	0	...
Vanuatu	20	13	63	59	13	31	22	25	...
Developed ADB Member Economies	**24,073**	**-17,727**	**42,938**	**64,576**	**86,197**	**50,230**	**82,275**	**67,044**	**85,400**
Australia	14,893	-25,093	35,211	53,997	63,195	45,051	39,226	44,480	58,048
Japan	10,688	5,460	7,441	10,648	19,752	5,252	40,954	20,420	25,877
New Zealand	-1,508	1,907	286	-70	3,249	-74	2,096	2,144	1,475
Developing ADB Member Economies[a]	**157,045**	**223,080**	**498,461**	**571,956**	**600,251**	**630,481**	**526,710**	**541,917**	**...**
All ADB Regional Members[a]	**181,118**	**205,353**	**541,399**	**636,532**	**686,447**	**680,710**	**608,985**	**608,961**	**...**
World	**1,460,994**	**1,546,409**	**1,857,433**	**2,134,350**	**1,838,186**	**2,394,019**	**2,480,344**	**2,085,130**	**...**

... = data not available, -0 or 0 = magnitude is less than half of unit employed, $ = United States dollars, ADB = Asian Development Bank.

a   For reporting economies only.

Sources: World Bank. World Development Indicators. http://data.worldbank.org/indicator/BX.KLT.DINV.CD.WD?locations=MH (accessed 24 July 2019).
For Taipei,China: Central bank of Taipei,China. https://www.cbc.gov.tw/ct.asp?xitem=1061&ctnode=535&mp=2 (accessed 24 July 2019).

Balance of Payments

Table 2.4.7: **Foreign Direct Investment, Net Inflows**
(% of GDP)

ADB Regional Member	2000	2005	2010	2013	2014	2015	2016	2017	2018
Developing ADB Member Economies									
Central and West Asia									
Afghanistan	1.2 (2002)	4.1	1.2	0.2	0.2	0.8	0.5	0.2	...
Armenia	5.5	6.0	5.7	3.1	3.5	1.7	3.2	2.2	2.0
Azerbaijan	2.5	33.8	6.3	3.5	5.9	7.6	11.9	7.0	3.0
Georgia	4.3	7.1	7.7	6.4	11.0	11.9	10.9	12.1	7.3
Kazakhstan	7.5	4.5	5.0	4.2	3.3	3.6	12.5	2.9	0.1
Kyrgyz Republic	-0.2	1.7	9.9	8.3	4.6	17.1	9.1	-1.4	...
Pakistan	0.4	1.8	1.2	0.6	0.8	0.6	0.9	1.0	1.0
Tajikistan	2.7	2.4	1.7	3.3	3.5	5.8	3.5	2.6	2.9
Turkmenistan	2.7	2.4	16.1	7.3	8.8	8.5	6.2	6.1	...
Uzbekistan	0.5	1.3	3.5	0.9	1.0	0.1	2.0	3.0	1.2
East Asia									
China, People's Republic of	3.5	4.6	4.0	3.0	2.6	2.2	1.6	1.4	1.5
Hong Kong, China	41.1	22.6	36.2	27.9	44.6	58.5	41.5	36.8	23.8
Korea, Republic of	2.0	1.5	0.8	0.9	0.6	0.3	0.8	1.1	0.8
Mongolia	4.7	7.4	23.5	16.4	2.8	0.8	-37.2	13.1	16.7
Taipei,China	1.5	0.4	0.6	0.7	0.5	0.5	1.7	0.6	1.2
South Asia									
Bangladesh	0.6	1.3	1.1	1.7	1.5	1.5	1.1	0.9	...
Bhutan	0.5 (2002)	0.8	4.7	1.1	1.2	0.3	0.5	-0.7	...
India	0.7	0.9	1.6	1.5	1.7	2.1	1.9	1.5	1.6
Maldives	3.6	4.6	8.4	11.0	9.0	7.3	10.3	10.1	...
Nepal	-0.0	0.0	0.5	0.4	0.2	0.2	0.5	0.8	...
Sri Lanka	1.0	1.1	0.8	1.3	1.1	0.8	1.1	1.6	...
Southeast Asia									
Brunei Darussalam	1.1 (2001)	1.8	3.5	4.3	3.3	1.3	-1.3	3.9	...
Cambodia	3.2	6.0	12.5	13.6	11.1	10.1	12.4	12.6	12.6
Indonesia	-2.8	2.9	2.0	2.6	2.8	2.3	0.5	2.0	1.9
Lao People's Democratic Republic	2.1	1.0	4.1	5.7	6.5	7.5	5.9	9.5	...
Malaysia	4.0	2.7	4.3	3.5	3.1	3.3	4.5	3.0	...
Myanmar	...	...	...	3.6	3.3	6.5	5.1	6.0	...
Philippines	1.8	1.6	0.5	1.4	2.0	1.9	2.7	3.3	3.0
Singapore	16.1	14.2	23.0	20.9	21.8	22.7	23.1	28.0	22.5
Thailand	2.7	4.3	4.3	3.8	1.2	2.2	0.7	1.8	2.6
Viet Nam	4.2	3.4	6.9	5.2	4.9	6.1	6.1	6.3	...
The Pacific									
Cook Islands	...	...	...	...	...	...	...	...	...
Fiji	0.0	5.8	5.7	5.8	7.8	4.4	7.9	7.4	...
Kiribati	1.1	2.3	-4.2	0.5	1.5	-0.5	1.0	0.4	...
Marshall Islands	111.8	2.3	-5.6	16.9	4.9	-3.0	-1.5	0.1	...
Micronesia, Federated States of	-0.1 (2001)	0.0	0.3	0.3	6.4	0.3	...	...	...
Nauru	...	3.2	3.0 (2009)	...	...	...	...	...	...
Niue	...	...	...	...	...	...	...	...	...
Palau	2.2	2.2	1.5	8.1	16.4	12.3	11.7	9.6	...
Papua New Guinea	2.8	0.7	0.2	0.1	-0.1	0.9	-0.2	-0.8	...
Samoa	-0.5	0.9	-0.2	1.8	2.9	3.4	0.3	1.1	...
Solomon Islands	0.7	0.1	23.8	5.3	2.0	3.1	3.4	...	...
Timor-Leste	0.2 (2002)	0.1	0.8	1.0	0.8	1.4	0.2	0.3	...
Tonga	4.9	2.3	1.2	1.4	3.0	3.2	1.4	-1.2	3.2
Tuvalu	-0.1 (2001)	-0.1	1.4	0.9	0.8	0.9	0.8	0.7	...
Vanuatu	7.4	3.4	9.0	7.4	1.6	4.1	2.7	2.8	...
Developed ADB Member Economies									
Australia	3.9	-3.6	2.9	3.6	4.4	3.7	3.2	3.3	4.2
Japan	0.2	0.1	0.1	0.2	0.4	0.1	0.8	0.4	0.5
New Zealand	-2.8	1.7	0.2	-0.0	1.6	-0.0	1.1	1.1	...
DEVELOPING ADB MEMBER ECONOMIES[a]	**4.4**	**3.8**	**4.1**	**3.3**	**3.3**	**3.3**	**2.7**	**2.6**	**2.1**
ALL ADB REGIONAL MEMBERS[a]	**2.0**	**1.8**	**2.8**	**2.7**	**2.8**	**2.8**	**2.4**	**2.2**	**2.0**

... = data not available, 0.0 = magnitude is less than half of the unit employed, ADB = Asian Development Bank, GDP = gross domestic product.

a   For reporting economies with data available for both foreign direct investment and GDP.

Sources: World Bank. World Development Indicators. http://data.worldbank.org/indicator/BX.KLT.DINV.CD.WD?locations=MH (accessed 24 July 2019).
For Taipei,China: Central bank of Taipei,China. https://www.cbc.gov.tw/ct.asp?xItem=1061&ctNode=535&mp=2 (accessed 24 July 2019).

Table 2.4.8: **Merchandise Exports**
($ million)

ADB Regional Member	2000	2005	2010	2013	2014	2015	2016	2017	2018
Developing ADB Member Economies									
Central and West Asia	**26,716**	**64,110**	**134,665**	**181,036**	**174,603**	**116,374**	**97,395**	**113,221**	**125,443**
Afghanistan	137	384	388	515	571	571	596	723	875
Armenia	300	974	1,041	1,479	1,547	1,485	1,792	2,238	2,412
Azerbaijan	1,745	7,649	26,374	31,703	28,260	15,586	13,211	15,152	20,794
Georgia	324	865	1,677	2,910	2,861	2,205	2,113	2,735	3,355
Kazakhstan	8,812	27,849	60,271	84,700	79,460	45,956	36,737	48,503	60,956
Kyrgyz Republic	505	674	1,756	2,007	1,884	1,483	1,573	1,764	1,765
Pakistan	8,335	14,453	19,261	23,383	25,715	23,526	20,859	20,566	21,296
Tajikistan	784	909	1,195	1,162	977	891	899	1,198	...
Turkmenistan	2,508	4,944	9,679	18,854	19,782	12,164	7,520	7,788	...
Uzbekistan	3,265	5,409	13,023	14,323	13,546	12,508	12,095	12,554	13,991
East Asia	**775,319**	**1,536,567**	**2,714,594**	**3,542,100**	**3,713,254**	**3,553,456**	**3,339,763**	**3,657,920**	**3,965,543**
China, People's Republic of	249,203	761,953	1,577,754	2,209,004	2,342,293	2,273,468	2,097,631	2,263,371	2,487,401
Hong Kong, China	201,855	289,325	390,134	458,959	473,654	465,092	462,269	497,340	530,472
Korea, Republic of	172,268	284,419	466,384	559,632	572,665	526,757	495,426	573,694	604,860
Mongolia	536	1,064	2,909	4,269	5,774	4,669	4,916	6,201	7,012
Taipei,China	151,458	199,807	277,413	310,236	318,869	283,470	279,521	317,313	335,798
South Asia	**56,445**	**119,305**	**276,096**	**364,634**	**353,306**	**310,212**	**320,174**	**346,730**	**385,742**
Bangladesh	4,780	8,259	16,099	27,619	29,807	30,588	33,352	33,462	35,612
Bhutan	103	214	535	511	539	561	488	566	604
India	45,297	103,496	249,951	325,099	310,742	267,550	275,233	300,440	336,879
Maldives	109	162	62	166	144	144	139	199	...
Nepal	701	823	830	826	943	833	653	699	745
Sri Lanka	5,456	6,351	8,618	10,413	11,130	10,536	10,309	11,364	11,901
Southeast Asia	**427,409**	**655,385**	**1,048,737**	**1,279,250**	**1,297,458**	**1,172,817**	**1,152,310**	**1,313,489**	**1,446,072**
Brunei Darussalam	3,906	6,247	8,887	11,436	10,601	6,338	4,917	5,585	6,575
Cambodia	1,397	2,908	3,903	7,044	8,170	9,336	10,273	11,224	12,963
Indonesia	62,124	85,660	157,779	182,552	175,981	150,366	145,186	168,811	180,215
Lao People's Democratic Republic	330	553	1,746	2,264	3,276	3,653	4,245	4,873	5,295
Malaysia	98,229	141,595	198,325	228,503	233,868	199,041	189,708	217,403	247,397
Myanmar	1,756	3,836	8,872	11,233	11,452	11,432	11,837	13,878	16,672
Philippines	38,078	41,255	51,498	56,698	62,102	58,827	57,406	68,713	69,307
Singapore	137,954	230,523	352,553	419,969	415,191	357,729	337,962	372,938	411,958
Thailand	69,152	110,360	192,937	227,518	226,601	214,077	214,195	234,947	252,207
Viet Nam	14,483	32,447	72,237	132,033	150,217	162,017	176,581	215,119	243,483
The Pacific	**2,813**	**4,304**	**7,010**	**7,803**	**10,721**	**10,052**	**9,924**	**11,645**	**11,793**
Cook Islands	9	5	5	11	18	14	14	20	17
Fiji	543	705	837	1,151	1,220	982	931	985	1,016
Kiribati	4	4	4	7	10	9	...	...	...
Marshall Islands	25	34	...	...	...	...	...	...	...
Micronesia, Federated States of	17	13	30	35	32	40	49	46	...
Nauru[a]	...	0	32	48	22	14	26	25	...
Niue	0	...	1	1	1	1	1	2	2
Palau	12	14	16	21	19	18	...	...	...
Papua New Guinea	2,089	3,311	5,737	5,951	8,794	8,425	8,202	9,958	10,060
Samoa	14	12	23	24	27	34	36	37	42
Solomon Islands	65	105	227	448	455	421	432	469	534
Timor-Leste	...	43	42	53	39	38	162	24	46
Tonga	9	10	8	14	19	18	21	19	13
Tuvalu	0	0	1	0	0	0	0	0	...
Vanuatu	26	46	48	39	63	39	50	60	64
Developed ADB Member Economies	**557,173**	**723,803**	**1,012,107**	**1,008,852**	**970,204**	**846,261**	**869,790**	**967,697**	**1,035,712**
Australia	63,980	106,211	212,027	252,894	239,708	187,525	192,140	230,950	257,436
Japan	479,320	595,696	767,825	714,931	689,916	624,681	643,753	697,951	737,877
New Zealand	13,873	21,896	32,255	41,026	40,579	34,054	33,897	38,797	40,399
DEVELOPING ADB MEMBER ECONOMIES[b]	**1,288,702**	**2,379,671**	**4,181,101**	**5,374,823**	**5,549,341**	**5,162,911**	**4,919,565**	**5,443,006**	**5,934,593**
ALL ADB REGIONAL MEMBERS[b]	**1,845,875**	**3,103,474**	**5,193,208**	**6,383,675**	**6,519,545**	**6,009,172**	**5,789,355**	**6,410,703**	**6,970,305**
WORLD	**6,439,934**	**10,433,968**	**15,142,190**	**18,699,578**	**18,797,999**	**16,400,565**	**15,845,543**	**17,518,078**	**19,324,970**

... = data not available, 0 = magnitude is less than half of unit employed, $ = United States dollars, ADB = Asian Development Bank.

a For 2002–2015, data were taken from the media release on International Merchandise Trade Statistics (IMTS Release No. 01/2016) of the Nauru Bureau of Statistics, published on 3 November 2016.
b For reporting economies only.

Sources: Economy sources; and International Monetary Fund. International Financial Statistics. http://data.imf.org/ (accessed 27 March 2019).
For world merchandise exports: International Monetary Fund. Direction of Trade Statistics.
http://data.imf.org/?sk=9D6028D4-F14A-464C-A2F2-59B2CD424B85 (accessed 20 May 2019).

External Trade

Table 2.4.9: **Growth Rates of Merchandise Exports**[a]
(%)

ADB Regional Member	2000	2005	2010	2013	2014	2015	2016	2017	2018
Developing ADB Member Economies									
Central and West Asia									
Afghanistan	-17.4	25.9	-3.7	24.4	10.9	–	4.5	21.2	21.1
Armenia	29.7	34.7	46.6	7.1	4.6	-4.0	20.6	24.9	7.8
Azerbaijan	87.7	...	25.3	-2.1	-10.9	-44.8	-15.2	14.7	37.2
Georgia	36.1	33.8	48.0	22.5	-1.7	-22.9	-4.2	29.5	22.6
Kazakhstan	50.1	38.6	39.5	-2.0	-6.2	-42.2	-20.1	32.0	25.7
Kyrgyz Republic	11.2	-6.5	5.0	4.1	-6.1	-21.3	6.1	12.1	0.0
Pakistan	4.8	14.9	12.0	2.6	10.0	-8.5	-11.3	-1.4	3.6
Tajikistan	13.9	-0.7	18.3	-14.4	-15.9	-8.9	0.9	33.3	...
Turkmenistan	115.5	28.3	3.8	-5.7	4.9	-38.5	-38.2	3.6	...
Uzbekistan	0.9	11.5	10.6	5.3	-5.4	-7.7	-3.3	3.8	11.4
East Asia									
China, People's Republic of	27.8	28.4	31.3	7.8	6.0	-2.9	-7.7	7.9	9.9
Hong Kong, China	16.1	11.6	22.5	3.7	3.2	-1.8	-0.6	7.6	6.7
Korea, Republic of	19.9	12.0	28.3	2.1	2.3	-8.0	-5.9	15.8	5.4
Mongolia	18.0	22.4	54.3	-2.6	35.3	-19.1	5.3	26.1	13.1
Taipei,China	22.6	8.6	35.1	1.3	2.8	-11.1	-1.4	13.5	5.8
South Asia									
Bangladesh	12.5	11.3	3.7	17.5	7.9	2.6	9.0	0.3	6.4
Bhutan	-11.3	35.8	6.5	-11.9	5.5	4.1	-13.0	16.0	6.6
India	22.2	25.0	43.1	6.3	-4.4	-13.9	2.9	9.2	12.1
Maldives	18.8	-10.5	-63.6	2.8	-13.0	-0.6	-3.2	43.0	...
Nepal	34.0	12.4	-4.9	-5.2	14.1	-11.6	-21.6	7.0	6.6
Sri Lanka	18.5	10.1	21.7	6.7	6.9	-5.3	-2.2	10.2	4.7
Southeast Asia									
Brunei Darussalam	53.1	23.3	23.9	-11.9	-7.3	-40.2	-22.4	13.6	17.7
Cambodia	23.6	12.3	24.4	23.9	16.0	14.3	10.0	9.3	15.5
Indonesia	27.7	19.7	35.4	-3.9	-3.6	-14.6	-3.4	16.3	6.8
Lao People's Democratic Republic	9.6	52.2	65.9	3.3	44.7	11.5	16.2	14.8	8.7
Malaysia	16.1	11.8	26.5	0.4	2.3	-14.9	-4.7	14.6	13.8
Myanmar	53.1	61.8	32.4	26.2	1.9	-0.2	3.5	17.2	20.1
Philippines	8.7	4.0	34.0	8.8	9.5	-5.3	-2.4	19.7	0.9
Singapore	20.3	15.7	30.5	1.1	-1.1	-13.8	-5.5	10.3	10.5
Thailand	18.0	14.6	27.3	-0.1	-0.4	-5.5	0.1	9.7	7.3
Viet Nam	25.5	22.5	26.5	15.3	13.8	7.9	9.0	21.8	13.2
The Pacific									
Cook Islands	154.4	-26.9	88.0	100.6	65.8	-20.3	-2.9	48.9	-14.2
Fiji	-12.1	1.4	24.9	-5.6	6.0	-19.5	-5.1	5.8	3.1
Kiribati	-59.1	58.2	-38.0	-4.9	51.9	-11.0	...	...	...
Marshall Islands	48.7	14.0	5.6 (2009)	...	...	...	...	...	...
Micronesia, Federated States of	...	-7.3	63.5	-33.3	-7.8	23.0	23.3	-5.6	...
Nauru	...	-69.8	249.5	-33.4	-53.4	-39.4	...	-4.1	...
Niue	...	...	1.0	47.7	1.4	-20.2	8.8	23.0	12.8
Palau	65.9	116.9	15.9	-0.5	-8.7	-5.3	...	...	...
Papua New Guinea	7.3	26.8	30.9	-5.9	47.8	-4.2	-2.6	21.4	1.0
Samoa	-24.9	0.6	114.4	-23.2	14.7	23.8	6.3	3.1	13.5
Solomon Islands	-48.1	22.3	37.4	-8.3	1.7	-7.6	2.7	8.6	13.7
Timor-Leste	...	-58.9	20.7	-30.7	-26.7	-1.7	321.2	-85.1	91.5
Tonga	-27.1	-35.2	7.1	-9.2	34.2	-6.5	21.1	-12.1	-31.2
Tuvalu	-91.5	-54.0	76.5	4.4	464.8	-12.0	7.2	-8.1	...
Vanuatu	2.8	-6.5	-14.8	-29.4	62.6	-38.0	28.8	20.2	5.8
Developed ADB Member Economies									
Australia	14.1	22.6	38.3	-1.4	-5.2	-21.8	2.5	20.2	11.5
Japan	14.8	5.4	32.6	-10.5	-3.5	-9.5	3.1	8.4	5.7
New Zealand	11.2	6.3	30.5	9.7	-1.1	-16.1	-0.5	14.5	4.1
DEVELOPING ADB MEMBER ECONOMIES[b]	**21.0**	**18.4**	**30.2**	**4.6**	**3.2**	**-7.0**	**-4.7**	**10.6**	**9.0**
ALL ADB REGIONAL MEMBERS[b]	**19.0**	**15.7**	**30.9**	**2.4**	**2.1**	**-7.8**	**-3.7**	**10.7**	**8.7**
WORLD	**13.7**	**13.6**	**22.2**	**2.2**	**0.5**	**-12.8**	**-3.4**	**10.6**	**10.3**

... = data not available, – = magnitude equals zero, ADB = Asian Development Bank.

a   Growth rates are based on the value of exports in United States dollars.
b   For reporting economies only.

Sources: Economy sources; and International Monetary Fund. International Financial Statistics. http://data.imf.org/ (accessed 27 March 2019).

Table 2.4.10:   Merchandise Imports
($ million)

ADB Regional Member	2000	2005	2010	2013	2014	2015	2016	2017	2018
Developing ADB Member Economies									
Central and West Asia	**24,868**	**58,649**	**109,356**	**163,205**	**157,857**	**138,055**	**128,493**	**141,951**	**144,635**
Afghanistan	1,176	2,470	5,154	8,724	7,729	7,723	6,534	7,065	7,407
Armenia	885	1,802	3,749	4,386	4,424	3,239	3,273	4,097	4,963
Azerbaijan	1,172	4,350	6,662	10,321	9,332	9,774	9,004	9,037	10,952
Georgia	710	2,488	5,236	8,023	8,602	7,300	7,294	7,939	9,121
Kazakhstan	5,040	17,353	31,127	48,806	41,296	30,568	25,377	29,600	32,534
Kyrgyz Republic	554	1,189	3,223	5,987	5,735	4,154	4,000	4,495	4,907
Pakistan	9,967	20,630	34,169	42,802	45,820	45,394	44,665	52,742	55,189
Tajikistan	675	1,330	2,657	4,121	4,297	3,436	3,031	2,775	...
Turkmenistan	1,742	2,947	8,204	16,090	16,638	14,051	13,177	10,189	...
Uzbekistan	2,947	4,091	9,176	13,947	13,984	12,417	12,138	14,012	19,562
East Asia	**739,620**	**1,407,134**	**2,513,437**	**3,272,375**	**3,314,814**	**2,877,443**	**2,743,744**	**3,145,101**	**3,565,346**
China, People's Republic of	225,094	659,953	1,396,244	1,949,989	1,959,235	1,679,565	1,587,926	1,843,793	2,135,637
Hong Kong, China	212,800	299,520	433,102	523,558	544,107	522,001	516,395	559,074	602,335
Korea, Republic of	160,481	261,238	425,212	515,586	525,515	436,499	406,193	478,478	535,202
Mongolia	615	1,177	3,200	6,358	5,237	3,798	3,358	4,337	5,875
Taipei,China	140,630	185,245	255,679	276,884	280,722	235,581	229,872	259,419	286,297
South Asia	**67,978**	**173,194**	**409,681**	**524,337**	**514,757**	**455,084**	**452,970**	**537,469**	**612,777**
Bangladesh	7,300	11,329	21,245	34,362	36,608	37,528	39,795	42,779	53,572
Bhutan[a]	193	466	810	864	936	977	1,046	1,044	1,001
India	51,372	149,753	368,166	463,402	448,486	388,189	383,609	460,836	524,596
Maldives	389	683	909	1,728	1,988	1,890	2,121	2,355	...
Nepal	1,526	2,094	5,110	5,981	7,323	7,565	7,204	9,474	11,409
Sri Lanka	7,198	8,869	13,441	17,999	19,417	18,935	19,195	20,982	22,200
Southeast Asia	**368,445**	**583,426**	**953,163**	**1,231,466**	**1,224,012**	**1,089,115**	**1,070,651**	**1,232,236**	**1,405,052**
Brunei Darussalam	1,107	1,448	2,535	3,613	3,596	3,235	2,671	3,083	4,167
Cambodia[a]	1,936	3,918	6,588	10,680	12,022	13,285	14,119	15,502	18,806
Indonesia	33,515	57,701	135,663	186,629	178,179	142,695	135,653	156,925	188,711
Lao People's Democratic Republic[a]	535	882	2,060	3,051	4,976	5,675	5,372	5,667	6,164
Malaysia	81,963	114,302	164,177	205,875	208,667	175,593	168,459	194,497	217,530
Myanmar	2,407	1,934	4,866	12,043	16,220	16,743	15,706	19,253	19,345
Philippines	34,491	47,418	54,933	62,411	65,398	71,067	84,108	96,093	112,841
Singapore	134,675	200,861	312,668	388,053	377,714	307,967	291,922	327,389	370,833
Thailand	62,180	118,200	184,834	227,079	209,392	187,079	177,662	200,820	229,967
Viet Nam	15,637	36,761	84,839	132,033	147,849	165,776	174,978	213,007	236,688
The Pacific	**2,639**	**4,445**	**7,231**	**11,640**	**9,825**	**7,794**	**6,985**	**8,195**	**7,474**
Cook Islands	51	81	91	116	121	110	106	135	134
Fiji	856	1,610	1,806	2,823	2,656	2,268	2,310	2,402	2,729
Kiribati	39	76	73	107	107	103	...	...	...
Marshall Islands	116	132	...	...	...	...	...	...	...
Micronesia, Federated States of	107	128	168	188	161	160	186	183	...
Nauru[b]	...	9	13	152	114	93	65	72	...
Niue	2	...	9	15	15	13	13	15	18
Palau	127	108	103	145	149	156	...	...	...
Papua New Guinea	999	1,519	3,522	6,196	4,548	3,005	2,381	3,363	2,853
Samoa	91	187	280	326	341	298	312	321	...
Solomon Islands	92	185	405	510	505	485	465	516	592
Timor-Leste	...	109	298	529	554	491	512	554	565
Tonga	70	121	158	198	219	209	229	238	228
Tuvalu	5	13	22	21	22	37	23	27	...
Vanuatu	84	165	284	314	314	367	382	370	355
Developed ADB Member Economies	**461,984**	**662,401**	**917,034**	**1,105,496**	**1,081,292**	**885,067**	**832,597**	**934,246**	**1,020,561**
Australia	67,806	118,836	193,071	232,685	227,859	200,643	189,075	220,953	227,242
Japan	379,884	516,697	692,242	832,440	810,886	647,744	607,043	672,032	748,967
New Zealand	14,294	26,868	31,721	40,372	42,547	36,680	36,479	41,261	44,352
DEVELOPING ADB MEMBER ECONOMIES[c]	**1,203,550**	**2,226,847**	**3,992,868**	**5,203,023**	**5,221,265**	**4,567,492**	**4,402,843**	**5,064,952**	**5,735,285**
ALL ADB REGIONAL MEMBERS[c]	**1,665,534**	**2,889,248**	**4,909,903**	**6,308,520**	**6,302,557**	**5,452,559**	**5,235,440**	**5,999,198**	**6,755,845**
WORLD	**6,608,013**	**10,688,594**	**15,398,542**	**18,821,237**	**18,916,839**	**16,586,436**	**16,149,680**	**17,739,316**	**19,553,220**

... = data not available, $ = United States dollars, ADB = Asian Development Bank.

a   Compilation methodology shifted from cost, insurance, and freight to free on board from 2004 onward for Bhutan; from 2005 onward for Cambodia; and from 2017 onward for the Lao People's Democratic Republic.
b   For 2002–2015, data were taken from the media release on International Merchandise Trade Statistics (IMTS Release No. 01/2016) of the Nauru Bureau of Statistics, published on 3 November 2016.
c   For reporting economies only.

Sources: Economy sources; and International Monetary Fund. International Financial Statistics. http://data.imf.org/ (accessed 27 March 2019).
For world merchandise exports: International Monetary Fund. Direction of Trade Statistics.
http://data.imf.org/?sk=9D6028D4-F14A-464C-A2F2-59B2CD424B85 (accessed 20 May 2019).

External Trade

Table 2.4.11:   Growth Rates of Merchandise Imports[a]
(%)

ADB Regional Member	2000	2005	2010	2013	2014	2015	2016	2017	2018
Developing ADB Member Economies									
Central and West Asia									
Afghanistan	16.2	13.5	54.5	-2.3	-11.4	-0.1	-15.4	8.1	4.8
Armenia	9.1	33.4	12.9	2.9	0.9	-26.8	1.1	25.2	21.1
Azerbaijan	13.1	...	6.9	1.3	-9.6	4.7	-7.9	0.4	21.2
Georgia	2.9	34.9	17.0	-0.4	7.2	-15.1	-0.1	8.8	14.9
Kazakhstan	37.9	35.8	9.6	5.3	-15.4	-26.0	-17.0	16.6	9.9
Kyrgyz Republic	-7.6	25.5	6.0	7.4	-4.2	-27.6	-3.7	12.4	9.2
Pakistan	5.7	33.7	2.5	-0.4	7.1	-0.9	-1.6	18.1	4.6
Tajikistan	1.8	11.7	3.4	9.1	4.3	-20.1	-11.8	-8.4	...
Turkmenistan	26.8	-6.4	-8.8	13.8	3.4	-15.5	-6.2	-22.7	...
Uzbekistan	-5.2	7.2	-2.8	8.8	0.3	-11.2	-2.2	15.4	39.6
East Asia									
China, People's Republic of	35.8	17.6	38.8	7.2	0.5	-14.3	-5.5	16.1	15.8
Hong Kong, China	18.5	10.5	24.7	3.8	3.9	-4.1	-1.1	8.3	7.7
Korea, Republic of	34.0	16.4	31.6	-0.8	1.9	-16.9	-6.9	17.8	11.9
Mongolia	19.8	15.5	49.7	-5.6	-17.6	-27.5	-11.6	29.2	35.5
Taipei,China	26.3	7.8	44.3	-0.1	1.4	-16.1	-2.4	12.9	10.4
South Asia									
Bangladesh	3.3	16.3	5.1	6.8	6.5	2.5	6.0	7.5	25.2
Bhutan	2.9	77.2	40.7	-9.2	8.3	4.4	7.0	-0.1	-4.1
India	2.8	35.4	30.7	-7.2	-3.2	-13.4	-1.2	20.1	13.8
Maldives	-3.4	21.3	-5.6	11.2	15.0	-4.9	12.2	11.1	...
Nepal	19.0	13.2	39.3	10.4	22.4	3.3	-4.8	31.5	20.4
Sri Lanka	20.5	10.7	31.8	-5.9	7.9	-2.5	1.4	9.3	5.8
Southeast Asia									
Brunei Darussalam	-16.7	1.5	5.6	1.4	-0.5	-10.0	-17.4	15.4	35.2
Cambodia	21.6	...	35.0	15.9	12.6	10.5	6.3	9.8	21.3
Indonesia	39.6	24.0	40.1	-2.6	-4.5	-19.9	-4.9	15.7	20.3
Lao People's Democratic Republic	-3.4	23.8	41.0	0.1	63.1	14.1	-5.3	5.5	8.8
Malaysia	25.3	8.7	33.1	4.8	1.4	-15.9	-4.1	15.5	11.8
Myanmar	3.3	-11.6	11.0	30.9	34.7	3.2	-6.2	22.6	0.5
Philippines	5.9	7.7	27.5	0.5	4.8	8.7	18.3	14.2	17.4
Singapore	21.3	15.4	26.9	0.6	-2.7	-18.5	-5.2	12.1	13.3
Thailand	23.3	25.1	37.7	-0.2	-7.8	-10.7	-5.0	13.0	14.5
Viet Nam	33.2	15.0	21.3	16.0	12.0	12.1	5.6	21.7	11.1
The Pacific									
Cook Islands	21.9	7.0	11.2	3.9	4.1	-9.3	-3.0	26.9	-0.4
Fiji	-8.3	11.5	16.9	25.4	-5.9	-14.6	1.9	4.0	13.6
Kiribati	-4.2	28.7	5.4	-1.2	0.0	-3.7	...	...	...
Marshall Islands	16.7	15.3	15.0 (2009)	...	...	...	...	...	...
Micronesia, Federated States of	...	-3.2	-1.8	-3.1	-14.3	-0.3	16.0	-1.4	...
Nauru	...	-27.0	-47.3	283.2	-25.3	-18.0	...	10.4	...
Niue	...	...	28.5	16.8	1.4	-15.4	5.2	13.1	17.8
Palau	-5.7	0.7	9.3	6.7	3.1	4.4	...	...	...
Papua New Guinea	-7.0	4.5	23.0	30.3	-26.6	-33.9	-20.8	41.3	-15.2
Samoa	-21.7	20.7	36.6	5.6	4.8	-12.7	4.8	2.7	...
Solomon Islands	-16.1	52.4	51.2	2.7	-1.0	-4.1	-4.1	11.1	14.8
Timor-Leste	...	-25.3	1.0	-21.1	4.7	-11.3	4.2	8.2	2.1
Tonga	-3.8	15.3	10.3	-0.5	10.4	-4.4	9.5	3.7	-4.0
Tuvalu	-36.0	13.3	59.2	1.2	7.0	66.4	-36.2	13.1	...
Vanuatu	-12.6	22.4	-2.5	5.8	-0.0	17.0	4.0	-3.1	-4.0
Developed ADB Member Economies									
Australia	3.5	14.4	23.4	-7.1	-2.1	-11.9	-5.8	16.9	2.8
Japan	22.7	13.6	25.8	-6.0	-2.6	-20.1	-6.3	10.7	11.4
New Zealand	-0.4	14.4	27.9	6.7	5.4	-13.8	-0.5	13.1	7.5
DEVELOPING ADB MEMBER ECONOMIES[b]	**24.4**	**16.3**	**32.7**	**2.9**	**0.4**	**-12.5**	**-3.6**	**15.0**	**13.2**
ALL ADB REGIONAL MEMBERS[b]	**22.7**	**15.7**	**31.2**	**1.3**	**-0.1**	**-13.5**	**-4.0**	**14.6**	**12.6**
WORLD	**13.6**	**13.2**	**21.4**	**1.5**	**0.5**	**-12.3**	**-2.6**	**9.8**	**10.2**

... = data not available, -0.0 or 0.0 = magnitude is less than half of unit employed, ADB = Asian Development Bank.

a   Growth rates are based on the value of imports in United States dollars.
b   For reporting economies only.

Sources: Economy sources; and International Monetary Fund. International Financial Statistics. http://data.imf.org/ (accessed 27 March 2019).

Table 2.4.12:   Trade in Goods[a]
(% of GDP)

ADB Regional Member	2000	2005	2010	2013	2014	2015	2016	2017	2018
Developing ADB Member Economies									
Central and West Asia									
Afghanistan	...	43.1	34.5	42.8	38.9	40.2	35.2	36.2	40.4
Armenia	62.0	56.6	51.7	52.7	51.4	44.8	48.0	55.0	59.3
Azerbaijan	55.3	90.6	62.4	56.7	50.0	47.8	58.7	59.2	67.6
Georgia	33.8	52.3	59.4	67.7	69.4	67.9	65.4	70.8	77.0
Kazakhstan	75.7	79.1	61.7	56.4	54.5	41.5	45.2	47.9	54.1
Kyrgyz Republic	77.3	75.7	103.8	109.0	102.0	84.4	81.8	81.3	82.4
Pakistan	23.1	29.3	30.6	30.0	28.7	25.8	23.6	24.2	27.1
Tajikistan	169.6	96.8	68.3	62.1	57.1	55.1	56.5	55.5	...
Turkmenistan	86.2	45.9	79.2	89.1	83.8	73.1	57.2	47.4	...
Uzbekistan	45.1	66.0	47.3	41.0	35.9	30.5	29.6	44.9	66.4
East Asia									
China, People's Republic of	39.2	62.2	48.9	43.5	41.2	35.9	33.1	33.8	34.0
Hong Kong, China	241.5	324.3	360.1	356.4	349.2	319.0	305.0	309.2	312.3
Korea, Republic of	57.8	58.4	77.9	78.4	74.0	65.7	60.1	64.8	66.3
Mongolia	101.2	88.8	85.0	84.5	90.1	72.1	74.0	92.2	99.3
Taipei,China	88.1	102.4	119.5	114.8	113.0	98.7	95.8	100.3	105.5
South Asia									
Bangladesh[b]	26.6	34.0	32.6	40.4	38.4	35.0	33.1	31.0	33.1
Bhutan[b]	67.3	83.1	84.9	76.5	75.3	74.7	69.1	63.7	...
India	20.0	30.2	36.3	41.1	37.2	30.5	28.8	29.0	31.0
Maldives	79.7	72.6	37.5	57.5	57.7	49.5	51.2	52.5	...
Nepal	41.7	35.3	36.5	37.4	41.0	40.4	37.4	39.8	43.7
Sri Lanka	75.7	62.4	38.9	38.2	38.5	36.6	35.8	36.7	38.3
Southeast Asia									
Brunei Darussalam	83.5	80.7	83.3	83.2	83.0	74.0	66.6	71.5	79.2
Cambodia[b]	90.9	108.5	93.3	116.4	120.9	125.3	121.9	120.5	129.3
Indonesia	58.0	50.1	38.9	40.5	39.8	34.0	30.1	32.1	35.4
Lao People's Democratic Republic[b]	52.9	52.8	56.5	44.5	62.2	64.8	60.8	62.6	63.8
Malaysia	192.1	178.3	142.1	134.4	130.9	124.3	118.9	129.1	129.7
Myanmar	...	...	...	37.5	41.7	45.0	42.6	49.8	...
Philippines	89.6	86.0	53.3	43.8	44.8	44.4	46.4	52.5	55.0
Singapore[c]	283.8	337.5	277.4	262.7	251.8	216.1	198.0	207.0	215.0
Thailand	103.9	120.7	110.7	108.2	107.0	100.0	95.0	95.7	95.5
Viet Nam	96.6	120.1	135.5	154.2	160.1	169.6	171.3	191.3	195.8
The Pacific									
Cook Islands	65.3	47.3	39.8	43.8	43.4	40.9	38.7	44.9	40.6
Fiji	83.3	77.7	84.2	94.9	79.8	69.4	65.8	64.3	...
Kiribati	63.6	72.0	49.3	61.5	65.3	65.6	...	...	...
Marshall Islands	125.4	118.1	...	...	...	...	...	...	...
Micronesia, Federated States of	53.0	56.5	66.7	70.4	60.7	63.4	70.8	63.2	...
Nauru	...	30.4	86.3	196.1	118.5	118.4	86.8	83.1	...
Niue	28.9	...	56.5	64.2	60.8	58.7	59.7	63.9	65.0
Palau	95.2	66.2	64.7	74.1	69.2	62.0	...	...	...
Papua New Guinea	88.3	99.3	65.0	57.1	57.5	52.6	51.0	56.2	51.4
Samoa	45.1	45.9	43.7	45.8	47.2	42.2	42.4	43.4	...
Solomon Islands	55.1	67.7	90.8	94.4	91.8	88.1	82.1	...	...
Timor-Leste	...	8.4	8.5	10.3	14.7	17.1	26.9	23.2	...
Tonga	41.9	49.6	44.6	48.2	54.5	57.0	61.7	56.1	50.6
Tuvalu	37.3	59.8	72.7	55.9	60.8	105.7	60.0	61.0	...
Vanuatu	40.5	53.5	47.4	43.9	46.2	53.4	53.7	48.9	...
Developed ADB Member Economies									
Australia	34.4	31.9	33.9	32.7	32.4	31.8	30.8	33.4	35.1
Japan	17.6	23.4	25.6	30.0	30.9	29.0	25.4	28.2	29.9
New Zealand	51.7	42.5	43.6	42.7	41.4	39.9	37.5	39.6	...
DEVELOPING ADB MEMBER ECONOMIES[d]	69.5	78.2	66.7	61.6	58.6	51.3	48.1	49.6	50.6
ALL ADB REGIONAL MEMBERS[d]	39.4	52.3	52.3	52.9	51.5	46.3	42.9	45.0	46.7

... = data not available, ADB = Asian Development Bank, GDP = gross domestic product.

a   The sum of merchandise exports and imports valued in United States dollars.
b   The compilation methodology shifted from cost, insurance, and freight to free on board from 2004 onward for Bhutan, from 2005 onward for Cambodia, and from 2017
    onward for the Lao People's Democratic Republic.
c   Prior to 2003, data excludes Indonesia.
d   For reporting economies only.

Sources: Economy sources; and International Monetary Fund. International Financial Statistics. http://data.imf.org/ (accessed 27 March 2019).

External Trade

Table 2.4.13:   Direction of Trade: Merchandise Exports
(% of total merchandise exports)

To From ADB Regional Member	Asia and the Pacific		Europe		North and Central America		Middle East		South America		Africa		Rest of the World	
	2000	2018	2000	2018	2000	2018	2000	2018	2000	2018	2000	2018	2000	2018
Developing ADB Member Economies														
Central and West Asia														
Afghanistan	35.8	69.7	50.3	2.5	2.7	1.0	8.7	26.5	2.2	0.0	0.3	0.2	0.0	0.0
Armenia	8.0	8.4	56.5	71.3	12.9	3.4	12.5	16.0	0.0	0.0	0.0	0.1	10.1	0.8
Azerbaijan	7.4	16.1	82.4	70.5	0.5	4.8	8.6	7.2	0.4	0.4	0.6	1.0	0.1	0.0
Georgia	16.1	38.5	75.5	50.2	2.7	5.3	4.0	4.9	0.1	0.6	1.4	0.5	0.3	0.0
Kazakhstan	12.4	27.2	48.9	68.1	14.8	1.8	2.5	2.1	0.1	0.1	0.1	0.6	21.2	0.0
Kyrgyz Republic	37.6	30.0	58.7	68.4	0.6	0.1	1.6	1.4	0.0	0.0	1.5	0.0	0.0	0.0
Pakistan	24.8	30.1	29.7	36.7	28.1	18.0	12.4	8.1	1.2	1.2	3.6	5.9	0.1	0.0
Tajikistan	16.6	44.0	80.1	48.4	0.1	0.3	1.7	5.3	0.7	0.1	0.8	1.9	0.0	0.0
Turkmenistan	6.0	90.7	81.2	7.5	1.1	0.1	10.2	1.5	0.0	0.1	0.2	0.0	1.3	0.0
Uzbekistan	60.5	39.5	30.4	25.0	0.0	0.1	8.9	2.3	0.1	0.1	0.0	0.0	0.0	33.0
East Asia														
China, People's Republic of	51.8	45.4	18.4	19.8	23.5	23.1	2.9	4.5	1.4	3.4	1.7	3.7	0.3	0.1
Hong Kong, China	53.9	76.1	16.7	10.6	26.1	9.4	1.4	2.3	1.1	0.8	0.7	0.8	0.1	0.0
Korea, Republic of	49.1	65.3	16.2	12.2	26.4	15.9	4.3	3.6	2.2	1.7	1.5	1.3	0.2	0.0
Mongolia	57.7	95.0	17.6	4.8	24.6	0.2	0.1	0.0	0.0	0.0	0.0	0.0	0.0	0.0
Taipei,China	53.6	73.3	15.7	9.4	26.1	13.6	1.7	1.8	1.1	0.8	0.9	0.6	0.8	0.4
South Asia														
Bangladesh	6.9	11.5	41.5	51.9	33.8	15.3	2.4	1.8	0.2	0.9	0.6	0.5	14.6	18.1
Bhutan	77.9	95.4	6.5	4.5	4.3	0.1	0.0	0.0	0.8	0.0	10.2	0.0	0.2	0.0
India	26.2	33.3	28.5	20.9	23.8	18.5	12.2	16.6	1.3	2.4	4.3	7.4	3.6	0.8
Maldives	36.9	47.9	18.6	42.0	44.4	9.5	0.0	0.4	0.0	0.0	0.0	0.2	0.0	0.0
Nepal	46.2	64.4	24.1	17.8	28.0	12.2	0.1	1.8	0.0	0.0	0.0	0.1	1.6	3.7
Sri Lanka	14.8	21.9	30.6	35.4	43.5	29.7	7.7	9.1	0.6	1.8	0.7	1.5	2.1	0.8
Southeast Asia														
Brunei Darussalam	87.0	98.3	0.5	0.4	12.4	0.9	0.1	0.1	0.0	0.0	0.0	0.2	0.0	0.0
Cambodia	28.2	28.1	17.3	39.3	54.4	30.1	0.0	1.0	0.0	0.8	0.0	0.3	0.0	0.4
Indonesia	64.1	70.9	15.1	11.3	15.1	11.6	3.4	2.9	0.9	1.2	1.4	2.1	0.1	0.0
Lao People's Democratic Republic	58.3	89.1	38.1	6.0	3.2	3.9	0.1	0.8	0.0	0.1	0.3	0.1	0.0	0.0
Malaysia	60.0	72.3	14.5	12.3	22.3	10.0	2.0	2.8	0.6	0.7	0.6	1.8	0.2	0.0
Myanmar	69.8	79.4	8.0	15.0	21.0	2.9	0.6	0.8	0.3	0.2	0.3	1.6	0.0	0.0
Philippines	48.8	66.6	18.7	13.8	31.7	17.5	0.5	1.1	0.2	0.7	0.1	0.4	0.0	0.0
Singapore	62.8	76.1	14.6	10.2	19.2	10.1	1.7	1.9	0.4	0.4	1.1	1.4	0.2	0.0
Thailand	53.0	67.0	17.6	12.0	23.3	13.2	3.1	3.3	0.6	1.8	1.7	2.6	0.7	0.3
Viet Nam	65.9	52.9	23.1	19.6	6.1	22.0	2.9	3.0	0.3	1.6	0.8	0.7	0.9	0.0
The Pacific														
Cook Islands	87.1	96.7	0.0	0.0	7.8	0.1	0.0	0.0	0.0	0.0	0.0	0.0	5.1	3.2
Fiji	56.0	72.7	20.2	4.4	23.7	22.4	0.0	0.3	0.1	0.0	0.0	0.2	0.0	0.0
Kiribati	85.3	89.0	2.8	1.8	0.1	9.0	0.0	0.0	11.8	0.0	0.0	0.1	0.0	0.0
Marshall Islands	0.0	39.4	42.3	34.8	57.7	3.4	0.0	19.0	0.0	1.1	0.0	2.2	0.0	0.0
Micronesia, Federated States of	42.1	92.7	0.3	0.2	57.4	5.3	0.0	0.0	0.0	1.7	0.0	0.0	0.2	0.0
Nauru	84.0	34.8	1.3	0.9	7.5	10.7	0.0	2.8	0.1	0.1	7.1	50.8	0.0	0.0
Niue	...	...	...	...	...	...	...	...	...	...	...	...	...	...
Palau	64.6	67.5	6.8	8.5	12.2	22.3	0.0	0.0	1.2	1.4	14.8	0.2	0.3	0.1
Papua New Guinea	72.0	86.0	19.9	11.4	6.9	1.5	0.2	0.1	0.0	0.9	1.1	0.1	0.0	0.1
Samoa	71.4	83.9	1.6	2.8	26.6	8.4	0.2	0.1	0.0	4.5	0.1	0.3	0.0	0.0
Solomon Islands	98.0	82.2	0.8	16.0	0.0	0.9	0.0	0.0	0.0	0.4	1.1	0.5	0.0	0.1
Timor-Leste[a]	75.5	70.5	17.1	11.5	6.7	16.6	0.0	0.5	0.0	0.0	0.6	0.8	0.0	0.0
Tonga	61.7	76.9	1.2	8.1	21.5	14.3	0.1	0.1	0.0	0.0	15.5	0.3	0.1	0.4
Tuvalu	4.8	52.8	78.8	3.9	0.6	6.1	0.0	0.3	8.4	33.0	5.6	3.9	1.7	0.1
Vanuatu	28.7	81.5	68.5	3.9	2.5	7.1	0.0	0.0	0.1	6.7	0.0	0.8	0.1	0.0
Developed Member Economies														
Australia	66.4	83.4	12.4	5.8	11.6	4.5	5.1	2.8	0.8	0.6	1.9	0.9	1.7	2.0
Japan	43.4	58.1	17.9	13.5	34.3	23.0	2.3	3.2	1.2	1.3	0.9	1.0	0.1	0.0
New Zealand	59.0	68.6	16.7	11.1	18.0	12.0	2.8	4.3	1.5	0.9	0.9	2.2	1.1	1.0
DEVELOPING ADB MEMBER ECONOMIES	52.8	56.5	17.8	16.9	23.6	17.4	2.9	4.2	1.1	2.1	1.3	2.6	0.6	0.3
ALL ADB REGIONAL MEMBERS	50.8	57.7	17.6	16.1	25.9	17.5	2.8	4.0	1.1	2.0	1.2	2.4	0.5	0.3
WORLD	24.5	33.6	42.4	38.1	25.2	18.1	3.0	4.1	2.2	2.5	1.8	2.6	0.9	1.1

0.0 = magnitude is less than half of unit employed, ADB = Asian Development Bank.

a For 2000, data refer to 2004.

Sources: International Monetary Fund. Direction of Trade Statistics. http://data.imf.org/?sk=9D6028D4-F14A-464C-A2F2-59B2CD424B85 (accessed 20 May 2019).
For the Cook Islands and Taipei,China: Economy sources.

Table 2.4.14: Direction of Trade, Merchandise Imports
(% of total merchandise imports)

From / To / ADB Regional Member	Asia and the Pacific 2000	Asia and the Pacific 2018	Europe 2000	Europe 2018	North and Central America 2000	North and Central America 2018	Middle East 2000	Middle East 2018	South America 2000	South America 2018	Africa 2000	Africa 2018	Rest of the World 2000	Rest of the World 2018
Developing ADB Member Economies														
Central and West Asia														
Afghanistan	93.4	64.9	3.3	4.2	0.1	1.4	3.0	28.3	0.0	0.2	0.2	0.9	0.0	0.0
Armenia	4.3	23.2	60.4	60.2	14.6	4.5	15.4	8.1	0.0	1.8	0.0	1.0	5.3	1.0
Azerbaijan	14.4	23.3	65.1	61.7	10.5	6.6	7.3	4.4	0.5	2.0	2.1	1.5	0.1	0.5
Georgia	17.8	26.7	66.7	62.6	10.2	4.2	4.2	4.2	0.9	2.0	0.1	0.4	0.1	0.0
Kazakhstan	11.7	29.2	78.5	63.6	6.3	5.2	1.1	1.0	1.0	0.5	0.5	0.4	0.8	0.0
Kyrgyz Republic	39.8	57.2	45.5	39.0	11.7	3.0	2.9	0.6	0.1	0.2	0.0	0.1	0.0	0.0
Pakistan	31.2	45.8	19.8	12.6	7.0	6.1	38.3	28.6	1.0	1.2	2.7	5.7	0.0	0.0
Tajikistan	56.5	49.8	40.6	38.4	0.1	1.5	1.6	9.5	0.0	0.8	1.1	0.0	0.0	0.0
Turkmenistan	17.5	27.4	58.9	64.9	3.5	4.8	13.5	2.1	0.1	0.9	0.0	0.0	6.4	0.0
Uzbekistan	43.4	44.8	47.3	46.2	1.5	7.8	5.0	0.9	2.6	0.3	0.1	0.0	0.0	0.0
East Asia														
China, People's Republic of	58.2	47.2	17.7	17.9	11.8	9.4	4.5	7.6	2.1	6.6	2.4	4.3	3.2	6.9
Hong Kong, China	80.5	82.1	10.3	9.5	7.6	5.6	0.8	1.4	0.5	0.8	0.3	0.6	0.0	0.0
Korea, Republic of	48.1	50.6	12.5	16.1	20.0	13.2	15.9	15.6	1.6	2.4	1.8	1.6	0.0	0.4
Mongolia	47.1	56.2	47.8	39.1	4.8	4.1	0.2	0.2	0.0	0.3	0.0	0.1	0.0	0.0
Taipei,China	58.9	62.6	13.6	12.1	19.3	13.4	4.8	9.6	1.0	1.3	2.3	0.9	0.0	0.0
South Asia														
Bangladesh	60.1	66.1	12.4	9.8	3.7	4.1	5.2	6.5	1.4	3.4	0.9	3.0	16.4	7.0
Bhutan	84.9	94.7	14.3	1.1	0.4	3.1	0.0	0.4	0.3	0.0	0.0	0.0	0.0	0.7
India	23.6	39.4	28.9	16.3	7.2	8.3	9.4	23.7	1.4	4.0	6.1	7.8	23.4	0.5
Maldives	76.0	63.8	10.6	13.1	3.7	2.3	8.9	19.7	0.1	0.6	0.4	0.5	0.4	0.0
Nepal	71.6	85.4	12.8	5.6	2.0	3.0	5.8	2.3	0.8	1.5	0.1	0.3	7.0	2.0
Sri Lanka	70.4	71.9	14.2	12.2	4.6	3.7	9.4	10.1	0.5	0.4	0.5	1.7	0.2	0.0
Southeast Asia														
Brunei Darussalam	75.1	82.7	12.7	7.3	11.2	8.9	0.3	0.3	0.1	0.5	0.0	0.1	0.5	0.1
Cambodia	88.5	93.4	8.3	4.5	2.8	1.6	0.1	0.2	0.1	0.1	0.0	0.1	0.2	0.1
Indonesia	60.5	73.6	14.1	9.6	12.3	6.5	8.4	5.1	1.5	1.9	2.3	3.2	0.9	0.0
Lao People's Democratic Republic	92.2	94.5	7.0	5.1	0.7	0.4	0.0	0.0	0.0	0.0	0.0	0.0	0.0	0.0
Malaysia	65.2	68.9	12.6	15.4	17.3	7.5	2.0	4.6	0.6	2.2	0.4	1.2	1.9	0.2
Myanmar	88.7	85.5	8.9	5.6	2.3	3.7	0.0	4.4	0.0	0.4	0.0	0.3	0.0	0.0
Philippines	58.4	77.2	10.8	9.3	19.4	7.7	10.5	4.7	0.7	0.9	0.2	0.2	0.0	0.0
Singapore	60.7	57.8	14.2	17.7	15.8	12.5	8.2	10.5	0.3	0.8	0.4	0.7	0.4	0.0
Thailand	60.2	65.8	12.7	13.0	12.6	7.5	10.2	9.3	1.1	1.5	1.3	1.4	2.0	1.4
Viet Nam	82.9	81.0	11.8	7.5	2.6	6.3	1.3	2.3	0.4	2.2	0.3	0.6	0.7	0.0
The Pacific														
Cook Islands	87.0	77.8	0.2	0.0	8.6	13.1	0.0	0.0	0.0	0.0	0.0	0.0	4.3	9.1
Fiji	84.6	91.2	3.8	4.6	5.5	3.2	0.1	0.6	0.3	0.1	0.2	0.2	5.5	0.2
Kiribati	86.3	89.8	2.3	2.2	11.4	6.5	0.0	0.0	0.0	1.3	0.0	0.2	0.0	0.0
Marshall Islands	0.1	74.2	99.8	21.3	0.0	2.3	0.0	1.2	0.0	0.6	0.0	0.4	0.0	0.0
Micronesia, Federated States of	98.0	70.9	1.7	0.3	0.0	18.3	0.0	0.0	0.0	0.1	0.0	0.2	0.2	10.3
Nauru	32.3	91.0	7.9	0.3	10.6	0.8	0.0	0.0	0.0	0.1	49.2	7.7	0.0	0.0
Niue	...	...	...	...	...	...	...	...	...	...	...	...	...	...
Palau	40.4	64.5	0.7	2.5	59.0	32.5	0.0	0.0	0.0	0.4	0.0	0.0	0.0	0.0
Papua New Guinea	94.1	92.5	3.2	3.4	2.3	3.4	0.0	0.2	0.2	0.1	0.1	0.4	0.0	0.0
Samoa	78.5	86.0	0.7	2.2	20.5	11.1	0.0	0.1	0.2	0.2	0.0	0.0	0.0	0.4
Solomon Islands	90.6	95.8	3.0	1.4	6.1	2.4	0.0	0.0	0.1	0.0	0.2	0.3	0.0	0.0
Timor-Leste[a]	94.0	82.5	5.3	5.7	0.6	8.3	0.0	0.4	0.1	2.9	0.0	0.1	0.0	0.1
Tonga	88.8	84.6	0.7	1.5	10.3	13.0	0.0	0.1	0.2	0.8	0.1	0.1	0.0	0.1
Tuvalu	66.0	87.4	32.4	3.2	0.2	6.5	0.0	0.3	1.0	0.9	0.0	1.6	0.4	0.0
Vanuatu	90.5	92.5	7.8	3.8	0.7	3.1	0.0	0.2	0.3	0.2	0.5	0.1	0.3	0.1
Developed ADB Member Economies														
Australia	49.5	61.5	23.5	20.1	22.1	12.2	2.8	2.0	0.8	0.8	0.9	1.2	0.4	2.3
Japan	46.4	54.7	15.1	15.4	22.2	13.8	13.0	12.3	2.0	2.6	1.3	1.1	0.1	0.0
New Zealand	53.1	60.6	18.8	19.4	19.6	12.1	5.6	5.9	1.1	1.2	1.2	0.5	0.5	0.3
DEVELOPING ADB MEMBER ECONOMIES	60.3	57.2	14.8	15.5	13.5	9.0	6.7	9.1	1.1	3.6	1.5	2.9	2.1	2.8
ALL ADB REGIONAL MEMBERS	56.6	57.1	15.3	15.6	15.9	9.6	7.9	9.1	1.3	3.4	1.4	2.6	1.5	2.4
WORLD	29.2	35.7	40.6	38.6	19.9	13.6	4.2	5.2	2.6	3.0	2.2	2.5	1.3	1.3

0.0 = magnitude is less than half of unit employed, ADB = Asian Development Bank.

a For 2000, data refer to 2004.

Sources: International Monetary Fund. Direction of Trade Statistics. http://data.imf.org/?sk=9D6028D4-F14A-464C-A2F2-59B2CD424B85 (accessed 20 May 2019). For the Cook Islands and Taipei,China: Economy sources.

International Reserves

Table 2.4.15:   International Reserves and Ratio to Imports

ADB Regional Member	International Reserves[a] ($ million)				Ratio to Imports[b] (months)			
	2000	**2005**	**2010**	**2018**	**2000**	**2005**	**2010**	**2018**
Developing ADB Member Economies								
Central and West Asia								
Afghanistan	7 (2002)	0	5,147	8,191	0.0 (2002)	0.0	12.5	14.2
Armenia	314	669	1,866	2,249	4.8	4.8	6.9	6.2
Azerbaijan	680	1,178	6,409	6,666	5.3	3.2	11.5	7.3
Georgia	116	479	2,264	3,289	1.4	2.2	5.4	4.6
Kazakhstan	2,096	7,070	28,275	30,927	3.6	4.7	10.3	11.2
Kyrgyz Republic	262	612	1,720	2,156	6.2	6.6	6.9	5.6
Pakistan	2,056	10,948	17,210	11,709	2.6	6.9	6.6	2.5
Tajikistan	94	189	403	1,284	1.2	2.0	1.7	5.6
Turkmenistan	1,808	4,457	...	...	15.8	18.1	...	...
Uzbekistan	1,273	2,900	14,600	28,077 (2017)	6.3	10.5	22.0	25.8 (2017)
East Asia								
China, People's Republic of	168,855	825,588	2,872,090	3,168,212	10.8	17.5	27.8	18.8
Hong Kong, China	107,560	124,278	268,743	424,630	7.9	6.1	8.4	8.5
Korea, Republic of	96,198	210,391	291,571	403,575	7.5	10.0	8.4	9.4
Mongolia	202	333	2,288	3,549	4.0	3.4	8.9	7.2
Taipei,China	111,370	257,952	387,207	466,792	9.7	17.0	18.4	19.6
South Asia								
Bangladesh	1,516	2,825	11,178	32,019	2.4	2.9	6.3	7.1
Bhutan	318	467	1,002	1,206 (2017)	20.6	12.2	15.1	14.1 (2017)
India	40,155	136,026	296,730	396,115	8.3	10.4	9.3	9.2
Maldives	123	189	364	768	4.3	3.5	3.5	3.3
Nepal	952	1,504	2,939	8,079	7.3	8.9	7.2	8.3
Sri Lanka	1,147	2,735	7,196	7,959 (2017)	1.9	3.7	6.4	4.6 (2017)
Southeast Asia								
Brunei Darussalam	382 (2001)	492	1,563	3,488 (2017)	4.2 (2001)	4.2	7.3	13.6 (2017)
Cambodia	611	1,159	3,802	14,628	3.8	3.5	6.9	9.3
Indonesia	29,268	34,731	96,211	120,654	8.7	6.5	9.7	8.0
Lao People's Democratic Republic	140	239	713	1,270 (2017)	3.1	3.3	4.2	2.7 (2017)
Malaysia	28,624	70,152	106,525	101,444	4.4	7.8	8.6	6.9
Myanmar	234	782	5,729	5,214 (2017)	1.3	5.3	16.0	4.0 (2017)
Philippines	15,063	18,494	62,373	79,193	4.2	5.9	14.0	9.4
Singapore	80,170	116,172	225,715	287,678	6.9	7.2	8.7	9.6
Thailand	32,661	52,065	172,129	205,641	6.3	5.9	12.4	10.7
Viet Nam	3,510	9,216	12,926	49,497 (2017)	3.0	3.2	2.0	2.9 (2017)
The Pacific								
Cook Islands	...	...	...	...	...	...	...	...
Fiji	412	321	721	947	6.4	2.8	5.6	2.3
Kiribati	0	0	8	8 (2017)	0.0	0.0	1.4	0.8 (2017)
Marshall Islands	0	0	5	5 (2017)	0.0	0.0	0.5	0.5 (2017)
Micronesia, Federated States of	113	50	56	204 (2017)	12.4	4.8	4.2	13.9 (2017)
Nauru	...	...	...	1	...	...	...	0.2
Niue	...	...	...	...	...	...	...	...
Palau	0	0	5	4	0.0	0.0	0.6	0.3
Papua New Guinea	343 (2002)	749	3,092	2,213	3.8 (2002)	5.9	10.5	10.3
Samoa	57 (2001)	77	189	170	5.7 (2001)	5.0	8.1	6.1
Solomon Islands	32	95	266	616	4.2	9.4	8.9	13.9
Timor-Leste	43 (2002)	84 (2006)	406	674	...	8.9 (2006)	15.9	13.2
Tonga	25	47	105	227	2.9	2.8	6.0	6.7
Tuvalu	0	0 (2006)	3	2 (2017)	0.0	0.0 (2006)	1.8	1.1 (2017)
Vanuatu	39	67	161	395 (2017)	6.1	6.2	8.1	15.2 (2017)
Developed ADB Member Economies								
Australia	18,817	43,257	42,268	53,875	3.5	4.5	2.6	2.9
Japan	361,639	846,896	1,096,185	1,270,466	12.9	21.9	21.0	21.0
New Zealand	3,952	8,893	16,723	20,684 (2017)	3.7	4.2	6.5	6.0 (2017)
DEVELOPING ADB MEMBER ECONOMIES[c]	**728,826**	**1,895,784**	**4,911,905**	**5,881,627**	**7.7**	**11.1**	**15.8**	**12.8**
ALL ADB REGIONAL MEMBERS[c]	**1,113,234**	**2,794,830**	**6,067,080**	**7,226,652**	**8.7**	**12.7**	**15.9**	**13.5**

... = data not available, 0 or 0.0 = magnitude is less than half of the unit employed, $ = United States dollars, ADB = Asian Development Bank.

a Data refer to international reserves with gold at national valuation, unless otherwise specified, end of year. For Afghanistan (up to 2007), Bhutan, Kiribati, Nauru, Palau, Samoa, Solomon Islands (up to 2011), Tonga, Turkmenistan, and Vanuatu, data refer to international reserves without gold.
b Merchandise imports from the balance of payments were used in the calculation.
c For reporting economies only.

Sources: For international reserves: International Monetary Fund. International Financial Statistics. http://data.imf.org/ (accessed 27 March 2019); for Taipei,China: economy source. For the reserves-to-imports ratio: Asian Development Bank estimates using data from the International Monetary Fund's International Financial Statistics and economy sources.

Table 2.4.16: Net Official Development Assistance from All Sources to Developing Economies[a]
($ million)

ADB Regional Member	2000	2005	2010	2012	2013	2014	2015	2016	2017
Developing ADB Member Economies									
Central and West Asia									
Afghanistan	136	2,815	6,235	6,667	5,153	4,943	4,267	4,069	3,804
Armenia	216	173	320	271	280	267	347	326	256
Azerbaijan	141	210	156	287	-71	217	70	78	116
Georgia	172	293	589	659	646	564	449	463	446
Kazakhstan	185	225	212	132	91	93	83	64	59
Kyrgyz Republic	193	238	372	470	539	627	770	516	461
Pakistan	550	1,477	2,933	2,017	2,194	3,616	3,754	2,950	2,283
Tajikistan	112	226	388	394	391	356	427	343	317
Turkmenistan	36	29	44	38	36	34	24	33	29
Uzbekistan	185	169	198	256	295	325	448	457	638
East Asia									
China, People's Republic of	1,749	1,798	672	-181	-657	-947	-332	-792	-1,045
Hong Kong, China	...	...	...	...	...	...	...	...	...
Korea, Republic of	...	...	...	...	...	...	...	...	...
Mongolia	186	195	287	447	431	317	236	326	764
Taipei,China	...	...	...	...	...	...	...	...	...
South Asia									
Bangladesh	976	1,252	1,327	2,154	2,634	2,423	2,570	2,505	3,758
Bhutan	47	79	97	162	137	131	97	52	119
India	1,383	1,876	2,831	1,682	2,456	2,992	3,174	2,679	3,161
Maldives	18	72	88	57	22	23	27	27	43
Nepal	311	407	767	770	873	884	1,225	1,063	1,268
Sri Lanka	222	1,040	559	491	403	492	427	357	297
Southeast Asia									
Brunei Darussalam	...	...	...	...	...	...	...	...	...
Cambodia	346	453	681	808	808	803	679	728	856
Indonesia	1,645	2,489	1,324	69	69	-382	-33	-111	277
Lao People's Democratic Republic	234	241	389	411	423	474	471	399	480
Malaysia	49	29	-6	18	-113	20	-1	-52	-29
Myanmar	106	145	355	505	3,936	1,384	1,169	1,537	1,543
Philippines	553	588	582	-3	192	677	515	284	160
Singapore	...	...	...	...	...	...	...	...	...
Thailand	701	-165	-20	-131	29	355	59	228	250
Viet Nam	1,485	1,693	2,770	4,113	4,086	4,216	3,157	2,895	2,392
The Pacific									
Cook Islands	4	7	14	21	16	28	26	17	19
Fiji	29	66	76	105	91	94	102	117	146
Kiribati	17	27	24	66	65	81	65	61	77
Marshall Islands	47	56	25	84	94	56	57	13	73
Micronesia, Federated States of	97	105	64	143	143	117	81	51	98
Nauru	4	9	28	36	29	23	31	23	26
Niue	3	21	15	20	18	14	20	14	15
Palau	39	24	29	15	35	23	14	18	22
Papua New Guinea	275	268	514	670	657	582	591	532	533
Samoa	29	43	124	117	113	94	94	89	131
Solomon Islands	68	197	333	305	290	201	190	176	187
Timor-Leste	231	185	290	284	259	250	212	224	232
Tonga	16	33	66	78	81	80	68	83	87
Tuvalu	4	9	14	25	28	34	50	24	27
Vanuatu	35	40	109	102	91	100	187	129	132
DEVELOPING ADB MEMBER ECONOMIES[b]	12,837	19,139	25,876	24,633	27,294	26,678	25,867	22,992	24,506
DEVELOPING ECONOMIES WORLDWIDE[c]	48,993	107,452	129,264	133,752	151,138	161,730	153,220	158,218	163,144

... = data not available, $ = United States dollars, ADB = Asian Development Bank.

a Net official development assistance refers to concessional flows to developing economies and multilateral institutions provided by official agencies, including state and local governments, or by their executing agencies, administered with the objective of promoting the economic development and welfare of developing economies, and containing a grant element of at least 25%. Net flow takes into account principal repayments for loans, offsetting entries for forgiven debt, and recoveries made on grants.
b For reporting economies only.
c Includes data for all developing economies as reported in the Organisation for Economic Co-operation and Development's OECD.Stat database.

Source: Organisation for Economic Co-operation and Development. OECD.Stat. http://stats.oecd.org (accessed 22 April 2019).

Table 2.4.17:   Net Other Official Flows from All Sources to Developing Economies[a]
($ million)

ADB Regional Member	2000	2005	2010	2012	2013	2014	2015	2016	2017
Developing ADB Member Economies									
Central and West Asia									
Afghanistan	...	56.9	71.2	29.1	60.5	-24.2	127.4	97.2	56.1
Armenia	16.9	7.8	288.3	133.4	112.1	103.6	111.1	197.2	157.6
Azerbaijan	314.3	226.5	179.9	411.8	391.0	630.1	801.8	1,114.7	1,738.5
Georgia	62.7	86.3	250.2	146.6	-0.7	2.9	342.4	486.6	262.1
Kazakhstan	-41.7	-502.3	2,247.2	606.9	1,548.0	549.5	1,256.7	441.4	-853.7
Kyrgyz Republic	-4.0	56.3	18.3	73.7	69.7	16.5	0.4	-43.2	-6.0
Pakistan	-592.9	127.4	345.3	414.3	-236.7	-97.1	-343.9	1,102.3	377.7
Tajikistan	0.7	22.8	6.4	9.2	6.6	-5.5	68.1	13.6	15.6
Turkmenistan	130.3	-74.1	647.4	-333.2	135.4	1,143.9	2,356.6	926.1	532.3
Uzbekistan	272.1	-48.7	16.0	122.9	754.6	743.9	530.5	1,204.2	383.0
East Asia									
China, People's Republic of	-1,782.4	423.1	3,196.3	1,474.0	742.1	343.0	1,215.8	139.9	1,227.3
Hong Kong, China	...	...	...	...	...	...	...	...	...
Korea, Republic of	...	...	...	...	...	...	...	...	...
Mongolia	-8.5	-14.6	159.3	283.9	255.0	509.8	213.3	756.4	-210.6
Taipei,China	...	...	...	...	...	...	...	...	...
South Asia									
Bangladesh	-30.5	186.8	35.1	129.3	187.7	247.0	417.9	1,421.5	2,337.4
Bhutan	-1.1	4.8	24.0	3.7	-5.0	-6.0	-2.8	8.0	3.1
India	-196.4	2,322.3	5,967.5	4,011.4	3,010.8	4,029.7	1,811.5	1,935.6	1,188.9
Maldives	-4.8	44.0	-33.9	-105.3	13.3	-3.7	-8.1	-24.7	-23.8
Nepal	23.7	-8.3	-6.9	3.9	16.2	-2.4	-7.4	0.7	-2.3
Sri Lanka	-22.7	39.8	189.3	491.3	436.0	350.5	320.8	312.6	132.3
Southeast Asia									
Brunei Darussalam	...	...	...	...	...	...	...	...	...
Cambodia	-0.4	7.6	-5.0	33.4	89.3	96.3	84.6	-12.3	84.1
Indonesia	100.1	1,443.8	1,783.7	-2,036.8	120.8	-1,715.7	3,775.4	3,708.7	2,934.5
Lao People's Democratic Republic	-8.8	59.4	-120.5	29.7	4.6	194.8	73.1	38.6	74.7
Malaysia	519.9	-1,369.3	159.2	552.9	-126.4	1,339.4	-231.8	-1,494.5	-739.8
Myanmar	20.1	-31.5	30.9	-32.7	227.2	107.6	427.5	100.6	96.4
Philippines	499.6	-945.9	-680.3	603.5	-1,245.5	1,029.6	1,148.5	203.1	-32.2
Singapore	...	...	...	...	...	...	...	...	...
Thailand	-2,112.2	1,629.6	-71.5	1,474.9	2,454.4	-349.0	138.7	-39.3	-1,051.6
Viet Nam	-546.4	248.4	2,815.4	2,005.8	4,828.3	2,133.3	2,782.1	580.6	-1,345.9
The Pacific									
Cook Islands	-0.2	-0.3	9.7	7.1	4.9	-1.3	-0.6	-1.2	1.8
Fiji	-11.8	1.2	14.2	20.3	73.6	66.1	-11.4	40.6	48.3
Kiribati	0.1 (2002)	0.2	0.5	0.8	0.6	0.2	0.2	0.3	0.1
Marshall Islands	-0.2	-0.1	-0.6	-57.2	-21.1	146.2	7.6	36.7	17.1
Micronesia, Federated States of	-0.1	0.3	0.8	3.5		1.1	0.2	2.3	1.5
Nauru	-5.6	0.2	0.3	0.3	-0.1	...	...	62.5	19.4
Niue	7.5	...	...	...	...	...	...	0.0	...
Palau	-1.5	-2.1	0.1 (2008)	14.7	6.4	-11.1	0.3	6.6	9.9
Papua New Guinea	85.4	-9.1	4,892.3	843.2	1,025.2	-2,991.6	19.4	-320.7	-267.2
Samoa	0.4	-0.1	4.1	-5.7	4.2	-0.9	-1.3	5.6	1.3
Solomon Islands	1.2	-11.7	59.2	0.6	37.4	25.0	0.7	19.1	0.5
Timor-Leste	417.8	1.1	4.6	2.0	5.7	9.9	7.8	24.8	11.8
Tonga	0.0	0.4	0.3	1.0	0.3	0.0	2.1	2.5	1.2
Tuvalu	...	0.5 (2006)	-0.1	0.2	0.2	0.2	0.2	0.2	0.1
Vanuatu	-16.2	0.8	1.3	2.6	1.7	0.8	0.7	0.9	2.1
DEVELOPING ADB MEMBER ECONOMIES[b]	**-2,915.4**	**3,980.2**	**22,499.3**	**11,370.6**	**14,987.2**	**8,612.3**	**17,436.0**	**13,055.7**	**7,183.3**
DEVELOPING ECONOMIES WORLDWIDE[c]	**9,856.9**	**9,605.9**	**70,855.8**	**38,758.7**	**38,935.3**	**22,461.4**	**50,604.3**	**29,589.4**	**21,222.0**

... = data not available, 0.0 = magnitude is less than half of unit employed, $ = United States dollars, ADB = Asian Development Bank.

a   Net other official flows refer to official sector transactions with economies on the Development Assistance Committee List of Official Development Assistance Recipients, which do not meet the conditions for eligibility as official development assistance, either because they are not primarily aimed at development or because they have a grant element of less than 25%. The Development Assistance Committee List of Official Development Assistance Recipients is available at http://www.oecd.org/dac/financing-sustainable-development/development-finance-standards/daclist.htm. Also includes net export credits. Net flow takes into account principal repayments for loans, offsetting entries for forgiven debt, and recoveries made on grants.

b   For reporting economies only.

c   Includes data for all developing economies as reported in the Organisation for Economic Co-operation and Development's OECD.Stat database.

Source: Organisation for Economic Co-operation and Development. OECD.Stat. http://stats.oecd.org (accessed 22 April 2019).

Table 2.4.18: Net Private Flows from All Sources to Developing Economies[a]
($ million)

ADB Regional Member	2000	2005	2010	2012	2013	2014	2015	2016	2017
Developing ADB Member Economies									
Central and West Asia									
Afghanistan	21	-14	-21	-12	26	32	-5	-5	3
Armenia	-21	35	-69	-91	208	-0	57	179	85
Azerbaijan	219	1,082	798	326	869	-129	436	404	107
Georgia	23	-32	22	182	52	-59	1,249	190	360
Kazakhstan	603	2,252	-1,511	194	2,947	1,251	3,090	-86	-3,041
Kyrgyz Republic	12	7	23	15	18	10	6	-23	4
Pakistan	60	833	-75	298	-172	155	131	192	707
Tajikistan	-8	-1	18	15	47	4	-8	-2	-42
Turkmenistan	124	1	-46	43	103	42	-11	285	106
Uzbekistan	-10	-84	39	153	-117	-478	110	108	435
East Asia									
China, People's Republic of	923	21,125	46,301	17,987	53,925	61,702	17,154	42,121	36,602
Hong Kong, China	...	...	...	...	...	...	...	...	...
Korea, Republic of	...	...	...	...	...	...	...	...	...
Mongolia	3	-2	22	417	511	42	216	586	66
Taipei,China	...	...	...	...	...	...	...	...	...
South Asia									
Bangladesh	93	186	-3	858	-105	249	100	-380	230
Bhutan	-8	1	18	107	-163	9	16	-0	-1
India	1,099	4,548	19,976	14,426	6,292	10,655	7,288	14,813	18,564
Maldives	-4	8	38	38	-16	100	112	17	-1
Nepal	-4	-2	-11	78	115	7	-3	6	53
Sri Lanka	98	35	218	199	447	427	387	482	387
Southeast Asia									
Brunei Darussalam	...	...	...	...	...	...	...	...	...
Cambodia	9	9	256	276	310	399	380	403	412
Indonesia	606	4,012	3,348	10,084	7,291	13,343	9,678	10,235	11,158
Lao People's Democratic Republic	14	0	172	363	59	50	-19	44	72
Malaysia	-872	2,064	6,573	9,684	9,719	6,165	3,689	2,134	2,839
Myanmar	-70	17	260	357	534	566	865	356	452
Philippines	330	3,496	2,424	4,785	2,510	4,839	1,908	2,738	4,121
Singapore	...	...	...	...	...	...	...	...	...
Thailand	32	10,944	6,394	5,356	6,096	10,076	-2,337	2,760	1,304
Viet Nam	237	224	2,038	3,412	5,002	3,467	2,790	4,758	4,515
The Pacific									
Cook Islands	-31	-29	-0	-1	3	-2	-2	-1	0
Fiji	6	51	-3	163	2	49	53	-15	45
Kiribati	0	1	-0	0	0	3	3	-9	-1
Marshall Islands	108	2,737	974	2,179	-1,048	-365	2,245	9	570
Micronesia, Federated States of	-0 (2001)	0	3	4	93	320	798	714	453
Nauru	4	2	2 (2009)	...	...	...	...	-0	0
Niue	12	-1	...	-0	...	0	0	0	0
Palau	18	1	3	7	2	6	7	9	10
Papua New Guinea	-27	238	-40	3,063	879	65	-2,931	211	134
Samoa	1	30	17	14	-36	37	3	8	6
Solomon Islands	-15	-17	3	-463	4	23	11	-1	-8
Timor-Leste	54 (2001)	0	-3	3	25	2	17	-41	15
Tonga	-7	2	-10	0	1	1	-1	-0	0
Tuvalu	-4	-1	...	-0	-2	-1	0	0	0
Vanuatu	41	11	31	86	43	15	-5	1	-1
DEVELOPING ADB MEMBER ECONOMIES[b]	**3,668**	**53,771**	**88,180**	**74,604**	**96,474**	**113,076**	**47,476**	**83,201**	**80,720**
DEVELOPING ECONOMIES WORLDWIDE[c]	**75,170**	**173,009**	**324,145**	**300,041**	**251,386**	**414,308**	**116,530**	**128,651**	**229,598**

... = data not available, -0 or 0 = magnitude is less than half of unit employed, $ = United States dollars, ADB = Asian Development Bank.

a Net private flows refer to the sum of direct investments and portfolio investments.
b For reporting economies only.
c Includes data for all developing economies as reported in the Organisation for Economic Co-operation and Development's OECD.Stat database.

Source: Organisation for Economic Co-operation and Development. OECD.Stat. http://stats.oecd.org (accessed 22 April 2019).

Table 2.4.19:   Aggregate Net Resource Flows from All Sources to Developing Economies[a]
($ million)

ADB Regional Member	2000	2005	2010	2012	2013	2014	2015	2016	2017
Developing ADB Member Economies									
Central and West Asia									
Afghanistan	157	2,858	6,285	6,684	5,239	4,951	4,389	4,162	3,863
Armenia	211	216	539	313	600	371	515	703	498
Azerbaijan	673	1,519	1,135	1,024	1,189	718	1,308	1,596	1,961
Georgia	258	347	861	987	698	508	2,040	1,139	1,069
Kazakhstan	746	1,975	948	933	4,586	1,893	4,430	419	-3,836
Kyrgyz Republic	201	302	413	559	627	653	776	450	459
Pakistan	17	2,437	3,203	2,730	1,786	3,673	3,541	4,244	3,368
Tajikistan	105	248	413	418	444	355	487	354	290
Turkmenistan	290	-44	645	-253	274	1,220	2,370	1,244	667
Uzbekistan	447	37	253	532	933	590	1,089	1,770	1,456
East Asia									
China, People's Republic of	889	23,346	50,169	19,280	54,011	61,098	18,037	41,469	36,784
Hong Kong, China	...	...	...	...	...	...	...	...	...
Korea, Republic of	...	...	...	...	...	...	...	...	...
Mongolia	180	179	468	1,147	1,196	869	665	1,668	619
Taipei,China	...	...	...	...	...	...	...	...	...
South Asia									
Bangladesh	1,039	1,625	1,360	3,141	2,717	2,918	3,088	3,546	6,325
Bhutan	38	85	140	273	-32	133	110	60	121
India	2,286	8,746	28,774	20,120	11,760	17,676	12,274	19,428	22,914
Maldives	10	124	93	-10	19	119	131	19	18
Nepal	331	397	749	851	1,005	888	1,215	1,070	1,319
Sri Lanka	298	1,115	966	1,181	1,286	1,269	1,135	1,152	816
Southeast Asia									
Brunei Darussalam	...	...	...	...	...	...	...	...	...
Cambodia	354	470	932	1,117	1,207	1,298	1,144	1,120	1,352
Indonesia	2,352	7,945	6,456	8,116	7,481	11,245	13,420	13,833	14,369
Lao People's Democratic Republic	239	301	441	803	487	719	526	482	627
Malaysia	-304	724	6,726	10,255	9,480	7,524	3,457	588	2,070
Myanmar	56	131	646	829	4,697	2,058	2,460	1,993	2,091
Philippines	1,383	3,138	2,326	5,385	1,457	6,546	3,572	3,225	4,249
Singapore	...	...	...	...	...	...	...	...	...
Thailand	-1,380	12,409	6,302	6,700	8,579	10,081	-2,139	2,949	502
Viet Nam	1,176	2,166	7,623	9,531	13,916	9,816	8,729	8,233	5,561
The Pacific									
Cook Islands	-27	-23	23	28	23	25	23	15	20
Fiji	24	118	87	289	166	210	144	143	239
Kiribati	17	28	24	67	66	84	68	52	77
Marshall Islands	156	2,793	998	2,205	-975	-163	2,309	58	660
Micronesia, Federated States of	97	105	68	150	236	438	879	767	552
Nauru	2	12	28	36	29	23	31	85	45
Niue	23	20	15	20	18	14	20	14	15
Palau	55	22	32	37	44	18	21	33	42
Papua New Guinea	333	498	5,366	4,576	2,562	-2,344	-2,320	422	400
Samoa	30	73	145	126	81	130	95	103	139
Solomon Islands	55	169	395	-158	331	249	202	194	179
Timor-Leste	649	186	292	288	290	262	238	207	259
Tonga	10	35	57	79	83	82	70	85	88
Tuvalu	-0	8	14	26	26	34	50	25	27
Vanuatu	60	52	142	191	136	117	182	131	134
DEVELOPING ADB MEMBER ECONOMIES[b]	**13,536**	**76,890**	**136,553**	**110,607**	**138,756**	**148,366**	**90,779**	**119,248**	**112,409**
DEVELOPING ECONOMIES WORLDWIDE[c]	**134,020**	**290,067**	**524,265**	**472,551**	**441,459**	**598,499**	**320,354**	**316,459**	**413,964**

... = data not available, -0 or 0 = magnitude is less than half of unit employed, $ = United States dollars, ADB = Asian Development Bank.

a Aggregate net resource flows refer to the sum of net official development assistance, net other official flows, and net private flows.
b For reporting economies only.
c Includes data for all developing economies as reported in the Organisation for Economic Co-operation and Development's OECD.Stat database.

Source: Organisation for Economic Co-operation and Development. OECD.Stat. http://stats.oecd.org (accessed 22 April 2019).

Table 2.4.20: Total External Debt of Developing Economies[a]
($ million)

ADB Regional Member	Total External Debt				External Debt, Public and Publicly Guaranteed			
	2000	2005	2010	2017	2000	2005	2010	2017
Developing ADB Member Economies								
Central and West Asia								
Afghanistan	0	979 (2006)	2,436	2,552	0	920 (2006)	1,976	1,982
Armenia	1,018	1,970	6,307	10,335	684	924	2,560	5,228
Azerbaijan	1,585	2,247	7,279	15,254	794	1,491	3,839	12,663
Georgia	1,826	2,151	8,790	15,756	1,274	1,531	3,274	6,054
Kazakhstan	12,890	43,857	119,145	167,485	3,623	2,177	3,845	21,295
Kyrgyz Republic	1,938	2,257	4,118	8,161	1,220	1,665	2,446	3,908
Pakistan	33,022	34,018	62,801	84,523	27,192	30,089	43,403	60,049
Tajikistan	1,141	1,125	3,561	5,881	755	829	1,806	3,092
Turkmenistan	2,627	1,153	529	781	2,271	878	359	226
Uzbekistan	4,948	4,632	7,802	17,708	3,766	3,626	3,423	8,208
East Asia								
China, People's Republic of	145,666	283,310	734,465	1,710,235	94,489	84,212	94,003	201,724
Hong Kong, China	208,260	470,288	879,034	1,692,317 (2018)	...	...	...	...
Korea, Republic of	135,208	161,956	355,911	440,599 (2018)	52,128	39,665	120,636	...
Mongolia	960	1,396	5,928	28,199	833	1,267	1,782	7,492
Taipei,China	34,757	86,732	101,581	191,161 (2018)	23	222	8,035	168 (2018)
South Asia								
Bangladesh	15,603	18,506	26,881	47,155	14,992	17,441	21,453	31,367
Bhutan	212	657	935	2,636	202	636	919	2,565
India	101,131	121,195	290,428	513,209	81,196	54,726	100,563	196,176
Maldives	203	362	917	1,365	185	300	628	1,260
Nepal	2,878	3,191	3,789	4,963	2,826	3,112	3,509	4,299
Sri Lanka	9,250	11,300	21,684	50,142	7,945	9,658	16,430	32,575
Southeast Asia								
Brunei Darussalam	...	...	...	...	...	...	...	...
Cambodia	1,946	2,769	3,825	11,898	1,853	2,666	2,874	6,380
Indonesia	144,032	142,120	198,269	354,352	70,025	77,705	103,388	195,691
Lao People's Democratic Republic	2,531	3,279	6,554	14,498	2,474	2,354	3,751	8,374
Malaysia	41,946	64,911	133,800	200,364 (2016)	19,125	34,387	61,858	65,721 (2016)
Myanmar	6,239	7,288	10,187	16,139	5,692	6,429	8,616	14,837
Philippines	58,456	58,693	65,358	73,080	33,744	35,364	45,094	35,440
Singapore	220,298	300,359	...	...	...	...	...	...
Thailand	79,830	58,467	106,358	129,765	29,462	12,602	15,929	24,458
Viet Nam	12,785	18,530	44,902	104,079	11,584	16,219	32,764	51,782
The Pacific								
Cook Islands	59	68	99	70 (2018)	...	...	...	...
Fiji	195	303	607	899	174	185	426	753
Kiribati	8	11	14	42 (2018)	...	...	...	...
Marshall Islands	105	92	105	83	...	...	...	...
Micronesia, Federated States of	63	62	86	80 (2016)	...	...	...	...
Nauru	...	...	...	...	...	...	...	...
Niue	...	...	...	...	...	...	...	...
Palau	58	60	66	88 (2018)	...	...	...	...
Papua New Guinea	2,325	1,871	5,987	17,367	1,454	1,264	1,042	2,299
Samoa	139	169	325	443	138	167	299	416
Solomon Islands	156	167	231	350	121	144	125	97
Timor-Leste	0	0	77 (2012)	50	0	0	0	36
Tonga	74	89	154	169	65	80	144	159
Tuvalu	4	10 (2006)	16	26	...	...	...	...
Vanuatu	112	100	178	393	73	72	102	287
DEVELOPING ADB MEMBER ECONOMIES[b]	1,024,241	1,547,430	3,087,716	5,734,288	453,258	410,618	649,443	941,342
DEVELOPING ECONOMIES WORLDWIDE[c]	2,269,263	3,043,004	5,591,470	9,383,642	1,206,268	1,223,350	1,656,407	2,639,996

... = data not available, $ = United States dollars, ADB = Asian Development Bank.

a Refers to the sum of public and publicly guaranteed long-term debt, private nonguaranteed long-term debt, use of International Monetary Fund credit, and estimated short-term debt.
b For reporting economies only.
c Refers to all low- and middle-income countries as classified by the World Bank. For developing member economies not covered by the World Bank, data are from economy sources.

Sources: World Bank. International Debt Statistics Online. http://data.worldbank.org/data-catalog/international-debt-statistics (accessed 19 July 2019); and Asian Development Bank estimates using economy sources.

External Indebtness

Table 2.4.21:   **Total External Debt of Developing ADB Member Economies**
(% of GNI)

ADB Regional Member	Total External Debt				External Debt, Public and Publicly Guaranteed			
	2000	2005	2010	2017	2000	2005	2010	2017
Developing ADB Member Economies								
Central and West Asia								
Afghanistan	...	13.8 (2006)	15.2	12.1	...	13.0 (2006)	12.4	9.8
Armenia	51.8	38.6	64.9	85.9	34.8	18.1	26.3	43.6
Azerbaijan	31.8	19.4	14.6	39.1	15.9	12.9	7.7	32.4
Georgia	57.5	33.2	77.9	109.8	40.1	23.7	29.0	42.4
Kazakhstan	75.7	84.7	92.6	118.4	21.3	4.2	3.0	14.7
Kyrgyz Republic	150.5	95.1	91.7	111.2	94.8	70.2	54.5	53.3
Pakistan	45.2	30.4	34.1	26.3	37.2	26.9	23.6	18.7
Tajikistan	138.4	50.3	51.1	71.3	91.6	37.1	25.9	37.5
Turkmenistan	96.3	15.3	2.6	1.9	83.3	11.6	1.7	0.6
Uzbekistan	36.5	32.4	19.3	35.0	27.8	25.4	8.4	13.6
East Asia								
China, People's Republic of	12.2	12.5	12.1	14.0	7.9	3.7	1.6	1.7
Hong Kong, China	120.3	257.7	376.5	444.5 (2018)	...	...	...	...
Korea, Republic of	23.6	17.4	31.1	25.5 (2018)	9.1	4.3	10.5	...
Mongolia	84.8	56.5	89.7	285.5	73.6	51.2	27.0	76.3
Taipei,China	10.3	22.5	22.1	31.9 (2018)	0.0	0.1	1.7	0.1
South Asia								
Bangladesh	28.3	25.5	21.6	18.1	27.2	24.1	17.2	12.0
Bhutan	48.2	81.3	62.4	113.3	46.1	78.7	61.4	110.8
India	22.1	15.1	17.7	19.8	17.5	6.7	6.1	7.5
Maldives	34.2	32.0	40.3	32.2	31.1	26.5	27.6	28.2
Nepal	52.2	39.1	23.5	20.1	51.2	38.2	21.8	17.1
Sri Lanka	57.8	46.9	38.6	59.1	49.6	40.1	29.3	38.0
Southeast Asia								
Brunei Darussalam	...	...	...	...	...	...	...	...
Cambodia	55.1	46.1	35.7	57.2	52.4	44.4	26.8	30.7
Indonesia	93.5	52.3	27.0	36.0	45.4	28.6	14.1	19.9
Lao People's Democratic Republic	152.4	122.8	98.2	90.8	149.0	88.2	56.2	52.5
Malaysia	48.7	47.3	54.2	69.6 (2016)	22.2	25.1	25.1	22.8 (2016)
Myanmar	70.1	60.8	20.6	24.5	63.9	53.7	17.4	22.9
Philippines	61.6	48.0	27.2	19.4	35.5	28.9	18.7	9.4
Singapore	16.0	...	...	...	...	...	...	...
Thailand	64.4	32.3	32.5	29.8	23.8	7.0	4.9	5.6
Viet Nam	38.5	32.8	40.3	48.8	34.9	28.7	29.4	24.3
The Pacific								
Cook Islands[a]	64.3	37.4	41.0	18.8 (2018)	...	...	...	...
Fiji	11.3	9.9	20.0	18.7	10.1	6.1	14.0	15.2
Kiribati[a]	7.1 (2001)	7.1	6.3	11.8	...	...	...	...
Marshall Islands	70.5	50.9	52.1	30.5	...	...	...	...
Micronesia, Federated States of	26.4	23.9	27.9	20.8 (2016)	...	...	...	...
Nauru	...	...	...	...	...	...	...	...
Niue	...	...	...	...	...	...	...	...
Palau[a]	40.0	32.3	36.2	31.1 (2018)	...	...	...	...
Papua New Guinea	70.4	41.3	45.7	85.6	44.0	27.9	8.0	10.6
Samoa	51.7	38.6	52.0	53.5	48.8 (2001)	39.1	48.0	51.0
Solomon Islands	35.9	40.3	46.5	28.6	27.7	34.7	25.2	7.9
Timor-Leste	0.0	0.0	0.0	1.9	0.0	0.0	0.0	1.6
Tonga	36.7	34.0	40.3	39.1	32.2	30.3	37.6	36.3
Tuvalu[a]	29.0	45.7 (2006)	49.1	45.4	...	...	...	...
Vanuatu	43.3	27.2	26.3	46.0	28.2	19.5	15.2	34.1

... = data not available, 0.0 = magnitude is less than half of unit employed, ADB = Asian Development Bank, GNI = gross national income.

a   For total external debt as a percentage of GNI, gross domestic product is used in lieu of GNI.

Sources: World Bank. International Debt Statistics Online. http://data.worldbank.org/data-catalog/international-debt-statistics (accessed 19 July 2019); and Asian Development Bank estimates using economy sources.

Table 2.4.22: Total External Debt of Developing ADB Member Economies
(% of exports of goods, services, and primary income)

ADB Regional Member	2000	2005	2010	2012	2013	2014	2015	2016	2017
Developing ADB Member Economies									
Central and West Asia									
Afghanistan	...	...	89.0	110.6	162.7	119.6	147.9	187.1	186.7
Armenia	182.6	101.3	193.5	189.5	196.7	188.8	222.0	228.8	192.4
Azerbaijan	72.9	26.9	25.2	28.9	29.0	36.1	64.6	81.2	72.2
Georgia	183.7	89.1	191.5	170.8	161.9	169.3	206.8	223.1	181.3
Kazakhstan	123.0	139.8	174.7	144.4	160.5	176.9	277.6	357.3	287.1
Kyrgyz Republic	328.5	234.4	181.2	170.9	176.8	219.9	307.6	325.8	313.3
Pakistan	326.5	172.1	218.5	194.2	189.9	197.9	224.9	262.6	286.0
Tajikistan	163.0 (2002)	89.0	158.3	130.8	130.3	162.7	203.2	235.5	216.2
Turkmenistan	...	...	...	...	...	...	...	...	...
Uzbekistan	...	...	...	...	...	...	...	127.6	118.0
East Asia									
China, People's Republic of	71.9	34.9	42.1	48.6	57.9	65.5	51.3	58.4	63.8
Hong Kong, China[a]	76.8	121.2	149.2	145.6	152.0	166.2	168.8	177.6	190.4
Korea, Republic of[a]	64.7	46.6	62.6	55.6	56.4	56.3	59.5	60.4	58.9
Mongolia	153.3	93.6	173.2	345.0	423.4	345.4	422.4	453.7	410.0
Taipei,China[a]	19.3	35.9	29.9	29.2	38.4	39.6	39.1	45.2	42.4
South Asia									
Bangladesh	214.0	163.4	123.5	102.8	100.2	99.6	103.4	102.8	120.1
Bhutan	...	188.8 (2006)	154.0	194.2	233.9	270.6	269.1	346.9	353.1
India	161.9	75.6	81.1	86.5	89.1	91.8	108.1	102.2	101.0
Maldives	43.4	73.1	45.6	35.7	30.9	32.1	30.6	36.6	39.2
Nepal	212.5	224.2	212.7	175.1	159.5	142.2	154.8	167.2	165.7
Sri Lanka	141.7	141.9	189.8	260.5	258.5	250.2	257.3	265.4	260.1
Southeast Asia									
Brunei Darussalam	...	...	...	...	...	...	...	...	...
Cambodia	102.8	67.6	62.7	72.0	68.8	66.0	71.1	76.3	73.1
Indonesia	197.1	146.5	117.6	118.2	127.8	145.8	175.8	186.8	177.0
Lao People's Democratic Republic	493.1	430.1	284.0	249.8	259.1	231.6	252.2	259.6	248.6
Malaysia	36.7	38.9	57.2	73.7	72.8	74.0	86.0	94.5	...
Myanmar	290.9	189.9	129.7	115.7	99.8	99.2	101.6	103.0	106.4
Philippines	189.8	152.4	106.7	92.4	86.9	92.1	93.5	87.4	74.4
Singapore	104.5	87.6	...	...	...	...	...	...	...
Thailand	92.8	44.4	45.7	47.0	46.9	46.7	46.2	42.1	40.6
Viet Nam	73.1	50.1	56.0	49.4	45.8	44.8	44.8	45.2	45.7
The Pacific									
Cook Islands[a]	...	...	61.3	45.8	35.6	39.3	32.8	27.2	24.9
Fiji	19.0	17.9	32.2	31.4	33.9	35.6	37.2	39.5	36.0
Kiribati[a]	16.3	17.6	14.9	11.1	9.8	7.4	15.8	23.5	21.0
Marshall Islands[a]	141.1	98.0	98.9	70.7	66.4	68.9	63.0	63.7	52.7
Micronesia, Federated States of[a]	100.3	98.2	91.8	69.3	65.7	65.9	52.0	49.0	...
Nauru	...	...	...	...	...	...	...	...	...
Niue	...	...	...	...	...	...	...	...	...
Palau[a]	82.4	64.0	62.5	48.4	43.1	43.0	35.1	46.0	51.7
Papua New Guinea	98.2	51.3	98.2	217.7	337.3	227.4	238.7	230.1	169.0
Samoa	...	114.8	161.1	177.7	179.4	184.4	182.6	162.7	154.5
Solomon Islands	121.3	108.1	68.9	35.0	33.7	30.5	35.9	40.3	53.6
Timor–Leste	...	...	0.0	1.9	2.5	3.6	6.4	4.5	5.7
Tonga	...	167.6	283.9	190.4	171.0	200.0	137.5	130.9	121.3
Tuvalu[a]	85.9	54.9 (2006)	65.0	36.7	61.7	87.3	82.2	68.5	71.4
Vanuatu	63.9	49.0	48.9	46.2	47.6	44.8	74.7	68.2	...

... = data not available, ADB = Asian Development Bank.

a External debt as a percentage of exports of goods, services, and primary income was derived using balance-of-payments data.

Sources: World Bank. International Debt Statistics Online. http://data.worldbank.org/data-catalog/international-debt-statistics (accessed 19 July 2019); and Asian Development Bank estimates using economy sources.

External Indebtness

Table 2.4.23: Total Debt Service Paid by Developing ADB Member Economies

ADB Regional Member	Debt Service Payment ($ million)				Debt Service Payment (% of exports of goods, services, and primary income)			
	2000	2005	2010	2017	2000	2005	2010	2017
Developing ADB Member Economies								
Central and West Asia								
Afghanistan	0	11 (2006)	10	54	...	...	0.4	4.0
Armenia	48	142	969	1,451	8.7	7.3	29.7	27.0
Azerbaijan	138	242	415	2,252	6.4	2.9	1.4	10.7
Georgia	126	195	803	2,555	12.7	8.1	17.5	29.4
Kazakhstan	3,392	13,158	39,474	27,966	32.4	41.9	57.9	47.9
Kyrgyz Republic	178	143	557	778	30.2	14.8	24.5	29.9
Pakistan	2,871	2,466	4,310	6,739	28.4	12.5	15.0	22.8
Tajikistan	66	73	695	711	...	5.8	30.9	26.1
Turkmenistan	472	310	155	46	...	...	...	...
Uzbekistan	907	795	618	1,941	...	...	...	12.9
East Asia								
China, People's Republic of	26,610	27,469	51,992	204,171	13.1	3.4	3.0	7.6
Hong Kong, China	...	...	...	...	...	...	...	...
Korea, Republic of	22,905	7,224	2,843	...	11.0	2.1	0.5	...
Mongolia	41	45	239	3,868	6.6	3.0	7.0	56.2
Taipei,China[a, b]	45	11,006	3,630	9,218 (2018)	0.0	4.6	1.1	2.1 (2018)
South Asia								
Bangladesh	773	812	1,129	2,168	10.6	7.2	5.2	5.5
Bhutan	7	7	87	79	...	...	14.4	10.5
India	10,668	23,922	24,413	51,160	17.1	14.9	6.8	10.1
Maldives	20	31	81	122	4.2	6.3	4.0	3.5
Nepal	103	120	188	254	7.6	8.5	10.6	8.5
Sri Lanka	791	441	1,408	4,086	12.1	5.5	12.3	21.2
Southeast Asia								
Brunei Darussalam	...	...	...	...	...	...	...	...
Cambodia	13	30	65	638	0.7	0.7	1.1	3.9
Indonesia	16,696	20,281	31,569	67,981	22.8	20.9	18.7	34.0
Lao People's Democratic Republic	41	136	302	780	8.0	17.8	13.1	13.4
Malaysia	6,441	9,381	5,575	10,385 (2016)	5.6	5.6	2.4	4.9 (2016)
Myanmar	20	24	249	792	1.0	0.6	3.2	5.2
Philippines	7,066	9,528	11,461	11,111	22.9	24.7	18.7	11.3
Singapore	...	...	...	...	...	...	...	...
Thailand	14,013	18,044	10,965	15,057	16.3	13.7	4.7	4.7
Viet Nam	1,306	946	1,873	13,545	7.5	2.6	2.3	5.9
The Pacific								
Cook Islands[a, b]	4	4	3	7	...	...	2.0	2.4
Fiji	26	15	26	58	2.6	0.9	1.4	2.3
Kiribati[b]	1	1	1	1	1.7	1.9	0.9	0.5
Marshall Islands[b]	22	4	9	8	29.8	4.8	8.1	5.0
Micronesia, Federated States of[b]	23	2	5	6 (2016)	36.1	3.9	5.3	3.9 (2016)
Nauru	...	...	...	...	...	...	...	...
Niue	...	...	...	...	...	...	...	...
Palau	...	...	...	...	...	...	...	...
Papua New Guinea	305	308	812	2,787	12.9	8.4	13.3	27.1
Samoa	6	6	11	26	...	3.9	5.3	8.9
Solomon Islands	9	14	21	26	7.1	9.1	6.2	3.9
Timor-Leste	0	0	0	1	...	...	0.0	0.1
Tonga	5	5	5	14	...	9.8	9.3	9.9
Tuvalu	...	...	...	...	...	...	...	...
Vanuatu	3	3	6	10	1.6	1.6	1.7	2.1 (2016)

... = data not available, 0 or 0.0 = magnitude is less than half of unit employed, $ = United States dollars; ADB = Asian Development Bank.

a Refers to principal repayments on long-term debt plus interest on short-term and long-term debt.
b Debt service payment as a percentage of exports of goods, services, and primary income was derived using balance-of-payments data.

Sources: World Bank. International Debt Statistics Online. http://data.worldbank.org/data-catalog/international-debt-statistics (accessed 19 July 2019); and Asian Development Bank estimates using economy sources.

Table 2.4.24: **International Tourist Arrivals**[a]
('000)

ADB Regional Member	2000	2005	2010	2015	2016	2017	2018*
Developing ADB Member Economies							
Central and West Asia[b]	**3,404**	**5,514**	**7,947**	**15,116**	**10,799**	**13,017**	...
Afghanistan	...	...	...	...	...	...	...
Armenia	45	319	687	1,192	1,260	1,495	1,652
Azerbaijan	576 (2002)	693	1,280	1,922	2,045	2,454	...
Georgia	387	...	1,067	3,012	3,297	4,069	4,757
Kazakhstan	1,471	3,143	2,991	4,560 (2014)	...	...	...
Kyrgyz Republic	59	319		855	3,051	3,853	4,568	...
Pakistan	557	798	907	965 (2014)	...	...	...
Tajikistan	4	...	160	414	344	431	1,250
Turkmenistan	3	...	...	...	...	...	...
Uzbekistan	302	242	...	...	...	...	...
East Asia	**48,126**	**71,322**	**90,571**	**107,630**	**114,159**	**113,170**	**119,106**
China, People's Republic of	31,229	46,809	55,665	56,886	59,270	60,740	62,900
Hong Kong, China	8,814	14,773	20,085	26,686	26,553	27,885	29,263
Korea, Republic of	5,322	6,023	8,798	13,232	17,242	13,336	15,347
Mongolia	137	339	456	386	404	469	529
Taipei,China	2,624	3,378	5,567	10,440	10,690	10,740	11,067
South Asia[b]	**4,187**	**5,460**	**8,169**	**17,653**	**19,700**	**21,270**	...
Bangladesh	199	208	303	643	830	1,026	...
Bhutan	8	14	41	155	210	255	274
India	2,649	3,919	5,776		13,284	14,570	15,543	...
Maldives	467	395	792	1,234	1,286	1,390	1,484
Nepal	464	375	603	539	753	940	1,173
Sri Lanka	400	549	654	1,798	2,051	2,116	2,334
Southeast Asia[b]	**35,458**	**48,971**	**70,431**	**104,181**	**110,706**	**120,392**	**96,984**
Brunei Darussalam	...	126	214	218	219	259	278
Cambodia	...	1,333	2,508	4,775	5,012	5,602	6,201
Indonesia	5,064	5,002	7,003		9,963	11,072	12,948	...
Lao People's Democratic Republic	191	672	1,670	3,543	3,315	3,257	3,770
Malaysia	10,222	16,431	24,577	25,721	26,757	25,948	25,832
Myanmar	208	660	792	4,681	2,907	3,443	...
Philippines	1,992	2,623	3,520	5,361	5,967	6,621	7,128
Singapore	6,062	7,079	9,161	12,052	12,914	13,909	...
Thailand	9,579	11,567	15,936	29,923	32,530	35,483	38,277
Viet Nam	2,140	3,478	5,050	7,944	10,013	12,922	15,498
The Pacific[b]	**759**	**1,112**	**1,351**	**1,652**	**1,666**	**1,711**	...
Cook Islands	73	88	104	125	146	161	169
Fiji	294	545	632	755	792	843	870
Kiribati	5	4	5	4	6	6	...
Marshall Islands	5	9	5	6	10	6	...
Micronesia, Federated States of	21	19	45	31	30	...	...
Nauru	58	81	...	...	...	...	...
Niue	...	...	6	8	8	10	...
Palau	58	81	85	164	138	123	116
Papua New Guinea	58	69	140	201	156	143	...
Samoa	88	102	122	128	134	146	...
Solomon Islands	5	9	21	22	22	26	28
Timor-Leste	...	...	40	62	66	74	75
Tonga	35	42	47	54	61	62	...
Tuvalu	1	1	2	2	2	2	...
Vanuatu	58	62	97	90	95	109	116
Developed ADB Member Economies	**11,475**	**14,544**	**16,918**	**30,226**	**35,678**	**41,061**	**44,124**
Australia	4,931	5,463	5,872	7,450	8,269	8,815	9,246
Japan	4,757	6,728	8,611	19,737	24,039	28,691	31,192
New Zealand	1,787	2,353	2,435	3,039	3,370	3,555	3,686
DEVELOPING ADB MEMBER ECONOMIES[b]	**91,934**	**132,379**	**178,469**	**246,232**	**257,030**	**269,560**	**230,388**
ALL ADB REGIONAL MEMBERS[b]	**103,409**	**146,923**	**195,387**	**276,458**	**292,708**	**310,621**	**274,512**
WORLD	**676,655**	**808,570**	**951,522**	**1,195,053**	**1,240,866**	**1,327,800**	**1,402,789**

... = data not available, | = marks break in the series, * = provisional or preliminary, ADB = Asian Development Bank.

a For Australia; Japan; the Kyrgyz Republic; the Republic of Korea; Taipei,China; Tajikistan; and Viet Nam: Data refer to international visitor arrivals at frontiers (including tourists and same-day visitors). For the rest of the economies: Data refer to international tourist arrivals at frontiers (overnight visitors only, i.e., excluding same-day visitors).
b For reporting economies only.

Source: United Nations World Tourism Organization. 2019. *World Tourism Barometer and Statistical Annex, May 2019.* Volume 17; and past volumes.

Table 2.4.25: **International Tourism Receipts**
($ million)

ADB Regional Member	2000	2005	2010	2015	2016	2017	2018*
Developing ADB Member Economies							
Central and West Asia[a]	**679**	**1,528**	**3,631**	**7,470**	**8,607**	**10,097**	**10,862**
Afghanistan	...	...	75	79	49	2	...
Armenia	38	223	646	936	968	1,120	1,208
Azerbaijan	63	78	657	2,309	2,714	3,012	2,634
Georgia	97	241	659	1,868	2,111	2,704	3,222
Kazakhstan	356	701	1,005	1,534	1,549	1,781	2,255
Kyrgyz Republic	15	73	160	426	432	429	...
Pakistan	81	182	306	317	322	352	390
Tajikistan	2 (2002)	2	2	1	4	8	9
Turkmenistan	...	...	...	...	...	...	...
Uzbekistan	27	28	121	...	458	689	1,144
East Asia	**32,707**	**50,550**	**87,307**	**110,966**	**108,301**	**97,977**	**106,573**
China, People's Republic of	16,231	29,296	45,814	44,969	44,432	38,559	40,386
Hong Kong, China	5,868	10,294	22,200	36,150	32,846	33,339	36,703
Korea, Republic of	6,834	5,806	10,328	15,214	17,332	13,368	15,319
Mongolia	36	177	244	246	316	396	461
Taipei,China	3,738	4,977	8,721	14,387	13,375	12,315	13,704
South Asia[a]	**4,247**	**8,974**	**17,244**	**27,288**	**29,202**	**35,104**	**35,557**
Bangladesh	50	75	81	150	214	337	...
Bhutan	10	19	40	94	91	103	102
India	3,460	7,493	14,490	21,013	22,427	27,365	28,568
Maldives	321	826	1,713	2,569	2,506	2,744	3,028
Nepal	158	132	344	481	446	630	...
Sri Lanka	248	429	576	2,981	3,518	3,925	3,859
Southeast Asia[a]	**25,502**	**34,986**	**68,423**	**108,628**	**116,925**	**130,557**	**138,726**
Brunei Darussalam	155 (2001)	191	...	147	144	177	...
Cambodia	304	840	1,519	3,131	3,208	3,636	4,362
Indonesia	4,975	4,522	6,958	10,761	11,206	13,139	14,110
Lao People's Democratic Republic	114	147	382	724	716	761	...
Malaysia	5,011	8,847	18,115	17,584	18,075	18,323	19,143
Myanmar	162	67	72	2,120	2,197	1,969	...
Philippines	2,156	2,287	2,645	5,272	5,143	6,986	7,461
Singapore	5,142	6,209	14,178	16,617	18,944	19,738	20,528
Thailand	7,483	9,576	20,104	44,922	48,792	56,938	63,042
Viet Nam	...	2,300	4,450	7,350	8,500	8,890	10,080
The Pacific[a]	**416**	**839**	**1,292**	**1,653**	**1,505**	**1,585**	**...**
Cook Islands	36	91	111	154	179	183	...
Fiji	189	485	634	805	863	926	956
Kiribati	3	4	4	2	3	4	...
Marshall Islands	3	3	4	1	5	...	...
Micronesia, Federated States of	17	16	24	25	...	...	...
Nauru	...	...	...	...	...	...	...
Niue	...	...	...	...	...	...	...
Palau	53	60	73	149	141	116	...
Papua New Guinea	7	4	2	2	1	2	...
Samoa	41	73	132	142	148	166	...
Solomon Islands	4	2	44	51	56	67	...
Timor-Leste	...	...	31	51	58	73	...
Tonga	7	15	16	43	51	48	48
Tuvalu	...	1	...	...	...	...	...
Vanuatu	56	85	217	228	...	...	...
Developed ADB Member Economies	**14,934**	**31,526**	**52,305**	**68,587**	**77,539**	**86,379**	**97,154**
Australia	9,289	18,423	32,584	34,246	37,040	41,732	45,035
Japan	3,373	6,630	13,199	24,982	30,679	34,054	41,115
New Zealand	2,272	6,473	6,522	9,359	9,820	10,593	11,004
DEVELOPING ADB MEMBER ECONOMIES[a]	**63,550**	**96,877**	**177,897**	**256,005**	**264,540**	**275,320**	**292,722**
ALL ADB REGIONAL MEMBERS[a]	**78,484**	**128,403**	**230,202**	**324,592**	**342,079**	**361,699**	**389,876**
WORLD	**475,510**	**703,779**	**975,302**	**1,222,092**	**1,246,391**	**1,345,624**	**1,447,749**

... = data not available, * = provisional or preliminary, $ = United States dollars, ADB = Asian Development Bank.

a   For reporting economies only.

Source: United Nations World Tourism Organization. 2019. *World Tourism Barometer and Statistical Annex, May 2019.* Volume 17; and past volumes.

V. Transport and Communications

Transport and Communications features a discussion on air passenger traffic and carrier departures, as well as internet usage and penetration rates in Asia and the Pacific. Other data topics covered in the statistical tables include container port traffic; road and rail networks; motor vehicle ownership, injuries, and fatalities; fixed telephone subscriptions; and mobile telephone subscriptions.

Asia and the Pacific is the world's busiest region for air passenger air traffic

Asia and the Pacific is the busiest region in the world in terms of air passenger traffic, as measured by the UN International Civil Aviation Organization. The region accounted for about 34% of global air passenger traffic in 2017, with an increase of nearly 11% over 2016. By comparison, Europe accounted for about 27% of global air passenger traffic in 2017, North America about 23%, the Middle East about 9%, Latin America and the Caribbean about 5%, and Africa about 2% (ICAO 2017).

This growth in air passenger traffic across Asia and the Pacific is reflected in the significant growth in air carrier departures in ADB developing member economies. In 31 of the 38 regional economies with available data, air carrier departures increased from 2000 to 2017 (Table 2.5.6). The economies with the highest average annual growth rates in air carrier departures over this period were Bangladesh (51.8%), Vanuatu (48.3%), and Viet Nam (47.8%). The most notable average annual declines in air carrier departures were observed in Fiji (–3.6%), Turkmenistan (–2.9%), and Uzbekistan (–1.6%).

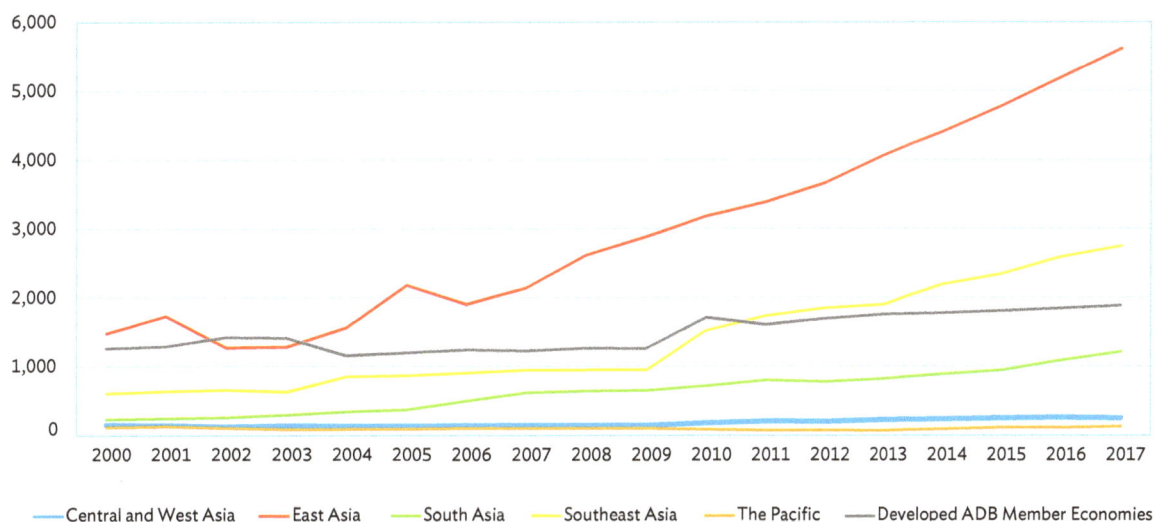

Figure 2.5.1: Air Carrier Departures by Subregion within Asia and the Pacific
('000)

ADB = Asian Development Bank.
Note: This chart treats unavailable data for economies as 0 for calculating the total number of take offs by subregion
Source: Table 2.5.6, Key Indicators for Asia and the Pacific 2019.

The developing member economies with the most air carrier departures in 2017 were the PRC (4.36 million); India (1.03 million); Indonesia (0.92 million); Taipei,China (0.51 million); and the Republic of Korea (0.50 million). By contrast, the most air carrier departures in 2000 were in Taipei,China (0.59 million); the PRC (0.57 million); the Republic of Korea (0.23 million); India (0.20 million); and Malaysia (0.17 million).

In terms of the subregions, annual growth in air carrier departures was most pronounced in South Asia (25.1%), Southeast Asia (20.8%), and East Asia (16.6%) as shown in Figure 2.5.1. Much lower annual growth rates were observed in Central and West Asia (3.8%), ADB's developed member economies (2.9%), and the Pacific (0.5%).

Internet use is spreading across Asia and the Pacific, with nearly half of all households connected to the internet in 2017; yet, a gender digital divide persists

According to the International Telecommunications Union, the proportion of households in Asia and the Pacific with internet access rose from about 28% in 2010 to more than 48% by 2017. However, a gender gap persists in terms of internet penetration rates for men and women in Asia and the Pacific. In 2017, the rates for males and females were 47.9% and 39.7%, respectively (ITU 2017).

From 2010 to 2017, of the 46 regional economies with available data, the largest gains in terms of internet users per 100 population were in Kazakhstan (44.8), Brunei Darussalam (41.9), and Armenia (39.7) as can be observed in Figure 2.5.2.

The eight economies with the highest internet use penetration rates per 100 population in 2017 were all high-income economies: the Republic of Korea (95.1); Brunei Darussalam (94.9); Taipei,China

Figure 2.5.2: Proportion of Internet Users in Select Economies of Asia and the Pacific
(per 100 population)

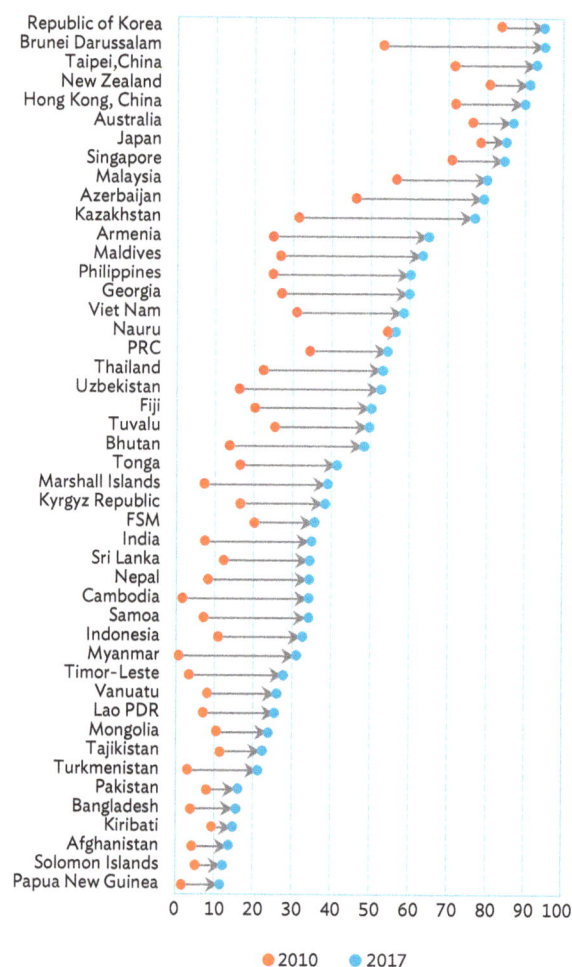

FSM = Federated States of Micronesia, Lao PDR = Lao People's Democratic Republic, PRC = People's Republic of China.
Note: Only economies with available data for both 2010 and 2017 are included.
Source: Table 2.5.9, Key Indicators for Asia and the Pacific 2019.

(92.8); New Zealand (90.8); Hong Kong, China (89.4); Australia (86.5); Japan (84.6); and Singapore (84.4).

Data Issues and Comparability

Issues with the data organization, collection, compilation, and dissemination affect the availability, quality, and timeliness of road statistics. Some subregions, especially the Pacific, have incomplete or no data. The most recent road data are usually 2–3 years old at the time of review.

Most data on telephone and internet subscriptions come from questionnaires sent by the International Telecommunication Union to participating economies. Other information and reports are sourced from national ministries in charge of telecommunications, and staff estimates.

Table 2.5.1:   Road Indicators—Network[a]
(km)

ADB Regional Member	Primary	Class I	Class II	Class III	Below III	Other	Year[b]
Developing ADB Member Economies							
Central and West Asia							
Afghanistan	–	10	2,549	–	1,461	–	2015
Armenia	–	147	721	58	40	–	2013
Azerbaijan	–	544	905	–	–	–	2017
Georgia	–	90	1,058	–	–	–	2017
Kazakhstan	–	557	5,407	6,389	475	–	2010
Kyrgyz Republic	–	–	303	1,324	136	–	2013
Pakistan	357	1,116	275	2,442	1,138	–	2015
Tajikistan	–	20	978	–	914	–	2015
Turkmenistan	–	60	–	2,120	24	–	2008
Uzbekistan	–	1,195	1,101	670	–	–	2008
East Asia							
China, People's Republic of	8,437	230	1,855	321	5	–	2015
Hong Kong, China	…	…	…	…	…	…	
Korea, Republic of	457	423	40	–	–	–	2017
Mongolia	–	8	2,593	233	1,480	–	2017
Taipei,China	…	…	…	…	…	…	
South Asia							
Bangladesh	–	321	1,680	44	5	–	2017
Bhutan	–	7	116	–	47	–	2017
India	90	7,067	1,071	3,556	117	–	2015
Maldives	…	…	…	…	…	…	
Nepal	…	–	218	1,082	13	–	2013
Sri Lanka	–	60	545	45	–	–	2017
Southeast Asia							
Brunei Darussalam	…	…	…	…	…	…	
Cambodia	–	–	633	1,321	–	–	2017
Indonesia	409	603	3,045	–	–	34	2010
Lao People's Democratic Republic	–	–	244	2,307	306	–	2010
Malaysia	795	61	817	–	–	–	2010
Myanmar	–	320	575	1,702	1,928	–	2015
Philippines	–	665	2,048	687	–	–	2017
Singapore	13	6	–	–	–	–	2015
Thailand	572	4,075	848	27	–	–	2017
Viet Nam	–	1,202	1,915	–	–	–	2017
The Pacific							
Cook Islands	…	…	…	…	…	…	
Fiji	…	…	…	…	…	…	
Kiribati	…	…	…	…	…	…	
Marshall Islands	…	…	…	…	…	…	
Micronesia, Federated States of	…	…	…	…	…	…	
Nauru					…		
Niue							
Palau	…	…	…	…	…	…	
Papua New Guinea	…	…	…	…	…	…	
Samoa	…	…	…	…	…	…	
Solomon Islands	…	…	…	…	…	…	
Timor-Leste	…	…	…	…	…	…	
Tonga	…	…	…	…	…	…	
Tuvalu	…	…	…	…	…	…	
Vanuatu	…	…	…	…	…	…	
Developed ADB Member Economies							
Australia	…	…	…	…	…	…	
Japan	1,138	–	–	–	–	–	2015
New Zealand	…	…	…	…	…	…	

… = data not available, - = magnitude equals zero, ADB = Asian Development Bank, km = kilometer.

a The road network refers to the Asian Highway that consists of highway routes of international importance within Asia, including highway routes substantially crossing more than one subregion; highway routes within subregions that connect neighboring subregions; and highway routes located within member states that provide access to (a) capital cities; (b) main industrial and agricultural centers; (c) major air, sea, and river ports; (d) major container terminals and depots; and (e) major tourist attractions. "Primary" class in the classification refers to access-controlled motorways. Access-controlled motorways are used exclusively by automobiles. Motorcycles, bicycles, and pedestrians will not be allowed to enter the motorway to ensure traffic safety and the high running speed of automobiles.
Class I refers to asphalt, cement, or concrete roads with four or more lanes.
Class II refers to double bituminous-treated roads with two lanes.
Class III is regarded as the minimum desirable standard usually described as a two-lane (narrow) road.
Roads classified below Class III are road sections below the minimum desirable standard.
b The year data was received by the Secretariat of the United Nations Economic and Social Commission for Asia and the Pacific.

Source: United Nations Economic and Social Commission for Asia and the Pacific (ESCAP). ESCAP Online Statistical Database. http://data.unescap.org/escap_stat/ (accessed 24 July 2019).

Table 2.5.2:   Road Indicators—Vehicles

ADB Regional Member	Number of Registered Vehicles, 2016						
	Total	(per 1,000 people)[b]	By type[a]				
			Four-Wheeled Vehicles	Two- and Three-Wheeled Vehicles	Heavy Trucks	Buses	Others
Developing ADB Member Economies							
Central and West Asia							
Afghanistan	655,357 (2013)	25.2	407,608	68,090	81,416	20,589	77,654
Armenia	300,091 (2010)	98.6	247,723	28	40,924	11,396	20
Azerbaijan	1,330,551	136.4	1,136,983	3,290	141,525	30,958	17,795
Georgia	1,126,470	302.2	919,199	63,083	93,497	50,691	–
Kazakhstan	4,383,120	246.3	3,835,609	9,692	439,167	98,652	–
Kyrgyz Republic	993,000 (2015)	168.4	...	...	...	...	...
Pakistan	18,352,500	93.9	2,835,400	13,538,200	259,900	229,200	1,489,800
Tajikistan	439,972	50.9	380,496	4,546	39,261	15,669	–
Turkmenistan	...	...	...	...	...	...	...
Uzbekistan	...	...	...	...	...	...	...
East Asia							
China, People's Republic of[c]	294,694,457	213.1	...	...	...	...	...
Hong Kong, China	...	...	...	...	...	...	...
Korea, Republic of	25,680,967	501.6	17,338,160	2,180,688	3,492,173	892,539	1,777,407
Mongolia	841,537	272.4	547,299	42,751	175,648	6,823	69,016
Taipei,China[d,e]	21,704,365 (2017)	921.4	6,763,422	13,755,582	1,086,382	34,188	64,791
South Asia							
Bangladesh	2,879,708	17.9	613,149	1,980,246	158,379	64,608	63,326
Bhutan[e]	86,981 (2017)	119.6	56,232	9,786	12,891	681	7,391
India	210,023,289 (2015)	163.7	38,523,053	154,297,746	4,461,059	1,970,786	10,770,645
Maldives	92,983	196.8	14,314	75,053	3,438	178	–
Nepal	2,339,169 (2015)	83.7	187,014	1,547,312	56,250	52,388	496,205
Sri Lanka	6,795,469	320.5	717,674	4,815,617	762,912	104,104	395,162
Southeast Asia							
Brunei Darussalam	349,279 (2010)	903.0	...	...	...	...	...
Cambodia	3,751,715	246.0	97,239	2,714,193	57,321	5,972	876,990
Indonesia	128,398,594	496.3	...	...	...	...	...
Lao People's Democratic Republic	1,850,020	280.9	370,043	1,422,869	52,443	4,665	–
Malaysia	27,613,120	873.8	13,123,638	12,667,041	1,191,310	59,977	561,154
Myanmar[e]	6,381,136 (2017)	119.5	516,707	5,391,505	59,680	28,383	384,861
Philippines	9,251,565	89.6	3,434,329	5,329,770	407,357	29,794	50,315
Singapore	933,534	166.5	727,533	142,439	45,224	18,338	–
Thailand	37,338,139	553.5	15,003,774	20,497,296	1,055,717	157,799	623,553
Viet Nam	50,666,855	546.6	3,033,527	47,131,928	...	...	501,400
The Pacific							
Cook Islands	12,453 (2014)	676.8	5,085	6,846	491	31	–
Fiji	110,763	0.1	...	...	...	...	...
Kiribati[e]	3,706 (2017)	32.8	2,547	757	4	398	–
Marshall Islands	2,116 (2013)	39.5	1,917	52	26	63	58
Micronesia, Federated States of	5,673	55.4	5,436	25	55	62	95
Nauru	...	...	...	...	...	...	...
Niue	...	...	...	...	...	...	...
Palau	7,102 (2013)	408.2	...	...	...	...	...
Papua New Guinea	100,993	11.9	66,017	1,289	22,072	11,615	–
Samoa	25,235	128.8	23,557	95	1,184	326	73
Solomon Islands	...	...	...	...	...	...	...
Timor-Leste[e]	146,596 (2016)	115.6	24,438	108,409	1,120	207	12,422
Tonga	8,154 (2012)	79.4	6,039	184	1,882	49	–
Tuvalu	...	...	...	...	...	...	...
Vanuatu	...	...	...	...	...	...	...
Developed ADB Member Economies							
Australia	18,326,236	757.6	16,946,125	828,965	430,997	96,582	23,567
Japan	81,602,046	642.6	...	...	...	...	...
New Zealand	3,656,300	779.1	...	...	...	...	...

... = data not available, – = magnitude equals zero; ADB = Asian Development Bank.

a   Figures refer to the same year indicated in the column for "Total" unless otherwise specified.
b   Calculated by dividing the total number of registered vehicles by the midyear population in thousands.
c   The "per 1,000 people" calculation used end-of-year population data instead of midyear data.
d   The "Heavy Trucks" category includes a combination of heavy and light trucks.
e   For 2017, data only covers 1 January to April 30.

Sources: World Health Organization. 2018. *Global Status Report on Road Safety 2018*. Geneva. For number of registered vehicles per 1,000 people in 2016: Asian Development Bank estimates. For Armenia and Brunei Darussalam: World Health Organization. 2013. *Global Status Report on Road Safety 2013*. Geneva. For Taipei,China: Government of Taipei,China, Directorate-General of Budget, Accounting and Statistics. 2018. *Statistical Yearbook 2017*. Nantou City. https://eng.dgbas.gov. tw/public/data/dgbas03/bs2/yearbook_eng/Yearbook2017.pdf (accessed 26 July 2019).

Transport

Table 2.5.3:   Road Indicators—Safety

ADB Regional Member	Estimated Road Traffic Deaths, 2016		Road User Deaths, 2016 (%)				
	Total	Death Rate (per 100,000 population)	Four-Wheeled Vehicles	Two- and Three- Wheeled Vehicles	Cyclists	Pedestrians	Others
Developing ADB Member Economies							
Central and West Asia							
Afghanistan	5,230	15	...	...	...	...	...
Armenia	499	17	59.6	1.5	0.4	34.8	3.7
Azerbaijan	845	9	51.8	0.9	0.9	42.0	4.3
Georgia	599	15	44.9	0.5	0.7	26.5	27.4
Kazakhstan	3,158	18	59.8	4.3	1.7	30.9	3.3
Kyrgyz Republic	916	15	27.6	2.1	0.2	40.0	30.0
Pakistan	27,582	14	...	...	...	...	...
Tajikistan	1,577	18	57.4	...	2.3	40.3	–
Turkmenistan	823	15	...	...	...	...	...
Uzbekistan	3,617	12	...	...	...	...	...
East Asia							
China, People's Republic of	256,180	18	...	...	...	...	...
Hong Kong, China	...	...	...	...	...	...	...
Korea, Republic of	4,990	10	...	20.5	5.9	39.9	33.7
Mongolia	499	17	39.3	18.6	1.2	28.7	12.2
Taipei,China	...	...	...	...	...	...	...
South Asia							
Bangladesh	24,954	15	...	...	...	...	...
Bhutan	139	17	...	...	...	...	...
India	299,091	23	17.9	39.6	1.7	10.4	30.4
Maldives	4	1	–	75.0	–	25.0	–
Nepal	4,622	16					
Sri Lanka	3,096	15	6.2	50.8	8.1	29.2	5.7
Southeast Asia							
Brunei Darussalam	...	...	...	...	...	...	...
Cambodia	2,803	18	6.2	73.5	2.3	9.6	8.4
Indonesia	31,726	12	4.9	73.6	3.2	15.5	2.7
Lao People's Democratic Republic	1,120	17	...	...	...	...	...
Malaysia	7,374	24	...	...	...	...	...
Myanmar	10,540	20	10.8	64.8	3.1	14.2	7.1
Philippines	12,690	12	0.3	4.7	0.1	1	93.9
Singapore	155	3	7.8	44.0	14.2	33.3	0.7
Thailand	22,491	33	12.3	74.4	3.5	7.6	2.3
Viet Nam	24,970	26	...	...	...	...	...
The Pacific							
Cook Islands	3	17	20.0	80.0	–	–	–
Fiji	86	10	63.3	...	...	36.7	–
Kiribati	5	4	40.0	20.0	–	40.0	–
Marshall Islands	...	...	...	...	...	...	...
Micronesia, Federated States of	2	2	50.0	–	–	50.0	–
Nauru	...	...	...	...	...	...	...
Niue	...	...	...	...	...	...	...
Palau	...	...	...	...	...	...	...
Papua New Guinea	1,145	14	52.5	...	...	47.5	–
Samoa	22	11	41.2	–	5.9	47.1	5.9
Solomon Islands	104	17	...	...	...	...	...
Timor–Leste	161	13	...	...	...	...	...
Tonga	18	17	66.7	–	–	27.8	5.6
Tuvalu	...	...	...	...	...	...	...
Vanuatu	43	16	...	...	...	...	...
Developed ADB Member Economies							
Australia	1,351	6	60.9	19.3	2.2	14.0	3.5
Japan	5,224	4	32.4	17.2	15.1	35.0	1.0
New Zealand	364	8	68.5	15.9	1.5	7.6	6.4

... = data not available, – = magnitude equals zero; ADB = Asian Development Bank.

Source: World Health Organization. 2018. *Global Status Report on Road Safety 2018*. Geneva.

Table 2.5.4:   Rail Indicators

ADB Regional Member	Rail Lines, Total Route (km)				Rail Network, Length per Land Area (km per km^2 '000)			
	2000	2005	2010	2017	2000	2005	2010	2017
Developing ADB Member Economies								
Central and West Asia								
Afghanistan	...	...	...	...	...	...	...	...
Armenia	843.0	711.0 (2004)	826.07	685.6	29.6	29.7 (2006)	29.0	24.1
Azerbaijan	2,116.0	2,122.0	2,079.1	2,132.0	25.6	25.7	25.2	25.8
Georgia	1,562.0	1,336.0	1,566.4	1,285.0	22.5	19.2	22.5	18.5
Kazakhstan	13,545.0	14,204.0	14,184.1	16,040.3	5.0	5.3	5.3	5.9
Kyrgyz Republic	417.0	417.0	417.2	424.0	2.2	2.2	2.2	2.2
Pakistan	7,791.0	7,791.0	7,791.0	7,791.0	10.1	10.1	10.1	10.1
Tajikistan	533.0	617.0	620.7	620.0	3.8	4.4	4.4	4.5
Turkmenistan	2,521.0	2,529.0	3,115.0	3,840.0	5.4	5.4	6.6	8.2
Uzbekistan	3,645.0	4,014.0	4,227.2	4,642.0	8.6	9.4	9.9	10.9
East Asia								
China, People's Republic of	58,656.0	62,200.0	66,239.0	67,278.0	6.2	6.6	7.2	7.2
Hong Kong, China	...	...			...	...	...	...
Korea, Republic of	3,123.0	3,392.0	3,618.3	4,191.7	32.4	35.0	37.2	43.0
Mongolia	1,810.0	1,810.0	1,814.0	1,810.0	1.2	1.2	1.2	1.2
Taipei,China	1,190.0	1,336.0	1,743.0	1,835.0	33.2	37.2	48.6	51.1
South Asia								
Bangladesh	2,745.0	2,855.0	2,835.0	...	21.1	21.9	21.8	...
Bhutan	...	...	...	...	...	...	...	...
India	62,759.0	63,485.0	63,974.0	67,368.0	21.1	21.4	21.5	22.7
Maldives	...	...	...	...	...	...	...	...
Nepal	...	...	...	...	...	...	...	...
Sri Lanka	...	1,463.0 (2007)	1,148.3 (2011)	1,561.7 (2016)	...	23.3 (2007)	18.3 (2011)	24.9 (2016)
Southeast Asia								
Brunei Darussalam	...	...	...	...	...	...	...	...
Cambodia	601.0	650.0 (2004)	...	...	3.4	3.7 (2004)	...	...
Indonesia	...	3,370.0 (2006)	4,684.0 (2010)	...	...	1.9 (2006)	2.6	...
Lao People's Democratic Republic	...	...	...	...	...	...	...	...
Malaysia	1,636.0	1,667.0	2,209.7	...	5.0	5.1	6.7	...
Myanmar	...	...	...	...	...	...	...	...
Philippines	...	...	479.0 (2008)	509.0 (2016)	...	...	1.6 (2008)	1.7 (2016)
Singapore	...	...	...	...				
Thailand	4,044.0	4,429.0 (2007)	4,458.0	...	7.9	8.7 (2007)	8.7	...
Viet Nam	3,142.0	3,147.0	2,576.6	2,367.0	10.1	10.1	8.3	7.6
The Pacific								
Cook Islands	...	...	...	...	...	...	...	...
Fiji	...	...	...	...	...	...	...	...
Kiribati	...	...	...	...	...	...	...	...
Marshall Islands	...	...	...	...	...	...	...	...
Micronesia, Federated States of	...	...	...	...	...	...	...	...
Nauru	...	...	...	...	...	...	...	...
Niue	...	...	...	...	...	...	...	...
Palau	...	...	...	...	...	...	...	...
Papua New Guinea	...	...	...	...	...	...	...	...
Samoa	...	...	...	...	...	...	...	...
Solomon Islands	...	...	...	...	...	...	...	...
Timor-Leste	...	...	...	...	...	...	...	...
Tonga	...	...	...	...	...	...	...	...
Tuvalu	...	...	...	...	...	...	...	...
Vanuatu	...	...	...	...	...	...	...	...
Developed ADB Member Economies								
Australia	9,499.0	9,528.0	8,615.4	...	1.2	1.2	1.1	...
Japan	29,799.0	20,052.3	20,140.3	16,976.4	81.8	55.0	55.2	46.6
New Zealand	...	...	...	...	...	...	...	...

... = data not available; ADB = Asian Development Bank; km = kilometer; km^2 = square kilometer.

Sources: World Bank. World Development Indicators. http://data.worldbank.org/indicator (accessed 25 July 2019) and Asian Development Bank estimates. For Taipei,China: National Development Council. 2018. *Statistical Data Book*. https://ws.ndc.gov.tw/Download.ashx?u=LzAwMS9hZG1pbmlzdHJhdG9yLzExL3JlbGZpbGUvNTgxNy8zMTc2MTc2MS82NDA0ZDUzOC1kZDc1LTQ0ZmMtYWYwMS1jODRkN2lxMjFYjMucGRm&n=VGFpd2FuIFN0YXRpc3RpY2FsIERhdGEgQm9vayAyMDE4LnBkZg%3d%3d&icon=..pdf (accessed 26 July 2019).

Table 2.5.5:   Railways—Passengers Carried and Goods Transported

ADB Regional Member	Passengers Carried (passenger-km million)				Goods Transported (t-km million)			
	2000	2005	2010	2017	2000	2005	2010	2017
Developing ADB Member Economies								
Central and West Asia								
Afghanistan	...	...	...	...	...	...	...	...
Armenia	47	27	50	25	354	654	346	689
Azerbaijan	493	878	917	467	5,770	10,374 (2007)	8,250	4,633
Georgia	453	720	654	597	3,912	6,127	6,228	2,963
Kazakhstan	10,215	12,129	15,448	19,241	124,983	171,855	213,174	206,258
Kyrgyz Republic	44	60 (2006)	99	43	337	752 (2007)	738	935
Pakistan	18,495	24,238	20,619 (2011)	22,476	3,612	5,014	1,757 (2011)	5,031
Tajikistan	73	52 (2006)	33	28	1,326	1,274 (2007)	808	165
Turkmenistan	943	1,435 (2006)	1,811	2,340	7,588	10,441 (2006)	11,765	13,327
Uzbekistan	2,163	2,012	2,905	4,294	15,441	18,007	22,282	22,940
East Asia								
China, People's Republic of	441,468	583,320	791,158	685,213	1,333,606	1,953,336	2,451,185	2,146,466
Hong Kong, China	...	...	...	...	...	...	...	...
Korea, Republic of	28,097	31,004	33,012	21,935	10,621	10,108	9,452	8,229
Mongolia	1,070	1,289 (2006)	2,440	973	4,293	8,361 (2007)	20,574	13,493
Taipei,China	12,269 (2001)	19,066 (2008)	20,931	29,004	1,010 (2001)	933 (2008)	873	515
South Asia								
Bangladesh	3,941	4,164	7,305	...	777	817	710	...
Bhutan	...	...	...	...	...	...	...	...
India	430,666	575,702	903,465	1,149,835	305,201	407,398	600,548	620,175
Maldives	...	...	...	...	...	...	...	...
Nepal	...	...	...	...	...	...	...	...
Sri Lanka	3,208	4,358	4,574 (2011)	7,407 (2015)	127 (2003)	135	154 (2011)	127 (2015)
Southeast Asia								
Brunei Darussalam	...	...	...	...	...	...	...	...
Cambodia	45	45	...	...	92 (2003)	...	...	...
Indonesia	19,228	14,345	20,340	25,654	4,997	4,390 (2006)	7,166 (2012)	...
Lao People's Democratic Republic	...	...	...	...	...	...	...	...
Malaysia	1,220	2,152	2,415	2,029	916	1,177	1,483	1,234
Myanmar	4,451	4,163 (2004)	...	...	1,222	885 (2004)	...	...
Philippines	123	83 (2004)	...	384 (2016)	...	1 (2004)	...	...
Singapore	...	...	...	...	...	...	...	...
Thailand	9,935	9,195	8,187	9,195	2,247	4,037	2,701	...
Viet Nam	3,200	4,558	4,378	3,657	1,921	2,928	3,901	3,574
The Pacific								
Cook Islands	...	...	...	...	...	...	...	...
Fiji	...	...	...	...	...	...	...	...
Kiribati	...	...	...	...	...	...	...	...
Marshall Islands	...	...	...	...	...	...	...	...
Micronesia, Federated States of	...	...	...	...	...	...	...	...
Nauru	...	...	...	...	...	...	...	...
Niue								
Palau	...	...	...	...	...	...	...	...
Papua New Guinea	...	...	...	...	...	...	...	...
Samoa	...	...	...	...	...	...	...	...
Solomon Islands	...	...	...	...	...	...	...	...
Timor-Leste	...	...	...	...	...	...	...	...
Tonga	...	...	...	...	...	...	...	...
Tuvalu	...	...	...	...	...	...	...	...
Vanuatu	...	...	...	...	...	...	...	...
Developed ADB Member Economies								
Australia	1,265	1,290	1,500	...	33,592	46,164	64,172	...
Japan	240,657	245,957	244,591	197,254	21,800	22,632	20,255	21,265 (2016)
New Zealand	...	...	...	...	4,078	...	...	...

... = data not available; ADB = Asian Development Bank; km = kilometer; t = metric ton.

Sources: World Bank. World Development Indicators. http://data.worldbank.org/indicator (accessed 25 July 2019). For Taipei,China: Government of Taipei,China, Directorate-General of Budget, Accounting and Statistics. 2018. *Statistical Yearbook 2017*. Nantou City. https://eng.dgbas.gov.tw/public/data/dgbas03/bs2/yearbook_eng/Yearbook2017.pdf (accessed 26 July 2019).

Table 2.5.6:   Air Transport

ADB Regional Member	Carrier Departure Worldwide (takeoffs)				Freight (t-km million)				Passenger Carried ('000)			
	2000	2005	2010	2017	2000	2005	2010	2017	2000	2005	2010	2017
Developing ADB Member Economies												
Central and West Asia												
Afghanistan	3,409	...	21,677	23,682	7.8	...	108.0	25.1	150	...	1,999	1,859
Armenia	4,406	5,939	8,761	...	8.8	7.0	6.0	...	298	556	705	...
Azerbaijan	8,012	12,470	9,885	25,365	47.2	11.9	7.8	751.1	546	1,134	797	2,331
Georgia	1,906	4,673	2,803	4,985	2.0	2.8	0.9	0.3	118	249	164	323
Kazakhstan	8,041	17,302	33,483	65,009	11.8	15.8	42.4	49.3	461	1,160	3,098	5,653
Kyrgyz Republic	6,051	5,228	7,371	27,097	3.7	2.0	1.3	0.0	241	226	376	1,127
Pakistan	63,956	48,905	64,932	66,346	340.3	407.9	333.0	249.9	5,294	5,364	6,588	9,920
Tajikistan	3,953	6,987	5,710	5,283	2.0	3.7	1.0	4.0	168	479	617	796
Turkmenistan	21,858	14,094	3,221	11,068	11.9	10.1	6.2	6.0	1,284	1,654	301	1,280
Uzbekistan	30,075	22,183	22,924	21,730	79.6	71.6	153.7	126.8	1,745	1,639	2,114	2,582
East Asia												
China, People's Republic of	572,921	1,349,269	2,377,789	4,359,033	3,900.1	7,579.4	17,193.9	23,323.6	61,892	136,722	266,293	551,235
Hong Kong, China	79,182	122,705	158,255	243,518	5,111.5	7,763.9	10,373.4	12,415.2	14,378	20,230	28,348	45,580
Korea, Republic of	226,910	221,424	280,427	496,326	7,651.3	7,432.6	12,942.7	11,002.2	34,331	33,888	36,988	84,045
Mongolia	6,200	5,332	6,528	5,277	8.4	6.1	3.9	8.4	254	295	391	603
Taipei,China[a]	586,560	479,499	360,409	509,181	1.3	1.8	2.3	2.4	48,407	44,268	41,091	65,979
South Asia												
Bangladesh	6,313	7,399	19,300	61,902	193.9	183.5	164.4	61.7	1,331	1,634	1,819	3,786
Bhutan[b]	1,138	2,467	3,053	7,927	–	0.3	0.4	0.8	34	49	182	293
India	198,426	330,484	623,197	1,029,961	547.7	774.0	1,631.0	2,407.3	17,299	27,879	64,374	139,822
Maldives[c]	5,970	4,520	4,971	33,904	13.2	0.0	...	7.7	315	82	1,025	1,486
Nepal	12,130	6,255	45,990	33,767	17.0	6.9	6.5	6.0	643	480	918	780
Sri Lanka	5,206	19,712	20,921	41,272	255.7	310.4	339.0	398.6	1,756	2,818	3,008	5,342
Southeast Asia												
Brunei Darussalam	12,739	11,808	12,333	10,743	140.2	134.1	148.5	132.6	864	978	1,263	1,172
Cambodia[b]	...	3,207	5,105	14,372	...	1.2	0.0	0.9	...	169	278	1,305
Indonesia	159,027	320,724	520,932	916,471	408.5	439.8	665.7	1,056.0	9,916	26,836	59,384	110,253
Lao People's Democratic Republic	6,411	9,002	11,374	9,731	1.7	2.5	0.1	1.5	211	293	444	1,196
Malaysia	169,263	176,152	302,185	432,454	1,863.8	2,577.6	2,564.7	1,261.6	16,561	20,369	34,239	58,189
Myanmar	10,329	26,460	20,485	65,028	0.8	2.7	2.1	5.5	438	1,504	924	2,854
Philippines	44,547	58,944	205,318	369,158	289.9	322.7	460.2	756.9	5,756	8,057	22,575	44,087
Singapore	71,042	77,119	131,722	213,198	6,004.9	7,571.3	7,121.4	7,006.9	16,704	17,744	24,860	37,680
Thailand	101,591	124,347	201,306	445,736	1,712.9	2,002.4	2,938.7	2,393.3	17,392	18,903	28,781	71,192
Viet Nam	28,999	54,415	109,176	264,548	117.3	230.2	426.9	453.3	2,878	5,454	14,378	42,593
The Pacific												
Cook Islands	...	...	...	...	...	...	...	...	...	...	...	...
Fiji	57,776	41,886	26,127	22,075	90.8	92.1	77.1	102.6	586	871	1,259	1,558
Kiribati	...	...	...	5,005	...	...	...	...	...	...	...	67
Marshall Islands[c]	2,324	3,083	3,480	2,756	0.2	0.3	...	0.7	16	26	...	47
Micronesia, Federated States of	...	...	...	...	...	...	...	...	...	...	...	...
Nauru	...	...	342	842	...	...	6.3	7.9	...	...	30	45
Niue	...	...	...	...	...	...	...	...	...	...	...	...
Palau	...	...	...	...	...	...	...	...	...	...	...	...
Papua New Guinea	27,512	19,606	32,741	53,696	22.3	21.1	28.5	29.2	1,100	819	1,405	1,865
Samoa[c]	10,877	11,439	12,492	13,433	2.2	1.8	0.0	0.0	164	267	271	135
Solomon Islands	11,481	12,318	7,388	14,365	1.0	0.8	2.5	3.8	75	91	143	428
Timor-Leste	...	...	...	...	...	...	...	...	...	...	...	...
Tonga[d]	3,814	5,255	...	...	0.0	0.0	...	...	52	75	...	...
Tuvalu	...	...	...	...	...	...	...	...	...	...	...	...
Vanuatu	1,402	1,580	17,212	12,920	1.8	1.8	0.2	2.3	102	112	248	339
Developed ADB Member Economies												
Australia	382,514	342,509	572,906	672,349	1,730.7	2,444.6	2,938.3	1,982.6	32,578	44,657	60,641	74,257
Japan	645,087	651,858	934,487	1,035,522	8,672.0	8,549.2	7,698.8	10,684.6	109,123	102,279	109,617	123,898
New Zealand	240,046	209,469	207,872	184,762	817.1	781.5	468.6	1,336.0	10,781	11,952	13,295	16,272

... = data not available, 0.0 = magnitude is less than half of unit employed, ADB = Asian Development Bank, km = kilometer, t = metric ton.

a   Carried departure worldwide is based on the number of aircraft movements, both domestic and international. Freight is based on million ton.
b   For the freight indicator, data for 2000 refer to 2002.
c   For all indicators, data for 2010 refer to 2009.
d   For all indicators, data for 2005 refer to 2004.

Sources: World Bank. World Development Indicators. http://databank.worldbank.org/data/reports.aspx?source=world-development-indicators (accessed 24 July 2019). For Taipei,China: Government of Taipei,China, Directorate-General of Budget, Accounting and Statistics. 2018. *Statistical Yearbook 2017*. Nantou City. https://eng.dgbas.gov.tw/public/data/dgbas03/bs2/yearbook_eng/Yearbook2017.pdf (accessed 26 July 2019).

Transport

Table 2.5.7:   Container Port Traffic
(teu '000)

ADB Regional Member	2000	2005	2006	2007	2008	2009	2010	2012	2013	2014	2015	2016	2017
Developing ADB Member Economies													
Central and West Asia													
Afghanistan	...	...	...	...	...	...	...	...	...	...	...	...	...
Armenia	...	...	...	...	...	...	...	...	...	...	...	...	...
Azerbaijan	...	...	...	...	...	...	...	...	...	...	...	...	...
Georgia	...	...	...	185	254	182	210	210	226	256	222	222	222
Kazakhstan	...	...	...	...	...	...	...	...	...	...	...	...	...
Kyrgyz Republic	...	...	...	...	...	...	...	...	...	...	...	...	...
Pakistan	...	1,686	1,777	1,936	1,938	2,058	2,149	2,222	2,262	2,535	2,756	2,756	2,986
Tajikistan	...	...	...	...	...	...	...	...	...	...	...	...	...
Turkmenistan	...	...	...	...	...	...	...	...	...	...	...	...	...
Uzbekistan	...	...	...	...	...	...	...	...	...	...	...	...	...
East Asia													
China, People's Republic of	41,000	67,245	84,811	103,823	115,942	108,800	142,970	166,511	175,936	186,679	195,277	199,552	213,720
Hong Kong, China	...	22,602	23,539	23,998	24,494	21,040	23,600	23,100	22,290	22,300	20,114	19,580	20,770
Korea, Republic of	9,030	15,113	15,514	17,086	17,418	15,700	19,456	22,618	23,711	24,819	25,354	26,153	27,427
Mongolia	...	...	...	...	...	...	...	...	...	...	...	...	...
Taipei,China	...	12,791	13,102	13,720	12,971	11,352	12,937	13,878	14,047	15,050	14,492	14,885	14,865
South Asia													
Bangladesh	456	809	902	978	1,091	1,182	1,350	1,427	1,489	1,643	2,045	2,377	2,587
Bhutan	...	...	...	...	...	...	...	...	...	...	...	...	...
India	2,451	4,982	6,141	7,398	7,672	8,014	8,923	10,072	10,626	11,323	11,882	12,086	13,259
Maldives	...	...	...	48	54	56	50	55	80	84	84	82	83
Nepal	...	...	...	...	...	...	...	...	...	...	...	...	...
Sri Lanka	1,733	2,455	3,079	3,687	3,687	3,464	4,100	4,321	4,310	4,908	5,185	5,550	6,000
Southeast Asia													
Brunei Darussalam	...	...	...	...	90	86	93	109	122	128	128	125	125
Cambodia	...	...	...	253	259	208	224	224	230	342	392	400	485
Indonesia	3,798	5,503	4,316	6,583	7,405	7,255	9,692	11,543	11,862	11,620	11,979	12,479	13,860
Lao People's Democratic Republic	...	...	...	...	...	...	...	...	...	...	...	...	...
Malaysia	4,642	12,198	13,419	14,829	16,094	15,923	18,142	20,898	21,377	22,645	24,260	24,570	24,719
Myanmar	...	...	...	170	180	164	335	474	567	717	827	1,026	1,070
Philippines	3,032	3,634	3,676	4,351	4,471	4,307	5,087	5,642	5,826	6,176	7,210	7,621	8,197
Singapore	17,100	23,192	24,792	28,768	30,891	26,593	29,147	32,347	33,388	34,688	31,710	32,668	33,600
Thailand	3,179	5,115	5,574	6,339	6,726	5,898	7,553	8,414	8,891	9,420	9,522	9,940	10,732
Viet Nam	1,190	2,537	3,000	4,009	4,394	4,937	5,968	8,362	8,967	10,189	11,479	11,853	12,284
The Pacific													
Cook Islands	...	...	...	...	...	...	...	...	...	...	...	...	...
Fiji	...	...	...	...	...	...	87	82	88	260	89	89	89
Kiribati	...	...	...	...	...	...	...	...	...	...	...	...	...
Marshall Islands	...	...	...	...	...	...	...	...	...	...	...	...	...
Micronesia, Federated States of	...	...	...	...	...	...	...	...	...	...	...	...	...
Nauru	...	...	...	...	...	...	...	...	...	...	...	...	...
Niue	...	...	...	...	...	...	...	...	...	...	...	...	...
Palau	...	...	...	...	...	...	...	...	...	...	...	...	...
Papua New Guinea	...	...	...	282	255	262	283	279	279	279	279	279	276
Samoa	...	...	...	...	...	...	...	23	24	27	28	28	28
Solomon Islands	...	...	...	...	...	...	...	...	...	...	...	...	...
Timor-Leste	...	...	...	...	...	...	...	...	...	...	...	...	...
Tonga	...	...	...	...	...	...	...	...	...	...	...	...	...
Tuvalu	...	...	...	...	...	...	...	...	...	...	...	...	...
Vanuatu	...	...	...	...	...	...	...	...	...	...	...	...	...
Developed ADB Member Economies													
Australia	3,543	5,191	5,742	6,290	6,102	6,200	6,412	7,251	7,180	7,405	7,634	7,690	7,694
Japan	13,100	17,055	18,470	19,165	18,944	16,286	19,548	20,834	21,050	21,139	20,577	20,785	21,904
New Zealand	1,067	1,603	1,807	2,312	2,318	2,325	2,526	2,822	2,891	3,003	3,173	3,165	3,227

... = data not available, – = magnitude equals zero, ADB = Asian Development Bank, teu = twenty-foot equivalent unit.

Sources: World Bank. World Development Indicators. http://data.worldbank.org/indicator (accessed 24 July 2019). For Taipei,China for 2005–2007: United Nations Conference on Trade and Development. 2008 and 2010. Review of Maritime Transport. New York, New York: United Nations Publications. For Taipei,China for 2010–2017: United Nations Conference on Trade and Development. UNCTADstat. http://unctadstat.unctad.org/EN/Index.html (accessed 24 July 2019).

Table 2.5.8: **Access to Fixed Telephone, Mobile Phones, and Internet**
('000)

ADB Regional Member	Telephone Subscribers		Mobile Phone Subscribers		Fixed Broadband Subscribers	
	2000	2017	2000	2017	2000	2017
Developing ADB Member Economies						
Central and West Asia						
Afghanistan	29.0	118.8	25.0 (2002)	23,929.7	0.2 (2004)	29.4
Armenia	533.4	505.2	17.5	3,488.5	0.0 (2001)	315.3
Azerbaijan	801.2	1,688.3	420.4	10,127.0	1.0 (2002)	1,805.2
Georgia	508.8	713.8	194.7	5,502.4	0.4 (2001)	770.9
Kazakhstan	1,834.2	3,686.6	197.3	26,693.3	1.0 (2003)	2,576.1
Kyrgyz Republic	376.1	362.3	9.0	7,369.9	0.0 (2002)	258.0
Pakistan	3,053.5	2,940.2	306.5	144,525.6	14.6 (2005)	1,829.7
Tajikistan	218.5	479.0	1.2	9,904.0	0.0 (2003)	6.0
Turkmenistan	364.4	682.0	7.5	9,377.0	...	5.0
Uzbekistan	1,655.0	3,444.3	53.1	24,265.5	2.8 (2003)	3,320.2
East Asia						
China, People's Republic of	144,829.0	193,757.0	85,260.0	1,469,882.5	22.7	394,190.0
Hong Kong, China	3,925.8	4,249.4	5,447.3	18,394.8	444.5	2,658.1
Korea, Republic of	25,863.0	26,844.7	26,816.4	63,658.7	3,870.0	21,195.9
Mongolia	117.5	292.6	154.6	3,886.2	0.0 (2001)	285.1
Taipei,China	12,642.2	13,565.1	17,873.8	28,777.4	229.0	5,713.6
South Asia						
Bangladesh	491.3	707.6	279.0	150,945.0	43.7 (2007)	7,300.5
Bhutan	14.1	21.4	0.0	730.6	...	16.7
India	32,436.1	23,234.7	3,577.1	1,168,902.3	50.0 (2001)	17,856.0
Maldives	24.4	20.4	7.6	900.1	0.2 (2002)	36.5
Nepal	266.9	861.3	10.2	36,096.4	1.0 (2006)	503.2
Sri Lanka	767.4	2,603.2	430.2	28,199.1	0.3 (2001)	1,220.5
Southeast Asia						
Brunei Darussalam	80.5	72.0	95.0	544.7	1.9 (2001)	41.2
Cambodia	30.9	132.9	130.5	18,573.0	0.1 (2002)	133.6
Indonesia	6,662.6	11,053.3	3,669.3	435,193.6	4.0	6,215.9
Lao People's Democratic Republic	40.9	1,125.5	12.7	3,711.8	0.0 (2003)	27.2
Malaysia	4,628.0	6,578.2	5,121.7	42,338.5	4.0 (2001)	2,687.8
Myanmar	271.4	556.1	13.4	47,946.7	0.2 (2005)	111.6
Philippines	3,061.4	4,163.3	6,454.4	115,825.0	10.0 (2001)	3,399.3
Singapore	1,946.0	1,991.7	2,747.4	8,381.9	69.0	1,475.7
Thailand	5,591.1	3,466.0	3,056.0	121,530.0	1.6 (2001)	8,208.0
Viet Nam	2,542.7	4,385.4	788.6	120,016.2	1.1 (2002)	11,269.9
The Pacific						
Cook Islands	...	...	...	...	...	...
Fiji	86.4	76.0	55.1	1,033.9	7.0 (2005)	12.1
Kiribati	3.4	0.8	0.3	46.1	0.3 (2005)	0.1
Marshall Islands	4.0	0.0	0.4	16.0	...	1.0
Micronesia, Federated States of	9.6	6.9	–	23.1	0.0 (2003)	3.8
Nauru	1.8	0.0	1.2	10.0	...	1.0 (2010)
Niue	1.1	1.0 (2015)	0.4	...	...	...
Palau	6.9 (2002)	7.2 (2015)	2.5 (2002)	23.7 (2015)	0.1 (2004)	1.2 (2015)
Papua New Guinea	64.8	158.0	8.6	4.0	3.0 (2008)	18.0
Samoa	8.5	8.5	2.5	124.2	0.0 (2004)	1.7
Solomon Islands	7.7	7.4	1.2	465.3	0.2 (2004)	1.2
Timor-Leste	2.0 (2003)	2.4	20.1 (2003)	1,556.6	0.0 (2003)	3.3
Tonga	9.7	14.7	0.2	107.9	0.0 (2002)	3.0
Tuvalu	0.7	2.0	0.5 (2004)	8.0	0.1 (2004)	0.5
Vanuatu	6.6	4.5	0.4	228.0	0.0 (2003)	4.5
Developed ADB Member Economies						
Australia	10,050.0	8,460.0	8,562.0	27,553.0	122.8 (2001)	7,922.0
Japan	61,957.1	63,954.5	66,784.4	172,790.0	854.7	40,532.5
New Zealand	1,831.0	1,790.0	1,542.0	6,400.0	4.7	1,583.0

... = data not available, 0.0 = magnitude is less than half of unit employed, – = magnitude equals zero, ADB = Asian Development Bank.

Source: International Telecommunication Union. World Telecommunication/ICT Indicators Database. http://www.itu.int/en/ITU-D/Statistics/Pages/stat/default.aspx (accessed 24 July 2019).

Communications

Table 2.5.9:   Access to Fixed Telephone, Mobile Phones, and Internet
(per 100 people)

ADB Regional Member	Fixed Telephone				Mobile Cellular				Fixed Broadband				Internet Users[a]			
	2000	2005	2010	2017	2000	2005	2010	2017	2000	2005	2010	2017	2000	2005	2010	2017
Developing ADB Member Economies																
Central and West Asia																
Afghanistan[b]	0.1	0.2	0.1	0.3	–	4.8	35.5	67.4	...	0.0	0.0	0.1	0.0	1.2	4.0	13.5
Armenia	17.4	19.9	20.6	17.2	0.6	10.7	134.3	119.0	...	0.1	3.3	10.8	1.3	5.3	25.0	64.7
Azerbaijan	9.9	12.8	16.7	17.2	5.2	26.3	100.7	103.0	...	0.0	5.3	18.4	0.1	8.0	46.0	79.0
Georgia	10.8	12.7	26.3	18.2	4.1	26.2	94.0	140.7	...	0.1	4.3	19.7	0.5	6.1	26.9	59.7
Kazakhstan	12.2	17.4	24.7	20.3	1.3	34.7	118.3	146.6	...	0.0	5.3	14.2	0.7	3.0	31.6	76.4
Kyrgyz Republic	7.6	8.7	9.0	6.0	0.2	10.7	97.3	121.9	...	0.0	0.4	4.3	1.0	10.5	16.3	38.0
Pakistan	2.2	3.4	3.6	1.5	0.2	8.3	58.2	73.4	...	0.0	0.5	0.9	1.3	6.3	8.0	15.5
Tajikistan	3.5	4.1	4.8	5.4	0.0	3.9	77.7	111.0	...	...	0.1	0.1	0.0	0.3	11.6	22.0
Turkmenistan	8.1	8.4	10.2	11.8	0.2	2.2	62.9	162.8	...	...	0.0	0.1	0.1	1.0	3.0	21.3
Uzbekistan	6.7	6.8	6.6	10.8	0.2	2.7	73.2	76.0	...	0.0	0.4	10.4	0.5	3.3	15.9	52.3
East Asia																
China, People's Republic of	11.3	26.5	21.6	13.7	6.6	29.8	63.2	104.3	0.0	2.8	9.3	28.0	1.8	8.5	34.3	54.3
Hong Kong, China	58.9	55.6	62.1	57.7	81.7	125.1	196.3	249.8	6.7	24.3	30.9	36.1	27.8	56.9	72.0	89.4
Korea, Republic of	54.6	49.1	57.6	52.7	56.6	78.7	102.5	124.9	8.2	25.0	34.7	41.6	44.7	73.5	83.7	95.1
Mongolia[c]	4.9	6.2	7.1	9.5	6.4	22.1	92.5	126.4	0.0	0.1	2.8	9.3	1.3	9.0	10.2	23.7
Taipei,China	57.9	64.1	71.1	57.4	81.8	98.1	120.5	121.8	1.0	19.2	23.0	24.2	28.1	58.0	71.5	92.8
South Asia																
Bangladesh[d]	0.4	0.7	0.8	0.4	0.2	6.3	44.6	91.7	...	0.0	0.3	4.4	0.1	0.2	3.7	15.0
Bhutan	2.5	5.0	3.6	2.6	–	5.5	54.2	90.5	...	...	1.2	2.1	0.4	3.8	13.6	48.1
India[e]	3.1	4.4	2.9	1.7	0.3	7.9	61.1	87.3	0.0	0.1	0.9	1.3	0.5	2.4	7.5	34.5
Maldives[f]	8.7	10.1	7.8	4.7	2.7	63.9	135.6	206.3	0.1	1.0	4.3	8.4	2.2	6.9	26.5	63.2
Nepal[g]	1.1	1.9	3.1	2.9	0.0	0.9	34.0	123.2	...	0.0	0.2	1.7	0.2	0.8	7.9	34.0
Sri Lanka[e]	4.1	6.4	17.7	12.5	2.3	17.2	85.9	135.1	0.0	0.1	1.1	5.8	0.6	1.8	12.0	34.1
Southeast Asia																
Brunei Darussalam[e]	24.2	23.0	20.6	16.8	28.5	63.8	111.9	127.1	0.6	2.2	5.6	9.6	9.0	36.5	53.0	94.9
Cambodia[f]	0.3	0.2	2.5	0.8	1.1	8.0	57.0	116.0	0.0	0.0	0.2	0.8	0.0	0.3	1.3	34.0
Indonesia	3.1	6.0	16.9	4.2	1.7	20.7	87.1	164.9	0.0	0.0	0.9	2.4	0.9	3.6	10.9	32.3
Lao People's Democratic Republic	0.8	1.6	1.7	16.4	0.2	11.4	64.1	54.1	...	0.0	0.1	0.4	0.1	0.9	7.0	25.5
Malaysia[e]	20.0	17.0	16.4	20.8	22.1	76.2	120.4	133.9	0.0	1.9	7.5	8.5	21.4	48.6	56.3	80.1
Myanmar	0.6	1.0	1.0	1.0	0.0	0.3	1.2	89.8	...	0.0	0.0	0.2	0.0	0.1	0.3	30.7
Philippines[h]	3.9	3.9	3.6	4.0	8.3	40.3	88.7	110.4	0.0	0.1	1.9	3.2	2.0	5.4	25.0	60.1
Singapore	49.7	41.1	39.3	34.9	70.2	97.6	145.5	146.8	1.8	14.6	26.4	25.8	36.0	61.0	71.0	84.4
Thailand[e]	8.9	10.8	10.2	5.0	4.9	46.6	106.7	176.0	0.0	0.8	4.8	11.9	3.7	15.0	22.4	52.9
Viet Nam[i]	3.2	10.1	16.2	4.6	1.0	11.4	126.1	125.6	0.0	0.2	4.1	11.8	0.3	12.7	30.7	58.1
The Pacific																
Cook Islands	...	...	...	...	...	...	...	...	...	...	...	...	...	...	...	...
Fiji	10.7	13.7	15.1	8.4	6.8	24.9	81.2	114.2	...	0.9	2.7	1.3	1.5	8.5	20.0	50.0
Kiribati	4.0	4.5	8.2	0.7	0.4	0.7	10.3	39.6	...	0.3	0.8	0.1	1.8	4.0	9.1	14.6
Marshall Islands[j]	7.7	10.6		4.5	0.9	1.3	29.3	30.1	...	...	2.4	1.9	1.5	3.9	7.0	38.7
Micronesia[k], Federated States of	9.0	11.7	8.2	6.6	0.1	13.3	26.6	21.9	...	0.0	1.0	3.6	3.7	11.9	20.0	35.3
Nauru[l]	17.9	17.8	–	–	12.0	...	61.8	88.0	...	...	9.5	...	3.0	...	54.0	57.0
Niue	55.3	62.4	61.3	61.4	21.6	37.9	...	...	...	...	...	...	26.5	51.7	77.0	...
Palau[m]	35.4	40.1	34.1	33.8	12.6	30.4	70.9	111.5	...	0.5	1.2	5.7	...	27.0	...	...
Papua New Guinea	1.2	1.0	1.7	1.9	0.2	1.2	26.9	48.7	...	...	0.1	0.2	0.8	1.7	1.3	11.2
Samoa	4.9	10.8	4.3	4.3	1.4	13.3	48.3	63.2	...	0.0	0.1	0.9	0.6	3.4	7.0	33.6
Solomon Islands	1.9	1.6	1.6	1.2	0.3	1.3	21.9	76.1	...	0.1	0.5	0.2	0.5	0.8	5.0	11.9
Timor-Leste	...	0.2	0.3	0.2	...	3.2	42.6	120.1	...	0.0	0.0	0.3	0.0	0.1	3.0	27.5
Tonga[f]	9.9	13.6	29.8	13.6	0.2	29.6	52.1	99.9	0.0	0.6	1.1	2.8	2.4	4.9	16.0	41.2
Tuvalu	7.0	8.9	11.4	17.9	–	13.0	15.2	71.5	...	1.5	2.3	4.0	5.2	...	25.0	49.3
Vanuatu	3.6	3.3	3.0	1.6	0.2	6.1	71.9	82.5	...	0.0	0.2	1.6	2.1	5.1	8.0	25.7
Developed ADB Member Economies																
Australia[e]	52.7	50.0	48.0	34.6	44.9	91.0	101.7	112.7	0.6	10.0	24.9	32.4	46.8	63.0	76.0	86.5
Japan	48.6	45.2	51.0	50.2	52.4	75.2	95.9	135.5	0.7	18.2	26.5	31.8	30.0	66.9	78.2	84.6
New Zealand	47.4	41.8	43.0	38.0	40.0	85.4	107.8	136.0	0.1	7.8	25.0	33.6	47.4	62.7	80.5	90.8

... = data not available, 0.0 = magnitude is less than half of unit employed, – = magnitude equals zero, ADB = Asian Development Bank.

a The reference population differs across countries. For example, some countries refer to population of people aged 6 years and older, some refer to 7 years and older, and others refer to ages from 16 to 74 years. The details are provided in the documentation of the International Telecommunication Union.

b For fixed telephone, the figure for 2005 refers to 2003. For internet users, the figure for 2000 refers to 2001.

c For fixed broadband, the figure for 2000 refers to 2001. For internet users, the figure for 2005 refers to 2007.

d For fixed broadband, the figure for 2005 refers to 2007.

e For fixed broadband, the figure for 2000 refers to 2001.

f For fixed broadband, the figure for 2000 refers to 2002.

g For fixed broadband, the figure for 2005 refers to 2006.

h For fixed broadband, the figure for 2000 refers to 2001 and the figure for 2010 refers to 2011.

i For fixed telephone, the figure for 2005 refers to 2006. For fixed broadband, the figure for 2000 refers to 2002.

j For fixed telephone, the figure for 2005 refers to 2004 and the figure for 2017 refers to 2014. For mobile celluar, the figure for 2010 refers to 2014. For fixed broadband, the figure for 2010 refers to 2013.

k For mobile cellular, the figure for 2000 refers to 2002.

l For fixed telephone, the figure for 2017 refers to 2014. For internet users, the figure for 2000 refers to 2001 and the figure for 2010 refers to 2011.

m For fixed telephone, the figure for 2000 refers to 2002. For moblie cellular, the figure for 2000 refers to 2002 and the figure for 2017 refers to 2015.

Source: International Telecommunication Union. World Telecommunication/ICT Indicators Database. http://www.itu.int/en/ITU-D/Statistics/Pages/stat/default.aspx (accessed 24 July 2019).

VI. Energy and Electricity

Energy and Electricity comprises statistics on energy demand, supplies and uses of primary energy, and electricity consumption and generation. The discussion focuses on trends across the region in energy efficiency, global share of energy production, and energy imports.

All five of Asia and the Pacific's most populous economies increased their energy efficiency between 2000 and 2016.

From 2000 to 2016, Asia and the Pacific's five most populous economies—the PRC, India, Indonesia, Pakistan, and Bangladesh—all increased their energy efficiency, measured by the amount of GDP per unit use of energy (i.e., one petajoule), as seen in Figure 2.6.1. The largest increases in GDP per petajoule among these five economies were in India ($76.1 million at constant 2011 PPP), Bangladesh ($73.7 million), and the PRC ($57.5 million).

In absolute terms, the most energy efficient among the top five most populous economies in 2016 were Bangladesh ($290.2 million at constant 2011 PPP per petajoule) and Indonesia ($280.5 million). The global average for GDP per unit of energy use in 2016 was $204.0 million at constant 2011 PPP. For regional developing member economies, the average was $190.9 million at constant 2011 PPP. For ADB's three developed member economies in Asia and the Pacific, the average was $251.0 million at constant 2011 PPP.

Figure 2.6.1: Energy Use by the Five Most Populous Economies in Asia and the Pacific
(GDP per unit use of energy)

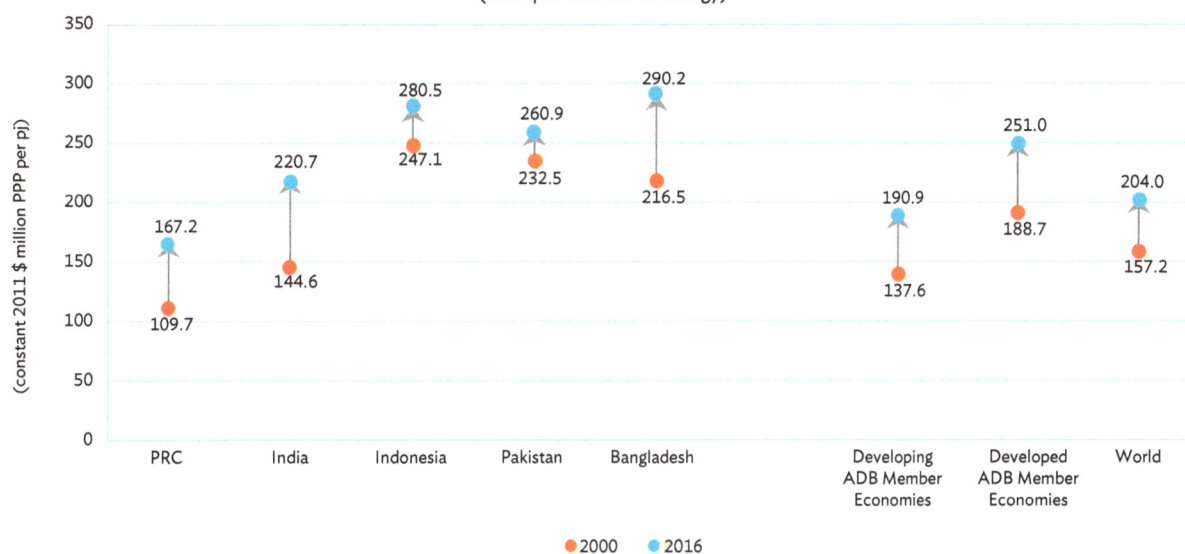

● 2000   ● 2016

$ = United States dollars, ADB = Asian Development Bank, GDP = Gross Domestic Product, PJ = petajoule, PPP = purchasing power parity, PRC = People's Republic of China.
Source: Table 2.6.3, Key Indicators for Asia and the Pacific 2019.

The PRC is becoming a global energy production powerhouse

Asia and the Pacific's energy production comprised 33.7% of the global total in 2016, compared with 24.6% in 2000 (Figure 2.6.2, Table 2.6.4). The increase during the review period was mainly driven by expanded energy production in the PRC, which saw its global share of energy production rise from 9.9% in 2000 to 16.6% in 2016.

The PRC accounted for 49.3% of energy generated in Asia and the Pacific in 2016, up from 40.2% in 2000. The region's next largest energy producers, and their respective shares of regional production, were India (12.1% in 2016, down from 15.5% in 2000), Indonesia (9.8% in 2016, up from 8.0% in 2000), and Australia (8.5% in 2016, down from 9.6% in 2000).

Nearly two-thirds of regional economies were net energy importers in 2016.

In 2016, 14 regional economies were net energy exporters, while 29 were net energy importers. Compared with their respective status in 2000 (or the earliest year for which data are available), the Lao People's Democratic Republic, Mongolia, and Timor-Leste had all switched from being net energy importers to being net energy exporters by 2016. Conversely, Viet Nam, which had been a net energy exporter in 2000, was a net energy importer in 2016.

The oil- and gas-rich economies of Timor-Leste, Brunei Darussalam, and Azerbaijan led the region in terms of energy exports as a share of domestic energy use in 2016 (Figure 2.6.3). Energy exports from Timor-Leste in 2016 were equivalent to 1,412.5% of the economy's domestic energy use. For Brunei Darussalam and Azerbaijan, these percentages were 410.5% and 305.9%, respectively.

Figure 2.6.2: Energy production by global region and by economy in Asia and the Pacific, 2016
(petajoules, %)

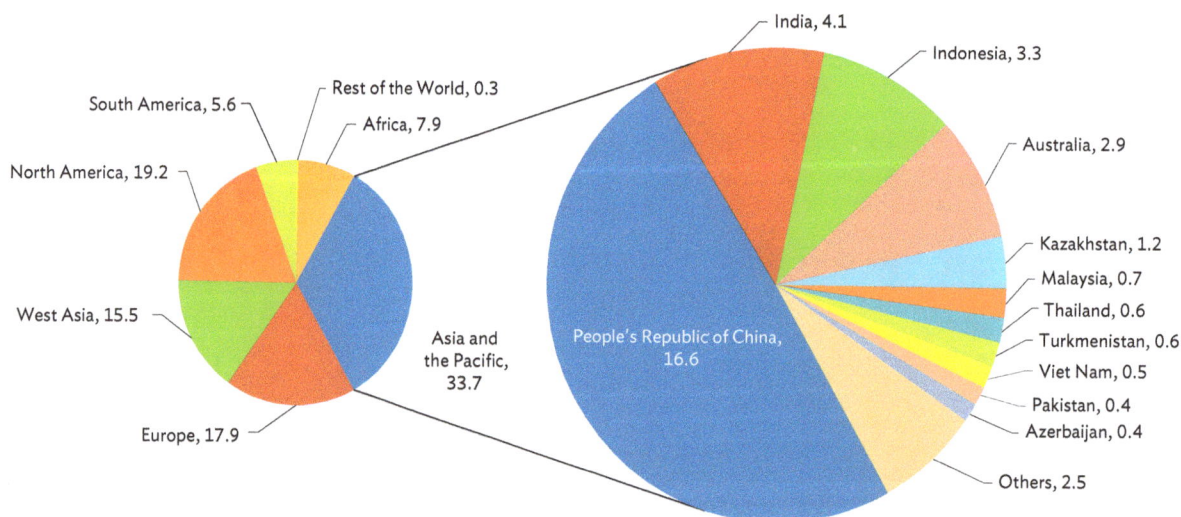

Source: Table 2.6.4, Key Indicators for Asia and the Pacific 2019.

Figure 2.6.3: Net Energy Imports as Share of Energy Use in Select Economies of Asia and the Pacific
(%)

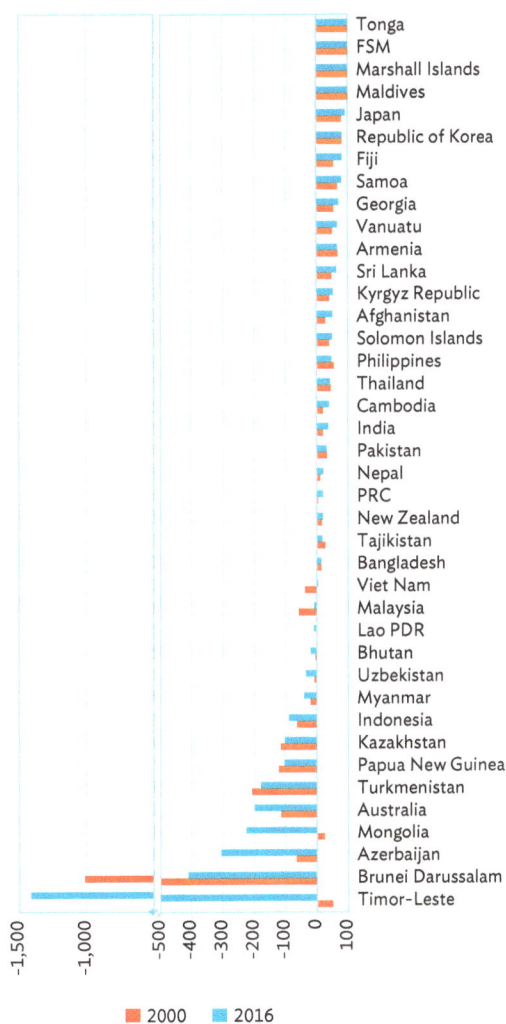

■ 2000 ■ 2016

FSM = Federated States of Micronesia, Lao PDR = Lao People's Democratic Republic, PRC = People's Republic of China.
Note: The chart includes economies with available data for 2000 (or the earliest year) and 2016. For Timor-Leste, the earliest year for which data are vailable is 2002.
Source: Table 2.6.4, Key Indicators for Asia and the Pacific 2019.

The island economies of the Federated States of Micronesia, Maldives, the Marshall Islands, and Tonga relied on imports for 100% of their energy use in both 2000 and 2016.

Data Issues and Comparability

Energy data are compiled by the United Nations Statistics Division (UNSD) using standard procedures that follow the definitions of the United Nations International Recommendations for Energy Statistics.[4] The UNSD Annual Questionnaire on Energy Statistics to the UN member economies is the primary source of information. Additional sources of information for the UNSD energy database include national, regional, and international statistical publications. These include, but are not limited to, publications from the International Energy Agency, the Statistical Office of the European Communities (Eurostat), the International Atomic Energy Agency, the Organization of the Petroleum Exporting Countries, and the Organización Latinoamericana de Energía. The UNSD prepares estimates where official data are incomplete or inconsistent. For the indicator on GDP per unit use of energy, the energy statistics adopt the territory principle, while national accounts are being compiled on the residency principle, which could be a potential source of inconsistency, although in practice differences are not huge (UN 2016).

Data for the household electrification indicator are lacking. Data are posted over a varied range of years, i.e., different starting and ending years, depending on data availability. These data may therefore not be comparable, limiting possibilities for analysis.

[4] For the full definitions of the International Recommendations for Energy Statistics, go to https://unstats.un.org/UNSD/energy/ires/.

Table 2.6.1:   Electricity Production and Sources

ADB Regional Member	Total Electricity Production (billion kWh)		Sources of Electricity (% of total)							
			Combustible Fuels[a]		Hydropower		Solar		Others[b]	
	2000	2016	2000	2016	2000	2016	2000	2016	2000	2016
Developing ADB Member Economies										
Central and West Asia										
Afghanistan	0.7	1.1 (2017)	25.0	15.3 (2017)	75.0	84.7 (2017)	–	–	–	–
Armenia	6.0	7.8 (2017)	45.2	37.0 (2017)	21.2	29.2 (2017)	–	0.0	33.7	33.8 (2017)
Azerbaijan	18.7	25.0	91.8	91.9	8.2	7.9	–	0.1	–	0.1
Georgia	7.4	11.5 (2017)	21.1	19.4 (2017)	78.9	79.9 (2017)	–	–	–	–
Kazakhstan	51.6	106.6	85.4	88.8	14.6	10.9	–	0.1	–	0.3
Kyrgyz Republic	16.0	13.3	14.4	13.3	85.6	86.7	–	–	–	–
Pakistan	65.8	123.1	70.1	66.0	29.3	26.1	–	–	0.6	7.9
Tajikistan	14.2	18.1 (2017)	2.3	5.6 (2017)	97.7	94.4 (2017)	–	–	–	–
Turkmenistan	9.8	22.5	100.0	100.0	–	–	–	–	–	–
Uzbekistan	46.9	58.3	87.5	79.7	12.5	20.3	–	–	–	–
East Asia										
China, People's Republic of	1,355.6	6,142.5	82.4	72.2	16.4	19.4	–	1.0	1.2	7.3
Hong Kong, China	31.3	37.0 (2017)	100.0	100.0 (2017)	–	–	–	…	…	…
Korea, Republic of	290.1	562.6	60.5	68.5	1.9	1.2	0.0	0.9	37.6	29.3
Mongolia	2.9	5.7	100.0	100.0 (2017)	–	–	–	–	–	–
Taipei,China	184.8	273.6 (2018)	…	…	…	…	…	…	…	…
South Asia										
Bangladesh	15.8	64.3	94.0	98.9	6.0	0.9	–	0.3	–	0.0
Bhutan	1.8	8.0	–	–	100.0	100.0	–	–	–	0.0
India	560.8	1,432.4	83.4	83.0	13.3	8.6	–	0.9	3.3	7.6
Maldives	0.1	0.6	100.0	99.2	–	–	–	0.8	–	…
Nepal	1.7	4.2	1.6	–	98.4	99.8	–	0.0	–	0.1
Sri Lanka	7.0	14.4	54.0	67.7	46.0	29.4	0.0	0.5	0.0	2.4
Southeast Asia										
Brunei Darussalam	2.8	4.3	100.0	100.0	–	–	–	0.0	–	–
Cambodia	0.3	5.6	85.9	53.1	14.1	46.8	–	0.1	–	–
Indonesia	99.5	233.4	83.5	86.2	13.8	9.2	–	0.0	2.7	4.6
Lao People's Democratic Republic	4.0	25.1	9.1	28.4	90.9	71.6	–	0.0	–	–
Malaysia	69.2	156.7	89.3	87.0	10.7	12.8	–	0.2	–	–
Myanmar	5.1	17.9	63.0	45.5	37.0	54.5	–	…	–	–
Philippines	45.3	93.4 (2017)	57.1	76.2 (2017)	17.2	10.3 (2017)	–	1.3 (2017)	25.6	12.2 (2017)
Singapore	31.7	51.6	100.0	100.0	–	–	–	–	–	–
Thailand	106.1	191.3	94.3	94.4	5.7	3.6	–	1.8	0.0	0.2
Viet Nam	26.6	191.6 (2017)	45.2	53.5 (2017)	54.8	46.4 (2017)	–	–	–	0.1 (2017)
The Pacific										
Cook Islands	0.0	0.0	100.0	90.7 (2017)	–	–	–	9.3 (2017)	–	–
Fiji	0.7	0.9	39.8	46.6	60.2	53.0	–	–	–	0.4
Kiribati	0.0	0.0	100.0	84.0	–	–	–	16.0	–	–
Marshall Islands	0.1	0.1	100.0	97.7	–	–	–	2.3	–	–
Micronesia, Federated States of	0.1	0.1	99.8	96.9	–	0.2	0.2	3.0	–	–
Nauru	0.0	0.0	100.0	98.9	–	–	–	1.1	–	–
Niue	0.0	0.0	100.0	97.9	–	–	–	2.1	–	–
Palau	0.1	0.1	100.0	100.0	–	–	–	–	–	–
Papua New Guinea	2.4	4.4	52.9	67.9	39.2	22.6	–	–	7.8	9.4
Samoa	0.1	0.1	50.4	67.5	49.6	22.0	–	10.4	–	0.1
Solomon Islands	0.1	0.1	100.0	97.9	–	–	–	2.1	–	–
Timor-Leste	0.1 (2002)	0.4	100.0 (2002)	100.0	–	–	–	…	–	–
Tonga	0.0	0.1	100.0	92.1	–	–	–	7.8	–	0.0
Tuvalu	0.0	0.0	100.0	63.0	–	–	–	37.0	–	–
Vanuatu	0.0	0.1	100.0	79.5	–	9.9	–	2.8	–	7.8
Developed ADB Member Economies										
Australia	210.2	256.6	92.0	86.9	8.0	6.0	0.0	2.4	0.0	4.8
Japan	1,070.3	1,058.0	58.6	82.6	9.0	8.0	0.0	4.8	32.3	4.5
New Zealand	39.2	43.0	29.8	17.3	62.3	59.8	–	0.1	7.8	22.6

… = data not available, – = magnitude equals zero, 0.0 = magnitude is less than half of unit employed, ADB = Asian Development Bank, kWh = kilowatt-hour.

a   Electricity from combustible fuels refers to the production of electricity from the combustion of fuels that are capable of igniting or burning, which would include coal, natural gas, oil, and other combustible fuels.

b   Includes chemical heat, geothermal, nuclear, tide, other marine electricity, wind, wave, and other sources of energy.

Sources: United Nations. Energy Statistics Database. http://data.un.org/Explorer.aspx?d=EDATA (accessed 17 July 2019). For Taipei,China: Government of Taipei,China; Directorate-General of Budget, Accounting and Statistics; Official communication, 17 May 2018.

Table 2.6.2: Electric Power Consumption and Electrification

ADB Regional Member	Electric Power Consumption (per capita kWh)		Household Electrification Rate (% of households)	
	2000	2016	2000	2016
Developing ADB Member Economies				
Central and West Asia				
Afghanistan	30	123	25.0 (2005)	71.5 (2015)
Armenia	1,170	1,815	98.9	100.0
Azerbaijan	1,914	2,117	99.5 (2006)	
Georgia	1,542	2,817	...	...
Kazakhstan	2,773	4,275	...	...
Kyrgyz Republic	1,891	1,715	100.0 (2002)	99.8 (2012)
Pakistan	320	469	89.2 (2006)	92.7 (2018)
Tajikistan	2,146	1,499	99.0 (2002)	99.2 (2017)
Turkmenistan	1,526	2,602	99.6	...
Uzbekistan	1,669	1,526	99.7 (2002)	...
East Asia				
China, People's Republic of	993	3,867	...	...
Hong Kong, China	5,446	5,930 (2017)	...	...
Korea, Republic of	5,597	10,345	...	...
Mongolia	970	1,910 (2017)	67.3	...
Taipei,China	7,956	11,212 (2018)	...	...
South Asia				
Bangladesh	98	335	32.0	62.4 (2014)
Bhutan	675	2,727	41.1 (2003)	72.0 (2007)
India	300	809	67.9 (2006)	88.2
Maldives	487	1,247	83.8	99.8 (2017)
Nepal	54	181	24.6 (2001)	90.5
Sri Lanka	290	600	...	...
Southeast Asia				
Brunei Darussalam	7,561	8,690	...	...
Cambodia	29	384	16.6	56.1 (2014)
Indonesia	374	825	90.7 (2003)	96.0 (2012)
Lao People's Democratic Republic	120	714 (2017)	46.3 (2002)	...
Malaysia	2,637	4,694	...	...
Myanmar	70	292	47.0 (2002)	55.6
Philippines	469	497 (2017)	76.6 (2003)	92.7 (2017)
Singapore	7,233	8,672	...	...
Thailand	1,558	2,816	...	...
Viet Nam	284	1,706	89.1 (2002)	96.1 (2005)
The Pacific				
Cook Islands	1,389	1,867 (2017)	97.0 (2006)	99.5
Fiji	749	965	...	84.0 (2009)
Kiribati	169	218	...	92.6 (2015)
Marshall Islands	1,517	1,320	...	90.0 (2011)
Micronesia, Federated States of	705	418	...	72.8 (2013)
Nauru	2,902	1,770	100.0 (2002)	100.0 (2013)
Niue	...	...	...	98.7
Palau	4,481	4,000	99.0 (2005)	98.3 (2015)
Papua New Guinea	390	483	...	19.5 (2010)
Samoa	516	690	98.0 (2006)	96.4
Solomon Islands	139	145	14.0 (2005)	55.1 (2015)
Timor-Leste	52 (2002)	273	27.0 (2002)	38.0 (2009)
Tonga	369	527	89.0 (2006)	97.0
Tuvalu	309	722	94.0 (2005)	97.3
Vanuatu	224	235	...	57.8
Developed ADB Member Economies				
Australia	9,390	9,478	...	...
Japan	7,533	7,725	...	...
New Zealand	9,016	8,348	...	...

... = data not available, ADB = Asian Development Bank, kWh = kilowatt-hour.

Sources: For Electric Power Consumption: United Nations. Energy Statistics Database. http://data.un.org/Explorer.aspx?d=EDATA (accessed 17 July 2019); and for Taipei,China: Asian Development Bank estimates using economy source. For Household Electrification Rate: World Bank. International Development Association Results Measurement System. http://data.worldbank.org/data-catalog/IDA-results-measurement. (accessed 17 July 2019); United States Agency for International Development. Demographic and Health Surveys Program. STAT Compiler. http://www.statcompiler.com/ (accessed 17 July 2019); and Secretariat of the Pacific Community. National Minimum Development Indicators. http://www.spc.int/nmdi/MdiHome.aspx (accessed 17 July 2019).

Table 2.6.3:   Use of Energy

ADB Regional Member	Energy Use (PJ)				GDP per Unit Use of Energy (constant 2011 $ million PPP per PJ)			
	2000	2005	2010	2016	2000	2005	2010	2016
Developing ADB Member Economies								
Central and West Asia								
Afghanistan	32 (2002)	36	137	143	717.7 (2002)	783.2	356.1	434.7
Armenia	84	105	119	131	106.9	152.1	162.1	182.9
Azerbaijan	485	573	486	598	76.4	119.8	302.1	263.2
Georgia	120	135	140	204	119.8	151.6	188.8	169.1
Kazakhstan	1,560	2,352	3,363	3,335	94.9	103.1	97.5	125.1
Kyrgyz Republic	101	114	115	162	100.6	107.3	132.2	124.0
Pakistan	2,082	2,642	3,094	3,597	232.5	233.8	236.1	260.9
Tajikistan	141	148	143	166	52.3	78.9	112.6	145.3
Turkmenistan	625	805	951	1,158	38.5	38.4	53.2	76.5
Uzbekistan	2,130	2,050	1,809	1,574	29.2	39.3	67.0	119.0
East Asia								
China, People's Republic of	42,461	68,833	101,618	118,484	109.7	108.0	125.0	167.2
Hong Kong, China	570	579	544	590	397.8	481.5	621.2	676.7
Korea, Republic of	7,854	8,764	10,441	11,762	124.2	140.3	144.1	152.6
Mongolia	87	104	164	294	128.3	146.9	127.5	116.9
Taipei,China	...	...	...	...	...	...	...	...
South Asia								
Bangladesh	998	1,191	1,493	1,864	216.5	232.4	248.9	290.2
Bhutan	44	48	57	66	46.1	61.9	82.0	99.8
India	19,808	22,706	29,193	36,886	144.6	172.4	188.2	220.7
Maldives	6	9	13	21	456.5	328.5	336.6	294.8
Nepal	349	388	446	536	104.7	111.3	120.3	124.5
Sri Lanka	296	324	360	467	351.6	390.3	478.6	519.7
Southeast Asia								
Brunei Darussalam	73	76	136	124	374.6	398.6	230.2	245.0
Cambodia	142	144	223	317	118.5	181.5	161.9	172.4
Indonesia	4,970	7,087	8,322	10,021	247.1	218.3	245.8	280.5
Lao People's Democratic Republic	58	68	100	244	228.3	263.6	263.5	168.2
Malaysia	1,959	2,745	2,965	3,527	193.0	173.7	200.1	227.1
Myanmar	538	619	663	836	111.9	178.2	281.5	335.6
Philippines	1,551	1,469	1,631	2,126	212.4	280.7	321.6	351.5
Singapore	756	805	1,109	910	279.0	331.9	334.5	521.9
Thailand	3,075	4,067	4,945	5,794	188.1	185.4	183.3	187.0
Viet Nam	1,262	1,756	2,319	3,006	163.0	163.5	168.2	183.7
The Pacific								
Cook Islands	1	1	1	1	...	...	...	...
Fiji	22	24	21	33	246.1	254.3	301.1	237.1
Kiribati	1	1	1	1	167.9	180.8	180.3	230.4
Marshall Islands	2	2	2	2	75.5	84.2	91.2	99.0
Micronesia, Federated States of	2	2	2	2	167.5	172.8	170.8	172.0
Nauru	1	1	1	1	...	...	66.1	169.0
Niue	–	–	–	–	...	...	...	...
Palau	3	3	3	3	78.6	92.4	81.6	101.4
Papua New Guinea	99	126	141	184	154.5	135.1	160.9	175.2
Samoa	3	3	4	5	251.8	320.0	251.4	230.9
Solomon Islands	5	6	6	6	149.9	131.6	164.6	217.7
Timor-Leste	...	4	4	8	...	1,617.3	2,461.9	1,153.1
Tonga	1	2	2	2	451.3	249.9	259.5	285.3
Tuvalu	–	–	–	–	...	...	...	...
Vanuatu	2	2	3	3	261.2	273.2	232.2	257.5
Developed ADB Member Economies	26,942	27,355	27,187	24,245	188.7	200.4	207.2	251.0
Australia	4,540	4,762	5,417	5,451	149.3	166.9	168.9	198.0
Japan	21,655	21,847	20,938	17,845	198.4	208.5	218.7	271.2
New Zealand	747	746	832	949	145.1	176.9	168.6	176.6
DEVELOPING ADB MEMBER ECONOMIES[a]	94,359	130,919	177,290	209,194	137.7	140.7	154.1	190.9
ALL ADB REGIONAL MEMBERS[a]	121,301	158,274	204,477	233,439	149.0	151.0	161.2	197.1
WORLD	404,363	463,300	517,492	551,579	157.2	165.2	176.9	204.0

... = data not available, – = magnitude equals zero, $ = United States dollars, ADB = Asian Development Bank, GDP = gross domestic product, PJ = petajoule, PPP = purchasing power parity.

a   Includes only reporting economies with data corresponding to the year heading.

Sources: For Energy Use: United Nations Statistics Division. Official communication, 25 July 2019. For GDP per Unit Use of Energy: Asian Development Bank estimates.

Table 2.6.4:   Energy Production and Imports

ADB Regional Member	Energy Production (PJ)				Energy Imports, Net (% of energy use)			
	2000	2005	2010	2016	2000	2005	2010	2016
Developing ADB Member Economies								
Central and West Asia								
Afghanistan	18	23	41	70	28.0	36.1	70.1	51.0
Armenia	27	36	52	44	67.9	65.7	56.3	66.4
Azerbaijan	803	1,155	2,759	2,427	-65.6	-101.6	-467.7	-305.9
Georgia	55	53	58	60	54.2	60.7	58.6	70.6
Kazakhstan	3,367	5,131	6,770	6,737	-115.8	-118.2	-101.3	-102.0
Kyrgyz Republic	60	61	53	77	40.6	46.5	53.9	52.5
Pakistan	1,403	2,020	2,253	2,438	32.6	23.5	27.2	32.2
Tajikistan	103	115	115	136	27.0	22.3	19.6	18.1
Turkmenistan	1,928	2,584	1,982	3,230	-208.5	-221.0	-108.4	-178.9
Uzbekistan	2,307	2,446	2,309	2,134	-8.3	-19.3	-27.6	-35.6
East Asia								
China, People's Republic of	40,783	63,831	88,642	94,591	4.0	7.3	12.8	20.2
Hong Kong, China	...	...	...	...	...	...	...	...
Korea, Republic of	1,420	1,776	1,855	2,117	81.9	79.7	82.2	82.0
Mongolia	66	138	655	959	24.1	-32.7	-299.4	-226.2
Taipei,China	...	...	...	...	...	...	...	...
South Asia								
Bangladesh	857	1,027	1,304	1,597	14.1	13.8	12.7	14.3
Bhutan	46	53	73	79	-4.5	-10.4	-28.1	-19.7
India	15,763	18,212	22,888	23,301	20.4	19.8	21.6	36.8
Maldives	–	–	–	–	100.0	100.0	100.0	100.0
Nepal	310	349	384	422	11.2	10.1	13.9	21.3
Sri Lanka	156	163	184	169	47.3	49.7	48.9	63.8
Southeast Asia								
Brunei Darussalam	813	848	775	633	-1,013.7	-1,015.8	-469.9	-410.5
Cambodia	114	105	152	191	19.7	27.1	31.8	39.7
Indonesia	8,129	11,351	16,854	18,885	-63.6	-60.2	-102.5	-88.5
Lao People's Democratic Republic	57	64	98	267	1.7	5.9	2.0	-9.4
Malaysia	3,082	3,770	3,450	3,787	-57.3	-37.3	-16.4	-7.4
Myanmar	648	927	969	1,175	-20.4	-49.8	-46.2	-40.6
Philippines	695	762	924	1,106	55.2	48.1	43.3	48.0
Singapore	...	...	25	28	...	...	97.7	96.9
Thailand	1,700	2,144	2,952	3,283	44.7	47.3	40.3	43.3
Viet Nam	1,733	2,612	2,747	2,880	-37.3	-48.7	-18.5	4.2
The Pacific								
Cook Islands	...	...	...	–	...	...	...	100.0
Fiji	10	9	5	6	54.5	62.5	76.2	81.8
Kiribati	–	–	1	1	100.0	100.0	–	–
Marshall Islands	–	–	–	–	100.0	100.0	100.0	100.0
Micronesia, Federated States of	–	–	–	–	100.0	100.0	100.0	100.0
Nauru	...	– (2006)	–	–	...	100.0 (2006)	100.0	100.0
Niue	–	–	–	–	...	...	...	...
Palau	...	...	...	...	...	...	...	...
Papua New Guinea	220	174	95	376	-122.2	-38.1	32.6	-104.3
Samoa	1	1	1	1	66.7	66.7	75.0	80.0
Solomon Islands	3	3	3	3	40.0	50.0	50.0	50.0
Timor-Leste	2 (2002)	201	186	121	50.0 (2002)	-4,925.0	-4,550.0	-1,412.5
Tonga	–	–	–	–	100.0	100.0	100.0	100.0
Tuvalu	...	...	...	...	...	...	...	...
Vanuatu	1	1	1	1	50.0	50.0	66.7	66.7
Developed ADB Member Economies	**14,738**	**16,282**	**18,586**	**18,561**				
Australia	9,731	11,451	13,606	16,322	-114.3	-140.5	-151.2	-199.4
Japan	4,379	4,260	4,211	1,481	79.8	80.5	79.9	91.7
New Zealand	628	571	769	758	15.9	23.5	7.6	20.1
DEVELOPING ADB MEMBER ECONOMIES[a]	**86,680**	**122,145**	**161,615**	**173,332**				
ALL ADB REGIONAL MEMBERS[a]	**101,418**	**138,427**	**180,201**	**191,893**				
WORLD	**412,155**	**476,738**	**530,597**	**568,988**				

... = data not available, – = magnitude equals zero, ADB = Asian Development Bank, PJ = petajoule.

a   Includes only reporting economies with data corresponding to the year heading.

Sources: For Energy Production: United Nations Statistics Division. Official communication, 25 July 2019. For Net Energy Imports: Asian Development Bank estimates.

Table 2.6.5:   Retail Prices of Fuel Energy
($/L)

ADB Regional Member	Gasoline (Premium)				Diesel			
	2000	2005	2010	2018	2000	2005	2010	2018
Developing ADB Member Economies								
Central and West Asia								
Afghanistan	...	...	...	...	...	...	...	...
Armenia	0.51	0.73	1.01	0.93	0.34	0.60	0.92	0.95
Azerbaijan	...	...	...	...	...	...	...	...
Georgia	0.52	0.46 (2003)	1.03	0.94	0.38	0.70	1.00	0.96
Kazakhstan	0.35	0.47	0.58	0.45	0.30	0.39	0.53	0.56
Kyrgyz Republic	...	...	...	...	...	...	...	...
Pakistan	0.48	0.82	0.80	0.73 (2016)	0.22	0.54	0.83	0.77 (2016)
Tajikistan	...	...	...	...	...	...	...	...
Turkmenistan	...	...	...	...	...	...	...	...
Uzbekistan	0.44	0.33 (2004)	...	...	...	...	...	...
East Asia								
China, People's Republic of	...	...	...	...	...	...	...	...
Hong Kong, China	1.32	1.60	1.75	1.93	0.80	1.00	1.25	1.72
Korea, Republic of	1.10	1.40	1.48	1.44	0.54	1.05	1.30	1.26
Mongolia	0.33	0.56	1.01	0.66	0.38	0.81 (2006)	0.96	0.98
Taipei,China	0.57	0.73	0.94	0.93	0.41	0.59	0.82	0.86
South Asia								
Bangladesh	...	...	...	...	...	...	...	...
Bhutan	...	...	...	...	...	...	...	...
India	0.58	0.86	1.05	...	0.32	0.64	0.83	...
Maldives	...	...	...	...	...	...	...	...
Nepal	0.58	0.87	1.22	1.00	0.33	0.58	0.95	0.85
Sri Lanka	0.65	0.80	1.02	0.77	0.32	0.50	0.65	0.62
Southeast Asia								
Brunei Darussalam	...	...	...	...	...	...	...	...
Cambodia	...	...	...	...	...	...	...	...
Indonesia	0.14	0.30	0.50	0.62 (2017)	0.07	0.27	0.50	...
Lao People's Democratic Republic	...	...	...	...	...	...	...	...
Malaysia	0.29	0.40	0.67	0.59 (2017)	0.18	0.29	0.57	0.53 (2017)
Myanmar	...	1.84 (2007)	1.41	0.67	...	1.62 (2007)	1.37	0.67
Philippines	0.37	0.57	0.96	1.03	0.28	0.51	0.76	0.81
Singapore	0.82	0.92	1.35	1.83	0.33	0.56	0.89	1.16
Thailand	0.39	0.59	1.12 (2009)	...	0.32	0.50	0.90	0.88
Viet Nam	...	...	0.99 (2011)	...	...	...	0.93 (2011)	0.68 (2015)
The Pacific								
Cook Islands	...	...	...	...	...	...	...	...
Fiji	...	...	...	...	...	...	...	...
Kiribati	...	...	...	...	...	...	...	...
Marshall Islands	...	...	...	...	...	...	...	...
Micronesia, Federated States of	...	...	...	...	...	...	...	...
Nauru	...	...	...	...	...	...	...	...
Niue	...	...						
Palau	...	...	...	...	...	...	...	...
Papua New Guinea	...	...	...	...	...	...	...	...
Samoa	...	...						
Solomon Islands	...	0.86 (2007)	1.14	1.12	...	0.86 (2007)	1.15	1.15
Timor-Leste	...	...	...	...	...	...	...	...
Tonga	...	...	...	...	...	...	...	...
Tuvalu	...	...	...	...				
Vanuatu	0.78	1.23	1.50	...	...	...	...	...
Developed ADB Member Economies								
Australia	0.49	0.82	1.09	0.97	...	0.87	1.09	1.01
Japan	1.05	1.23	1.64	1.45	0.76	0.91	1.28	1.16
New Zealand	0.51	0.97	1.34	1.55	0.33	0.64	0.85	0.99

... = data not available, $ = United States dollars, ADB = Asian Development Bank, L = liter.

Source: Economy sources.

VII. Environment

Environment includes a discussion on deforestation and greenhouse gas emissions. Indicators related to land use, forest resources, air and water pollution, and per capita freshwater resources are presented in the statistical tables.

The amount of forested land is declining in about one-third of Asia and Pacific economies.

An estimated 1.6 billion people use forests for all or part of their livelihoods, while millions more depend on forest resources for clean air and fresh water. By absorbing and storing massive amounts of carbon dioxide (CO_2), forests play a crucial role in the fight against climate change.[5]

In 2016, 15 of the 46 regional economies with available data reported an increase in total forested land, 14 economies reported a decrease, and 17 reported no change (Table 2.7.2).

The region's highest rates of deforestation in 2016 were in Pakistan (2.9%), Myanmar (1.9%), and Timor-Leste (1.6%) as shown in Figure 2.7.1. The highest rates of negative deforestation (i.e., reforestation) occurred in the Philippines (–3.0%), Azerbaijan (–2.3%), and the Lao People's Democratic Republic (–1.0%).

Figure 2.7.1: Deforestation Rates in Select Economies of Asia and the Pacific, 2016
(%)

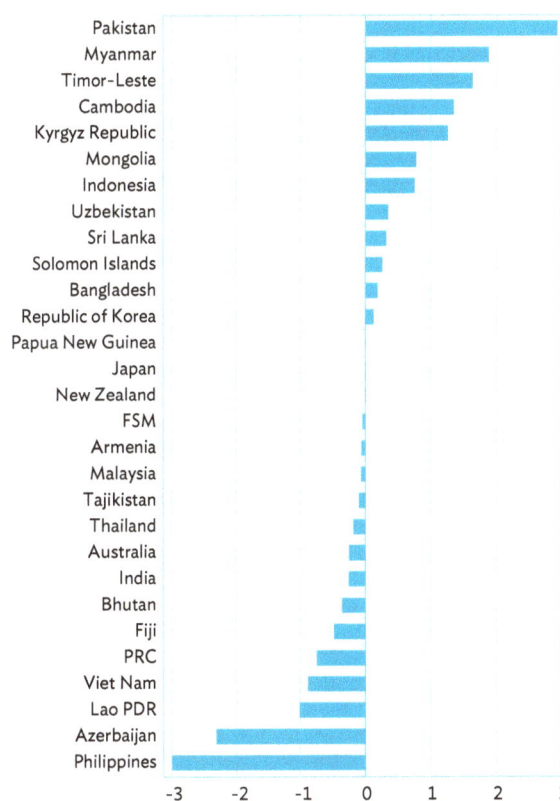

FSM = Federated States of Micronesia, Lao PDR = Lao People's Democratic Republic, PRC = People's Republic of China.

Note: A negative deforestation rate implies an increase in the forested area compared with the previous year (i.e., "reforestation"). Deforestation rates for Afghanistan; Brunei Darussalam; the Cook Islands; Georgia; Kazakhstan; Kiribati; Maldives; the Marshall Islands; Nepal; Palau; Samoa; Singapore; Taipei,China; Tonga; Turkmenistan; Tuvalu; and Vanuatu are zero.

Source: Table 2.7.2, Key Indicators for Asia and the Pacific 2019.

---

5   For more information about the role of forests in the Earth's environment, go to https://www.un-redd.org/forest-facts.

Carbon emissions per capita increased in about 85% of Asia and Pacific economies between 2000 and 2014.

In 2014, Asia and the Pacific accounted for nearly half (47.7%) of all global CO_2 emissions. The region's highest emitters were the PRC (28.5% of global emissions), India (6.2%), Japan (3.4%), the Republic of Korea (1.6%), and Indonesia (1.3%). Together, these five economies accounted for more than 90% of the region's total emissions (ADB 2018). Rising living standards in Asia and the Pacific have been associated with rising CO_2 emissions as power generation and the use of energy-consuming goods, such as cars and air-conditioning units, increase (ADB 2013).

From 2000 to 2014, only 7 of the 47 regional economies with available data were successful in reducing CO_2 emissions on a per capita basis (Figure 2.7.2). Among this group, the largest reductions occurred in Nauru (3.9 thousand tons of CO_2 emissions per capita), Australia (1.9 thousand tons), and Singapore (1.9 thousand tons). The largest increases occurred in Brunei Darussalam (7.8 thousand tons of CO_2 emissions per capita), Kazakhstan (6.4 thousand tons), and the PRC (4.8 thousand tons).

Data Issues and Comparability

Data on greenhouse gases (GHGs) have been compiled from the Emissions Database for Global Atmospheric Research, a joint project of the European Commission Joint Research Centre and the Netherlands Environmental Assessment Agency. This database applies a technology-based emissions factor approach consistently for all economies. It utilizes a consistent set of activity data for calculating various substances, GHGs, and air pollutants; and relies on the spatial allocation of emissions on a 0.1-degree by 0.1-degree grid.

There may be substantial uncertainty in data for individual economies—especially for methane, nitrous

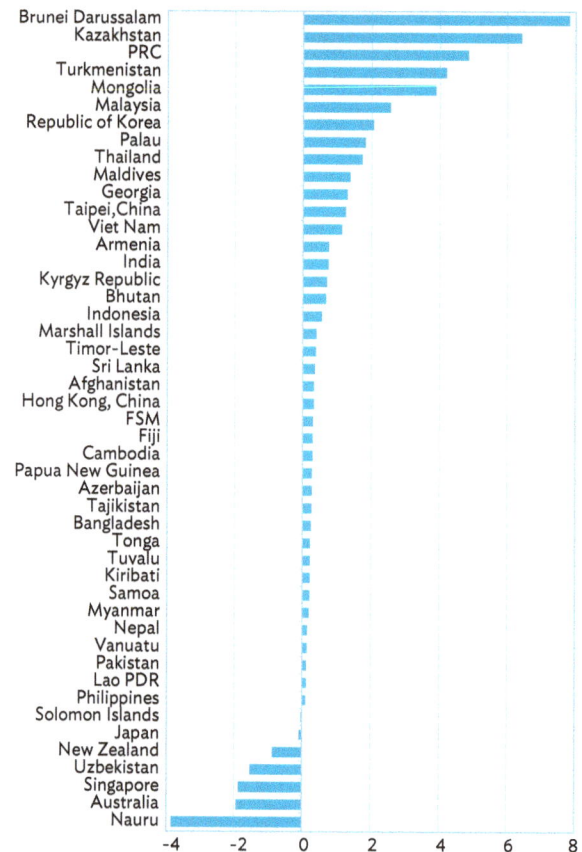

Figure 2.7.2: Change in Carbon Dioxide Emissions in Select Economies of Asia and the Pacific, 2000–2014
(t '000 per capita)

t = metric ton, FSM = Federated States of Micronesia, Lao PDR = Lao People's Democratic Republic, PRC = People's Republic of China.

Note: Only economies with available data for both 2000 and 2014 are included. For Taipei,China, data refer to 2001 and 2015.

Source: ADB estimates using Table 2.7.2 and Table 2.1.1, Key Indicators for Asia and the Pacific 2019.

oxide, and other GHGs—due to the limited accuracy of international activity data and the emission factors selected for calculating emissions on an economy level. However, since Intergovernmental Panel on Climate Change methodologies are consistently used, and data are based on international information sources, there is sound basis for comparability.[6]

The Food and Agriculture Organization of the UN monitors land use and forestry data, using its own expert sources, country reports, satellite imagery, and official data gathered through questionnaires conducted by the organization.

---

[6] For more information on the methodologies of the Emissions Database for Global Atmospheric Research, go to http://edgar.jrc.ec.europa.eu/methodology.php.

Table 2.7.1: Agriculture Land Use
(% of total land area)

ADB Regional Member	Agricultural Land				Arable Land				Permanent Cropland			
	2000	2005	2010	2016	2000	2005	2010	2016	2000	2005	2010	2016
Developing ADB Member Economies												
Central and West Asia												
Afghanistan	57.8	58.1	58.1	58.1	11.8	12.0	11.9	11.8	0.1	0.2	0.2	0.3
Armenia	46.5	56.4	60.9	58.9	15.8	16.0	15.8	15.7	1.3	1.8	1.9	2.0
Azerbaijan	57.4	57.6	57.7	57.7	22.1	22.3	22.8	24.2	2.9	2.7	2.8	2.9
Georgia	43.2	36.3	35.4	34.5	11.4	6.8	5.7	5.0	3.9	1.6	1.8	1.6
Kazakhstan	79.8	78.6	80.4	80.4	11.2	10.6	10.6	10.9	0.1	0.0	0.0	0.0
Kyrgyz Republic	55.9	56.0	55.3	55.0	7.1	6.7	6.7	6.7	0.3	0.4	0.4	0.4
Pakistan	47.6	46.7	45.7	47.8	40.3	39.1	38.1	40.3	0.9	1.0	1.1	1.0
Tajikistan	32.7	33.4	34.0	34.1	5.6	5.4	5.3	5.3	0.7	0.8	1.0	1.0
Turkmenistan	75.5	74.2	72.4	72.0	4.1	4.3	4.1	4.1	0.1	0.1	0.1	0.1
Uzbekistan	64.2	62.9	62.7	62.9	10.5	10.3	10.2	10.3	0.8	0.8	0.8	0.9
East Asia												
China, People's Republic of	55.6	55.1	54.8	56.2	12.6	12.0	11.4	12.7	1.2	1.3	1.5	1.7
Hong Kong, China	6.7	6.7	5.2	4.8	4.8	4.8	3.3	2.9	1.0	1.0	1.0	1.0
Korea, Republic of	20.5	19.4	18.2	17.4	17.8	17.0	15.5	14.6	2.1	1.9	2.1	2.3
Mongolia	84.0	73.0	73.1	71.5	0.8	0.4	0.4	0.4	0.0	0.0	0.0	0.0
Taipei,China	24.0	23.5	23.0	22.4	17.5	17.0	16.9	16.6	6.5	6.5	6.1	5.8
South Asia												
Bangladesh	72.2	71.5	71.0	70.6	64.1	60.8	59.9	59.6	3.5	6.1	6.5	6.4
Bhutan	13.3	15.6	13.6	13.6	2.7	4.4	2.6	2.6	0.5	0.5	0.3	0.2
India	60.9	60.6	60.4	60.4	54.1	53.6	52.8	52.6	3.1	3.4	4.1	4.4
Maldives	30.0	30.0	26.3	26.3	10.0	10.0	13.0	13.0	16.7	16.7	10.0	10.0
Nepal	29.6	29.3	28.8	28.7	16.4	15.9	15.2	14.7	0.8	0.9	1.1	1.5
Sri Lanka	37.5	40.0	41.8	43.7	14.6	17.5	19.1	20.7	15.9	15.5	15.6	15.9
Southeast Asia												
Brunei Darussalam	1.9	2.1	2.5	2.7	0.4	0.4	0.8	0.9	0.8	0.9	1.1	1.1
Cambodia	27.0	30.3	30.9	30.9	21.0	21.0	21.5	21.5	0.8	0.9	0.9	0.9
Indonesia	26.0	28.6	30.7	31.5	11.3	12.7	13.0	13.0	8.6	9.9	11.6	12.4
Lao People's Democratic Republic	7.8	8.6	9.6	10.3	4.0	5.0	6.1	6.6	0.4	0.4	0.6	0.7
Malaysia	21.1	21.7	22.5	26.3	2.6	2.9	2.6	2.7	17.6	18.0	19.0	22.7
Myanmar	16.5	17.2	19.2	19.5	15.2	15.4	16.5	16.7	0.9	1.4	2.2	2.4
Philippines	37.7	38.1	40.6	41.7	16.9	16.8	17.8	18.7	15.8	16.3	17.8	17.9
Singapore	1.8	1.1	1.1	0.9	1.5	1.0	0.9	0.8	0.3	0.1	0.1	0.1
Thailand	38.8	38.4	41.2	43.3	30.6	29.8	30.8	32.9	6.6	7.1	8.8	8.8
Viet Nam	28.2	32.4	34.7	39.3	19.9	20.5	20.8	22.6	6.2	9.8	11.9	14.6
The Pacific												
Cook Islands	20.0	11.4	5.6	6.3	7.5	5.2	2.9	4.2	12.5	6.2	2.7	2.1
Fiji	23.4	23.4	23.3	23.3	9.3	9.3	9.0	9.0	4.5	4.5	4.7	4.7
Kiribati	42.0	42.0	42.0	42.0	2.5	2.5	2.5	2.5	39.5	39.5	39.5	39.5
Marshall Islands	66.7	72.2	72.2	63.9	5.6	11.1	11.1	11.1	44.4	44.4	44.4	36.1
Micronesia, Federated States of	32.1	32.1	31.4	31.4	3.6	3.6	2.9	2.9	24.3	24.3	24.3	24.3
Nauru	20.0	20.0	20.0	20.0	–	–	–	–	20.0	20.0	20.0	20.0
Niue	18.5	18.5	19.2	19.2	3.8	3.8	3.8	3.8	10.8	10.8	11.5	11.5
Palau	10.9	10.9	10.9	10.9	2.2	2.2	2.2	2.2	4.3	4.3	4.3	4.3
Papua New Guinea	2.2	2.3	2.6	2.6	0.5	0.5	0.7	0.7	1.4	1.3	1.5	1.5
Samoa	17.0	14.8	12.4	12.4	4.9	3.9	2.8	2.8	11.0	9.5	7.8	7.8
Solomon Islands	2.7	3.2	3.8	3.9	0.5	0.6	0.7	0.7	2.0	2.3	2.9	2.9
Timor-Leste	22.7	25.9	25.0	25.6	8.1	11.4	10.1	10.4	4.5	4.4	4.8	5.0
Tonga	41.7	41.7	44.4	45.8	20.8	20.8	23.6	25.0	15.3	15.3	15.3	15.3
Tuvalu	66.7	56.7	60.0	60.0	–	–	–	–	66.7	56.7	60.0	60.0
Vanuatu	14.4	15.0	15.3	15.3	1.6	1.6	1.6	1.6	9.3	9.9	10.3	10.3
Developed ADB Member Economies												
Australia	59.3	57.9	51.9	48.2	6.2	6.4	5.5	6.0	0.0	0.0	0.1	0.0
Japan	14.4	12.9	12.6	12.3	12.3	12.0	11.7	11.5	1.0	0.9	0.9	0.8
New Zealand	58.5	44.5	43.3	40.5	5.7	1.6	1.9	2.2	0.2	0.2	0.3	0.3

– = magnitude equals zero, 0.0 = magnitude is less than half of unit employed, ADB = Asian Development Bank.

Source: Food and Agriculture Organization of the United Nations. FAOSTAT Database. http://www.fao.org/faostat/en/#data/RL (accessed 21 May 2019).

Pollution

Table 2.7.2:   Deforestation and Pollution

ADB Regional Member	Deforestation Rate[a] (average % change)		Carbon Dioxide Emissions[b] (t '000)		Nitrous Oxide Emissions (t '000 CO_2 equivalent)	
	2000	2016	2000	2014	2000	2012
Developing ADB Member Economies						
Central and West Asia						
Afghanistan	–	–	774	9,809	3,317	3,424
Armenia	0.06	-0.06	3,465	5,530	462	1,023
Azerbaijan	-0.23	-2.30	29,508	37,488	2,030	2,673
Georgia	-0.03	–	4,536	8,988	2,437	2,352
Kazakhstan	0.17	–	118,099	248,315	14,865	17,822
Kyrgyz Republic	-0.26	1.26	4,635	9,608	1,452	1,567
Pakistan	1.91	2.92	106,449	166,298	26,350	30,651
Tajikistan	-0.05	-0.10	2,237	5,189	1,110	1,848
Turkmenistan	–	–	37,539	68,423	3,046	4,924
Uzbekistan	-0.52	0.35	121,829	105,214	9,610	13,192
East Asia						
China, People's Republic of	-1.13	-0.74	3,405,180	10,291,927	414,138	587,166
Hong Kong, China	...	...	40,440	46,223	513	476
Korea, Republic of	0.13	0.12	447,561	587,156	18,576	14,979
Mongolia	0.69	0.77	7,506	20,840	5,058	3,548
Taipei,China	–	– (2017)	230,022 (2001)	271,013 (2015)	3,845 (2001)	4,506 (2015)
South Asia						
Bangladesh	0.18	0.18	27,869	73,190	20,770	26,683
Bhutan	-0.38	-0.36	396	1,001	281	555
India	-0.22	-0.25	1,031,853	2,238,377	207,700	239,755
Maldives	–	–	451	1,335	12	27
Nepal	2.30	–	3,069	8,031	4,232	4,598
Sri Lanka	0.42	0.32	10,238	18,394	2,044	2,174
Southeast Asia						
Brunei Darussalam	0.40	–	4,712	9,109	395	342
Cambodia	1.20	1.35	1,977	6,685	3,295	16,685
Indonesia	1.89	0.75	263,419	464,176	94,933	93,139
Lao People's Democratic Republic	0.67	-1.01	939	1,955	3,265	8,987
Malaysia	0.36	-0.06	125,734	242,821	13,822	15,310
Myanmar	1.23	1.88	10,088	21,632	31,300	26,783
Philippines	-0.68	-2.99	73,307	105,654	12,365	12,762
Singapore	–	–	49,006	56,373	6,635	1,909
Thailand	-1.80	-0.18	181,271	316,213	18,677	30,833
Viet Nam	-2.06	-0.87	53,645	166,911	19,746	34,494
The Pacific						
Cook Islands	-0.47	–	...	...	...	...
Fiji	-0.28	-0.48	843	1,170	343	344
Kiribati	–	–	29	62	3	4
Marshall Islands	–	–	77	103	0	0
Micronesia, Federated States of	-0.05	-0.05	125	150	11	11
Nauru	...	...	84	48	0	0
Niue	...	...	...	...	...	...
Palau	-0.38	–	249	260	0	0
Papua New Guinea	0.01	0.01	2,666	6,318	1,613	1,234
Samoa	-2.46	–	143	198	37	40
Solomon Islands	0.25	0.26	150	202	2,425	2,656
Timor-Leste	1.29	1.63	–	469	164	226
Tonga	–	–	95	121	22	22
Tuvalu	–	–	7	11	1	1
Vanuatu	–	–	84	154	118	109
Developed ADB Member Economies						
Australia	-0.02	-0.25	329,443	361,262	75,581	54,247
Japan	0.03	0.01	1,220,528	1,214,048	30,411	24,911
New Zealand	-0.48	-0.00	32,981	34,664	11,549	11,880

continued on next page

Table 2.7.2: **Deforestation and Pollution** (*continued*)

ADB Regional Member	Methane Emissions (t '000 CO_2 equivalent)		Other Greenhouse Gases[c] (t '000 CO_2 equivalent)	
	2000	2012	2000	2012
Developing ADB Member Economies				
Central and West Asia				
Afghanistan	9,384	13,763	126	349
Armenia	2,565	3,426	112	710
Azerbaijan	9,955	19,955	464	1,142
Georgia	4,137	5,019	3	227
Kazakhstan	38,779	71,350	14,065	30,363
Kyrgyz Republic	3,486	4,291	93	68
Pakistan	117,125	158,337	757	1,159
Tajikistan	3,304	5,408	798	367
Turkmenistan	21,241	22,009	124	595
Uzbekistan	37,233	47,333	298	989
East Asia				
China, People's Republic of	1,043,400	1,752,290	104,677	251,254
Hong Kong, China	2,695	3,147	155	150
Korea, Republic of	30,916	32,625	14,934	8,968
Mongolia	9,218	6,257	26,233	2,216 (2010)
Taipei,China	12,215 (2001)	5,449 (2015)	6,304 (2001)	3,052 (2015)
South Asia				
Bangladesh	89,247	105,142	686	1,329
Bhutan	1,032	1,770	644	488
India	561,733	636,396	56,626	153,658
Maldives	34	52	...	...
Nepal	21,206	23,982	2,443	7,995
Sri Lanka	9,606	11,864	441	91
Southeast Asia				
Brunei Darussalam	3,882	4,539	101	427
Cambodia	14,985	35,915	23,021	73,300
Indonesia	170,032	223,316	63,048	2,556
Lao People's Democratic Republic	7,219	15,011	13,588	136,841
Malaysia	29,309	34,271	5,144	3,866
Myanmar	66,942	80,637	78,176	406,274
Philippines	49,911	57,170	12,487	3,891
Singapore	1,684	2,386	1,889 (2001)	3,299
Thailand	83,564	106,499	8,756	45,556
Viet Nam	75,430	113,564	5,782	25,707
The Pacific				
Cook Islands	...	...	...	...
Fiji	705	715	9	52
Kiribati	13	16	–	–
Marshall Islands	6	8	...	...
Micronesia, Federated States of	28	30	...	...
Nauru	3	3	...	...
Niue	...	...	...	...
Palau	1	1	...	...
Papua New Guinea	2,001	2,143	1,949	2,188
Samoa	116	133	-0	0
Solomon Islands	1,394	1,449	0	0
Timor-Leste	450	732	–	-0
Tonga	58	61	-0	...
Tuvalu	3	3	-0	0
Vanuatu	267	254	0	-0
Developed ADB Member Economies				
Australia	128,133	125,588	520,911	174,653
Japan	47,496	38,957	51,527	71,746
New Zealand	26,584	28,658	1,506	1,764

... = data not available, – = magnitude equals zero, -0 or 0 = magnitude is less than half of unit employed, ADB = Asian Development Bank, CO_2 = carbon dioxide, t = metric ton.

a Rate refers to percentage change over previous year. A negative value indicates that the deforestation rate is decreasing (i.e., reforestation).
b Data from the World Bank are expressed in kilotons, while data provided in the table are expressed in thousands of metric tons, using a conversion factor of 1 kiloton = 1,000 metric tons.
c Other greenhouse gas emissions refer to hydrofluorocarbons, perfluorocarbons, and sulphur hexafluoride.

Sources: Food and Agriculture Organization of the United Nations. FAOSTAT Database. http://www.fao.org/faostat/en/#data/RL (accessed 25 July 2019); and World Bank. World Development Indicators Online. http://data.worldbank.org/indicator (accessed 25 July 2019). For Taipei,China: Government of Taipei,China, Directorate-General of Budget, Accounting and Statistics. Statistical Yearbook 2017. https://eng.dgbas.gov.tw/public/data/dgbas03/bs2/yearbook_eng/Yearbook2017.pdf (accessed 22 May 2019).

Freshwater

Table 2.7.3:   Freshwater Resources

ADB Regional Member	Internal Renewable Freshwater Resources		Annual Freshwater Withdrawals	Water Productivity[a]
	(m³ billion per year)	(m³ per inhabitant per year)	(m³ billion)	(constant 2010 $ per m³)
	2017	2017[b]		
Developing ADB Member Economies				
Central and West Asia	**370**	**1,155**		
Afghanistan	47	1,327	20 (2000)	...
Armenia	7	2,341	3 (2017)	3.5 (2015)
Azerbaijan	8	826	13 (2017)	4.4 (2012)
Georgia	58	14,859	2 (2008)	6.2 (2008)
Kazakhstan	64	3,535	21 (2016)	7.4 (2010)
Kyrgyz Republic	49	8,094	8 (2006)	0.5 (2006)
Pakistan	55	279	184 (2008)	0.9 (2008)
Tajikistan	63	7,114	11 (2006)	0.4 (2006)
Turkmenistan	1	244	28 (2004)	0.4 (2004)
Uzbekistan	16	512	53 (2016)	0.5 (2005)
East Asia[c]	**2,913**	**1,948**		
China, People's Republic of	2,813	1,952	594 (2015)	15.0 (2015)
Hong Kong, China	...	...	...	...
Korea, Republic of	65	1,272	29 (2005)	30.8 (2005)
Mongolia	35	11,313	0 (2016)	12.3 (2009)
Taipei,China	...	...	...	...
South Asia	**1,880**	**1,209**		
Bangladesh	105	638	36 (2008)	2.9 (2008)
Bhutan	78	96,582	0 (2008)	3.9 (2008)
India	1,446	1,080	648 (2010)	2.6 (2010)
Maldives	0	69	...	...
Nepal	198	6,763	9 (2006)	1.4 (2006)
Sri Lanka	53	2,529	13 (2005)	3.2 (2005)
Southeast Asia	**4,985**	**7,699**		
Brunei Darussalam	9	19,827	...	...
Cambodia	121	7,535	2 (2006)	4.1 (2006)
Indonesia	2,019	7,648	223 (2016)	4.0 (2000)
Lao People's Democratic Republic	190	27,763	3 (2005)	1.4 (2005)
Malaysia	580	18,341	11 (2005)	18.3 (2005)
Myanmar	1,003	18,793	33 (2000)	0.5 (2000)
Philippines	479	4,565	85 (2016)	2.3 (2009)
Singapore	1	105	...	...
Thailand	225	3,252	57 (2007)	5.5 (2007)
Viet Nam	359	3,762	82 (2005)	1.0 (2005)
The Pacific[c]	**892**	**78,701**		
Cook Islands	...	...	...	...
Fiji	29	31,530	0 (2005)	35.7 (2005)
Kiribati	...	...	...	...
Marshall Islands	...	...	...	...
Micronesia, Federated States of	...	...	...	...
Nauru	...	...	...	...
Niue	...	...	...	...
Palau	...	...	...	...
Papua New Guinea	801	97,079	0 (2005)	27.3 (2005)
Samoa	...	...	...	...
Solomon Islands	45	73,123	...	...
Timor-Leste	8	6,339	1 (2004)	1.6 (2004)
Tonga	...	...	...	...
Tuvalu	...	...	...	...
Vanuatu	10	36,206	...	...
Developed ADB Member Economies	**1,249**	**7,974**		
Australia	492	20,123	16 (2016)	78.4 (2015)
Japan	430	3,373	81 (2009)	67.4 (2009)
New Zealand	327	69,486	5 (2010)	28.2 (2010)
DEVELOPING ADB MEMBER ECONOMIES[c]	**11,040**	**2,740**		
ALL ADB REGIONAL MEMBERS[c]	**12,289**	**2,936**		

... = data not available, 0 = magnitude is less than half of unit employed, $ = United States dollars, ADB = Asian Development Bank, m³ = cubic meter.

a   Gross domestic product in constant 2010 United States dollars per cubic meter of total freshwater withdrawal.
b   Regional aggregates are weighted averages estimated using population.
c   For reporting economies only.

Sources: Food and Agriculture Organization of the United Nations. AQUASTAT Database. http://www.fao.org/nr/water/aquastat/data/query/index.html (accessed 25 July 2019); and World Bank. World Development Indicators Online. http://data.worldbank.org/indicator (accessed 25 July 2019).

VIII. Government and Governance

Government and Governance presents statistics on government taxes, revenues, and expenditure; government net lending/net borrowing; and government expenditures on health, education, and social protection. The section also includes data on the time and cost required to register a new business in each economy, as well as the latest global rankings for Transparency International's Corruption Perceptions Index. The discussion here focuses on government taxes as a share of GDP, as well as the number of days required to start a business.

In 2018, the share of taxes collected by government as a proportion of GDP was 20% or higher in around one third of the 23 economies with available data

Government taxes comprise value-added tax, sales tax, import duties, income tax, profit tax, property tax, capital gains tax, and compulsory social security charges, among others. The total government tax take as a share of GDP was 20.0% or higher in 8 of the 23 economies with available data for 2018 (Figure 2.8.1).

From 2017 to 2018, the proportion of government taxes to GDP rose in 13 of the 23 reporting economies. In 8 economies, there was a decrease in the proportion of government taxes to GDP, and in 2 economies the proportion remained unchanged. The largest increases during the review period were observed in Tonga (4.9 percentage points), Mongolia (2.6 percentage points), and Uzbekistan (2.4 percentage points). The largest decreases were observed in Nauru (–5.4 percentage points), Bangladesh (–1.7 percentage points), and Maldives (–1.1 percentage points).

Figure 2.8.1: Government Taxes as a Proportion of Gross Domestic Product in Select Economies of Asia and the Pacific
(%)

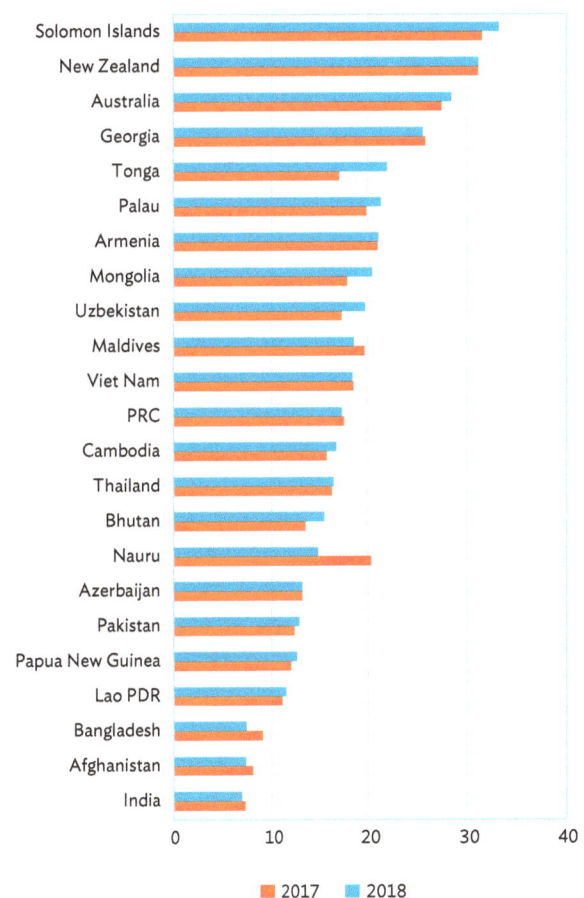

Lao PDR = Lao People's Democratic Republic, PRC = People's Republic of China.
Note: Only economies with data for both 2017 and 2018 are included in the chart. Data refer to general government, except for Bangladesh, Bhutan, Cambodia, India, the Lao People's Democratic Republic, Maldives, Nauru, Palau, Solomon Islands, Tonga, and Viet Nam, where data refer to central government.
Source: Table 2.8.2, Key Indicators for Asia and the Pacific 2019.

Economies in Asia and the Pacific are spurring entrepreneurial activity by reducing the number of days required to start a business.

Reducing the amount of time required to start a business can act as an incentive to entrepreneurial activity. Shorter start-up times are associated with simplified registration procedures and reduced opportunities for bribes (World Bank 2019b).

From 2005 to 2018, of the 37 regional economies with available data, 30 reduced the number of days required to start a business, 4 reported an increase, and 3 had no change (Figure 2.8.2). On a subregional basis, the average number of days required to start a business were reduced as follows: Southeast Asia (25.8 days), the Pacific (25.6 days), South Asia (22.8 days), Central and West Asia (33.0 days), and East Asia (20.5 days). Among ADB's developed member economies in Asia and the Pacific, the average reduction was 2.8 days.

By individual economy, the largest reductions from 2005 to 2018 were achieved in Timor-Leste (154.0 days), Brunei Darussalam (116.0 days), and Azerbaijan (109.5 days). The three most populous economies of the region achieved significant reductions in the number of days required to start a business between 2013 and 2018 for which data are available—the PRC (from 32.4 to 8.6 days), India (from 32.7 to 16.5 days), and Indonesia (from 75.5 to 19.6 days).

The high-income economies of New Zealand (0.5 days); Hong Kong, China (1.5 days); and Singapore (1.5 days) had the shortest amount of time required to start a business among the 37 economies reporting for 2018 (Figure 2.8.2). The longest delays in starting a business in 2018 were incurred in the Lao People's Democratic Republic (174.0 days), Cambodia (99.0 days), and Papua New Guinea (41.0 days).

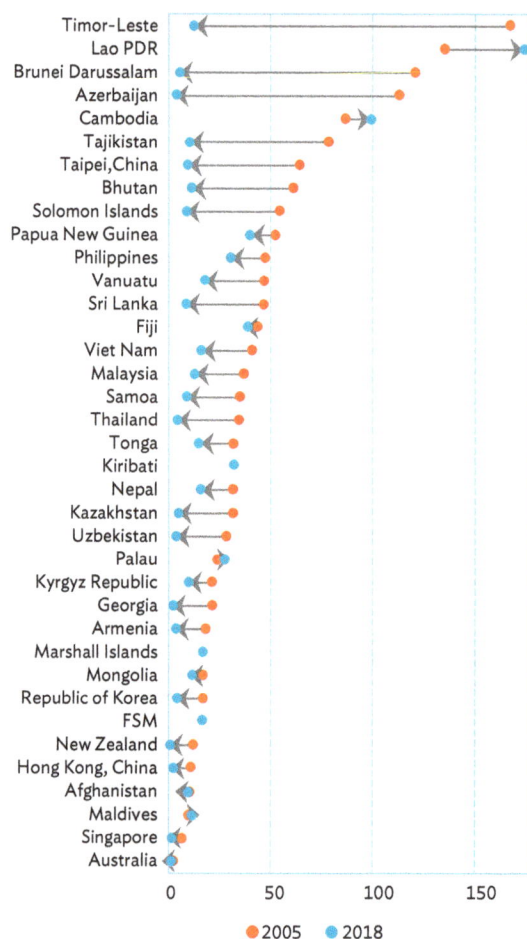

Figure 2.8.2: Time Required to Start a Business in Select Economies of Asia and the Pacific
(days)

● 2005   ● 2018

FSM = Federated States of Micronesia, Lao PDR = Lao People's Democratic Republic.
Note: Only economies with data for both 2005 and 2018 are included in the chart. Initial year for Brunei Darussalam is 2006.
Source: Table 2.8.6, Key Indicators for Asia and the Pacific 2019.

Data Issues and Comparability

Most economies generally follow the IMF's Government Finance Statistics (GFS) guidelines, with some economies still using the 1986 version, while others have switched to the 2001 or 2014 GFS guidelines. The comparability of the data is limited by variations in the concepts and definitions used in different versions of the GFS framework.

Furthermore, there is no single framework for an extended time series available in most economies using the 2014 guidelines, with most economies recording their transactions on a cash basis (and a few on an accrual basis).

Data on government expenditures and revenue are derived from economy sources and are therefore not standard throughout Asia and the Pacific. Data refer to general government for some economies, and central government for other economies.

Statistics on the time and cost for registering new businesses, and on perceived corruption, are taken from nonofficial sources. Common procedures are used in all economies, and the researchers producing these data have refined their procedures over several surveys. However, because of the subjective nature of many of the data, they can only be used to give a broad idea of trends, levels, and rankings. Therefore, small changes from one year to the next should be interpreted with caution.

Table 2.8.1:   Government Net Lending/Net Borrowing[a]
(% of GDP)

ADB Regional Member	2010	2011	2012	2013	2014	2015	2016	2017	2018
Developing ADB Member Economies									
Central and West Asia									
Afghanistan[b]	0.8	-1.2	-0.6	-2.7	-1.8	-1.3	0.5	-0.4	–
Armenia	-5.0	-2.8	-1.5	-1.5	-1.9	-4.8	-5.5	-4.8	-1.6
Azerbaijan	-10.8	-13.0	-13.1	-13.6	-13.4	-12.4	-5.5	-6.3	-9.0
Georgia	-4.5	-0.9	-0.6	-1.1	-2.0	-1.1	-1.4	-0.9	-0.8
Kazakhstan	5.0	8.3	6.0	5.0	3.5	-2.2	-2.8	-3.0	...
Kyrgyz Republic	-4.8	-4.8	-6.5	-0.8	0.0	-1.0	-3.7	-2.6	...
Pakistan[c]	-6.0	-6.4	-8.6	-8.1	-4.7	-5.2	-4.5	-5.8	-6.5
Tajikistan	-7.1	-5.8	-3.4	-5.4	-3.8	-7.8	-10.4	...	...
Turkmenistan	2.0	3.5	6.4	1.5	0.9	-0.7	...	...	...
Uzbekistan	...	...	...	8.4	7.8	6.8	4.0	1.5	3.2
East Asia									
China, People's Republic of	-1.6	-1.1	-1.6	-1.9	-1.8	-3.4	-3.8	-3.7	-4.2
Hong Kong, China[d]	4.1	3.8	3.5	0.7	4.2	1.4	4.7	6.3	...
Korea, Republic of	...	...	1.1	1.4	1.3	1.2	2.5	2.6	...
Mongolia	-3.2	-11.8	-15.5	-8.3	-11.5	-10.9	-23.0	-11.1	-4.1
Taipei,China	-2.6	-1.5	-2.8	-1.0	-0.8	0.2	-0.3	-0.1	...
South Asia									
Bangladesh[c]	-1.7	-0.9	-0.5	-1.3	-2.3	-2.2	-2.7	-3.0	-1.9
Bhutan[c]	1.5	-2.0	-1.1	-4.0	3.6	1.4	-1.0	-3.3	-0.3
India[d]	-4.8	-5.9	-4.9	-4.5	-4.1	-3.9	-3.5	-3.5	-3.4
Maldives	-12.9	-5.8	-6.7	-3.5	-2.4	-6.7	-10.4	-3.0	-5.5
Nepal[e]	-1.4	-1.0	-0.6	1.7	1.8	1.1	1.4	-3.1	...
Sri Lanka	-6.3	-5.8	-5.3	-5.3	-5.6	-7.6	-5.3	-5.4	-5.3
Southeast Asia									
Brunei Darussalam[f]	15.6	25.6	15.7	10.1	-0.7	-14.5	-21.7	-9.9	...
Cambodia	-4.5	-5.4	-4.4	-2.7	-1.3	-0.9	-0.4	-1.0	0.2
Indonesia	-0.6	-0.7	-1.5	-1.8	-2.6	-3.0	-1.9	-2.0	...
Lao People's Democratic Republic[g]	-0.9	-0.9	-0.7	-4.9	-3.3	-3.7	-4.9	-4.4	-6.0
Malaysia	-5.0	-4.6	-4.4	-3.8	-3.3	-3.1	-3.0	-2.9	...
Myanmar[d]	...	...	-4.4	-3.2	-2.5	-4.4	-3.0	-3.1	...
Philippines	-3.5	-1.8	-1.9	-1.2	-0.5	-1.3	-2.3	-2.2	...
Singapore[d]	7.5	9.1	8.5	8.1	7.1	4.2	5.1	7.7	...
Thailand[g]	-0.7	-0.6	-0.8	0.6	-0.7	0.1	0.4	-0.3	0.3
Viet Nam[h]	-2.1	-0.5	-3.4	-5.0	-4.4	-4.3	-4.2	-3.5	-3.5
The Pacific									
Cook Islands[c]	2.9	9.6	0.8	14.2	-2.9	-7.8	1.4	8.7	...
Fiji	-2.6	-1.7	-1.4	-0.9	-2.4	-2.0	-0.8	-0.9	...
Kiribati[c]	...	-6.9	3.5	20.3	44.7	56.1	21.6	17.0	...
Marshall Islands[g]	0.3	2.1	-0.7	0.7	2.8	2.8	4.0	4.5	...
Micronesia, Federated States of[g]	0.5	-0.6	0.9	2.9	11.2	10.4	7.3	14.6	...
Nauru[c]	0.1	...	7.9	1.5	25.0	8.9	23.5	10.4	9.0
Niue	...	...	...	...	...	...	...	...	...
Palau[g]	10.0	8.8	9.3	5.1	8.1	10.0	9.2	7.8	8.2
Papua New Guinea	...	...	...	...	...	...	...	-2.4	-2.5
Samoa[c]	...	...	-8.1	-3.9	-4.8	-3.7	0.7	-0.6	...
Solomon Islands	7.3	7.9	6.0	4.5	2.7	1.0	-4.1	-2.9	1.9
Timor-Leste	...	...	...	-3.3	-11.8	3.8	-6.9	5.5	...
Tonga[c]	...	...	...	...	...	...	2.7	4.4	3.0
Tuvalu	...	...	11.5	26.6	29.0	40.0	4.8	...	...
Vanuatu	...	...	-1.6	-0.2	1.2	6.9	2.5	1.9	...
Developed ADB Member Economies									
Australia[c]	-5.5	-4.8	-4.3	-2.7	-2.9	-2.9	-2.7	-2.3	-1.1
Japan[d]	-8.9	-9.0	-8.2	-7.2	-5.0	-3.4	-3.4	-2.8	...
New Zealand[c]	-3.4	-7.5	-2.7	-1.9	-0.9	-0.1	0.6	1.2	1.1

... = data not available, | = marks break in series, – = magnitude equals zero, ADB = Asian Development Bank, GDP = gross domestic product.

a   In general, economies follow the guidelines of the International Monetary Fund on Government Finance Statistics (GFS). Some economies still use the 1986 version of the GFS guidelines, while others have switched to the 2001 or 2014 guidelines. The comparability of the data in this table is limited by variations in the concepts and definitions used in different versions of the GFS framework. Data refer to government net lending/net borrowing as classified in the GFS 2001 or GFS 2014 framework, except for Bhutan; Brunei Darussalam; India, Maldives; Nauru; Pakistan; the People's Republic of China; Taipei,China; Tajikistan; Turkmenistan; and Viet Nam, where data refer to overall budgetary surplus/deficit as classified in the GFS 1986 framework. Data refer to general government, except for Bangladesh; Bhutan; Brunei Darussalam; Cambodia; the Cook Islands; the Federated States of Micronesia; Fiji; India; the Lao People's Democratic Republic; Malaysia; Maldives; the Marshall Islands; Nauru; Nepal; Palau; the Philippines; Solomon Islands; Sri Lanka; Taipei,China; Timor-Leste; Tonga; Tuvalu; Vanuatu; and Viet Nam, where data refer to central government. For Azerbaijan: Data are based on the state budget. For Cambodia: Data refer to central government excluding extra budgetary central government. For the Kyrgyz Republic: For 2010–2013, data refer to central government. For Pakistan: Data refer to the consolidated federal and provincial governments. For the People's Republic of China: Data refer to consolidated central and local governments. For Turkmenistan: For 2010, data refer to central government.
b   For 2005–2011, GFS data are based on fiscal year beginning 21 March. For 2012, data cover 9 months from 21 March to 20 December. For 2013 onward, data are based on fiscal year ending 20 December. National accounts data for 2005–2017 are based on fiscal year beginning 21 March, and for 2018 on fiscal year ending 20 December.
c   Data are based on fiscal year ending 30 June.
d   Data are based on fiscal year beginning 1 April.
e   Data are based on fiscal year ending 15 July.
f   For 2005 onward, data are based on fiscal year beginning 1 April. Data are derived as excess of revenue over expenditure (ordinary plus charged) less the sum of contribution to a development fund, contribution to a government trust fund, and capital and currency adjustments.
g   Data are based on fiscal year ending 30 September.
h   Taxes include local government taxes.

Sources: Economy sources. For Fiji; Hong Kong, China; Kiribati (2011–2013 and 2017); the Kyrgyz Republic; Nepal; and Sri Lanka (2010–2013): International Monetary Fund. Government Finance Statistics. https://data.imf.org/ (accessed May–June 2019). For Nauru: International Monetary Fund. Staff Country Reports. Republic of Nauru: 2017 Article IV. http://www.imf.org/en/Publications/CR/Issues/2017/04/03/Republic-of-Nauru-2017-Article-IV-Consultation-Press-Release-Staff-Report-and-Statement-by-44794 (accessed 6 June 2019).

Table 2.8.2: Government Taxes[a]
(% of GDP)

ADB Regional Member	2010	2011	2012	2013	2014	2015	2016	2017	2018
Developing ADB Member Economies									
Central and West Asia									
Afghanistan[b]	9.2	8.7	7.4	7.5	6.7	7.2	7.1	8.1	7.3
Armenia	17.7	17.8	19.2	22.0	22.2	21.3	21.5	21.0	21.1
Azerbaijan	12.4	12.3	12.7	13.2	14.2	16.2	14.9	13.3	13.3
Georgia	23.5	25.2	25.5	24.8	24.8	25.2	25.8	25.8	25.6
Kazakhstan	19.6	21.7	16.9	19.5	17.8	13.6	12.4	14.2	...
Kyrgyz Republic	15.0	16.1	18.1	17.6	20.4	19.7	19.5	19.6	...
Pakistan[c]	10.0	9.4	10.2	9.8	10.2	11.0	12.4	12.5	13.0
Tajikistan	18.0	19.5	19.6	20.8	22.7	21.9	20.6	...	...
Turkmenistan	...	17.5	20.2	17.7	17.0	15.6	...	...	...
Uzbekistan	...	...	...	21.1	20.4	20.3	20.0	17.3	19.7
East Asia									
China, People's Republic of	17.8	18.4	18.7	18.6	18.6	18.2	17.6	17.6	17.4
Hong Kong, China[d]	13.5	14.2	13.7	13.4	15.5	14.4	13.6	14.3	...
Korea, Republic of	...	...	18.0	17.3	17.3	17.6	18.4	19.0	...
Mongolia	24.2	24.3	21.1	21.9	19.1	17.7	16.0	17.9	20.5
Taipei,China	7.6	8.4	8.4	8.0	8.4	8.7	8.9	8.8	...
South Asia									
Bangladesh[c]	10.2	10.6	10.3	9.7	9.6	8.9	8.8	9.1	7.4
Bhutan[c]	13.3	13.6	15.1	14.6	13.5	13.9	13.1	13.6	15.5
India[d]	7.3	7.2	7.5	7.3	7.3	6.9	7.2	7.3	6.9
Maldives	8.8	12.1	15.5	17.5	19.1	19.4	19.6	19.7	18.6
Nepal[e]	13.4	13.3	13.9	15.3	15.9	16.7	18.7	21.0	...
Sri Lanka	11.3	11.3	10.4	10.5	10.1	12.4	12.2	12.4	...
Southeast Asia									
Brunei Darussalam[f]	...	...	...	...	...	...	...	...	...
Cambodia	7.3	7.6	11.6	12.1	14.6	14.6	14.8	15.8	16.8
Indonesia	12.1	12.2	12.5	12.5	12.1	12.0	11.6	11.2	...
Lao People's Democratic Republic[g]	13.8	14.3	13.6	13.7	13.8	13.5	12.9	11.1	11.5
Malaysia	13.3	14.8	15.6	15.3	14.8	14.1	13.6	13.0	...
Myanmar[d]	...	...	6.6	7.3	7.8	7.5	7.8	7.2	...
Philippines	12.1	12.4	12.9	13.3	13.6	13.6	13.7	14.2	...
Singapore[d]	12.8	13.1	13.6	13.3	13.6	13.1	13.4	14.2	...
Thailand[g]	16.1	17.7	16.8	18.4	17.3	17.6	16.8	16.3	16.5
Viet Nam[h]	22.4	22.3	19.0	19.1	18.2	18.0	17.9	18.6	18.5
The Pacific									
Cook Islands[c]	27.0	26.4	23.8	28.1	25.3	23.5	26.3	26.0	...
Fiji	21.8	23.0	23.2	23.6	22.7	23.7	23.5	25.0	...
Kiribati[c]	...	18.3	19.0	18.6	18.4	22.7	25.5	22.8	...
Marshall Islands[g]	16.8	16.5	15.7	15.8	17.0	13.5	17.5	17.9	...
Micronesia, Federated States of[g]	12.0	12.0	11.6	12.1	19.0	12.4	12.9	17.7	...
Nauru[c]	...	...	8.1	15.3	14.9	18.8	22.5	20.3	14.9
Niue	...	...	...	...	...	...	...	...	...
Palau[g]	17.0	18.0	18.5	18.6	19.3	20.2	19.7	19.9	21.4
Papua New Guinea	...	...	...	...	...	...	...	12.1	12.7
Samoa[c]	...	...	20.9	23.5	24.9	23.6	24.3	25.0	...
Solomon Islands	28.4	32.5	33.8	33.7	32.7	32.8	30.3	31.6	33.3
Timor-Leste	...	...	...	1.9	3.1	4.0	6.3	5.6	...
Tonga[c]	...	...	...	...	...	...	20.3	17.1	22.0
Tuvalu	...	...	28.5	34.7	30.1	33.1	28.0	...	...
Vanuatu	...	...	16.5	17.2	17.3	16.3	16.3	17.1	...
Developed ADB Member Economies									
Australia[c]	25.6	25.3	26.0	27.0	27.1	27.3	27.8	27.5	28.5
Japan[d]	15.7	16.4	16.7	17.4	18.7	18.8	18.5	19.0	...
New Zealand[c]	29.1	28.6	29.3	30.5	29.6	30.7	30.9	31.2	31.2

... = data not available, | = marks break in series, ADB = Asian Development Bank, GDP = gross domestic product.

a   In general, economies follow the guidelines of the International Monetary Fund on Government Finance Statistics (GFS). Some economies still use the 1986 version of the GFS guidelines, while others have switched to the 2001 or 2014 guidelines. The comparability of the data in this table is limited by variations in the concepts and definitions used in different versions of the GFS framework. Data refer to government taxes as classified in the GFS 2001 or GFS 2014 framework, except for Bhutan; Brunei Darussalam; India, Maldives; Nauru; Pakistan; the People's Republic of China; Taipei,China; Tajikistan; Turkmenistan; and Viet Nam, where data refer to tax revenue as classified in the GFS 1986 framework. Data refer to general government, except for Bangladesh; Bhutan; Brunei Darussalam; Cambodia; the Cook Islands; the Federated States of Micronesia; Fiji; India; the Lao People's Democratic Republic; Malaysia; Maldives; the Marshall Islands; Nauru; Nepal; Palau; the Philippines; Solomon Islands; Sri Lanka; Taipei,China; Timor-Leste; Tonga; Tuvalu; Vanuatu; and Viet Nam, where data refer to central government. For Azerbaijan: Data are based on the state budget. For Cambodia: Data refer to central government excluding extra budgetary central government. For the Kyrgyz Republic: For 2010–2013, data refer to central government. For Pakistan: Data refer to the consolidated federal and provincial governments. For the People's Republic of China: Data refer to consolidated central and local governments. For Turkmenistan: For 2010, data refer to central government.

b   For 2005–2011, GFS data are based on fiscal year beginning 21 March. For 2012, data cover 9 months from 21 March to 20 December. For 2013 onward, data are based on fiscal year ending 20 December. National accounts data for 2005–2017 are based on fiscal year beginning 21 March, and for 2018 on fiscal year ending 20 December.

c   Data are based on fiscal year ending 30 June.

d   Data are based on fiscal year beginning 1 April.

e   Data are based on fiscal year ending 15 July.

f   For 2005 onward, data are based on fiscal year beginning 1 April. Data are derived as excess of revenue over expenditure (ordinary plus charged) less the sum of contribution to a development fund, contribution to a government trust fund, and capital and currency adjustments.

g   Data are based on fiscal year ending 30 September.

h   Taxes include local government taxes.

Sources: Economy sources. For Fiji; Hong Kong, China; Kiribati (2011–2013 and 2017); the Kyrgyz Republic; Nepal; and Sri Lanka (2010–2013): International Monetary Fund. Government Finance Statistics. https://data.imf.org/ (accessed May–June 2019). For Nauru: International Monetary Fund. Staff Country Reports. Republic of Nauru: 2017 Article IV. http://www.imf.org/en/Publications/CR/Issues/2017/04/03/Republic-of-Nauru-2017-Article-IV-Consultation-Press-Release-Staff-Report-and-Statement-by-44794 (accessed 6 June 2019).

Table 2.8.3: Government Revenue[a]
(% of GDP)

ADB Regional Member	2010	2011	2012	2013	2014	2015	2016	2017	2018
Developing ADB Member Economies									
Central and West Asia									
Afghanistan[b]	23.6	22.5	19.0	26.9	24.1	23.9	25.2	24.6	26.9
Armenia	23.2	24.0	24.4	24.2	24.4	23.8	23.8	22.9	23.1
Azerbaijan	26.9	30.1	31.6	33.5	31.2	32.2	29.0	23.5	28.2
Georgia	28.3	28.2	28.9	27.7	27.9	28.2	28.4	28.9	28.8
Kazakhstan	25.5	27.6	26.3	24.2	23.2	17.6	17.6	20.4	...
Kyrgyz Republic	22.6	24.1	25.0	25.1	35.4	35.6	33.1	33.9	...
Pakistan[c]	14.2	12.5	12.8	13.3	14.5	14.4	15.0	15.5	15.2
Tajikistan	19.3	21.1	21.5	22.7	25.1	25.0	23.4	...	...
Turkmenistan	15.8	18.1	21.0	18.4	17.9	16.6	11.7	14.9	14.1
Uzbekistan	...	...	...	30.3	29.0	27.6	27.5	24.3	27.8
East Asia									
China, People's Republic of	20.2	21.3	21.8	21.8	21.9	22.2	21.6	21.0	20.4
Hong Kong, China[d]	22.3	23.8	23.5	21.5	23.6	21.7	24.6	25.8	...
Korea, Republic of	...	...	33.3	32.3	32.3	32.2	32.6	33.2	...
Mongolia	32.0	32.2	29.3	31.0	28.2	25.8	24.4	26.1	28.7
Taipei,China	10.7	11.8	11.0	11.5	10.9	11.6	11.1	11.1	...
South Asia									
Bangladesh[c]	13.0	13.9	13.7	12.9	11.5	10.6	10.2	10.5	8.3
Bhutan[c]	27.4	20.8	20.7	20.0	19.7	19.9	17.8	18.6	21.4
India[d]	10.6	9.0	9.3	9.4	9.3	9.2	9.4	9.1	8.8
Maldives	19.3	22.6	22.0	23.3	26.4	26.4	27.0	26.6	25.1
Nepal[e]	18.1	18.5	18.7	19.5	20.6	21.1	23.3	24.4	...
Sri Lanka	13.0	13.2	12.2	12.0	11.5	13.3	14.1	13.7	13.4
Southeast Asia									
Brunei Darussalam[f]	49.0	55.3	46.8	37.9	31.1	24.2	17.7	26.1	...
Cambodia	13.8	12.5	16.3	17.9	19.1	18.5	19.8	20.4	21.6
Indonesia	16.6	16.8	17.0	16.9	16.8	15.1	14.4	14.1	...
Lao People's Democratic Republic[g]	21.7	21.5	20.8	20.9	20.9	20.3	16.2	13.9	15.0
Malaysia	19.4	20.3	21.4	20.9	19.9	18.6	17.0	16.1	...
Myanmar[d]	...	...	9.8	11.2	13.9	11.8	11.7	10.7	...
Philippines	13.4	14.0	14.5	14.8	15.1	15.4	15.2	15.6	...
Singapore[d]	16.8	17.0	17.5	17.2	18.0	18.0	18.5	20.5	...
Thailand[g]	20.6	21.3	20.4	22.2	21.3	22.1	21.5	20.9	21.5
Viet Nam[h]	26.7	25.5	22.3	22.8	22.0	23.5	24.3	25.6	25.6
The Pacific									
Cook Islands[c]	38.3	40.6	39.0	42.2	38.8	39.7	39.2	38.8	...
Fiji	24.3	25.6	25.6	26.1	25.9	27.4	26.1	27.9	...
Kiribati[c]	...	64.4	77.9	92.2	112.1	127.8	99.9	104.3	...
Marshall Islands[g]	60.0	57.0	50.8	53.5	58.6	57.9	61.9	70.0	...
Micronesia, Federated States of[g]	67.7	64.8	66.2	62.6	65.7	66.3	69.1	79.1	...
Nauru[c]	39.2	...	31.9	39.1	60.0	64.7	94.1	92.6	74.7
Niue	...	...	...	...	...	...	...	...	...
Palau[g]	46.7	45.2	45.0	41.2	43.8	41.0	41.5	40.2	44.7
Papua New Guinea	...	...	...	...	...	...	...	15.2	17.1
Samoa[c]	...	...	30.2	31.7	36.0	32.0	32.6	34.0	...
Solomon Islands	36.5	42.4	43.9	44.8	42.6	44.7	38.8	39.3	41.3
Timor-Leste	...	...	...	15.6	21.3	47.0	58.1	52.4	...
Tonga[c]	...	...	...	...	...	...	26.1	22.6	29.9
Tuvalu	...	...	105.3	123.3	140.4	184.0	161.5	...	...
Vanuatu	...	...	21.8	21.4	23.4	31.1	30.8	30.9	...
Developed ADB Member Economies									
Australia[c]	32.3	31.7	32.3	33.7	33.7	34.2	34.8	34.5	35.6
Japan[d]	30.2	31.5	32.0	33.1	34.9	35.6	35.4	35.7	...
New Zealand[c]	36.9	38.3	36.7	37.8	36.7	37.5	37.6	37.6	37.3

... = data not available, | = marks break in series, ADB = Asian Development Bank, GDP = gross domestic product.

a In general, economies follow the guidelines of the International Monetary Fund on Government Finance Statistics (GFS). Some economies still use the 1986 version of the GFS guidelines, while others have switched to the 2001 or 2014 guidelines. The comparability of the data in this table is limited by variations in the concepts and definitions used in different versions of the GFS framework. Data refer to government revenue as classified in the GFS 2001 or GFS 2014 framework, except for Bhutan; Brunei Darussalam; India, Maldives; Nauru; Pakistan; the People's Republic of China; Taipei,China; Tajikistan; Turkmenistan; and Viet Nam, where data refer to total government revenue as classified in the GFS 1986 framework. Data refer to general government, except for Bangladesh; Bhutan; Brunei Darussalam; Cambodia; the Cook Islands; the Federated States of Micronesia; Fiji; India; the Lao People's Democratic Republic; Malaysia; Maldives; the Marshall Islands; Nauru; Nepal; Palau; the Philippines; Solomon Islands; Sri Lanka; Taipei,China; Timor-Leste; Tonga; Tuvalu; Vanuatu; and Viet Nam, where data refer to central government. For Azerbaijan: Data are based on the state budget. For Cambodia: Data refer to central government excluding extra budgetary central government. For the Kyrgyz Republic: For 2010–2013, data refer to central government. For Pakistan: Data refer to the consolidated federal and provincial governments. For the People's Republic of China: Data refer to consolidated central and local governments. For Turkmenistan: For 2010, data refer to central government.

b For 2005–2011, GFS data are based on fiscal year beginning 21 March. For 2012, data cover 9 months from 21 March to 20 December. For 2013 onward, data are based on fiscal year ending 20 December. National accounts data for 2005–2017 are based on fiscal year beginning 21 March, and for 2018 on fiscal year ending 20 December.

c Data are based on fiscal year ending 30 June.

d Data are based on fiscal year beginning 1 April.

e Data are based on fiscal year ending 15 July.

f For 2005 onward, data are based on fiscal year beginning 1 April. Data are derived as excess of revenue over expenditure (ordinary plus charged) less the sum of contribution to a development fund, contribution to a government trust fund, and capital and currency adjustments.

g Data are based on fiscal year ending 30 September.

h Taxes include local government taxes.

Sources: Economy sources. For Fiji; Hong Kong, China; Kiribati (2011–2013 and 2017); the Kyrgyz Republic; Nepal; and Sri Lanka (2010–2013): International Monetary Fund. Government Finance Statistics. https://data.imf.org/ (accessed May–June 2019). For Nauru: International Monetary Fund. Staff Country Reports. Republic of Nauru: 2017 Article IV. http://www.imf.org/en/Publications/CR/Issues/2017/04/03/Republic-of-Nauru-2017-Article-IV-Consultation-Press-Release-Staff-Report-and-Statement-by-44794 (accessed 6 June 2019).

Table 2.8.4: Government Expenditure[a]
(% of GDP)

ADB Regional Member	2010	2011	2012	2013	2014	2015	2016	2017	2018
Developing ADB Member Economies									
Central and West Asia									
Afghanistan[b]	29.5	25.5	24.7	23.9	25.5	25.4	28.2	27.4	26.8
Armenia	28.2	26.8	25.9	25.7	26.3	28.6	29.3	27.7	24.7
Azerbaijan	37.7	43.2	44.7	47.1	44.6	44.6	34.4	29.8	37.2
Georgia	32.8	29.1	29.5	28.8	29.8	29.3	29.8	29.7	29.6
Kazakhstan	20.4	19.3	20.3	19.1	19.8	19.8	20.5	23.4	...
Kyrgyz Republic	27.5	29.0	31.5	25.9	35.4	36.5	36.9	36.5	...
Pakistan[c]	20.4	18.9	21.2	19.8	20.4	20.2	20.3	21.6	21.6
Tajikistan	25.1	27.4	25.1	28.5	28.8	33.6	33.8	...	...
Turkmenistan	13.8	14.6	14.7	16.9	17.0	17.3	14.1	17.7	13.5
Uzbekistan	...	...	...	25.4	24.7	24.3	23.6	22.8	24.6
East Asia									
China, People's Republic of	21.8	22.4	23.4	23.6	23.7	25.6	25.4	24.7	24.5
Hong Kong, China[d]	18.1	20.0	20.0	20.8	19.3	20.3	19.9	19.5	...
Korea, Republic of	...	...	32.2	30.9	31.0	31.1	30.2	30.7	...
Mongolia	35.2	44.0	44.8	39.3	39.8	36.8	47.3	37.1	32.8
Taipei,China	13.3	13.3	13.7	12.5	11.7	11.4	11.4	11.2	...
South Asia									
Bangladesh[c]	14.8	14.8	14.2	14.2	13.7	12.7	12.9	13.4	10.2
Bhutan[c]	35.6	34.8	35.8	34.7	29.0	27.6	29.4	31.3	32.3
India[d]	15.4	14.9	14.2	13.9	13.4	13.1	12.9	12.5	12.2
Maldives	33.2	31.3	29.8	27.0	29.1	34.0	37.3	30.1	31.3
Nepal[e]	19.5	19.5	19.3	17.8	18.8	20.1	21.9	27.5	...
Sri Lanka	19.3	19.0	17.5	17.3	17.0	20.9	19.5	19.1	18.7
Southeast Asia									
Brunei Darussalam[f]	33.3	29.7	31.0	27.8	31.8	38.7	39.4	36.0	...
Cambodia	18.3	17.9	20.7	20.6	20.5	19.4	20.2	21.4	21.4
Indonesia	17.2	17.5	18.4	18.7	18.5	17.8	16.9	16.5	...
Lao People's Democratic Republic[g]	22.7	22.4	21.5	25.7	24.2	24.1	21.1	18.3	21.0
Malaysia	24.4	25.0	25.8	24.7	23.2	21.7	20.0	19.0	...
Myanmar[d]	...	...	14.2	14.4	16.4	16.2	14.7	13.7	...
Philippines	16.9	15.8	16.4	16.1	15.6	16.7	17.4	17.9	...
Singapore[d]	9.3	7.9	9.0	9.2	10.9	13.8	13.5	12.8	...
Thailand[g]	21.3	21.9	21.2	21.6	22.0	21.9	21.1	21.2	21.2
Viet Nam[h]	27.2	25.4	28.2	28.8	26.4	28.2	28.7	29.2	29.2
The Pacific									
Cook Islands[c]	35.5	31.0	35.7	28.0	41.7	47.5	37.8	30.1	...
Fiji	27.0	27.3	27.0	26.9	28.4	29.4	28.0	26.5	...
Kiribati[c]	...	71.3	74.5	71.9	67.4	71.7	78.3	87.4	...
Marshall Islands[g]	59.8	54.9	51.5	52.8	55.8	55.2	57.9	65.5	...
Micronesia, Federated States of[g]	67.2	65.4	65.3	59.8	54.5	55.9	61.8	64.5	...
Nauru[c]	83.6	...	44.7	57.4	51.8	72.3	91.6	99.9	94.5
Niue	...	...	...	...	...	...	...	...	...
Palau[g]	...	...	...	...	...	...	...	...	...
Papua New Guinea	...	...	...	...	...	...	...	17.6	19.6
Samoa[c]	...	...	38.3	35.7	40.8	35.7	31.9	34.7	...
Solomon Islands	29.1	34.4	37.9	40.2	39.9	43.7	42.9	42.1	39.3
Timor-Leste	...	...	...	18.9	33.1	43.2	65.0	46.9	...
Tonga[c]	...	...	...	...	...	...	23.4	18.2	26.8
Tuvalu	...	...	92.0	93.3	106.7	117.0	121.9	...	...
Vanuatu	...	...	23.4	21.6	22.2	24.2	28.4	29.1	...
Developed ADB Member Economies									
Australia[c]	37.8	36.5	36.7	36.4	36.6	37.2	37.4	36.9	36.7
Japan[d]	39.1	40.4	40.2	40.4	39.8	39.0	38.8	38.5	...
New Zealand[c]	40.3	45.7	39.4	39.7	37.7	37.7	37.0	36.4	36.2

... = data not available, | = marks break in series, ADB = Asian Development Bank, GDP = gross domestic product.

a   In general, economies follow the guidelines of the International Monetary Fund on Government Finance Statistics (GFS). Some economies still use the 1986 version of the GFS guidelines, while others have switched to the 2001 or 2014 guidelines. The comparability of the data in this table is limited by variations in the concepts and definitions used in different versions of the GFS framework. Data refer to government expenditure as classified in the GFS 2001 or GFS 2014 framework, except for Bhutan; Brunei Darussalam; India, Maldives; Nauru; Pakistan; the People's Republic of China; Taipei,China; Tajikistan; Turkmenistan; and Viet Nam, where data refer to total government expenditure as classified in the GFS 1986 framework. Data refer to general government, except for Bangladesh; Bhutan; Brunei Darussalam; Cambodia; the Cook Islands; the Federated States of Micronesia; Fiji; India; the Lao People's Democratic Republic; Malaysia; Maldives; the Marshall Islands; Nauru; Nepal; Palau; the Philippines; Solomon Islands; Sri Lanka; Taipei,China; Timor-Leste; Tonga; Tuvalu; Vanuatu; and Viet Nam, where data refer to central government. For Azerbaijan: Data are based on the state budget. For Cambodia: Data refer to central government excluding extra budgetary central government. For the Kyrgyz Republic: For 2010–2013, data refer to central government. For Pakistan: Data refer to the consolidated federal and provincial governments. For the People's Republic of China: Data refer to consolidated central and local governments. For Turkmenistan: For 2010, data refer to central government.
b   For 2005–2011, GFS data are based on fiscal year beginning 21 March. For 2012, data cover 9 months from 21 March to 20 December. For 2013 onward, data are based on fiscal year ending 20 December. National accounts data for 2005–2017 are based on fiscal year beginning 21 March, and for 2018 on fiscal year ending 20 December.
c   Data are based on fiscal year ending 30 June.
d   Data are based on fiscal year beginning 1 April.
e   Data are based on fiscal year ending 15 July.
f   For 2005 onward, data are based on fiscal year beginning 1 April. Data are derived as excess of revenue over expenditure (ordinary plus charged) less the sum of contribution to a development fund, contribution to a government trust fund, and capital and currency adjustments.
g   Data are based on fiscal year ending 30 September.
h   Taxes include local government taxes.

Sources: Economy sources. For Fiji; Hong Kong, China; Kiribati (2011–2013 and 2017); the Kyrgyz Republic; Nepal; and Sri Lanka (2010–2013): International Monetary Fund. Government Finance Statistics. https://data.imf.org/ (accessed May–June 2019). For Nauru: International Monetary Fund. Staff Country Reports. Republic of Nauru: 2017 Article IV. http://www.imf.org/en/Publications/CR/Issues/2017/04/03/Republic-of-Nauru-2017-Article-IV-Consultation-Press-Release-Staff-Report-and-Statement-by-44794 (accessed 6 June 2019).

Table 2.8.5: Government Expenditure by Economic Activity[a]
(% of GDP)

ADB Regional Member	Health			Education			Social Protection		
	2010	2015	2018	2010	2015	2018	2010	2015	2018
Developing ADB Member Economies									
Central and West Asia									
Afghanistan[b]	1.7	1.2	1.7	4.4	3.5	3.2	1.3	1.4	2.2
Armenia	1.6	1.7	1.3	3.2	2.9	2.5	7.1	7.7	7.0
Azerbaijan	1.0	1.3	0.9	2.8	3.0	2.5	2.6	3.4	2.7
Georgia	2.2	2.9	3.0	2.9	3.4	3.8	6.9	7.8	7.1
Kazakhstan	2.5	2.1	2.6 (2017)	3.5	3.3	3.4 (2017)	4.5	4.5	4.7 (2017)
Kyrgyz Republic	2.8 |	3.5	3.4 (2017)	2.1 |	7.0	7.2 (2017)	4.8 |	10.8	10.0 (2017)
Pakistan	...	...	...	...	...	...	...	...	...
Tajikistan	1.4	2.1	2.2	4.0	5.2	5.6	3.5	5.4	4.5
Turkmenistan	...	...	...	...	...	...	...	...	...
Uzbekistan	...	2.5	2.3	...	6.0	5.4	...	7.4	6.3
East Asia									
China, People's Republic of	1.2	1.7	1.7	3.0	3.8	3.6	2.2	2.8	3.0
Hong Kong, China[c]	2.4	3.2	2.9 (2017)	3.5	3.4	3.5 (2017)	2.4	2.9	2.8 (2017)
Korea, Republic of	0.2	0.3	0.2 (2017)	2.8	3.0	3.2 (2017)	4.3	5.3	5.4 (2017)
Mongolia	2.5	2.5	2.5	5.1	3.0	2.8	11.1	7.6	7.4
Taipei,China	0.2	0.1	0.1 (2017)	1.7	1.5	1.5 (2017)	3.1	3.3	3.4 (2017)
South Asia									
Bangladesh[d]	0.8	0.7	0.3 (2017)	2.0	2.0	2.5 (2017)	0.9	0.7	0.8 (2017)
Bhutan[d]	3.0	2.6	2.8	6.7	5.5	6.2	3.1	3.0	1.9
India[c]	1.0 (2011)	1.2	1.3 (2016)	4.4 (2011)	4.4	4.6 (2016)	1.4 (2011)	1.8	1.8 (2016)
Maldives	3.0	3.5	...	5.0	4.7	...	1.7	5.2	...
Nepal[e]	1.5	1.4	1.7 (2017)	3.9	3.7	4.1 (2017)	0.8	0.7	1.4 (2017)
Sri Lanka	1.2	1.6	1.5 (2017)	1.6	2.1	1.9 (2017)	1.7	2.6	2.0 (2017)
Southeast Asia									
Brunei Darussalam[c]	1.8	...	...	3.6	...	...	0.8	...	...
Cambodia	1.3	1.3	1.2	1.6	2.0	2.5	0.5	0.8	0.9
Indonesia	1.0	1.1	1.4 (2017)	3.4	3.3	2.7 (2017)	0.1	0.3	1.2 (2017)
Lao People's Democratic Republic	...	...	...	...	...	...	...	...	...
Malaysia	2.0	2.0	1.9 (2017)	6.1	4.8	4.4 (2017)	...	...	...
Myanmar[c]	0.7 (2012)	1.0	0.8 (2017)	1.5 (2012)	2.1	1.8 (2017)	0.4 (2012)	0.8	0.8 (2017)
Philippines[f]	0.3	0.8	1.0	2.5	2.9	4.1	1.7	1.4	2.6
Singapore[c]	1.2	2.1	2.2 (2017)	3.0	2.9	2.8 (2017)	1.1	1.8	1.0 (2017)
Thailand[g]	...	1.1	1.3	...	3.8	3.1	...	2.5	3.0
Viet Nam	...	...	...	...	...	...	...	...	...
The Pacific									
Cook Islands[d]	3.9	3.0	2.7 (2017)	4.0	3.5	2.7 (2017)	3.9	4.2	3.7 (2017)
Fiji	...	...	...	...	...	...	...	...	...
Kiribati[d]	...	9.9	11.2 (2017)	...	9.9	11.0 (2017)	...	1.4	1.3 (2017)
Marshall Islands[g]	7.8	7.6	12.0 (2017)	19.6	16.7	15.5 (2017)	–	–	3.6 (2017)
Micronesia, Federated States of	...	...	...	...	...	...	...	...	...
Nauru	...	...	...	...	...	...	...	...	...
Niue	...	...	...	...	...	...	...	...	...
Palau	...	...	...	...	...	...	...	...	...
Papua New Guinea	...	...	...	...	...	...	...	...	...
Samoa[d]	3.6	5.4	3.8	5.8	4.5	4.5	1.1	2.1	1.2
Solomon Islands	...	...	...	...	...	...	...	...	...
Timor-Leste	0.9	1.9	2.2 (2017)	1.7	3.4	3.8 (2017)	3.6	6.0	6.2 (2017)
Tonga	...	...	...	...	...	...	...	...	...
Tuvalu	8.5 (2012)	9.4	9.6 (2016)	16.0 (2012)	23.2	20.4 (2016)	6.1 (2012)	18.3	9.1 (2016)
Vanuatu	2.9 (2011)	2.4	2.1 (2017)	6.2 (2011)	5.4	5.6 (2017)	0.0 (2011)	0.1	0.0 (2017)
Developed ADB Member Economies									
Australia[d]	6.7	6.8	7.0	5.9	5.4	5.4	9.9	10.4	9.6
Japan[c]	6.9	7.4	7.4 (2017)	2.8	2.6	2.5 (2017)	2.2	2.5	2.6 (2017)
New Zealand[d]	7.0	6.9	6.6	6.8	6.3	5.7	12.5	11.5	10.6

... = data not available, – = magnitude equals zero, 0.0 = magnitude is less than half of unit employed, ADB = Asian Development Bank, GDP = gross domestic product.

a In general, economies follow the guidelines of the International Monetary Fund on Government Finance Statistics (GFS). Some economies still use the 1986 version of the guidelines, while others have switched to the 2001 or 2014 guidelines. The comparability of the data in this table is limited by variations in the concepts and definitions used in different versions of the GFS framework. The table refers to government expenditure by economic activity as classified in the GFS 2001 or GFS 2014 framework, except for Bhutan; Brunei Darussalam; Maldives; the People's Republic of China; and Taipei,China, where data refer to health, education, and social security and welfare, as classified in the GFS 1986 framework. Data refer to general government, except for Bangladesh; Bhutan; Brunei Darussalam; Cambodia; the Cook Islands; Malaysia; Maldives; the Marshall Islands; Nepal; the People's Republic of China; the Philippines; Samoa; Sri Lanka; Taipei,China; Timor-Leste; Tuvalu; and Vanuatu, where data refer to central government. For the Kyrgyz Republic: Data for 2010–2013 refer to expenditure of the budgetary central government, while data for 2014 onward refer to expenditure of the general government.
b For 2005–2011, GFS data are based on fiscal year beginning 21 March. For 2012, data cover 9 months from 21 March to 20 December. For 2013 onward, data are based on fiscal year ending 20 December. National accounts data for 2005–2017 are based on fiscal year beginning 21 March, and for 2018 on fiscal year ending 20 December.
c Data are based on fiscal year beginning 1 April.
d Data are based on fiscal year ending 30 June.
e Data are based on fiscal year ending 15 July.
f For 2000–2013, data on education include expenditure on recreation, culture, and religion.
g Data are based on fiscal year ending 30 September.

Source: Economy sources.

Table 2.8.6: Indicators for Business Startups

ADB Regional Member	Cost of Business Startup Procedure (% of GNI per capita)			Time Required to Start Business (days)		
	2005	2010	2018	2005	2010	2018
Developing ADB Member Economies						
Central and West Asia[a]	**28.0**	**11.3**	**4.5**	**40.1**	**12.9**	**7.1**
Afghanistan	75.2	26.7	6.4	9.5	9.5	8.5
Armenia	6.1	3.1	0.8	18.0	14.0	3.5
Azerbaijan	12.3	3.1	1.3	113.0	8.0	3.5
Georgia	13.7	5.0	2.2	21.0	3.0	2.0
Kazakhstan	9.9	1.0	0.3	31.0	25.0	5.0
Kyrgyz Republic	10.4	3.7	1.9	21.0	14.0	10.0
Pakistan	...	...	6.8	...	...	16.5
Tajikistan	85.1	36.9	18.0	79.0	16.0	11.0
Turkmenistan	...	...	...	...	...	...
Uzbekistan	11.5	10.8	3.1	28.0	14.0	4.0
East Asia[a]	**8.3**	**6.0**	**3.9**	**27.5**	**13.0**	**7.0**
China, People's Republic of	...	...	0.4	...	...	8.6
Hong Kong, China	3.4	2.0	1.1	11.0	6.0	1.5
Korea, Republic of	15.7	14.7	14.6	17.0	14.0	4.0
Mongolia	9.6	3.2	1.3	17.0	17.0	11.0
Taipei,China	4.4	4.0	1.9	65.0	15.0	10.0
South Asia[a]	**37.7**	**24.0**	**12.5**	**37.0**	**31.8**	**14.3**
Bangladesh	...	...	21.2	...	...	19.5
Bhutan	16.9	6.1	3.5	62.0	46.0	12.0
India	...	...	14.4	...	...	16.5
Maldives	14.0	9.4	4.0	9.0	12.0	12.0
Nepal	69.9	46.6	22.2	31.0	31.0	16.5
Sri Lanka	50.0	33.9	9.4	46.0	38.0	9.0
Southeast Asia[a]	**50.9**	**41.4**	**12.7**	**63.8**	**55.6**	**38.0**
Brunei Darussalam	8.9 (2006)	13.6	1.2	121.5 (2006)	108.5	5.5
Cambodia	276.1	127.5	47.4	87.0	102.0	99.0
Indonesia	...	...	6.1	...	...	19.6
Lao People's Democratic Republic	25.6	13.3	6.6	135.0	86.0	174.0
Malaysia	26.6	17.5	11.6	37.5	17.5	13.5
Myanmar	...	157.7 (2012)	24.8	...	77.0 (2012)	14.0
Philippines	23.9	22.1	20.3	47.0	37.0	31.0
Singapore	0.9	0.7	0.4	6.0	2.5	1.5
Thailand	17.3	7.7	3.1	35.0	34.0	4.5
Viet Nam	27.6	12.1	5.9	41.0	36.0	17.0
The Pacific[a]	**59.4**	**37.1**	**28.4**	**47.3**	**39.5**	**21.6**
Cook Islands	...	...	...	...	...	...
Fiji	28.4	23.8	15.9	44.0	44.0	40.0
Kiribati	40.3	47.1	36.1	31.0	31.0	31.0
Marshall Islands	22.4	17.6	10.6	17.0	17.0	17.0
Micronesia, Federated States of	127.6	137.8	141.7	16.0	16.0	16.0
Nauru	...	...	...	...	...	...
Niue	...	...	...	...	...	...
Palau	4.7	5.7	2.9	24.0	28.0	28.0
Papua New Guinea	27.7	27.0	20.5	52.0	52.0	41.0
Samoa	46.4	9.8	7.3	35.0	9.0	9.1
Solomon Islands	135.5	78.5	28.1	55.0	55.0	9.0
Timor-Leste	125.4	5.7	0.6	167.0	110.0	13.0
Tonga	11.7	7.0	6.5	32.0	25.0	16.0
Tuvalu	...	...	...	...	...	...
Vanuatu	83.5	48.2	42.0	47.0	47.0	18.0
Developed ADB Member Economies[a]	**1.1**	**0.6**	**2.8**	**7.5**	**1.5**	**4.7**
Australia	1.9	0.7	0.7	3.0	2.5	2.5
Japan	...	...	7.5	...	...	11.2
New Zealand	0.2	0.4	0.2	12.0	0.5	0.5
DEVELOPING ADB MEMBER ECONOMIES[a]	**42.0**	**27.5**	**14.0**	**46.0**	**33.8**	**19.6**
ALL ADB REGIONAL MEMBERS[a]	**39.7**	**26.1**	**13.2**	**43.9**	**32.1**	**18.6**
WORLD	**84.5**	**45.1**	**23.9**	**50.7**	**35.7**	**20.1**

... = data not available, ADB = Asian Development Bank, GNI = gross national income.

a   Arithmetic average of reporting economies only.

Source: World Bank. Doing Business Online. http://data.worldbank.org/indicator (accessed 9 July 2019).

Governance

Table 2.8.7:   Corruption Perceptions Index[a]

ADB Regional Member	2000	2005	2010	2012	2013	2014	2015	2016	2017	2018	Rank in 2017[b]	Rank in 2018[b]
Developing ADB Member Economies												
Central and West Asia												
Afghanistan	...	2.5	1.4 |	8	8	12	11	15	15	16	177	172
Armenia	2.5	2.9	2.6 |	34	36	37	35	33	35	35	107	105
Azerbaijan	1.5	2.2	2.4 |	27	28	29	29	30	31	25	122	152
Georgia	2.4 (2002)	2.3	3.8 |	52	49	52	52	57	56	58	46	41
Kazakhstan	3.0	2.6	2.9 |	28	26	29	28	29	31	31	122	124
Kyrgyz Republic	...	2.3	2.0 |	24	24	27	28	28	29	29	135	132
Pakistan	2.3 (2001)	2.1	2.3 |	27	28	29	30	32	32	33	117	117
Tajikistan	...	2.1	2.1 |	22	22	23	26	25	21	25	161	152
Turkmenistan	...	1.8	1.6 |	17	17	17	18	22	19	20	167	161
Uzbekistan	2.4	2.2	1.6 |	17	17	18	19	21	22	23	157	158
East Asia												
China, People's Republic of	3.1	3.2	3.5 |	39	40	36	37	40	41	39	77	87
Hong Kong, China	7.7	8.3	8.4 |	77	75	74	75	77	77	76	13	14
Korea, Republic of	4.0	5.0	5.4 |	56	55	55	56	53	54	57	51	45
Mongolia	...	3.0	2.7 |	36	38	39	39	38	36	37	103	93
Taipei,China	5.5	5.9	5.8 |	61	61	61	62	61	63	63	29	31
South Asia												
Bangladesh	0.4 (2001)	1.7	2.4 |	26	27	25	25	26	28	26	143	149
Bhutan	...	6.0 (2006)	5.7 |	63	63	65	65	65	67	68	26	25
India	2.8	2.9	3.3 |	36	36	38	38	40	40	41	81	78
Maldives	...	3.3 (2007)	2.3 |	...	...	...	...	36	33	31	112	124
Nepal	...	2.5	2.2 |	27	31	29	27	29	31	31	122	124
Sri Lanka	3.7 (2002)	3.2	3.2 |	40	37	38	37	36	38	38	91	89
Southeast Asia												
Brunei Darussalam	...	...	5.5 |	55	60	...	...	58	62	63	32	31
Cambodia	...	2.3	2.1 |	22	20	21	21	21	21	20	161	161
Indonesia	1.7	2.2	2.8 |	32	32	34	36	37	37	38	96	89
Lao People's Democratic Republic	...	3.3	2.1 |	21	26	25	25	30	29	29	135	132
Malaysia	4.8	5.1	4.4 |	49	50	52	50	49	47	47	62	61
Myanmar	...	1.8	1.4 |	15	21	21	22	28	30	29	130	132
Philippines	2.8	2.5	2.4 |	34	36	38	35	35	34	36	111	99
Singapore	9.1	9.4	9.3 |	87	86	84	85	84	84	85	6	3
Thailand	3.2	3.8	3.5 |	37	35	38	38	35	37	36	96	99
Viet Nam	2.5	2.6	2.7 |	31	31	31	31	33	35	33	107	117
The Pacific												
Cook Islands	...	...	...	...	...	...	...	...	...	...	...	...
Fiji	...	4.0	...	...	...	...	...	...	...	...	...	...
Kiribati	...	3.3 (2007)	3.2 |	...	...	...	...	...	...	...	...	...
Marshall Islands	...	...	...	...	...	...	...	...	...	...	...	...
Micronesia, Federated States of	...	...	...	...	...	...	...	...	...	...	...	...
Nauru	...	...	...	...	...	...	...	...	...	...	...	...
Niue	...	...	...	...	...	...	...	...	...	...	...	...
Palau	...	...	...	...	...	...	...	...	...	...	...	...
Papua New Guinea	...	2.3	2.1 |	25	25	25	25	28	29	28	135	138
Samoa	...	4.5 (2007)	4.1 |	...	...	52	...	...	...	...	...	...
Solomon Islands	...	2.8 (2007)	2.8 |	...	...	...	...	42	39	44	85	70
Timor-Leste	...	2.6 (2006)	2.5 |	33	30	28	28	35	38	35	91	105
Tonga	...	1.7 (2007)	3.0 |	...	...	...	...	...	...	...	...	...
Tuvalu	...	...	...	...	...	...	...	...	...	...	...	...
Vanuatu	...	3.1 (2007)	3.6 |	...	...	...	...	...	43	46	71	64
Developed ADB Member Economies												
Australia	8.3	8.8	8.7 |	85	81	80	79	79	77	77	13	13
Japan	6.4	7.3	7.8 |	74	74	76	75	72	73	73	20	18
New Zealand	9.4	9.6	9.3 |	90	91	91	88	90	89	87	1	2

... = data not available, | = marks break in the series, ADB = Asian Development Bank.

a   For 2000–2011, scores relate to perceptions of the degree of corruption as seen by business people and country analysts, and are not comparable over time; scores range from 0 (highly corrupt) to 10 (very clean). From 2012 onward, an updated methodology was used to calculate scores, and these are presented on a scale from 0 (highly corrupt) to 100 (very clean). Due to the differences in methodology, scores prior to 2012 should not be compared with scores from 2012 onward.

b   Based on the Transparency International Index, an economy's rank indicates its position relative to the Corruption Perceptions Index of other economies of the world; 2017 and 2018 rankings compare 180 economies.

Source: Transparency International. Corruption Perception Index 2018. https://www.transparency.org/cpi2018 (accessed 23 May 2019).

References

ADB. 2013. *Asian Development Outlook 2013*. Manila.

ADB. 2018. *Key Indicators for Asia and the Pacific 2018*. Manila.

ADB. 2019. *Asian Development Outlook 2019: Strengthening Disaster Reliance*. Manila.

International Civil Aviation Organization (ICAO). 2017. *The World of Air Transport 2017*. Montreal. https://www.icao.int/annual-report-2017/Pages/the-world-of-air-transport-in-2017.aspx.

International Telecommunications Union (ITU). 2017. *ICT Facts and Figures 2017*. Geneva. https://www.itu.int/en/ITU-D/Statistics/Documents/facts/ICTFactsFigures2017.pdf.

UN. 2016. *Energy Statistics Compilers Manual*. New York.

UN. 2019a. Department of Economic and Social Affairs, Population Division. *World Population Prospects, 2019 Revision*. New York. https://population.un.org/wpp/Publications/Files/WPP2019_Highlights.pdf.

UN. 2019b. Conference on Trade and Development. *World Investment Report 2019*. Geneva.

World Bank. 2019a. *Migration and Development Brief 31*. Washington, DC.

World Bank. 2019b. *Doing Business 2019: Training for Reform*. Washington, DC. https://www.worldbank.org/content/dam/doingBusiness/media/Annual-Reports/English/DB2019-report_web-version.pdf.

PART III

Global Value Chains

The Evolving Dynamics of Domestic Value-Added in Asia

Snapshot

- Domestic value-added via forward linkages measures the amount of domestic value-added that is generated from the production of total exports. It can be used to describe the evolving dynamics of production networks within Asia and the Pacific.

- The share of domestic value-added flowing to and from Asia increased from 2000 to 2018, highlighting the increasing role of the region as a source of, and destination for, domestic value-added. Meanwhile, Asia's connection to North America, as measured by domestic value-added flows, had diminished by 2018.

- Intraregional trade matters for Asia, with the region retaining up to 33.5% of its generated domestic value-added within its own economies in 2018. This share of intraregional outflows is equivalent to 39.0% of total value-added inflows to Asia.

- While dynamics vary by sector, by 2018, the People's Republic of China had surpassed other subregions and individual economies as Asia's source hub for intraregional domestic value-added outflows when considering all sectors. Meanwhile, Southeast Asia plus Fiji emerged as the region's largest destination for intraregional domestic value-added inflows.

Global value chain (GVC) statistics have been included in *Key Indicators for Asia and the Pacific* (*Key Indicators*) since 2015. This flagship publication began by highlighting the GVC statistics of 11 Asian economies and covered the years 2000, 2005, and 2011. In *Key Indicators 2016*, the GVC statistical assessment expanded to 13 Asian economies and covered 2008 and 2015, while the 2017 edition embraced 23 economies of the Asia and Pacific region and covered 2014–2016. In *Key Indicators 2018*, GVC statistics were presented for 25 economies from across the region, assessing the years 2010 and 2017.

Across its first 4 years, the GVC chapter of *Key Indicators* has featured some insightful analyses of the importance of value chains to international trade and commerce. *Key Indicators 2015* documented the exponential growth in trade in intermediates in 11 Asian economies, while the 2016 edition discussed the increasing localization of production in 13 Asian economies. *Key Indicators 2017* emphasized the increase in the domestic content in exports as a mitigating factor to the global trade slowdown. A year later, in *Key Indicators 2018,* some stylized facts were presented to highlight the participation of Asian economies in GVCs, using the decomposition developed by Wang, Wei, and Zhu (2018). It presented variations in forward and backward GVC participation across economies, across sectors, and over time.

In 2019, *Key Indicators* utilizes domestic value-added via forward linkages (DVA_F) to discuss the evolution of global value chains in Asia. DVA_F measures the amount of domestic value-added that is generated from the production of total exports (Wang, Wei, and Zhu 2018). The discussion encompasses 25 economies of Asia and the Pacific included in the 2019 release of the ADB multi-regional input-output tables (MRIOTs), and covers 2000 and 2007–2018. The MRIOTs provide a 35-sector breakdown for each economy. However, for simplicity, the analysis in this chapter aggregates results into 5 major sectors.[1]

---

[1] The data presented in this Part III are not official statistics. Production and trade data from various sources were integrated into the input–output economic analysis framework and adjusted as required to conform to specific macroeconomic concepts. As such, data and statistics presented here could differ from relevant official statistics.

Asia's Role in Sending and Receiving Domestic Value-Added in Exports

Figure 3.1.1 uses DVA_F to shed light on Asia's role as a source of, and destination for, domestic value-added generated in exports production across the world.

A growing share of the world's total DVA_F is from Asia. In 2000, Asia's share in the world's total DVA_F was 23.0%. At 35.7%, Japan was the largest contributor to Asia's domestic value-added generation, followed by the People's Republic of China (PRC), which contributed 16.8% of Asia's total. From 2001 to 2018, Asia's share in the world's total DVA_F increased to 30.2%. Additionally, the PRC overtook Japan as the leading source of DVA_F in Asia. By 2018, the PRC was generating 44.2% of Asia's total DVA_F, while only 13.8% of that total was generated in Japan.

Likewise, Asia's role as a destination for DVA_F has also grown. In 2000, less than 19.7% of total world DVA_F went to Asia. By 2018, this share had grown to 26.0%. Of the total domestic value-added that was sent to Asia in 2000, 28.7% went to Japan, while only 14.2% went to the PRC. In 2018, by contrast, the PRC was the biggest destination for DVA_F in Asia, receiving 32.8% of the region's total. Japan was the second largest single destination for DVA_F sent to Asia, receiving 15.3% of the total.

Figure 3.1.1 also shows that Asia plays a larger role as an exporter of value-added than as an importer of value-added. Across all years, in 2000 and 2007–2018, the share of world DVA_F generated in Asia is bigger than the share of world DVA_F that is sent to Asia.

Figure 3.1.1: Asia's Role in the Global Transfer of Domestic Value-Added in Exports

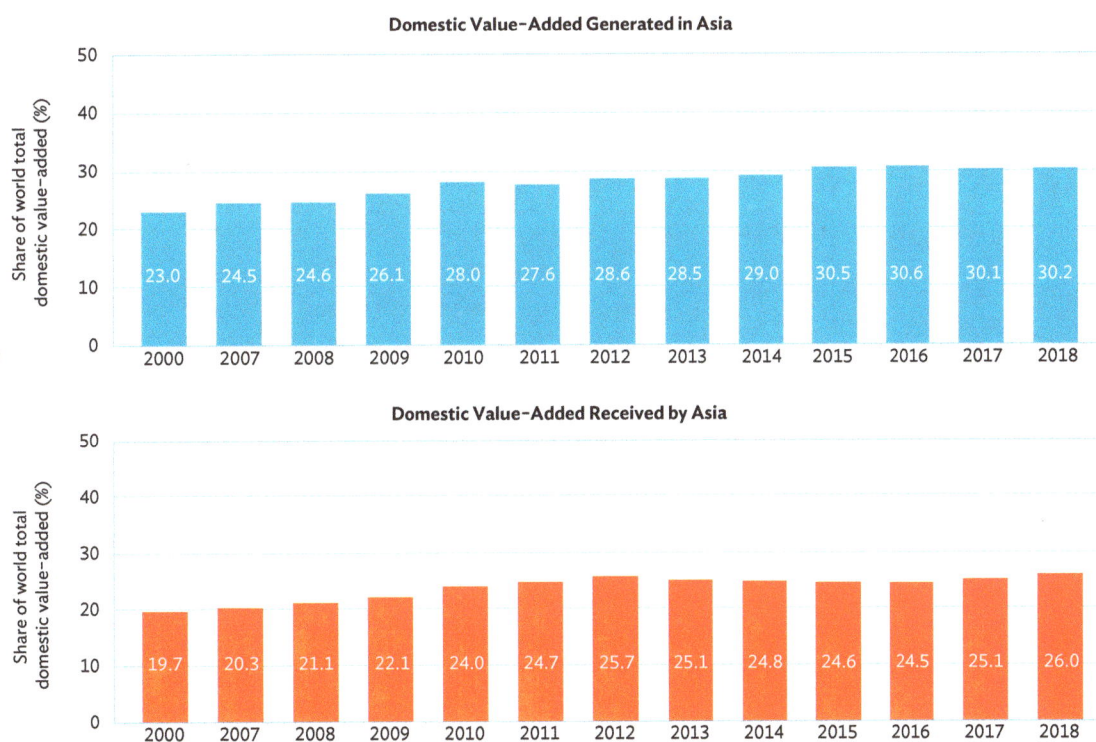

Domestic Value–Added Generated in Asia

Year	Share of world total domestic value-added (%)
2000	23.0
2007	24.5
2008	24.6
2009	26.1
2010	28.0
2011	27.6
2012	28.6
2013	28.5
2014	29.0
2015	30.5
2016	30.6
2017	30.1
2018	30.2

Domestic Value–Added Received by Asia

Year	Share of world total domestic value-added (%)
2000	19.7
2007	20.3
2008	21.1
2009	22.1
2010	24.0
2011	24.7
2012	25.7
2013	25.1
2014	24.8
2015	24.6
2016	24.5
2017	25.1
2018	26.0

Source: Asian Development Bank estimates based on Wang, Wei, and Zhu (2018) using Asian Development Bank Multi–Regional Input–Output Tables (2000, 2007–2018).

Where Does Asia's Domestic Value-Added Go?

The first part of Figure 3.1.2 shows domestic value-added generated in Asia's production of exports, and breaks it down by destination.

A large proportion of DVA_F originating from Asia flows to economies within the region. The share of Asia's total DVA_F that is sent within Asia has been fairly stable, from 32.0% in 2000 to 33.5% in 2018. The share of DVA_F from Asia that goes to Europe has also been stable at 15.4% in 2000 and 16.4% by 2018.

On the other hand, significant changes can be seen in the shares of domestic value-added flowing from Asia to North America (defined here as the United States and Canada) and to the rest of the world (defined here as economies in the ADB MRIOTs that are not in Asia, Europe, or North America). The proportion of DVA_F sent from Asia to North America decreased substantially, from 21.3% in 2000 to 13.4% in 2018. Meanwhile, the proportion of Asia's total DVA_F that was sent to the rest of the world grew from 31.3% in 2000 to 36.7% in 2018.

Figure 3.1.2: Transfer of Domestic Value-Added in Exports by Region

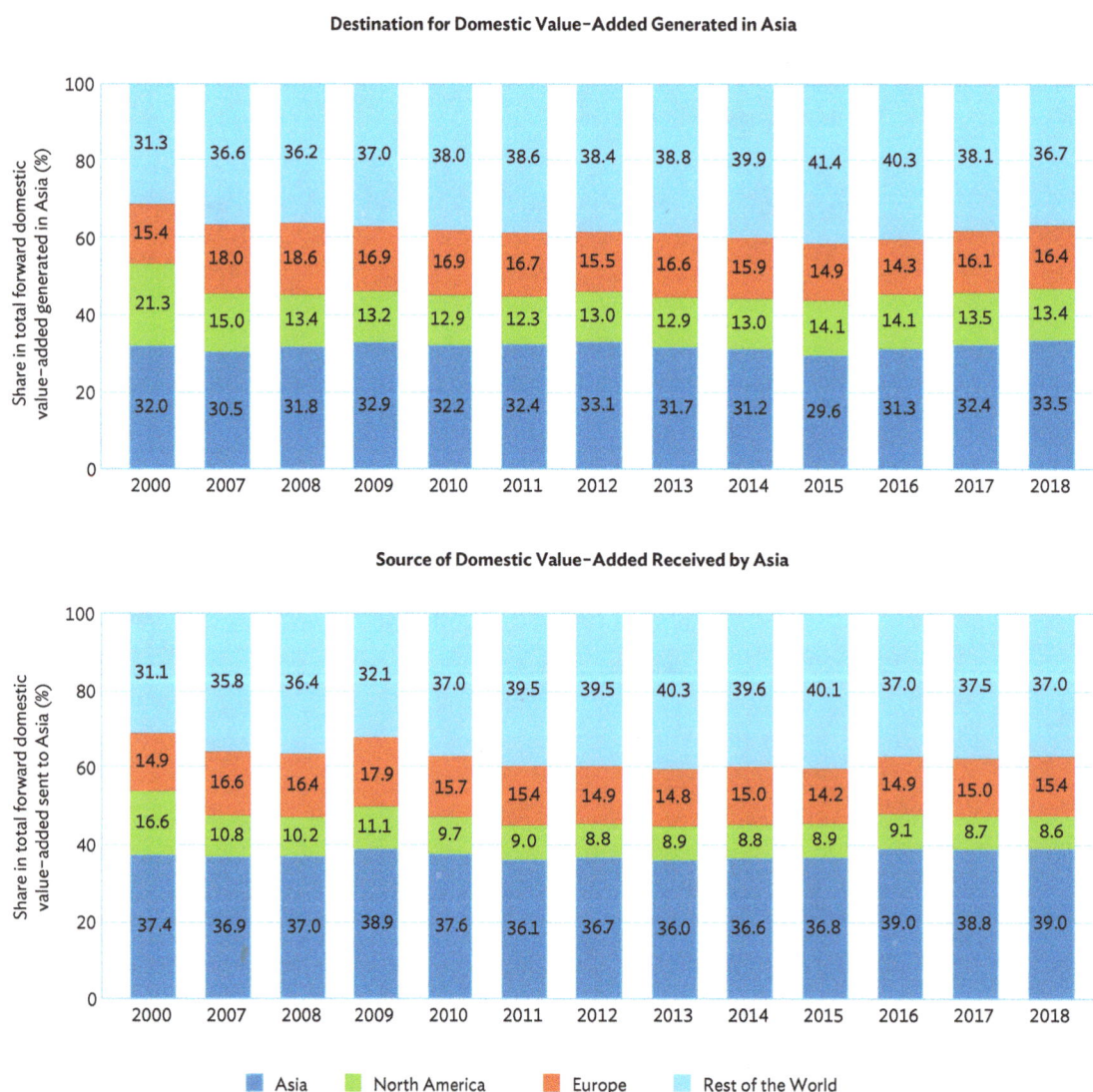

Destination for Domestic Value-Added Generated in Asia

Source of Domestic Value-Added Received by Asia

Legend: ■ Asia ■ North America ■ Europe ■ Rest of the World

Source: Asian Development Bank estimates based on Wang, Wei, and Zhu (2018) using Asian Development Bank Multi-Regional Input-Output Tables (2000, 2007–2018).

Where Does the Domestic Value-Added Received by Asia Come From?

The second part of Figure 3.1.2 presents domestic value-added in exports sent to Asia, and breaks it down by source.

The largest sources of domestic value-added sent to Asia are Asia itself and economies across the rest of the world. By 2018, the share of DVA_F received by Asia from within Asia was 39.0%, while the share from the rest of the world was 37.4%. The share of domestic value-added sent to Asia from within Asia remained fairly stable over the period assessed, ranging from a low of 36.0% in 2013 to a high of 39.0% in both 2016 and 2018. On the other hand, the share of DVA_F sent to Asia from the rest of the world has fluctuated, ranging from a low of 31.1% in 2000 to a high of 40.3% in 2013.

North America's proportion of the total domestic value-added that is sent to Asia appears to be in decline. From 16.6% in 2000, this figure fell to 8.6% in 2018. Meanwhile, Europe's contribution to domestic value-added sent to Asia remained fairly constant over the period assessed, from 14.9% in 2000 to 15.4% in 2018.

In summary, Figure 3.1.1 underlines the global importance of Asia as both a source of domestic value-added sent to other parts of the globe, and as a destination for domestic value-added generated around the world. Figure 3.1.2 highlights the declining role of North America as a destination for DVA_F generated in Asia, and as a source of DVA_F received by Asia.

The Evolving Dynamics of Domestic Value-Added within Asia

A focus on DVA_F flows within Asia can give insights into the evolving role of Asian subregions as sources of, and destinations for, intraregional DVA_F. The Sankey diagrams below are used to demonstrate how DVA_F flows from source (on the left axis) to destination (on the right axis). The sizes of the nodes are proportional to each nodes' share of total DVA_F flows. The thickness of the arcs connecting the nodes is proportional to the value of the flow of DVA_F.

For simplicity, economies in Asia have been organized into four subregions: Central & West Asia, East Asia, South Asia, and Southeast Asia plus Fiji. India, Japan, and the PRC are reported separately from the subregions to which they would otherwise belong. Central & West Asia includes Kazakhstan, the Kyrgyz Republic, and Pakistan. East Asia includes Hong Kong, China; Mongolia; the Republic of Korea; and Taipei,China. Fiji is grouped with economies from Southeast Asia, namely Brunei Darussalam, Cambodia, Indonesia, the Lao People's Democratic Republic, Malaysia, the Philippines, Singapore, Thailand, and Viet Nam. South Asia includes Bangladesh, Bhutan, Maldives, Nepal, and Sri Lanka.

Figure 3.1.3 shows that, in 2000, Japan was the largest single source of DVA_F outflows within the region, exceeding even the combined contributions of the four economies making up East Asia. In that year, 46.1% of Japan's DVA_F sent within Asia went to East Asia, 33.3% went to Southeast Asia plus Fiji, and 17.4% went to the PRC. Following Japan as sources of intraregional DVA_F in 2000 are East Asia and Southeast Asia plus Fiji, which accounted for 23.5% and 21.3% of total Asian DVA_F outflow to the region, respectively.

In terms of intraregional DVA_F inflows in 2000, East Asia was the largest destination for DVA_F from other parts of Asia, absorbing 30.0% of these inflows. Japan was the largest source of DVA_F inflows into East Asia. Southeast Asia plus Fiji came a close second as a destination for intraregional DVA_F flows. In 2000, 26.5% of intraregional DVA_F inflows went to Southeast Asia plus Fiji, with Japan also being this subregion's main source of intraregional DVA_F inflows.

Figure 3.1.3: Intraregional Flow of Asia's Domestic Value-Added Generated in Exports, All Sectors

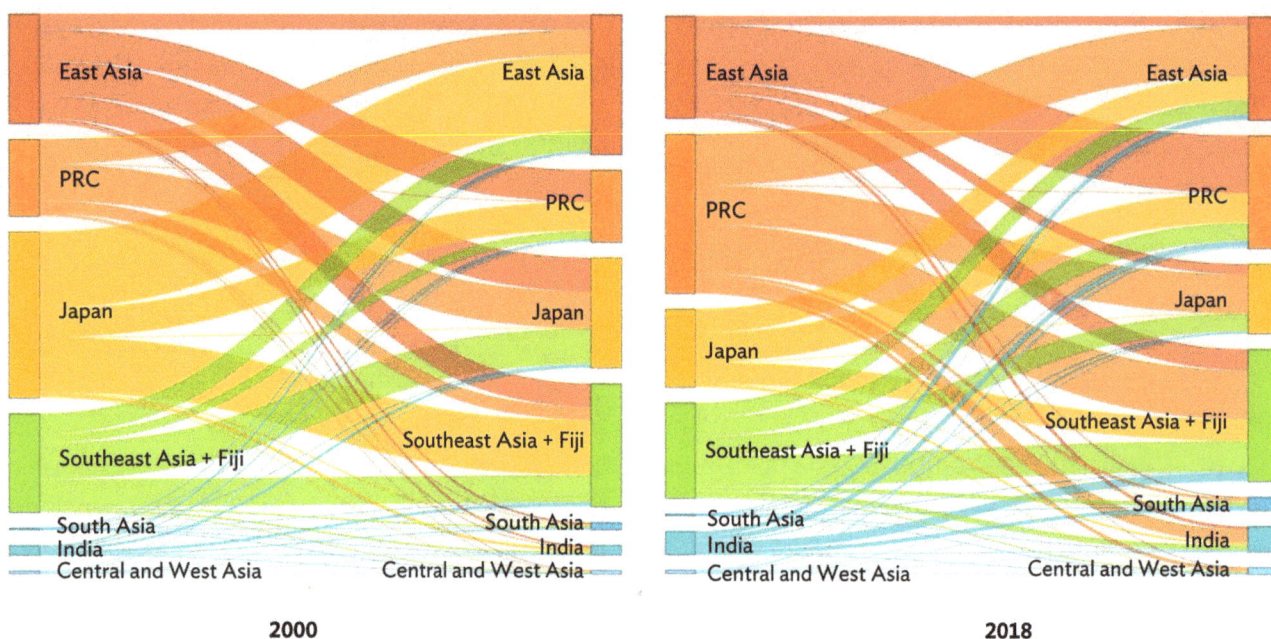

2000   2018

PRC = People's Republic of China
Source: Asian Development Bank estimates based on Wang, Wei, and Zhu (2018) using Asian Development Bank Multi-Regional Input-Output Tables
           (2000, 2007-2018).

By 2018, Asia's top source of, and destination for, intraregional DVA_F had changed. The PRC became the largest source of intraregional DVA_F, accounting for 34.4% of total DVA_F flowing within Asia. The PRC's top destination for DVA_F within the region also changed, from Japan in 2000 to East Asia and followed by Southeast Asia plus Fiji in 2018, reflecting the PRC's stronger links to the latter subregion. Moreover, data for 2018 show that India became an important intraregional destination for DVA_F from the PRC.

Meanwhile, Japan's contribution to intraregional DVA_F outflows decreased by 18.8 percentage points from 2000 to 2018. While its proportion of total intraregional DVA_F outflows stood at only 16.8% in 2018, Japan's outflows were more diversified. Southeast Asia plus Fiji and East Asia also observed smaller shares of total intraregional DVA_F outflows in 2018. India's increasing role as a source of intraregional DVA_F was also noticeable, with a large portion of its DVA_F being sent to Southeast Asia plus Fiji.

A look at the destinations for intraregional DVA_F in 2018 shows that Southeast Asia plus Fiji became the largest destination within Asia. Most intraregional DVA_F flowing into Southeast Asia plus Fiji came from the PRC, followed by Southeast Asia plus Fiji itself. While Japan was once the top source of intraregional DVA_F inflows to Southeast Asia plus Fiji, by 2018 it was only the third biggest source for that subregion. In 2018, the PRC was the second largest destination for intraregional DVA_F inflows, with 51.0% of those inflows coming from East Asia.

Overall, a comparison between 2000 and 2018 shows that the PRC has overtaken Japan as a source of, and destination for, intraregional DVA_F. Moreover, in 2018, the PRC was playing a larger role as an exporter of intraregional DVA_F than as an importer of intraregional DVA_F. Meanwhile, Southeast Asia plus Fiji has always been a larger exporter of intraregional DVA_F than an importer of intraregional DVA_F.

In summary, Asia has different hubs of intraregional DVA_F. As a source of intraregional DVA_F, the PRC emerges as the hub. In terms of destination for intraregional DVA_F, Southeast Asia plus Fiji can be defined as Asia's hub.

There are differences when looking at intraregional DVA_F flows by sector. Source and destination hubs also vary according to which sector is being examined and they change over time. Figure 3.1.4 shows results specific to the primary sector, while Figure 3.1.5 and Figure 3.1.6 show results for the low-technology industrial sector and the medium- to high-technology industrial sector, respectively. Figure 3.1.7 and Figure 3.1.8 demonstrate the flows of intraregional DVA_F for the business services sector and the personal and public services sector, respectively.

Primary sector

In 2000, Southeast Asia plus Fiji was Asia's major generator of primary sector intraregional DVA_F, accounting for 51.4% of the region's total, compared to the PRC's 30.1%. Almost half (49.9%) of the intraregional DVA_F generated in Southeast Asia plus Fiji's production of primary sector exports was sent to Japan, while 19.7% was sent to East Asia, and 16.8% was sent within the subregion. The PRC was Asia's second largest generator of primary sector intraregional DVA_F in 2000 and its main destinations within Asia were Japan (48.6%), East Asia (29.6%), and Southeast Asia plus Fiji (18.4%).

Japan was the biggest destination for primary sector intraregional DVA_F in 2000, with 46.5% of Asia's total intraregional inflows. Most primary sector intraregional DVA_F sent to Japan was generated in Southeast Asia plus Fiji and the PRC at 55.2% and 31.5%, respectively. The next two biggest destinations in 2000 were East Asia and Southeast Asia plus Fiji, with both having similar DVA_F inflow breakdowns.

By 2018, the PRC had overtaken Southeast Asia plus Fiji as Asia's largest source of intraregional DVA_F generated in primary sector exports. It generated 46.3% of intraregional DVA_F in the primary sector, of which 38.5% went to Southeast Asia plus Fiji, 26.5% went to East Asia, and 23.1% went to Japan. Meanwhile, Southeast Asia plus Fiji's primary sector DVA_F outflows had become more diversified by 2018. In 2000, almost half of its intraregional DVA_F in the primary sector was sent to Japan (49.9%), but this share has gone down to 25.3% in 2018 as increasing proportions of intraregional DVA_F generated in the subregion were sent to the subregion itself (30.8%), East Asia (16.3%) and the PRC (16.3%).

The roles of East Asia and Japan as producers also shrank in the period from 2000 to 2018, while India's role grew slightly. India exported a smaller share of its primary sector DVA_F to Japan in 2018 than in 2000, with Southeast Asia plus Fiji becoming its top intraregional destination in 2018.

Southeast Asia plus Fiji had become Asia's top destination for intraregional primary sector DVA_F by 2018, receiving 33.7% of intraregional DVA_F in the primary sector. A bulk of its inflows (52.9%) came from the PRC and 35.4% came from within the subregion itself. Japan (21.5%) and East Asia (20.4%) were the second and third biggest destinations for primary sector intraregional DVA_F inflows in 2018.

Overall, in terms of the primary sector, Asia's source hubs for intraregional DVA_F shifted from Southeast Asia plus Fiji in 2000 to the PRC in 2018, although Southeast Asia plus Fiji remained a major contributor for the region. On the other hand, the main destination hub within Asia shifted from Japan in 2000 to Southeast Asia plus Fiji in 2018.

Figure 3.1.4: Intraregional Flow of Asia's Domestic Value-Added Generated in Exports, Primary Sector

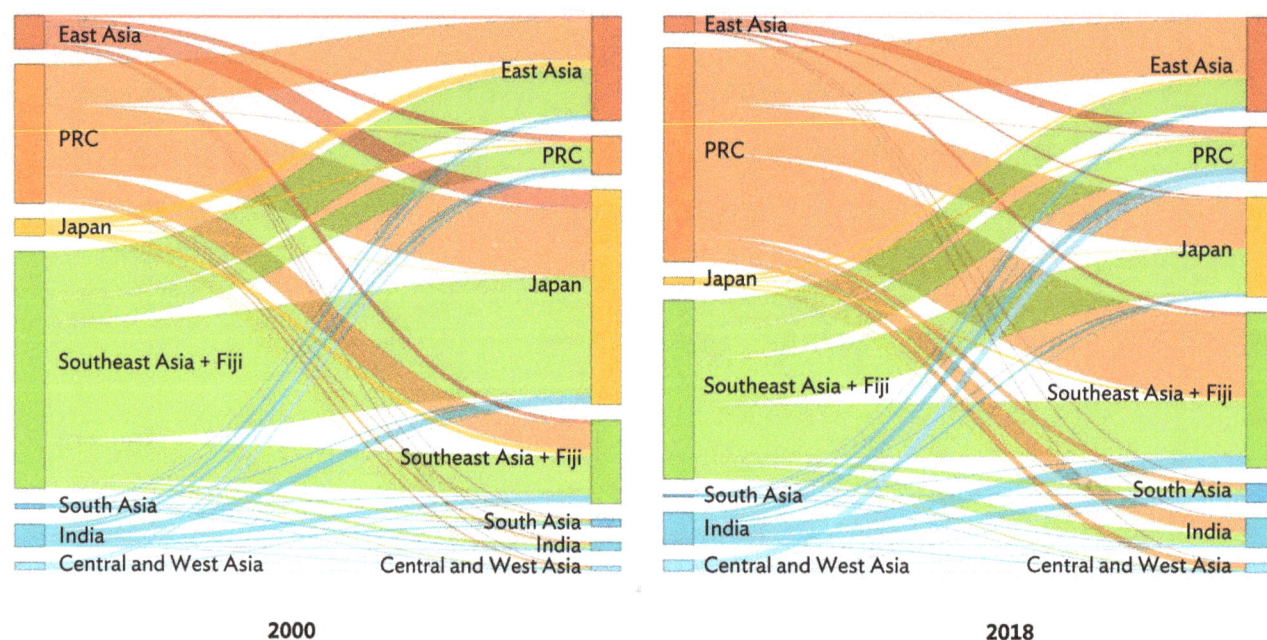

2000

2018

PRC = People's Republic of China
Source: Asian Development Bank estimates based on Wang, Wei, and Zhu (2018) using Asian Development Bank Multi-Regional Input-Output Tables
           (2000, 2007–2018).

Low-technology industrial sector

In 2000, the major sources of, and destinations for, intraregional DVA_F flows in the low-technology industrial sector were the PRC, Japan, East Asia, and Southeast Asia plus Fiji.

The sources of intraregional DVA_F generated in the sector were more or less evenly distributed in 2000, with the PRC contributing 27.8%, Japan contributing 27.4%, East Asia contributing 21.3%, and Southeast Asia plus Fiji contributing 20.3% of Asia's total. The PRC was a major source of low-technology industrial intraregional DVA_F for Japan, East Asia, and Southeast Asia plus Fiji, while Japan was a key source for East Asia, Southeast Asia plus Fiji, and the PRC. Within Asia, East Asia sent most of its low-technology DVA_F to the PRC, Japan, Southeast Asia plus Fiji, and within the subregion itself. Lastly, Southeast Asia plus Fiji's was a major source for Japan, itself, East Asia, and the PRC.

Looking at intraregional destinations for low-technology industrial DVA_F in 2000, Japan was the largest, receiving 31.5% of total intraregional inflows. Most of Japan's low-technology intraregional DVA_F at this time came from the PRC, followed by Southeast Asia plus Fiji and East Asia. Meanwhile, East Asia was the second largest intraregional destination in 2000, absorbing 26.7% of Asia's total low-technology industrial DVA_F, most of it coming from Japan.

By 2018, the PRC had emerged as Asia's source hub, generating 42.2% of low-technology industrial intraregional DVA_F and replacing Japan as the top source. Southeast Asia plus Fiji was the second largest source in 2018, generating 24.8% of the total. At the same time, the contribution of Japan and East Asia to low-technology industrial DVA_F declined considerably.

In terms of intraregional destinations in 2018, Southeast Asia plus Fiji became the largest receiver of Asia's low-technology industrial DVA_F. Other

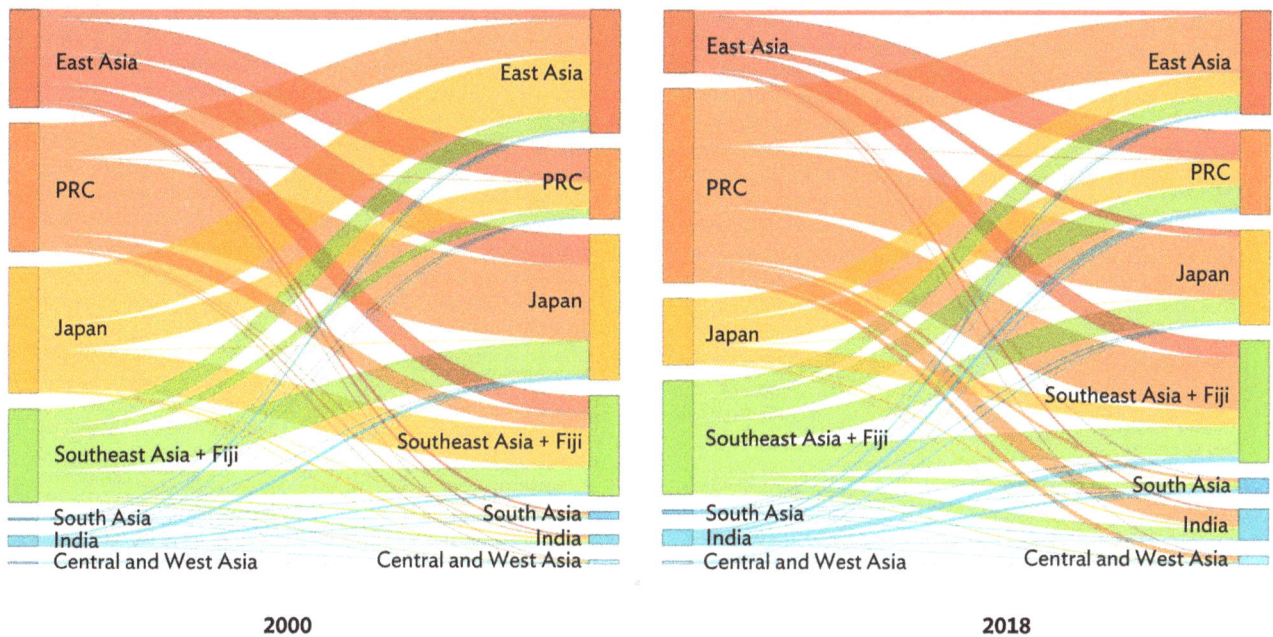

Figure 3.1.5: Intraregional Flow of Asia's Domestic Value-Added Generated in Exports, Low-Technology Industrial Sector

2000

2018

PRC = People's Republic of China
Source: Asian Development Bank estimates based on Wang, Wei, and Zhu (2018) using Asian Development Bank Multi-Regional Input-Output Tables
          (2000, 2007–2018).

noticeable changes in the low-technology industrial sector were the growth in the shares of intraregional DVA_F received by India and by economies in South Asia and Central & West Asia. The combined share of these three destinations was only at 4.6% in 2000, but it grew to 11.9% in 2018.

Medium- to high-technology industrial sector

In 2000, Asia's largest intraregional source of medium- to high-technology industrial DVA_F was by far Japan (45.3%), while its largest destination was East Asia (31.2%).

By 2018, Japan's role as the region's major source had been assumed by East Asia, with that subregion and the PRC increasing their intraregional contributions to total medium- to high-technology DVA_F generation to 32.4% and 28.8%, respectively. Japan's share had been reduced to 22.4% by that time.

From the destination perspective, over 60.0% of the sector's intraregional DVA_F in 2000 flowed into East Asia and Southeast Asia plus Fiji, while another 35.3% was received by the PRC and Japan combined. In 2018, the PRC was the region's top destination of medium- to high-technology industrial DVA_F, absorbing 33.4% of the total intraregional inflows in the sector.

For the medium- to high-technology manufacturing sector, the two largest intraregional DVA_F flows in 2000 were from Japan to East Asia and from Japan to Southeast Asia plus Fiji. These two flows made up 35.7% of the sector's intraregional DVA_F flows. In 2018, the two largest intraregional DVA_F flows were from East Asia to the PRC and from Japan to the PRC, amounting to a combined 29.5% of total intraregional DVA_F flows.

Also worth noting is the increase in medium- to high-technology industrial DVA_F received by India,

Figure 3.1.6: Intraregional Flow of Asia's Domestic Value-Added Generated in Exports, Medium- to High-Technology Industrial Sector

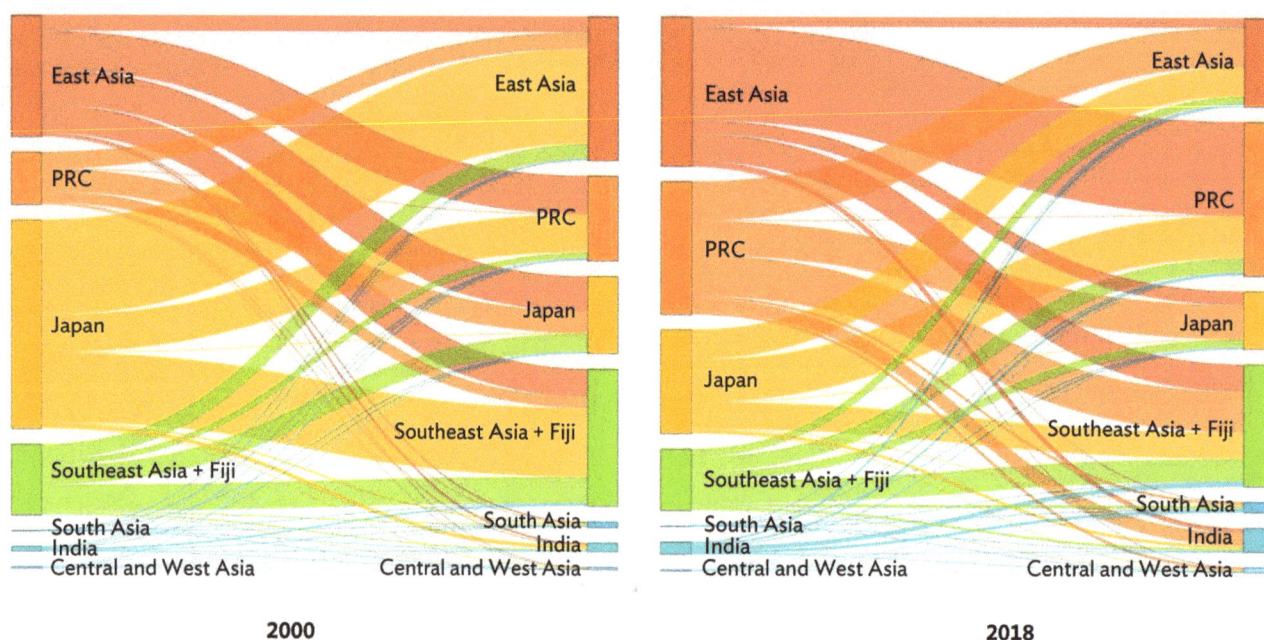

2000   2018

PRC = People's Republic of China
Source: Asian Development Bank estimates based on Wang, Wei, and Zhu (2018) using Asian Development Bank Multi-Regional Input-Output Tables
           (2000, 2007-2018).

South Asia, and Central & West Asia by 2018. Most of the inflows of this DVA_F to India came from the PRC.

In summary, the results highlight Japan's decreasing role as a source of DVA_F in the medium- to high-technology industrial sector within Asia. In 2000, Japan was Asia's main hub in terms of DVA_F generation, but the Sankey diagram for 2018 implies that the region is diversifying its source of DVA_F in this sector. Moreover, unlike the scenarios in the primary and low-technology industrial sectors, the PRC emerged as a destination hub for intraregional DVA_F generated in the medium- to high-technology industrial sector.

Business services sector

Japan was Asia's source hub of intraregional DVA_F in the business services sector in 2000. Its economy generated 37.2% of Asia's intraregional DVA_F for this sector, 47.5% of which was sent to East Asia and another 34.4% of which went to Southeast Asia plus Fiji. These two major destinations for Japan's intraregional DVA_F in business services were also the biggest recipients of Asia's total intraregional DVA_F flows for the sector in 2000: East Asia absorbing 32.4% and Southeast Asia plus Fiji absorbing 27.0%.

By 2018, Japan's and East Asia's roles as the source hubs of intraregional flows in business services had diminished, as other economies boosted their DVA_F generation in the sector. Particularly, the PRC and Southeast Asia plus Fiji became the two largest sources of intraregional DVA_F flows for the sector, respectively contributing 33.8% and 21.3% to the sector's total intraregional outflows.

On the destination side, the share of business services intraregional DVA_F received by the PRC noticeably increased, growing from 13.9% in 2000 to 20.0% in 2018. Meanwhile, the shares received by East

Figure 3.1.7. Intraregional Flow of Asia's Domestic Value-Added Generated in Exports, Business Services Sector

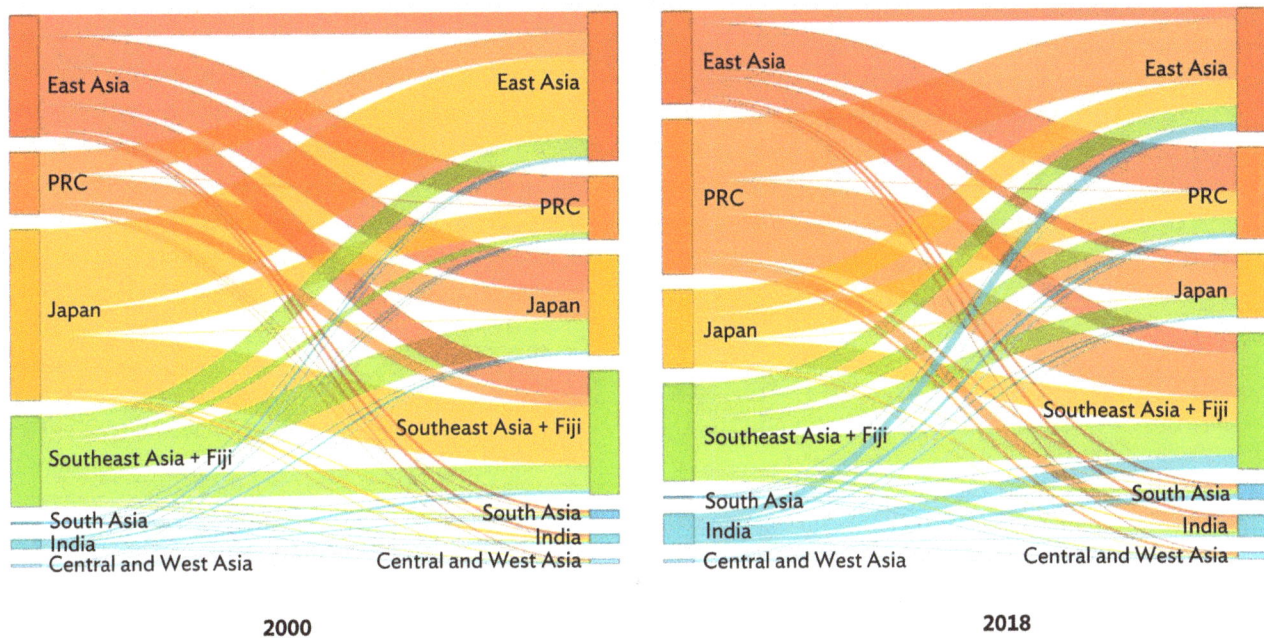

2000

2018

PRC = People's Republic of China
Source: Asian Development Bank estimates based on Wang, Wei, and Zhu (2018) using Asian Development Bank Multi-Regional Input-Output Tables (2000, 2007–2018).

Asia and Japan decreased by 5.4 and 8.0 percentage points, respectively, from 2000 to 2018. Intuitively, as the PRC's economy grew through the early part of the millennium, more business services were being demanded to support the growing economic activity.

Overall, the business services sector in Asia saw a shift in sources of intraregional DVA_F and a persistence in destination hubs over time. In 2000, intraregional DVA_F outflows in the sector came mostly from Japan and East Asia. By 2018, the contributions of the PRC and Southeast Asia plus Fiji to intraregional DVA_F outflows had expanded. While the PRC absorbed a considerable amount of intraregional inflows in 2018, East Asia and Southeast Asia remained the destination hubs of business services intraregional DVA_F flows.

Personal and public services sector

Japan was Asia's leader in terms of intraregional DVA_F generation in the personal and public services sector in 2000. At this time, Japan's intraregional DVA_F flows in the sector went to East Asia, Southeast Asia plus Fiji, and the PRC, representing 17.5%, 13.6%, and 8.3% of total intraregional outflows, respectively.

By 2018, Japan's position as the leading source in the sector had been assumed by the PRC, while the outflows of intraregional DVA_F were also more evenly distributed between East Asia, Japan, Southeast Asia plus Fiji, and India (which is positioned as a key source of intraregional DVA_F compared to its contribution in other sectors). The largest single outflow in 2018 was sent from India to the PRC, representing 11.9% of total intraregional outflows.

Figure 3.1.8: Intraregional Flow of Asia's Domestic Value-Added Generated in Exports, Personal and Public Services Sector

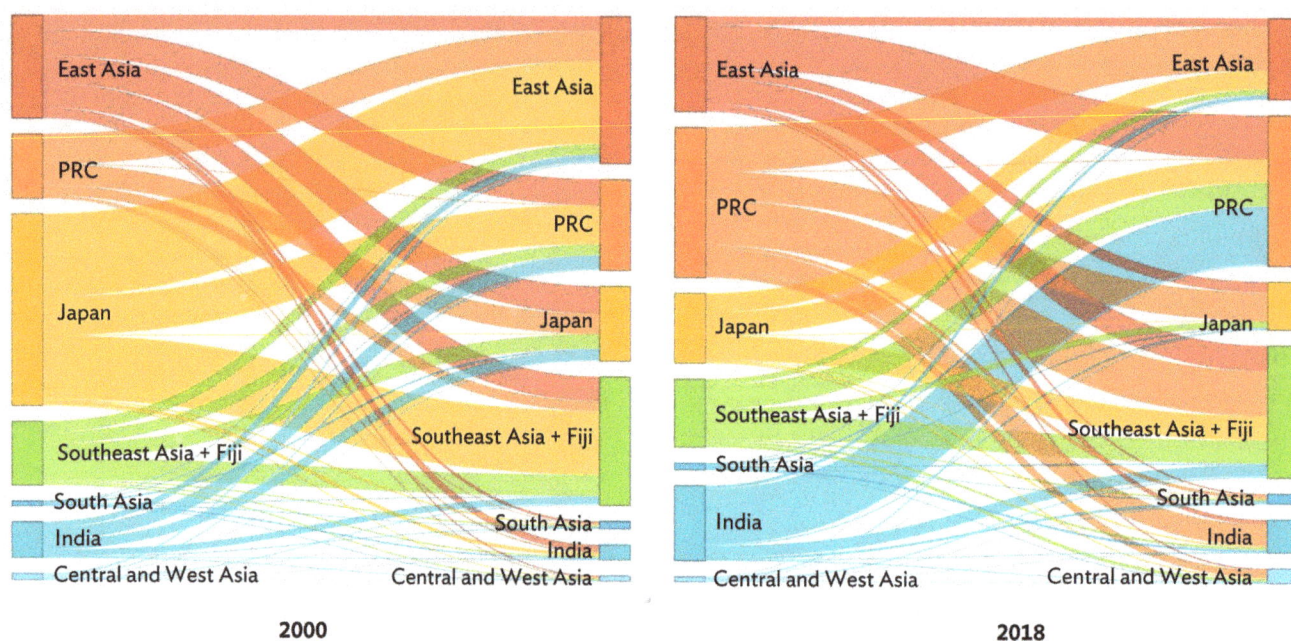

2000

2018

PRC = People's Republic of China
Source: Asian Development Bank estimates based on Wang, Wei, and Zhu (2018) using Asian Development Bank Multi-Regional Input-Output Tables (2000, 2007–2018).

In terms of the sector's intraregional DVA_F inflows, East Asia and Southeast Asia plus Fiji were the top two destinations in 2000. By 2018, East Asia's share in the region's total personal and public services intraregional DVA_F inflows had fallen, as was the case with Japan's share. Those two shares combined fell from 47.2% of total sectoral intraregional DVA_F flows in 2000 to 27.6% in 2018. Surpassing Southeast Asia plus Fiji as the top destination for intraregional DVA_F in the sector was the PRC.

In short, the PRC has become a dominant player in intraregional DVA_F flows in the personal and public services sector. The source hub shifted from Japan in 2000 to the PRC in 2018. The destination hub changed from East Asia in 2000 to the PRC in 2018, with Southeast Asia plus Fiji remaining a major destination of personal and public services sector intraregional DVA_F inflows.

Conclusion

The analysis in this chapter shows that Asia's role as a source of, and destination for, domestic value-added in exports increased from 2000 to 2018. DVA_F generated in Asia went up from 23.0% of the world's total in 2000 to 30.2% in 2018. Moreover, an increasing share of world DVA_F was absorbed by Asia. In 2000, the region received 19.7% of the world's total DVA_F, and this has risen to 26.0% of total DVA_F by 2018. Comparing Asia's share in world DVA_F generation against its share in world DVA_F absorption, it can be said that the region plays a larger role as an exporter of domestic value-added than as an importer of value-added.

In 2018, almost a third of the DVA_F generated in Asia stayed within the region. This represented 39.0% of the total domestic value-added that was sent to the region. It is therefore clear that intraregional trade matters for Asia. The data also show that Asia's connection to North America is weakening, as represented by the declining shares of DVA_F that the region sends to North America, and by North America's shrinking share of DVA_F inflows into Asia.

Focusing on intraregional trade, the PRC has surpassed Japan and took over as the region's leading source of intraregional DVA_F, while Southeast Asia plus Fiji is now larger than East Asia as a destination for intraregional DVA_F. The changing dynamics and patterns of intraregional DVA_F flows can vary by sector, but the growth of the PRC as a source and the persistence of Southeast Asia plus Fiji as a major destination is evident across all five sectors assessed here.

References

Asian Development Bank. *Key Indicators for Asia and the Pacific*. Manila (4 years: 2015–2018).

Asian Development Bank. 2000, 2007—2018. Multiregional Input-Output Tables.

Z. Wang, S. Wei, and K. Zhu. 2018. Quantifying International Production Sharing at the Bilateral and Sector Levels. *NBER Working Paper* No. 19677. Cambridge, MA: National Bureau of Economic Research.

Global Value Chain Tables for Economies of Asia and the Pacific

Table 3.2.1a: Value-Added Decomposition of Exports—Primary Sector				
ADB Regional Member	**Exports**	**VAX_G**	**RDV_B**	**FVA**	**PDC**
	($ million)	(% share in exports)			
Bangladesh					
2008	338.39	92.05	0.07	5.91	1.97
2018	518.39	92.47	0.09	6.15	1.29
Bhutan					
2008	106.48	94.37	0.01	4.94	0.68
2018	114.07	92.96	0.01	6.47	0.57
Brunei Darussalam					
2008	5,742.14	93.74	0.01	4.12	2.13
2018	3,476.43	87.97	0.01	8.06	3.97
Cambodia					
2008	374.62	89.92	0.14	6.93	3.02
2018	1,083.54	89.32	0.22	6.73	3.72
China, People's Republic of					
2008	23,336.67	86.30	2.53	7.26	3.91
2018	29,476.22	89.97	2.74	4.80	2.49
Fiji					
2008	55.08	69.06	0.01	26.10	4.84
2018	202.83	74.60	0.01	21.46	3.94
Hong Kong, China					
2008	91.73	51.29	0.26	32.25	16.20
2018	114.11	60.57	0.22	28.40	10.81
India					
2008	20,874.68	93.22	0.63	4.21	1.95
2018	24,219.99	94.10	0.92	3.46	1.52
Indonesia					
2008	39,409.50	92.38	0.80	4.19	2.62
2018	53,853.96	88.33	1.21	6.12	4.34
Japan					
2008	2,677.27	59.09	1.36	25.17	14.38
2018	3,611.63	60.32	1.36	24.93	13.39
Kazakhstan					
2008	37,320.47	85.28	0.12	8.84	5.76
2018	26,849.79	90.14	0.08	5.38	4.40
Korea, Republic of					
2008	681.64	82.02	0.39	14.94	2.66
2018	919.36	82.18	0.78	13.09	3.96
Kyrgyz Republic					
2008	163.73	85.94	0.02	11.27	2.76
2018	303.62	79.76	0.10	15.91	4.23
Lao People's Democratic Republic					
2008	743.10	84.64	0.01	10.07	5.29
2018	1,675.22	89.32	0.06	7.55	3.07

continued on next page

Table 3.2.1a: continued

Table 3.2.1a: Value-Added Decomposition of Exports—Primary Sector					
ADB Regional Member	**Exports**	**VAX_G**	**RDV_B**	**FVA**	**PDC**
	($ million)	(% share in exports)			
Malaysia					
2008	18,279.10	91.11	0.26	5.61	3.02
2018	15,115.99	86.40	0.78	8.01	4.81
Maldives					
2008	19.44	56.36	0.01	37.19	6.43
2018	39.46	58.30	0.01	33.94	7.75
Mongolia					
2008	1,713.82	74.44	0.01	16.26	9.30
2018	5,611.65	75.09	0.01	18.22	6.68
Nepal					
2008	75.93	92.18	0.05	7.11	0.66
2018	75.64	91.04	0.08	8.41	0.48
Pakistan					
2008	1,026.92	95.80	0.13	3.19	0.89
2018	2,202.50	96.60	0.11	2.68	0.62
Philippines					
2008	1,463.20	89.75	0.19	7.18	2.87
2018	1,718.85	90.55	0.23	6.83	2.39
Singapore					
2008	128.28	59.01	0.10	34.31	6.58
2018	33.38	64.74	0.10	26.09	9.07
Sri Lanka					
2008	478.14	89.96	0.06	7.77	2.21
2018	833.74	89.44	0.03	8.88	1.65
Taipei,China					
2008	1,517.44	70.98	0.09	25.94	2.98
2018	1,690.25	76.31	0.13	19.36	4.20
Thailand					
2008	3,503.27	84.89	0.38	10.33	4.40
2018	10,896.53	87.35	0.20	9.37	3.08
Viet Nam					
2008	9,186.97	74.31	0.19	18.82	6.67
2018	21,582.55	62.26	1.23	27.54	8.97

0.00 = magnitude is less than half of unit employed, $ = United States dollars, FVA = foreign value-added, PDC = pure double counted terms, RDV_B = domestic value-added first exported then returned home, VAX_G = domestic value-added absorbed abroad.

Source: ADB Multi Region Input–Output Tables Database.

ADB Regional Member	Exports ($ million)	VAX_G	RDV_B	FVA	PDC
			(% share in exports)		
Bangladesh					
2008	13,165.14	81.44	0.02	16.59	1.94
2018	30,780.11	83.39	0.04	14.78	1.79
Bhutan					
2008	235.81	84.88	0.00	11.10	4.03
2018	309.14	82.87	0.00	11.25	5.88
Brunei Darussalam					
2008	42.87	68.15	0.01	25.13	6.71
2018	111.81	58.91	0.01	34.55	6.54
Cambodia					
2008	2,470.62	62.66	0.00	34.85	2.49
2018	6,213.53	64.81	0.01	32.71	2.48
China, People's Republic of					
2008	362,219.77	84.75	0.54	12.86	1.84
2018	621,135.34	89.27	1.17	8.06	1.50
Fiji					
2008	190.63	73.09	0.00	22.34	4.57
2018	501.82	73.87	0.00	22.12	4.01
Hong Kong, China					
2008	7,806.17	57.18	0.07	33.06	9.69
2018	7,211.08	47.12	0.07	44.38	8.43
India					
2008	37,943.29	82.32	0.28	14.48	2.91
2018	85,694.44	87.32	0.30	10.36	2.03
Indonesia					
2008	55,887.16	81.35	0.22	14.74	3.69
2018	101,845.06	78.40	0.17	16.98	4.46
Japan					
2008	44,857.60	82.17	1.71	10.52	5.60
2018	53,193.78	81.54	1.23	11.77	5.45
Kazakhstan					
2008	1,586.26	81.45	0.14	13.79	4.62
2018	1,542.36	84.94	0.32	11.86	2.88
Korea, Republic of					
2008	33,791.40	68.84	0.39	21.90	8.87
2018	41,683.97	70.09	0.57	20.36	8.98
Kyrgyz Republic					
2008	196.11	59.75	0.03	32.79	7.43
2018	256.30	67.81	0.03	27.76	4.40
Lao People's Democratic Republic					
2008	229.39	88.40	0.01	8.84	2.76
2018	3,375.41	89.77	0.02	7.79	2.42
Malaysia					
2008	41,269.46	69.95	0.14	21.88	8.03
2018	47,960.66	62.99	0.16	28.03	8.83

Table 3.2.1b: Value-Added Decomposition of Exports—Low-Technology Manufacturing Sector

continued on next page

Table 3.2.1b: continued

Table 3.2.1b: Value-Added Decomposition of Exports—Low-Technology Manufacturing Sector					
ADB Regional Member	**Exports**	**VAX_G**	**RDV_B**	**FVA**	**PDC**
	($ million)	(% share in exports)			
Maldives					
2008	35.57	57.93	0.01	28.01	14.05
2018	341.48	58.77	0.00	33.05	8.18
Mongolia					
2008	150.51	78.42	0.01	16.69	4.88
2018	178.88	69.31	0.03	23.41	7.24
Nepal					
2008	243.92	77.35	0.02	20.66	1.98
2018	253.26	73.03	0.04	24.19	2.75
Pakistan					
2008	10,881.98	90.67	0.08	6.95	2.30
2018	14,666.02	91.89	0.09	6.25	1.77
Philippines					
2008	12,285.20	83.26	0.07	13.92	2.75
2018	15,376.28	84.53	0.11	12.86	2.49
Singapore					
2008	7,211.76	41.76	0.07	47.19	10.97
2018	10,832.82	54.40	0.07	38.00	7.53
Sri Lanka					
2008	3,716.59	78.24	0.02	18.79	2.96
2018	6,899.54	84.54	0.01	13.70	1.75
Taipei,China					
2008	21,222.35	54.91	0.13	32.19	12.77
2018	23,679.74	58.87	0.14	29.53	11.46
Thailand					
2008	27,907.45	71.88	0.18	22.23	5.71
2018	44,742.74	77.00	0.14	17.72	5.15
Viet Nam					
2008	22,308.23	69.42	0.04	26.56	3.98
2018	95,023.80	59.90	0.06	33.84	6.20

0.00 = magnitude is less than half of unit employed, $ = United States dollars, FVA = foreign value-added, PDC = pure double counted terms, RDV_B = domestic value-added first exported then returned home, VAX_G = domestic value-added absorbed abroad.

Source: ADB Multi Region Input–Output Tables Database.

Table 3.2.1c: Value-Added Decomposition of Exports—Medium- and High-Technology Manufacturing Sector

ADB Regional Member	Exports ($ million)	VAX_G	RDV_B	FVA	PDC
			(% share in exports)		
Bangladesh					
2008	437.51	83.46	0.09	12.41	4.04
2018	655.83	84.64	0.04	14.49	0.84
Bhutan					
2008	117.74	77.64	0.02	20.10	2.24
2018	85.30	80.20	0.01	18.07	1.71
Brunei Darussalam					
2008	3,345.81	92.96	0.01	4.77	2.27
2018	2,952.44	89.43	0.01	7.34	3.22
Cambodia					
2008	31.89	67.36	0.04	23.96	8.64
2018	110.87	69.18	0.04	25.37	5.41
China, People's Republic of					
2008	906,218.76	71.63	1.67	20.30	6.40
2018	1,603,200.92	77.87	3.17	13.78	5.18
Fiji					
2008	25.49	59.20	0.01	32.77	8.03
2018	55.30	61.20	0.00	35.27	3.53
Hong Kong, China					
2008	6,993.56	26.00	0.04	49.30	24.66
2018	11,353.30	22.24	0.02	57.74	19.99
India					
2008	77,400.96	62.79	0.49	22.50	14.22
2018	171,380.59	74.39	0.53	17.55	7.54
Indonesia					
2008	53,993.70	75.32	0.43	16.87	7.38
2018	77,088.29	66.99	0.35	22.61	10.05
Japan					
2008	607,682.84	77.99	1.23	14.54	6.24
2018	696,067.45	75.23	0.91	17.12	6.74
Kazakhstan					
2008	12,979.44	85.19	0.24	8.79	5.79
2018	12,036.45	91.29	0.20	4.82	3.69
Korea, Republic of					
2008	390,437.58	57.99	0.37	29.92	11.72
2018	581,976.81	61.41	0.43	27.42	10.74
Kyrgyz Republic					
2008	594.47	56.58	0.01	28.68	14.73
2018	575.95	75.97	0.01	16.13	7.89
Lao People's Democratic Republic					
2008	8.32	45.87	0.02	36.19	17.93
2018	44.87	80.05	0.06	13.18	6.71
Malaysia					
2008	72,095.77	63.90	0.29	21.60	14.22
2018	79,526.61	53.21	0.42	30.14	16.23

continued on next page

Table 3.2.1c: continued

Table 3.2.1c: Value-Added Decomposition of Exports—Medium- and High-Technology Manufacturing Sector					
ADB Regional Member	Exports ($ million)	VAX_G	RDV_B	FVA	PDC
			(% share in exports)		
Maldives					
2008	1.07	60.83	0.01	33.84	5.32
2018	5.99	68.36	0.00	27.55	4.09
Mongolia					
2008	51.98	66.94	0.01	20.81	12.25
2018	125.01	73.67	0.01	19.76	6.56
Nepal					
2008	92.31	62.50	0.08	31.72	5.70
2018	102.57	58.35	0.11	37.01	4.52
Pakistan					
2008	969.27	75.96	0.09	17.98	5.97
2018	1,667.93	78.44	0.10	17.34	4.12
Philippines					
2008	32,928.51	49.98	0.10	29.57	20.34
2018	28,413.44	49.58	0.19	31.80	18.42
Singapore					
2008	133,314.31	28.70	0.07	48.96	22.26
2018	207,365.04	36.57	0.11	46.48	16.83
Sri Lanka					
2008	723.13	65.92	0.04	25.17	8.87
2018	537.30	50.63	0.03	40.05	9.30
Taipei,China					
2008	221,339.21	49.77	0.21	30.84	19.18
2018	287,430.37	52.66	0.26	30.12	16.96
Thailand					
2008	86,623.55	51.36	0.26	32.60	15.78
2018	104,159.38	53.91	0.21	33.64	12.24
Viet Nam					
2008	5,571.60	62.82	0.10	26.28	10.79
2018	41,596.58	43.80	0.08	36.22	19.90

0.00 = magnitude is less than half of unit employed, $ = United States dollars, FVA = foreign value-added, PDC = pure double counted terms, RDV_B = domestic value-added first exported then returned home, VAX_G = domestic value-added absorbed abroad.

Source: ADB Multi Region Input–Output Tables Database.

ADB Regional Member	Exports ($ million)	VAX_G	RDV_B	FVA	PDC
			(% share in exports)		
Bangladesh					
2008	1,921.39	95.86	0.05	3.00	1.09
2018	2,311.31	96.31	0.12	2.47	1.09
Bhutan					
2008	63.08	73.64	0.00	21.01	5.35
2018	219.67	82.34	0.00	13.28	4.38
Brunei Darussalam					
2008	569.44	74.86	0.00	19.02	6.12
2018	448.96	73.29	0.01	19.53	7.17
Cambodia					
2008	1,258.52	81.03	0.01	14.81	4.16
2018	3,320.72	80.54	0.01	14.83	4.62
China, People's Republic of					
2008	237,154.45	85.92	1.96	8.51	3.60
2018	455,895.60	89.52	3.64	4.47	2.37
Fiji					
2008	746.60	67.22	0.01	27.78	4.99
2018	1,737.95	72.63	0.01	22.20	5.17
Hong Kong, China					
2008	122,562.16	74.18	0.14	20.55	5.13
2018	187,584.58	75.73	0.16	19.56	4.55
India					
2008	105,866.03	87.85	0.74	8.24	3.16
2018	117,204.45	93.31	0.59	4.66	1.45
Indonesia					
2008	9,033.30	87.90	0.30	8.76	3.03
2018	13,175.41	87.45	0.29	9.16	3.10
Japan					
2008	203,055.59	87.43	1.49	7.91	3.17
2018	158,944.42	90.83	0.96	5.53	2.67
Kazakhstan					
2008	18,605.46	87.32	0.39	9.26	3.03
2018	15,218.99	90.78	0.56	6.23	2.42
Korea, Republic of					
2008	55,289.22	79.14	0.54	14.49	5.84
2018	83,176.89	82.17	0.50	12.47	4.87
Kyrgyz Republic					
2008	544.82	63.09	0.01	29.17	7.73
2018	431.87	70.02	0.02	22.43	7.53
Lao People's Democratic Republic					
2008	109.49	79.88	0.01	14.09	6.02
2018	897.23	87.02	0.02	9.65	3.31
Malaysia					
2008	36,864.23	77.55	0.19	16.39	5.87
2018	35,829.33	74.60	0.27	18.34	6.79

Table 3.2.1d: Value-Added Decomposition of Exports—Business Services Sector

continued on next page

Table 3.2.1d: continued

Table 3.2.1d: Value-Added Decomposition of Exports—Business Services Sector					
ADB Regional Member	**Exports**	**VAX_G**	**RDV_B**	**FVA**	**PDC**
	($ million)	(% share in exports)			
Maldives					
2008	1,341.86	67.60	0.00	24.54	7.85
2018	3,002.09	64.38	0.00	27.29	8.32
Mongolia					
2008	491.62	75.96	0.01	18.57	5.47
2018	820.45	78.34	0.04	15.97	5.66
Nepal					
2008	364.37	82.97	0.02	13.26	3.75
2018	531.93	78.97	0.05	17.09	3.89
Pakistan					
2008	2,612.58	92.41	0.10	5.58	1.91
2018	5,083.23	93.33	0.11	5.16	1.39
Philippines					
2008	14,646.65	90.22	0.11	7.42	2.25
2018	33,179.01	90.25	0.16	7.20	2.38
Singapore					
2008	114,405.78	58.10	0.09	31.59	10.22
2018	235,952.41	54.49	0.12	34.12	11.27
Sri Lanka					
2008	3,006.16	86.05	0.03	11.24	2.68
2018	6,224.95	89.12	0.02	8.59	2.27
Taipei,China					
2008	46,541.78	77.33	0.31	15.52	6.84
2018	79,081.81	78.42	0.33	14.96	6.29
Thailand					
2008	17,603.81	78.32	0.27	16.38	5.03
2018	87,145.81	84.64	0.15	12.19	3.02
Viet Nam					
2008	7,399.11	77.39	0.06	18.28	4.27
2018	29,713.37	73.76	0.10	21.20	4.95

0.00 = magnitude is less than half of unit employed, $ = United States dollars, FVA = foreign value-added, PDC = pure double counted terms, RDV_B = domestic value-added first exported then returned home, VAX_G = domestic value-added absorbed abroad.

Source: ADB Multi Region Input–Output Tables Database.

Table 3.2.1e: Value-Added Decomposition of Exports—Personal Services Sector					
ADB Regional Member	**Exports**	**VAX_G**	**RDV_B**	**FVA**	**PDC**
	($ million)		(% share in exports)		
Bangladesh					
2008	321.38	96.58	0.02	2.87	0.52
2018	2,292.50	96.71	0.07	2.43	0.79
Bhutan					
2008	4.32	86.60	0.00	11.07	2.33
2018	25.91	84.98	0.00	11.90	3.12
Brunei Darussalam					
2008	92.14	90.44	0.00	8.09	1.47
2018	56.10	83.25	0.00	15.38	1.37
Cambodia					
2008	85.35	79.46	0.01	15.00	5.53
2018	121.29	80.69	0.02	15.31	3.99
China, People's Republic of					
2008	11,855.53	87.49	0.61	9.80	2.10
2018	18,896.06	92.03	1.32	5.41	1.23
Fiji					
2008	15.99	81.35	0.01	14.70	3.93
2018	51.88	86.28	0.01	12.95	0.76
Hong Kong, China					
2008	958.03	85.87	0.18	10.94	3.01
2018	1,292.53	86.56	0.15	10.17	3.11
India					
2008	10,500.45	94.22	0.02	5.64	0.12
2018	12,006.52	97.94	0.01	2.03	0.02
Indonesia					
2008	1,638.51	89.10	0.21	9.00	1.69
2018	2,178.61	91.04	0.12	7.57	1.27
Japan					
2008	3,250.32	92.91	0.90	4.87	1.32
2018	3,400.89	93.24	0.45	5.39	0.92
Kazakhstan					
2008	605.55	83.48	0.04	15.20	1.29
2018	302.35	93.13	0.04	6.24	0.60
Korea, Republic of					
2008	6,059.60	82.84	0.80	11.19	5.17
2018	4,953.84	84.55	0.39	12.22	2.84
Kyrgyz Republic					
2008	182.15	77.06	0.00	18.99	3.94
2018	260.09	85.85	0.00	11.27	2.88
Lao People's Democratic Republic					
2008	1.69	85.49	0.00	13.91	0.61
2018	182.47	91.31	0.01	7.44	1.23
Malaysia					
2008	1,904.65	75.27	0.11	18.59	6.03
2018	1,882.24	76.04	0.08	22.00	1.88

continued on next page

Table 3.2.1e: continued

Table 3.2.1e: Value-Added Decomposition of Exports—Personal Services Sector					
ADB Regional Member	**Exports**	**VAX_G**	**RDV_B**	**FVA**	**PDC**
	($ million)	(% share in exports)			
Maldives					
2008	17.61	75.57	0.01	19.66	4.77
2018	99.61	76.98	0.01	16.83	6.18
Mongolia					
2008	4.22	83.33	0.01	10.93	5.73
2018	20.35	76.36	0.01	20.62	3.01
Nepal					
2008	307.68	91.47	0.02	6.51	2.00
2018	470.75	88.83	0.07	9.03	2.06
Pakistan					
2008	912.06	94.31	0.03	5.21	0.45
2018	1,366.55	95.21	0.03	4.43	0.32
Philippines					
2008	432.49	89.17	0.11	7.54	3.18
2018	1,571.10	88.67	0.11	8.27	2.94
Singapore					
2008	1,365.45	74.43	0.17	18.04	7.36
2018	1,764.75	79.42	0.15	14.04	6.38
Sri Lanka					
2008	66.59	83.28	0.03	11.47	5.22
2018	532.81	89.47	0.01	9.13	1.39
Taipei,China					
2008	1,229.35	84.14	0.11	14.30	1.45
2018	1,547.80	83.81	0.11	14.82	1.26
Thailand					
2008	2,219.64	82.94	0.10	15.37	1.59
2018	7,891.71	87.67	0.09	11.15	1.09
Viet Nam					
2008	249.78	84.41	0.03	14.69	0.88
2018	2,089.97	75.95	0.05	22.59	1.42

0.00 = magnitude is less than half of unit employed, $ = United States dollars, FVA = foreign value-added, PDC = pure double counted terms, RDV_B = domestic value-added first exported then returned home, VAX_G = domestic value-added absorbed abroad.

Source: ADB Multi Region Input–Output Tables Database.

ADB Regional Member	Exports ($ million)	VAX_G	RDV_B	FVA	PDC
			(% share in exports)		
Bangladesh					
2008	16,183.80	83.73	0.03	14.37	1.87
2018	36,558.14	85.19	0.05	13.10	1.66
Bhutan					
2008	527.43	83.84	0.01	13.05	3.10
2018	754.09	84.01	0.01	11.91	4.07
Brunei Darussalam					
2008	9,792.41	92.23	0.01	5.34	2.42
2018	7,045.74	87.15	0.01	8.97	3.88
Cambodia					
2008	4,221.00	70.93	0.02	25.91	3.14
2018	10,849.95	72.29	0.03	24.37	3.31
China, People's Republic of					
2008	1,540,785.17	77.26	1.46	16.46	4.83
2018	2,728,604.14	82.64	2.77	10.77	3.82
Fiji					
2008	1,033.78	68.42	0.01	26.61	4.96
2018	2,549.77	73.06	0.01	22.22	4.72
Hong Kong, China					
2008	138,411.64	70.85	0.13	22.65	6.37
2018	207,555.60	71.87	0.15	22.46	5.52
India					
2008	252,585.42	80.05	0.56	13.11	6.29
2018	410,505.99	84.34	0.50	11.08	4.07
Indonesia					
2008	159,962.18	82.48	0.44	12.46	4.62
2018	248,141.33	77.60	0.46	15.87	6.07
Japan					
2008	861,523.63	80.43	1.31	12.77	5.49
2018	915,218.17	78.31	0.94	14.78	5.97
Kazakhstan					
2008	71,097.18	85.70	0.21	9.10	4.99
2018	55,949.93	90.44	0.24	5.68	3.65
Korea, Republic of					
2008	486,259.44	61.49	0.40	27.35	10.76
2018	712,710.88	64.53	0.44	25.14	9.89
Kyrgyz Republic					
2008	1,681.29	64.14	0.01	26.57	9.28
2018	1,827.83	75.45	0.03	18.52	5.99
Lao People's Democratic Republic					
2008	1,092.00	84.66	0.01	10.42	4.92
2018	6,175.19	89.22	0.03	8.03	2.72
Malaysia					
2008	170,413.22	71.36	0.23	18.79	9.62
2018	180,314.83	63.08	0.35	25.29	11.28

Table 3.2.1f: Value-Added Decomposition of Exports—All Sectors

continued on next page

Table 3.2.1f: continued

Table 3.2.1f: Value-Added Decomposition of Exports—All Sectors					
ADB Regional Member	**Exports**	**VAX_G**	**RDV_B**	**FVA**	**PDC**
	($ million)	(% share in exports)			
Maldives					
2008	1,415.57	67.30	0.00	24.75	7.94
2018	3,488.63	64.13	0.00	27.63	8.23
Mongolia					
2008	2,412.15	74.85	0.01	16.84	8.30
2018	6,756.34	75.31	0.02	18.12	6.56
Nepal					
2008	1,084.21	83.02	0.03	14.15	2.80
2018	1,434.15	80.32	0.06	16.67	2.95
Pakistan					
2008	16,402.81	90.60	0.08	7.05	2.27
2018	24,986.22	91.88	0.09	6.36	1.67
Philippines					
2008	61,756.06	67.36	0.10	20.52	12.01
2018	80,258.69	74.73	0.16	17.01	8.09
Singapore					
2008	256,425.58	42.44	0.08	40.99	16.49
2018	455,948.40	46.44	0.12	39.76	13.69
Sri Lanka					
2008	7,990.62	80.81	0.02	15.81	3.36
2018	15,028.33	85.67	0.02	12.10	2.22
Taipei,China					
2008	291,850.12	54.80	0.22	28.40	16.59
2018	393,429.97	58.44	0.27	26.93	14.37
Thailand					
2008	137,857.72	60.31	0.25	27.59	11.85
2018	254,836.17	70.95	0.17	21.77	7.10
Viet Nam					
2008	44,715.69	71.01	0.08	23.50	5.41
2018	190,006.28	58.99	0.20	31.55	9.27

0.00 = magnitude is less than half of unit employed, $ = United States dollars, FVA = foreign value-added, PDC = pure double counted terms, RDV_B = domestic value-added first exported then returned home, VAX_G = domestic value-added absorbed abroad.

Source: ADB Multi Region Input–Output Tables Database.

ADB Regional Member	VAX_G	DVA_B	DVA_F	VAX_B	VAX_F
	Value-Added Export Measure to Gross Exports Ratio (%)				
Bangladesh					
2008	92.05	92.14	576.35	92.05	576.17
2018	92.47	92.58	614.35	92.47	614.03
Bhutan					
2008	94.37	94.38	103.02	94.37	103.01
2018	92.96	92.97	101.77	92.96	101.76
Brunei Darussalam					
2008	93.74	93.75	115.11	93.74	115.10
2018	87.97	87.97	121.78	87.97	121.78
Cambodia					
2008	89.92	90.06	160.15	89.92	160.01
2018	89.32	89.56	130.93	89.32	130.71
China, People's Republic of					
2008	86.30	89.34	795.09	86.30	780.55
2018	89.97	92.91	1,060.01	89.97	1,028.86
Fiji					
2008	69.06	69.07	138.08	69.06	138.07
2018	74.60	74.61	106.92	74.60	106.91
Hong Kong, China					
2008	51.29	51.55	41.54	51.29	41.35
2018	60.57	60.81	56.72	60.57	56.52
India					
2008	93.22	93.87	145.23	93.22	144.32
2018	94.10	95.07	181.09	94.10	179.81
Indonesia					
2008	92.38	93.23	131.05	92.38	130.14
2018	88.33	89.61	133.29	88.33	132.01
Japan					
2008	59.09	60.50	185.77	59.09	182.29
2018	60.32	61.75	178.10	60.32	175.28
Kazakhstan					
2008	85.28	85.40	72.87	85.28	72.76
2018	90.14	90.22	75.55	90.14	75.47
Korea, Republic of					
2008	82.02	82.47	615.83	82.02	612.36
2018	82.18	83.05	659.56	82.18	655.35
Kyrgyz Republic					
2008	85.94	85.96	120.59	85.94	120.56
2018	79.76	79.87	64.54	79.76	64.47
Lao People's Democratic Republic					
2008	84.64	84.64	80.81	84.64	80.81
2018	89.32	89.38	102.76	89.32	102.69
Malaysia					
2008	91.11	91.43	227.88	91.11	227.24
2018	86.40	87.27	196.85	86.40	195.72

Table 3.2.2a: Value-Added Exports by Various Measures—Primary Sector

continued on next page

Table 3.2.2a: continued

Table 3.2.2a: Value-Added Exports by Various Measures—Primary Sector					
ADB Regional Member	**VAX_G**	**DVA_B**	**DVA_F**	**VAX_B**	**VAX_F**
	Value-Added Export Measure to Gross Exports Ratio (%)				
Maldives					
2008	56.36	56.37	476.05	56.36	476.02
2018	58.30	58.31	200.75	58.30	200.74
Mongolia					
2008	74.44	74.45	67.39	74.44	67.38
2018	75.09	75.10	55.54	75.09	55.53
Nepal					
2008	92.18	92.23	178.84	92.18	178.77
2018	91.04	91.12	208.30	91.04	208.15
Pakistan					
2008	95.80	95.93	525.26	95.80	524.76
2018	96.60	96.70	386.78	96.60	386.39
Philippines					
2008	89.75	89.96	344.45	89.75	344.02
2018	90.55	90.79	363.22	90.55	362.64
Singapore					
2008	59.01	59.09	53.15	59.01	53.06
2018	64.74	64.89	123.45	64.74	123.26
Sri Lanka					
2008	89.96	90.02	147.15	89.96	147.07
2018	89.44	89.47	148.06	89.44	148.02
Taipei,China					
2008	70.98	71.04	115.30	70.98	115.05
2018	76.31	76.43	122.36	76.31	122.11
Thailand					
2008	84.89	85.29	207.57	84.89	206.87
2018	87.35	87.59	165.93	87.35	165.62
Viet Nam					
2008	74.31	74.54	108.94	74.31	108.75
2018	62.26	63.60	105.04	62.26	103.97

DVA_B = domestic value-added exports by backward industrial linkages, DVA_F = domestic value-added exports by forward industrial linkages, VAX_B = value-added exports by backward industrial linkages, VAX_F = value-added exports by forward industrial linkages, VAX_G = domestic value-added absorbed abroad.

Source: ADB Multi Region Input–Output Tables Database.

Table 3.2.2b: Value-Added Exports by Various Measures—Low-Technology Manufacturing Sector					
ADB Regional Member	**VAX_G**	**DVA_B**	**DVA_F**	**VAX_B**	**VAX_F**
	Value-Added Export Measure to Gross Exports Ratio (%)				
Bangladesh					
2008	81.44	81.46	40.62	81.44	40.61
2018	83.39	83.43	47.87	83.39	47.85
Bhutan					
2008	84.88	84.88	92.92	84.88	92.92
2018	82.87	82.87	80.15	82.87	80.15
Brunei Darussalam					
2008	68.15	68.15	155.49	68.15	155.48
2018	58.91	58.91	55.57	58.91	55.56
Cambodia					
2008	62.66	62.66	49.41	62.66	49.40
2018	64.81	64.81	50.14	64.81	50.14
China, People's Republic of					
2008	84.75	85.16	62.48	84.75	61.77
2018	89.27	90.37	63.66	89.27	62.30
Fiji					
2008	73.09	73.09	55.56	73.09	55.56
2018	73.87	73.87	57.01	73.87	57.00
Hong Kong, China					
2008	57.18	57.22	56.37	57.18	56.28
2018	47.12	47.13	49.77	47.12	49.69
India					
2008	82.32	82.56	50.61	82.32	50.35
2018	87.32	87.59	47.88	87.32	47.65
Indonesia					
2008	81.35	81.54	47.40	81.35	47.26
2018	78.40	78.54	46.55	78.40	46.44
Japan					
2008	82.17	83.99	138.62	82.17	136.18
2018	81.54	82.85	128.10	81.54	126.42
Kazakhstan					
2008	81.45	81.56	206.51	81.45	206.05
2018	84.94	85.22	119.03	84.94	118.65
Korea, Republic of					
2008	68.84	69.26	74.59	68.84	74.14
2018	70.09	70.69	95.77	70.09	95.05
Kyrgyz Republic					
2008	59.75	59.78	46.14	59.75	46.12
2018	67.81	67.84	53.64	67.81	53.62
Lao People's Democratic Republic					
2008	88.40	88.40	72.19	88.40	72.18
2018	89.77	89.78	74.34	89.77	74.33
Malaysia					
2008	69.95	70.08	30.75	69.95	30.68
2018	62.99	63.13	29.95	62.99	29.85

continued on next page

Table 3.2.2b: continued

Table 3.2.2b: Value-Added Exports by Various Measures—Low-Technology Manufacturing Sector					
ADB Regional Member	**VAX_G**	**DVA_B**	**DVA_F**	**VAX_B**	**VAX_F**
	Value-Added Export Measure to Gross Exports Ratio (%)				
Maldives					
2008	57.93	57.94	200.90	57.93	200.88
2018	58.77	58.77	156.19	58.77	156.18
Mongolia					
2008	78.42	78.43	59.41	78.42	59.40
2018	69.31	69.34	171.99	69.31	171.95
Nepal					
2008	77.35	77.36	53.16	77.35	53.15
2018	73.03	73.06	58.45	73.03	58.41
Pakistan					
2008	90.67	90.75	33.02	90.67	32.99
2018	91.89	91.98	33.30	91.89	33.27
Philippines					
2008	83.26	83.33	60.97	83.26	60.91
2018	84.53	84.64	67.60	84.53	67.50
Singapore					
2008	41.76	41.81	46.97	41.76	46.88
2018	54.40	54.44	73.67	54.40	73.52
Sri Lanka					
2008	78.24	78.25	58.74	78.24	58.72
2018	84.54	84.55	66.21	84.54	66.20
Taipei,China					
2008	54.91	55.02	49.75	54.91	49.61
2018	58.87	58.99	66.09	58.87	65.88
Thailand					
2008	71.88	72.04	55.94	71.88	55.76
2018	77.00	77.13	64.40	77.00	64.26
Viet Nam					
2008	69.42	69.45	43.64	69.42	43.61
2018	59.90	59.93	40.20	59.90	40.15

DVA_B = domestic value-added exports by backward industrial linkages, DVA_F = domestic value-added exports by forward industrial linkages, VAX_B = value-added exports by backward industrial linkages, VAX_F = value-added exports by forward industrial linkages, VAX_G = domestic value-added absorbed abroad.

Source: ADB Multi Region Input–Output Tables Database.

Table 3.2.2c: Value-Added Exports by Various Measures—Medium- and High-Technology Manufacturing Sector

ADB Regional Member	VAX_G	DVA_B	DVA_F	VAX_B	VAX_F
	Value-Added Export Measure to Gross Exports Ratio (%)				
Bangladesh					
2008	83.46	83.56	122.95	83.46	122.88
2018	84.64	84.67	130.74	84.64	130.68
Bhutan					
2008	77.64	77.66	30.05	77.64	30.04
2018	80.20	80.22	48.71	80.20	48.71
Brunei Darussalam					
2008	92.96	92.97	48.60	92.96	48.59
2018	89.43	89.44	47.11	89.43	47.10
Cambodia					
2008	67.36	67.40	96.63	67.36	96.59
2018	69.18	69.22	93.63	69.18	93.57
China, People's Republic of					
2008	71.63	73.23	46.88	71.63	45.89
2018	77.87	80.96	43.84	77.87	42.22
Fiji					
2008	59.20	59.21	68.51	59.20	68.50
2018	61.20	61.20	75.00	61.20	74.99
Hong Kong, China					
2008	26.00	26.00	8.27	26.00	8.26
2018	22.24	22.21	4.63	22.24	4.62
India					
2008	62.79	63.26	43.64	62.79	43.31
2018	74.39	74.91	38.50	74.39	38.24
Indonesia					
2008	75.32	75.74	53.99	75.32	53.70
2018	66.99	67.32	45.88	66.99	45.65
Japan					
2008	77.99	79.18	51.96	77.99	51.17
2018	75.23	76.11	49.41	75.23	48.83
Kazakhstan					
2008	85.19	85.42	57.93	85.19	57.77
2018	91.29	91.48	67.47	91.29	67.33
Korea, Republic of					
2008	57.99	58.34	42.78	57.99	42.50
2018	61.41	61.82	45.44	61.41	45.12
Kyrgyz Republic					
2008	56.58	56.59	51.80	56.58	51.79
2018	75.97	75.98	75.48	75.97	75.46
Lao People's Democratic Republic					
2008	45.87	45.88	137.87	45.87	137.85
2018	80.05	80.11	208.85	80.05	208.77
Malaysia					
2008	63.90	64.18	38.83	63.90	38.66
2018	53.21	53.62	36.55	53.21	36.27

continued on next page

Table 3.2.2c: continued

Table 3.2.2c: Value-Added Exports by Various Measures—Medium- and High-Technology Manufacturing Sector					
ADB Regional Member	**VAX_G**	**DVA_B**	**DVA_F**	**VAX_B**	**VAX_F**
	Value-Added Export Measure to Gross Exports Ratio (%)				
Maldives					
2008	60.83	60.83	388.78	60.83	388.76
2018	68.36	68.36	161.81	68.36	161.80
Mongolia					
2008	66.94	66.95	69.18	66.94	69.17
2018	73.67	73.68	106.10	73.67	106.08
Nepal					
2008	62.50	62.58	49.98	62.50	49.93
2018	58.35	58.47	58.66	58.35	58.57
Pakistan					
2008	75.96	76.06	66.90	75.96	66.83
2018	78.44	78.54	69.24	78.44	69.16
Philippines					
2008	49.98	50.08	31.08	49.98	31.02
2018	49.58	49.76	34.62	49.58	34.50
Singapore					
2008	28.70	28.74	23.86	28.70	23.80
2018	36.57	36.62	26.99	36.57	26.91
Sri Lanka					
2008	65.92	65.96	64.63	65.92	64.60
2018	50.63	50.65	68.52	50.63	68.50
Taipei,China					
2008	49.77	49.98	40.98	49.77	40.81
2018	52.66	52.91	45.92	52.66	45.69
Thailand					
2008	51.36	51.62	32.52	51.36	32.36
2018	53.91	54.12	35.30	53.91	35.18
Viet Nam					
2008	62.82	62.93	67.12	62.82	67.02
2018	43.80	43.88	42.92	43.80	42.80

DVA_B = domestic value-added exports by backward industrial linkages, DVA_F = domestic value-added exports by forward industrial linkages, VAX_B = value-added exports by backward industrial linkages, VAX_F = value-added exports by forward industrial linkages, VAX_G = domestic value-added absorbed abroad.

Source: ADB Multi Region Input–Output Tables Database.

Table 3.2.2d: Value-Added Exports by Various Measures—Business Services Sector

ADB Regional Member	VAX_G	DVA_B	DVA_F	VAX_B	VAX_F
	Value-Added Export Measure to Gross Exports Ratio (%)				
Bangladesh					
2008	95.86	95.92	239.05	95.86	238.97
2018	96.31	96.44	387.45	96.31	387.21
Bhutan					
2008	73.64	73.64	116.40	73.64	116.39
2018	82.34	82.34	96.24	82.34	96.24
Brunei Darussalam					
2008	74.86	74.86	108.36	74.86	108.36
2018	73.29	73.30	90.73	73.29	90.72
Cambodia					
2008	81.03	81.03	84.61	81.03	84.61
2018	80.54	80.55	92.33	80.54	92.31
China, People's Republic of					
2008	85.92	88.30	148.33	85.92	145.34
2018	89.52	93.51	188.74	89.52	182.09
Fiji					
2008	67.22	67.23	65.56	67.22	65.55
2018	72.63	72.63	72.90	72.63	72.89
Hong Kong, China					
2008	74.18	74.32	72.99	74.18	72.86
2018	75.73	75.89	74.13	75.73	73.98
India					
2008	87.85	88.62	102.39	87.85	101.59
2018	93.31	93.91	153.14	93.31	152.22
Indonesia					
2008	87.90	88.21	256.58	87.90	255.48
2018	87.45	87.75	273.11	87.45	272.01
Japan					
2008	87.43	89.01	150.07	87.43	147.58
2018	90.83	91.87	182.08	90.83	179.99
Kazakhstan					
2008	87.32	87.72	121.52	87.32	121.09
2018	90.78	91.36	132.87	90.78	132.27
Korea, Republic of					
2008	79.14	79.79	170.09	79.14	168.99
2018	82.17	82.76	164.62	82.17	163.54
Kyrgyz Republic					
2008	63.09	63.10	68.71	63.09	68.69
2018	70.02	70.04	98.59	70.02	98.55
Lao People's Democratic Republic					
2008	79.88	79.89	133.14	79.88	133.13
2018	87.02	87.04	117.33	87.02	117.31
Malaysia					
2008	77.55	77.74	103.44	77.55	103.14
2018	74.60	74.88	109.88	74.60	109.39

continued on next page

Table 3.2.2d: continued

Table 3.2.2d: Value-Added Exports by Various Measures—Business Services Sector					
ADB Regional Member	VAX_G	DVA_B	DVA_F	VAX_B	VAX_F
	Value-Added Export Measure to Gross Exports Ratio (%)				
Maldives					
2008	67.60	67.61	57.03	67.60	57.03
2018	64.38	64.39	49.52	64.38	49.52
Mongolia					
2008	75.96	75.97	103.01	75.96	103.00
2018	78.34	78.37	180.29	78.34	180.24
Nepal					
2008	82.97	82.99	103.94	82.97	103.92
2018	78.97	79.01	92.58	78.97	92.52
Pakistan					
2008	92.41	92.51	168.92	92.41	168.75
2018	93.33	93.44	141.67	93.33	141.50
Philippines					
2008	90.22	90.35	125.37	90.22	125.18
2018	90.25	90.43	96.38	90.25	96.17
Singapore					
2008	58.10	58.23	62.48	58.10	62.37
2018	54.49	54.66	61.90	54.49	61.76
Sri Lanka					
2008	86.05	86.08	96.29	86.05	96.26
2018	89.12	89.14	98.14	89.12	98.12
Taipei,China					
2008	77.33	77.70	116.37	77.33	115.91
2018	78.42	78.79	97.67	78.42	97.26
Thailand					
2008	78.32	78.60	172.18	78.32	171.50
2018	84.64	84.79	104.20	84.64	103.96
Viet Nam					
2008	77.39	77.45	108.50	77.39	108.40
2018	73.76	73.85	108.06	73.76	107.86

DVA_B = domestic value-added exports by backward industrial linkages, DVA_F = domestic value-added exports by forward industrial linkages, VAX_B = value-added exports by backward industrial linkages, VAX_F = value-added exports by forward industrial linkages, VAX_G = domestic value-added absorbed abroad.

Source: ADB Multi Region Input–Output Tables Database.

Table 3.2.2e: Value-Added Exports by Various Measures—Personal Services Sector					
ADB Regional Member	**VAX_G**	**DVA_B**	**DVA_F**	**VAX_B**	**VAX_F**
	Value-Added Export Measure to Gross Exports Ratio (%)				
Bangladesh					
2008	96.58	96.61	350.46	96.58	350.36
2018	96.71	96.79	149.60	96.71	149.51
Bhutan					
2008	86.60	86.61	107.47	86.60	107.46
2018	84.98	84.98	64.54	84.98	64.54
Brunei Darussalam					
2008	90.44	90.44	122.74	90.44	122.74
2018	83.25	83.25	82.86	83.25	82.86
Cambodia					
2008	79.46	79.47	91.86	79.46	91.85
2018	80.69	80.70	117.87	80.69	117.84
China, People's Republic of					
2008	87.49	88.06	205.06	87.49	201.71
2018	92.03	93.33	314.38	92.03	304.72
Fiji					
2008	81.35	81.37	115.76	81.35	115.74
2018	86.28	86.29	99.41	86.28	99.40
Hong Kong, China					
2008	85.87	86.09	393.42	85.87	392.68
2018	86.56	86.74	482.12	86.56	481.19
India					
2008	94.22	94.21	113.42	94.22	113.22
2018	97.94	97.94	149.35	97.94	148.98
Indonesia					
2008	89.10	89.29	132.67	89.10	132.19
2018	91.04	91.16	144.49	91.04	144.10
Japan					
2008	92.91	93.86	510.76	92.91	502.46
2018	93.24	93.70	511.39	93.24	505.45
Kazakhstan					
2008	83.48	83.47	79.01	83.48	78.92
2018	93.13	93.15	89.47	93.13	89.40
Korea, Republic of					
2008	82.84	83.84	173.07	82.84	171.78
2018	84.55	84.98	317.63	84.55	315.56
Kyrgyz Republic					
2008	77.06	77.06	59.47	77.06	59.47
2018	85.85	85.85	71.43	85.85	71.43
Lao People's Democratic Republic					
2008	85.49	85.49	67.72	85.49	67.72
2018	91.31	91.32	73.64	91.31	73.64
Malaysia					
2008	75.27	75.36	80.17	75.27	80.01
2018	76.04	76.07	96.16	76.04	95.87

continued on next page

Table 3.2.2e: continued

Table 3.2.2e: Value-Added Exports by Various Measures—Personal Services Sector					
ADB Regional Member	**VAX_G**	**DVA_B**	**DVA_F**	**VAX_B**	**VAX_F**
	Value-Added Export Measure to Gross Exports Ratio (%)				
Maldives					
2008	75.57	75.58	109.29	75.57	109.28
2018	76.98	76.99	129.06	76.98	129.05
Mongolia					
2008	83.33	83.34	451.55	83.33	451.49
2018	76.36	76.37	258.70	76.36	258.65
Nepal					
2008	91.47	91.49	68.27	91.47	68.25
2018	88.83	88.91	62.57	88.83	62.52
Pakistan					
2008	94.31	94.34	90.55	94.31	90.52
2018	95.21	95.24	89.41	95.21	89.37
Philippines					
2008	89.17	89.29	123.89	89.17	123.73
2018	88.67	88.79	105.55	88.67	105.38
Singapore					
2008	74.43	74.67	168.81	74.43	168.46
2018	79.42	79.67	123.88	79.42	123.62
Sri Lanka					
2008	83.28	83.31	315.67	83.28	315.58
2018	89.47	89.48	112.12	89.47	112.10
Taipei,China					
2008	84.14	84.22	275.78	84.14	274.91
2018	83.81	83.87	259.72	83.81	258.90
Thailand					
2008	82.94	83.02	95.46	82.94	95.24
2018	87.67	87.75	85.86	87.67	85.74
Viet Nam					
2008	84.41	84.43	111.05	84.41	110.98
2018	75.95	75.98	78.20	75.95	78.07

DVA_B = domestic value-added exports by backward industrial linkages, DVA_F = domestic value-added exports by forward industrial linkages, VAX_B = value-added exports by backward industrial linkages, VAX_F = value-added exports by forward industrial linkages, VAX_G = domestic value-added absorbed abroad.

Source: ADB Multi Region Input–Output Tables Database.

Table 3.2.2f: Value-Added Exports by Various Measures—All Sectors					
ADB Regional Member	VAX_G	DVA_B	DVA_F	VAX_B	VAX_F
	Value-Added Export Measure to Gross Exports Ratio (%)				
Bangladesh					
2008	83.73	83.76	83.76	83.73	83.73
2018	85.19	85.24	85.24	85.19	85.19
Bhutan					
2008	83.84	83.85	83.85	83.84	83.84
2018	84.01	84.02	84.02	84.01	84.01
Brunei Darussalam					
2008	92.23	92.24	92.24	92.23	92.23
2018	87.15	87.15	87.15	87.15	87.15
Cambodia					
2008	70.93	70.95	70.95	70.93	70.93
2018	72.29	72.32	72.32	72.29	72.29
China, People's Republic of					
2008	77.26	78.71	78.71	77.26	77.26
2018	82.64	85.41	85.41	82.64	82.64
Fiji					
2008	68.42	68.43	68.43	68.42	68.42
2018	73.06	73.06	73.06	73.06	73.06
Hong Kong, China					
2008	70.85	70.98	70.98	70.85	70.85
2018	71.87	72.02	72.02	71.87	71.87
India					
2008	80.05	80.61	80.61	80.05	80.05
2018	84.34	84.84	84.84	84.34	84.34
Indonesia					
2008	82.48	82.92	82.92	82.48	82.48
2018	77.60	78.06	78.06	77.60	77.60
Japan					
2008	80.43	81.74	81.74	80.43	80.43
2018	78.31	79.25	79.25	78.31	78.31
Kazakhstan					
2008	85.70	85.91	85.91	85.70	85.70
2018	90.44	90.68	90.68	90.44	90.44
Korea, Republic of					
2008	61.49	61.89	61.89	61.49	61.49
2018	64.53	64.97	64.97	64.53	64.53
Kyrgyz Republic					
2008	64.14	64.15	64.15	64.14	64.14
2018	75.45	75.48	75.48	75.45	75.45
Lao People's Democratic Republic					
2008	84.66	84.66	84.66	84.66	84.66
2018	89.22	89.25	89.25	89.22	89.22
Malaysia					
2008	71.36	71.59	71.59	71.36	71.36
2018	63.08	63.43	63.43	63.08	63.08

continued on next page

Table 3.2.2f: continued

Table 3.2.2f: Value-Added Exports by Various Measures—All Sectors					
ADB Regional Member	**VAX_G**	**DVA_B**	**DVA_F**	**VAX_B**	**VAX_F**
	Value-Added Export Measure to Gross Exports Ratio (%)				
Maldives					
2008	67.30	67.30	67.30	67.30	67.30
2018	64.13	64.14	64.14	64.13	64.13
Mongolia					
2008	74.85	74.86	74.86	74.85	74.85
2018	75.31	75.32	75.32	75.31	75.31
Nepal					
2008	83.02	83.05	83.05	83.02	83.02
2018	80.32	80.38	80.38	80.32	80.32
Pakistan					
2008	90.60	90.68	90.68	90.60	90.60
2018	91.88	91.97	91.97	91.88	91.88
Philippines					
2008	67.36	67.46	67.46	67.36	67.36
2018	74.73	74.90	74.90	74.73	74.73
Singapore					
2008	42.44	42.53	42.53	42.44	42.44
2018	46.44	46.55	46.55	46.44	46.44
Sri Lanka					
2008	80.81	80.83	80.83	80.81	80.81
2018	85.67	85.69	85.69	85.67	85.67
Taipei,China					
2008	54.80	55.02	55.02	54.80	54.80
2018	58.44	58.70	58.70	58.44	58.44
Thailand					
2008	60.31	60.56	60.56	60.31	60.31
2018	70.95	71.12	71.12	70.95	70.95
Viet Nam					
2008	71.01	71.09	71.09	71.01	71.01
2018	58.99	59.19	59.19	58.99	58.99

DVA_B = domestic value-added exports by backward industrial linkages, DVA_F = domestic value-added exports by forward industrial linkages, VAX_B = value-added exports by backward industrial linkages, VAX_F = value-added exports by forward industrial linkages, VAX_G = domestic value-added absorbed abroad.

Source: ADB Multi Region Input–Output Tables Database.

Table 3.2.3a: Revealed Comparative Advantage by Aggregate Sector (Traditional Method)		
ADB Regional Member	**2008**	**2018**
	(ratio)	
Bangladesh		
Business Services Sector	0.51	0.24
Low-Technology Manufacturing Sector	5.24	5.31
Medium- and High-Technology Manufacturing Sector	0.06	0.04
Personal Services Sector	1.11	2.97
Primary Sector	0.19	0.14
Bhutan		
Business Services Sector	0.51	1.09
Low-Technology Manufacturing Sector	2.88	2.58
Medium- and High-Technology Manufacturing Sector	0.47	0.25
Personal Services Sector	0.46	1.63
Primary Sector	1.79	1.54
Brunei Darussalam		
Business Services Sector	0.25	0.24
Low-Technology Manufacturing Sector	0.03	0.10
Medium- and High-Technology Manufacturing Sector	0.71	0.92
Personal Services Sector	0.52	0.38
Primary Sector	5.20	5.03
Cambodia		
Business Services Sector	1.27	1.14
Low-Technology Manufacturing Sector	3.77	3.61
Medium- and High-Technology Manufacturing Sector	0.02	0.02
Personal Services Sector	1.13	0.53
Primary Sector	0.79	1.02
China, People's Republic of		
Business Services Sector	0.66	0.62
Low-Technology Manufacturing Sector	1.51	1.44
Medium- and High-Technology Manufacturing Sector	1.23	1.29
Personal Services Sector	0.43	0.33
Primary Sector	0.13	0.11
Fiji		
Business Services Sector	3.07	2.54
Low-Technology Manufacturing Sector	1.19	1.24
Medium- and High-Technology Manufacturing Sector	0.05	0.05
Personal Services Sector	0.86	0.96
Primary Sector	0.47	0.81
Hong Kong, China		
Business Services Sector	3.77	3.37
Low-Technology Manufacturing Sector	0.36	0.22
Medium- and High-Technology Manufacturing Sector	0.11	0.12
Personal Services Sector	0.39	0.29
Primary Sector	0.01	0.01
India		
Business Services Sector	1.78	1.06
Low-Technology Manufacturing Sector	0.97	1.32
Medium- and High-Technology Manufacturing Sector	0.64	0.92
Personal Services Sector	2.32	1.39
Primary Sector	0.73	0.60
Indonesia		
Business Services Sector	0.24	0.20
Low-Technology Manufacturing Sector	2.25	2.59
Medium- and High-Technology Manufacturing Sector	0.70	0.68
Personal Services Sector	0.57	0.42
Primary Sector	2.18	2.21

continued on next page

Table 3.2.3a: continued

Table 3.2.3a: Revealed Comparative Advantage by Aggregate Sector (Traditional Method)		
ADB Regional Member	**2008**	**2018**
	(ratio)	
Japan		
Business Services Sector	1.00	0.65
Low-Technology Manufacturing Sector	0.34	0.37
Medium- and High-Technology Manufacturing Sector	1.47	1.68
Personal Services Sector	0.21	0.18
Primary Sector	0.03	0.04
Kazakhstan		
Business Services Sector	1.11	1.01
Low-Technology Manufacturing Sector	0.14	0.17
Medium- and High-Technology Manufacturing Sector	0.38	0.47
Personal Services Sector	0.47	0.26
Primary Sector	4.65	4.89
Korea, Republic of		
Business Services Sector	0.48	0.43
Low-Technology Manufacturing Sector	0.45	0.37
Medium- and High-Technology Manufacturing Sector	1.68	1.80
Personal Services Sector	0.69	0.33
Primary Sector	0.01	0.01
Kyrgyz Republic		
Business Services Sector	1.38	0.88
Low-Technology Manufacturing Sector	0.75	0.88
Medium- and High-Technology Manufacturing Sector	0.74	0.69
Personal Services Sector	6.04	6.74
Primary Sector	0.86	1.69
Lao People's Democratic Republic		
Business Services Sector	0.43	0.54
Low-Technology Manufacturing Sector	1.35	3.45
Medium- and High-Technology Manufacturing Sector	0.02	0.02
Personal Services Sector	0.09	1.40
Primary Sector	6.03	2.77
Malaysia		
Business Services Sector	0.92	0.74
Low-Technology Manufacturing Sector	1.56	1.68
Medium- and High-Technology Manufacturing Sector	0.88	0.97
Personal Services Sector	0.62	0.49
Primary Sector	0.95	0.86
Maldives		
Business Services Sector	4.04	3.21
Low-Technology Manufacturing Sector	0.16	0.62
Medium- and High-Technology Manufacturing Sector	0.00	0.00
Personal Services Sector	0.69	1.35
Primary Sector	0.12	0.12
Mongolia		
Business Services Sector	0.87	0.45
Low-Technology Manufacturing Sector	0.40	0.17
Medium- and High-Technology Manufacturing Sector	0.04	0.04
Personal Services Sector	0.10	0.14
Primary Sector	6.30	8.47
Nepal		
Business Services Sector	1.43	1.38
Low-Technology Manufacturing Sector	1.45	1.11
Medium- and High-Technology Manufacturing Sector	0.18	0.16
Personal Services Sector	15.81	15.55
Primary Sector	0.62	0.54

continued on next page

Table 3.2.3a: continued

Table 3.2.3a: Revealed Comparative Advantage by Aggregate Sector (Traditional Method)		
ADB Regional Member	**2008**	**2018**
	(ratio)	
Pakistan		
Business Services Sector	0.68	0.76
Low-Technology Manufacturing Sector	4.28	3.70
Medium- and High-Technology Manufacturing Sector	0.12	0.15
Personal Services Sector	3.10	2.59
Primary Sector	0.55	0.90
Philippines		
Business Services Sector	1.01	1.54
Low-Technology Manufacturing Sector	1.28	1.21
Medium- and High-Technology Manufacturing Sector	1.11	0.78
Personal Services Sector	0.39	0.93
Primary Sector	0.21	0.22
Singapore		
Business Services Sector	1.90	1.93
Low-Technology Manufacturing Sector	0.18	0.15
Medium- and High-Technology Manufacturing Sector	1.09	1.00
Personal Services Sector	0.30	0.18
Primary Sector	0.00	0.00
Sri Lanka		
Business Services Sector	1.60	1.54
Low-Technology Manufacturing Sector	3.00	2.89
Medium- and High-Technology Manufacturing Sector	0.19	0.08
Personal Services Sector	0.46	1.68
Primary Sector	0.53	0.57
Taipei,China		
Business Services Sector	0.68	0.75
Low-Technology Manufacturing Sector	0.47	0.38
Medium- and High-Technology Manufacturing Sector	1.58	1.61
Personal Services Sector	0.23	0.19
Primary Sector	0.05	0.04
Thailand		
Business Services Sector	0.54	1.27
Low-Technology Manufacturing Sector	1.30	1.11
Medium- and High-Technology Manufacturing Sector	1.31	0.90
Personal Services Sector	0.90	1.47
Primary Sector	0.23	0.44
Viet Nam		
Business Services Sector	0.70	0.58
Low-Technology Manufacturing Sector	3.21	3.15
Medium- and High-Technology Manufacturing Sector	0.26	0.48
Personal Services Sector	0.31	0.52
Primary Sector	1.82	1.16

Source: ADB Multi Region Input–Output Tables Database.

Table 3.2.3b: Revealed Comparative Advantage by Aggregate Sector (Value-Added Method)		
ADB Regional Member	**2008**	**2018**
	(ratio)	
Bangladesh		
Business Services Sector	0.84	0.67
Low-Technology Manufacturing Sector	3.06	3.58
Medium- and High-Technology Manufacturing Sector	0.14	0.11
Personal Services Sector	2.32	2.82
Primary Sector	0.92	0.72
Bhutan		
Business Services Sector	0.41	0.78
Low-Technology Manufacturing Sector	3.84	2.96
Medium- and High-Technology Manufacturing Sector	0.29	0.25
Personal Services Sector	0.29	0.68
Primary Sector	1.59	1.30
Brunei Darussalam		
Business Services Sector	0.17	0.15
Low-Technology Manufacturing Sector	0.06	0.08
Medium- and High-Technology Manufacturing Sector	0.65	0.87
Personal Services Sector	0.35	0.19
Primary Sector	4.70	4.89
Cambodia		
Business Services Sector	0.89	0.91
Low-Technology Manufacturing Sector	3.16	3.01
Medium- and High-Technology Manufacturing Sector	0.04	0.05
Personal Services Sector	0.73	0.47
Primary Sector	1.29	1.28
China, People's Republic of		
Business Services Sector	0.72	0.86
Low-Technology Manufacturing Sector	1.45	1.29
Medium- and High-Technology Manufacturing Sector	1.26	1.16
Personal Services Sector	0.56	0.65
Primary Sector	0.98	0.95
Fiji		
Business Services Sector	1.72	1.59
Low-Technology Manufacturing Sector	1.16	1.16
Medium- and High-Technology Manufacturing Sector	0.09	0.09
Personal Services Sector	0.73	0.71
Primary Sector	0.69	0.83
Hong Kong, China		
Business Services Sector	2.27	2.17
Low-Technology Manufacturing Sector	0.35	0.18
Medium- and High-Technology Manufacturing Sector	0.02	0.01
Personal Services Sector	1.07	1.07
Primary Sector	0.00	0.00
India		
Business Services Sector	1.33	1.20
Low-Technology Manufacturing Sector	0.73	0.89
Medium- and High-Technology Manufacturing Sector	0.60	0.73
Personal Services Sector	1.64	1.32
Primary Sector	0.96	0.89
Indonesia		
Business Services Sector	0.43	0.43
Low-Technology Manufacturing Sector	1.55	1.85
Medium- and High-Technology Manufacturing Sector	0.79	0.70
Personal Services Sector	0.46	0.42
Primary Sector	2.50	2.63

continued on next page

Table 3.2.3b: continued

Table 3.2.3b: Revealed Comparative Advantage by Aggregate Sector (Value-Added Method)		
ADB Regional Member	**2008**	**2018**
	(ratio)	
Japan		
Business Services Sector	1.08	0.93
Low-Technology Manufacturing Sector	0.68	0.71
Medium- and High-Technology Manufacturing Sector	1.61	1.83
Personal Services Sector	0.66	0.61
Primary Sector	0.05	0.06
Kazakhstan		
Business Services Sector	0.92	0.93
Low-Technology Manufacturing Sector	0.42	0.27
Medium- and High-Technology Manufacturing Sector	0.44	0.62
Personal Services Sector	0.22	0.14
Primary Sector	2.86	2.83
Korea, Republic of		
Business Services Sector	0.78	0.69
Low-Technology Manufacturing Sector	0.65	0.65
Medium- and High-Technology Manufacturing Sector	2.00	2.20
Personal Services Sector	0.97	0.87
Primary Sector	0.09	0.09
Kyrgyz Republic		
Business Services Sector	0.86	0.72
Low-Technology Manufacturing Sector	0.65	0.75
Medium- and High-Technology Manufacturing Sector	1.03	1.22
Personal Services Sector	2.81	3.45
Primary Sector	1.18	1.01
Lao People's Democratic Republic		
Business Services Sector	0.39	0.45
Low-Technology Manufacturing Sector	1.39	3.45
Medium- and High-Technology Manufacturing Sector	0.04	0.07
Personal Services Sector	0.03	0.62
Primary Sector	4.17	2.21
Malaysia		
Business Services Sector	0.78	0.80
Low-Technology Manufacturing Sector	0.81	0.95
Medium- and High-Technology Manufacturing Sector	0.83	0.98
Personal Services Sector	0.35	0.40
Primary Sector	2.19	1.84
Maldives		
Business Services Sector	2.00	1.55
Low-Technology Manufacturing Sector	0.58	1.81
Medium- and High-Technology Manufacturing Sector	0.02	0.02
Personal Services Sector	0.56	1.47
Primary Sector	0.62	0.25
Mongolia		
Business Services Sector	0.70	0.68
Low-Technology Manufacturing Sector	0.38	0.46
Medium- and High-Technology Manufacturing Sector	0.07	0.10
Personal Services Sector	0.30	0.26
Primary Sector	4.11	4.34
Nepal		
Business Services Sector	1.05	1.00
Low-Technology Manufacturing Sector	1.12	0.97
Medium- and High-Technology Manufacturing Pector	0.18	0.20
Personal Services Sector	6.52	6.54
Primary Sector	0.97	0.97

continued on next page

Table 3.2.3b: continued

Table 3.2.3b: Revealed Comparative Advantage by Aggregate Sector (Value-Added Method)		
ADB Regional Member	**2008**	**2018**
	(ratio)	
Pakistan		
Business Services Sector	0.74	0.73
Low-Technology Manufacturing Sector	1.87	1.61
Medium- and High-Technology Manufacturing Sector	0.16	0.19
Personal Services Sector	1.55	1.36
Primary Sector	2.33	2.63
Philippines		
Business Services Sector	1.10	1.24
Low-Technology Manufacturing Sector	1.39	1.31
Medium- and High-Technology Manufacturing Sector	0.88	0.63
Personal Services Sector	0.36	0.71
Primary Sector	0.78	0.74
Singapore		
Business Services Sector	1.63	1.61
Low-Technology Manufacturing Sector	0.24	0.28
Medium- and High-Technology Manufacturing Sector	1.05	1.02
Personal Services Sector	0.59	0.26
Primary Sector	0.00	0.00
Sri Lanka		
Business Services Sector	1.12	1.11
Low-Technology Manufacturing Sector	2.62	2.69
Medium- and High-Technology Manufacturing Sector	0.26	0.11
Personal Services Sector	0.91	1.19
Primary Sector	0.70	0.68
Taipei,China		
Business Services Sector	0.84	0.78
Low-Technology Manufacturing Sector	0.51	0.51
Medium- and High-Technology Manufacturing Sector	2.03	2.21
Personal Services Sector	0.59	0.45
Primary Sector	0.07	0.06
Thailand		
Business Services Sector	0.90	1.17
Low-Technology Manufacturing Sector	1.45	1.20
Medium- and High-Technology Manufacturing Sector	1.21	0.78
Personal Services Sector	0.71	0.96
Primary Sector	0.56	0.71
Viet Nam		
Business Services Sector	0.63	0.67
Low-Technology Manufacturing Sector	2.37	2.57
Medium- and High-Technology Manufacturing Sector	0.42	0.61
Personal Services Sector	0.24	0.37
Primary Sector	2.02	1.43

Source: ADB Multi Region Input–Output Tables Database.

Table 3.2.4.a: Vertical Specialization, Disaggregated—Bangladesh

	Exports	VS	FVA_FIN	FVA_INT	DDC	FDC
	($ million)	(% of gross exports)	(% of VS)			
Agriculture, Hunting, Forestry and Fishing						
2008	336.48	7.91	12.95	62.04	0.26	24.75
2018	511.74	7.49	28.27	54.47	0.29	16.97
Textiles and Textile Products						
2008	12,416.59	18.81	77.71	11.93	0.06	10.29
2018	29,725.79	16.76	76.42	12.70	0.15	10.73
Wholesale Trade and Commission Trade, Except of Motor Vehicles and Motorcycles						
2008	363.45	3.40	11.75	42.12	0.19	45.95
2018	484.15	4.17	14.36	36.46	0.22	48.96

$ = United States dollars, DDC = domestic value-added double counted in exports, FDC = foreign value-added double counted in exports, FVA_FIN = foreign value-added in exports for final consumption, FVA_INT = foreign value-added in intermediate exports, VS = vertical specialization.

Source: ADB Multi Region Input–Output Tables Database.

Table 3.2.4.b: Vertical Specialization, Disaggregated—Bhutan

	Exports	VS	FVA_FIN	FVA_INT	DDC	FDC
	($ million)	(% of gross exports)	(% of VS)			
Agriculture, Hunting, Forestry and Fishing						
2008	87.81	4.57	32.24	53.45	0.02	14.29
2018	51.82	3.57	37.13	53.25	0.01	9.61
Electricity, Gas and Water Supply						
2008	200.22	12.68	1.45	64.18	0.01	34.36
2018	276.44	16.27	1.23	61.86	0.01	36.91
Inland Transport						
2008	27.33	28.48	49.42	37.46	0.01	13.12
2018	61.34	24.23	31.11	47.21	0.00	21.68

$ = United States dollars, DDC = domestic value-added double counted in exports, FDC = foreign value-added double counted in exports, FVA_FIN = foreign value-added in exports for final consumption, FVA_INT = foreign value-added in intermediate exports, VS = vertical specialization.

Source: ADB Multi Region Input–Output Tables Database.

Table 3.2.4.c: Vertical Specialization, Disaggregated—Brunei Darussalam

	Exports	VS	FVA_FIN	FVA_INT	DDC	FDC
	($ million)	(% of gross exports)	(% of VS)			
Air Transport						
2008	207.28	30.32	50.43	34.41	0.03	15.13
2018	23.02	42.16	35.44	36.33	0.01	28.22
Coke, Refined Petroleum and Nuclear Fuel						
2008	3,220.03	6.70	4.53	65.28	0.04	30.15
2018	2,875.89	9.99	6.52	62.25	0.01	31.23
Mining and Quarrying						
2008	5,740.09	6.24	0.09	65.82	0.05	34.04
2018	3,454.15	11.93	0.35	66.34	0.01	33.30

$ = United States dollars, DDC = domestic value-added double counted in exports, FDC = foreign value-added double counted in exports, FVA_FIN = foreign value-added in exports for final consumption, FVA_INT = foreign value-added in intermediate exports, VS = vertical specialization.

Source: ADB Multi Region Input–Output Tables Database.

Table 3.2.4.d: Vertical Specialization, Disaggregated—Cambodia

	Exports	VS	FVA_FIN	FVA_INT	DDC	FDC
	($ million)	(% of gross exports)	(% of VS)			
Hotels and Restaurants						
2008	681.06	16.47	59.15	26.65	0.01	14.19
2018	1,404.68	17.33	56.81	26.36	0.02	16.81
Textiles and Textile Products						
2008	2,259.81	37.98	89.39	4.94	0.00	5.66
2018	5,621.83	35.73	84.16	9.64	0.00	6.19
Wholesale Trade and Commission Trade, Except of Motor Vehicles and Motorcycles						
2008	327.23	22.19	22.65	45.10	0.01	32.24
2018	1,143.43	20.62	30.37	37.66	0.03	31.95

$ = United States dollars, DDC = domestic value-added double counted in exports, FDC = foreign value-added double counted in exports, FVA_FIN = foreign value-added in exports for final consumption, FVA_INT = foreign value-added in intermediate exports, VS = vertical specialization.

Source: ADB Multi Region Input–Output Tables Database.

Table 3.2.4.e: Vertical Specialization, Disaggregated—China, People's Republic of

	Exports	VS	FVA_FIN	FVA_INT	DDC	FDC
	($ million)	(% of gross exports)		(% of VS)		
Basic Metals and Fabricated Metal						
2008	122,193.53	22.19	15.52	46.29	5.39	32.79
2018	190,846.81	18.31	22.79	43.47	5.67	28.08
Electrical and Optical Equipment						
2008	483,100.83	31.26	61.98	16.27	3.42	18.33
2018	860,708.64	21.58	53.41	20.10	5.91	20.58
Textiles and Textile Products						
2008	164,533.50	13.85	79.58	10.32	1.26	8.85
2018	266,740.74	8.36	75.72	12.38	1.96	9.94

$ = United States dollars, DDC = domestic value-added double counted in exports, FDC = foreign value-added double counted in exports, FVA_FIN = foreign value-added in exports for final consumption, FVA_INT = foreign value-added in intermediate exports, VS = vertical specialization.

Source: ADB Multi Region Input–Output Tables Database.

Table 3.2.4.f: Vertical Specialization, Disaggregated—Fiji

	Exports	VS	FVA_FIN	FVA_INT	DDC	FDC
	($ million)	(% of gross exports)		(% of VS)		
Agriculture, Hunting, Forestry and Fishing						
2008	38.32	18.72	36.53	49.36	0.01	14.11
2018	132.68	17.62	38.57	44.64	0.01	16.77
Food, Beverages and Tobacco						
2008	140.86	28.15	25.55	57.23	0.01	17.21
2018	354.47	27.24	48.94	36.65	0.01	14.40
Textiles and Textile Products						
2008	18.14	16.19	79.03	14.75	0.00	6.22
2018	48.18	14.67	77.35	15.44	0.01	7.21

$ = United States dollars, DDC = domestic value-added double counted in exports, FDC = foreign value-added double counted in exports, FVA_FIN = foreign value-added in exports for final consumption, FVA_INT = foreign value-added in intermediate exports, VS = vertical specialization.

Source: ADB Multi Region Input–Output Tables Database.

Table 3.2.4.g: Vertical Specialization, Disaggregated—Hong Kong, China

	Exports	VS	FVA_FIN	FVA_INT	DDC	FDC
	($ million)	(% of gross exports)		(% of VS)		
Air Transport						
2008	10,753.51	42.47	12.76	53.27	0.50	33.46
2018	15,530.05	33.86	22.52	47.82	0.54	29.11
Retail Trade, Except of Motor Vehicles and Motorcycles; Repair of Household Goods						
2008	14,308.98	11.16	61.33	29.24	0.52	8.91
2018	19,624.49	10.61	68.06	22.46	0.55	8.93
Wholesale Trade and Commission Trade, Except of Motor Vehicles and Motorcycles						
2008	70,779.38	26.85	50.96	35.99	0.38	12.66
2018	110,944.68	27.06	54.27	30.93	0.41	14.39

$ = United States dollars, DDC = domestic value-added double counted in exports, FDC = foreign value-added double counted in exports, FVA_FIN = foreign value-added in exports for final consumption, FVA_INT = foreign value-added in intermediate exports, VS = vertical specialization.

Source: ADB Multi Region Input–Output Tables Database.

Table 3.2.4.h: Vertical Specialization, Disaggregated—India

	Exports	VS	FVA_FIN	FVA_INT	DDC	FDC
	($ million)	(% of gross exports)		(% of VS)		
Chemicals and Chemical Products						
2008	15,279.64	29.32	10.95	52.69	0.69	35.67
2018	31,124.17	17.00	11.11	51.13	0.83	36.93
Renting of Machinery and Equipment and Other Business Activities						
2008	62,272.04	12.01	24.20	48.25	0.74	26.80
2018	77,353.52	4.29	49.74	29.95	1.10	19.21
Textiles and Textile Products						
2008	15,734.69	15.07	68.82	16.20	0.25	14.73
2018	32,503.56	10.60	64.09	19.48	0.34	16.08

$ = United States dollars, DDC = domestic value-added double counted in exports, FDC = foreign value-added double counted in exports, FVA_FIN = foreign value-added in exports for final consumption, FVA_INT = foreign value-added in intermediate exports, VS = vertical specialization.

Source: ADB Multi Region Input–Output Tables Database.

Table 3.2.4.i: Vertical Specialization, Disaggregated—Indonesia

	Exports	VS	FVA_FIN	FVA_INT	DDC	FDC
	($ million)	(% of gross exports)		(% of VS)		
Coke, Refined Petroleum and Nuclear Fuel						
2008	15,138.11	12.81	20.11	48.24	0.62	31.03
2018	17,243.89	47.01	22.07	46.27	0.44	31.22
Mining and Quarrying						
2008	35,512.98	7.04	1.39	58.93	1.21	38.47
2018	48,018.93	11.21	1.49	56.23	1.14	41.13
Textiles and Textile Products						
2008	9,021.33	26.61	72.40	15.27	0.26	12.07
2018	16,251.31	30.11	72.62	15.19	0.20	11.99

$ = United States dollars, DDC = domestic value-added double counted in exports, FDC = foreign value-added double counted in exports, FVA_FIN = foreign value-added in exports for final consumption, FVA_INT = foreign value-added in intermediate exports, VS = vertical specialization.

Source: ADB Multi Region Input–Output Tables Database.

Table 3.2.4.j: Vertical Specialization, Disaggregated—Japan

	Exports	VS	FVA_FIN	FVA_INT	DDC	FDC
	($ million)	(% of gross exports)		(% of VS)		
Electrical and Optical Equipment						
2008	174,821.94	18.15	34.48	29.34	3.28	32.90
2018	174,856.84	20.70	33.05	32.97	2.34	31.65
Machinery, Nec						
2008	65,815.51	15.48	62.34	20.51	1.45	15.70
2018	84,274.67	17.46	56.70	24.37	1.19	17.74
Transport Equipment						
2008	187,468.74	16.68	76.35	14.41	0.84	8.40
2018	217,689.94	19.57	70.06	19.34	0.73	9.86

$ = United States dollars, DDC = domestic value-added double counted in exports, FDC = foreign value-added double counted in exports, FVA_FIN = foreign value-added in exports for final consumption, FVA_INT = foreign value-added in intermediate exports, VS = vertical specialization.

Source: ADB Multi Region Input–Output Tables Database.

Table 3.2.4.k: Vertical Specialization, Disaggregated—Kazakhstan

	Exports	VS	FVA_FIN	FVA_INT	DDC	FDC
	($ million)	(% of gross exports)		(% of VS)		
Basic Metals and Fabricated Metal						
2008	7,641.83	11.21	0.55	45.29	0.67	53.48
2018	9,114.52	7.95	6.85	37.38	0.43	55.34
Coke, Refined Petroleum and Nuclear Fuel						
2008	4,103.30	18.42	24.60	47.39	0.31	27.69
2018	1,575.41	6.88	36.86	42.82	0.30	20.01
Mining and Quarrying						
2008	35,899.30	14.95	1.78	58.43	0.54	39.25
2018	25,750.38	9.75	3.57	49.86	0.40	46.16

$ = United States dollars, DDC = domestic value-added double counted in exports, FDC = foreign value-added double counted in exports, FVA_FIN = foreign value-added in exports for final consumption, FVA_INT = foreign value-added in intermediate exports, VS = vertical specialization.

Source: ADB Multi Region Input–Output Tables Database.

Table 3.2.4.l: Vertical Specialization, Disaggregated—Korea, Republic of

	Exports	VS	FVA_FIN	FVA_INT	DDC	FDC
	($ million)	(% of gross exports)		(% of VS)		
Electrical and Optical Equipment						
2008	141,978.97	35.59	39.39	26.12	1.20	33.29
2018	244,916.40	31.53	35.02	33.03	1.67	30.27
Textiles and Textile Products						
2008	14,903.61	29.04	21.70	41.94	0.81	35.56
2018	18,096.13	27.99	20.36	39.89	0.93	38.82
Transport Equipment						
2008	90,978.29	34.56	77.39	14.51	0.24	7.87
2018	101,412.83	33.18	73.47	16.33	0.33	9.87

$ = United States dollars, DDC = domestic value-added double counted in exports, FDC = foreign value-added double counted in exports, FVA_FIN = foreign value-added in exports for final consumption, FVA_INT = foreign value-added in intermediate exports, VS = vertical specialization.

Source: ADB Multi Region Input–Output Tables Database.

Table 3.2.4.m: Vertical Specialization, Disaggregated—Kyrgyz Republic

	Exports	VS	FVA_FIN	FVA_INT	DDC	FDC
	($ million)	(% of gross exports)	(% of VS)			
Agriculture, Hunting, Forestry and Fishing						
2008	159.36	13.46	40.77	40.29	0.01	18.92
2018	277.22	20.12	46.26	33.73	0.03	19.98
Basic Metals and Fabricated Metal						
2008	539.26	44.16	23.95	41.28	0.01	34.76
2018	541.43	23.52	28.13	37.81	0.01	34.05
Food, Beverages and Tobacco						
2008	62.26	24.94	63.34	20.70	0.01	15.95
2018	14.33	26.66	79.64	16.61	0.02	3.73

$ = United States dollars, DDC = domestic value-added double counted in exports, FDC = foreign value-added double counted in exports, FVA_FIN = foreign value-added in exports for final consumption, FVA_INT = foreign value-added in intermediate exports, VS = vertical specialization.

Source: ADB Multi Region Input–Output Tables Database.

Table 3.2.4.n: Vertical Specialization, Disaggregated—Lao People's Democratic Republic

	Exports	VS	FVA_FIN	FVA_INT	DDC	FDC
	($ million)	(% of gross exports)	(% of VS)			
Agriculture, Hunting, Forestry and Fishing						
2008	65.67	3.69	7.06	61.05	0.01	31.88
2018	609.01	3.24	8.46	47.04	0.09	44.42
Electricity, Gas and Water Supply						
2008	78.87	8.02	12.92	55.63	0.01	31.44
2018	2,197.53	6.52	16.75	54.39	0.02	28.83
Retail Trade, Except of Motor Vehicles and Motorcycles; Repair of Household Goods						
2008	43.93	13.75	23.52	45.99	0.00	30.48
2018	374.19	9.49	34.64	40.90	0.01	24.44

$ = United States dollars, DDC = domestic value-added double counted in exports, FDC = foreign value-added double counted in exports, FVA_FIN = foreign value-added in exports for final consumption, FVA_INT = foreign value-added in intermediate exports, VS = vertical specialization.

Source: ADB Multi Region Input–Output Tables Database.

Table 3.2.4.o: Vertical Specialization, Disaggregated—Malaysia

	Exports	VS	FVA_FIN	FVA_INT	DDC	FDC
	($ million)	(% of gross exports)	(% of VS)			
Electrical and Optical Equipment						
2008	28,208.83	46.29	29.63	25.38	0.82	44.18
2018	47,166.02	47.74	26.21	32.35	0.72	40.72
Machinery, Nec						
2008	1,439.81	39.24	39.31	31.82	0.39	28.48
2018	1,862.47	44.60	14.60	49.68	0.38	35.35
Mining and Quarrying						
2008	14,984.49	7.41	0.27	59.35	1.32	39.06
2018	9,931.14	10.11	-5.37	49.14	1.76	54.47

$ = United States dollars, DDC = domestic value-added double counted in exports, FDC = foreign value-added double counted in exports, FVA_FIN = foreign value-added in exports for final consumption, FVA_INT = foreign value-added in intermediate exports, VS = vertical specialization.

Source: ADB Multi Region Input–Output Tables Database.

Table 3.2.4.p: Vertical Specialization, Disaggregated—Maldives

	Exports	VS	FVA_FIN	FVA_INT	DDC	FDC
	($ million)	(% of gross exports)	(% of VS)			
Air Transport						
2008	19.15	44.55	7.17	73.17	0.00	19.66
2018	142.21	39.10	35.43	54.55	0.01	10.01
Hotels and Restaurants						
2008	1,246.27	32.62	39.79	37.60	0.00	22.60
2018	2,550.06	36.36	41.01	35.34	0.01	23.65
Other Supporting and Auxiliary Transport Activities; Activities of Travel Agencies						
2008	15.55	21.36	27.43	47.68	0.00	24.88
2018	78.02	26.39	29.06	41.69	0.01	29.24

$ = United States dollars, DDC = domestic value-added double counted in exports, FDC = foreign value-added double counted in exports, FVA_FIN = foreign value-added in exports for final consumption, FVA_INT = foreign value-added in intermediate exports, VS = vertical specialization.

Source: ADB Multi Region Input–Output Tables Database.

Table 3.2.4.q: Vertical Specialization, Disaggregated—Mongolia

	Exports	VS	FVA_FIN	FVA_INT	DDC	FDC
	($ million)	(% of gross exports)	(% of VS)			
Inland Transport						
2008	81.69	31.08	28.07	51.57	0.01	20.35
2018	137.89	37.27	23.69	57.14	0.01	19.16
Mining and Quarrying						
2008	1,516.30	27.41	1.28	61.38	0.01	37.33
2018	5,382.16	25.45	2.17	70.92	0.03	26.88
Textiles and Textile Products						
2008	69.31	21.12	49.42	25.02	0.00	25.56
2018	47.55	30.12	11.82	53.12	0.01	35.05

$ = United States dollars, DDC = domestic value-added double counted in exports, FDC = foreign value-added double counted in exports, FVA_FIN = foreign value-added in exports for final consumption, FVA_INT = foreign value-added in intermediate exports, VS = vertical specialization.

Source: ADB Multi Region Input–Output Tables Database.

Table 3.2.4.r: Vertical Specialization, Disaggregated—Nepal

	Exports	VS	FVA_FIN	FVA_INT	DDC	FDC
	($ million)	(% of gross exports)	(% of VS)			
Agriculture, Hunting, Forestry and Fishing						
2008	74.27	7.71	40.81	51.53	0.02	7.64
2018	72.56	8.76	52.58	42.20	0.01	5.21
Food, Beverages and Tobacco						
2008	73.06	13.87	70.02	26.27	0.01	3.70
2018	67.27	15.40	42.13	46.84	0.01	11.02
Retail Trade, Except of Motor Vehicles and Motorcycles; Repair of Household Goods						
2008	92.65	7.40	29.16	43.04	0.01	27.80
2018	139.16	8.63	32.10	40.21	0.01	27.68

$ = United States dollars, DDC = domestic value-added double counted in exports, FDC = foreign value-added double counted in exports, FVA_FIN = foreign value-added in exports for final consumption, FVA_INT = foreign value-added in intermediate exports, VS = vertical specialization.

Source: ADB Multi Region Input–Output Tables Database.

Table 3.2.4.s: Vertical Specialization, Disaggregated—Pakistan

	Exports	VS	FVA_FIN	FVA_INT	DDC	FDC
	($ million)	(% of gross exports)	(% of VS)			
Inland Transport						
2008	702.97	15.18	33.47	50.03	0.02	16.47
2018	1,403.40	13.05	37.26	46.10	0.02	16.61
Retail Trade, Except of Motor Vehicles and Motorcycles; Repair of Household Goods						
2008	948.93	5.54	46.70	34.58	0.05	18.68
2018	1,569.43	5.03	47.95	35.23	0.05	16.77
Textiles and Textile Products						
2008	8,280.53	9.30	47.33	26.13	0.03	26.51
2018	10,923.32	8.01	49.79	26.68	0.03	23.50

$ = United States dollars, DDC = domestic value-added double counted in exports, FDC = foreign value-added double counted in exports, FVA_FIN = foreign value-added in exports for final consumption, FVA_INT = foreign value-added in intermediate exports, VS = vertical specialization.

Source: ADB Multi Region Input–Output Tables Database.

Table 3.2.4.t: Vertical Specialization, Disaggregated—Philippines

	Exports	VS	FVA_FIN	FVA_INT	DDC	FDC
	($ million)	(% of gross exports)	(% of VS)			
Electrical and Optical Equipment						
2008	22,572.95	54.69	20.35	32.58	0.38	46.70
2018	19,077.94	54.07	31.57	27.78	0.27	40.38
Machinery, Nec						
2008	3,337.74	42.16	74.19	15.19	0.03	10.58
2018	1,888.97	43.84	75.65	13.39	0.03	10.93
Textiles and Textile Products						
2008	1,152.50	25.45	84.18	7.92	0.02	7.88
2018	1,063.53	26.09	75.03	10.10	0.04	14.82

$ = United States dollars, DDC = domestic value-added double counted in exports, FDC = foreign value-added double counted in exports, FVA_FIN = foreign value-added in exports for final consumption, FVA_INT = foreign value-added in intermediate exports, VS = vertical specialization.

Source: ADB Multi Region Input–Output Tables Database.

Table 3.2.4.u: Vertical Specialization, Disaggregated—Singapore					
	Exports	VS	FVA_FIN	FVA_INT	DDC	FDC
	($ million)	(% of gross exports)	(% of VS)			
Coke, Refined Petroleum and Nuclear Fuel						
2008	47,477.59	85.36	35.30	32.01	0.31	32.38
2018	60,863.33	84.03	41.11	34.38	0.46	24.04
Electrical and Optical Equipment						
2008	52,295.91	69.02	40.95	25.70	0.42	32.93
2018	80,083.25	60.99	36.35	30.04	0.68	32.93
Wholesale Trade and Commission Trade, Except of Motor Vehicles and Motorcycles						
2008	36,999.20	34.24	23.16	56.29	0.46	20.09
2018	92,310.49	40.21	23.52	54.57	0.74	21.17

$ = United States dollars, DDC = domestic value-added double counted in exports, FDC = foreign value-added double counted in exports, FVA_FIN = foreign value-added in exports for final consumption, FVA_INT = foreign value-added in intermediate exports, VS = vertical specialization.

Source: ADB Multi Region Input–Output Tables Database.

Table 3.2.4.v: Vertical Specialization, Disaggregated—Sri Lanka					
	Exports	VS	FVA_FIN	FVA_INT	DDC	FDC
	($ million)	(% of gross exports)	(% of VS)			
Agriculture, Hunting, Forestry and Fishing						
2008	382.56	10.79	38.59	39.03	0.02	22.36
2018	650.35	11.50	58.19	26.95	0.01	14.85
Inland Transport						
2008	885.84	18.87	35.40	48.55	0.01	16.03
2018	2,359.48	14.27	33.64	49.01	0.02	17.33
Other Community, Social and Personal Services						
2008	66.59	16.69	-17.64	86.38	0.03	31.23
2018	523.00	10.69	45.05	41.74	0.02	13.19

$ = United States dollars, DDC = domestic value-added double counted in exports, FDC = foreign value-added double counted in exports, FVA_FIN = foreign value-added in exports for final consumption, FVA_INT = foreign value-added in intermediate exports, VS = vertical specialization.

Source: ADB Multi Region Input–Output Tables Database.

Table 3.2.4.w: Vertical Specialization, Disaggregated—Taipei,China					
	Exports	VS	FVA_FIN	FVA_INT	DDC	FDC
	($ million)	(% of gross exports)	(% of VS)			
Electrical and Optical Equipment						
2008	115,872.72	42.43	23.51	34.86	1.15	40.48
2018	163,738.48	41.74	18.41	42.17	1.40	38.02
Textiles and Textile Products						
2008	8,433.89	43.61	30.75	36.15	0.31	32.79
2018	7,931.22	40.36	23.87	40.61	0.34	35.18
Wholesale Trade and Commission Trade, Except of Motor Vehicles and Motorcycles						
2008	26,369.52	12.50	24.96	44.91	1.03	29.09
2018	43,079.10	13.34	30.07	42.97	0.85	26.11

$ = United States dollars, DDC = domestic value-added double counted in exports, FDC = foreign value-added double counted in exports, FVA_FIN = foreign value-added in exports for final consumption, FVA_INT = foreign value-added in intermediate exports, VS = vertical specialization.

Source: ADB Multi Region Input–Output Tables Database.

Table 3.2.4.x: Vertical Specialization, Disaggregated—Thailand					
	Exports	VS	FVA_FIN	FVA_INT	DDC	FDC
	($ million)	(% of gross exports)	(% of VS)			
Basic Metals and Fabricated Metal						
2008	47,195.53	52.07	9.99	56.60	0.39	33.02
2018	48,431.32	44.24	14.69	55.84	0.44	29.02
Food, Beverages and Tobacco						
2008	11,002.08	29.04	54.51	33.08	0.16	12.25
2018	20,488.10	21.57	57.71	29.37	0.21	12.71
Textiles and Textile Products						
2008	5,806.75	27.28	69.96	15.12	0.11	14.81
2018	7,305.76	26.84	51.52	21.51	0.18	26.79

$ = United States dollars, DDC = domestic value-added double counted in exports, FDC = foreign value-added double counted in exports, FVA_FIN = foreign value-added in exports for final consumption, FVA_INT = foreign value-added in intermediate exports, VS = vertical specialization.

Source: ADB Multi Region Input–Output Tables Database.

Table 3.2.4.y: Vertical Specialization, Disaggregated—Viet Nam						
	Exports	VS	FVA_FIN	FVA_INT	DDC	FDC
	($ million)	(% of gross exports)	(% of VS)			
Agriculture, Hunting, Forestry and Fishing						
2008	2,803.16	20.93	33.17	49.51	0.19	17.13
2018	9,450.53	34.28	39.94	44.61	0.27	15.18
Food, Beverages and Tobacco						
2008	10,004.24	26.08	62.46	29.67	0.06	7.80
2018	36,444.90	38.61	55.40	30.80	0.13	13.68
Mining and Quarrying						
2008	6,383.81	27.49	0.48	70.39	0.27	28.86
2018	12,132.03	38.25	3.96	65.08	0.62	30.34

$ = United States dollars, DDC = domestic value-added double counted in exports, FDC = foreign value-added double counted in exports, FVA_FIN = foreign value-added in exports for final consumption, FVA_INT = foreign value-added in intermediate exports, VS = vertical specialization.

Source: ADB Multi Region Input–Output Tables Database.

Definitions

This section contains the definitions of statistical indicators that are covered in Part I - Sustainable Development Goals (SDGs), Part II - Regional Trends and Tables, and Part III - Global Value Chains (GVCs). The definitions are taken mostly from the Asian Development Bank's Development Indicators Reference Manual, including websites and publications of international and private organizations such as the Food and Agriculture Organization of the United Nations (FAO); International Labour Organization (ILO); International Monetary Fund (IMF); International Telecommunication Union (ITU); Organisation for Economic Co-operation and Development (OECD); Transparency International; United Nations Children's Fund (UNICEF); United Nations

Educational, Scientific and Cultural Organization (UNESCO); United Nations Population Division (UNPD); United Nations Statistics Division (UNSD); World Bank; World Health Organization (WHO); and United Nations World Tourism Organization (UNWTO). The definitions for GVCs are taken from ADB's Key Indicators for Asia and the Pacific 2015. The SDG indicators are arranged according to their respective goals and targets before they are defined, while the indicators for the Regional Trends and Tables are grouped according to their themes and subtopics before they are defined. In many instances, the indicators themselves, rather than their growth rates or ratios to another indicator, are defined.

Sustainable Development Goals

Goals and Targets	Statistical Indicators	Definition
Goal 1. End poverty in all its forms everywhere		
Target 1.1: By 2030, eradicate extreme poverty (currently measured as people living on less than $1.90 a day) for all people everywhere.	1.1.1.a: Proportion of the population living below the international poverty line, by sex, age, employment status, and geographical location (urban or rural)	Proportion of the population living on less than $1.90 a day, measured at 2011 international prices, adjusted for purchasing power parity (PPP). Note: The PPP conversion factor for private consumption is the number of units of a country's currency required to buy the same amount of goods and/or services in the domestic market as a United States (US) dollar would buy in the US.
	1.1.1.b: Proportion of the employed population living below the international poverty line, by sex	Proportion of the employed population living in households with per capita consumption or income below the international poverty line of $1.90. Note: The proportion of working poor in total employment (also known as the working poverty rate) combines data on household income or consumption with labor force framework variables measured at the individual level, and sheds light on the relationship between household poverty and employment. The numbers are International Labour Organization modeled estimates. Employed persons refer to all persons of working age who, during a short reference period such as a day or a week, performed work for others in exchange for pay or profit.
Target 1.2: By 2030, reduce at least by half the proportion of men, women, and children of all ages living in poverty in all its dimensions, according to national definitions.	1.2.1: Proportion of the population living below the national poverty line, by sex, age, and geographical location (urban or rural)	Percentage of the total population living below the national poverty line. Note: National poverty rates are defined at country-specific poverty lines in local currencies, which are different in real terms across countries and different from the international poverty line of $1.90 a day. Thus, national poverty rates cannot be compared across countries or with the poverty rate of $1.90a day.

(continued on next page)

Goals and Targets	Statistical Indicators	Definition
Goal 2. End hunger, achieve food security and improved nutrition, and promote sustainable agriculture		
Target 2.1: By 2030, end hunger and ensure access by all people, in particular the poor and people in vulnerable situations, including infants, to safe, nutritious, and sufficient food all year round.	2.1.1: Prevalence of undernourishment	Proportion of the population whose habitual food consumption is insufficient to provide the dietary energy levels that are required to maintain a normal active and healthy life. Note: Undernourishment is defined as the condition by which a person has access, on a regular basis, to amounts of food that are insufficient to provide the energy required for conducting a normal, healthy, and active life, given his or her own dietary energy requirements.
Target 2.2: By 2030, end all forms of malnutrition, including achieving, by 2025, the internationally agreed targets on stunting and wasting in children under 5 years of age, and address the nutritional needs of adolescent girls, pregnant and lactating women, and older persons.	2.2.1: Prevalence of stunting—height for age <-2 standard deviation from the median of World Health Organization (WHO) Child Growth Standards—among children under 5 years of age	Prevalence of stunting—height-for-age <-2 standard deviation from the median of WHO Child Growth Standards—among children under 5 years of age. Note: Stunting refers to the impaired growth and development that children experience from poor nutrition, repeated infection, and inadequate psychosocial stimulation.
	2.2.2.a: Prevalence of malnutrition—weight for height <-2 standard deviation from the median of WHO Child Growth Standards—among children under 5 years of age (wasting)	Prevalence of wasting—weight for height <-2 standard deviation from the median of WHO Child Growth Standards—among children under 5 years of age. Note: Child wasting refers to a child who is too thin for his or her height, and is the result of recent rapid weight loss or the failure to gain weight.
	2.2.2.b: Prevalence of malnutrition—weight for height >+2 standard deviation from the median of WHO Child Growth Standards—among children under 5 years of age (overweight)	Prevalence of overweight—weight for height >+2 standard deviation from the median of WHO Child Growth Standards—among children under 5 years of age. Note: Child overweight refers to a child who is too heavy for his or her height.
Target 2.a: Increase investment, including through enhanced international cooperation, in rural infrastructure, agricultural research and extension services, technology development, and plant and livestock gene banks in order to enhance agricultural productive capacity in developing countries, in particular least developed countries.	2.a.1: The agriculture orientation index for government expenditures	The Agriculture Orientation Index for Government Expenditures is defined as the agriculture share of government expenditure, divided by the agriculture value-added share of gross domestic product (GDP), where "agriculture" refers to the agriculture, forestry, fishing, and hunting sector. The measure is a currency-free index, calculated as the ratio of these two shares. National governments are requested to compile government expenditures according to the international Classification of Functions of Government and agriculture value-added share of GDP according to the System of National Accounts. Note: Government expenditure is all expense and acquisition of nonfinancial assets associated with supporting a particular sector, as defined in the Government Finance Statistics Manual 2014 developed by the International Monetary Fund.

(continued on next page)

Goals and Targets	Statistical Indicators	Definition
	2.a.2: Total official flows (official development assistance plus other official flows) to the agriculture sector	Gross disbursements of total official development assistance (ODA) and other official flows from all donors to the agriculture sector. Note: The Development Assistance Committee (DAC) defines ODA as those flows to countries and territories on the DAC List of ODA Recipients and to multilateral institutions which are (i) provided by official agencies, including state and local governments, or by their executive agencies; (ii) each transaction is administered with the promotion of the economic development and welfare of developing countries as its main objective; and (iii) each transaction is concessional in character and conveys a grant element of at least 25% (calculated at a rate of discount of 10%). Other official flows are defined as transactions by the official sector, which do not meet the conditions for eligibility as ODA, either because they are not primarily aimed at development or because they are not sufficiently concessional. They also exclude officially supported export credits.
Goal 3. Ensure healthy lives and promote well-being for all at all ages		
Target 3.1: By 2030, reduce the global maternal mortality ratio to less than 70 per 100,000 live births.	3.1.1: Maternal mortality ratio	Number of maternal deaths during a given time period per 100,000 live births during the same time period. Note: The term maternal deaths refers to the annual number of female deaths from any cause related to, or aggravated by, pregnancy or its management (excluding accidental or incidental causes) during pregnancy and childbirth or within 42 days of termination of pregnancy, irrespective of the duration and site of the pregnancy, expressed per 100,000 live births, for a specified time period.
	3.1.2: Proportion of births attended by skilled health personnel	Percentage of deliveries attended by health personnel trained in providing lifesaving obstetric care, including giving the necessary supervision, care, and advice to women during pregnancy, labor, and the post-partum period; conducting deliveries on their own; and caring for newborns. Traditional birth attendants, even if they receive a short training course, are not included. Note: Having a skilled attendant at the time of delivery is an important lifesaving intervention for both mothers and babies. Not having access to this key assistance is detrimental to women's health and gender empowerment because it could cause the death of the mother or long-lasting disability, especially in marginalized settings.
Target 3.2: By 2030, end preventable deaths of newborns and children under 5 years of age, with all countries aiming to reduce neonatal mortality to at least as low as 12 per 1,000 live births and under-5 mortality to at least as low as 25 per 1,000 live births.	3.2.1: Under-5 mortality rate	The probability of a child born in a specific year or period dying before reaching the age of 5 years, if subject to age specific mortality rates of that period, expressed per 1,000 live births. Note: The under-5 mortality rate as defined here is, strictly speaking, not a rate (i.e., the number of deaths divided by the number of population at risk during a certain period of time) but a probability of death derived from a life table and expressed as a rate per 1,000 live births.
	3.2.2: Neonatal mortality rate	Probability that a child born in a specific year or period will die during the first 28 completed days of life, if subject to age-specific mortality rates of that period, expressed per 1,000 live births. Note: Neonatal deaths (deaths among live births during the first 28 completed days of life) may be subdivided into early neonatal deaths, occurring during the first 7 days of life, and late neonatal deaths, occurring after the seventh day but before the 28th completed day of life.

(continued on next page)

Goals and Targets	Statistical Indicators	Definition
Target 3.3: By 2030, end the epidemics of AIDS, tuberculosis, malaria, and neglected tropical diseases; and combat hepatitis, water-borne diseases, and other communicable diseases.	3.3.1: Number of new HIV infections per 1,000 uninfected population, by sex, age, and key populations	Number of new HIV infections per 1,000 person-years among the uninfected population.
	3.3.2: Tuberculosis incidence per 100,000 population	Estimated number of new and relapse tuberculosis cases (all forms of tuberculosis, including cases in people living with HIV) arising in a given year, expressed as a rate per 100,000 population.
	3.3.3: Malaria incidence per 1,000 population	The number of new cases of malaria per 1,000 people at risk each year.
Target 3.4: By 2030, reduce by one third premature mortality from noncommunicable diseases through prevention and treatment, and promote mental health and well-being.	3.4.1: Mortality rate attributed to cardiovascular disease, cancer, diabetes, or chronic respiratory disease	Probability of dying between the ages of 30 and 70 years from cardiovascular diseases , cancer, diabetes, or chronic respiratory diseases; defined as the percentage of 30-year-old people who would die before their 70th birthday from cardiovascular disease, cancer, diabetes, or chronic respiratory disease, assuming that a person would experience current mortality rates at every age and he or she would not die from any other cause of death (e.g., injuries or HIV/AIDS). Note: Probability of dying refers to the likelihood that an individual would die between two ages given current mortality rates at each age, calculated using life table methods. The probability of death between two ages may be called a mortality rate.
	3.4.2: Suicide mortality rate	The number of suicide deaths in a year, divided by the population and multiplied by 100,000. Note: The number of suicide deaths refers to crude suicide rates (per 100,000 population).
Target 3.6: By 2020, halve the number of global deaths and injuries from road traffic accidents.	3.6.1: Death rate due to road traffic injuries	Number of road traffic fatal injury deaths per 100,000 population.
Target 3.7: By 2030, ensure universal access to sexual and reproductive health care services, including for family planning, information and education, and the integration of reproductive health into national strategies and programs	3.7.1: Proportion of women of reproductive age (15-49 years) who have their need for family planning satisfied by modern methods	The percentage of women of reproductive age (15-49 years) who desire either to have no (additional) children or to postpone the next child, and who are currently using a modern contraceptive method.
	3.7.2: Adolescent birth rate (15-19 years) per 1,000 women in that age group	Annual number of births to females aged 15-19 years per 1,000 females in the respective age group.
Target 3.8: Achieve universal health coverage, including financial risk protection; access to quality essential healthcare services; and access to safe, effective, quality, and affordable essential medicines and vaccines for all	3.8.1: Coverage of essential health services (defined as the average coverage of essential services based on tracer interventions that include reproductive, maternal, newborn and child heath, infectious disease, noncommunicable diseases, and service capacity and access, among the general and the most disadvantaged population)	The indicator is an index reported on a unitless scale of 0 to 100, which is calculated as the geometric mean of 14 tracer indicators of health service coverage. Note: The index of health service coverage is computed as the geometric means of tracer indicators. The tracer indicators are organized by four broad categories of service coverage: (i) reproductive, maternal, newborn, and child health, (ii) infectious diseases, (iii) noncommunicable diseases, and (iv) service capacity and access.

(continued on next page)

Goals and Targets	Statistical Indicators	Definition
Target 3.9: By 2030, substantially reduce the number of deaths and illnesses from hazardous chemicals and air, water, and soil pollution and contamination.	3.9.1: Mortality rate attributed to household and ambient air pollution	Expressed as the number of deaths and death rate. Death rates are calculated by dividing the number of deaths by the total population (or indicated if a different population group is used, e.g., children under 5 years). Note: Evidence from epidemiological studies has shown that exposure to air pollution is linked to, among others, the important diseases taken into account in this estimate: - acute respiratory infections in young children (estimated under 5 years of age); - cerebrovascular diseases (stroke) in adults (estimated above 25 years of age); - ischemic heart diseases in adults (estimated above 25 years of age); - chronic obstructive pulmonary disease in adults (estimated above 25 years of age); and - lung cancer in adults (estimated above 25 years of age).
	3.9.2: Mortality rate attributed to unsafe water, unsafe sanitation, and lack of hygiene—exposure to unsafe water, sanitation, and hygiene for all (WASH) services	Number of deaths from unsafe water, unsafe sanitation, and lack of hygiene —exposure to unsafe water, sanitation and hygiene for all (WASH) services—in a year, divided by the population, and multiplied by 100,000.
Goal 4. Ensure inclusive and equitable quality education and promote lifelong learning opportunities for all		
Target 4.2: By 2030, ensure that all girls and boys have access to quality early childhood development, care, and preprimary education, so that they are ready for primary education.	4.2.2: Participation rate in organized learning (1 year before the official primary entry age), by sex	Percentage of children in the given age range who participate in one or more organized learning programs, including programs which offer a combination of education and care. Participation in early childhood education and primary education are both included. The age range will vary by country, depending on the official age for entry to primary education. Note: An organized learning program is one that consists of a coherent set or sequence of educational activities designed with the intention of achieving predetermined learning outcomes or the accomplishment of a specific set of educational tasks. Early childhood and primary education programs are examples of organized learning programs. The official primary entry age is the age at which children are obliged to start primary education, according to national legislation or policies.

(continued on next page)

Goals and Targets	Statistical Indicators	Definition
Target 4.c: By 2030, substantially increase the supply of qualified teachers, including through international cooperation for teacher training in developing countries, especially least developed countries and small island developing states.	4.c.1.a: Proportion of teachers in preprimary education who have received at least the minimum organized teacher training 4.c.1.b: Proportion of teachers in primary education who have received at least the minimum organized teacher training 4.c.1.c: Proportion of teachers in lower secondary education who have received at least the minimum organized teacher training 4.c.1.d: Proportion of teachers in upper secondary education who have received at least the minimum organized teacher training	Percentage of teachers by level of education taught (preprimary, primary, lower secondary, and upper secondary education) who have received at least the minimum organized pedagogical teacher training pre-service and in-service required for teaching at the relevant level in a given country. Note: Number of teachers in a given level of education who are trained is expressed as a percentage of all teachers in that level of education. A teacher is trained if they have received at least the minimum organized pedagogical teacher training pre-service and in-service required for teaching at the relevant level in each country.
Goal 5. Achieve gender equality and empower all women and girls		
Target 5.3: Eliminate all harmful practices, such as child, early, and forced marriage, and female genital mutilation.	5.3.1: Proportion of women aged 20–24 years who were married or in a union before age 15 and before age 18	Proportion of women aged 20-24 years who were married or in a union before age 15 and before age 18. Note: Both formal (i.e., marriages) and informal unions are covered under this indicator. Informal unions are generally defined as those in which a couple lives together (i.e., cohabits) for some time, intends to have a lasting relationship, but for which there has been no formal civil or religious ceremony.
Target 5.5: Ensure women's full and effective participation in, and equal opportunities for leadership at, all levels of decision-making in political, economic, and public life.	5.5.1: Proportion of seats held by women in national parliaments	The proportion of seats held by women in national parliaments, as of 1 February of reporting year, is currently measured as the number of seats held by women members in single or lower chambers of national parliaments, expressed as a percentage of all occupied seats. Note: National parliaments can be bicameral or unicameral. This indicator covers the single chamber in unicameral parliaments and the lower chamber in bicameral parliaments. It does not cover the upper chamber of bicameral parliaments. Seats are usually won by members in general parliamentary elections. Seats may also be filled by nomination, appointment, indirect election, rotation of members, and by-election. Seats refer to the number of parliamentary mandates, or the number of members of parliament.
	5.5.2: Proportion of women in managerial positions	Proportion of females in the total number of persons employed in senior and middle management. Senior and middle management correspond to major group 1 in International Standard Classification of Occupations (ISCO)-08 and ISCO-88, minus category 14 in ISCO-08 (hospitality, retail, and other services managers) and minus category 13 in ISCO-88 (general managers), since these comprise mainly managers of small enterprises. Note: The indicator provides information on the proportion of women who are employed in decision-making and managerial roles in government, large enterprises, and institutions, thus providing some insight into women's power in decision-making and in the economy (especially compared to men's power in those areas).

(continued on next page)

Goals and Targets	Statistical Indicators	Definition
Goal 6. Ensure availability and sustainable management of water and sanitation for all		
Target 6.1: By 2030, achieve universal and equitable access to safe and affordable drinking water for all.	6.1.1: Proportion of population using safely managed drinking water services	Proportion of population using an improved basic drinking water source that is located on premises, available when needed, and free of fecal (and priority chemical) contamination. Note: Improved drinking water sources include the following: piped water into a dwelling, yard, or plot; public taps or standpipes; boreholes or tubewells; protected dug wells; protected springs; packaged water; delivered water; and rainwater. "Located on premises": A water source is considered to be located on premises if the point of collection is within the dwelling, yard, or plot. "Available when needed": Households that are able to access sufficient quantities of water when needed. "Free from fecal (and priority chemical) contamination": Water that complies with relevant national or local standards. In the absence of such standards, reference is made to the WHO Guidelines for Drinking Water Quality (http://www.who.int/water_sanitation_health/dwq/guidelines/en/). E. coli or thermotolerant coliforms are the preferred indicator for microbiological quality, and arsenic and fluoride are the priority chemicals for global reporting. The WHO/UNICEF Joint Monitoring Programme (JMP) for Water Supply, Sanitation, and Hygiene estimates access to basic services for each country, separately in urban and rural areas, by fitting a regression line to a series of data points from household surveys and censuses. This approach was used to report on use of 'improved water' sources for Millennium Development Goal monitoring. The JMP is evaluating the use of alternative statistical estimation methods as more data become available. The JMP 2017 update and SDG baselines report describes in more detail how data on availability and quality from different sources can be combined with data on use of different types of supplies, as recorded in the current JMP database, to calculate the safely managed drinking water services indicator (https://washdata.org/report/jmp-2017-report-final).

(continued on next page)

Goals and Targets	Statistical Indicators	Definition
Target 6.2: By 2030, achieve access to adequate and equitable sanitation and hygiene for all, and end open defecation, paying special attention to the needs of women and girls and those in vulnerable situations.	6.2.1.a: Proportion of population using safely managed sanitation services	The proportion of population using a basic sanitation facility, including a handwashing facility with soap and water, that is not shared with other households and where excreta is safely disposed in situ or treated off-site. Note: Improved sanitation facilities include flush or pour-flush toilets to sewer systems, septic tanks or pit latrines, ventilated improved pit latrines, pit latrines with a slab, and composting toilets. "Safely disposed in situ": When pit latrines and septic tanks are not emptied, the excreta may still remain isolated from human contact and can be considered safely managed. For example, with the new SDG indicator, households that use twin pit latrines or safely abandon full pit latrines and dig new facilities (a common practice in rural areas) would be counted as using safely managed sanitation services. "Treated offsite": Not all excreta from toilet facilities conveyed in sewers (as wastewater) or emptied from pit latrines and septic tanks (as fecal sludge) reach a treatment site. For instance, a portion may leak from the sewer itself or, due to broken pumping installations, be discharged directly to the environment. Similarly, a portion of the fecal sludge emptied from containers may be discharged into open drains, to open ground or water bodies, rather than being transported to a treatment plant. And finally, even once the excreta reach a treatment plant, a portion may remain untreated due to dysfunctional treatment equipment or inadequate treatment capacity, and be discharged to the environment. For the purposes of SDG monitoring, adequacy of treatment will initially be assessed based on the reported level of treatment. "A handwashing facility with soap and water": A handwashing facility is a device to contain, transport, or regulate the flow of water to facilitate handwashing.
Target 6.4: By 2030, substantially increase water-use efficiency across all sectors and ensure sustainable withdrawals and supply of freshwater to address water scarcity and substantially reduce the number of people suffering from water scarcity.	6.4.2: Level of water stress; freshwater withdrawal as a proportion of available freshwater resources	Ratio of total freshwater withdrawn by all major sectors to total renewable freshwater resources, after taking into account environmental water requirements. Note: Total freshwater withdrawal is the volume of freshwater extracted from its source (rivers, lakes, aquifers) for agriculture, industries, and municipalities. Freshwater withdrawal includes primary freshwater (not withdrawn before), secondary freshwater (previously withdrawn and returned to rivers and groundwater, such as discharged wastewater and agricultural drainage water) and fossil groundwater. Main sectors, as defined by International Standard Industrial Classification standards, include agriculture, forestry and fishing, manufacturing, electricity industry, and services. Environmental water requirements are the quantities of water required to sustain freshwater and estuarine ecosystems. This indicator is also known as water withdrawal intensity. Total renewable freshwater resources are expressed as the sum of internal and external renewable water resources. Internal renewable water resources are defined as the long-term average annual flow of rivers and recharge of groundwater, generated from endogenous precipitation, for a given country. External renewable water resources refer to the flows of water entering the country, taking into consideration the quantity of flows reserved to upstream and downstream countries through agreements or treaties.

(continued on next page)

Goals and Targets	Statistical Indicators	Definition
Target 6.a: By 2030, expand international cooperation and capacity-building support to developing countries in water- and sanitation-related activities and programs, including water harvesting, desalination, water efficiency, wastewater treatment, recycling, and reuse technologies.	6.a.1: Amount of water- and sanitation-related ODA that is part of a government-coordinated spending plan	Proportion of total water- and sanitation-related ODA disbursements that are included in a government's budget.

Note:
The amount of water- and sanitation-related ODA is a quantifiable measurement as a proxy for "international cooperation and capacity development support" in financial terms.

A low value of this indicator (near 0%) would suggest that international donors are investing in water- and sanitation-related activities and programs in the country, outside the purview of the national government. A high value (near 100%) would indicate that donors are aligned with the national government and national policies and plans for water and sanitation. |
| **Goal 7. Ensure access to affordable, reliable, sustainable, and modern energy for all** | | |
| **Target 7.1:** By 2030, ensure universal access to affordable, reliable, and modern energy services. | 7.1.1: Proportion of population with access to electricity | Percentage of the population with access to electricity.

Note:
Access to electricity addresses major critical issues in all the dimensions of sustainable development. The target has a wide range of social and economic impacts, including facilitating development of household-based income-generating activities and lightening the burden of household tasks. |
| | 7.1.2: Proportion of population with primary reliance on clean fuels and technology | Number of people using clean fuels and technologies for cooking, heating, and lighting, divided by total population reporting any cooking, heating, or lighting, and expressed as a percentage. "Clean" is defined by the official emission rate targets and specific fuel recommendations (i.e., against unprocessed coal and kerosene) included in the WHO guidelines for indoor air quality: household fuel combustion. |
| **Target 7.2:** By 2030, increase substantially the share of renewable energy in the global energy mix. | 7.2.1: Renewable energy share in total final energy consumption | Percentage of final consumption of energy that is derived from renewable resources.

Note:
Renewable energy consumption includes consumption of energy derived from hydro, solid biofuels, wind, solar, liquid biofuels, biogas, geothermal, marine sources, and waste. Total final energy consumption is calculated from national balances and statistics as total final consumption minus nonenergy use. |
| **Target 7.3:** By 2030, double the global rate of improvement in energy efficiency. | 7.3.1: Energy intensity measured in terms of primary energy and GDP | Energy supplied to the economy per unit value of economic output.

Note:
Total energy supply, as defined by the International Recommendations for Energy Statistics, is made up of production, plus net imports, minus international marine and aviation bunkers plus-stock changes. GDP is the measure of economic output. For international comparison purposes, GDP is measured in constant terms at PPP. |
| **Goal 8. Promote sustained, inclusive, and sustainable economic growth, full and productive employment, and decent work for all** | | |
| **Target 8.1:** Sustain per-capita economic growth in accordance with national circumstances and, in particular, at least 7% GDP growth per annum in the least developed countries. | 8.1.1: Annual growth rate of real GDP per capita | Percentage change in the real GDP per capita between 2 consecutive years.

Note:
Real GDP per capita is calculated by dividing GDP at constant prices by the population of a country or area. The data for real GDP is measured in constant US dollars to facilitate the calculation of country growth rates and aggregation of the country data. |

(continued on next page)

Goals and Targets	Statistical Indicators	Definition
Target 8.2: Achieve higher levels of economic productivity through diversification, technological upgrading, and innovation, including through a focus on high-value-added and labor-intensive sectors.	8.2.1: Annual growth rate of real GDP per employed person	Annual percentage change in real GDP per employed person. Note: With the real GDP per employed person being a measure of labor productivity, this indicator represents a measure of labor productivity growth. It therefore provides information on the evolution, efficiency, and quality of human capital in the production process.
Target 8.5: By 2030, achieve full and productive employment and decent work for all women and men, including for young people and persons with disabilities, and equal pay for work of equal value.	8.5.2: Unemployment rate, by sex and age	Percentage of persons in the labor force who are unemployed. Note: Unemployed persons are defined as all those of working age (usually persons aged 15 and above) who were not in employment, carried out activities to seek employment during a specified recent period, and were currently available to take up employment given a job opportunity, where: (i) "not in employment" is assessed with respect to the short reference period for the measurement of employment; (ii) to "seek employment" refers to any activity when carried out, during a specified recent period comprising the past 4 weeks or 1 month, for the purpose of finding a job or setting up a business or agricultural undertaking; (iii) the point when the enterprise starts to exist should be used to distinguish between search activities aimed at setting up a business and the work activity itself, as evidenced by the enterprise's registration to operate or by when financial resources become available, the necessary infrastructure or materials are in place, or the first client or order is received, depending on the context; and (iv) "currently available" serves as a test of readiness to start a job in the present, assessed with respect to a short reference period comprising that used to measure employment (depending on national circumstances, the reference period may be extended to include a short subsequent period not exceeding 2 weeks in total, so as to ensure adequate coverage of unemployment situations among different population groups).
Target 8.6: By 2020, substantially reduce the proportion of youth not in employment, education, or training.	8.6.1: Proportion of youth (aged 15-24 years) not in education, employment, or training	Proportion of youth (aged 15-24 years) who are not in education, employment, or training, also known as "the NEET rate". It conveys the number of young persons not in education, employment, or training as a percentage of the total youth population.
Target 8.7: Take immediate and effective measures to eradicate forced labor, end modern slavery and human trafficking, and secure the prohibition and elimination of the worst forms of child labor, including recruitment and use of child soldiers, and, by 2025, end child labor in all its forms.	8.7.1: Proportion of children aged 5-17 years engaged in child labor	The number of children aged 5-17 years reported to be in child labor during the reference period (usually the week prior to the survey). The proportion of children in child labor is calculated as the number of children in child labor, divided by the total number of children in the population.

(continued on next page)

Goals and Targets	Statistical Indicators	Definition
Target 8.10: Strengthen the capacity of domestic financial institutions to encourage and expand access to banking, insurance, and financial services for all.	8.10.1: Number of commercial bank branches and ATMs per 100,000 adults	The number of commercial bank branches per 100,000 adults refers to the number of commercial banks branches reported by the central bank or the main financial regulator of the country every year. To make it comparable, this number is presented as a reference per 100,000 adults in the respective country. The number of ATMs per 100,000 adults, refers to the number of ATMs in the country for all types of institutions, such as commercial banks, non-deposit-taking microfinance institutions, deposit-taking micro finance institutions, credit unions, financial cooperatives, and others. This information is reported every year by the central bank or the main financial regulator of the country. To make it comparable, this number is presented as a reference per 100,000 adults in the respective country.
	8.10.2: Proportion of adults (aged 15 years and older) with an account at a bank or other financial institution or with a mobile-money service provider	Percentage of adults (aged 15+) who report having an account (of their own or held with someone else) at a bank or another type of financial institution or have personally used a mobile-money service in the past 12 months.
Goal 9. Build resilient infrastructure, promote inclusive and sustainable industrialization, and foster innovation		
Target 9.1: Develop quality, reliable, sustainable, and resilient infrastructure, including regional and transborder infrastructure, to support economic development and human well-being, with a focus on affordable and equitable access for all.	9.1.a: Passenger volume by road transport, measured in millions of passenger-kilometers	Passenger and freight volumes are the sums of the passenger and freight volumes reported for the road and rail carriers in terms of number of people and metric tons of cargo, respectively. Note: The International Transport Forum collects data on transport (rail and road) statistics on annual basis from all its member countries. Data are collected from transport ministries, statistical offices, and other institutions designated as official data sources. Although there are clear definitions for all the terms used in this survey, countries might have different methodologies to calculate passenger-kilometers and ton-kilometers. Methods could be based on traffic or mobility surveys, using very different sampling methods and estimating techniques, which could affect the comparability of the statistics.
	9.1.b: Freight volume by road transport, measured in millions of ton-kilometers	
	9.1.c: Passenger volume by rail transport, measured in millions of passenger-kilometers	
	9.1.d: Freight volume by rail transport, measured in millions of ton-kilometers	
Target 9.2: Promote inclusive and sustainable industrialization and, by 2030, significantly raise industry's share of employment and GDP, in line with national circumstances, and double its share in least developed countries.	9.2.1: Manufacturing value added as a proportion of GDP and per capita	Manufacturing value added (MVA) as a proportion of GDP is a ratio between MVA and GDP, both reported in constant 2010 US dollars. MVA per capita is calculated by dividing MVA in constant 2010 US dollars by the population of a country or area.
	9.2.2: Manufacturing employment as a proportion of total employment	Share of manufacturing employment in total employment.
Target 9.4: By 2030, upgrade infrastructure and retrofit industries to make them sustainable, with increased resource-use efficiency and greater adoption of clean and environmentally sound technologies and industrial processes, with all countries taking action in accordance with their respective capabilities.	9.4.1: Carbon dioxide (CO_2) emissions per unit of value added	CO_2 emissions per unit value added is an indicator calculated as ratio between CO_2 emissions from fuel combustion and the value added of associated economic activities. The indicator can be calculated for the whole economy (total CO_2 emissions to GDP) or for specific sectors, notably the manufacturing sector (CO_2 emissions from manufacturing industries per MVA). CO_2 emissions per unit of GDP are expressed in kilograms of CO_2 per constant 2010 US dollar PPP GDP. CO_2 emissions from manufacturing industries per unit of MVA are measured in kilograms of CO_2 equivalent per unit of MVA in constant 2010 US dollars.

(continued on next page)

Goals and Targets	Statistical Indicators	Definition
Target 9.5: Enhance scientific research and upgrade the technological capabilities of industrial sectors in all countries, in particular developing countries, including, by 2030, encouraging innovation and substantially increasing the number of research and development (R&D) workers per 1 million people and public and private R&D spending.	9.5.1: R&D expenditure as a proportion of GDP	Amount of R&D expenditure divided by the total output of the economy.
	9.5.2: Researchers (full-time equivalent) per million inhabitants	Number of R&D workers per 1 million people.
Target 9.a: Facilitate sustainable and resilient infrastructure development in developing countries through enhanced financial, technological, and technical support to African countries, least developed countries, landlocked developing countries, and small island developing states.	9.a.1: Total official international support (ODA plus other official flows) to infrastructure	Gross disbursements of total ODA and other official flows from all donors in support of infrastructure.
Target 9.b: Support domestic technology development, research, and innovation in developing countries, including by ensuring a conducive policy environment for, among other things, industrial diversification and value addition to commodities.	9.b.1: Proportion of medium- and high-tech industry value added in total value added	Ratio of the value added by medium- and high-tech (MHT) industry to total MVA. Note: Industrial development generally entails a structural transition from resource-based and low-tech activities to MHT activities. A modern, highly complex production structure offers better opportunities for skills development and technological innovation. MHT activities are also the high-value addition industries of manufacturing with higher technological intensity and labor productivity. Increasing the share of MHT sectors also reflects the impact of innovation.
Target 9.c: Significantly increase access to information and communications technology and strive to provide universal and affordable access to the Internet in least developed countries by 2020.	9.c.1.a: Proportion of the population covered by narrowband (2G) mobile networks 9.c.1.b: Proportion of the population covered by 3G mobile networks 9.c.1.c: Proportion of the population covered by LTE mobile networks	Proportion of the population covered by a mobile network, broken down by technology, refers to the percentage of inhabitants living within range of a mobile-cellular signal, irrespective of whether or not they are mobile-phone subscribers or users. This is calculated by dividing the number of inhabitants within range of a mobile-cellular signal by the total population and multiplying by 100. Note: Coverage refers to Long-Term Evolution (LTE), broadband (3G), and narrowband (2G) mobile-cellular technologies: 2G mobile population coverage refers to the percentage of inhabitants within range of a mobile networks with access to data communications (e.g. Internet) at downstream speeds below 256 Kbit/s. This includes mobile-cellular technologies such as general packet radio service, code division multiple access 2000 1x, and most enhanced data for global system for mobile communications evolution implementations. 3G population coverage refers to the percentage of inhabitants that are within range of at least a 3G mobile-cellular signal, irrespective of whether or not they are subscribers. LTE population coverage refers to the percentage of inhabitants that live within range of LTE/LTE-Advanced, mobile WiMAX/WirelessMAN or other more advanced mobile-cellular networks, irrespective of whether or not they are subscribers.

(continued on next page)

Goals and Targets	Statistical Indicators	Definition
Goal 10. Reduce inequality within and among countries		
Target 10.1: By 2030, progressively achieve and sustain income growth of the bottom 40% of the population at a rate higher than the national average.	10.1.1.a: Growth rates of household expenditure or income per capita among the bottom 40% of the population	The growth rate in the welfare aggregate of the bottom 40% of the population is calculated as the annualized average growth rate in per capita real consumption or income of the bottom 40% of the income distribution in a country from household surveys over a period of approximately 5 years.
	10.1.1.b: Growth rates of household expenditure or income per capita	The national average growth rate in the welfare aggregate is calculated as the annualized average growth rate in per capita real consumption or income of the total population in a country from household surveys over a period of approximately 5 years.
Goal 11. Make cities and human settlements inclusive, safe, resilient, and sustainable		
Target 11.1: By 2030, ensure access for all to adequate, safe, and affordable housing and basic services, and upgrade slums.	11.1.1: Proportion of the urban population living in slums, informal settlements, or inadequate housing	The proportion of the urban population living in slums, informal settlements, or inadequate housing to total urban population is currently being measured by the proportion of the urban population living in slums and informal settlements. This indicator has been monitored for the past 17 years by United Nations (UN)-Habitat in mostly developing countries, with a new component—inadequate housing or affordability—that applies largely to the developed countries. By integrating these two components, the indicator is now universal and can be monitored in both developing and developed regions. The inadequate housing component allows capturing housing informality in more developed countries and wealthier urban contexts. Note: This indicator is expected to be a composite one, with the main components being slums or informal settlements, and the added component being affordability defining inadequate housing.
Target 11.5: By 2030, significantly reduce the number of deaths and the number of people affected, and substantially decrease the direct economic losses relative to global GDP caused by disasters, including water-related disasters, with a focus on protecting the poor and people in vulnerable situations.	11.5.2: Direct economic loss in relation to global GDP, damage to critical infrastructure, and number of disruptions to basic services, attributed to disasters	Direct economic loss is the monetary value of total or partial destruction of physical assets existing in the affected area. Direct economic loss is nearly equivalent to physical damage. Note: The original national disaster loss databases usually register physical damage value (housing unit loss, infrastructure loss, etc.), which needs conversion to a monetary value according to the United Nations International Strategy for Disaster Reduction methodology. The converted global value is divided by global GDP (inflation adjusted, constant US dollars) calculated from the World Bank Development Indicators.
Target 11.6: By 2030, reduce the adverse per capita environmental impact of cities, including by paying special attention to air quality and municipal and other waste management.	11.6.2: Annual mean levels of fine particulate matter (PM), e.g., PM2.5 and PM10, in cities, measured in total (population weighted) micrograms per cubic meter	The mean annual concentration of fine suspended particles of less than 2.5 microns in diameters (PM2.5) is a common measure of air pollution. Note: The mean is a population-weighted average for urban population in a country and is expressed in micrograms per cubic meter.

(continued on next page)

Goals and Targets	Statistical Indicators	Definition
Goal 12. Ensure sustainable consumption and production patterns		
Target 12.2: By 2030, achieve the sustainable management and efficient use of natural resources.	12.2.1: Material footprint, material footprint per capita, and material footprint per GDP	Material footprint is the attribution of global material extraction to domestic final demand of a country. The total material footprint is the sum of the material footprint for biomass, fossil fuels, metal ores, and nonmetal ores. This indicator is calculated as raw material equivalent of imports plus domestic extraction minus raw material equivalents of exports. A global multi-regional input-output framework is employed for the attribution of the primary material needs of final demand.
	12.2.2: Domestic material consumption, domestic material consumption per capita, and domestic material consumption per GDP	Domestic material consumption (DMC) is a standard material flow accounting indicator and reports the apparent consumption of materials in a national economy. Note: DMC reports the amount of materials used in a national economy. DMC is a territorial (production side) indicator. DMC also presents the amount of material that needs to be handled within an economy, which is either added to material stocks of buildings and transport infrastructure, or used to fuel the economy as material throughput. DMC describes the physical dimension of economic processes and interactions. It can also be interpreted as long-term waste equivalent.
Goal 13. Take urgent action to combat climate change and its impacts		
Target 13.1: Strengthen resilience and adaptive capacity to climate-related hazards and natural disasters in all countries.	13.1.1.a: Number of persons affected by disasters	Number of people who were directly affected by disasters per 100,000 population. Note: Directly affected means people who have suffered injury, illness, or other health effects; who were evacuated, displaced, or relocated; or have suffered direct damage to their livelihoods, economic, physical, social, cultural, and/or environmental assets.
	13.1.1.b: Number of deaths due to disasters	The number of people who died during a disaster, or directly after, or as a direct result of the hazardous event.
	13.1.2: Number of countries that adopt and implement national disaster risk reduction strategies in line with the Sendai Framework for Disaster Risk Reduction 2015–2030	Number of countries that adopt and implement national disaster risk reduction strategies in line with the Sendai Framework for Disaster Risk Reduction 2015–2030. Note: The score of adoption and implementation of national disaster risk reduction strategies in line with the Sendai Framework was developed to monitor progress and achievement against Indicator 13.1.2. The score indicates compliance of alignment of national strategies with the Sendai Framework, based on self-assessments of the country and using 10 criteria for monitoring the progress of national disaster risk reduction strategies.
Goal 14. Conserve and sustainably use the oceans, seas, and marine resources for sustainable development		
Target 14.5: By 2020, conserve at least 10% of coastal and marine areas, consistent with national and international law and based on the best available scientific information.	14.5.1: Coverage of protected areas in relation to marine areas	The indicator measures the coverage of protected areas in relation to marine areas and shows temporal trends in the mean percentage of important sites for marine biodiversity (i.e., those that contribute significantly to the global persistence of biodiversity or key biodiversity areas) that are wholly covered by designated protected areas. Note: The International Union for Conservation of Nature (IUCN) defines a protected area as "a clearly defined geographical space, recognized, dedicated and managed, through legal or other effective means, to achieve the long-term conservation of nature with associated ecosystem services and cultural values."

(continued on next page)

Goals and Targets	Statistical Indicators	Definition
Goal 15. Protect, restore, and promote sustainable use of terrestrial ecosystems, sustainably manage forests, combat desertification, halt and reverse land degradation, and halt biodiversity loss		
Target 15.1: By 2020, ensure the conservation, restoration, and sustainable use of terrestrial and inland freshwater ecosystems and their services, in particular forests, wetlands, mountains, and drylands, in line with obligations under international agreements.	15.1.1: Forest area as a proportion of total land area	Size of forest cover in relation to total land area.
	15.1.2: Proportion of important sites for terrestrial and freshwater biodiversity that are covered by protected areas, by ecosystem type	Proportion of important sites for terrestrial and freshwater biodiversity that are covered by protected areas shows temporal trends in the mean percentage of each important site for terrestrial and freshwater biodiversity (i.e., those that contribute significantly to the global persistence of biodiversity) that is covered by designated protected areas.
Target 15.4: By 2030, ensure the conservation of mountain ecosystems, including their biodiversity, in order to enhance their capacity to provide benefits that are essential for sustainable development	15.4.1: Coverage by protected areas of important sites for mountain biodiversity	Coverage by protected areas of important sites for mountain biodiversity shows temporal trends in the mean percentage of each important site for mountain biodiversity (i.e., those that contribute significantly to the global persistence of biodiversity) that is covered by designated protected areas. Note: Protected areas, as defined by the IUCN (IUCN; Dudley 2008), are clearly defined geographical spaces, recognized, dedicated, and managed, through legal or other effective means, to achieve the long-term conservation of nature with associated ecosystem services and cultural values. Importantly, a variety of specific management objectives are recognized within this definition, spanning conservation, restoration, and sustainable use: "(i) Category Ia: Strict nature reserve; (ii) Category Ib: Wilderness area; (iii) Category II: National park; (iv) Category III: Natural monument or feature; (v) Category IV: Habitat/species management area; (vi) Category V: Protected landscape/seascape; (vii) Category VI: Protected area with sustainable use of natural resources."
Target 15.5: Take urgent and significant action to reduce the degradation of natural habitats, halt the loss of biodiversity and, by 2020, protect and prevent the extinction of threatened species.	15.5.1: Red List Index	The Red List Index measures changes in aggregate extinction risk across groups of species. It is based on genuine changes in the number of species in each category of extinction risk on the IUCN Red List of Threatened Species (IUCN 2015), which is expressed as changes in an index ranging from 0 to 1. Note: The Red List Index value ranges from 1 (all species are categorized as "Least Concern") to 0 (all species are categorized as "Extinct"), indicating how far the set of species has moved overall toward extinction. Threatened species are those listed on The IUCN Red List of Threatened Species in the categories Vulnerable, Endangered, or Critically Endangered (i.e., species that are facing a high, very high, or extremely high risk of extinction in the wild in the medium-term future).
Goal 16. Promote peaceful and inclusive societies for sustainable development; provide access to justice for all; and build effective, accountable, and inclusive institutions at all levels		
Target 16.1: Significantly reduce all forms of violence and related death rates everywhere.	16.1.1: Number of victims of intentional homicide per 100,000 population, by sex and age	Total count of victims of intentional homicide divided by the total population, expressed per 100,000 population. Intentional homicide is defined as the unlawful death inflicted upon a person with the intent to cause death or serious injury (International Classification of Crime for Statistical Purposes, ICCS 2015). Population refers to total resident population in a given country in a given year. Note: This indicator is widely used at national and international levels to measure the most extreme form of violent crime, providing a direct indication of lack of security.

(continued on next page)

Goals and Targets	Statistical Indicators	Definition
Target 16.3: Promote the rule of law at the national and international levels, and ensure equal access to justice for all.	16.3.2: Unsentenced detainees as a proportion of the overall prison population	Total number of persons held in detention who have not yet been sentenced, as a percentage of the total number of persons held in detention, on a specified date.
Target 16.5: Substantially reduce corruption and bribery in all their forms.	16.5.2: Proportion of businesses that had at least one contact with a public official and that paid a bribe to a public official, or were asked for a bribe by those public officials during the previous 12 months	Proportion of firms that were asked for a gift or informal payment when meeting with tax officials. Note: This indicator aims to ascertain whether or not firms have been solicited for gifts or informal payments (i.e., bribes) when meeting with tax officials. Paying taxes are required of formal forms in most countries, and the rationale for this indicator is to measure the incidence of corruption during this routine interaction.
Target 16.9: By 2030, provide legal identity, including birth registration, for all.	16.9.1: Proportion of children under 5 years of age whose births have been registered with a civil authority, by age	Proportion of children under 5 years of age whose births have been registered with a civil authority.
Goal 17. Strengthen the means of implementation and revitalize the Global Partnership for Sustainable Development		
Target 17.4: Assist developing countries in attaining long-term debt sustainability through coordinated policies aimed at fostering debt financing, debt relief, and debt restructuring, as appropriate, and address the external debt of highly indebted poor countries to reduce debt distress	17.4.1: Debt service as a proportion of exports of goods and services	Percentage of debt services (principle and interest payments) to the exports of goods and services. Debt services covered in this indicator refer only to public and publicly guaranteed debt.
Target 17.9: Enhance international support for implementing effective and targeted capacity-building in developing countries to support national plans to implement all the Sustainable Development Goals, including through North-South, South-South, and triangular cooperation.	17.9.1: Dollar value of financial and technical assistance (including through North-South, South-South, and triangular cooperation) committed to developing countries	Gross disbursements of total ODA and other official flows from all donors for capacity-building and national planning. Note: ODA refers to "those flows to countries and territories on the Development Assistance Committee List of ODA Recipients and to multilateral institutions which are (i) provided by official agencies, including state and local governments, or by their executive agencies; and (ii) each transaction is administered with the promotion of the economic development and welfare of developing countries as its main objective; and is concessional in character and conveys a grant element of at least 25% (calculated at a rate of discount of 10%). Other official flows (excluding officially supported export credits) are defined as transactions by the official sector that do not meet the conditions for eligibility as ODA, either because they are not primarily aimed at development or because they are not sufficiently concessional.

(continued on next page)

Goals and Targets	Statistical Indicators	Definition
Target 17.18: By 2020, enhance capacity-building support to developing countries, including for least developed countries and small island developing states, to increase significantly the availability of high-quality, timely, and reliable data disaggregated by income, gender, age, race, ethnicity, migratory status, disability, geographic location, and other characteristics relevant in national contexts.	17.18.3: Number of countries with a national statistical plan that is fully funded and under implementation, by source of funding	Count of countries that are either (i) implementing a strategy, (ii) designing a strategy, or (iii) awaiting adoption of a strategy in the current year. Note: The indicator is based on the annual Status Report on National Strategies for the Development of Statistics. In collaboration with its partners, PARIS21 reports on country progress in designing and implementing national statistical plans. This indicator can be disaggregated by geographical area. Regional-level aggregates are based on the total count of national strategies.
Target 17.19: By 2030, build on existing initiatives to develop measurements of progress on sustainable development that complement GDP, and support statistical capacity-building in developing countries.	17.19.1: Dollar value of all resources made available to strengthen statistical capacity in developing countries	US dollar value of ongoing statistical support in developing countries. Note: The indicator is based on the Partner Report on Support to Statistics, which is designed and administered by PARIS21 to provide a snapshot of the US dollar value of ongoing statistical support in developing countries.
	17.19.2: Number of countries that have conducted at least one population and housing census in the past 10 years	Countries that have conducted at least one population and housing census in the past 10 years. This includes countries that compile their detailed population and housing statistics from population registers, administrative records, sample surveys, other sources, or a combination of those sources.

Regional Trends and Tables

Indicator	Definition
PEOPLE	
Population	
Midyear Population	Estimates of the midyear de facto population. De facto population includes all persons physically present in the country during the census day, including foreign, military, and diplomatic personnel and their accompanying household members; and transient foreign visitors in the country or in harbors.
Growth Rates in Population	Number of people added to (or subtracted from) a population over a given period of time because of natural increase and net migration, expressed as a percentage of the population at the given period of time.
Net International Migration Rate	Number of immigrants minus the number of emigrants over a period, divided by the person-years lived by the population of the receiving country over that period. It is expressed as net number of migrants per 1,000 population.
Urban Population (as % of total population)	Population living in urban areas, defined in accordance with the national definition or as used in the most recent population census. Because of national differences in the characteristics that distinguish urban from rural areas, the distinction between urban and rural populations is not amenable to a single definition that would be applicable to all countries. National definitions are most commonly based on size of locality. Population that is not urban is considered rural. The estimated population living in urban areas at midyear as a percentage of the total midyear population in a country.
Age Dependency Ratio	Ratio of the nonworking-age population to the working-age population. Since countries define working age differently, a straightforward application of the definition will lead to noncomparable data. The Asian Development Bank therefore uses the following United Nations definition that can be calculated directly from an age distribution: $$\frac{\text{Population aged } (0\text{--}14) + (65 \text{ and over}) \text{ years}}{\text{Population aged } (15\text{--}64) \text{ years}} \times 100$$
Labor Force and Employment	
Labor Force Participation Rate	Percentage of the labor force to the working-age population. The labor force is the sum of those employed and unemployed but seeking work. The labor force participation rate measures the extent of the economically active working-age population in an economy. It provides an indication of the relative size of the supply of labor available for the production of goods and services in the economy. It must be noted that the definition of working-age population varies across countries.
Employment in Agriculture	Employment in agriculture, including forestry and fishing, that corresponds to division 1 (International Standard of Industrial Classification [ISIC] revision 2), tabulation categories A and B (ISIC revision 3), and category A of ISIC revision 4.
Employment in Industry	Employment in industry includes mining and quarrying; manufacturing; electricity, gas, steam, and air-conditioning supply; water supply; sewage, waste management, and remediation activities; and construction.
Employment in Mining and Quarrying	Employment in mining and quarrying that corresponds to division 2 (ISIC revision 2), tabulation category C (ISIC revision 3), and category B of ISIC revision 4.
Employment in Manufacturing	Employment in manufacturing that corresponds to division 3 (ISIC revision 2), tabulation category D (ISIC revision 3), and category C of ISIC revision 4.
Employment in Electricity, Gas, Steam, and Air-Conditioning Supply; Water Supply; Sewerage, Waste Management and Remediation Activities	Employment in electricity, gas, steam, and air-conditioning supply; water supply; sewerage, waste management, and remediation activities that corresponds to division 4 (ISIC revision 2), tabulation category E (ISIC revision 3), and categories D and E of ISIC revision 4.
Employment in Construction	Employment in construction that corresponds to division 5 (ISIC revision 2), tabulation category F (ISIC revisions 3), and category F of ISIC revision 4.

(continued on next page)

Indicator	Definition
Employment in Service	Employment in service includes wholesale and retail trade; repair of motor vehicles and motorcycles; accommodation and food service activities; transportation and storage; information and communication; financial and insurance activities; real estate activities; and other services.
Employment in Wholesale and Retail Trade; Repair of Motor Vehicles and Motorcycles	Employment in wholesale and retail trade; repair of motor vehicles and motorcycles that corresponds to division 6 (subdivisions 61 and 62, ISIC revision 2); tabulation category G (ISIC revision 3); and category G of ISIC revision 4.
Employment in Accommodation and Food Service Activities	Employment in accommodation and food service activities that corresponds to division 6 (subdivision 63, ISIC revision 2); tabulation category H (ISIC revision 3); and category I of ISIC revision 4.
Employment in Transportation and Storage	Employment in transport and storage that corresponds to division 7 (subdivision 71, ISIC revision 2); tabulation category I (sub-categories 60–63, ISIC revision 3); and category H of ISIC revision 4.
Employment in Information and Communication	Employment in information and communication that corresponds to division 7 (subdivision 72, ISIC revision 2); tabulation category I (subcategory 64, ISIC revision 3); and category J of ISIC revision 4.
Employment in Financial and Insurance Activities	Employment in financial and insurance activities that corresponds to division 8 (subdivisions 81–82, ISIC revision 2), tabulation category J (ISIC revision 3), and category K of ISIC revision 4.
Employment in Real Estate Activities	Employment in real estate activities that corresponds to division 8 (subdivision 83, ISIC revision 2); tabulation category K (subcategory 70, ISIC revision 3); and category L of ISIC revision 4.
Employment in Other Services	Employment in other services that corresponds to divisions 9 and 0 (ISIC revision 2), tabulation categories L to Q (ISIC revision 3), and categories M to U of ISIC revision 4.
Poverty Indicators	
Proportion of Population below $1.90 a Day (2011 PPP)	Percentage of the population living on less than $1.90 a day at 2011 purchasing power parity (PPP).
Proportion of Population below $3.20 a Day (2011 PPP)	Percentage of the population living on less than $3.20 a day at 2011 PPP.
Income Ratio of Highest 20% to Lowest 20%	Income or consumption share that accrues to the richest 20% of the population, divided by the income or consumption share of the lowest 20% of the population.
Gini Coefficient or Index	Measure of the degree to which an economy's income distribution diverges from perfect equal distribution. A value of zero (0) implies perfect equality while a value of one (1) implies perfect inequality.
Human Development Index	Composite index of long and healthy life (measured by life expectancy at birth), knowledge (measured by expected years of schooling and mean years of schooling), and decent standard of living (measured by gross national income per capita in United States [US] PPP dollars).
Social Indicators	
Life Expectancy at Birth	Number of years that a newborn is expected to live if prevailing patterns of mortality at the time of his or her birth are to stay the same throughout his or her life.
Crude Birth Rate	Ratio of the total number of live births in a given period to the midyear total population of the same period, expressed per 1,000 people.
Crude Death Rate	Ratio of the number of deaths occurring within a given period to the midyear total population of the same period, expressed per 1,000 people.
Total Fertility Rate	Number of children that would be born to a woman if she were to live to the end of her childbearing years and bear children in accordance with current age-specific fertility rates.
Primary Education Completion Rate	Total number of new entrants in the last grade of primary education, regardless of age, expressed as a percentage of the total population at the theoretical entrance age to the last grade of primary education. This indicator is also known as "gross intake ratio to the last grade of primary." The ratio can exceed 100% due to overaged and underaged children who enter primary school late, early, and/or repeat grades.

(continued on next page)

Indicator	Definition
Adult Literacy Rate	The percentage of the population aged 15 years and older who can both read and write (with understanding) a short simple statement on his or her everyday life. Generally, literacy also encompasses numeracy, i.e., the ability to make simple arithmetic calculations.
Primary Pupil–Teacher Ratio	Average number of pupils (students) per teacher at the primary level of education in a given school year. This indicator is used to measure the level of human resources input in terms of number of teachers in relation to the size of the primary pupil population.
Secondary Pupil–Teacher Ratio	Average number of pupils (students) per teacher at the secondary level of education in a given school year. This indicator is used to measure the level of human resources input in terms of number of teachers in relation to the size of the secondary pupil population.
Physicians	Physicians, including general and specialist medical practitioners, expressed in terms of the number per 1,000 people.
Hospital Beds	In-patient beds for both acute and chronic care available in public, private, general, and specialized hospitals and rehabilitation centers expressed in terms of the number per 1,000 people.
Number of Adults Living with HIV	All adults, defined as men and women aged 15 years and older, with HIV infection, whether or not they have developed symptoms of AIDS, estimated to be alive at the end of a specific year.

ECONOMY AND OUTPUT

National Accounts

Indicator	Definition
Gross Domestic Product	Unduplicated market value of the total production activity of all resident producer units within the economic territory of a country during a given period. It is calculated without making deductions for depreciation of fabricated assets or for depletion and degradation of natural resources. Transfer payments are excluded from the calculation of gross domestic product (GDP). GDP can be calculated using the production, expenditure, and income approaches. Production-based GDP is the sum of the gross value added by all resident producers in the economy, plus any taxes and minus any subsidies not included in the value of the products. Gross value added is the net output of an industry after adding up all outputs and subtracting intermediate inputs. Income-based GDP is the sum of the compensation of employees, mixed income, operating surplus, consumption of fixed capital, and taxes, less subsidies on production and imports. Expenditure-based GDP is the sum of final consumption expenditure of households, nonprofit institutions serving households, and the government; gross capital formation; and exports minus imports of goods and services. GDP can be measured at current prices (the prices of the current reporting period), and constant prices (obtained by expressing values in terms of a base period and chain volume measure).
GDP at PPP	Measures obtained by using PPP to convert the GDP into a common currency, and by valuing them at a uniform price level. They are the spatial equivalent of a time series of GDP for a single country expressed at constant prices. At the level of GDP, they are used to compare the economic size of countries.
GDP at Current US Dollar	GDP at local currency units are obtained from the economy sources and are converted to US dollars using the official exchange rates from the International Monetary Fund (IMF). The exchange rates used are expressed as the average rate for a period of time (average of period), calculated as annual averages based on the monthly averages (local currency units relative to the US dollar).
GDP per Capita at PPP	GDP at PPP, divided by the midyear population.

(continued on next page)

Indicator	Definition
GNI per Capita, Atlas Method	The gross national income (GNI) converted to US dollars using the World Bank Atlas method, divided by the midyear population. GNI is the sum of value added by all resident producers, plus any product taxes (less subsidies) not included in the valuation of output, plus net receipts of primary income (compensation of employees and property income) from abroad. GNI, calculated in national currency, is usually converted to US dollars at official exchange rates for comparisons across economies, although an alternative rate is used when the official exchange rate is judged to diverge by an exceptionally large margin from the rate actually applied in international transactions. To smooth fluctuations in prices and exchange rates, a special Atlas method of conversion is used by the World Bank. This applies a conversion factor that averages the exchange rate for a given year and the 2 preceding years, adjusted for differences in rates of inflation between the country, and through 2000, the G-5 countries (France, Germany, Japan, the United Kingdom, and the US). From 2001, these countries include the Euro area, Japan, the United Kingdom, and the US.
GDP per Capita at Current US Dollar	GDP at current US dollar value, divided by the midyear population.
Agriculture Value Added	The gross output of the agriculture sector, less the corresponding value of intermediate consumption. The industrial origin of value added is determined by ISIC revision 4, where agriculture corresponds to ISIC Section A and includes agriculture, forestry, and fishing.
Industry Value Added	The gross output of industry sectors, less the corresponding value of intermediate consumption. The industrial origin of value added is determined by ISIC revision 4, where industry corresponds to ISIC Sections B–F and includes mining and quarrying (B); manufacturing (C); electricity, gas, steam, and air-conditioning supply (D); water supply; sewerage, waste management, and remediation activities (E); and construction (F).
Services Value Added	The gross output of services sectors, less the corresponding value of intermediate consumption. The industrial origin of value added is determined by ISIC revision 4, where services corresponds to ISIC Sections G–U and includes wholesale and retail trade; repair of motor vehicles and motorcycles (G); transport and storage (H); accommodation and food service activities (I); information and communication (J); financial and insurance activities (K); real estate activities (L); professional, scientific, and technical activities (M); administrative and support service activities (N); public administration and defense; compulsory social security (O); education (P); human health and social work activities (Q); arts, entertainment, and recreation (R); other service activities (S); activities of households as employers; undifferentiated goods- and services-producing activities of households for own use (T); and activities of extraterritorial organizations and bodies (U).
Household Consumption Expenditure	Market value of all goods and services, including durable products (such as cars, washing machines, and home computers), purchased or received as income in kind by households. It excludes purchases of dwellings, but includes imputed rent for owner-occupied dwellings. It also includes payments and fees to governments to obtain permits and licenses. The expenditure of nonprofit institutions serving households is generally included for most economies.
Government Consumption Expenditure	Includes all current outlays on purchases of goods and services (including wages and salaries of government employees). It also includes most expenditure on national defense and security, but excludes government military expenditures that are part of public investment.
Gross Capital Formation	Total value of gross fixed capital formation, changes in inventories, and acquisitions less disposals of valuables. Gross fixed capital formation is the total value of a producer's acquisitions, less disposals of tangible goods (such as buildings) and intangible goods (such as computer software) that are intended for use in production during several accounting periods, plus certain specified expenditure on services that add to the value of nonproduced assets. Changes in inventories are changes in stocks of produced goods and goods for intermediate consumption, and the net increase in the value of work in progress. Valuables are goods (such as precious metals and works of art) that are not used in production, but are acquired as stores of value in the expectation that they will retain or increase their value over time.
Exports of Goods and Services	Consist of sales, bartering, or gifts or grants of goods and services from residents to nonresidents. The treatment of exports in the System of National Accounts is generally identical with that in the balance of payments accounts as described in the IMF's Balance of Payments Manual.

(continued on next page)

Indicator	Definition
Imports of Goods and Services	Consist of purchases, bartering, or receipts of gifts or grants of goods and services by residents from nonresidents. The treatment of imports in the System of National Accounts is generally identical with that in the balance of payments accounts as described in the IMF's Balance of Payments Manual.
Gross Domestic Saving	Difference between GDP and final consumption expenditure, where final consumption expenditure is the sum of the final consumption of household, nonprofit institutions serving households, and the government.
Production	
Agriculture Production Index	Relative level of the aggregate volume of agricultural production for each year in comparison with the base period. It is based on the sum of price-weighted quantities of different agricultural commodities produced after deductions of quantities used as seed and feed weighted in a similar manner. The resulting aggregate therefore represents disposable production for any use, except as seed and feed.
Manufacturing Production Index	An index covering production in manufacturing. The exact coverage, the weighting system, and the methods of calculation vary from country to country, but the divergences are less important than, for example, in the case of price and wage indexes.
MONEY, FINANCE, AND PRICES	
Prices	
Consumer Price Index	An index that measures changes in prices against a reference period of a basket of goods and services purchased by households. Based on the purpose of the consumer price index, different baskets of goods and services can be selected. For macroeconomic purposes, a broad-based basket is used to represent the relative price movement of household final consumption expenditure.
Food and Nonalcoholic Beverages Price Index	An index that covers food and nonalcoholic beverages purchased by the household mainly for consumption or preparation at home including services for food processing for own consumption. The index corresponds to Classification of Individual Consumption by Purpose (COICOP) Version 1999 division 01. Excluded are food and nonalcoholic beverages that are provided as part of a food-serving service under hotels and restaurants (COICOP division 11).
Alcoholic Beverages, Tobacco, and Narcotics Price Index	An index that covers the purchase of alcoholic beverages, tobacco, and narcotics, regardless of where these are consumed, but not provided as part of a food-and-beverage-serving service under hotels and restaurants. Services for the production of alcohol for own consumption are also included. The index corresponds to COICOP division 02. Excluded are alcoholic beverages purchased for immediate consumption in hotels, restaurants, cafes, bars, kiosks, street vendors, automatic vending machines, etc. classified under restaurants, cafes, and the like (COICOP Group 11.1.1).
Clothing and Footwear Price Index	An index that covers all clothing materials, garments, articles and accessories, footwear and related services, including cleaning, repair, and hire of clothing and footwear, and the purchase of secondhand clothing and footwear. The index corresponds to COICOP division 03.
Housing, Water, Electricity, Gas, and Other Fuels Price Index	An index that covers goods and services for the use of the house or dwelling and its maintenance and repair; the supply of water and miscellaneous services related to the dwelling; and energy used for heating or cooling. The index corresponds to COICOP division 04.
Furnishings, Household Equipment, and Routine Household Maintenance Price Index	An index that covers a wide range of products to equip the house or dwelling and the household durables, semidurables, and nondurables as well as some household services. Includes all kinds of furniture (including lightning equipment, household textiles, glassware, tableware and household utensils), major and smaller electric household appliances, tools and equipment for house and garden, and goods for routine household maintenance. The index also includes the repair, installation, and rental services of the goods. Domestic services by paid staff in private service, supplied by enterprises or self-employed persons, window-cleaning and disinfecting services, as well as dry-cleaning and laundering of household textiles and carpets, are also included. The index corresponds to COICOP division 05.

(continued on next page)

Indicator	Definition
Health Price Index	An index that covers health services provided during an overnight stay, services that do not require an overnight stay, diagnostic imaging services, medical laboratory services, patient emergency transportation, and emergency rescue services. The index also includes medicines and health products, covering all products that are separately invoiced from health services, except when administered under the direct supervision of a health care professional during an overnight stay. The index corresponds to COICOP division 06.
Transport Price Index	An index that covers four main categories of goods and services for transportation: (i) purchase of vehicles covers motor cars, motor cycles, bicycles, and animal-drawn vehicles; (ii) goods and services for the operation of the personal transport equipment cover parts and accessories for personal transport equipment, fuels and lubricants, and the repair and maintenance of personal transport equipment including expenditures for parking spaces in garages or in public places, expenditures for tolls, and expenditures to acquire a driving certificate; (iii) transport services provided by the market, structured by the mode of transport; and (iv) transport services of goods covers postal and courier services, removal and storage services, and the delivery of any kinds of goods when charged separately. The index corresponds to COICOP division 07. It excludes purchases of recreational vehicles such as camper vans, caravans, trailers, aeroplanes, and boats that are classified under the Recreation and Culture Price Index.
Communication Price Index	An index that covers three main groups of goods and services: (i) information and communication equipment, including equipment for the capture, recording, and reproduction of sound and vision; software; and information and communication services; (ii) information and communication services including telephones and other communication services, internet access services, television and radio licenses, fee and subscription services including streaming services of films and music; and (iii) repair, maintenance, and rental of information and communication equipment. The index corresponds to COICOP division 08.
Recreation and Culture Price Index	An index that covers a wide range of goods and services for recreation, sport, and culture and is structured into eight groups: (i) recreation durables such as photographic equipment, other major durables for recreation, such as camper vans, boats, yachts, aeroplanes, and the like; (ii) nonmajor durable recreational goods such as games and toys, including video game computers, celebration articles, equipment for sport, camping, and open-air recreation; (iii) garden products and plants and flowers and purchases of pets and expenditures for pets, excluding veterinary services; (iv) recreational services cover rental, maintenance, and repair of goods, veterinary and other services for pets, recreational and leisure services, such as amusement parks, games of chance and expenditures for sporting services, both expenditures for practicing sports as well as expenditures for attendance of sport events; (v) cultural goods such as musical instruments and audio-visual media; (vi) cultural services such as cinemas, theatres, concerts, museums, and other cultural sites, and photographic services; (vii) newspapers, all kinds of books, stationery and drawing materials; and (viii) package holidays that include transportation, accommodation, food provision, or tour guide. The index corresponds to COICOP division 09.
Education Price Index	An index that covers educational services only. It includes: (i) education by radio or television broadcasting as well as e-learning and correspondence courses; (ii) admission and registration fees as well as tuition fees; and (iii) other education-related fees such as camps and/or field trips, course fees, diploma fees, examination fees, graduation fees, laboratory fees, physical education fees, etc. The index corresponds to COICOP division 10. It excludes expenditures on other education-related goods and services such as school uniforms, education support services, such as health-care services, transport services (except in the case of excursions that are part of the normal school program), text books and academic journals, stationery, catering services, and accommodation services.
Restaurants and Hotels Price Index	An index that covers services provided by restaurants, cafes, and similar facilities, either with full or limited- or self-service, or by canteens, cafeterias, or refectories at work or at school and other educational establishment's premises. It also includes catering services and accommodation services. The index corresponds to COICOP division 11.

(continued on next page)

Indicator	Definition
Miscellaneous Goods and Services Price Index	An index that covers insurance and financial services. It also includes personal care, prostitution, personal effects not elsewhere classified, social protection, financial services not elsewhere classified, and other services not elsewhere classified. The index corresponds to COICOP division 12.
Wholesale Price Index	A measure that reflects changes in the prices paid for goods at various stages of distribution up to the point of retail. It can include prices of raw materials for intermediate and final consumption, prices of intermediate or unfinished goods, and prices of finished goods. The goods are usually valued at purchasers' prices.
Producer Price Index	A measure of the change in the prices of goods and services, either as they leave their place of production or as they enter the production process. A measure of the change in the prices received by domestic producers for their outputs or of the change in the prices paid by domestic producers for their intermediate inputs.
GDP Deflator	A measure of the annual rate of price change in the economy as a whole for the period shown, obtained by dividing GDP at current prices by GDP at constant prices.
Money and Finance	
Money Supply	Refers to the total amount of money in circulation in a specific country. Money supply can be measured in different ways: M1 (Narrow Money) is a measure of money supply that includes all coins and notes (M0) as well as personal money in current accounts. M2 (Intermediate Money) is the sum of M1 and personal money in deposit accounts. M3 (Broad Money) is the sum of M2 and government and other deposits. According to the Organization for Economic Co-operation and Development, M3 includes currency, deposits with an agreed maturity of up to 2 years, deposits redeemable at notice of up to 3 months and repurchase agreements, money market fund shares or units, and debt securities up to 2 years. Not all countries publish the same types of aggregates, and even when aggregates are the same name (e.g., M1, M2, M3, etc.), their asset composition often differs significantly. Cross-country differences in national definitions of lowered-ordered aggregates also arise from differences in the maturity categories of nontransferable deposits included in a particular money aggregate. For example, the definition of M2 in one country may include time deposits with maturities of 1 year or less, whereas another country's M2 definition may include time deposits with maturities of 2 years or less. When the monetary policy strategy consists of monetary aggregate targeting, the choice of the definition of the targeted aggregate is guided mainly by two considerations. The aggregate should be sufficiently sensitive to interest rate changes for the central bank to be able to control it and display a stable relationship over time to the movement of the overall price level.
Interest Rate on Savings Deposits	Rate paid by commercial and similar banks for savings deposits.
Interest Rate on Time Deposits	Rate paid by commercial and similar banks for time deposits.
Lending Interest Rate	Bank rate that usually meets the short- and medium-term financing needs of the private sector. This rate is normally differentiated according to creditworthiness of borrowers and objectives of financing.
Yield on Short-Term Treasury Bills	Rate at which short-term securities are issued or traded in the market.
Domestic Credit Provided by Banking Sector	Includes all credits to various sectors on a gross basis, except credit to the central government, which is net. The banking sector includes monetary authorities, deposit money banks, and other banking institutions for which data are available (including institutions that do not accept transferable deposits but do incur such liabilities as time and savings deposits). Examples of other banking institutions are savings and mortgage loan institutions and building and loan associations.
Ratio of Bank Nonperforming Loans to Total Gross Loans	Value of nonperforming loans divided by the total value of the loan portfolio (including nonperforming loans before the deduction of loan loss provisions). The amount recorded as nonperforming should be the gross value of the loan as recorded in the balance sheet, not just the amount that is overdue.
Stock Market Price Index	Index that measures changes in the prices of stocks traded in the stock exchange. The price changes of the stocks are usually weighted by their market capitalization.

(continued on next page)

Indicator	Definition
Stock Market Capitalization	The share price multiplied by the number of shares outstanding (including their various classes) for listed domestic companies. Investment funds, unit trusts, and companies whose only business goal is to hold shares of other listed companies are excluded. Data are end-of-year values converted to US dollars using corresponding end-of-year foreign exchange rates. Also known as market value.
Exchange Rates	
Official Exchange Rate	The exchange rate determined by national authorities or the rate determined in the legally sanctioned exchange market. It is calculated as an annual average based on the monthly averages (local currency units relative to the US dollar).
Purchasing Power Parity Conversion Factor	Number of units of country B's currency that are needed in country B to purchase the same quantity of an individual good or service, which one unit of country A's currency can purchase in country A.
Price Level Index	Ratio of the relevant PPP to the exchange rate. It is expressed as an index on a base of 100. A price level index (PLI) greater than 100 means that, when the national average prices are converted at exchange rates, the resulting prices tend to be higher on average than prices in the base country (or countries) of the region (and vice versa). At the level of GDP, PLIs provide a measure of the differences in the general price levels of countries. PLIs are also referred to as comparative price levels.
GLOBALIZATION	
Balance of Payments	
Trade in Goods Balance	Difference between exports and imports of goods.
Trade in Services Balance	Difference between exports and imports of services.
Current Account Balance	Sum of net exports of goods, services, net income, and net current transfers.
Workers' Remittances and Compensation of Employees, Receipts	Consist of (i) Current transfers from migrant workers who are residents of the host country to recipients in their country of origin. To count as a resident, the worker must have been living in the host country for more than 1 year. (ii) Compensation of employees of migrants who have lived in the host country for less than 1 year. (iii) Migrants' transfers, defined as the net worth of migrants who are expected to remain in the host country for more than 1 year, which are transferred from one country to another at the time of migration.
Foreign Direct Investment	Refers to net inflows of investment to acquire a lasting management interest (10% or more of voting stock) in an enterprise operating in an economy other than that of the investor. It is the sum of equity capital, reinvestment of earnings, other long-term capital, and short-term capital as shown in the balance of payments.
External Trade	
Merchandise Exports or Imports	Covering all movable goods, with a few specified exceptions, the ownership of which changes between a resident and a foreigner. For merchandise exports, it represents the value of the goods and related distributive services at the customs frontier of the exporting economy, i.e., the free on board (FOB) value. Merchandise imports, on the other hand, are reported in cost, insurance, and freight (CIF) values.
Trade in Goods	Sum of merchandise exports and merchandise imports.
Direction of Trade	
Direction of Trade: Merchandise Exports and Imports	The direction of trade represents the value of merchandise exports and imports disaggregated according to a country's primary trading partners. Imports are reported on a CIF basis and exports are reported on an FOB basis, with the exception of a few countries for which imports are also available FOB. Time series data includes estimates derived from reports of partner countries for nonreporting and slow-reporting countries.

(continued on next page)

Indicator	Definition
International Reserves	
International Reserves	External assets that are readily available to, and controlled by, monetary authorities for meeting balance-of-payments financing needs, for intervention in exchange markets to affect the currency exchange rate, and for other related purposes (such as maintaining confidence in the currency and the economy, and serving as a basis for foreign borrowing).
	Consist of monetary gold, special drawing rights holdings, reserve position in the IMF, currency and deposits, securities (including debt and equity securities), financial derivatives, and other claims (loans and other financial instruments).
Ratio of International Reserves to Imports	International reserves outstanding at the end of the year as a proportion of imports of goods from the balance of payments during the year, where imports of goods are expressed in terms of a monthly average. It is a useful measure for reserve needs of countries with limited access to capital markets.
Capital Flows	
Net Official Development Assistance	Concessional flows to developing economies and multilateral institutions provided by official agencies, including state and local governments, or by their executing agencies, administered with the objective of promoting the economic development and welfare of developing economies, and containing a grant element of at least 25%. Net flow takes into account principal repayments for loans, offsetting entries for forgiven debt, and recoveries made on grants.
Net Other Official Flows	Official sector transactions with countries on the Development Assistance Committee List of Official Development Assistance Recipients, which do not meet the conditions for eligibility as official development assistance, either because they are not primarily aimed at development, or because they have a grant element of less than 25%. The Development Assistance Committee list of recipients of official development assistance is available at http://www.oecd.org/dac/financing-sustainable-development/development-finance-standards/daclist.htm. Net flow takes into account principal repayments for loans, offsetting entries for forgiven debt, and recoveries made on grants.
Net Private Flows	Sum of direct investment and portfolio investment.
	Direct investment is a category of international investment made by a resident entity in one economy (direct investor) with the objective of establishing a lasting interest in an enterprise that is resident in an economy other than that of the investor (direct investment enterprise). "Lasting interest" implies the existence of a long-term relationship between the direct investor and the enterprise and a significant degree of influence by the direct investor on the management of the direct investment enterprise. Direct investment involves both the initial transaction between the two entities and all subsequent capital transactions between them and among affiliated enterprises, both incorporated and unincorporated.
	Portfolio investment is the category of international investment that covers investment in equity and debt securities, excluding any such instruments that are classified as direct investment or reserve assets.
Aggregate Net Resource Flows	Sum of net official development assistance, net other official flows, and net private flows.
External Indebtedness	
Total External Debt	Debt owed to nonresidents repayable in currency, goods, or services. It is the sum of public, publicly guaranteed, and private nonguaranteed long-term debt, use of IMF credit, and short-term debt. Short-term debt includes all debt having an original maturity of 1 year or less and interest in arrears on long-term debt.
Public and Publicly Guaranteed Debt	Comprises long-term external obligations of public debtors, including the national government, political subdivisions (or an agency of either), and autonomous public bodies, and external obligations of private debtors that are guaranteed for repayment by a public entity.
External Debt as a Percentage of GNI	Total external debt as a percentage of GNI.
	GNI is the sum of value added by all resident producers plus any product taxes (less subsidies) not included in the valuation of output, plus net receipts of primary income (compensation of employees and property income) from abroad.

(continued on next page)

Indicator	Definition
External Debt as a Percentage of Exports of Goods and Services and Primary Income	Total external debt as a percentage of exports of goods, services, and primary income. Exports of goods, services, and primary income constitute the total value of exports of goods and services, receipts of compensation of nonresident workers, and investment income from abroad.
Total Debt Service Paid	The sum of principal repayments and interest actually paid in currency, goods, or services on long-term debt, interest paid on short-term debt, and repayments (repurchases and charges) to the IMF.
Total Debt Service Paid as a Percentage of Exports of Goods and Services and Primary Income	Total debt service paid as a percentage of exports of goods, services, and primary income.
Tourism	
International Tourist Arrivals	The number of tourists (overnight visitors) who travel to a country other than that in which they usually reside, and outside their usual environment, for a period not exceeding 12 months, and whose main purpose of visit is other than the activity remunerated from within the country visited. In some cases, data may also include same-day visitors when data on overnight visitors are not available separately. Data refer to the number of arrivals and not to the number of people.
International Tourism, Receipts	The receipts earned by a destination country from inbound tourism and covering all tourism receipts resulting from expenditures made by visitors from abroad. These include lodging, food and drinks, fuel, transport in the country, entertainment, shopping, etc. This concept includes receipts generated by overnight visits as well as by same-day trips. It does, however, exclude the receipts related to international transport by contracted residents of the other countries (for instance ticket receipts from foreigners travelling with a national company).
TRANSPORT AND COMMUNICATIONS	
Transport	
Road Traffic Deaths	Death caused by a road traffic crash and occurring within 24 hours (the Federated States of Micronesia, Kiribati, Solomon Islands, Timor-Leste, Tonga); 7 days (Azerbaijan, Bhutan, the People's Republic of China, Tajikistan, Turkmenistan, Viet Nam); 30 days (Armenia, Australia, Cambodia, Fiji, India, Indonesia, Japan, Kazakhstan, the Republic of Korea, the Lao People's Democratic Republic, Malaysia, Mongolia, Myanmar, Nepal, New Zealand, Papua New Guinea, Singapore, Sri Lanka, Uzbekistan); unlimited time period (Afghanistan, the Cook Islands, Georgia, Maldives, the Philippines, Samoa, Thailand); within a year (the Kyrgyz Republic); no definition for other countries.
Road Network	Refers to the Asian Highway that consists of highway routes of international importance within Asia, including highway routes substantially crossing more than one subregion; highway routes within subregions that connect neighboring subregions; and highway routes located within member states that provide access to: (a) capital cities; (b) main industrial and agricultural centers; (c) major air, sea, and river ports; (d) major container terminals and depots; and (e) major tourist attractions.
Motor Vehicles	Include cars, buses, freight vehicles, and two- and three-wheeled vehicles.
Container Port Traffic	Measures the flow of containers from land to sea transport modes, and vice versa, in 20-foot equivalent units, a standard-size container. Data refer to coastal shipping as well as international journeys. Transshipment traffic is counted as two lifts at the intermediate port (once to offload and again as an outbound lift) and includes empty units.
Air Transport, Passengers Carried	Air passengers carried include both domestic and international aircraft passengers of air carriers registered in the country.
Air Transport, Carrier Departures Worldwide	Registered carrier departures worldwide are domestic takeoffs and takeoffs abroad of air carriers registered in the country.
Air Transport, Freight	Air freight is the volume of freight, express, and diplomatic bags carried on each flight stage (operation of an aircraft from takeoff to its next landing), measured in metric tons multiplied by kilometers traveled.
Rail Lines	Rail lines are the length of railway route available for train service, irrespective of the number of parallel tracks.
Rail Network	Length of rail lines divided by the land area.

(continued on next page)

Indicator	Definition
Railways, Passengers Carried	Passengers carried by railway are the number of passengers transported by rail multiplied by kilometers traveled.
Railways, Goods Transported	Goods transported by railway are the volume of goods transported by railway, measured in metric tons multiplied by kilometers traveled.
Communications	
Telephone Subscribers	Fixed-telephone subscriptions refer to the sum of active number of analogue fixed telephone lines, voice-over-IP subscriptions, fixed wireless local loop subscriptions, ISDN voice-channel equivalents, and fixed public payphones.
Mobile Phone Subscribers	The proportion of individuals who used a mobile telephone in the 3 months prior to data collection. A mobile (cellular) telephone refers to a portable telephone subscribing to a public mobile telephone service using cellular technology, which provides access to the PSTN. This includes analogue and digital cellular systems and technologies such as IMT-2000 (3G) and IMT- Advanced. Users of both postpaid subscriptions and prepaid accounts are included.
Fixed-Broadband Subscribers	Fixed-broadband subscriptions refer to fixed subscriptions to high-speed access to the public internet (a TCP/IP connection), at downstream speeds equal to, or greater than, 256 kilobits per second. This includes cable modem, DSL, fiber-to-the-home/building, other fixed (wired)- broadband subscriptions, satellite broadband and terrestrial fixed wireless broadband. This total is measured irrespective of the method of payment. It excludes subscriptions that have access to data communications (including the Internet) via mobile-cellular networks. It should include fixed WiMAX and any other fixed wireless technologies. It includes both residential subscriptions and subscriptions for organizations.
Internet Users	The frequency of internet use by individuals who used the internet from any location in the 3 months prior to data collection. The internet can be used via a personal computer, digital tablet device, mobile or cell phone, personal digital assistant, games machine, digital television, etc.
ENERGY AND ELECTRICITY	
Energy	
GDP per Unit of Energy Use	The ratio of GDP to total energy use (measured per petajoule) with GDP converted to 2011 constant international dollars using PPP rates. An international dollar has the same purchasing power over GDP as a US dollar has in the US.
Energy Production	Primary energy production that is the capture or extraction of fuels or energy from natural energy flows, the biosphere, and natural reserves of fossil fuels within the national territory in a form suitable for use. Inert matter removed from the extracted fuels and quantities reinjected, flared, or vented are not included. The resulting products are referred to as primary products.
Energy Use	Energy production plus imports minus exports, minus international marine bunkers, minus international aviation bunkers, minus stock changes. Also referred to as energy supply.
Energy Imports, Net	Energy imports, net estimated as energy use less production, both measured in petajoules.
Electricity	
Electricity Production	Gross production, which is the sum of the electrical energy production by all the generating units and/or installations concerned (including pumped storage), measured at the output terminals of the main generators. Also referred to as electricity generation.

(continued on next page)

Indicator	Definition
Sources of Electricity	Refers to the different types of technology and/or processes for the generation or production of electricity, including: (i) electricity from combustible fuels, which refers to the production of electricity from the combustion of fuels that are capable of igniting or burning, i.e., reacting with oxygen to produce a significant rise in temperature; (ii) hydroelectricity, which refers to electricity produced from devices driven by fresh, flowing, or falling water; (iii) nuclear electricity, which refers to electricity generated by nuclear plants; and (iv) other electricity, which includes solar, wind, wave, tidal, other marine electricity, geothermal, electricity generated from chemical heat, and electricity from other sources not elsewhere specified.
Electric Power Consumption Per Capita	Total electricity consumption divided by midyear population, where consumption refers to energy-industries-own-use and final consumption. Energy-industries-own-use refers to the consumption of electricity for the direct support of the production and preparation for use of fuels and energy. Final consumption refers to the consumption of electricity by manufacturing, construction and nonfuel mining, transport, and households and other consumers (nonenergy use being irrelevant for electricity).
Household Electrification Rate	Percentage of households with an electricity connection.
ENVIRONMENT	
Land	
Agricultural Land or Area	Land area that is arable, under permanent crops, and/or under permanent meadows and pastures.
Arable Land	Land under temporary agricultural crops (double-cropped areas are counted only once), temporary meadows for mowing or pasture, land under market, and kitchen gardens and land temporarily fallow (less than 5 years). The abandoned land resulting from shifting cultivation is not included. Data for arable land are not meant to indicate the amount of land that are potentially cultivable.
Permanent Cropland	Land cultivated with long-term crops that do not have to be replanted for several years (such as cocoa and coffee); land under trees and shrubs producing flowers, such as roses and jasmine; and nurseries (except those for forest trees, which should be classified under "forestry"). Permanent meadows and pastures are excluded from land under permanent crops.
Deforestation Rate	Rate of permanent conversion of natural forest area into other uses, including shifting cultivation, permanent agriculture, ranching, settlements, and infrastructure development. Deforested areas do not include areas logged but intended for regeneration or areas degraded by fuel-wood gathering, acid precipitation, or forest fires. A negative rate indicates reforestation or increase in forest area.
Pollution	
Carbon Dioxide Emissions	Carbon dioxide emissions, largely by-products of energy production and use, account for the largest share of greenhouse gases, which are associated with global warming. Anthropogenic carbon dioxide emissions result primarily from fossil fuel combustion and cement manufacturing. In combustion, different fossil fuels release different amounts of carbon dioxide for the same level of energy used: oil releases about 50% more carbon dioxide than natural gas, while coal releases about twice as much. Cement manufacturing releases about half a metric ton of carbon dioxide for each metric ton of cement produced. Data for carbon dioxide emissions include gases from the burning of fossil fuels and cement manufacture but excludes emissions from land use such as deforestation.
Nitrous Oxide Emissions	Nitrous oxide emissions are mainly from fossil fuel combustion, fertilizers, rainforest fires, and animal waste. Nitrous oxide is a powerful greenhouse gas, with an estimated atmospheric lifetime of 114 years, compared with 12 years for methane. The per-kilogram global warming potential of nitrous oxide is nearly 310 times that of carbon dioxide within 100 years.
Methane Emissions	Methane emissions are those stemming from human activities such as agriculture and from industrial methane production. A kilogram of methane is 21 times as effective at trapping heat in the earth's atmosphere as a kilogram of carbon dioxide within 100 years.
Other Greenhouse Gases	By-product emissions of hydrofluorocarbons, perfluorocarbons, and sulfur hexafluoride.

(continued on next page)

Indicator	Definition
Freshwater	
Internal Renewable Water Resources	Internal renewable water resources (IRWR) refer to the long-term average annual flow of rivers and recharge of aquifers generated from endogenous precipitation. Double-counting of surface water and groundwater resources is avoided by deducting the overlap from the sum of the surface water and groundwater resources. IRWR in billion cubic meters per year refers to surface water produced internally, plus groundwater produced internally deducted by the overlap between surface water and groundwater. IRWR in cubic meters per inhabitant per year is calculated as total annual IRWR divided by total population.
Annual Freshwater Withdrawals	Sum of surface water withdrawal and groundwater withdrawal. Total water withdrawal summed by sector deducted by: desalinated water produced, direct use of treated wastewater, and direct use of agricultural drainage water.
Water Productivity	Water productivity is the ratio of the net benefits from crop, forestry, fishery, livestock, and mixed agricultural systems to the amount of water used to produce those benefits. It is calculated as GDP in constant US dollar prices, divided by annual total water withdrawal.
GOVERNMENT AND GOVERNANCE	
Government Finance	
Government Net Lending / Net Borrowing	Net lending (+) / net borrowing (−) is a summary measure indicating the extent to which government is either putting financial resources at the disposal of other sectors in the economy or abroad, or utilizing the financial resources generated by other sectors in the economy or resources from abroad. It may be viewed as an indicator of the financial impact of government activity on the rest of the economy and the rest of the world. Net lending (+) / net borrowing (−) is a balancing item calculated as the net operating balance (revenue minus expense) minus the net investment in nonfinancial assets. It is also equal to the net acquisition of all financial assets minus the net incurrence of all liabilities from transactions. For economies following the IMF's Government Finance Statistics 1986 framework, the indicator refers to the overall budgetary surplus/deficit measured as the difference between total revenue (including grants) and total expenditure (including net lending).
Government Taxes	Taxes are compulsory, unrequited amounts receivable by government units from institutional units. Certain compulsory receivables, such as fines, penalties, and most social security contributions are not considered to be taxes. For economies following the IMF's Government Finance Statistics 1986 framework, tax revenues are compulsory transfers to the central government for public purposes, which includes social security contributions.
Government Revenue	Government revenue is an increase in net worth resulting from a transaction. Revenue transactions have counterpart entries either in an increase in assets or in a decrease in liabilities, thereby increasing net worth. General government units have four types of revenue: (i) compulsory levies in the form of taxes and certain types of social contributions; (ii) property income derived from the ownership of assets; (iii) sales of goods and services; and (iv) other transfers receivable from other units. For economies following the IMF's Government Finance Statistics 1986 framework, total revenue (including grants) consists of current and capital revenues. Current revenue is the revenue accruing from taxes as well as all current nontax revenues, except transfers received from foreign governments and international institutions. Capital revenue constitutes the proceeds from the sale of nonfinancial capital assets.

(continued on next page)

Indicator	Definition
Government Expenditure	Government expenditure is the sum of expense and the net investment in nonfinancial assets. Expense is a decrease in net worth resulting from a transaction. The major types of expense are compensation of employees, use of goods and services subsidies, grants, social benefits, and other expense. The acquisition of a nonfinancial asset by purchase or barter is not an expense because it has no effect on net worth. Similarly, amounts payable on loans extended and repayments on loans incurred are not classified as expense. Nonfinancial assets are economic assets other than financial assets. Nonfinancial assets are stores of value and provide benefits either through their use in the production of goods and services or in the form of property income and holding gains. These assets are classified as fixed assets, inventories, valuables, and nonproduced assets. For economies following the IMF's Government Finance Statistics 1986 framework, total expenditure (including net lending) consists of current and capital expenditures. Current expenditure comprises purchases of goods and services by the central government, transfers to noncentral government units and to households, subsidies to producers, and interest on public debt. Capital expenditure covers outlays for the acquisition or construction of capital assets and for the purchase of intangible assets, as well as capital transfers to domestic and foreign recipients. Loans and advances for capital purposes are also included.
Government Expenditure on Education	Government expenditure on education includes expenditure on services provided to individual pupils and students as well as expenditure on services provided on a collective basis. Expenditure on education is allocated to preprimary and primary education, secondary education, postsecondary nontertiary education, tertiary education, subsidiary services to education, education not definable by level, and research and development (R&D) education. For economies following the IMF's Government Finance Statistics 1986 framework, the indicator refers to government expenditure on education affairs and services.
Government Expenditure on Health	Government expenditure on health includes expenditure on services provided to individual persons and services provided on a collective basis. Expenditure on health is allocated to medical products, appliances, and equipment; outpatient services; hospital services; public health services; R&D health; and health not elsewhere classified. For economies following the Government Finance Statistics 1986 framework, the indicator refers to government expenditure on health affairs and services.
Government Expenditure on Social Protection	Government expenditure on social protection includes expenditure on services and transfers provided to individual persons and households as well as expenditure on services provided on a collective basis. Expenditure on social protection is allocated to sickness and disability, old age, survivors, family and children, unemployment, housing, social exclusion not elsewhere classified, and R&D social protection. For economies following the IMF's Government Finance Statistics 1986 framework, the indicator refers to government expenditure on social security and welfare affairs and services.

(continued on next page)

Indicator	Definition
Governance	
Cost of Business Start-Up Procedure	Cost to register a business normalized by presenting it as a percentage of GNI per capita. It includes all official fees and fees for legal or professional services if such services are required by law or commonly used in practice. Fees for purchasing and legalizing company books are included if these transactions are required by law. Although value-added tax registration can be counted as a separate procedure, value-added tax is not part of the incorporation cost. Company law, commercial codes, and specific regulations and fee schedules are used as sources for calculating costs. In the absence of fee schedules, a government officer's estimate is taken as an official source. In the absence of a government officer's estimate, estimates by incorporation experts are used. If several incorporation experts provide different estimates, the median reported value is applied. In all cases, the cost excludes bribes.
Time Required to Start Up a Business	Number of calendar days needed to complete the procedures to legally operate a business. If a procedure can be accelerated at additional cost, the fastest procedure, independent of cost, is chosen.
Corruption Perceptions Index	Ranks countries and territories based on how corrupt or otherwise their public sector is perceived to be. It is a composite index—a combination of polls—drawing on corruption-related data collected by a variety of reputable institutions. The index reflects the views of observers from around the world, including experts living and working in the countries and territories evaluated. From 2000 to 2011, scores ranged from 10 (highly clean) to 0 (highly corrupt). From 2012 onwards, calculation of the score has used an updated methodology and is now presented on a 100 (very clean) to 0 (highly corrupt) scale. Due to this difference in methodology, scores from years prior to and including 2011 should not be compared with scores from 2012 onward. A country's rank indicates its position relative to the other countries or territories included in the index. It is important to keep in mind that a country's rank can change simply because new countries enter the index or others drop out.

Global Value Chains

Indicator	Definition
Business Services Sector	Consists of the sectors: Sale, Maintenance, and Repair of Motor Vehicles and Motorcycles; Retail Trade, Except of Motor Vehicles and Motorcycles; Repair of Household Goods; Hotels and Restaurants; Inland Transport; Water Transport; Air Transport; Other Supporting and Auxiliary Transport Activities; Activities of Travel Agencies; Post and Telecommunications; Financial Intermediation; Real Estate Activities; Renting of Machinery and Equipment; and Other Business Activities.
Domestic Value-Added via Backward Linkages (DVA_B)	Value-added that is originated from all domestic sectors that are embedded in the exports of a particular sector in the source economy, regardless of where it is ultimately absorbed.
Domestic Value-Added via Forward Linkages (DVA_F)	Domestic value-added that is exported via all forward linkages, regardless of where it is ultimately absorbed. Alternatively, this refers to domestic value-added that is originated from a particular sector and ultimately embodied in exports (regardless of where these exports are finally consumed).
Domestic Value-Added Absorbed Abroad (VAX_G)	All domestic value-added embodied in gross exports and ultimately absorbed abroad.
Domestic Value-Added First Exported then Returned Home (RDV_B)	Domestic value-added that is first exported, but then returned to the home economy for domestic consumption. This would happen, for example, when the Philippines exports electronic parts to the People's Republic of China for the final assembly of laptops, which are then returned to the Philippines for consumer purchase.
Foreign Value-Added (FVA)	Imported inputs of goods and services in the overall exports of an economy.
Global Value Chains (GVCs)	A network of interlinked stages of production for goods and services that straddles international borders. Typically, a GVC involves combining imported and domestically produced goods and services into products that are then exported for use as intermediates in the subsequent stage of production or as final consumption products.
GVC Participation	There are various ways to measure the participation of economies in GVCs. A simple metric is the share of foreign value-added in total exports. It reflects the extent to which an economy uses foreign inputs in producing exports. A more rigorous measure is vertical specialization.
Low-Technology Industrial Sector	Consists of the sectors: Food, Beverages, and Tobacco; Textiles and Textile Products; Leather, Leather Products, and Footwear; Wood and Products of Wood and Cork; Pulp, Paper, Paper Products, Printing, and Publishing; Rubber and Plastics; Manufacturing, NEC; Recycling; Electricity, Gas, and Water Supply; and Construction.
Medium- and High-Technology Industrial Sector	Consists of the sectors: Coke, Refined Petroleum, and Nuclear Fuel; Chemicals and Chemical Products; Other Nonmetallic Minerals; Basic Metals and Fabricated Metals; Machinery, NEC; Electrical and Optical Equipment; and Transport Equipment.
Personal and Public Services Sector	Consists of the sectors: Public Administration and Defense; Compulsory Social Security; Education; Health and Social Work; Other Community, Social, and Personal Services; and Private Households with Employed persons.
Primary Sector	Consists of the sectors: Agriculture, Hunting, Forestry, and Fishing; and Mining and Quarrying.
Pure Double-Counted Terms (PDC)	In a GVC, some goods or services may cross the same national border on three or more occasions.
Revealed Comparative Advantage (RCA)	Traditional method: Introduced by Bela Balassa, this index represents the relative advantage an economy has in the export of any given good or service. An economy is said to have an RCA in a product if it exports more than its "fair share", or a share that is equal to or greater than the share of the product to total world trade. Value-added method: Based on Wang, Wei and Zhu (2018), this measure is similar to the traditional RCA method, except that it is based on DVA_F rather than gross exports. An economy is said to have an RCA in a product if its DVA_F matches or exceeds the share of the product's DVA_F in total global value-added in exports.
Value-Added Exports via Backward Linkages (VAX_B)	Value-added that is originated from all domestic sectors and ultimately absorbed abroad via the exports of a particular sector in the source economy. For example, the domestic value-added of Japanese automobile exports includes that of all Japanese sectors (e.g., business services, computers) used as inputs.

(continued on next page)

Indicator	Definition
Value-Added Exports via Forward Linkages (VAX_F)	Domestic value-added that is originated from a particular sector and ultimately absorbed abroad via the exports of all sectors in the source economy. For example, besides direct export, the value-added of the Japanese business services sector may be exported as an input to Japanese automobiles. This indicator is useful in understanding the contribution of a given sector to the economy's aggregate exports.